The Calling
of Sociology

Selected Papers of Edward Shils, Volume III

Edward Shils

The Calling of Sociology
and
Other Essays on
the Pursuit of Learning

The University of Chicago Press
Chicago and London

The University of Chicago Press, Chicago 60637
The University of Chicago Press, Ltd., London
© 1980 by The University of Chicago
All rights reserved. Published 1980
Printed in the United States of America
84 83 82 81 80   5 4 3 2 1

Library of Congress Cataloging in Publication Data

Shils, Edward Albert, 1911–
    The calling of sociology and other essays on the
pursuit of learning.

    (His Selected papers of Edward Shils; 3)
    1. Sociology.   2. Sociology—United States.
I. Title.
AC8.S5337 vol.3 [HM51] 082s [301] 79–15048
ISBN 0–226–75323–9

Contents

I **The Place of Sociology**

    1.   The Calling of Sociology 3

II **The Trend of Sociology**

    2.   The Contemplation of Society in America 95
    3.   The Confluence of Sociological Traditions 134
    4.   Tradition, Ecology, and Institution in the History of Sociology 165

III **Sociology and Society**

    5.   Social Science and Social Policy 259
    6.   Learning and Liberalism 289
    7.   The Pursuit of Knowledge and the Concern for the Common Good 356

IV **The Ethics of Sociology**

    8.   Social Inquiry and the Autonomy of the Private Sphere 421
    9.   Social Science as Public Opinion 452
    10. The Legitimacy of Social Inquiry 465

Part One

The Place of Sociology

1   The Calling of Sociology

The Establishment and Reception of Sociology

From Heterogeneity to Unity

The concerns of counselors to princes, of philosophers who would be kings, of disenchanted and optimistic moralists, of rueful critics of conquest and revolution, and of reformers alarmed at the state of their societies provided the rudiments of the sociological outlook. They provided that detachment in intimate participation which is the platform of sociological observation; they provided the first elements of the belief that objectively reported observations could change the opinion and conduct of those who count in society. Distinct families of tradition began to be formed, linking with each other and then drawing away again. The coalescence of those traditions of preacademic thought and observation, which retrospectively may now be seen as the sources of sociology, has occurred only recently—certainly no earlier than the present century. The heterogeneous rudiments of sociology first took shape before the emergence of universities; even after the universities were formed, the ancestral constituents and prefigurations of sociology existed outside them. Nonetheless, sociology could not have become the pervasive power in contemporary sensibility which it is now, without having become a subject of the modern academic syllabus. The outlook which now dominates sociological inquiry, even among those sociologists who believe that they are its antagonists, could not have emerged had it not been for the assimilation of sociology into the universities. It had to become an academic subject before it could come into the possession of its present, larger public. It had to become academic—academic in its home, academic in its style—to acquire such coherence and diffusion as it now possesses.

The scatter of concrete sociological interests was, until relatively recently, the bane of thoughtful sociologists and the butt of critics of sociology. Assembled into a single university department, the diversity of the traditions which have gone into it revealed its motleyness. It was not a motleyness which went deep; and the instinct of the university teachers and administrators who brought those apparently random things together was a sound one. For a time, it appeared that

This is a revised and enlarged version of an essay that originally appeared in Talcott Parsons and Edward Shils, eds., *Theories of Society* (New York: Macmillan, The Free Press of Glencoe, 1961; copyright © 1961 by the Free Press of Glencoe), pp. 1403–48.

sociology was just a collection of the rejects and sweepings, cast off by the other, older academic social sciences—which were also not academic in their origins. It is not, however, in the nature of the best academic minds to tolerate randomness indefinitely—even though many accept it, some glory in it, and many more are incapable of overcoming it.

The establishment of sociology as a coherent subject, the creation of the general outlook which underlies it and of the general theory to which it aspires, and the nurturance of the comprehensive sociological sensibility which is its product and its source, all owe a tremendous amount—as does almost everything in the modern learned world—to the great age of the German university. It is not that sociology prospered in the German universities. For most of its history in the German universities—which has coincided mainly with a period of decline of those institutions from their once great condition—academic sociology was an arid subject. It was a thing of definitions and classifications, as dry as dust and as lifeless. There was, however, a valid impulse in those efforts. They were an attempt to make sociology into a coherent body of thought, unified around certain fundamental problems and the fundamental concepts which were entailed in these problems. The problem was the formation of a coherent order, of the concert of human actions and their disaggregation. The effort was not very successful. Max Weber, the greatest mind of German sociology, did not teach sociology except in the last years of his life. Academic German sociologists never succeeded in going beyond the taxonomic into the dynamic. The impulse which the German university tradition gave to the attempt to unify their subject-matter exhausted itself with the attainment of classification. They did not know how to go farther; but, more important, they did not have the impetus to go farther. They lacked the curiosity about particular actions and about man and society in general to go farther. The quality of imagination and the contemplative intensity of those scholars who had sociology in their care were too slight. The empirical achievement of sociology was still too scattered and many-named, the scope of academic sociological interest still too narrow, to give the sociological sensibility the substantial and differentiated stimulation which it needed.

Nonetheless, the German tradition of the systematic treatise and textbook which ordered a whole body of knowledge—although it was often performed with scholastic pedantry and was regarded by some sociologists as the end-state of sociological development—was one source of the movement to bring, into a single differentiated discipline with a central outlook, the wide diversity of scattered traditions which have gone into the making of sociology. The mere coexistence, within a single department of a characteristic American university of the twentieth century, of criminology, family studies, human ecology and urban sociology, the study of ethnic groups and of social status, political sociology, rural sociology, and the many other small dominions of the American academic sociological empire would, in the course of time, by an imperceptible, osmotic process, have drawn them into a somewhat greater unity. But, independently of this possibility and more important, was the effort to systematize the subject as a whole which arose from the Germanic university tradition of comprehensive textbooks and systematic treatises. For many decades, the efforts, although persistent, were unavailing. The sociological outlook—that vision of society as an incessant interplay of creativity, discipline, refusal, and revolt, against a shifting scene of primordial, civil, sacred, and personal objects—was still far from articulation.

By the end of the 1930s, sociology presented a picture of disarray. In the United States, there was already in existence a vast and heterogeneous body of particular inquiries, with practically nothing in common except their lively curiosity about contemporary America and their aspiration toward observational discipline. In Great Britain, the output was far smaller; on a microscopic scale, the situation was as in the United States. In other countries, empirical studies of contemporary conditions were rare within the universities. Analytically, the coherent sociological standpoint began to be precipitated in the inquiries of the pupils of Park, Mayo, Roethlisberger, Warner, Lazarsfeld, Dollard, and others. It was hesitant and uncertain, and its movements were uncoordinated. The promulgation of a substantive sociological theory had made scarcely any progress since Weber and Durkheim. In Germany, in France, in Italy, and in Great Britain, the theoretical movement of the first part of the century had come practically to a halt. In the United States, exertions were more deliberate, but the results were not impressive. False starts, from psychoanalysis and the behaviorist theory of learning, ran into the ground or evaporated into the air. Talcott Parsons' *The Structure of Social Action* was the turning point. It was this work which brought the greatest of the partial traditions into a measure of unity. It precipitated the sociological outlook which had been implicit in the most interesting of the empirical inquiries; it made explicit the affinities and complementarity of the sociological traditions which had arisen out of utilitarianism, idealism, and positivism. It redirected sociology into its classical path, and, in doing so, it began the slow process of bringing into the open the latent dispositions which had underlain the growth of sociological curiosity.

From the University to a Wider Public

In its largely inchoate state, sociology in the 1920s scarcely engaged the public mind in the United States. *Middletown* was, perhaps, the first work of academic sociology which came forward to meet the growing desire for the self-understanding of society. It left no lasting impact, other than the awareness that such efforts were possible and would be welcomed. *Recent Social Trends* and *The American Dilemma* refreshed the memory of *Middletown* and prepared the way for a more general reception of sociology.

Except, however, for the occasional trajectory of an isolated report across the field of public attention, sociology lived mainly within the walls of the university, emerging only to make observations and then returning to digest and assimilate the fruit of the outer world into an academic discipline. In the United States, it led a quiet, crudely respectable life, largely confined to the universities, where it was popular among students and disesteemed among the practitioners of the other academic disciplines. In Great Britain, it hardly found academic tolerance until the end of the Second World War, and its infiltration into the larger public occurred only much later. In Germany, too, in the universities, sociology—after the First World War and until the beginning of the Nazi regime, when it went into exile—led a fruitlessly solitary, usually neglected, sometimes dimly stormy career. The best fruit of German sociology ripened only when it was transplanted to America. The seed of sociological understanding could not grow unless it was fertilized by empirical research and by the diversification of its objects; the German universities offered little opportunity or motive for this kind of research. In France, its university establishment was still scant and scattered; it had indeed regressed somewhat after the death of Durkheim and his best protégés, but, insofar as it existed, it had its existence within the universities.

So, for many years, sociology lived its life, despised and scarcely noticed or tolerated by publicists, amateurs and professors of philosophy, economics, students of literature, ancient and modern, and of the great oriental civilizations. Social and civic reformers knew of it and valued it. Even when it obtained academic establishment, its lot was not a happy one. Its intellectual right to existence was often denigrated, even when it was allowed academic survival. Many had been the debates in Germany about the possible existence of sociology—debates which often ended in negative conclusions. Sociologists themselves used to feel the pressure of this contempt and they expended much energy in attempting to justify their existence— not by works, but by the demonstration that they had a proper place in the hierarchy of the sciences, that they were practitioners of a branch of learning which had an important subject-matter and a logically defensible claim to respect. They spent much time in the assertion of methodological principles which received neither reinforcement nor guidance from a matrix of experience.[1]

1. It was at this stage of sociological development that Henri Poincaré said that sociology was a science which produced a new methodology every year

Even in pragmatic America, the country of a legendarily untheoretical culture, sociology could not resist the feeling of obligation to prove itself by the argument that the fully assembled family of the sciences necessarily required the existence of sociology. No one was convinced by these arguments—the sociologists no more than the professors of other disciplines with a longer history and more glorious achievements, in the strength of which their own mediocre effort could seek protection. By an obdurate persistence, sociologists finally found their vocation in research. In Great Britain and France and then in the United States, utilitarian and humanitarian concerns with the poor had opened the way to empirical sociological inquiries. The roaring flood of immigrants to the large cities of the United States had early disturbed the Victorian calm. Humanitarian social workers were alarmed by squalor and delinquency; and sociologists had to share this alarm, to which they added intellectual curiosity and the pleasure of the discovery of particular things. At the end of the second decade of the twentieth century, the crisis in the relations between Negroes and whites—which had been uncovered and aggravated by the northward urban movement—gave sociologists a further extension of their domain. It also gave them a parochial self-confidence which muted their larger intellectual uncertainties. Within the universities of the United States—but much less in Europe—a sympathetic skepticism replaced disparagement among the neighboring disciplines of sociology: the traditional humanistic departments took abhorrent note of the sociological goings-on, and the real sciences showed a patient condescension.

In the 1930s, American sociology underwent a marked expansion at its periphery. Its population grew, and so did its output. It was helped by the Great Depression, by the influx of German and Austrian refugees, and by the coming of intellectual age of the first generation of the offspring of the Eastern European immigrants—mainly Jewish— of thirty years before. Research became more sophisticated through the development of a new statistical discipline, and through improvement in interviewing techniques under the influence of pschology, market research, and the emergent public opinion polling industry. Substance became a little more sophisticated under the impact of psychoanalysis, Marxism, and a greater knowledge of Emile Durkheim's and Max Weber's writings. These developments owed much to the influence of the Central European refugees and, above all, to indigenous developments in American intellectual life.

The Second World War gave sociologists the evidence they desired for their usefulness. Their employment, in many military and civilian

---

but never produced any results. Because there was so little substance, theory remained empty and directionless. Because there were no results, the methodological self-justifications of sociology remained empty and, quite naturally, possessed no persuasive powers.

roles, as sociologists, conferred on them the conviction of full-fledged intellectual citizenship which they had hitherto lacked. To this growth of a sense of belonging to the central domain of the intellectual cosmos, there corresponded a growing belief, among public officials, civic reformers, publicists, and the educated public at large, that sociology had something to contribute to the national life.

Sociology moved forward in the academic hierarchy. Its practitioners often took their place among the leading lights of their universities. The other disciplines became more deferential or at least suspended their derogation and replaced it by attentive distrust, furtive curiosity, or sheer resignation; sometimes they became positively eager to receive its collaboration. Political science became eager to learn from sociology. Anthropology, solid in its knowledge of facts and linked with the real sciences through physical anthropology, began to assimilate a little of it. Even the proud economists were willing to tolerate its right of existence and to allow that it might have something to say. A few American sociologists became known and respected throughout the academic world. A few sociologists indeed became public figures in America, although not on the same order as famous scientists, literary men, and publicists; and their fame has spread to Great Britain, Germany, and Italy—and even self-satisfied but discontented France has heard of them. Sociologists joined with publicists as commentators on the condition of their society.

Sociologists as criminologists, demographers, and as investigators of those below the "poverty line" had been known to governments before the Second World War. President Herbert Hoover had not been ashamed to lend his benediction to and rest his hopes on the President's Commission on Recent Social Trends, which was guided by sociologists—Howard Odum and William Ogburn—a political scientist—Charles Merriam—and an economist—Wesley Mitchell. In the Second World War, sociologists found a demand for their sociological services. They have never looked back. Governmental support for sociological research which is at best only marginally connected with policy, particularly for research done on a contractual basis for governmental departments on matters of direct concern to policy, has increased greatly. It is now accepted as normal that academic sociologists should do research which governments ostensibly regard as "relevant" to their various purposes. Sociologists are invited to be consultants and advisors to governmental bodies; their direct and tangible influence has probably not been great. Sociologists are employed by governmental commissions to study the causes of crime and delinquency, of the increase of violence, of the effects of pornography, of riots and conflicts between ethnic groups. Their discoveries probably have had little influence on the policies adopted by their patrons; they have, however, entered into public opinion and have helped form the image which Americans have of their own society. As the numbers of university and college graduates have increased, the numbers of those who have read sociology there, picked up its phrases and even its outlook, have increased. Sociology with its virtues and its vices has become part of public opinion.

The simple fact of the prominence of sociology in the United States would have made it, willy-nilly, a presence in Europe, with its preoccupation with American things. But the force comes not just—or even primarily—from the outside. Within each of the European countries, a wave of deeper opinion has carried sociology forward toward academic establishment and public attention and credence.

Thus, sociology—which had once been an earnest, uncouth subject, a discipline which flourished in the American Middle West, a dreary scholastic classificatory scheme of the German universities—invaded the atmosphere breathed by the most refined intellectuals of the United States and Europe. In Great Britain, in response to the demands of the young and the beliefs of their elders, it became established in the universities and in the organs of intellectual opinion. It became a proper subject for the intellectual reviews and the superior Sunday papers. It became an instrument for the criticism of governmental policies and for contemplating, appreciating, and criticizing the qualities of social classes. It became an organ for discovering one's fellow-man, more esteemed than the classics and the study of literature. It became a justification for bohemian emancipation. The improvised sociology of wartime increased attention to social affairs after the war, and—probably most important—the change in fundamental sensibility and moral dissatisfaction opened the way for the admission of sociology into the theater of public intellectual life.

In France, too, it became a vehicle of public intellectual discourse, and disillusioned and still believing Marxists sought in it solace for a lost faith or reinforcement for a persisting faith. The French government, with unprecedented beneficence, offers funds for sociological investigations—of a combination of concreteness, contemporaneity, and curiosity which had been almost unknown in France since Diderot went to the workshops to study the technology of his time and statisticians and reformers conducted surveys of the "dangerous classes." In Italy and Germany, sociology has already made its way in private and public administration and in its claims on the public purse and attention. Intellectual awakening and discontent, commercial enterprise, and youthful spirits have combined to explore critically the contemporary environment, studiously and enthusiastically. In Poland, in the most inhospitable environments, what was once a proper academic discipline has become the breath of life, the cord which binds to a fresh reality. It became a favored subject and even a recruiting ground for radicals. The claim of sociology to an ample place in the modern *Weltanschauung* has an especial force and poignancy in Poland. The grounds for a reception which has extended sociology from an academic subject into a part of the universal dialogue were more transparent in Poland than anywhere else in the world. In Poland after 1956, sociology—whatever the limitations of its intellectual achievement—became a critique of lifeless dogma; it was a declaration of the will to live, to live in conviviality with one's fellow man. Even in the dismal Soviet Union, a correspondingly dismal sociology has been fostered to survey beliefs and conduct. The more spirited sociology of the last decades of the Tsarist regime has not been allowed to come to life again, but in a more particular form and under an unacknowledged influence from American sociology the older tradition of empirical surveys has been allowed to revive.

The criticism of sociology from the outside has dwindled very markedly. There is still criticism. It is not what it once was—neither in volume, in acerbity of tone, nor in the objects criticized. Fifty years ago, sociology was belittled for not being scientific. It was scorned because it could not make its case for a place in a problematical classification of the sciences. It used to be accused of gathering "mere" facts without regard to their meaning. It used to be charged with only rediscovering what every intelligent man already knew— and doing so only with great effort and high costs. It was derided for its preoccupation with the trivial. It was ridiculed for its propensity to cumbersome terminology of sometimes obscure and sometimes too obvious reference. It was abhorrent to humanists, who were apprehensive that its "scientific" procedures would destroy what is essential in the human being, would falsify his nature and degrade him. Sociology used to be accused of abolishing individuality, of degrading man by an inhumane determinism. It was charged that it aspired to the erection of a Machiavellian regime of scientists. It was said to be an incubator of radicals. The poverty of its historical knowledge and imagination was underscored; its excessive and unthinking readiness to obliterate the uniqueness of historical events by cramping them in general categories was often bemoaned. Much of this criticism is now silent. Most of the criticism of sociology now comes from within the established sociology.

Somehow, for no good reason—since what was then valid in the criticisms still retains some validity—most of these accusations have evaporated. It is not that sociologists have confronted these criticisms and refuted them by reasoned argument, or that the actual development of sociology has rendered them completely nonsensical. They have simply faded away. The critics and those who accepted their criticisms were ordinarily not very knowledgeable about the then existing sociology or perceptive of its deficiencies; the silence of their heirs is no more reasonable than the volubility of the preceding generation of critics. Sociology, by the magnitude of its exertions and the grand scale of its academic establishment, by some of its achievements, by the groping towards its true vocation, and above all in consequence of the desire of the larger educated public to contemplate itself and its society in a presumably scientific way, has simply succeeded in imposing itself on its critics. Only a few echoes of the older arguments still resounded after the Second World War, and they became faint.

A rearguard action expresses apprehension about the literary inelegance of sociology and its imperialistic relationship with the treasuries of private foundations and governments. Sociologists are now accused—and often rightly so—of not presenting their thought in readily intelligible and grammatically correct language. But their intellectual right to do what they are doing, and the interest and value of their results, go, on the whole, unchallenged.

Most of these external complaints belong to the past. They did not help sociology to outgrow its faults when the faults were more obvious and the criticisms more harsh and numerous. The criticisms to which sociology and sociologists are subjected nowadays are rather different from the older criticisms. They are criticisms of the failures of sociology in the very things in which it was successful. Sociologists are now criticized for having claimed too much for the intellectual and practical value of their investigations, theories, and proposals for policy when they served as consultants of governments and as contributors to the making of policy. The criticism is directed not against a fledgling and disregarded academic or amateur discipline but against one which is financially well looked after and to which weighty public responsibilities have been given. The criticisms which are leveled against sociology are criticisms of a worldly success which is not quite matched by intellectual accomplishment.

Intellectual Discipline and Moral Sentiment

Sociology has, then, withstood the contumely of its traditional academic critics. It has outlived them and come to enjoy the acceptance of a new generation. How has sociology, after all the sterile travail of its deliberate search for citizenship in the intellectual community, and despite its own present conflicts, uncertainties, and imperfections, succeeded in gaining its now nearly unchallenged reception?

The first, most obvious, and most rational of the explanations is the actual improvement of sociology. Sociology has progressed, and not just in its institutional prominence and financial prosperity. It has, in fact, made some intellectual progress. Even one whom present-day sociology often appalls by naiveté and crudity cannot disregard the evidence of intellectual improvement. Understanding is now richer in its perception of possibilities and in its estimates of why one rather than another is realized. The accumulation of systematic inquiries on particular phenomena—such, for example, as the structure of the lower-class family in Western industrial societies—and the widened perspective of possibilities which a growing intellectual amity with history and anthropology has engendered, have made for more subtlety in interpretation. This age of the triviality and evasions of the "mass media" is also the age of a greater desire to know unpleasant things about one's own society; many reasonable persons have become suspicious of high-flown allegations of motives. Psychoanalysis has certainly contributed to this. The increased distrust of authority makes for an eagerness for disclosures that things are different from what self-interested authorities might allege them to be; sociologists share in this culture of distrust.

Sociology has increased its sophistication in observation and in the analysis of observation. Its ties with the more advanced disciplines of mathematics and statistics have become more intimate. It has, furthermore, come out of the dull isolation which it once thought it needed for its self-respect and mingled with the subject-matters of other fields, with the weighty topics of politics, science, and religion.

Sometimes hand-in-hand with this more refined and more realistic understanding and this more complete technology, sometimes moving at its own self-determined pace, theoretical reflection has also developed. Whereas half a century ago, there was a scatter of insightful surmises and the implicit standpoint of the sociological outlook, there is now a constant effort to bring these scattered estimates and hypotheses into a reasoned relationship with each other and to articulate the underlying premises of this coherence. Many sociologists do not like the theory which has been put forward with this intention, and there is much criticism of its detailed formulations. Much of the criticism is, however, permeated by the theoretical outlook which it disavows in detail.

These are some of the intellectual grounds for the reception of sociology. There are others, some less admirable, some more so. The popularity of sociology as an undergraduate subject in many American, French, British, and German universities must in part be a function of the very modest demands made on intelligence and diligence by much of the pedagogy of sociology. This, in turn, has both increased the professional sociological population and expanded the public which has some familiarity with the words, ideas, and famous names of sociology. For another—a smaller, but intellectually not insignificant—part of the youth of America and of Europe, sociology is a substitute for Marxism or a complement to it. Civil servants, politicians and businessmen, because of fantasies of scientific omnipotence, or because of their excessive affluence, or because of a humble desire to understand better the situation in which decisions are made and actions taken, have also encouraged the development of sociology. They have invoked its aid and counsel, supported its inquiries, and endowed its study.

Sociology has, in short, been accepted, in varying degrees and ways, throughout the educated world. I myself think that this recent reception of sociology is a historically unique phenomenon which corresponds to a great movement, and even progress, of the human race. Sociology has found its reception because it is an organ of the experience of a broader life, a life which reaches out towards other human beings. It is one major manifestation of the current of life, in a society in which the sense of affinity of human beings with each other has passed, very fragmentarily, from the thoughts of philosophers into actual existence. Sociology has arrived by becoming in some respects, an organ of the ties which characterize the most recent phase of modern society. Sociology has come into its present estate partly because of its own development has borne a rough correspondence to the development of the consciousness of the Western part of mankind in its moral movement.

The latest phase of modern society—called, by its derogators, "mass society"—has some dreadful features in which sociology shares. It contains an aspiration toward a scientistic technocracy, and sociology shares in this. The vulgarity of "mass society" is more rampantly visible than in the more hierarchical societies of the past; and sociology shares in this vulgarity. "Mass society" has been profoundly ravaged by the communistic, fascist, and national socialist ideologies, and their fellow-travelers; sociology has certainly shared to some extent in these ideologies. Sometimes it has even gloried in this alienation and contributed to it.

Nonetheless, this is far from the whole story. Modern society is, despite all its conflicts and disorders, more of a consensual society than its predecessors were. It is also a society in which personal attachments, for better or for worse, play a greater part than in most societies in the past, one in which the individual person is appreciated, in which there is a concern for his well-being—not just in a veterinary sense but as a moral personality. The humanitarianism of the present age, which extends beyond the boundaries of national societies, the growing acknowledgment as well as demand for the moral equality of races, the welfare policies and dreams of states, the very desire to please, the greater concern for the claims of the living than for the claims of the dead—all of these features, wise and silly, of contemporary Western, and, increasingly, of the modern sector of non-Western, societies disclose a concern with the happiness of the individual human being and an appreciation, however dim and muddled and at times perverse, of the moral dignity of his interior life. The beliefs in the solubility of all social problems and in the possibility of the elimination of all the disorders of the spirit which accompany this concern are also integral parts of this general outlook. Essential to it all is the belief that a judicious combination of organization, benevolent intentions, and scientific knowledge, including the knowledge gained by sociological study, is the right path to earthly redemption.

There are also very contrary tendencies in contemporary societies. There is a widespread cultivation of an overpowering preoccupation with the self. There is a widespread antinomianism and denial of the legitimacy of authority. There is a wanton disregard of the achievements and counsels of the past. There is much frivolity and an attendant sacrilegious attitude towards *la vie sérieuse*. Sociology in its development runs closely parallel both to this deep and broad flow of the river of modern life and to its deeply destructive countercurrents.

From a distant and almost police-like concern with the "condition of the poor," from a concern with numbers as clues to national wealth and power, from a desire to "unmask" and discredit the hopes and fantasies of the human race, sociology has advanced to a fundamental orientation which was incipiently present in its classics and is now tentatively elaborated in a strong current of sociological theory. This orientation appreciates not just the animality or mechanical properties of man, but his cognitive, moral, and appreciative humanity as well. This has corresponded to developments, in these categories, throughout the morally and intellectually sensitive sections of the human race. Sociology is a part of this growth in humanity. Yet alongside of these categories which are integrated into a belief in the scientific potentialities of sociology, there is also a dialectically contrary anticipation that when sociology becomes scientific it will be exactly applicable to the eradication of the afflictions of humanity.

These orientations are manifested both in the technique of sociology and in its theoretical orientation. The popularity of the interview is not simply a product of scientific necessity. It is not merely a technique of research; it is also an act of human conviviality and consensus. In both of these, there is an appreciation of the profound fellowship of human beings—what, long ago, Franklin Giddings, perhaps without quite knowing all he was talking about, called the "consciousness of kind." The basic technique of sociological research—the interview—despite all its distortions and corruptions in market research and public opinion polls, is one of the ways in which this fellowship is expressed. The books which come forth from this kind of research are collaborative in a sense much more important than that of the widely practiced team-research; they are collaborations of the investigator and those he studies. The elaboration of the theory of action spins out the threads of conviviality and consensus. It accepts the human being as an object of sociological study through an act of communion between object and subject. This act of communion is acknowledged through the promulgation of categories of person, society, and culture, which are as applicable to the analyst as to the object analyzed, as applicable to the act of analysis as to the actions analyzed.

Sociology also requires detachment; its human subjects must be seen from the "outside" as well as from the "inside." The detachment which is indispensable for observation and analytical judgment is capable of extension to the point where it overcomes fellow-feeling. Fellow-feeling is capable of extension to the point where it overcomes detachment. A third component is perspective, which sets observations into a wider setting. Here too fellow-feeling and detachment are called for, and the deficiencies or excesses of either or both can deform perspective. There is always a danger of leaning too much, or even of falling, in one direction or the other.

What I have been saying here is that sociology is a part of modern society. It has grown up with the growth of the self-consciousness of modern society. It is a more acute form of the interest of modern men—and women—in themselves and in the society and the epoch in which they live. Sociology is a refinement of a curiosity which is much braoder than sociology; sociology is simply its more acute form.

Sociology may be understood, in some respects, sociologically. It must also be seen as a cognitive or intellectual undertaking and it is to be assessed accordingly; that is in fact just what its practitioners have done as soon as they became self-conscious about having been sociological M. Jourdains. This entailed assessing what they were doing and saying, according to the most valid criteria known to them, namely, the criteria applied to works which purported to be scientific.

Sociology as it stands today is the confluence of a variety of traditions, intellectual, moral, and political. It stems from the empirical inventory first developed in Great Britain from the seventeenth to the nineteenth centuries. It stems from German idealism, from French positivism, from British utilitarianism, and from the scientism contained in the two latter outlooks. It would not have been possible without the pedantic, systematizing pedagogy of the German university and the open, adventurous helter-skelter of the American university. It could not exist without the humanitarianism of modern society, without the fundamental moral revolution which asserted that in some indefinable way all human beings possess a quality which entitles them to the respect and consideration of their fellows. It could not have come into existence without those empirical inquiries which so often seemed to lead nowhere, and which nonetheless played a great part in sharpening our awareness of social reality, particularly of parts of society usually quite unknown to the educated classes. It was certainly aided by the growing belief of rulers that they would benefit in their exercise of authority by the use of sociology.

The ungainly ill-assortedness of sociology and its academic isolation were, in a sense, preconditions of its present condition. The former gave it a variety of experience and such an anomalous heterogeneity that a desire for unity was generated. The latter placed it in the stream of tradition in which the unity of a discipline was a prized object of striving. The existence within a single department of persons of different intellectual interests resulted in a sense of obligation to become a unitary subject; the mutual influences of scholars with diverse substantive interests gave rise to similar desires.

In Germany, it was only in the schematic work of Max Weber that this unifying intention was even partially successful. It was as successful as it was in his case because it arose from an intellectual experience of very varied empirical and historical research, and was guided by a conviction that there were elements common to the heterogeneous subject-matters which could be called sociological. He had, however, no immediate impact and his task has not yet been wholly fulfilled. Nonetheless, there does now exist a sociological orientation which is pervasive throughout the whole field. It is not a systematic theory, although such a theory does exist. It is rather a proto-system of insights, ambiguously phrased propositions, hard-won and often painfully elaborated categories, and a sensibility. It is a body of "tacit knowledge." The explicit ratiocinative attainment up to the present moment, important though it is, is as nothing compared to this knowledge. The actual formulations, employing different idioms, fall short of the insight and understanding which enter into them.

The shaping of this orientation is the major achievement of sociology thus far. Its scientifically established general truths are at best very few, and they are not at the center of sociological thought. The achievements of sociology in concrete descriptive research are, likewise, more important for the general orientation which they exemplify in increasingly nuanced form than the particular details which convey them and which are often only of transient interest.

The general orientation is not the goal of sociology; but it is its most important product and precondition. Whatever the present achievements and defects of sociology, much is owed to its academic establishment. Teaching and training have imposed discipline on it; at the same time, the expansion of academic provision has increased the numbers of its practitioners beyond the intellectual level of the subject. It has not yet become rigorous and systematic enough to be codifiable; it has still to be assimilated rather than learned. The capacity to assimilate an unarticulated outlook is probably less common and less widely distributed in society than the capacity to learn a codified discipline. This results in slovenly teaching and learning and too much room is left open for arbitrariness. Slovenliness permits an easier entry of political and other prejudice. The fact however that sociology is now carried on in universities, with their tradition of trying to keeping political values and objectives apart from the criteria of scientific truth, imposes a discipline on sociology which it might otherwise escape. Indeed, even being in a university is not a guarantee against the danger of mixing up these two realms, a danger arising from and aided by the importance of the "tacit component" in sociological knowledge.

Sociology across the Disciplines

Sociology and Science

Sociology was born in the scientific age, but it has not been wholly a creation of the scientific spirit. The problems of sociology are old problems; at least the fundamental problems are older than the scientific age. They were first perceived and promulgated without a thought of being scientific in the contemporary sense of the word. The fundamental problems of the conditions of the establishment, maintenance, and mutation of social order, of the conditions of the effectiveness of authority, of the assimilation of the individual organism into culture and collectivity, are all much older than the modern scientific outlook. These, and others like them, have remained the proper problems of sociology into the scientific age. Furthermore, the efforts to elicit general principles or laws from particular observations and concrete experience, and to do so within an intellectual tradition, are, of course, older than scientific research as we now understand it.

Nonetheless, sociology has been tremendously influenced, to its advantage and disadvantage, by the model formed by a reflection of the natural sciences. The advantages it has gained from the scientific environment in modern culture in general, and its proximity to scientific work in the universities in particular, have been tremendous. From science, it has learned the virtue of self-discipline in observation and analysis. It has learned to criticize the quality of its observations. It has learned to try to control and order its observation—not only the specific techniques but, even more, the ideal of detached, dispassionate observation. It has learned to be painstaking in defining and delineating the objects of its inquiries; it has learned the advantages of specifying the categories of events which it would investigate and to stabilize the procedures of investigation. It has learned the fruitfulness of disciplined, routinized assessment of the data gathered through modes of observation controlled by rules. The life of sociology in the setting of an academic community has caused sociologists to attempt to be somewhat more responsible about the ways in which they proceed. But even if this setting had not had such an effect, the ubiquitous visibility of scientific standards would have made for such pressure.

From science, sociology has acquired the ideal of a theory intimately, dialectically, and systematically related to its observations. These are all important acquisitions; and, to the extent that sociology has moved forward it has done so by taking to heart the standards learned and adapted from the prevailing sciences.

Insofar as a science is a moving and yet coherent body of empirically supported propositions, which enjoy their validity within a particular and developing theoretical framework and which sustain that framework, sociology is certainly not a science today. The empirically more or less verified propositions at a level of low particularity are many; as they rise toward generality, they become fewer—not because the structure of any science requires it, but because of the deficient clarity and coherence of the analytical scheme which explicitly or implicitly guides these inquiries, and because the techniques of research have still not been sufficiently well adapted to the observation of more abstractly formulated variables.

Nor, for that matter, has whatever theory exists become sufficiently articulated and explicit. The gap between general theory and actual observation is still considerable, although the sociological outlook which inheres in the theory runs beyond the boundaries of the explicit theoretical formulation and has entered increasingly into research activity. The sociological outlook, however, is at least as ambiguous as the existing theory; and the task of establishing a firm correspondence of ''index-terms'' and ''concept-terms'' has still some considerable distance to go before it is resolved.

Sociology has begun to approximate the condition of science with respect to its observational and ''processing'' procedures, although—even on the level of particularity—results are too often indeterminate; artifacts produced by the technique of observation become the objects of idolatry. Pride in technical rigor often displaces reflection about the substance of the subjects studied. It is in its relations to theory that sociological research is least satisfactory scientifically. Sociological theory itself does not perform the functions of a scientific theory, either in the sense of guiding research by precise direction or in the sense of itself precisely incorporating the most significant results of research. This applies equally to general theory and to those theories of ''middle principles'' which some of the critics of general sociological theory have suggested as the best way toward science.

Despite these critical remarks, it must nonetheless be acknowledged that sociology has become more scientific over the years, and in a way which not only gratifies a scientistic idol, but which represents a genuine intellectual advance. Every decade of the past half-century has seen some work which is an improvement over what has gone before. Observations are better made; new and better techniques of observation are devised and applied; particular inquiries are more dominated by the sociological outlook which is being fostered by theoretical reflection.

Continuity too has increased, although the efforts to improve observations result in a situation in which it is difficult to fit more refined measures made at a later date with cruder ones made at an earlier date. Sociology has become increasingly a collective enterprise. I refer not to the fact of organized team-research, but to the sense in which sociologists, theorists as much as investigators of particular problems, have come to regard themselves as members of a community, engaged in a common effort over an unending span of time. The idea of an all-sufficient "system of sociology" created by one sociologist to last forever and to be incapable of change has passed away. No sociologist nowadays believes that he starts from scratch or that his work is the final word on the subject he treats. There are *virtuosi*, but—at least, in principle—they accept their place in the tradition of their subject. Their achievement lies in deepening its interpretation, in extending it, in fortifying it—but not through any entirely disjunctive act of creation. This sense of responsibility to the future of a subject which derives from its past is a quality which brings sociology closer to science than it was in its period of isolated individual achievement when there were many starts—some false, some true, but most of which ran off into nothingness. Cumulativeness of a self-revising, self-deepening sort is essential to science; and this has now become characteristic of sociology.

This increased cumulativeness is partly a result of the location of sociology's center in academic institutions, which laid emphasis on and which contributed to disciplined continuity. Through its academic establishment sociology is forced to be more continuous since its tradition becomes somewhat more focused in the syllabus of the courses of sociological study and through the steady transmission of knowledge from teacher to student. The traditions of sociology have also become less disjunctively heterogeneous than they used to be. Sociology is at once more catholic and less eclectic than in the past. There is by no means a complete consensus among the most creative workers in the field and their most productive followers; but the formation of the loose consensus necessary to constitute a scientific community has been under way for some time and it has continued to move despite intermittent regressions.

There is probably nothing in the nature of the subject-matter of sociology that would prevent it from becoming more scientific than it is now. The assertion that the meaningful or subjective aspects of social actions and the institutions of which they are parts render precise observation and generalization inherently impossible has not been demonstrated. The very fact that sociology has become somewhat more precise and more cumulative in the past half-century is evidence that the subject-matter does permit an increase in its scientific features. What has been achieved in the past half-century renders it reasonable to think that in the next half-century the scientific features of sociology will become more prominent. Whether they will also become more central is another matter.

Let us assume that, in the course of time, sociology does succeed in formulating and demonstrating laws of universal validity—the like of which it does not know at present. Would this place sociology among the natural sciences and cut off any links which it has with the humanistic disciplines? On the contrary, it would show that the conventional distinction between scientific and humanistic disciplines has been ill-conceived. The discernment of universal regularities has grown much farther in linguistics than in sociology. Does this make linguistics less humanistic than sociology? Being humanistic is a property of the nature of the subject-matter and of the attitude of those who study it. Being scientific is a property of the stability and orderliness of observations, the rigor of analysis of the data of observation and of the logical structure of the propositional system into which the results of the analysis are cast. Sociology could never become a natural science like physics or astronomy, even if its logical structure should become indistinguishable from that of physics or astronomy. The nature of the basic categories of action precludes the complete identification of the two kinds of discipline though it does not stand in the way of an identity of logical structure or even, conceivably, an approximately equal measure of reliability of demonstration.

In its purely cognitive respects, sociology could, in principle, be a science like any other science. Sociology is not, however an exclusively cognitive undertaking. It is also a moral relationship between the human beings studied and the student of the human beings studied. This is easily evident in the situation of the field-worker who must establish a relationship of trust with his interviewees and informants, who must call forth sentiments like friendship and affection in them and in himself. Naturally, a considerable element of detachment too must be present; otherwise the cognitive interest would be suppressed by the inevitable conviviality. Quite apart from the dangers of impeding or deforming the acquisition of knowledge or the impropriety of deception and manipulation, there are other problems which are raised by this relationship. Sociologists have not yet resolved them; they have scarcely begun to consider them. They must do so.

The treatment of persons long dead through historical research would appear to avoid the difficulties of dealing with the living. The treatment of the recently dead certainly does not avoid the problems of the moral obligations of sociologists to those human beings whom they study. Nor does the theoretical treatment of classes of anonymous individuals avoid them. These variations make the problems more complicated; they do not dissolve them. The sociologist is still dealing with human beings with a moral dignity given by their constitution and acknowledged by the theory which makes their understanding possible. The sociologist's work is part of society, not only through its dependence on certain cultural and institutional preconditions but also through the relationship of the sociologist to those whom he studies and through the consequences which his knowledge, once promulgated, might have.

I am not sure what bearing this moral feature of sociological theory has on its status in the intellectual cosmos. It does not prevent the growth of sociology into a scientific theory. It cannot prevent the exploitation of the knowledge presented by sociological theory for the manipulation of human action through the control of the situation of the actors—any more than the status of electronics or pharmacology as sciences can prevent their exploitation for the destruction of privacy and the manipulation of conduct.

Sociology and the Humanistic Study of Man   *which may be equally scientific*

In exerting themselves to increase the persuasiveness of their works by enhancing their accuracy of observation and analysis, sociologists accepted that this end of greater truthfulness and hence persuasiveness could be best achieved by their work becoming scientific like the natural sciences, as they understood them. Efforts to establish the dignity of social sciences—and then sociology—as a science like physics or astronomy had been underway since the seventeenth century. In the nineteenth century the acquisition of a name for some of the diverse activities, which, looking backwards, are now seen as adumbrations of sociology, gave a greater proto-disciplinary self-consciousness to the cultivators of these diverse subjects. Throughout the nineteenth century, sociologists were concerned to become scientific and thus to attain a degree of intellectual dignity which they thought they must possess.

To attain this end, sociologists were placed under constraints. They had distinguished themselves from other intellectual activities which were not scientific in the sense in which they wished to be. Those disciplines which seemed to them to be "unscientific," i.e., to depend on individual judgment, to be "subjective," had to be avoided. The procedures used by these disciplines had to be discarded and new and better ones adopted—or at least, espoused. The subject-matters of these other "unscientific" disciplines had to be avoided too, partly because the scientific techniques which sociologists were developing apparently could not be applied in them. It was also necessary to eschew attendance to those subject-matters because that would impair the capacity of sociology to attain the desired end. These other disciplines—philology and history—had already become established as recognized categories of intellectual activity; those who wished to establish sociology would have declared their superfluity if they undertook to cultivate these same subject-matters sociologically. It would furthermore have been difficult to match these already existent disciplines by saying something new about their subject-matters and by doing so by methods which would be as rigorous as those already being applied in these fields.

As a result of these not always deliberate considerations regarding procedure and subject-matter, sociology found itself dealing with a subject-matter which would be important in itself, which could be treated scientifically, and which was not already being treated in that way. This was particularly the case in the United States, where the needs of economy in the use of resources in universities and colleges meant that sociology had to be distinctive if it was to be accepted as an academic subject with a wide range of subjects taught and investigated. The situation was less pressing in France and in Germany, where the practitioners of sociology, which was only slightly established or not established at all as an academic subject, did not have to draw such a sharply delineated boundary around themselves. Furthermore, at least in Germany, the wide meaning of *Wissenschaft* permitted a greater catholicity in the choice of procedures and hence of subject-matters. As a result, sociology in France, at least during the lifetime of Durkheim, was enabled to attract gifted young scholars who were attempting to enter careers in other fields since there were very few opportunities for appointment as teachers of sociology. In Germany, a similar situation obtained; sociologists there could scarcely be professional academic sociologists. They were, if academic, practitioners of other disciplines; they could not be sociologists holding academic appointments to teach and do research in that field.

This had very momentous consequences for the future of sociology. Although some of the greatest sociologists were Europeans, American sociologists were the only ones who lived in a safe academic situation. They were therefore subject to a combination of motives and conditions which forced them to confine themselves to particular and distinctive subject-matters while pursuing the ideal of becoming more scientific. In consequence of this, sociology had to distinguish itself from the humanistic disciplines.

The relations between sociologists and those who have taken responsibility for the scholarly custody of man's past and his achievements in symbolic objectivations have, consequently, been neither fruitful, amicable, nor reasonable. Mutual distrust, derogation, and avoidance have been the common traits of the relationship. Defensive ignorance has played a larger part in aggravating this relationship than awareness of each other's procedures and objects. A genuine desire to understand the other side has been rare. The situation has been at its worst in the United States not only for the reasons already given which account for the attitudes of the sociologists but also because, until quite recently, it was only there that sociology was prominent enough to be noticed by the practitioners of the humanistic disciplines. In Europe, for the most part, the mention of sociology usually called forth a response of unsympathetic blankness. But there, sociologists also more often had the traditional humanistic education, and this made them a little more tolerable. In America, sociologists have wished to see themselves as scientists—which means being tough-minded, "objective," and skeptical of "intuition" with its overtones of effeminacy and mysticism. Sociologists have usually been unsympathetic with existing religious institutions, and they have not had much sympathy with religious belief. They have usually been poorly educated in history. The techniques of fieldwork and the demand for reliable quantitative information have turned sociologists away from historical studies. The fact that history dealt with individuals and, even worse, with rulers, while sociology studied the humble masses also created a distance between sociology and history. The strict training of historians to care above all for specific and particular details and their avoidance of generalizations made them averse to the generalizing disposition, however repressed, of sociologists. Sociologists have generally not been "bookish." This was especially true of the years between about 1920 and 1950. The literature of sociology as it increased in volume made the reading of works other than sociological ones more and more difficult, especially if a sociologist believed that he must "keep up with the literature." There would be little time to appreciate the objects of humanistic study if one wished to be a scientific sociologist.

An important current of sociological opinion has been "progressive," and has therefore, quite apart from methodological observations, looked upon the past as erroneous, superstitious, and, in any case, dead. Sociologists have not been much interested in traditions except in a negative way, with an emphasis on their breakdown; whereas traditions are very much of the stock-in-trade of the humanistic disciplines. The "progressive" attitude of sociology toward the past has been reinforced by the increased prominence of sample surveys of the opinions and activities of living persons as a major sociological activity. Humanistic scholarship has, up until quite recently, studiously avoided the contemporary. Sociologists have recognized the relevance of statistical procedures, which humanistic scholars associated with science and which only a few humanistic scholars had applied in their research. Sociologists have thought of the humanists as antiquarians, moralists, or aesthetes, in contrast with their own unsentimental, scientific, evaluatively neutral selves. To these more intellectual differences, sociologists have added a few others. They were uncouth in their literary style at a time when the humanistic disciplines had not yet sunk to the same level of jargon and vague abstraction; this difference is now being eradicated, jargon and vague abstraction having made great advances in the humanities. Then, too, feeling scientifically inferior, many sociologists were aggressive against disciplines which they regarded as even more vulnerable than their own to the criticism of being insufficiently scientific. Some of the animus of sociologists against the humanistic academic disciplines has arisen from the institutional necessities of sociology at a particular stage of its career.

The academic humanists have been not any better from their side. For a long time, they were eager to see sociology, in its pride and its apparent worldly success, cast down in humiliation. The very indifference, if not animosity, of sociologists against the past and its works and against historical study, the sociologists' ignorance of literary and artistic achievements with which the academic humanists dealt, were an affront to the dignity of their disciplines. Humanists lived in an atmosphere of dusty books and footnotes citing recondite monographs and forgotten minor authors; many sociologists seldom read books published more than a few years earlier. Books were not so often regarded by them as part of the apparatus of their science, and humanists exaggerated this and felt aggrieved about it. Besides, sociology, despite all its imperfections—which have been real enough—prospered in the most obvious ways. Its population increased, and its wealth even more, while the humanistic disciplines were yielding in prominence and honor. The humanistic departments of the universities saw an increasing proportion of students turn toward the natural sciences and the social sciences. Departments of sociology attracted many students who, in the past, would have concentrated their academic attention on English literature and history. Sociology became a major beneficiary of the reallocation of university funds, while the humanistic departments suffered a measure of attrition. Funds from private foundations and from governments went in great sums to the social sciences, while the humanistic disciplines were relatively neglected. Even though humanistic research is not as costly as scientific research—including research in the social sciences—still, the indulgence enjoyed by sociology has made it a plausible object for resentment, especially when there appeared to be so many substantive grounds for denying the legitimacy of its intellectual claims and its financial enjoyments.

It cannot be said that this episode of the academic history of the twentieth century has been to the credit of anyone. The acrimony and vanity of the discussion have obscured the genuine affinities and differences of these two domains of intellectual work. There are genuinely significant differences in the activities of sociologists and humanistic scholars. There will continue to be real differences: the techniques of humanistic research—such as paleography, the production of critical editions of literary texts, the establishment of the authenticity of manuscripts, the dating of paintings by chemical analysis and of archaeological artefacts by the use of radioactive carbon, the decipherment of hitherto unknown scripts, archaeological excavation, the study of inscriptions and coins, the establishment of detailed biographical accounts of individuals—will probably never take a place among the techniques of sociology.

Sociology too is concerned with the establishment of the validity of observations, but the immediate objects observed have been rather different. Sociology in its latest phase—ever since it became convinced that it would have to occupy itself with primary observation—has been concerned with the actions and beliefs of living persons. The humanistic disciplines have drawn their objects from the whole range of human history and even pre-history. Let us omit, for the moment, the far greater attention of the humanistic disciplines to the symbolic objectivations of man's intellectual and expressive powers, which makes it more feasible to extend backward the span of historical interest. Certain technical preoccupations of the humanistic studies correspond to their substantive preoccupation with the concrete individualities of persons or works and with actions and beliefs in the past.

This difference is, to some extent, a product of a historical accident. The conditions which gave rise to sociology were conditions in which the existence of the "nameless masses" had been discovered; the humanistic disciplines arose out of a stream of traditions which included the study of particular texts, the practice of hagiography, the celebration of greatness, and the exhumation of past things. Humanistic biography has largely concentrated on the understanding of the thematic coherence and the inner diversity of a unique career and a unique personality. Sociology has been less concerned with the distinctiveness of the structure of the individual's life; the "life-history" is not so much used by sociologists as it once was, and, when it has been used, the individual's history has been used illustratively.

This is one aspect of the difference between the two fields; it is not a historical accident but is constitutional to sociology. Sociology has been concerned with classes of individuals and not with particular individuals. Therein lies one major difference. Sociology has an abstractness of interest, a determination to see particular events as instances of classes of events, or as variants or composites of classes, or as subclasses. Sociologists have traditionally conducted case studies; but they have done so to illustrate the operation of more general classes of variables. They have assembled many case studies, in each of which justice is done to individual uniqueness; but they do so with the intention of transcending uniqueness and of establishing the distribution of individual variations and the connections between the several distributions.[2]

There is nothing in the constitution of sociology which would prohibit the writing of a biography of a person, living or dead; and, if the sociologist were literarily talented, scholarly, and imaginative, he could write a book which would be much like a good biography. Insofar, however, as he remained a sociologist, he might well adduce some general propositions to explain particular or recurrent events in the life of the subject, or to cite particular events or sequences of events as illustrative of general propositions. Indeed, this tendency would most likely dominate the work as a whole. Perhaps it would detract from the interest of the biography.

The fundamental disposition of an intelligent and sympathetic sociological biographer would necessarily approximate, in practice, the outlook which underlies and arises from the sociological theory of action. It would resemble too the disposition of the intelligent and sympathetic nonsociological biographer, except that the former would be somewhat more articulately sensitive to factors in the social situation of the subject. Both of them would have to be guided by an outlook common to both of them—assuming, of course, that they were both realistically sympathetic and imaginative. The fact that the biographer is interested in a particular man—one with a name which enjoys some fame and who is often a marked, although always imperfect, individuality—does not represent any fundamental departure form the paths of sociology. Individuality, creativity, force of

2. This distinction should not be regarded as one which makes a profound disjunction between sociology and the humanistic disciplines. Humanistic scholars treat general categories, such as landscape paintings or allegories or naturalistic novels or epic poems. Furthermore, the enunciation of a judgment with respect to a particular work of literature or art involves—in different ways—the use of general categories and standards, and their application, through judgment, to particular instances. It is very similar to sociological analysis in this regard. Moreover, the effort of sociology progressively to translate its orientation into an articulate theory, and its occasionally and relatively greater self-consciousness in the deployment of its general categories, does not distinguish it from one of the greatest fields of humanistic achievement, namely, linguistics. Its rhythmic movement into and away from abstraction is not a criterion which separates it from philosophy, which is far more self-containedly abstract and less frequently in contact with the particular and the concrete.

character are just as much legitimate themes and problems of sociological inquiry as they are of humanistic study—even if sociology does not usually express the same intensity of interest in biographical particularity.

Sociology does not often, however, take upon itself the description and explanation of the individuality of one particular human being or the task of giving a causal explanation of his creative achievement. The description and causal explanation of the action and creation of a particular individual are less often the concern—and are, therefore, less likely to be the successful achievement—of the sociologist.[3]

Much more important, sociology does not share the deeply rooted tradition of the appreciation and contemplation of greatness of an individual life or of created works of art or literature or thought which dominates the humanistic disciplines. This is a tradition which survives in great strength, even though humanistic research frequently falls far short of this standard, as in much literary-historical scholarship, or it goes off into the quite other direction of scientific generalization, as in contemporary linguistics.

Insofar as sociology has been interested in "the social problem," i.e., the poor, the outcasts, and the failures and in the discrepancies between asseveration of the ideal and actual performance, it has had rather a different bent from humanistic studies. These have often dwelt on great accomplishments and famous persons and works. Yet there is really no inherent incompatibility between sociology and humanistic studies in this respect. There is nothing in sociology aside from certain contingent traditions which have caused it to turn in this direction. And for their part, the humanistic studies have long had a great tradition of embittered contemplation of the failures of rulers and of the vanity and wantonness of the great of the earth. The introduction of psychoanalysis into biographical studies introduced a new mode of breaking the facade of dignity; the introduction of Marxism had a similar effect. "Psychohistory" has helped to close this particular gap between humanistic studies and sociology with uncertain benefit.

Much more important in closing the gap and a much weightier achievement has been the development of sociological history on the part of historians. The "social history" which was practiced by J. H.

3. Insofar as it has been their concern, sociologists have not been any more successful than humanists—indeed, rather less so. General sociological categories are still too nebulous and unstable, their explanatory powers are still too indeterminate, for this task to be carried out better by a sociologist than by a very superior biographer who is not a sociologist but who has a sure touch. Even if our categories and hypotheses were better than they are, the task of passing from general categories and propositions to the description and explanation of a particular individual event or to an individual constellation of events would still require an act of practiced judgment, which a good theoretical orientation can support but cannot supply or compel.

Green and Karl Lamprecht did not have much impact on historical studies. The work of Marc Bloch and Lucien Febvre did. The great French historians improvised the sociological component of their historical research. Others in Great Britain and the United States have more deliberately drawn upon sociological studies of the family and of social stratification. Historians of occidental antiquity, particularly Professor Arnaldo Momigliano, and of China and Japan have likewise drawn upon sociology and above all on the writings of Max Weber. The separation of historical studies from sociology has been much narrowed. The initiative has been taken primarily by the historians, although the activities of a few sociologists and anthropologists must not be disregarded.

There was a time, not so many decades ago, when the differences between sociological and historical studies seemed ineradicable. Serious historians with their reverence for meticulous documentation and their abstention—at least in principle—from any generalizations seemed insuperably separated from sociologists. The quantitative treatment of the details of contemporary life and the general categories of the sociologists seemed to be utterly antithetical to whatever serious historians did or wished to do.

This separation was supported by the methodological distinction between "nomothetic" and "ideographic" disciplines, between those disciplines which aim at generalizations and those which aim at the reconstruction of temporally and structurally unique events. Even at the height of its power, there were many qualifications introduced into this distinction which was in principle impermeable. When it turned out the sociologists were also historians in the sense that they dealt with contemporary society with the aid of general categories of uncertain scope of generality, one of the barriers was dismantled. Historians too found that some of their sources permitted more or less the same kinds of quantitative treatment of actions or events as those used by sociologists to study contemporary actions of a similar kind. Perhaps even more important was the subtle change in the attitude of historians. A sociological sensibility developed among them. Their perspective changed; they became more imaginative about similarities and differences among epochs and among societies. The writings of Max Weber were of some effectiveness in this change but they were so because they were sought out. They were sought out because sensibility and imagination had changed. This change owes something to the existence of sociology, but it would not have occurred without an expansion of sociological sensibility to the interplay of individuals and to the larger formations of states, cities, strata, and institutions. Sociology itself has been borne along by this sensibility.

The separation of the humanistic disciplines from sociology was and remains a result of their specialization respectively on culture and on social structure and society. Of course such a distinction is analytically reasonable. It is also tenable in practice: it is possible to concentrate on an intellectual or artistic or philosophical work without regard to its reference to society or the social conditions under which it was created or the social conditions of its propagation or its effect on society. It is also possible to concentrate the attention on some social institution to the disregard of its cultural content. In fact, however, social institutions or even elementary social relationships cannot be understood or even described without considering the norms or rules—which are matters of belief—which enter into them both ideally and in practice.

Sociologists have on the whole held to their part of the tacit bargain. Most of them abstained from dealing with culture to the extent that that was at all possible; they certainly refrained from dealing with elaborate beliefs and with works of artistic and literary expression, as well as with works of scientific and scholarly character. Max Weber, Max Scheler, and Emile Durkheim were exceptional in their generation. Pitirim Sorokin was the same in his. Historians of literature, art, science and scholarship also adhered to their part of the bargain. Nonetheless the walls began to crumble. Historians of intellectual and artistic works began to introduce elements of social history, the history of the organization of guilds of artists, of patronage, of the audiences of the works. Literary historians found a place for material bearing on the organization of publishing and the distribution of literary works. The separation was therefore never a complete one. Marxist writers like Hausenstein, Plekhanov, Bukharin, Hauser, Antal, and Lukàcs had never respected the division of labor although they were usually very crude in their "imputations." Nonetheless, the substantive separation was maintained. History, political history, the history of religious and educational institutions, and even social history were regarded as within the humanities; so were linguistics, aesthetics, and the history of art. The history of philosophy and the history of science were likewise counted among the humanities, and sociologists by their traditions and their training respected the rights of their humanistic colleagues.

Despite the self-restraint on both sides of the line, the boundary has turned out to be very shadowy. One of the results of the cultivation of the traditions of sociological analysis which grew out of German idealism was that cultural systems, and the institutions which maintain and are formed by cultural systems, have come more and more into the foreground of attention. Sociologists formed under the inspiration of Max Weber and Emile Durkheim have increasingly given themselves over to the assimilation of the achievements of the more humanistic disciplines of the history of art, of science, of literature, of religious beliefs, and even of languages. They have done so, moreover, not within the utilitarian and evolutionist schemes of analysis which treated the subject-matters of these disciplines as sociological epiphenomena. They no longer regard it as their task to "explain" religious ideas or scientific conceptions as products of the "relationships of production" or of the conflict of classes, etc., although this error has not been entirely expunged. A Durkheimian-Mannheimian "sociologism" now reinforced by Marxism still persists; it would derive the criteria of validity or of merit from sociological analysis.

The unification will never be complete. There is no good reason why it should be. Different tasks require different techniques; different interests require different logical structures. Substantive specialization will stand in the way of complete unification too, and that is unlikely ever to be overcome completely. The persistence of these differences and this specialization certainly do not, however, entail any necessary conflict between sociology and the humanistic disciplines, other than that which arises from the jealousies, vanities, and hypersensitivities of human beings. Sociology and the humanistic disciplines are bound together by an indissoluble tie. It is the tie of their common subject-matter and their common appreciation of the human qualities of the moral, intellectual, and aesthetic powers of the human beings who are their subject-matter.

Certainly, there will be sociologists in the future who will work on human beings outside these categories—just as there will be humanistic scholars who will be either extremely specialized or extremely technical, and insensitive to the human qualities of their subject-matter. This will not damage the awareness of the humanism of sociology.

Sociology is properly humanistic because it attempts to understand whatever man does in categories which acknowledge his humanity: his need for cognitive comprehension reaching out to the widest reaches of existence; his capacity for rational judgment and action, for affectionate attachment, for aesthetic expression, creation, and response, for moral decision. Naturally, there is not a complete consensus among sociologists in this respect. There are sociologists who deny or disregard it, just as there are philologists and archaeologists and historians who lose sight of the connections between the objects they hold in their hands or before their minds and the humanity of the creators, recipients, and users of those objects. The best tradition of sociology is humanistic; and the general sociological theory and the sociological orientation which represent the present phase of this tradition continue and make more articulate this humanism. Behaviorism has never been at the center of sociology. The fact that sociology attempts to observe precisely, and to express with precision, events which by their nature have imprecise boundaries, does not diminish the essential humanistic disposition of the tradition of sociology which comes primarily from Max Weber. The fact that sociology is often and increasingly quantitative does not diminish its humanistic component—which is necessitated by the task it takes upon itself—any more than does the fact that it seeks, with growing frequency but still relatively rarely, to express its theoretical constructions in mathematical form. The more refined rhetoric which sociology might come to use, as and if it becomes more mathematical, will not change the nature of the variables with which sociology deals or of the concepts which refer to them. Man does not have to be reduced to a biological organism or to an electronic mechanism for the regularities of his action to be described mathematically. The efforts of sociology to attain determinate laws in its propositions no more deprive it of that status than the regularities of linguistics or the uniformities discerned by comparative religious studies deprive the subject-matter of these disciplines of their dignity.

The humanistic orientation is simply not a function of busying one's self with books of novels, poems, or philosophical ideas. It is not bookishness. The humanistic orientation is not exclusively concentrated on the past; it certainly does not believe in the avoidance of rigorous analytical procedures; it does not require lucubrative compilation or undisciplined impression. These qualities, alone or in combination, are found in both sociological and humanistic faculties; and they are neither decisive for nor constitutive of the nature of the intellectual disciplines in which they are found.

Whatever the relations hitherto of sociology and the humanistic disciplines, it is now clear that the boundaries which became set for all sorts of good and poor reasons, should no longer be regarded as ordained by divine will or the nature of reality or the structure of the human mind. On both sides of the boundary, the two ways of studying human conduct and human achievements have been starving and deforming themselves in isolation from each other. I do not counsel an amalgamation by decree. On each side of the boundary, disciplines have developed which have their own literature and their own traditions through which distinguished or perhaps even great works have been produced. Any deliberate reorganization on a large scale, even if it could be brought about, would suffer from all of the defects of contrivance. Human beings and their disciplines cannot be rendered perfect by decree—for one thing, we do not know what perfection is. Nonetheless, some reciprocal permeation is needed. It is in fact already underway and it should continue, without doctrinaire annunciations.

Some Philosophical-Anthropological Observations

The Self-Interpretation of Man: The Extension of the Traditional Self-Interpretation

Sociological analysis is a variant in a contemporary idiom of the great efforts of the human mind to render judgment on man's vicissitudes on earth. At its best, it springs from an aspiration which is ultimately as profound, if less far-reaching, than that of theology. Uncommitted in a theological sense, it is more modest in its intention than the grandiose fusion of eschatology and the diagnosis of contemporaneity which has come down to us under the name of philosophy of history. It does not aspire to go beyond the boundaries of historical time. Sociology would, however, be no less unfaithful to its traditions, its tasks, and its possibilities if it were to confine itself to the diagnosis of the contemporary situation. Sociology and the "diagnosis of our time" are, when they are decently conducted, very intimate with each other. They are not identical. Sociology is much the more capacious, because it can transcend the role of *laudator temporis acti* which tradition has rendered an almost inevitable standpoint for the analysis of the present. Sociology has often suffered from the conceptual limitations arising from preoccupation with its own society and its own epoch; it has often suffered from a lighthearted acceptance of the convention that a good intellectual is under obligation to denounce his own times and his own society. Despite this temporal and territorial particularism, its aspiration has at times been broader. One of the dominant types of sociological theory of the present century has sought to transcend the local and periodic and to enter into a more trans-historical stratum of being.

Is this not what the moral philosophers have sought to do? Is the oracular "Know thyself" a recommendation to understand one's self as a particular bundle of motives and powers, alive in a Greek polis; or did it command those who read it to understand themselves as human beings? Cicero's reflections on friendship might well have been insufficiently catholic and too much preoccupied with the claims and weaknesses of friendship in Rome when the dangers of life in the dying Republic placed such strains on loyalty and affection. It was not, however, his intention to speak only of his age and country; he sought to speak of man, and, if he failed, it was more a result of the narrowness of his knowledge than of the narrowness of his intention.

The situation of sociology is similar in many respects. Even the sociological theory which would confine itself to "middle principles" is aware of the possibility of more general principles, less restricted in the historical and territorial range of their validity. It recommends "middle principles" because it does not yet believe that sociologists are ready to ascend to the loftier heights of a trans-local, trans-epochal generality. This more self-limiting theory, like the more abstract general theory, appreciates the aspiration of sociology to attain a coherent view of man's nature, of the meaning of the society which is given by man's nature, and by the exigencies of coexistence, and of the transformations which these can undergo within the scope of the limited potentialities so far known in the course of evolution and history.

Sociology is a continuation and elaboration of the permanent and necessary effort of man to understand himself and his species. It goes beyond the classical moralists, by directing the exertion of self-interpretation to the societies in which individuals live as well as to the earlier task of individual self-interpretation.

Sociology is an address to the task of understanding of man as a collective entity—of man's capacities which make him into a political animal, and of the network of human actions and creations which link the present and the past and the spatially dispersed into a reality as real as concrete individual biological existence. Sociology attempts to cast the results and procedures of this collective self-interpretation into a disciplined, systematic form. Insofar as it is a science—which it is not very much at present—then it differs from the sciences of the external world and from large parts of the biological sciences; it differs from them not just in the sense that its subject-matter is different and human, but also in the sense that it has taken upon itself a task different from that of the natural sciences of physics, chemistry, and biology. It is part of the vast, unorganized collective effort of the human mind to understand itself as a collectivity. To understand itself, it needs to know the temptations to which it yields, the resistances which it can erect against temptation, the sources of its weaknesses and strengths, of its impulses and its disciplines. These are good reasons for being as scientific as possible.

Sociological self-understanding—which is an elaboration of old traditions which are not accidents in the life of our species—does not stand in a continuous line of the tradition from classical ethical philosophy through Renaissance humanism and the French moralists from Montaigne to Alain. It overlaps these, but its sources are different and more heterogeneous. It has, for example, received a powerful impetus from Darwinism, and it might in the future derive much from neurology and the theory of servomechanisms. Nonetheless, the very constitution of the impulse which generates sociological exertion compels adherence to the basic task of self-understanding of man as an organism with moral, cognitive, and rational capacities and ideals.

Sociology enters the endless stream of man's effort to assess himself at a point where the stream has broadened and somewhat changed its course. Sociology, traditionally, has been agnostic where it has not been overtly hostile to religious beliefs and institutions; and it proceeds, even at its best, muted on the religious side. By virtue of this noncommittal attitude on the reality of a relationship between divinity and man, it refuses certain traditional religious currents in the self-understanding of man. Except for this ultimate religious "unmusicality," however, it has at its best absorbed the main substance of traditional self-interpretation, added to it the knowledge of the animal in man. It has immensely enriched and complicated the inheritance through its openness to the Darwinian increment and by its assimilation of some of the most general lines of psychoanalytical interpretation.

Through its reception of the Hegelian variant of idealism, it has widened its range tremendously. This is what has made the self-interpretation of man sociological. The traditional self-interpretation of man saw man as an instance of a category, but not as a knot in a network. To the extent that it saw man as a member of a collectivity, it saw him as a beneficiary of the advantages and a victim of the disadvantages of that membership. Society did not quite come into the picture of the objects of self-interpretation. Sociology has partially closed the gap left by Aristotle between the *Ethics* and the *Politics*. It was only natural that it should do so, because, in the age in which it has flourished, the consensual capacities of man have grown proportionately with his individuality. With this growth, the problems of self-interpretation have been complicated and deepened.

The strivings and writhings of collective humanity; the accumulation, transmission, assimilation, and transformation of the fruits and by-products of these movements, transcending generations and localities; and the precipitation of multitudinous individual actions into determinate social orders—these have become integral to our conception of man. Man is not simply an organism bounded by an epidermis and set into a physical-biological environment. He is not just an intelligence and a moral capacity formed into an individuality. He is also part of an entity beyond the boundaries of skin and person; he enters into a system of such organisms over space and through time. He has a memory, and he has the capacity to incorporate the images of others into an intermittently open self. These form an entity with an extension beyond the individual life-span and beyond the experiences of particular individuals. Its observations, concrete and particular, and abstract and general, on man in this broader view, are what sociology adds to the traditional self-interpretation of man. I speak here of sociology in its best aspirations.

Technological Sociology

Sociology is not simply the traditional self-interpretation of man, broadened by subsequent intellectual developments. It also shares in the modern scientific movement, and it attempts to act accordingly.

Disciplined, detached observation, emancipation from prejudice, the intellectual control of arbitrariness in judgment, the desire for a generalized picture of the world, the postulate of regularity in the sequence of events—these are all articles of the constitution of the scientific community; and, by virtue of acceptance of these rules, sociology becomes one of the dominions of that community. But the scientific community is a confederation without a central government. Not all the intellectual dominions need adhere rigorously or absolutely to the same rules. They can vary their conduct within the framework of the constitution of the community, according to their own traditions and the tasks which these traditions set.

There is one variant of the sociological self-interpretation of man and society which diverges markedly from the older contemplative tradition. That is a conception of society and of man's place in it which stresses the ordering of society in the light of a progressive growth of rational-empirical knowledge. It is a conception which regards knowledge as an instrument and guide to action, which no resistance can withstand. Ignorance, superstition, tradition are adventitious growths which will wither away as knowledge grows, so that society will become one vast self-knowing entity, propelling itself on the basis of its self-knowledge. Alternatively, the expanded knowledge will accumulate at certain crucial positions in society from which the rest of society can be ruled for its benefit by an enlightened despot-cum-social-engineer. The second alternative has been very attractive to sociologists.

This technological aspiration would put sociology to use in the way in which the knowledge of genetics is put to use in animal and plant breeding, or chemical knowledge in industry, or physiology and pharmacology in the practice of the profession of medicine. The Comtian maxim, *savoir pour prévoir pour pourvoir,* drew its inspiration from a tradition at least as old as Francis Bacon; it did not run into the ground with Auguste Comte. It has continued to be one current of the tradition of sociology ever since; it comes recurrently to the surface and at times it has one large part of the stream to itself.

There are profound ambivalences in this technological interpretation. It conceives of man, in one of the alternative interpretations, as an organism which has no limits to its cognitive capacities; it has the capacity to go on learning scientifically more and more about itself and the universe, learning of its right ends from its scientific knowledge and "applying" that scientific knowledge to attain those ends. This capacity is assumed to exist among all human beings. A variant interpretation conceives of society as an aggregate of egotistic actors, each concerned to attain his own ends and capable of acting realistically, with the aid of scientific knowledge, to attain those ends. This variant interpretation sees society as a gigantic market, each actor bargaining with each other actor as his needs dictate. A third alternative interpretation of man and society in this technological sociology involves these limitless cognitive capacities in some persons in crucial positions with the rest of the population pliant and submissive to those who know scientifically how to manipulate them with a benevolent intention.

To be technological in the first sense entails conceiving of man as at present irrational and traditional and having unawakened cognitive powers which are capable of being aroused and released by a rationalistic, scientific education. Man's cognitive powers will, in consequence of this education, replace all his present dispositions. To be technological in the second sense means to be manipulative; it means that events to be controlled are treated as having no affinity with the manipulator; man is seen as being incapable of exercising rational judgment or of appreciating the truth of valid empirical knowledge. The third alternative leads to placing this scientific knowledge at the disposal of government.

The manipulative conception of man and society entails the perception of the object of the manipulation as a discrete entity having no social relationship with the manipulator except with regard to the manipulative actions themselves. It denies the object's capacities for and claims for moral regard by the manipulating person, and it thus denies the mutuality which is implicit in the sociological theory which is based on the acknowledgment of the moral, cognitive, and rational capacities of human beings. Manipulative actions involve the suppression of certain of the features of the relationship between manipulator and manipulated which are fundamental to a major strand of the sociological tradition, namely, the identities of the sociologist and the subject-matter of his study.

The technological self-interpretation of man and society accepts either a mechanistic, conventionally behavioristic conception of man as incapable of valid reasoning and as unable to make choices guided by moral standards. Or it sees them as capable of rational decisions based on scientific knowledge and obdurately resistant to considerations of moral obligation.

A sociology which conforms entirely to either of the divergent postulates of the technology of control is one which sees the relationship between controller and controlled as wholly devoid of any moral and cultural content. A manipulative relationship would not be a social relationship since it would have no shared culture. But human relationships, except when some human beings are actually coercing other human beings, by shooting or binding or beating them, do have some common culture. I emphasize both the community and the culture—in fact, the existence of the latter presupposes the existence of the former. Authority could not be exercised without some common culture, and a technologically used sociological knowledge could only be used by authority within a common cultural matrix.

I do not wish to deny that the type of sociology derived from behaviorism or from a scientistic utilitarianism has some element of truth in it. But it is a mistake to think that those elements contain all that is important and can be known about human beings and the societies they form. It should also be made clear that not all sociologists who espouse this kind of sociology are in favor of manipulation or that they have sought to construct their kind of sociology so that it could be used as a technological instrument to some end which the manipulator does not share with those he manipulates. Nonetheless, there is a kind of sociology which is congenial to the manipulative procedure. Many sociologists—and social psychologists in particular—like to think that the knowledge they acquire will find use in the improvement of human life; they think that improvements are to be brought about by manipulation in which the manipulated persons' ends are data and not of normative significance. They are not hostile towards other human beings but their conception of them prevents them from taking human beings seriously. It prevents them from understanding the consensual element in the relationships between human beings and in the organization of societies.

The sociology formed and adapted to technology is probably not wholly incorrect: there are undoubtedly human situations which can be ameliorated only by manipulation, or coped with only by coercion; and the scientific improvement of sociology might well make these actions more efficacious. The technological application of sociology, quite apart from its distortion and partiality, can hardly claim to be fitting for a democratic liberal society which respects the dignity of individual existence. Sociology would be a moral monstrosity if, after its decent adolescence, it were in its riper years to develop into a tool for technocrats to rule the human race—presumably for its benefit—or into a belief that society should become one vast market in which every relationship had to be negotiated by a great number of wholly independent actors.

Sociology, Consensus, and the Illumination of Opinion

Sociology will not make any serious progress as long as it proceeds on the basis of a belief that a "stimulus-response" model, however ingenious, is adequate for understanding. Although the techniques of sociological research have gained much from the assimilation of features of the behavioristic tradition and although it might gain much from the prospective assimilation of the knowledge of thought-processes from research on computers, it will become paralyzed if it does not allow for the higher mental functions such as are exercised in intellectual, moral, and aesthetic creativity. Not only the intellectual traditions which have gone into the formation of sociology, but also the immanent necessities of present-day sociological research, the sheer need to do justice to the depth of the subject-matter, require a movement toward a theory which accords a proper place to moral, cognitive, and rational capacities.

Such a theory would be a self-interpretation since the act of its construction is of a piece with the objects of its contemplation. Its categories for describing man's nature must include the capacity for the construction of a theory about man and society and about the universe too. This itself is an acknowledgment of the continuity between the theorist and the subject-matter of the theory. It is a construction which, in rational self-consciousness, acknowledges the rational powers of man, even if it does not give them a monopoly or disregard their limitations. It acknowledges man's cognitive and aesthetic propensities; otherwise its own striving would be senseless. It acknowledges man's need for a cognitive order in the universe, a need which is more than an instrument of biological adaptation. Sociological theory, even in its present rudimentary state, is not just a theory like any other theory; it is also a social relationship between the theorist and the subject-matter of his theory. It is a relationship grounded in the sense of affinity.

Sociological theory cannot be an exclusively cognitive product which has no bearing on action. It can and does enter into action; but it does so through a process of illumination which modifies the disposition of the actor who shares it. Its efficacy necessitates the sharing of the insights it affords between those who promulgate them and those who receive them. The understanding of the social system which it conveys, heightening, as it does, the awareness of the unity which binds—as well as the separateness which separates!—would, if it were "applied," work through collective self-transformations. Collective self-transformations are those which would be decided upon consensually, by tacit understanding and by deliberation, and in which the adaptations of the actions of individual to individual would be made within the context of a perceived affinity. The kind of sociological theory I am speaking of here is a consensual intellectual construction. In a sociological interview, the person studied shares his knowledge of his own experiences and observations with the interviewer; the sociologist in his analysis attempts to understand those experiences as the interviewed person experienced and understood them. Thus sociological research is a sharing of knowledge between the person studied and the person studying. The acquisition of sociological knowledge is bound within but not exhausted by this consensus. The promulgation of sociological knowledge, at the next stage past the acquisition of data, also operates within a deeper consensus in which the sociologist arrives at a state of knowledge which the person studied does not have about himself but which he possesses the capacity to understand—at least potentially—because the categories in which his actions and beliefs are analyzed are congruous with the categories in which he apprehends society and the universe. Not everything which a sociologist understands about a society is identical with its own self-understanding, but that is what he has to begin with. And what he discovers about it which it does not already know is, in principle, assimilable by it into self-understanding.

The self-understanding of a society is not likely ever to be a wholly consensual affair; it is far more likely to be an act performed by only a few persons in that society. But those few persons to interpret their society correctly must see themselves as parts of it and not as isolated observers who have no affinity with it. This does not mean that they must approve of all that goes on in their society or that they must avoid reference to conflicts, exploitation, manipulation, and coercion. It does mean that the sociologist who interprets his society is also interpreting it to itself and that he is at the same time interpreting himself as part of it.

It is unlikely that, in the foreseeable future, mankind will dispense entirely with coercion and the threat of it in the internal life of its societies; it is also unlikely that deception or manipulation will disappear in the relationships of adults, to say nothing of the relationships of adults and children. Indeed, manipulation is rendered more probable because modern knowledge in pharmacology and neurology makes it more feasible. It is imperative intellectually for sociological theory of the kind I am speaking about to comprehend these instrumental, coercive, deceptive, and manipulative actions and to find a place for them in its analytical schema. It would be untruthful if it did not and it would also do harm to self-understanding.

The sociological theory here under discussion—both on the level of relatively concrete middle principles and on that of more abstract analysis—is a discipline fundamentally alien to technological application; it is not capable of becoming a technological science. It is not a discipline the propositions of which, if they are articulated, may be simply reformulated from, "If, under conditions A, B, and C, D is changed into D^1, then E will change into E^1 and if D is changed to D^2, then E will change into E^2" to the form, "If A, B, and C exist, and we wish to produce E^1 from E, then we must change D to D^1 and if we wish to produce E^2 from E, then we must change D to D^2." Technological propositions in this latter form assume that "we" and "D" belong to different classes of events. Sociology of the type derived from Max Weber's fragmentary program asserts, on the contrary, that the relationships between "ourselves" and "D" are as such of the same class as the relationships among A, B, C, D, and E, etc. The relationship between "D" and "ourselves" must insofar as "we" are not "D," therefore, be, in at least some measure, a consensual relationship. It can also contain coercive or manipulative elements as well, although not to the exclusion of the consensual element. In any case, a large part of the relationship which we undertake for the transformation of our collective situation will be one in which the consensual element will be very important.

There is no sharp disjunction separating technological sociology from consensual sociology; nor is there any sharper disjunction between consensual sociology and oppositional sociology. They all come from the same family of traditions. Oppositional sociology and consensual sociology are historically closely linked with each other. The sociology which grew up at the University of Chicago contained intertwined elements of both and it also contained the seed of technological sociology as well. As sociology has developed, the differences have become more discernible but even now their partial identities are still visible.

The ease of transition from one to the other was fostered by the sympathy which many leading sociologists of the first fifty years of this century had for positivism and pragmatism. The positivistic and the instrumentalist-pragmatist traditions which have guided the opinion of sociologists have made it appear as if a technological application of sociology, like the technological applications of the physical and biological sciences, was the fitting and harmonious by-product of the striving for sociological knowledge. Many of the best figures of the history of sociology have accepted this idiom, and they did indeed give much effort to the improvement of the condition of their society. Their idiom did not correspond completely to their practice. They were not manipulative in the way in which later technological sociologists have been; they attempted to illuminate the public mind by the results of their research and thus to improve their society by increasing the rationality—and thus self-evidently, the virtue—of their fellow citizens.

Oppositional Sociology and the Critique of Society

Sociology is not a normative discipline according to the sensible but simplistic view which distinguishes between "norm" and "fact." Indeed, all the main strands of sociology proceed on the basis of a belief in the existence of autonomous criteria of truth which are universally valid. Oppositional sociology not only has the same fundamental epistemological presuppositions as consensual and technological sociology, it also shares many of the substantive views of consensual sociology. They grew up together but they are in many respects very different, particularly in substantive matters.

Sociology has not been precluded by some of the fundamental categories of its better traditions from taking a critical and even hostile view of various features of the society in which it has been conducted. The powerful impulsion given by Hobbes and the individualism which came from him contained an oppositional tendency which the moderate political views of the utilitarians of the nineteenth and early twentieth centuries did not eradicate. Durkheim did not fully overcome such elements in his inheritance from St. Simon and Comte. For many years, sociology was viewed by some of its adherents as an intellectual activity outside the existing social order and as necessarily at odds with it, perhaps even subversive of it. Sociologists conceived of their subject as a necessarily dissensual factor in society dissolving traditional beliefs. Sociologists in their observations and theories emphasized the dissensual processes, toward which they took a tone of fascinated and severe disapproval. Conflict, frustrated lives, dereliction, loneliness, and failure became central figures in the portraits which sociologists painted of their societies.

It has been a proud boast of some sociologists that sociology is an "oppositional" science, meaning thereby that sociology is a factually documented denunciation of the society in which it is carried on. Some of those who take pride in the oppositional character of sociology are former or quasi-Marxists, but the oppositional tendency in sociology is much older and broader than Marxism. The oppositional conception of society came into sociology much earlier than the first contacts of sociology with Marxism. Marxism and late nineteenth-century German sociology both drank from wells of inspiration provided by German romanticism and by the radical Hegelian version of alienation. Rationalism and scientism, from Bacon to Descartes, although not producing a direct and substantive influence on sociology, helped to create the still prevailing culture of sociology.

Sociology as an "oppositional science" has varied in the extent and ways in which it has regarded itself as "outside" the societies which it has studied. It has often intimated a moral condemnation of the society which it has analyzed; the tradition of condemnation or opposition is a heterogeneous one.

The "oppositional" character of sociology covers a wide variety of types of opposition to existing arrangements. Some of the opposition has been more far-reaching and intellectually deeper than others. For much of the history of sociology in the nineteenth century, as a subject with a name although for much of the time without an institutional site, the various streams of the sociological tradition did recognize themselves and each other as more and as less oppositional. There were progressivistic "meliorists," there were also "pessimists" who found little to their satisfaction in existing arrangements, and there were moralists who wished to change or restore one institution or another. Sociology in Western countries was however practically never found in conjunction in the same persons with revolutionary political attitudes. Both in European and in American sociology, the oppositional attitudes have been present in the outlook of scholars who have had nothing of the revolutionary in their makeup and who, in fact, have often been liberal or conservative in their politics.

In Europe as well as in America, the major sociologists were conservatives, secularists, progressivists, rationalists, socialists, or aesthetes, and they all found their contemporary societies wanting. Herbert Spencer was an individualistic liberal, Frederic Le Play was a conservative, Ferdinand Tönnies was a socialist, Emile Durkheim was a rationalist and secularist, Max Weber was a liberal nationalist; yet on certain important points regarding the character of modern society in the nineteenth century they were in agreement. They agreed that European societies were in a state of moral disorder; they thought that these societies had gone too far in releasing the egoistical impulses of individuals; they thought that these societies lacked the common faith—or consensus—and the self-restraint needed for their well-being and that of the individuals within them. They did not accept the prevailing movements of democracy and liberalism as adequate to deal with the problems of an individualistic, irreligious society. Nor did they believe in the efficacy of the surviving traditional authorities. Their criticisms were sometimes made from a conservative standpoint, but in a certain fundamental respect the same criticisms were also made by the rationalists, secularists, and socialists.

The critical attitudes were exacerbated by the crudity of the categories of sociological analysis. The categories of sociological analysis have always been cruder than the reality they dichotomized; there has been much exaggeration of the preponderance of these disintegrative processes. What was not *Gemeinschaft* had to be *Gesellschaft;* what was not *solidarité organique* had to be *solidarité mécanique.* These fundamental, dichotomous concepts were usually intended by their authors to be no more than what later came to be called "ideal types"; the sociologists undoubtedly knew that reality was more complicated. Nonetheless, the distintegrative alternative of the simplified view was in fact accepted by many sociologists as the dominant feature of modern society, with elements of the integrative alternative continuing to exist only residually and transiently.

The most weighty figures of American sociology before the great upsurge which preceded the Second World War were William Graham Sumner, Robert Park, William I. Thomas, and Charles H. Cooley. With the exception of Sumner, who expected nothing reasonable from any society and demanded only individual freedom—and who, therefore, found himself at home in the freebooting capitalistic America of the turn of the century—all of these men practiced a sociological analysis which was in accordance with a severely critical assessment of the American society which was taking form during their lifetime. They were liberals of various sorts who regarded, especially in the United States, the times as being out of joint. The age of the trusts, of "the shame of the cities," the great flood of immigration, and the anxiety these called up in intellectual circles, gave an imprint to their work. They were liberals, warmhearted and empathic, with a genuine feeling for the other man—Sumner perhaps less so than others. They were not populists. They were certainly not Marxists. They were, however, the children of their age and, at a time when the names of politics and politicians stank in the nostrils of sensitive Americans, their noses too were wrinkled. Of course, as children of their age, they came under the all-permeating Darwinian influence. They therefore thought in terms of natural processes of evolutionary growth. Darwinism and liberalism combined to persuade them that governments, like the owl of Minerva, take their flight only when the shade of night has fallen. Their alienation was a patriotic one, like that of the upright Romans who mourned the decline of republican virtue.

The older types of "oppositional sociology" in Europe and America were not identical with the oppositional sociology which has clamored for attention in recent decades. The older types of "oppositional" sociologists were not wholly alienated from their own societies; they might have been alienated from many of their politicians, and most of them were critical of the avarice and hedonism which they associated with contemporary economic organization. They saw defects in their societies which they thought should be eliminated by reforms based on scientific knowledge. They did not regard the deficiencies which their research uncovered in their societies as representative of all features of those societies. They did not think that the microcosm of poverty, distress, neglect, and crime which sociologists investigated were wholly representative of all the major features of their respective societies. Most of the earlier oppositional sociologists were also confident, perhaps naively so, that these "problems" could be "solved" and that a scientific sociology would play its due part in this by making the "responsible" sections of society, that is, those who acted disinterestedly on behalf of the whole, aware of the facts of the situation and their causes.

Opposition toward the prevailing practice of politics and a critical attitude towards political institutions for falling short of the ideal are not inherent in sociological analysis; nor is a critical attitude towards the system of the private ownership of the instruments of production. An attitude of detachment from existing beliefs and institutions is perhaps a deeper source of opposition, and this attitude of detachment is inherent in the effort to see society as it really is. By a slight extension of this necessary detachment, the beliefs which are current in a society are especially susceptible to disparagement at the hands of sociologists, and religious beliefs above all others. Similarly, with respect to the judgment of institutions.

Sociology became a discipline in the time of secularization, when the traditional interpretation of Christian belief was in retreat before the ravages of advancing scientific knowledge in fields which did not include sociology. Sociology placed itself within this scientific movement. Myths, superstitions, folk adages, theological systems, and moral beliefs all came under the fire of sociology. Comte and Spencer incorporated this critical attitude into the character of sociology. A believed-in myth is different from a myth asserted to be untrue by an observer; a belief held on the grounds that it is believed to be true is different from a belief which an observer regards as being held for quite different reasons or motives; a belief believed to be true is different from a belief asserted by an observer to be wrong and to be held on grounds other than cognitive ones. The secularistic, agnostic attitude towards traditional beliefs set sociology at odds with the cultures it studied.

Sociology would not have been justified in the minds of its practitioners if it did not go beyond what laymen believed about their societies. If what sociologists discovered about "the causes of crime" was identical with what was already generally believed in society about that matter, there would have been no justification for sociology in the eyes of sociologists. Sociologists in their effort to describe any phenomenon of society had obviously to perceive things which were not perceived by the members of that society. There was nothing wrong with this, except that it placed sociologists "outside" the society which they studied and it led them to believe that there is something amiss with a society which has wrong beliefs about itself.

A physiologist who studies the pancreas and who arrives at conclusions which are not generally shared in society has no problems such as a sociologist has when he arrives at a conclusion about society. There are no generally entertained opinions about the pancreas. The physiologist does not feel himself superior to the pancreas because he has views about it which are intellectually superior to those which the pancreas has about itself. Nor is he in conflict with persons in whom the pancreas functions because those persons practically never have any views about the pancreas in their conception of the world and of themselves; they are willing to accept what the physiologist tells them about the pancreas.

The sociologist's task is to discover hitherto unknown things about society—that they seldom do so is to the discredit of sociology but it is certainly not intentional. When he does discover something hitherto unknown about society, it is by definition different from what has hitherto been believed by many persons. Those with wrong beliefs about such things as the nature of the relations between members of different social classes, about how the institutions of their society work, their motives for performing various actions, the consequences of their actions, and many other things about which they have opinions to which they attribute importance are automatically derogated for being wrong. The student of Assyriology, of logic and metaphysics, or of the founding of Rome has only his own professional colleagues to contend with; he ordinarily does not enter into relations with the laity through his espousal of substantive views about his subject-matter as the sociologist does. The sociologist is committed from the beginning to having different views from the persons whom he is studying, both about themselves and about their society.

If to this is added the combination of secularism and detachment of the sociologist in the consideration of beliefs and the further tendency to reduce most motives to motives of self-aggrandizement and practically all beliefs to self-deception and the deception of others, there seems to be a further element of alienation of sociologists from those whom they study added to the constitutive attitude of detachment. All of this is accentuated when sociologists study their own society or their own type of society. Thus sociologists, however uninterested they are in literature, history, and art, are the heirs of romanticism, overlaid by ethical repugnance for what they regard as the injustice of bourgeois society.

Nonetheless, not all of recent sociology is equally "oppositional." The more radical oppositional sociology of recent years is more hostile to types of society prevailing in the West but, in being so, it only accentuates certain traditions within sociology more generally; it joins to that inheritance an admixture of Marxism and political animus.

The opposition of the radical oppositional sociologist is threefold: his fundamental categories of analysis make him alien to the persons he studies; his subject-matter is predominantly the phenomena of alienation in society; he himself takes an ethically and politically alienated attitude toward the society which is his subject-matter. The last attitude implicitly employs a utopian ideal as a standard for assessing the condition of contemporary society; he judges it from the standpoint of ideals such as perfect equality, or perfect rationality, perfect communication, unqualified legitimacy, or perfect *Gemeinschaft*. The dominant tradition of sociology was able to recognize that there were other elements in society; all was not disorganization, coercion, and deception. The radical oppositional sociology proceeded as if that was all there was to society while the former was always more or less aware that there were other aspects of society than those it investigated. Radical oppositional sociology has concentrated on "conflict" and the "poor" and treated the rest of society either as the victim of "false consciousness" which permits it to obscure and transfigure conflict or as the deliberate manipulator and beneficiary of poverty as a device for assuring its own ascendancy.

The early focus of empirical sociological research on poverty and the miseries of the poor left a precipitate which has lasted long after these subjects ceased to preoccupy many sociologists. After first focusing attention on the condition of the miserable, the homeless, the parentless, the criminal, the isolated and neglected, the insulted and the injured, sociologists later generalized this condition into one which was put forward as representative of all modern society. As the subject-matter of sociology was extended and even shifted from the poor into the other sections of society, and to problems other than the description of poverty and its attendant troubles, the original disposition remained more or less intact. A great efflorescence of empirical inquiry took place in America in the 1930s, during the Great Depression which coincided with the time of an awakening interest, among American sociologists, in Marxism and psychoanalysis, and the reawakening interest in European sociology. Very few of the investigators of that period underwent all these influences simultaneously, and not many bore them directly; but they pervaded the intellectual atmosphere and could not be avoided. They increased the sophistication of American social science; but they also extended the orientation which, at least in urban sociological studies, had already been very much alive, albeit in a more callow form. Empirical inquiry in the second half of the 1930s—in industrial sociology, in the study of race relations, in the interest in mass communications, and in the introduction of psychoanalytic conceptions of personality—differentiated and accentuated but did not otherwise change the basic attitude of disapprobation towards modern Western societies.

The numerous investigations into industrial sociology, mass communications, criminality and delinquency, educational institutions, social stratification, urban communities, adolescents, and the aged which became more numerous in the 1930s and 1940s slipped easily into a state of mind which found "society" at the root of whatever evils beset human life. Such a potentiality had always existed in the distinctive belief of sociologists in the formative influence of "environment." The depression of the 1930s entered into sociological consciousness. Sociology became a dense documentation and a running commentary on the shortcomings of society as a whole. The radicalism which in recent years has gained adherents among sociologists more than among other social scientists has not been a wholly new departure. It was not simply a product of the eager reception of Marxism by sociologists in Western countries. It was rather a continuation and intensification of tendencies which had been present in both sociological research and sociological theory since early in the nineteenth century, and no less in the United States than it had been in Europe. From a sympathetic attitude towards the poor, there unfolded a belief in the wickedness and corruption of the other parts of society which allowed a curable poverty to occur. The intimation of wickedness was not always prominent; in some cases it was absent. In any case, the remediability of the evils of human life in society came increasingly to be assumed by sociologists. If society is the root of all evil, then the modification and indeed the transformation of society would eliminate evil.

This has frequently not been a result of a personal attitude; it has been a product of the traditional setting of the problems of inquiry and of the establishment of a certain set of subject-matters as the appropriate ones for investigation. The power of the tradition in accordance with which sociologists have worked has dominated their own not always especially strong or clearly defined moral and intellectual inclinations.

The result has been an outlook which has radically distrusted the inherited order of society. This is an outlook which has something to be said for it on the moral side, and it has many intellectual achievements to its credit. It is nonetheless defective intellectually, and it will not survive dispassionate reflection on experience or systematic study. A good deal of empirical sociological research and some sociological theory have their point of departure in a view of modern society which is damaged by an error. Society is not just a "congeries of atomized individuals"; nor is "the family relationship . . . an affair of money and nothing more" in bourgeois society. Contemporary society does not consist of anonymous "faces in the crowd"; political life is not just a scene in which self-interested pressure groups determine every policy. Yet these are notions which many sociologists have believed. Just as men of letters and artists have, for decades, indeed for nearly two centuries, enjoyed without serious reflection the prerogative of despising their fellow men and of being revolted by their own society in the name of genius and perfection, so sociologists have accepted, no more reflectively or truthfully, the romantic view of the iniquity of their own society. Much of the resistance against a more realistic sociological theory comes from this obstinately oppositional sociology. This strand of sociology simply takes for granted the view of society in its present condition as a state of nature, in the Hobbesian sense, in which human beings act in concern only when their "interests" dictate it.

My criticism of the oppositional outlook of much of the sociological work of recent years does not rest on political grounds. My primary reason for criticizing the oppositional type of sociology is that, despite the paraphernalia of systematic empirical research and learned theory, it presents a distorted picture of contemporary society and of society in general. It greatly overestimates the extent to which there is a war of each against all in society; it overestimates correspondingly the role of deception, manipulation, and coercion, and the degree of deliberate concerting of action by the "elite" against the rest of society. It is not that these observations are entirely untrue; they just do not represent the reality of modern societies.

Oppositional sociology, although it contains a harshly disapproving judgment about the society of which it is a part, has grown out of a reformative impulse. Although it has most recently been sympathetic with revolutionary movements, it has only in extreme and rare instances attempted to be the cognitive arm of revolution. Because it has so much in common with the reformative sociology, it too has, until recently, regarded its audience as the students of sociology and the wider public which is interested in the portrayal of its own society. In its moderate and unpolitical form, oppositional sociology is a major part of the subject. And since empirical research is now so widely taught and practiced and since technological sociology provides for the employment of so many sociologists, technological sociology and oppositional sociology have settled down together very comfortably. This, despite the severe strictures uttered by the most vigorous spokesmen of oppositional sociology against the triviality of quantitative empirical research.

Oppositional sociology, consistently with its criticism of the sociology which discerns some measure of consensus in society and which sees its social calling within a consensual framework, is in fact very congenial to a scientistic and technocratic outlook. It would influence civil servants to change society by the exercise of their bureaucratic power or it would influence students to transform the society by violent revolutionary action to some extent and much more by entry into influential positions in the media of mass communication and the civil service.

A Note on Marxism, Sociology, and the Critique of Society

The greatest popularity of sociology in Europe occurred in the quarter century after the Second World War, and it coincided with the erosion of traditional Marxism, partly as a result of the moral discredit of its association with the tyranny of the Soviet Union and of its intellectual insufficiency in dealing with the history of the last decades. Lively young men and women who had been, or who might otherwise have been, drawn to traditional Marxism turned to sociology. The failure of the old type of Marxism to satisfy, and the readiness to replace it by sociology, testified to an aspiration to enter into serious contact with contemporary society, and to the potentiality within sociology to provide a critical self-assessment of contemporary society which might turn towards radicalism. The traditional Marxism and even its occasional reanimation by a few leading communists like Bukharin had appealed to a handful of sociologists in the 1930s by its critical attitude towards contemporary liberal-democratic society and by its grand scope. It facilitated the location of the self in one's own epoch and society, on the largest map available at the time to uneducated and unsophisticated but alert minds. It provided a standard for criticizing that society. Sociology shared some of these qualities. It had, after all, grown out of some of the same sources as Marxism; and it was, as a contemporary of Marxism, a response to the same yearning. Traditional Marxism failed to gain or hold the imagination of morally sensitive and intelligent young persons because its political implications became too abhorrent and because its present embodiment and its chief exponents were too obviously contradictory to its enduring critical dispositions.

Sociology, both in its theory and in concrete analyses, has possessed, in contrast with Marxism, a critical potentiality all the greater by the flexibility of its traditions. It is more matter-of-fact, it exercises greater scruples about evidence, it is less bound by the obligation to justify particular policies and arrangements. It is far richer in the variety of topics covered by its literature. It creates no strain to justify arguments for which evidence is lacking; it allows for tentativeness. It also opens out in many directions into vast bodies of literature. It permits the pleasure of search and discovery and of large perspectives as well as intimate discernment. In all these respects, sociology, without the aid of Marxism, would seem to have an attractiveness much superior to Marxism intellectually.

Yet the ascendancy of sociology over Marxism did not last very long. The emergence of the "new left" was accompanied by a revival of Marxism of a relatively new kind. The "young Marx" who had been known to scholars of Marxism for more than a third of a century succeeded the more positivistic Marx. This "young Marx" satisfied the need to be Marxist, to be revolutionary, and to reject the fundamental categories of human conduct as they appeared to be effective in liberal democratic society. The refurbished conception of alienation, which had played only a supplementary role in traditional Marxism, became more central in the new Marxism. This resurrection of the "young Marx" was not entirely in opposition to sociology. It could not, in fact, be carried out without the aid of sociology. The romantic conception of the depersonalization of human life in the large urban centers of capitalistic society acquired a new life in the sociological beliefs of the "new left." The ideas of Tönnies and Simmel, and especially Max Weber's ideas about the tendencies of modern societies towards bureaucracy, had only to be touched up here and there by Marxist language to realize once more in acute form the oppositional potential of some of the main currents of sociology and to be turned into an internecine animosity against the academic sociology which had given it sustenance. The Marxist sociology of the present day which is the sociology of academic sociologists adhering to the "new left" is really not very different in substance from much of the sociology it denounces.

All this testifies to the fine balance of affirmation and criticism, of consensus and alienation within the dominant tradition of academic sociology. There is so much in the tradition of academic sociology—not just in the observations of empirical research but also in the traditions of theory and in the traditional ethos of sociology—which can be turned in nearly an opposite direction by a slight reemphasis.

Sociology as a Solvent Power

Sociology, Tradition, Authority

The solvent potentiality of sociology in the face of tradition and authority comes from a more serious source than mere rebelliousness or antinomianism. The myth-making needs of man are too great, his excitation by authority is too pronounced, for him to be able to picture things as they appear to an observer disciplined by training and experience to view certain major events sympathetically and yet without the passions they arouse in the untrained. Despite the counter-tendencies of philistinism in many human beings, there are strong inclinations among them to transfigure, glorify, or denigrate sacred things and great powers. Some men much of the time, many men some of the time, must be awestruck or sacrilegious. Those who have power over others are bound by the difficulties of finding out the truth and by their own vanity to paint for themselves a picture of their subordinates or constituents which is likely to be at variance with the facts. Those who are subordinated to authority are under similar compulsions to distort and obscure, out of self-abasing submissiveness or resentment. There are naturally great variations in the capacity of the agents and patients of authority to perceive truthfully the reality in which they live, just as all human beings, however disciplined, have difficulties in understanding themselves and others. The justification for sociology, when it is at its best, is that it aspires to assimilate and advance the best understanding which human beings can acquire in the course of their intelligent and sympathetic confrontation of life's problems and tasks. Whatever else sociology might be, it is the cultivation of a humane detachment.

Most of the great modern sociologists seem to have been agnostic in matters of religion. Yet at least two of them, Max Weber and Emile Durkheim, made very valuable contributions to the understanding of religion, which even religious believers can understand and learn from. They combined the detachment necessary for sociological analysis with a sympathy for attachment to sacred things. A detachment which has no appreciation of attachments to sacred objects would be worse than useless for the sociological study of religion and its surrogates. This empathic detachment is bound to keep sociology, however consensual its fundamental categories are, in a less than perfect consensus with much of the human race. Sociology is forced by this detachment to have somewhat strained relations with the believing sections of the race. It is also likely to have similarly strained relations with those who enjoy or who are sensitive to authority.

It is not that sociology irritates by its detachment from what men think is sacred in the universe or in their own lives, but rather that its results must diverge cognitively at certain points from what many of the best intelligences and spirits among human beings have perceived and experienced. It is the divergence from the established view of authority and tradition that generates a certain measure of isolation of sociology from the rest of the culture and the institutions which carry it.

Some of this strain is historically accidental. It is an inheritance of earlier strains between the traditions which have brought sociology to its present position and the beliefs against which the proponents of the traditions from which sociology grew, at one time contended. Some of the present disposition against tradition and authority is a result of sociology's historical share in a tradition of intellectual development much broader than sociology; another part is inherent in the sociological enterprise proper. Some of that disposition was inevitable and is also unavoidable for sociology even at its best. Some of it is also damaging to the capacities of sociology.

It is certainly reasonable to expect the historically adventitious part of the strain to be eliminated or reduced over the next decades. It is of a piece with that phase and outlook of sociology which caused it to be designated as an "oppositional science," or which caused it to be put forward as a "social technology." It is legitimate, moreover, to desire the rhetoric and mood of sociology to become more compassionate and less impelled by the bitterness of a disappointed rationalism in its contemplation of the poor human race. This too would aid in the diminution of the extraneous sources of strain.

Can sociology ever cease to be an implicit criticism of traditional beliefs and authorities? Can it ever give up its implicit critique of the vanity of princes and the magic of priests? The answer to these questions can be put in a simple and extreme form: If ever the time should come when the results of sociological analysis will be identical—for whatever cause—with what is believed by adult human beings in that society in which sociology so prospers, then sociology will no longer maintain its distance; in such a situation of identity, sociology will cease to imply at least some measure of distrust toward beliefs and

institutions which most people share and on behalf of which authorities speak. This condition is unlikely ever to occur, because of
both the nature of men and the nature of any concentrated intellectual
activity. The sociological enterprise would make no sense whatsoever
if sociology could not in some measure transcend the knowledge
which the widest human experience and the most discriminating sifting of tradition render available. Even now, when sociology is still a
rather feeble subject, filled with prejudices and vague notions, it com-
petes at its highest peaks quite impressively with the best that the
sober judgment and mature wisdom of the ages has brought forth.
There is no ground to think that it cannot, from the nature of things, do
better in the future. Even if ordinary human understanding
improves—which is by no means a hopeless prospect—sociological
analysis, as its better traditions become consolidated and as it attracts
better minds to their cultivation, is also likely to improve in the same
measure. Even with our best hopes realized, a gap is likely to persist.

As long as this gap exists, then the observations, insights, and
generalizations of sociology will inevitably assert that things are not
quite what they seem. They will impugn the grounds which human
beings adduce to justify their conduct. They will disclose an image of
the world different in some important respects from what the ordinary, and even the very intelligent, unsociological man sees. Some of
these disenchanting insights will be absorbed by many people, and the
gap will be narrowed thereby.

A gap will remain, however. If one thinks, as I do, that earthly
authority—exercising it, submitting to it, or being fascinated by it—is
one of the most mind-disturbing things in all human experience; if one
thinks that authority upsets the mind, affects one's inmost image of
one's self, of man, and of the world; then the very difference between
the states of mind induced by attachment to or repulsion from authority and the detached and dispassionate states of mind induced by the
exercise of sociological analysis means that different images of man,
the world, and the authoritative self will almost inevitably persist.

Sociology can divest itself of the quasi-Marxist, populistic,
rationalistic, anti-authoritarianism and blindness to the nature and
working of tradition which it has inherited; and it would, on the
whole, gain immeasurably thereby. It will in that event also find the
idiom, just as it has already begun to find the analytical categories,
which can give expression to a closer sense of affinity with those who
exercise authority or generally receive traditional beliefs. Fundamentally, however, the problem which confronts sociology here is the
problem of its relationship to religion, since authority and tradition are
at bottom, although not entirely, religious phenomena. They are religious phenomena in the sense that they claim validity through the
embodiment of, or through contact with, something ultimately, ir-

reducibly, and transcendently important. They contain the vital and touch on the source of the vital. There is much else to authority and tradition than this religious element; they are also supported by expediency, convenience, pig-headed complacency, and vain self-esteem—but they would not be the profound forces in the world which they have been and continue to be if they were not affected by this sense of the ultimately vital. The cleavage between sociological analysis and the religious belief, whether it be theological, political, or traditional, seems unbridgeable—and the gap might well remain a permanent one.

Sociological analysis still has forward steps to make in the appreciation of religious phenomena and the diversity of their manifestations. Sociologists can become much more religiously musical than they—except for Max Weber—have ever been. Sociologists might even become genuinely religious persons. Sociological analysis, as long as it remains within the most general outlines of its present fundamental framework, excludes any affirmation of the reality of miracles and revelations. It has no place at present for divine intervention in the affairs of man. These are hypotheses with which it at present dispenses. This refusal, which is seldom avowed because it is so much taken for granted, is the barrier between sociological analysis and the religious interpretation of events. Sociological analysis can make peace with rational natural law or with the natural law based on the theory of moral sentiments, but it cannot make a completely comfortable home with natural law based on a religion of revelation. It need not war with it, it need not carry on polemics, it need not regard it as its task to make men believe that religious beliefs are illusory. It can coexist in a spirit of reverence with a religion based on revelation, but there will always be a gap between them; and for genuinely religious persons, and not just stick-in-the-mud religious philistines, there must be some awareness of the sociological denial of the final claims of religion in general or of any of the great world religions of revelation in particular.

The same obtains for the relations between sociological analysis and the outlook of the politician at the pinnacle of authority or of the revolutionary outsider preoccupied with the subversion of the prevailing system of authority and with his own accession to its seat. The experience of authority at the extreme partakes of the nature of religious experience. It is a contact with the weightiest determinants of man's life. It is a confrontation which reaches toward the order which intrigues and overpoweringly excites. Although the idiom in which modern politicians and revolutionaries speak is not the cognitive idiom of religion—and this makes it appear easier to bridge the gap—the experience is of the same family as the religious experience. Powerful authority makes claims of the same order as those arising from religious experience. Sociological analysis can try to penetrate these states of mind by empathy, but it cannot easily accredit them according to their own standards. Sociology is agnostic vis-à-vis the order of being with which religions, authorities, and traditions purport to be in contact. The ultimate grounds of their validity are events which do not have the same reality to sociology as they have for those who espouse them. Their cognitive claims go beyond what sociology can acknowledge, however sympathetic it wishes to be.

These, then, are the outer limits of the extent to which sociology can become incorporated into the beliefs of society or can take an affirmative position with respect to traditional beliefs and authorities. The development of sociological analysis will only make this fundamental difference more explicit, in a way in which particular empirical inquiries are not likely to. "Theories of the middle range," because they avoid fundamentals, can enter into a more harmonious relationship with the thoughts of those who accept traditional beliefs or who exercise or seek to exercise authority.

Past and Present

The sense of the past. The interest in the past is not merely the product of contact between man's cognitive powers and the "stock" of events which are available to the play of those powers and which happen to have occurred in the past. It is the expression of a need to be in contact with the past, to feel continuous with it, to be in its presence. The need is a part of the need for the cognitive map which "locates" the self in the order of the universe. It is more than that. It is the sense that the existing self is only a fragment or stage in a larger being, which might be familial, neighborly, ethnic, national, or human. This larger being has a past which is as much a part of it as anything contemporary. Many human beings believe that in the past resides a value which is not exhausted by the virtue of having been the parent of the present. Of course, historians study the past to understand why the present is as it is, but they also study it, and many are fascinated by the results of their studies, because for them the past has a value of its own. Of course, many professional historians do not have this sense, any more than newspaper vendors have the great journalist's eagerness to be in the center of important events, or than many professional sociologists possess a consensual disposition, or than clergymen have a vivid sense of the divinely numinous. The writing of history has, however, been sustained by the great historians who do have that sense, and by the readers of their works who, in varying degrees, act under the same fascination. Even the least traditional societies possess, very unevenly distributed within the population, some attachment to the past, and the belief that vital matters, of great concern to the present, occurred there.

On the whole, it may be said that neither concrete empirical sociology nor theoretical sociology has been especially well endowed with a "sense of the past." Here again, Max Weber is an outstanding exception. Neither in the mental constitution of sociologists nor in their assessment of the societies which they have studied have the power and fascination of the past been prominent. The predominant conception of modern society as cut loose from tradition and veering towards traditionlessness gives adequate evidence of this deficient appreciation of pastness. A striking feature of almost all of contemporary sociological literature is the pervasive absence of any analysis of the nature and mechanisms of tradition. This omission only confirms the insensateness of sociologists to the significance of the past to other human beings, and their own deficient sense of the past.

The "oppositional" traditions of sociology, its friendliness toward the scientific spirit, its association with progressivistic ideas, are closely associated with this blindness to tradition. Exposure to the influence of romanticism encouraged the devaluation of modern society; it led to an idealization of "traditional" societies. Nonetheless, even this did not promote an analysis of traditional attachments, perhaps because the animus was directed against the modern society, and traditionality was only a stick with which to beat the modern dog. The fundamental distinction between *Gemeinschaft* and *Gesellschaft,* which still underlies so much of sociological analysis, called for a more direct consideration of the nature of tradition and the mechanisms of its transmission and reception. But it never became more than a residual category employed for purposes of delineating a problematical picture of modern society.

It is not so difficult to understand why American, French, and British sociology managed to avoid the issue. Their empiricism, their rationalism, and their commitment to enlightened improvement help to account for their failure. It is more difficult to understand the failure of German sociology to do more than it did. The profound influence of romanticism on German intellectual life, and the predominance of historical scholarship in the circles in which the fledgling sociology moved, should have been conducive to a greater appreciation of tradition and the traditional disposition. Even Max Weber's grandiose analysis of traditional authority leaves the question little further advanced than where he found it, at least as far as fundamentals are concerned.

Will the prospective development of sociological analysis overcome this deficiency? As long as the theory of middle principles preponderates, and as long as the preponderant concern of that theory is modern or contemporary Western—and, above all, contemporary American society—then this lack is not very likely to be made good. The traditional sense is not tangible enough in these situations to impose itself on the techniques of inquiry now in use, and the theory in question will operate only in a matrix of concrete observation.

As the theory which seeks only middle principles moves beyond Western societies into the African and Asian societies which are more overt in their attachment to the past and in their acknowledgment of the validity of sheer pastness, then some improvement might be expected. As long, however, as the focus is on the process of modernization—as it has been since sociologists took to the study of these societies—then the decay of tradition, rather than its maintenance and reproduction, will be accorded primacy. Mankind's attachment to the past thus will continue unstudied as long as this attitude prevails among sociologists.

The root of the deficiency goes very deeply into the constitution of contemporary sociology. It is improbable that it will yield readily. Sociological propositions are largely synchronic. Where they have not been so, it has largely been by virtue of the interest in personality structure—mainly of Freudian inspiration; and they have therefore extended themselves at most to a two-generational relationship occurring within the lifetime of a single generation. Those who find the situation intellectually unsatisfactory take refuge in a more uncritical historicism, adducing "history" as a residual genetic variable.

Pastness as the property of an object, of an individual action, of a symbol, or of a collectivity, has not yet been accorded a place in sociology. This need not remain the case; and the correction of the foundations of sociological theory in a way which would do justice to pastness should not be an insuperable task. Like much in general sociological theory, this step will depend as much on a matrix of sensibility as it does on the deductive powers.

The study of history is not in itself the therapy which sociology needs, although that is an important part of the cure. It is not just facts about the past that sociology needs, but a better sense of the past and a better sympathy with the sense of the past as it occurs in daily life and on exalted occasions. In the century-long *querelle des anciens et modernes,* there is so much that was right and humane on the modern side that one is reluctant to criticize its conclusions. But one of these conclusions is a presumed disjunction between the old and the modern. This has produced the disjunction between the archaic and the modern that has coincided with the equally deep disjunction between *Gemeinschaft* and *Gesellschaft* which came from a very different source. The preoccupation with this erroneous conception of modernity is probably the root of the trouble.

This brings us once more to the phenomena of primordiality and sacredness. Sociology will not come to grips with man's attachment to the past, and therewith of one of the most massive determinants of the continuity and stability of any order of society, until it has acquired a better, more sympathetic relationship with the phenomena of age, kinship, and religion. This is where the inherited conception of modern society has had disastrous results. The notion of a society which is disjunctive with past human experience—of an individuated society, in which the family has shrunken to its nuclear minimum and in which "secularism" is universal and all-pervasive—is an exaggeration of certain tendencies in modern society.

The growth of a general sociological theory will make sociologists more aware that, human beings being what they are, the historicism which is inherent in a doctrine of self-sufficient middle principles exaggerates and absolutizes certain tendencies in modern Western society that can never be completely fulfilled. The restoration of the affinity of the "archaic" and the "modern" would also require a more overt confrontation with the attachment to the past in modern society.

The myth-building which attachment to the past generates, the cosmological constructions which arise from the need to locate and objectivize the sacred, the morally irrational and repulsive emanations which come from the attachment to the primordial properties of objects—these are all contrary to the agnostic, secular, individualistic, liberal, and humane postulates of sociology. It is difficult, if not impossible, for an educated sociologist to share completely these images and attachments. They are not in harmony with his own best traditions; they are certainly repugnant to his worst traditions. He must, however, come closer to them than he has hitherto. He must come at least close enough to discern and appreciate their effectiveness in the lives of those who regard them as real.

To recognize the mythogenic propensities of man without believing in the literal, cognitive truthfulness of the imagery of the myths; to appreciate man's propensity to attach himself transfiguringly to the past of his collectivity, without sharing that attachment; to prize the achievement and cultivation of moral, intellectual, and aesthetic individuality, while understanding how rare it is in human history—these and similarly demanding tasks lie as great burdens on the sociologists of the present day and the future. A complete consensus with those we study would bring with it the cessation of our sociological activity; inadequate consensus will condemn that activity to intellectual insignificance and moral perniciousness. The general sociological theory which is now taking form makes possible a greater approximation to this optimal consensus of student and studied. Before it can do so, however, it will require reformulation, and that will require a concurrent enrichment of sensibility.

Sociology and contemporaneity. The past lives in us, but we live in the present. The present is actual experience. It is the moment of sensation which is different from recollection, rational knowledge, and anticipation. In a culture in which experience and sensation are prized, contemporaneity is also prized. Contemporaneity acquires a value of its own, independently, but derivatively, of sensation and experience. Being up-to-date in knowledge, in association, not losing contact with oncoming generations which have been born later than one's own, the sensation of the extended self—these are valuable in themselves, as long as they do not become exclusive of all else.

Man's need for conviviality is not just a need for cooperation or protection; it is not merely a need for "company," or a response to the threat of loneliness. Our convivial need goes beyond personal relationships, beyond the enlivening presence of other human beings loved or enjoyed. We need to be members of a society larger than our own associations and contacts—and on other than ecological, economic, or other functional grounds. There is a need to be in contact with the persons and events we see and directly experience. This is part of what Aristotle meant when he said that man was a "political animal."

The growth of consensuality in contemporary Western society, with its many disfigurements, has brought with it this enhanced need for contemporaneity. It is a merit and a motive of contemporary sociology that it is an organ of the need for contemporaneity. The practice of sociological inquiry and the reception of its results are equally gratifying to this need. The more abstract and general sociology becomes, the less it satisfies this need directly. General sociological theory, quite apart from its intellectual merits and the enjoyment of an intellectual exercise which it affords, is a legitimate transcendence of this need for contemporaneity.

It would be a genuine loss to our cultural life and a crippling of our moral existence if sociology were to become exclusively concentrated on the construction of a general theory, however scientific. The diagnosis of the age, *Zeitdiagnostik*, has always been the concern of the moral and aesthetically sensitive, who are aware of the flow of time. *Zeitdiagnostik*—of which our own time offers so many so melancholy and so ridiculous instances—has always been the device for criticizing one's contemporaries and for being in contact with them at the same time. It has very frequently, except for a fairly short span of time between the seventeenth and nineteenth centuries and in limited areas, been a means of derogating the present by contrasting it polemically with the past. It has, however, always testified to the acuteness of the sensation of contemporaneity and the need to give expression to it. One current of historicism corresponded exactly to this need, and this has remained one of the grounds for its persistence.

General sociological theory is a turning away from this preoccupation with presentness. It is that, however, only in its logical structure and intention. A general sociological theory which is no longer a mixture of *ad hoc* insights into the present and general categories will offer both a map which charts the world in which we stand and an intellectual location on a larger, trans-historical map.

Sociology and the Growth of "The Larger Mind"

Contemporary Western societies do not enjoy a good press in the world today. Dismay about them is widespread. Nor is it only among intellectuals, or those who still praise the Soviet Union or communist China or Yugoslavia, that their name is darkened. Their favored chroniclers cannot divert their minds from perversity, corruption, decay, ineptitude, frustration, and failure, and they have formed the self-image of these societies. The decay of morals, the triumph of "interests," technology which has escaped from control, nightmarish bureaucracy, the loneliness of man are the worn-out coins of an inflated intellectual currency. Sociology has certainly contributed to this inflation. Can sociology, by the devices and traditions available to it, correct the self-image of the time, can it reinterpret its own traditions?

Contemporary Western societies certainly are not completely integrated societies. The very notion of complete integration is an utter impossibility as well as an undesirable state. But it should also be said that contemporary Western societies, with all those deficiencies which the hypersensitive and hypocritical moral conscience of literary intellectuals and the sharpened eye of the sociological cyclops discern, are probably more integrated than any societies which have preceded them in world history or which are contemporaneous with them in other parts of the world. They are more integrated in the sense that there is more mutual awareness, more perception of others, more imaginative empathy about the states of mind and motivations of others, more fellow-feeling. How else can we explain the still small, but nonetheless real and growing, respect for the rights of blacks, African and American; the increased responsiveness to the human claims of women and children—indeed, the very idea of the welfare state and the right of every miserable creature among us to such happiness as this vale of tears allows? These represent a new stage in human existence. There is a consensus which is constructed out of each individual's perception of the individuality of others, out of a civility which perceives and accepts the plain humanity of another person, out of a sense of nationality which acknowledges rights arising from a shared territoriality. Although it is all fairly meager so far, it is more than what has gone before. The discrepancies between what is and what ought to be are painful to contemplate—partly because standards as to what ought to be have become more demanding of observance.

The progress of humanity toward a more liberal, more rational, more humane consensus has been very slow. And every step towards it gives rise to a new danger. Every new virtue which renders it possible can all too readily become a vice which undoes it. Perceptiveness of the state of mind of another can become a maliciously prying destruction of privacy. Love can turn to tyranny and then to hatred. The appreciation of individuality can become a self-indulgent perversity. The sense of nationality can become a monstrous exclusiveness. Civility can become a harshly self-righteous belief in the primacy of government over all other institutions.

And still, and nonetheless, the forward movement is a real thing, unprecedented in human history. Sociological analysis, no less unique and no less without a great preparatory tradition, part of this movement towards a greater awareness of one's fellow-man and one's society. Without this movement, there would be no sociological analysis as we know it. There was no sociology in antiquity or the Middle Ages, such as we have now, and there was no sociology in the great civilizations of Asia or in the lesser ones of Africa. There have been great sages and shrewd observers, but for better or for worse they were not sociologists. There have been preparers of the way, sometimes greater than most of those who have recently followed that way; sociology is a new thing. It is no derogation of the past achievements of the mind of man to say that the realistic novel, as it appeared first and intermittently in the eighteenth century and then with greater density in the nineteenth and early twentieth centuries, depicting the shape of a human life and taking its place among the greatest genres of artistic creation, did not exist in Western antiquity or the Middle Ages, or that it did not exist in India or Africa, or even in China or Japan (although approximations thereto did exist in these countries). Nor is it a derogation of human greatness in the Western past or outside the West to insist that the vivid, curious, empathic appreciation of the details of the patterns of man's action and relationship with other human beings and the imagination about the shape of whole societies and their natural history are parts of this new phase of more intimate and more civil relationships.

In this "growth of the larger mind," as Charles Horton Cooley named it, sociology is intimately involved. It is its product and it contributes to it. It also contributes to its deformity.

Sociology, in principle, takes the other man as he is; it tries to find out what he does, what he thinks and feels. This curiosity can be a perverse intrusion into privacy, it can be part of a program of acquiring information to be used to manipulate. It is also an acknowledgment of the other's right to an independent moral existence. In trying to acquire the interviewed person's account of his own past as he sees it and in his own words, the sociologist is introducing the interviewed person into science as a morally meaningful being. This is one of the partially realized possibilities.

Sociological inquiry is a social relationship, but it is not and cannot be a relationship of love or friendship. The detachment which it demands from the investigator deprives it of the symmetry and spontaneity which affection demands. Rudiments of a personal relationship are formed and then restricted by detachment and by the limitations of time. Within the limits imposed by the primacy of the cognitive interest in the guidance of the relationship between sociologist and interviewee, the relationship offers the opportunity of the opening outward of the minds of men of all types toward other men, through the sociologist as an intermediary.

Through the medium of sociology, as it has through literary works and genre-paintings, the content of a human life flows outward into other minds and lives in a wider area. The "larger mind" is extended and deepened through the program of a sociology which retains some of the concreteness of the interviews and observations on which it rests. Of course this concreteness is often lost in the course of analysis; sometimes it is not sought or, if sought, is not attained.

The consensual orientation did not create the techniques of present-day sociological inquiry. It found many of them ready to hand in the social survey itself which came out of heterogeneous traditions. The traditions of political arithmetic, scientific and concerned with national power, and those of the surveys of poverty were much improved by the development of the technique of participant-observation. Academic psychology and market research added their mite. Psychoanalysis contributed the prolonged intensive interview. Journalists like Mayhew and Steffens also enabled sociologists to appreciate the value of the interview. Travelers, missionaries, ships' doctors, soldiers, colonial administrators who were the forerunners of social anthropology also affected the sociologists' awareness of the fruitfulness of interviewing.

There are risks which are run in the eagerness to be in communion with other human beings. The more rigorous scientific techniques which discipline this eagerness also suppress it to some extent. They certainly narrow its receptiveness and make it more superficial. There is a mixture of motives associated with contemporary social inquiry. The technological, the consensual, and the alienative dispositions are present at all levels of sociological inquiry; and sometimes it happens that the first and the last impulses get the better of the consensual components. The cultivation of the alienative approach to human conduct and to its organization in institutions and societies would impair the growth of sociology both as an intellectual undertaking and as a part of the moral life of its age. If the academic practice of sociology refuses to acknowledge its rootedness in consensual experience and if it stresses instead the technological and, by virtue of that, the alienative dispositions, which are very intimately connected, it will dry up the springs of its own vitality.

Sociological theory is not, and will not be in all likelihood for some time to come, a useful, rigorously deductive theory. It rests on a rich matrix of concrete knowledge of many societies and of many parts of these societies. The full range of experience and learning necessary for the construction of a universally applicable general theory of society is certainly beyond the capacities of any one man. No one could himself do the systematic research or acquire the experience of life which must underlie such a theoretical construction. It will rest on the work of many men, and much of that work must be concrete and based on firsthand experience and intimate confrontation with the human beings with whom it is concerned. The collation of information gathered for administrative and commercial purposes, useful though it is, cannot produce that enriched matrix of concrete understanding necessary for the guidance of sociological theory. Empirical research, conducted by techniques adapted from experimental psychology and intended for technological purposes, cannot produce it either—even though, within marked limits, that type of research can have definite cognitive value. These techniques cannot produce it because they are not conducted in the medium of empathy, which is an essential constituent of consensus and which can grow only from direct human contact.

The more exact techniques of sociological research, in their present state and probably rather far into the future, produce results which are indeterminate without the support of empathically acquired knowledge. In fact, most of the rigorous research conducted at present is interesting because of the results of empathy which accumulate in their interstices. Without that "supplement" of empathy, the results would be of little intellectual consequence.

The results of concrete sociological inquiry would be unusable in the construction of sociological theory if they did not have this effluvium of perceptions which influence the direction of mind of the theorist. This effluvium is the unarticulated knowledge which grows from the experiencing of other human beings, from experiencing them in all the fulness of consensual contact. If the concepts of sociology were perfectly explicit and precise, and if rules of deduction could be established to govern their elaboration and interconnection, there might be less need for this primitive dependence. Such a development does not, however, seem to be immediately on the schedule of progress of sociology. And as long as sociology does not become absorbed into or subjugated to neurology or cybernetics, the fact that it is continuous with the experiencing of human beings will incessantly engender a condition in which much of our understanding will be penumbral around the zone which we can make explicit. Even if human relationships and mutual understanding lose some of their present opacity, there will always be an area of shadows.

The richness of experience will always be beyond our capacities for articulation. Our articulations will always be challenged to extend themselves into the zone of the still unarticulable. To seek this extension will require the kind of contact with the object of inquiry—even when the inquiry is pursued at the levels of highest abstraction—which only consensuality can furnish.

Sociology, not always beneficially, is slowly entering into the broader current of opinion. It is doing so very unequally. As the subject becomes established in the universities, and as larger proportions of the population attend universities or acquire some of the higher culture available in universities, so sociology will pass beyond the condition of an academic speciality, practiced and thought about only in academic environments. It will become part of educated opinion. This educated opinion even now receives reinforcement from the creation of a body of sociological literature which is capable of being read and appreciated and which is even sought out by the educated public outside the universities.

Sociology has begun to play the same role as psychoanalysis did through its popular reception. It could be employed to "unveil" base motives and discredit their bearers. It could encourage an immoral manipulativeness. It could continue to propagate an image of society as a decayed state of nature. This is no more inevitable than it is desirable. Concrete research which discloses the motivations of human beings and the institutions in which those motivations operate can bring the persons described, and the whole class which they exemplify, closer to those whom it informs. The readers and students of concrete sociology can be brought into a more empathic, although still unilateral, relationship with their subjects. Concrete sociology, which has learned the art of exposition, can heighten the identification of its readers with those they read about and render plausible and vivid the actions and sentiments of human beings.

As sociologists spread their activities over the surface of the earth, they widen the consensual network, they thicken its strands, in a way in which the literature of travel, geography, and even social anthropology seldom did. The sociological knowledge of the "nature and causes of things" would change the structure of our relationships with the human beings we study and with the species at large.

Sociology and Policy

The Philosopher-King and Counselor of Princes

The line of thought from which contemporary sociology has come forth was occupied with problems of public policy in a way which, in the nineteenth and twentieth centuries, became less prominent. The

great figures of classical political philosophy considered the fundamental problems of policy from the point of view of men who had to
exercise authority and to make practical decisions. Even when they
themselves lived in remoteness from practical affairs, the clarification
of the standards for the judgment and guidance of public policy was
always close to the center of their attention. The rulers' problems,
reduced to fundamentals, were their problems. The problem of maintaining order through the exercise of princely authority was the point
of departure of classical political philosophy; in the age of mercantilism, it was concerned with the maintenance and extension of the
power of the state; and it was extended, by modern liberalism, to the
maintenance of liberty in a framework of order. Political philosophy
was regarded, by those who professed it, as a means of enlightening
rulers—and citizens—regarding their right ends and the appropriate
means. One of the greatest ancestors of modern empirical sociology,
Sir William Petty, viewed his task as the quantitative inventory of
what existed. This inventory was justified because it would enable the
prince to know the resources over which he could dispose to
safeguard and increase his power. Early economic theory accepted
the same task. Even after mercantilism gave way to liberalism,
economic theory was still intended to be a guide to policy.

A rather fundamental change occurred in the course of the
nineteenth century. The coming forward of the "oppositional science," and the first academic establishment of the embryonic sociology of the turn of the century, inhibited the readiness of sociologists
to take the standpoint of the ruler. They wished to influence rulers but
they increasingly wished to do it through the medium of an informed
and hence aroused public opinion. In the United States, an important
antecedent of urban sociology—the muckraking movement—was
strongly anti-political, and it left a lasting impact on sociological
studies there. The "survey movement" in America and the
"poverty-line" surveys in Great Britain were not intended so much
for the use or even counsel of administrators or legislators as they
were intended to prod the leaders of public opinion into a more solicitous attitude toward the hardships of the poor. The prevailing
liberalism of the age replaced princes and legislators by the leaders of
public opinion. "Science" became a new means of influencing rulers.

Except in Germany, where the "socialism of the chair" sought to
keep the social sciences in the service of the state, the forerunners of
sociology at the end of the century wished to make clear the difference between social science and social policy. They did so for all sorts
of reasons: they wished to establish the "scientific" dignity of their
discipline by dissociating it from political action; they thought that it
was enjoined by the nature of scientific knowledge. They also distrusted politicians, who, they thought, would do what is right only if

pressed hard to do it by a public whose opinion had been illuminated and aroused by scientific knowledge of social facts.

This general tendency toward the "de-politicization" of social science and of sociology in particular might in part have resulted from the "separation" of the various spheres of life in the liberal society of the nineteenth century. The relative autonomy of the spheres fostered a belief in the possibilities of separate fields of inquiry, with the resultant expulsion of political elements from sociology and economics. (In the present century, the academic separation of political science, sociology, and economics from one another, and their consequent de-politicization, never went as far in Germany as it did in the Western countries where liberalism had flourished.) Moreover, the nature of the ideal social order "prescribed" by liberal economic theory, which was the most impressive product of this intellectual division of labor, minimized the importance of large, central decisions. It would disperse decisions into a great multitude of autonomously acting organs. The intellectual preponderance of economic theory among the social sciences in the English-speaking world thus reinforced this tendency of each social science to deny the function and virtue of politicians.

The development of the universities of the nineteenth century and their relations with the world of affairs also appear to have been an important factor in the de-politicization of the social sciences. The great schemes of interpretation and judgment formulated by the masters who formed the traditions from which sociology emerged had grown up outside the universities and in a fairly close connection with politics and practical affairs. Except for Adam Smith, no major figure of social science outside Germany, until the latter part of the nineteenth century, was primarily a university teacher. The development of social sciences as sciences, and of sociology in particular, entailed making their scientific disinterestedness clear. If the practitioners of these sciences had been simply reformers or at worst agitators without an adequate scientific basis, they would have deprived their subjects of their academic legitimacy. Yet the matter was not entirely unambiguous.

In Germany social science had some connection with the theory of the state as the embodiment of the highest values, and professors of social science were civil servants sworn to loyalty to the state. When Germanic social science was introduced into the American universities by men who had had their training in Germany in the 1870s and 1880s, the German theory of the state found no echo. The administrative recipes which formed a large part of the syllabus of the *Staatswissenschaften* were accepted as useful by university teachers who thought that the main problems of public policy could be solved by the reform of the civil service. This was intended to be a curb on the depredations of politicians, not an improvement of the instruments for the service of the politicians by social scientists.

This period of university history in the United States coincided with a period of severe alienation of the educated from politics as practiced by professional politicians. The corruption of government at all levels attendant on industrial and urban expansion revolted the intellectuals. This led them to carry on a guerilla war of intermittent urban reform and scholarly journalistic exposure of the "malefactors of great wealth" and their political confederates. The American academic social scientists lost the sense of affinity with the rulers of their society which the great figures of the social science tradition had had in the first centuries of modern times.

This was the milieu into which sociology came. It was unaware of the breadth and depth of its great traditions, and all around itself it saw its social science colleagues in opposition. (There were exceptions in the Middle West, especially in Wisconsin, where the Progressive opposition formed the government, and academic social scientists were, once more, for a time the counselors of princes.) Political science became concerned with the reform of the civil service and the "neutralization" of politics. Political philosophy, too, fell victim to intradepartmental specialization and the moral temper of the age; it degenerated from the greatness of its past, renouncing the ancient aspiration of the political philosopher to counsel the prince and to make him into a philosopher.

Sociology did nothing to compensate for the political abdication of political science. In order to prove their right to existence, sociologists sought to find a sphere of events left untouched by the already accredited social sciences. The inherited distinction between the state and civil society fitted this need very well. Even though they found a justification for their independent existence in the numerous "social problems" which had arisen in connection with urbanization and immigration, they seldom expected them to be solved by governmental action. Some sociologists thought that political decisions were impotent to affect "social processes." The persistence of evolutionary, biologistic, instinctivist theories in French, British, and American sociology was not conducive to the formulation of a sociological theory in which knowledge and rational decision were important categories in the conception of action. Neither in substance nor in its general theoretical scheme did sociology concern itself much with politics, with political decisions, or with decision-making in other spheres. The "new history" to which sociologists felt akin was a revolt from political history and from the history of rulers—it was a denial of the relevance of political decisions in social life; it was a denial of their worthiness as objects of study.

This tendency to withhold themselves from concern with the problems which appear on the agenda of the makers of the highest policies was furthered by the desire of social scientists, especially sociologists, to be scientific. The vastly superior prestige of the natural sciences, and the inferiority feelings of the social sciences in the face of the condescension they received from both the scientific and the humanistic disciplines, led some sociologists to the conviction that their own salvation lay in becoming scientific. "Scientific" meant being "objective," totally cut off from the object by any tie of sympathy, deliberately indifferent to the fate of the object. To be scientific meant other things as well, but these are the aspects which concern us here.

The program of "ethical neutrality" involved not simply the denial, from the scientistic belief, that recommendations for policy could be based exclusively on statements of fact and that factual propositions could without anything else supply guiding norms for political action. It involved, for some social scientists, a belief that an utter detachment in matters of policy was incumbent on a social scientist, beyond even the boundaries of his scientific role. For such social scientists— and there were certainly some sociologists among them—it involved renunciation of the role of the citizen. There was no uniformity and much confusion about this, and they were often better in their conduct than a strict adherence to their doctrine would have caused them to be.

Logically, the proposition which asserts that judgments of fact alone cannot provide to judgments of value is correct; what was incorrect was the deduction that, becausae empirical knowledge alone can offer no ineluctible imperative in the determination of the ultimate ends of individual conduct or social policy, social scientists are not only not qualified to discuss questions of value and policy, but their very profession as social scientists forbids their serious involvement in evaluative problems in any way—and particularly in the selection of problems. Not many sociologists took this extreme position. They did take active roles in civic affairs, but with very few outstanding exceptions who included no sociologists they did not stand for public office. They tended towards the pole of criticism of politics from the outside rather than as participants on the inside of the affairs of the leading parties.

Social scientists did, nonetheless, serve on governmental commissions, testify before congressional committees, and participate in political and social reform movements, but on the whole, they were exceptions to the mood of their professions. Woodrow Wilson, as professor of political science and president of the United States, and Charles Merriam, who sought to be mayor of Chicago, were the great exceptions to the prevalent attitude among American university social scientists which rejected politics as unclean. Even among those who participated in reform politics, the improvement of politics consisted in their elimination. The "city-manager" movement which would take municipal affairs "out of politics" is illustrative of this attitude. This contemptuous and distrustful alienation from the holders of power and the makers of public decisions brought about a situation in which sociologists and other American academic social scientists abstained from politics. It is true that the two careers could not easily be combined; the repugnance was evident enough in the attitudes of social scientists and on the occasion of their amateur sorties into civil affairs.

The Return to Policy

Of course, sociology did not have a great deal to offer at that time to policy-makers, administrators, and those concerned with the public good. It was the First World War which showed, particularly in the United States, that academic social scientists might usefully serve governments and any other organizations interested in controlling and modifying human behavior. The work of psychologists in the assessment of aptitudes for the United States Army during the First World War gave rise to a new conception of the relevance of the scientific study of man to the exercise of authority. This wartime experience affected the development of psychology, and therewith of social sciences, toward personnel selection and social psychology. Places were found for political scientists, historians, and geographers in "political information" and in the fumbling organization of the peace. After the war, psychologists, inspired by their acceptance, extended their skills in testing, selection, and counseling; and many bodies, private and public, sought to employ them. The great extension of advertising and propaganda after the First World War, and the increased prestige of psychologists in associated activities, gave many opportunities in the world of affairs to academically trained social scientists. The turning by enterprisers toward industrial psychology—which was also accentuated by the war and particularly by the disturbances in industrial relations following the war—was another stimulus to the increasingly mature science of psychology and an additional invitation for the social sciences to think manipulatively about society. The private foundations began to think about what social scientists could do to aid them in the performance of the duties which their wealth laid upon them, namely, to promote human welfare by "solving social problems."

Today governments, political parties, the military, private business, civic and economic organizations compete with universities and research institutions as employers of social scientists. Naturally, the process has gone farther in the United States than elsewhere, but Great Britain, France, Germany, the Netherlands, Italy, and

Poland—in short, all the countries where sociology is moderately well established—have moved in this direction. Knowledge of the "facts" can always be useful to those who exercise authority, regardless of whether they wish to share that truth with those over whom their power is exercised so that they act conjointly, or whether they wish to induce through their monopoly particular patterns of behavior in other persons.

They engage the services of social scientists because to be scientific is to be worthy of deference, even though they will not bear that knowledge in mind when they make decisions; as governments incline more and more toward intervention into the economy and undertake comprehensive economic planning, and as the "welfare state" advances towards the "egalitarian state," a more specific knowledge of the human beings over whom authority plays appears desirable.

The growth of mass communications and the advertisement of consumer goods have generated a large demand for sociologists in private employment. Nowadays, almost any organization with a claim to respectability believes it needs a sociologist to help it with the tasks it has taken on itself. Mental hospitals, medical schools, housing authorities, institutions for the aged, scientific institutions, churches and missionary bodies—these are only a few of the bodies which think they have to gain from the labors of the sociologist. Social scientists, after many decades of abstention from the exercise of executive influence on human affairs, except from the outside, are now involved in it more numerously and more intricately than ever before.

At more exalted levels, they work primarily as consultants and advisors. At lower levels, they are providers of knowledge, sometimes simply descriptive or enumerative, sometimes more general, gathered by the techniques of contemporary social research and interpreted in the light of the prevailing sociological theory.

Three Types of Orientation to Policy

Philosophers and humanistic scholars in the past sought or accepted invitations to serve rulers in the hope that they could make the rulers wise and hence lead them to rule in accordance with ethical precepts. The present situation is different; the older function is in attrition.

Social scientists are not drawn upon nowadays for their wisdom as counselors in the clarification of fundamental alternatives, nor as guides in the choice from among these alternatives once discovered.

Sociologists have, over the years, taken three types of attitude toward authority. They have sought to serve it as unquestioning servants; they have felt repelled by it, denounced it and censured association with it; and they have regarded themselves as equal to it and equally part of the same society. These three attitudes correspond to three modes of use of sociological knowledge referred to earlier in this essay: the use of sociological knowledge as a part of the technological action performed by the powerful over those they control; the use of sociology as a disavowal of responsibility and as criticism from the outside; the use of sociology as part of the process of modification of the relationship of authority and subject through the enhancement of collective self-understanding and of the sense of affinity. These three modes may be summarized as technology, opposition, and consensuality. Each has its characteristic mode of research, its own conception of what sociological knowledge should be like at the height of its development, and its characteristic conception of the calling of sociology. Each has its own intellectual tradition, somewhat separate from the others' but frequently overlapping. Different though they are from each other in tone, emphasis, and feeling about what the world is and ought to be, they are also capable of joining with each other. One sometimes adopts the techniques of another, thus the knowledge gained by the techniques associated with social technology might also be applied consensually.

Technological sociology in the service of policy. Sociologists who entered the service of government were not looked to for basic truths about human behavior derived either from rigorous scientific research, from sociological theory, or from the slow accretion of wisdom. Social scientists have rather been viewed as instruments for descriptive reporting and for the provision of devices and "programs" concerning the most effective ways to carry out a given policy. For the most part, they have provided estimates, more or less accurate, of the magnitude of particular variables, descriptions of trends, inventories of activities and beliefs. They have told their employers about the attitudes held by their subjects about the various actions and policies of the political superiors who wish to control them. They have reported on the frequency of alleged intentions to perform particular actions, such as voting, changing residence, sowing a certain number of acres with certain types of seeds, etc. They have attempted to show that, under certain conditions, certain consequences would occur. These types of knowledge are presumably of interest to politicians and civil servants because they would be able, on the basis of such knowledge, to adapt their actions more realistically to the conditions which they must manipulate in order to attain their goals. Possessing this knowledge, they would at least, in principle, be able to elicit more cooperation or arouse less resistance from the subjects of their authority, and thus attain their goals more easily. In their very role as exercisers of authority, they are concerned with the future and with the consequences of particular changes in their own behavior on the behavior of others. Their decisions as to whether this many policemen should be assigned to a particular district, or whether such and such housing should be provided for a given group, or whether school classes should have a particular ethnic composition, take into account the probability that certain particular events would occur if they act in one way, while other particular events would occur if they act in different ways. According to a scientistic sociological ideal, the ruler should have available to him sociological propositions which predict that, given certain conditions in the subject population, if the ruler acts in a specified way he will call forth specified responses from his subjects. The ruler is the independent variable, the subjects are the dependent variables. Sociology, if it were an adequate technology, would tell the independent variable how modifications in itself would bring forth modifications in its dependent variables, i.e., the subjects of authority.

The point of departure of these predictions is an approximate description of the present and recently past situation. The inventories, the estimates of magnitude and explanatory analyses, with which sociological research workers furnish policy-makers are used by them as data for their own predictions or "interpretations." The social scientist might, indeed, accompany his inventory or his depiction of trends with his own estimate of the way in which one course of action or another, working on these magnitudes, will affect the realization of the ostensible goals of the policy; he might even present data which show, on the basis of a contrived test, how the population in question would respond to one kind of measure or arrangement as compared with another.[4] Here, the social scientist does not merely determine isolated magnitudes; he analyzes the causal relations of the variables. Because of the far from determinate character of presumably demonstrated causal connections in present-day sociological research, this part of the report is usually not entirely persuasive to anyone who does not already incline toward that conclusion, on the basis of his own experiences or because he thinks that it will be rhetorically useful in gaining the assent of others to the policy which he wishes to carry through. The description of what happened is more likely to be accepted than the explanation or theory of why it happened.

4. The significant difference between applied sociological research and other types of sociological research lies neither in the logical structure of the propositions with which an investigation concludes, in their subject-matter, nor even in the aims of the investigator. The term "applied research" in the social sciences refers to investigations performed for policy-makers who will presumably take the resulting propositions into account in their decisions. It is simply research, the results of which are allegedly to be applied in some way in practice by those who are responsible for the care of practical affairs. It is not applied research in the sense of the application of scientifically tested general principles obtained in "basic" or "pure" research to the explanation of concrete and particular situations or to the management or construction of concrete and particular constellations of actions. Applied social research of the latter type might indeed develop in the course of time, when there is a body of

Yet there is nothing forever fixed in this situation. Research techniques are improving. There is, despite all the intellectual squalor of much of sociology of the present day, a gradual improvement in skill and realism in interpretation of the observations made by these improved techniques. There will probably come a time when the interpretation of data made by the sociologist will increase its persuasiveness, even to a hardheaded and thoughtful administrator or politician, so that he will give it a heavier weighting in forming his judgment than is usually the case nowadays.

There is no doubt that "sociology" would then be more "useful" to authority than it has been through most of the present century. Throughout the earlier part of this century, it was barely competent to do more than give a very loose account of a trend or an existing state of affairs; its explanations of events left much uncertainty. As it improved in technique, its marginal function in the making of policy became more apparent. The long abdication of the philosopher from his role as counselor of princes was now being paid for. In the 1930s when economists and political scientists were recalled to the presence of the powerful, sociologists were called to the performance of intellectually menial, even if costly, functions in the provision of descriptive information. The executive used them to supplement its capacities in an important but still a relatively subsidiary function. They had their triumphs in the statistical offices of the government; they did not come close to policy. Sociologists were to help the maker of policy by estimating trends and magnitudes, but they entered into nothing more fundamental in the formation of policy. Given the technically undeveloped condition of sociological research, its theoretical backwardness, and the incivility of so much of the culture of the sociologist, there was little to regret. There would not have been any great advantage to policy had it been otherwise. Sociology, for its part, benefited from its relegation to menial offices.

The progress of research techniques, which has been such a considerable feature of the development in sociology in the past quarter of a century, and, particularly, the development of opinion surveys, with the concomitant improvement of sampling and interviewing, owes very much to the support of governmental bodies and commercial enterprises. Although practically all the theory underlying these improvements was created in universities, the techniques themselves

---

basic propositions, rigorously tested by systematic empirical procedures and systematically integrated into general theory. Since there are practically no such propositions in social science today, this type of applied social research cannot exist, at least for the time being.

The difference from applied research in the better established sciences, therefore, consists (a) in the absence of rigorously tested general propositions; and (b) in the absence of rigorous intellectual controls over the results of the manipulations introduced in accordance with those hypotheses.

were refined largely in the course of their application in the service of government and business. Without this experience, the capacity of sociologists to deal with large masses of data and their facility in resorting to such extensive bodies of data in order to test hypotheses would not be so advanced as it is. Content analysis, sociometric tests, attitude scaling, latent structure analysis, regression analysis, causal analysis were all helped on their way in the course of taking advantage of the opportunities for research on behalf of government and business enterprise.

The results of research done by use of these and other techniques are bound, in their scientific form, to have a restricted audience. They can be appreciated only by other sociologists with high academic qualifications in the universities, in government or in private business enterprises. Their chances of reaching and being understood by high civil servants or politicians who are not expert in their mastery of these techniques, are not great. At some point, if the results are to be assimilated into policy, they must be made intelligible to laymen.

But even if the results of this kind of research are not drawn into the formulation of policy, the financial support which is provided in anticipation of such a possibility will move sociologists forward on a scientific path. For much of this kind of research, quantitative descriptions have been more important than generalized substantive propositions. The substantive progress of sociological knowledge has not been commensurate with the progress of techniques, and the continued support of research intended to promote the ends of government is not likely to change this greatly, although this outcome is not inevitable. As things stand at present, existing sociological knowledge is, at best, more suitable as orientation for the formation of judgment than it is instrumental to the execution of policy. It is, however, the desire of sociologists who do this kind of research that sociological knowledge should be able to provide the latter service. The aim is to furnish precise particular predictions; it is not to construct and demonstrate the validity of general interpretative or theoretical principles.

The progress towards the provision of precise particular predictions is real but spotty. The increased financial resources which are now placed at the disposal of sociological research and the technical improvement have provided employment for many well qualified, gifted young men and women. The increasing intellectual complexity of research techniques and the intricacy of analysis which they permit challenge acute intelligences. It is possible that brilliant minds like these which have been attracted to mathematics, physics, econometrics, and linguistics will see, in this kind of technological sociology, an equally demanding and equally rewarding field for their talents. These talents will not always be content to work in the sphere of research techniques alone, nor will they always be satisfied with the improvement of description and the establishment of particular relationships. They will inevitably push forward into more theoretical analysis of the interconnections of the events before them. They might succeed in going beneath the surface of particular events. They might produce a science consisting in the first instance of "middle principles," or "theories of middle range." Sociology might at last move towards becoming the science of which some of its great nineteenth-century forerunners dreamed.

As such a science, sociology would permit the application of which genuine sciences are capable. Carrying on the scientistic tradition, its application would entail experimentation on its human subjects in the light of the scientific knowledge it has created. The scientific and the scientistic traditions and the patronage which now supports this development might well keep it on a technological course. The existing division of labor between policy-making and scientific "intelligence" would remain.

Although sociologists will often cross the line in their capacity as consultants, expert witnesses, and publicists, their governmental patrons are likely to keep them on the side of the line which justifies their support. Many sociologists will find this division of labor congenial to their own scientistic attitudes.

The scientific tradition is a tradition in which the subject-matter of research has been alien to the scientists who do the research. It is not the romantic revolutionary tradition of oppositional sociology; but it is a tradition of alienation nonetheless. The tradition of scientism—which is different from the practice of science—is a tradition of tidiness, of planned and ordered progress, of continuous improvement along clearly defined lines. It is impatient of inefficiency, of a plurality of ends, of compromise and slovenliness. It wants its principles to be clear and their application to be prompt and efficient. It likes comprehensiveness and the long-range view.

There is nothing in this view of the world which renders it logically compelling to those who practice sociology. There is, however, an inner affinity between the scientistic outlook and the practice of the physical sciences which makes their adhesion in the course of modern history more than adventitious. By no means all physical scientists have shared the scientistic outlook, but it is not an accident that it is prominent among those who have extended their activities into the public sphere. They are in favor of governmental planning, which appears to them to be more "scientific" than the mutual adjustment of a plurality of groups within society. They are trying to discover "solutions to practical social problems" and the politicians and civil servants are the ones to put these "solutions" into practice.

It is not merely the extra-scientific traditions of the scientific movement which cause me to think that the technological development of sociology under the patronage of the mighty accentuates the scientistic turn of sociology. The internal life of the subject will also play an influential part. One source of technical progress in sociology has hitherto come from psychology—the most scientific and the most scientistic of the various branches of the study of man. The fields of sociology which have benefited from these advances have been those closest to psychology, e.g., attitude studies, public opinion polling, small groups, industrial relations, organizational behavior, etc. The sociological theory which has been derived from these studies has been "psychologistic," i.e., it has reduced society to the behavior of individuals in precisely defined social situations. It has pronounced technological manipulative overtones. Some of the leading exponents of this kind of "reductionistic" sociology are explicit in their refusal to see anything wrong in manipulation.

For better or for worse, the experimental tradition of psychology and its early invitation to help in the tasks of personnel selection, propaganda, and advertising, and the increase in the sophistication of the study of learning processes have strengthened the manipulative orientation. Despite occasional efforts in a contrary direction, improvement of the condition of man and the increase in the efficiency of institutions through manipulation continue as a basic article of faith in the program of psychology. The sociology which is partly inspired by that psychology shares the belief in that article of faith.

The "terms of employment" exert a similar pressure. The large-scale employment of sociologists in market research, or in inquiries which resemble market research, on behalf of civic, political, and governmental organizations usually delimits the sphere of competence of the sociologist. There are situations in which he might be invited to discuss the fundamental issues of policy, or in which chance and intention enable him to discuss these issues as one who shares the responsibility for decision. On the whole, this is not so; and sociologists drawn into such service become used to accepting this division of functions. Sometimes it is because they conceive of themselves as scientists who have no special qualifications for discussing "evaluative" questions; sometimes they regard these questions as falling outside their responsibility as experts called upon by their employers only for a certain kind of judgment and no other. It should be added that not all manipulatively oriented research is done outside the universities. It is not just a function of the "terms of employment"; the general cultural tradition of the natural sciences and the aura of experimental psychology can produce similar results in sociology within universities.

By no means all sociological research done for government or private corporate bodies is designed to facilitate manipulation. For one thing, sociologists are not always, despite their intentions, able to design an inquiry so that the manipulable variable and the independent variable coincide. The separation of sociologists from policy-making has been so long and so great that, even though these sociologists might wish to make a policy more effective, many of them have been unable to design their inquiries in a way which will produce the necessary recipes.

The precise inventories, particular predictions, and ad hoc recommendations which emerge from this kind of research should not be considered as adding a totally new danger to human freedom. Social science in the service of authority, even if it produces knowledge which is used technologically for the deception and the manipulation of the subjects of authority, only comes upon an already long-sullied scene. It would not be technological sociology which brings about the degradation of man—that has been going on for a long time. Scientific sociological research might possibly make deception more skillful, it might make it more effective—just as developments in electronics make intrusions into privacy more effective, and perhaps more tempting, or as nuclear weapons make war more destructive.

The sociology used in this way would share the immorality of its use and would therefore merit our moral condemnation—but only insofar as the use or the intention was immoral. Not all manipulation is necessarily immoral—e.g., the education of children—and the scientific sociology which would serve such manipulation is not immoral either. The real deficiency of technological sociology, which would remain despite its scientific rigor, its moral naiveté, and its harmlessness (hitherto) is its failure to grasp that the true calling of sociology is to contribute to the self-understanding of society rather than to its manipulated improvement.

Oppositional sociology and policy. It was the Great Depression of 1939 which gave a marked twist to the "oppositional" tradition of American sociology, diverting part of it into the more radical course which it has since followed. A variety of currents of Marxism began to flow through the intellectual classes in the United States in the second half of the 1930s. After the Second World War and especially after 1956, dissident Marxism, enriched and reclothed by Max Weber, was ready to take up where liberal and populist criticism had left off. Psychoanalysis was added to the armament of criticism, especially through the writings of Karen Horney and Erich Fromm. Several of these traditions came together in the work of the Institute for Social Research under the leadership of Max Horkheimer and in the sociological discussions of "mass society." C. Wright Mills revived the ideas of Thorstein Veblen and adapted them to the newer beliefs.

This broad current of sociological research and analysis has continued and accentuated the oppositional tradition. It has passed from a partially "outside" position to one of much greater alienation; it alleges that contemporary society, except for a few dissident movements, is on a wholly wrong track and that there is nothing which can put it right short of a "total transformation." Romanticism, Marxism, psychoanalysis, Darwinism, and populism have coalesced to form a point of view which sees modern, and especially contemporary, society as the theater of a passionate struggle for power, of a war of each against all, saved from absolute chaos by deliberately maintained ignorance and stupefaction, by fear and repression.

Oppositional sociology—a large part of sociology—did not aim to make itself useful to the rulers of society. It was indeed more interested in making the wider public more aware of their deficiencies and of the deficiencies in their societies for which they were held responsible. It wished to influence public opinion, not academic opinion and not the opinion of officeholders. The moderately oppositional sociology was addressed in the first instance to the educated classes, which included academics such as philosophers, historians, and economists, because it was thought they were already concerned or could be aroused to the point of becoming concerned about "social conditions." The more radically oppositional sociologists addressed themselves to a very similar audience. When Werner Sombart was a young man and still a Marxist, he did not address himself primarily or directly to the working classes. Robert Michels, who belonged to a radical section of the German Social-Democratic party, does not seem to have addressed the first edition of his book on political parties to an audience of workingmen. C. Wright Mills, who was the main radical sociologist in the United States, also wrote for an educated public. There is no evidence that he intended his books for an audience of radical workingmen or workingmen who were to be brought over to a radical political outlook.

By the time Mills appeared on the sociological scene there were many established academic sociologists, but Mills does not appear to have addressed himself to them either; he did address himself to the younger teachers and students of the subject. He certainly did not address himself to governmental officeholders or to managers of business enterprises. He had neither the hope nor the desire that his writings should be used by persons in positions of economic or governmental power for the furtherance of their ends; he thought those ends inimical to the common good. Nothing was further from his mind than to serve those ends. He aimed at an indeterminate, obscurely circumscribed educated public whose members he wished to turn against their own society so that they would in some undefined way contribute to its revolutionary transformation. Mills, like Robert Lynd before him, held against his contemporary sociologists their unquestioning acceptance of the existing structure of society and their readiness to accept the stipulation by their patrons of the problems which they were to investigate. Mills thought that these vices were especially characteristic of contemporary American empirical sociology. He took it for granted that men of honor, such as he thought the radical sociologists he was hoping to create would be, would not betray their ideal by serving a social order as corrupt and oppressive as he thought contemporary Western societies and especially American society were.

Latter-day, radical oppositional sociology has renounced the aspiration to reach a wide lay audience such as Mills aimed at and reached. Some of its proponents sometimes assert that their proper audience should be the "poor," the "exploited," the "victims," but in fact this objective is very seldom pursued. If it were pursued, the result would be a certain kind of technological sociology in which the "user" would be the "exploited" rather than the "exploiter." Although its intended audience is even less inclined to read empirical and statistical sociological monographs and papers than are civil servants and politicians, radical oppositional sociology aims to be a counterpart of technological sociology which it so often denounces. As a matter of fact, oppositional sociologists—at least some of them—have closed ranks with the technological sociologists.

The temptations of employment and forthcomingness of those in positions of authority in government and in academic life have brought the exponents of radical oppositional sociology closer to the service of governmental policy. They have, in doing so, also come much closer to technological sociology. Studies of class and ethnic conflict, of bureaucratic and professional shortcomings, of deviance and "dropping out" all find governmental and private sponsors who believe that sociology offers information and insight which will make the actions of governments more effective, their policies more consistent and more far-reachingly conceived. The macrosociological ideas of radical oppositional sociology can, it turns out, be adapted to the procedures and problems of technological sociology. The problems in which the makers of policy, or rather their agents who commission research projects, are interested also interest this combination of radical oppositional and technological sociology, so that it too can be drawn as closely to the service of public authorities as the technological sociology which has no grandiose oppositional beliefs. In principle, the practitioners of radical oppositional sociology are opposed to what they regard as the corruption of financial support by private and public authorities; in fact, however, many of them adapt their schemes of research to this necessity and opportunity.

There are various reasons for this apparent infidelity of radical oppositional sociology to its own conception of itself. For one thing, the radical oppositional sociologists, despite the radicalism of their opposition to contemporary liberal-democratic society, have been brought up intellectually in a period in which sociology has reached a relatively advanced state of institutionalization. Those who are trained in sociology learn something about the techniques of sociological research, and if they wish to make a professional career as sociologists, as teachers or as research workers, the pressure for conformity with expectations is too strong for most of them. If they wish to do research, and wish to have it supported financially, they are under pressure to formulate their proposals in the scientific idiom. It is not that there are no grants and fellowships for speculative macrosociological work of a radical orientation, but most of the funds available for the support of sociology is for scientific microsociology. Radical oppositional sociologists are poured into the mold.

Their acceptance of the technological form is not wholly uncongenial to them. Some of the governmental officials themselves are sympathetic with the radical oppositional view and they welcome the alliance. Furthermore, present-day radical oppositional sociology does not regard the traditional stereotype of the revolutionary as an "outcast" as inevitable. The prospect and promise of what Professor Helmut Schelsky has called the "long march through the institutions" are inviting. Technological sociology in the service of the "long march" is a not wholly unpleasing arrangement for the radical oppositional sociologist who wishes to earn a livelihood, to be a professional sociologist, and at the same time to be faithful to some part of his ideal.

Consensual sociology. "Pure science" of the type which has developed in the present century could be indirectly defined as scientific communication which has as its audience only other scientists; the audience for the results of "applied research" is made up of their intended "users." Philosophical speculation of the type which was carried on by Aristotle, Plato, and Cicero was not addressed exclusively or even primarily to other persons who gave their time mainly to the study of philosophy; as some parts of philosophy became more complex and required more philosophical training for their comprehension, their audience became more restricted. Literary works have with very few exceptions never been addressed primarily to audiences made up of other writers; literary criticism has not been intended only for literary critics or the authors of literary works. Historiography has practically invariably been for audiences far broader than those made up primarily of other historians; it is only in the past two centuries that very learned monographs and papers in history have been addressed primarily to audiences of other historians, no less specialized in area and epoch than the papers and monographs which are offered to them. Before sociology became an academic subject, works which bore the name of sociology, or which retrospectively were designated as falling within sociology, necessarily were addressed to audiences which did not consist of persons specializing in sociology.

Sociology is now in a different situation. The many professional sociologists teaching in universities and other educational institutions and the many sociologists employed in research institutions offer a possibility of self-containment. Sociology—like certain other intellectual disciplines, scientific and scholarly—has the possibility and the danger of becoming an entirely academic affair. By academic here, I do not mean anything pejorative but rather being produced by academics for academics and not having to leave the fenced-in fold of academic institutions. Sociology might become a branch of learning like Indology in the West in the sense that its products would not reach outside the universities. (There are rare exceptions in Indian studies in the West, such as van Buitenen's translation of the *Mahābhārata* or Basham's *The Wonder That Was India,* in which the results of decades of specialized academic study are translated or sublimated into forms accessible to laymen.)

Sociology throughout its short history has never been a cloistered subject. Its forerunners were not academics, and they had no academic audience of sociologists. They wished to move intellectual opinion for purposes of understanding the world better and improving the beliefs of the larger public and, through this means, improving society. Sociological works were written not for other sociologists, academic or lay, but for a public interested in "the social question." Some sociological works, especially criminological works in the nineteenth century which helped to form the tradition of empirical, quantitative research, were written both for a larger public and for specialized members of the intellectual-practical professions, such as judges or civil servants. Some sociological works like Simmel's *Soziologie* and *Uber soziale Differenzierung* and Tönnies' *Gemeinschaft und Gesellschaft* were written for both academic and lay audiences; they could not have been written for an audience of academic sociologists because none existed at that time. The audience for sociological works probably was vaguely envisaged in the intentions of their authors. *Die protestantische Ethik* was certainly not written with the expectation that it would be read mainly by other sociologists, since there was no profession of academic sociologists in Germany in 1904. It was however first published in a journal of the social sciences, the *Archiv für Sozialwissenschaft und Sozialpolitik,* most of the contributors to which were academics, and its readership was presumably mostly academic economists, economic historians, lawyers, theologians, and church historians. *Wirtschaft und Gesellschaft* was intended primarily for academic audiences. It was one part of a systematic compendium of economics, broadly understood; it was like an encyclopaedia or other works of reference but it also had the character of a textbook and was thus intended for a then still nonexistent audience of university students of sociology. Max Weber adhered to a very exigent ideal of *Wissenschaftlichkeit;* at the same time he was also very interested in the problems of the application of social science to social policy and often addressed himself to lay audiences. He regarded it as one of his tasks to clarify the issues of policy and to make the educated lay public and university students, university teachers, and publicists and politicians "face the facts." In general, most German, French, and British sociologists of the end of the last century and the first decades of the present century wrote with the intention of instructing a larger public beyond the boundaries of academic sociology, insofar as it existed. Durkheim was probably the first sociologist who wrote as if there were an audience of academic sociologists; he was in fact addressing himself to an academic audience in many disciplines while hoping to create an audience of specialized sociologists of wide culture.

The dominant tradition of American sociology, at least for a very long part of its history, accepted that sociologists should address themselves to an audience wider than the academic world, while at the same time seeking to be strictly scientific. That combination was intended to be a merit which sociology shared with the other social sciences; it was not thought that being scientific in social matters would entail unintelligibility to the laity. Other intellectual activities like journalism and philosophy also sought to communicate the results of their observation to a larger public beyond the circle of their own practitioners; the social sciences alone aspired to do this with results which had been established by systematic and hence scientific methods. For most of the history of American sociology there was no insuperable obstacle in the path to the wider public—at least none which was visible at that time. Sociologists like Cooley, Sumner, Park, and Giddings wrote in a clear English style, their work was not technical in the sense that only the long-trained and initiated could decipher it. Except for the books published by the University of Chicago Press, most major sociological works were published by commercial publishers who did not, as far as I know, think that their primary audiences for these books would be university students and teachers of sociology. Charles Cooley's books were published by

Scribner's, Giddings by Macmillan. Among the most famous sociological works of the period between the wars, the Lynds' *Middletown* was published by Harcourt Brace, Ogburn's *Social Change* was published by B. W. Huebsch. Thomas and Znaniecki's *The Polish Peasant in Europe and America* was republished by A. A. Knopf.

The sociologists thought that it was part of their task to share their knowledge with the public. The public was vaguely conceived; as far as I can make out, it was thought of as made up of civic-minded, educated persons, the leaders of their communities, local, ethnic, and religious. Most of the sociologists seemed to think that sharing their knowledge with a very wide nonacademic public was a means of elevating the quality of their society by providing the cognitive basis for an improving social action. It was the intention of sociologists to reach this wider audience, regardless of whether they were interested in sharing their discoveries about society with the "public"—as many scientists did in the nineteenth century—or whether they wished to "guide public opinion" by pointing to certain inevitable trends to which wisdom counseled adaptation through discarding old traditions, or whether they wished to contribute to the "solution of social problems" by accurately describing "social conditions" to the public which would then take action in order to "solve" them.

There were sociologists who did not quite approve of this. The "young Turks", Read Bain, George Lundberg, and Nels Anderson, in their manifesto of 1929 obviously thought that sociologists should renounce this inclination to address themselves to a wider, unscientific public; they thought that sociologists should make their discipline into a really scientific one so that when they were successful, in times yet to come, their knowledge would be scientific enough to confer genuine benefit on society. They did not say how this anticipated knowledge of society would bring about its benefits. They presumably thought that it would be applied by "social engineers" to the rest of society, in the same way in which mechanical engineers apply their knowledge of the strength of materials in the fabrication of machines. About two decades after the "manifesto," Lundberg wrote *Can Science Save Us?* In that book, he seemed to think that the salvationary effects of social science would be accomplished through "social technology"; the members of the society had simply to know enough about the merits of science and of the "scientific approach" to render themselves amenable to authorities possessing and applying scientific knowledge to the control of the other members of society.

The situation in recent years has seen changes in the situation of sociology in many respects. Governments now support a very much larger proportion of all sociological research and, in absolute terms, a

greatly increased amount of it, with the expectation—at least per-
functorily expressed—that it will contribute to the "solution of social
problems." A much larger proportion of sociologists than ever in the
past are now engaged in what its patrons allege to hope will be
"technological sociology." There is also, because of the greatly enlarged number of sociologists, a "pure," strictly professional public
of practicing sociologists which consumes the literary output of
sociologists in books and in papers in sociological journals; they have
not only their own institutions of publication into which the layman
does not enter as author or reader, they have their own idiom, which
outsiders cannot understand. The technical development of sociology
has made for self-enclosure.

Those sociologists who are engaged in "policy research" are not
happy except about the funds they receive. They complain that their
reports are disregarded or, when regarded, not adequately acted
upon. Those sociologists who live almost entirely within their professional boundaries include the practitioners of a highly recondite
theory and the practitioners of a highly recondite methodology.
Within the larger enclosure of professional sociology, each of the two
groups prospers in its self-sustaining isolation. There are occasional
crossings of the boundaries. Sometimes the highly recondite
methodologists also do technological sociological research; most of
them intend that their kind of sociology should ultimately become
technological. Sometimes the boundary between the two separate
realms of "pure" sociology is crossed and the theoretical and the
methodological come together.

In each of these realms of professional sociology the "pure"
sociologists write their works for each other or for any other
sufficiently qualified person such as might be found in the adjacent
academic social sciences like political science or anthropology or
economics and an unusual high civil servant or lawyer who is still
fresh enough from his own academic studies to be abreast of the latest
developments of his subject. This confinement to the community of
sociologists is the intention of some and the fate of many sociologists.
They are not always happy with their restricted audience of peers and
would like to be publicly acclaimed and influential.

This self-confinement to the community of sociologists is not always the result of deliberate choice. As long as there is a major
discrepancy between the degree of mathematical and statistical mastery of the academic sociologist and that of the laity, the audience of
those sociologists whose work is highly mathematical or statistical
will perforce be restricted. It might be that in remote years to come,
the scientific education of the wider public will be so excellent and its
mathematical and statistical facility so great that it will be able to read

mathematical sociology with the ease with which the educated public of seventy or sixty years ago could read Charles Cooley, William Graham Sumner, and John Dewey. That is not the case now and it is not likely to be the case in the reasonably near future. If the average level of mathematical and statistical knowledge rises in the future, the level of professional academics, especially in disciplines like sociology the practice of which will then meet strict scientific standards, will rise to correspondingly higher levels. It might therefore be the case that if sociology becomes mathematically and statistically scientific it will be compelled by its own intellectual achievements to be either a handmaiden to social technology or a self-contained academic discipline or both. It will in any case be inaccessible to the nongovernmental laity.

To write in prose rather than in numbers or in mathematical symbols does not necessarily make a sociologist accessible to the educated laity. Let me take as an example the writings of one of the most important sociologists in the entire history of the subject, Professor Talcott Parsons. He is one of the most devoted and unswerving pursuers of the deeper truth about society in general and modern society in particular. He is a scholar of much learning and sober judgment; in the assessment of important situations and trends of modern societies, he has very realistic views. For many years he has given his great talents to the systematic differentiation of the fundamental variables of action, elaborating them with an unceasing determination to be consistent, pursuing a goal which has never been attained in sociology previously. In the course of this titanic undertaking, at times with the aid of collaborators and more recently with the reinforcement of former pupils who have been won to his way of proceeding, the sociological theory of action has now reached a degree of complexity which begins to approximate that of the model of the DNA molecule. This observation, it should be obvious, says nothing about the intellectual validity of Professor Parsons' analysis of society.

Regardless of whether a theory of this degree of multifarious and ramified complexity is the right way to advance the fortunes of sociology as a special intellectual discipline—it is no serious criticism of *Kritik der reinen Vernunft* to say that it makes far greater demands on a reader than *Zur Genealogie der Moral*—there are high barriers against its diffusion to the educated laity. The abstractness of the theory of action as well as the multiplicity and complexity of relationships of its variables seem to be sufficient to deter any but the most resolutely devoted initiates within the sociological profession from pursuing it in all its meticulously worked-out refinement. A further obstacle is the high frequency of neologisms and a daunting stylistic inelegance.

The literary cumbersomeness and ineptitude of many sociologists have long been the laughingstock of literate persons. The literary barbarism of sociology, which is repugnant aesthetically, helps to isolate sociology from the wider public. The combination of the opacity resulting from literary awkwardness with the opacity which results from great abstractness and complexity, almost wholly unrelieved by any illustrative concreteness, increases the isolation and the corresponding self-containedness of verbally expressed sociology.

But only a quite modest part of sociology has reached this condition. There are other parts of sociology which are still written in prose and which use only fairly elementary statistical and no mathematical techniques. These kinds of sociology can, in principle, still be addressed to a general public. There is still a large amount of sociology which is capable of being read by such an audience. Writers like Raymond Aron, François Bourricaud, S. N. Eisenstadt, Ralf Dahrendorf, Morris Janowitz, S. M. Lipset, T. H. Marshall, David Martin, Robert Merton, Robert Nisbet, W. G. Runciman, and Helmut Schelsky clearly are in this class. They write about important phenomena, they write with the best existing knowledge of society as their point of departure, and they write in a prose style which is, generally, intelligible and in some cases even agreeable to an educated layman who wishes to be informed about and reflect on the problems of society.

The sociology which reaches the wider public comes to it in fragments. A few weeklies like *New Society* report bits of research in generally accessible form. Newspapers and newsmagazines occasionally summarize the results of something which journalists think interesting or entertaining or sensational enough to present to their large, undifferentiated mass of readers. Not many sociological books attain this degree of publicity. These authors are few in comparison with the numerous sociologists who address themselves to each other and who do research which is read by even a very small number of their professional colleagues.

This handful of sociologists, respected though they are in their own countries and internationally, are not regarded by the practitioners of the newer trends of sociology as moving on the path to the future in their subjects. They do not have a "systematic" theory; their concepts are not rigorously "derived" in a systematic manner. They know little of mathematical models and do not care about them; such models do not appear in their work. They do not write in accordance with the rules of deductive theory nor in accordance with the terminology of an allegedly distinctive "approach," such as that of ethnomethodological or of phenomenological sociology. They can be read by the lay public without writing as "popularizers" or with the intention of exciting or alarming.

There are some sociologists today who disapprove of sociologists

who do not write "for the profession." Their conception of the profession makes them look upon it as a custodian of scientific values
which would be debilitated by contact with a public not made of
professional sociologists. Underlying this view is the fear that discourse addressed to a wider public would be demagogic—they sometimes call it "emotive"—and would yield easily to any temptation to
fall short of scientific standards. They also believe that this line of
sociology is not what is needed in order to make sociology into an
intellectually sound discipline. They regard themselves above all as
under obligation to that ideal; they investigate, analyze, and write for
their own fellow sociologists, senior and junior, in order to move
towards it. They are not averse to public appreciation or governmental action which is influenced by their works but that is not their
primary concern; their concern is to advance their subject as well as
they can and that entails the acceptance and incorporation of their
work by their fellow sociologists.

Yet these contemporary sociologists who disapprove of works
which are only "intellectual" and not "really professional" are seldom interested in confining the radius of their works to colleagues in
their own disciplines or neighboring academic disciplines. Most of
them would be pleased to influence through their sociological work
the policies espoused and pursued by governments. Many of these
sociologists are entirely ready to extend their influence beyond
academic sociology, by serving as consultants to governmental
bodies, as expert witnesses, or through the selection, design, and
execution of sociological investigations, the results of which, they
hope, will be taken conscientiously into account in the construction of
new policies and in the "evaluation" of policies. Their aim is primarily to influence government, and not the public, through their works
and expertise. In the United States most of them are Democrats, with
tinctures of radicalism and populism; they wish to promote the interests of "the people" but they think that governmental action is essential in that promotion. Their belief in scientific integrity and in the
ideal of the advancement of the "social good" issues in their conviction that government is the proper audience for sociological work.

Thus, even if an intellectually sophisticated sociology were available to the educated laity and even if the educated laity desired to have
it, the internal tendencies within the profession of sociology are not
propitious. The audience might be there but, insofar as it is, it might
wait in vain.

The existence of an audience outside of professional and academic
sociology is not the sole criterion of consensual sociology. One reason
for calling it consensual is that it rests on the affinity between the

sociologist and the subject-matter of his investigation. It has often been said that the distinctiveness of the social sciences lies in the possibility of empathic understanding—*Verstehen*—in contrast with the absence of such a possibility in the natural sciences. Be that as it may and whatever may be the adequacy of *Verstehen* as a technique of research, there is no doubt that the phenomenon it refers to is a social relationship between the sociologist and his subject-matter.

It is certainly possible to act and speak as if there is no social relationship between the social scientist and the persons he studies. The relationship with remote or dead persons is not entirely different.

Nonetheless, there are elements of a fundamental identity shared by the sociologists and the individual human beings in the society he studies. The sociologist might be more intelligent, he might be more learned and have more capacity to perceive particular events in general categories, but his capacity for the appreciation of an ideal—in the cases of some sociologists, truth, in the case of the same or other sociologists, equality or community—his capacity for the disinterested cultivation of the ideal, must also be seen to exist in his subjects. The belief that one's subjects are motivated and can only be motivated by the desire to maximize their own income, power, and status and cannot be influenced by ideal considerations—that when the latter seem to be present, they are no more than "false consciousness"—is a block in the path of a realistic understanding of society. A sociologist who takes seriously his own intellectual undertaking, who thinks himself capable of appreciating and of acting in accordance with criteria of cognitive validity but who thinks that the persons who are his subject-matter are incapable, at least minimally, of doing the same, is committing himself to error. If, as a citizen, a sociologist thinks himself capable of appreciating the ideal of justice, while thinking that the persons he studies can act only on the basis of "interests" or myths or sensual impulse, he is damaging his prospect of understanding.

Let me put it somewhat differently: the subject of sociological investigation should be able to understand the results of the investigation, if he has the necessary capacity and training to assess particular events in general categories, if he has sufficient ratiocinative capacity and freedom from blinding passions to receive them. Of course, not every one can understand complex events equally well, not every one is equally gifted in abstract conception and reasoning, but human beings must be viewed in categories which allow for the existence of these capacities.

Very few human beings are saints but many have an occasional apprehension of sanctity; not many human beings can write great novels but very many more have the capacity to appreciate great novels. The adequacy of a conception of human beings and of the society and culture which they form and are formed by may be judged by its capacity to perceive and describe the creative person as well as the philistine and the bohemian. A conception of human beings which sees them only as the creatures of their culture or which sees them only as capable of self-protecting and self-aggrandizing action and concerned only with their own income, power, or status may be useful enough for describing many actions of many human beings. It will certainly be unable to describe the most influential and greatest actions which call forth the assent and cooperation of many. Such a conception, embodied in propositional form, may have what social scientists call "predictive" capacity but it will not be satisfactory intellectually.

It will also be morally defective because, apart from its scientific or cognitive product, it will generate a morally poor relationship of the sociologist to his society. This conception of individual and society makes the sociologist into an "outsider" who is not a member of a community of diverse human beings. It is a view which will be accepted by one who regards himself as an "outsider." If a sociologist conceives of society as an aggregation of individuals held together by identity of individual and familial "interests," fear of coercion, "false consciousness," and exploitative manipulation by the powerful, he puts himself outside and above the species. If he insists that such self-elevation is alien to his intentions, and if he accepts that he seeks the truth about what he studies, how can he deny altogether those propensities in other human beings and their occasional expression? And what kind of moral relationship can he have with the human beings who have allowed him to observe them or whom he has observed without their permission, if he conceives of them in that way?

Sociologists have sometimes expressed pride in being "outsiders" vis-à-vis the society which they study. Of course there is some justification for this. Detachment is necessary. The sociologist must have a larger perspective than those he studies; he must not become embroiled, while doing his work, in the partisanship which exists in every society. But to be completely an "outsider" is impossible, and belief that one is or should be is self-stultifying. A sociologist is part of his own society and he becomes, in a segmental and "unnatural" way, a part of any society of living persons which he studies. (The problem is somewhat but not wholly different in the study of societies of the past.)

These remarks about the fundamental affinity between sociological observers and the sociologically observed do not imply either that sociologists must approve morally of all that they study. It does not mean that sociologists must avoid political sympathy with any one political current in society. There is no necessary incompatibility between the practice of consensual sociology and political partisanship; there is an incompatibility between consensual sociology and ideological zeal which treats adversaries who are also the subjects of inquiry as having nothing fundamental in common with oneself as a sociologist.

Consensual sociology differs from technological sociology partly in its substantive conception of human beings and of society. (In many of its fundamental substantive conceptions, technological sociology has more in common with radical oppositional sociology when they both treat the same subject-matter. Both of them regard manipulation, coercion, and deception as the chief elements of social life and policy; they use somewhat different terminology.) Consensual sociology accepts the existence of consensus in varying degrees and forms but it also accepts its fragility and partiality. Unlike oppositional sociology, which denies the possibility of consensus in large modern societies and regards conflict among the mutually alienated as the fundamental feature of such societies, consensual sociology accommodates both consensus and conflict as well as their limits and their interdependence.

A third feature of consensual sociology is that its audience lies outside of the sociological profession as well as inside it. For this to be so, sociology must be intelligible to intelligent persons even as its knowledge becomes more scientific in the sense that its assertions become better founded on valid evidence. It also implies that sociologists will address themselves to both these audiences and that they will have something to tell the members of these audiences, something important that they did not know before. Of course, no intellectual discourse directed toward individual and collective self-understanding could ever become so widely extended as to become the common possession of the entire adult population of any society of the foreseeable future. A complete consensus of self-understanding throughout society is only a construction which is difficult to develop because it seems so far from what is realizable. Many human beings are not interested in understanding themselves as individuals and as members of society; they have other tasks and interests. Others are not intellectually capable of doing so or they have insufficient educational preparation for assimilating elaborate ideas and for incorporating them critically into their outlook.

Any kind of sociology is bound to be more abstract than daily experience, and it is required to treat aspects of society which are beyond the limits and to some extent below the surface of ordinary experience. After all, who has ever actually experienced a class-system running over the length and breadth of a society; who has ever seen an empire or a dictatorship or a democratic or an aristocratic republic? Only bits and pieces of such large structures may be seen and experienced by any single individual, even the most widely traveled and the most observant. There is bound to be some difficulty in assimilating this abstractness and remoteness from the everyday experience of human beings, even where the understanding which has been conveyed has been demonstrated by the rules accepted in the best sociological circles. The more "scientific" or the more theoretical the type of sociology, the further it will be from the idiom of daily experience—and not just because of stylistic barbarism.

The three types of sociology treated here are in similar situations with respect to remoteness and abstractness. Oppositional sociology also goes below the surface and beyond the radius of daily experience, while technological sociology reports unobserved regularities and connections which might well not be known to those who participate in them. It is in these respects that the laity have something to learn from sociology, but this does not mean that they will. There are too many obstacles, inherent in the nature of social life and in the structure of any realistically imaginable society, to permit the fulfillment of the ideal which is implicit in the conception of consensual sociology.

There is bound to be a major inequality in the distribution of sociological knowledge. In a society of equals, with a comprehensive consensus, equality of capacity and opportunity for enlightenment, and without any concentration of authority except for specified and terminable tasks, valid sociological knowledge, universally diffused, would be an important constituent of individual and collective self-knowledge and self-government. None of these conditions is likely to be achieved in the reasonably imaginable future.

The traditional pattern of diffusion of sociological knowledge which gave rise to the idea of a consensual sociology was always limited. Surveys of the population living near the poverty line were usually intended to call the attention of the public to conditions which fell short of prevailing moral standards. Once public opinion was aroused, some members of the public, including employers and politicians, would perhaps change their conduct—so it was hoped—and thus alleviate to some extent the undesirable conditions which the survey had discovered and disclosed. But not all of the expected effect was to be achieved in this way. Insofar as the results of this type of sociological research were incorporated into action, the incorporation usually occurred among the "leaders" of society who were mainly moderately oppositional leaders close to the center of their local societies. Insofar as these leaders were successful in their undertakings, they exerted influence on wealthy persons to provide funds for the support of certain kinds of institutions or they persuaded employers to modify their policies or they influenced local and state politicians to modify or establish certain kinds of provident institutions. To a considerable extent, the diffusion of works of social science, although it does not begin with a technological intention, ends in social technology, within the traditional framework of the exercise of legitimate political authority. Much of it falls into the pattern implied by William Graham Sumner's definition of "social welfare" as what is done when A and B get together to decide what C should do for D. A and B are the lay public which is the audience for sociological works; C is increasingly the government and D is the part of the citizenry which is to be protected, provided for, guided or regulated, and restrained by government. The Benthamite ideal is realized in this process of the flow of knowledge into action. Consensual sociology—as technological sociology—ends when it is effectively accepted in legislative and administrative action.

There is however a substantial difference between the two patterns of the flow from discovery to policy.

Even though consensual sociology is most unlikely ever to fulfil its ideal calling, it can still retain something of that calling, which distinguishes it from technological sociology and from oppositional sociology. Consensual sociology is a substantive type of sociological investigation which cannot be wholly absorbed into the scientific and theoretical types of academic sociology; it cannot be simply a popularization of their results. It is closer to the level of concrete description, and such theory as it employs is a means of understanding and not an end sought for its own sake. It might up to some point employ the theory which is developed by academic theorists but never as an end in itself; and it will employ it selectively, using only those parts which are illuminating, without regard for the theory as a systematic whole. The same may be said about its relation to the accomplishments of scientific sociology. It might employ some of the models which have been elaborated there but it will do so by infusing them into the relatively concrete descriptive data. Unless the two main types of academic sociology are drawn upon in this way, the task of consensual sociology cannot be entered upon; its contribution to the furtherance of the consensus between the sociologists and the lay public, even to the small degree that such a thing is possible, cannot be made without this.

Even the contribution of consensual sociology to policy may occur mainly through its culmination in legislative and administrative action, and even if its diffusion to a wider public is necessarily limited to a relatively small part of the entire electorate, it seems to be a very worthwhile thing. The criterion by which it is to be judged is not primarily its merit as a set of intellectual achievements, nor its exact utility as a cognitive component in the execution of government policies. Consensual sociology is a phenomenon of moral value; it is a constituent of public rationality—and by public here I do not mean governmental. Its task is the extension and elevation of the public life of society by improving the citizen's understanding of the collective life in which he is involved and by improving the quality of discussion among citizens. Its task is to enhance the quality of citizenship and to delimit its sphere. The oppositional ideal of turning sociology into an organ of criticism of government and the social order, quite apart from the traditional intellectual limitation of the oppositional outlook, which begins with the postulate of the repudiation of all that exists, can only disorder the mind and render rational public discussion impossible. Technological sociology does not undertake to improve the quality of citizenship except insofar as its results are used by governments to do so through manipulation in the educational system. Consensual sociology alone could contribute directly to the improvement of the quality of public discourse. This is an objective of great value.

It is an objective which is very far from attainment. Part of this is attributable simply to the patent intellectual shortcomings of sociology. In this respect the other kinds of sociology have also been unsuccessful: technological sociology has very few successes which can be traced back to its scientific merits; oppositional sociology has by no means persuaded the lay public to turn against its own society, although among the increasing number of university graduates in sociology it has had some success.

Consensual sociology cannot and should not lay claim to the kind of success in the influence over policy that technological sociology aspires to and that it could have if it were scientific. Consensual sociology will probably never match technological sociology in scientific precision and rigor. The kinds of problems of collective self-interpretation with which consensual sociology should be concerned do not lend themselves to a degree of precision similar to that attainable in the study of more narrowly conceived problems.

For these and for other reasons consensual sociology can at best add a tincture to opinion. It can give it tone and tendency; it cannot determine its precise content. It leaves to the human beings to whom it is addressed the freedom of interpretation and judgment which is needed in the public life of a reasonably decent society. It recognizes its own limitations and the limitations in human powers more generally. These are important virtues in an age which is tempted by scientistic aspirations and beliefs in the total transformation of societies.

Part Two

The Trend of Sociology

2   The Contemplation of Society
in America

I

To think of the American universities and of their professors of
sociology of fifty and sixty years ago brings with it the tone of an old
photograph of Woodrow Wilson. Into our mind's eye come men
dressed in garments of iron, with high stiff collars, with sagging fedoras
or unyieldingly rigid flat straw hats. Weighty watch-chains hang across
their inevitable vests. The visages are usually as stiff as their apparel.
Long heads, high domes, strong jaws, firm chins prevail, with a
sprinkling of round-headed and bearded men with the air of patrician
European professors. Self-conscious dignity and remoteness from the
world around them seem to stand out.

They seem very far away now. They now look like men to whom it
would be very difficult for us to talk, very difficult to reach with an
understanding of the problems which preoccupy our contemporaries,
educated in the idiom of latter-day sociologists and political scientists.
They seem very proper, very serious, learned, dry, unsubtly
intelligent—really rather conventional intellectually.

These sociologists were worthy men, who believed in their calling
as university professors. They were, almost to a man, appalled by the
development of American cities. Respectable sober citizens, they
were aware that the life in the poorer areas of the cities was far from
the life of the American small town which they remembered. This was
the centerpiece of their picture of American society. It was common
and fundamental to them. There were a few men of great erudition
among them, who were erudite on the old German and French model,
who had read widely in the literature in their own fields and much else
as well. Almost all of them had studied subjects other than sociology
when they were young. They had studied literature, philosophy, and
the Bible. Some had been journalists; some had been clergymen.
Many of the then older generation had studied in Germany. They
were, in a peculiarly distant way, men of the world, who regarded
great affairs as their natural concern. They were critical of government and society in all sorts of respects, but they were not radical.
They were probably more abreast of the established culture of their
time than all but a few of those who succeeded them over the next half

This is a revised and enlarged version of an essay that originally appeared in
Arthur M. Schlesinger, Jr., and Morton G. White, eds., *Paths of American
Thought* (Boston: Houghton Mifflin, 1963).

a century. The avant-garde of Greenwich Village and the Left Bank appealed to scarcely any except the anthropologists Alexander Goldenweiser, Paul Radin, Edward Sapir, and Ruth Benedict, who in age and bearing belong rather to the next generation. The sociologists were scholars; they read widely and they regarded manuscripts and books with the critical reverence which had been characteristic of German and French erudition of the preceding century. Although they were moving into an age in which sociologists created their own data by interviews and direct observation, they still respected the traditional sources of knowledge: books and governmental statistics. They inclined towards the concreteness, descriptive and statistical, of historical scholarship. The institutional descriptions of the historical school of economics and *Staatswissenschaften* and the social survey, the ethnographic monograph and the articles of the city reporter were their models. They were intensely in earnest about their subjects, about their place in the hierarchy of the sciences, in university courses of study, and in the furtherance of social order and the common good. They came out of a tradition of Darwinism and the German historical and philological disciplines. Almost to a man, they wished their subjects to become more scientific, because they wished them to enjoy the respect which the natural sciences enjoyed in the esteem of their university colleagues and of the educated public, and to possess the precision, the reliability, and the power of prediction attributed to the natural sciences.

Their desire has not been fulfilled. The social sciences have not yet become sciences according to the simplified model that the seniors of about a half-century ago held before themselves. But even if their goal, towards which some of the best minds in social science still aspire, has not been realized, the work of the decades which separate us from them has disciplined our mode of understanding, modified and in some respects enriched our conception of the social world, and become a vital sector of contemporary culture.

It has recently become stylish, among some of the critics of the American social sciences, to speak as if the past half-century has been witness to a sequence of misguided and wasted efforts. The simplest answer to these critics is an invitation to read the best and the average literature of the early 1920s. They will see how much more differentiated the understanding of the complexities of individual action and social structure has become, how much more intimate observation has become, how much deeper analysis has become and how much more systematic. They will also see that sociology and its companions in anthropology, political science, and psychology have become, not more blind to some of the great problems of the age, but, rather, no less concerned, and in a more disciplined way, than they used to be. The treatment of almost any subject fifty years ago seems very simple by contrast with the treatment it now receives. Sociology was obviously much cruder in its techniques of observation and analysis. It was more simplistic in its theory, less ambitious and more unsystematic. Much of what was then called theory in American sociology was prolegomena to theory rather than theory about the working of particular classes of social things and their relationships. It consisted to a large extent of declaratory aspirations, definitions, and classifications. *Aperçus* and discursive reflections were most of its best substance. The human detachment and a greater readiness to take things on their face value which we sense in the photographed faces of its practitioners of those days correspond to that distant relationship to vital realities we can still see in their writings. There was more respect for privacy and a more benign conception of what went on in individual minds and in institutions.

Most of the sociology of the older generation of the 1920s has disappeared from the memory of most sociologists of the present generation, and it is not wrong in many cases that it should have done so. Some of it still lives on and is still very relevant to present-day interests and the present-day idiom. Books like *The Polish Peasant in Europe and America* by W. I. Thomas and Florian Znaniecki, *Human Nature and the Social Order* by Charles Cooley, the writings of Robert Park and of a few others are still intelligible and still not exhausted. Much of what has happened since, however different it is, would be inconceivable without the laborious efforts of that serious generation. What was essential in the tradition has not been lost, although its context has been changed. The fundamental outlook of Robert Park, W. I. Thomas, Charles Cooley, John Dewey, and George Herbert Mead has been assimilated into the new intellectual line of the succeeding decades. The conception of man as a restless, outgoing, instrumentally rational, end-seeking, value-internalizing organism, developed by Dewey from a Darwinian inspiration, has continued at the center of American social science. The conception of society as an anonymous moral order, of institutions bearing traditions and changing them, of a perpetual strain towards and away from consensus, of conflicts among individuals and groups for a better standing and a larger share, and this within an ecological setting of scarcity of place, time, and resources, still persists despite many changes in nomenclature and many new intellectual influences. Every new influence has had to adapt itself to these initial points of departure, which despite limitations has been rich in its capacity for extension. Much assimilation has been possible. The conception of a consensual order, an order of shared values, brought into the foreground by Thomas, Park, and Cooley, from an ultimately Hegelian and German romantic inspiration, has provided a framework which—however complicated and differentiated, and even transformed, by subsequent criticism, research, and theory—has endured into the present. The conception of an individual capable of conformity, withdrawal, rebellion, disorganization, intelligence and creativity, within a moral order—loose and differentiated, but an order nonetheless—was a great achievement. It was an achievement of which even the founders were uncertain and often unaware.

The simultaneous tasks of establishing the academic responsibility of their subject and of embarking on the quite novel experience of disinterested, direct investigation in their own society distracted and scattered their attention onto a variety of concerns which have not always been worthy of remembrance. This generation of earnest academic personalities were intensely serious men where learning and civility were concerned. A professor did not run the risk of making a fool of himself, in those days, without having a serious intellectual reason for doing so.

What were they serious about? It should be recalled that sociologists were few in number; anthropologists were even fewer. They were isolated bands of newcomers in the American universities. Even in the newer institutions of the Middle West, they had to exist in the midst of members of academically longer-established subjects with recognized achievements. This made them—especially the sociologists—solicitous about the legitimacy of their subject; and it caused them to engage in activities which no longer retain any interest for us. They were concerned to show that the realistic study of society had a proper place in the classification of the sciences and in the ranks of university subjects. They felt that their subjects could satisfy these requirements by becoming natural sciences like the physical or mathematical sciences; alternatively they could be legitimately different from the natural sciences by virtue of the differences in their subject matters and in the intellectual procedures which these entailed.

But far from all their efforts was abstract self-justification. They were not just concerned with academic respectability. As men with a sense of civic responsibility and concern about the well-being of their society, they also attended to a variety of public problems. Immigrants, from abroad and from the American countryside, were much on their minds; like other conservative and liberal intellectuals, they wished to see the newcomers well and happily assimilated into an orderly and seemly American society. The Negro, too, became an early object of their interest. Juvenile delinquency and broken families attracted a curiosity which was impelled by compassion and abhorrence. These considerations came together in urban sociological studies at the Unversity of Chicago. In the state universities of the Middle West, at Minnesota, Wisconsin, Iowa, and Illinois, the society of the agricultural population was inventoried and analyzed. Church attendance, family budgets, farm ownership and succession, educational attainments, club memberships and farm cooperatives were studied—rather more quantitatively and with less vivid empathy than in the urban studies. The anthropologists studied American Indians. The political scientists studied urban politics and governmental administration in the United States. They were meticulous and scholarly. They were solid and old-fashioned; they did not "let themselves go" because they respected facts too much and because they did not wish to go astray. There were exceptions, of course. Franz Boas, Edward Sapir, Arthur F. Bentley, Thorstein Veblen dared to leave the beaten path and to penetrate a bit more deeply, to see the general beyond the particular, the abstract beyond the concrete, but they too respected concrete facts and were critical of evolutionary schemes.

They knew about societies other than that of the United States. They had traveled; those who had been missionaries brought back some insight into Asian and African societies. Some of them had studied the older anthropological or ethnographic literature, but William Graham Sumner was the only sociologist who had continued that tradition. After his death only his pupil, Albert G. Keller, carried it on while the rest of the American sociologists fixed their attention primarily on the United States. The remarkable study of Thomas and Znaniecki on Polish society was intended as background for the understanding of Polish immigrants in Chicago. Park and his pupils sometimes turned their minds to colonies, and they did so in a worldwide ecological perspective. But these were exceptions.

Theoretical treatises—on society in general or on particular classes of phenomena—were practically nonexistent, as would be expected in such an atmosphere. Such theoretical exertions as there were, found their way into textbooks—as in the case of the *Introduction to the Science of Sociology,* by Robert Park and Ernest Burgess—or into the monographs and papers which reported on field observation, again, largely the products·of the department of sociology of the University of Chicago, and of the universities to which its graduates went as teachers.

The analysis of politics had come down in the world. The dethronement of Aristotle and the growth of the great law schools, where the emerging legal order was studied, had left the study of the polity a collection of fragments. The expansive propensities of sociology had not yet begun to evince themselves in that time when sociology was quietly struggling to keep itself alive and to prove its right to exist. Thus, at the end of the First World War, the sociological study of politics was little cultivated. The great studies of government institutions like those of A. Lawrence Lowell and Woodrow Wilson were done without the benefit of sociology. Graham Wallas had labored in America for a short time but his work had no academic consequence. Only Walter Lippmann was inspired by it, and it was only in his *Public Opinion* that the expansion of sociology into the study of politics was foreshadowed.

Sociologists, eager to delimit an autonomous territory of their own and aware of the majestic connections of the *Staatswissenschaften* in the German universities, deliberately eschewed the political. There was another reason for the avoidance: generally, sociologists who were liberals and inclined towards social reforms did not have much confidence in politics. They regarded society as a part of the process of the natural order of things, controlled by forces deeper than the human will. Power and authority, as part of this natural process, did not impress them much. The sociological social science of the turn into the third decade was a part of the general revolt—humanitarian, antiauthoritarian, and even realistic—against the ascendancy of kings and rulers. *The New History* of James Harvey Robinson had pulled down the monarchs and the conquerors as the determinants of life and had installed the workaday activities of mankind as ethically and intellectually more worthy of the scholar's attention. Social scientists were too close to an older and fruitless contest between the "individual" and "society," or as it was put in the terminology of those days "social forces," and they had, in the main, come down on the side of "social forces." Politics were epiphenomenal to "social forces," according to historians like Charles Beard and Robinson, and sociologists were sympathetic with this view.

The study of politics was, therefore, left to political science, which, into the early 1920s, continued to be largely a subject for research in books and public documents in libraries. The municipal reform movements—which had begun with the lofty ambition of making politics conform with the ideals of German university social science—were petering out. The description of the machinery of government continued to be a major subject for political scientists. Those of a more worldly outlook concerned themselves with those treasure-troves of well-intentioned legalists, international treaties and the League of Nations. "Comparative government" was the study of modern European constitutions since 1870, and its sociological potential, visible in the works of Lowell and Bryce, was not appreciated by either sociologists or political scientists. Michels' study of political parties was scarcely known in the United States until the latter part of the third decade. Political theory was almost entirely the drabbest, most dun-colored paraphrase and mortification of the ideas of the great men of the past. Political theory had ceased to be a body of real, still-relevant problems. The disparagement of metaphysics and the emptying of belief in natural law made political philosophy into a dusty museum. The empirical study of politics had not yet risen to the point where, as it did later, it could even pretend to replace the philosophy of politics by the science of politics.

The adumbrations of realistic study could, however, already be seen at Columbia where Charles Beard had opened a view path and mainly at Chicago, that somber city where, free from the inhibitions of the older universities in the East, young men would knock at any door. In the 1920s, Charles Merriam, an amorphous, tentacular mind, himself a veteran of the last phases of the heroic municipal reform movements of the prewar period, encouraged or initiated studies in voting behavior, local and state political leadership, the public image of government, the political machine, and the psychology of political participation, passion, and indifference. At Columbia, the learned ex-journalist Franklin Giddings and W. F. Ogburn gave their patronage to political studies which were beyond the conventional boundaries. There Peter Odegaard, in his study of the temperance movement, let out the first tiny rivulet of what later became the central theme of American political studies and even of American political philosophy—of politics as the battleground of interests, pressing for fulfillment, of politics as the study of "who gets what, when and how." At Columbia, too, the first awkward studies of voting were started by Ogburn and carried forward by Stuart Rice, to show that "interests"—and not "ideals"—were the determinants of political conduct. The remote, abstract idealism of the common good could offer no sufficient counterattraction to the call of a new scientistic tough-mindedness.

At Cornell, George Catlin, an expatriated British national, tried in two ambitious books to establish the systematic legitimacy of realistic political science, drawing on the prematurely harvested fruits of psychology, sociology, and anthropology. They did not catch on. They were too broad for the concrete and particular events with which the new political science was concerned and too alien to the inherited conventions of the old political science.

Anthropology was dominated by Franz Boas, Robert Lowie, and A. L. Kroeber. It was in accordance with the mood of the time that anthropology was the meticulous study of the North American Indian—a study skeptical of every generalization, and distrustful, above all, of evolutionary schemes which gave meaning to the course of man's existence on earth. It was solid, matter-of-fact, and "scientifically" disciplined by its own procedures and its intimate and austere neighborhood with physical anthropology, archaeology, and linguistics. It had little to do with sociology, even though at Chicago the two were bound together administratively by being in the same department.

Throughout the country, the universities were small by present standards. Postgraduate students were relatively few, and teachers, in so far as they did research, did so with scarcely any assistance other than that provided by a student assistant and students working on their dissertations. The support of sociological research by funds outside the universities was rare; Thomas had had such support for *The Polish Peasant*. *The Negro in Chicago*, the survey of race relations in the early 1920s, and the studies of Americanization which were supported by the Carnegie Corporation at about the same time were rare phenomena. The Local Community Research Committee at Chicago was still to be established. The great philanthropic foundations had not turned to the social sciences as a means for solving social problems. The paucity of students and the administratively amateur organization of research and the sparceness of its financial provision meant that there was a low density of work on any particular subject. The social map was only faintly and grazingly explored.

Such was the position of the contemplation of society at the end of the first quarter of the century. Nowadays we see that Dos Passos' *Manhattan Transfer*, Scott Fitzgerald's *The Great Gatsby*, Dreiser's *An American Tragedy*, Eliot's *The Waste Land*—the "new spirit in life and literature"—left a precipitate which, forty years later, tinctured the tone of contemporary American social science. In their own decade, however, social scientists had nothing to do with the somber or desperate apprehensions which the leading literary figures of the time experienced when they thought about modern society. Like their literary contemporaries, social scientists were attempting to free themselves from the inhibiting burden of the puritanism and idealism of the Victorian age. But they were doing so shyly, awkwardly, and provincially. Nonetheless, the First World War had occurred, and America had been involved in it. When it was over, the United States began to enter on a new intellectual course.

II

The new pattern of contact with European scholarship which was to transform American intellectual life in the second third of the century came only after a lull in the relationship. The lull was the decade of the 1920s. Of the older generation, which came to maturity before 1914, many had spent a year or more in study in Germany. They knew German and had read Ratzel, Gierke, Tönnies, Simmel, Ratzenhofer, and Gumplowicz. They knew French and had to read Durkheim and Tarde. The period when American academics could read no language other than their own was still to come.

In outlook and style, the older generation still bore some of the imprint of the placid earnestness of the German universities of those years before the First World War, when, it was later alleged, *la vie était belle et douce*. Of course, they did not believe that life was wholly beautiful and sweet. Giddings and Park had been journalists. Park and Thomas knew the miseries of the newly arrived "greenhorns," of homeless men, alcoholics, women deserted by their husbands, unmarried mothers and illegitimate children; they knew about industrial conflict, about socialism, about revolutionary movements; they knew about unemployment and industrial accidents and diseases. The political scientists knew about the corruption of the public services. They had lived in the age of the muckrakers and they knew about the "trusts." But they and those who came to maturity in the 1920s did not anticipate that any of these things were harbingers of the apocalypse. They were not nervous, quakingly uneasy, or eager, from a safe position, to see the world in flames. They were not worried about the destiny of their civilization. They were not narrow-minded men nor were they ignorant of the affairs of the great world, but the Russian Revolution, the nationalism of Asia and the Middle East, did not intrude immediately into their imagination as to what the world was really like, or what it was likely to become.

III

By the time of the American entry into the First World War, psychoanalysis had already found a sympathetic if not sophisticated reception in literary circles of a slightly radical bent. It was for them a part of the emancipation from puritanism. The name, the notions, and, to some extent, the writings of Freud had begun also to be known among American social scientists. Alfred Kroeber and William Ogburn quite early took a critical and detached interest in psychoanalysis. Alexander Goldenweiser dipped into it. By the middle of the 1920s, Professor Harold Lasswell, then little more than a youth, was devoted seriously to the elaboration of the implications of psychoanalysis for the understanding of conduct beyond the zone where it is interesting to psychiatrists; in doing so he had the sponsorship of Charles Merriam. Margaret Mead was then beginning her pioneering work, strongly tinged by psychoanalysis. It cannot, however, be said that these adventurous undertakings had a resounding echo in the 1920s.

As in so many other spheres of American life, it was the participation in the First World War that started the chain of events which ultimately transformed the style of the sociological sciences. Psychology had become a proper university subject before the turn of the century; when it rejected introspection and replaced it by experimentation, it acquired credentials as a science. The subject progressed steadily. The employment of psychologists in the Adjutant General's Office of the Department of War was an important event for the development of sociology, although sociologists had no part in that particular event. With one stroke, psychology became established as a science which had pertinent practical things to relate about human beings. Once they had classified a substantial proportion of the recruits to the United States Army as mentally inferior, psychologists were greatly enhanced in their self-confidence. Mental testing went forward at a great rate in the decade which followed the war. It was much aided by the growing belief among businessmen in the merits of "scientific management." The popularity of Taylorism—although Taylor had not been a psychologist—gave the psychologists the sense that they had discovered their calling. Psychologists began to regard the industrial working force as one of the objects fit for their studies. The expansion of their numbers and influence went on apace.

From tests of mental capacities and vocational aptitudes, they proceeded to attitudes toward social questions and toward classes of human beings. The simplistic theses of Watsonian behaviorism seemed to fortify the affinity between experimental work in the laboratories and the understanding and management of human action in the workshop, the marketplace, and the schoolroom. Psychologists appeared increasingly outside academic laboratories in the exercise of their profession, studying the attitudes of the students, advising employers regarding the productivity and discipline of their labor force. The systematic development of scales and questionnaires for the study of attitudes, and the statistical treatment of the resultant data, were the products of this expanded establishment of psychology. The growth of advertising was only an indirect consequence of the war; but the close links which it effected with psychology in market research owed much to wartime experience. The originators of market research had had some of their baptism of fire, and perhaps even their inspiration, in the quasi-psychological propaganda issuing from the Committee on Public Information.

Another extra-academic influence of · ultimately intellectual importance—greater than its original intention—arose from the concern with the well-being of the rural population. Farmers were at that time a far more influential section of American society than they are now and much attention was given to them. Sociologists joined in this. Rural sociology, in the second decade, had made progress in an unspectacular way. It was solid, matter-of-fact, quantitative, and without theoretical pretensions. One part of its concern was carried by the Institute of Social and Religious Research—this was the concern for the health of the church in the countryside and in small towns. In the early 1920s, the Institute decided to extend its interests to a somewhat larger community and engaged a young divine-turned-sociologist to conduct a study of the town of Muncie, Indiana.

The result was *Middletown*, which was the first sociological inquiry to attract wide and enduring public attention; a popular version written by Stuart Chase was a landmark in the installation of sociology as a constituent of public opinion. *Middletown* itself was factual, comprehensive, courageous, and pedestrian. It vaguely conceived of itself—at least post facto—as an anthropological monograph, on the Boasian model. It was indeed introduced to the world by Clark Wissler, an eminent anthropologist who had worked on American Indians. It ignored, for all practical purposes, the ideas and the procedures of the urban sociology which Professors Park and Burgess had instituted at Chicago. This had always dealt with segments of the society of Chicago. *Middletown,* as an "anthropological" inquiry, studied, for the first time, the full round of life of all sectors of the population of an entire urban community. It did so by combining the ambition of an ethnographer with the methods of the Institute of Social and Religious Research. The techniques of the latter had been in the process of formation from the time of Eden's *Condition of the Poor,* Le Play's *Les Ouvriers européens,* Engels' studies of family budgets, the *Reports of H.M. Poor Law Commissioners,* and the *Survey of London Life and Labour* of Charles Booth. Its comparison between an existing town and the same town a half-century earlier underscored the theme of Chicago sociologists, which was the movement from *Gemeinschaft* to *Gesellschaft.* It is difficult to say what effect *Middletown* had on the susequent development of sociology in the United States. *Middletown* was in many respects a prefiguration of the future. It espoused and confirmed the claim of social research that prosaic, patient, quantitative analysis was the road to progress. Though it pointed to and followed the direction of progress, the genre of *Middletown* did not have any imitators. When Lloyd Warner came to his own anthropological study of Newburyport, *Middletown* was not taken as a model. Social science was becoming both too scientific and too imbued also with a desire to be theoretical for this type of comprehensive sociological inventory of an entire community to be regarded as a fit thing to do.

What was living sociologically in *Middletown* was reinforced by the influence of a very different and somewhat later work, which also owed much to extra-academic initiative and patronage. This was the report of the President's Committee on Recent Social Trends. Its genius was Herbert Hoover, then United States secretary of commerce. He had been an engineer, much more learned than most engineers, with a widely ranging curiosity and the intellectual discipline of a scholar-engineer. He was a rationalist who thought that the future lay with the scientific management of human affairs. As secretary of commerce, he had already sponsored the earlier survey of *Recent Economic Changes.* As president, he invited a committee, with W. F. Ogburn as its research director (at that time he was professor at the University of Chicago, where he had come from Columbia University), to inquire into the major changes which had occurred in all spheres of American life—economic, administrative, religious, sumptuary, educational, familial, etc.—since the latter part of the

nineteenth century. It was an ideal theater for Ogburn's talents: no
theoretical adventures, a minimum of generalization, with every effort
guided by an ideal of rigorous documentation and quantitative demonstration. No investigation of "political arithmetic" of a comparable
magnitude and thoroughness had ever been undertaken and successfully carried out hitherto. No similar study has ever been undertaken since. Like *Middletown*, but for different reasons, *Recent
Social Trends* was the culmination of a great line of inquiry. Although
it helped to change the intellectual climate in which sociology worked,
Recent Social Trends brought forth no immediate progeny; it was the
last and greatest instance of its species. It was perhaps too historical
and too atheoretical for the kind of intellectual taste which flourished
over subsequent decades. The theory of "cultural lag" which pervaded it seemed too simplistic; the failure of institutions to keep
abreast of technological innovation did not satisfy the interest in
particular social processes such as stratification and mobility, the integration and disintegration of particular institutions, socialization, the
relations of ethnic groups and the influence of mass communications
which were engaging the interests of sociologists. Perhaps it was also
too macrosociological in its outlook. It did not become alive again
until a desire to construct "social indicators" appeared about four
decades later. Nonetheless it did set a standard of rigorous quantitative documentation which has remained and become stronger in
sociology. This was the lasting influence left behind by *Recent Social
Trends* and *Middletown*.

IV

Thus it was that sociology came into the second third of the century.
Its first European contact was behind it. Out of the large and vague
historical perspectives of European sociology and its efforts to establish the autonomous dignity of its subject-matter, it had retained in a
variety of formulations the distinction between *Gemeinschaft* and
Gesellschaft. In its open, pragmatic, active curiosity about the immediate environment, American sociology had gone far beyond its
European forebears. Although, like European sociology, it still
spoke of "methodology," unlike the European it had begun to develop a passion to observe and for the techniques of observation.
"Methodology" in American sociology came to mean techniques of
observation and quantitative analysis, and not the epistemology and
logic of the social sciences.

    In the 1920s and in the first years of the Great Depression, the lines
which linked American and European sociology had become attenuated. They were never dropped. The older generation of Park,
Giddings, Ross, Cooley, Dunning, and Boas knew the writings of their

German teachers and colleagues. But to their pupils, the great figures who had been their teachers' masters were little more than names which had little connection with what the new stage of the subject demanded. The German and French masters of their teachers were either too archaic or too remote, in their real concerns, from the work which American sociologists wanted to do in this period. The inability to read French and German also had a part in this. Although most of the famous European figures of sociology continued for a time to be viewed with a distant respect, they left no direct impact on the sociology of the 1920s.

For the American generation born in the second decade of this century, European sociology appeared in a guise which did not last well. Their older teachers had been preoccupied with the establishment of sociology as a separate, self-sufficient discipline; and they had chosen from Europe what they thought would accredit this claim. Thus, in Simmel, they fastened onto the opening chapter of his *Soziologie,* in which he wondered confusedly over the distinction between the "form" and "content" of social relationships; in Max Weber, they found of the greatest interest the opening chapter of *Wirtschaft und Gesellschaft,* in which he tried, in German textbook style, to define the basic elements of the subject matter of sociology; in Durkheim, they were interested primarily in his definition of a "social fact." There was not much nutriment in these concerns for a sociology interested in the concrete observable activities of individuals and institutions.

An extended translation by Howard Becker of von Wiese's elaborate classification of social relations appeared at the beginning of the thirties; it was lifeless from the moment it came into the world. The empirical sociology of the time would not hear of that kind of theory, which was only a system of nomenclature. Karl Mannheim's *Ideologie und Utopie,* which appeared in English translation a few years later, aroused some excitement; but it never penetrated into the work of the generation which dominated the professional sociology of the 1930s. It was too abstract, too historical.

The substantive potentialities of the best of European sociology had, of course, scarcely been taken up in Europe. Few Germans had read much of Max Weber beyond the first chapter of *Wirtschaft und Gesellschaft,* the first essay on "Die Protestantische Ethik und der Geist des Kapitalismus" in the first volume of the *Gesammelte Aufsätze zur Religionssoziologie,* and a few of the essays from *Wissenschaftslehre.* The Americans did no more, although, very early on, Professor Frank Knight translated Max Weber's posthumously published lectures on universal economic and social history, in which he put his powerful classificatory apparatus to work. It was too compartive and too historical for American sociologists of the time.

The "daring" ideas in which Roberto Michels criticized the insufficiency of democracy in large societies, Carl Schmitt's conception of politics as an engagement of irreconcilable enemies, Marx, Weber, Pareto, Sombart, Sorel, Mannheim—all those who dealt in the coin of revolution, of violence, of oppression and hierarchy, those who, whether they were right or wrong, at least looked over the whole terrain of society and out over a broad horizon—these writers did become known in the thirties, but they did not penetrate widely into sociological research or theory. Carl Friedrich and William Yandell Elliott, political scientists at Harvard, knew these European writers, but their own writings did not turn American sociologists and political scientists onto their direction. Only two men, Professors Lasswell and Parsons, in different ways, took up European social science, assimilated it into their own thought, and made it fruitful in the study of modern society.

There were a few other sociologists and political scientists who were in their maturity in the 1920s and who knew European sociology. They were Theodore Abel, Howard Becker, and Louis Wirth. Abel's dissertation was concerned primarily with German conceptions of the subject-matter, the jurisdiction, and the divisions of sociology. Becker was the translator and adapter of von Wiese's classificatory system; Wirth knew the writers Park had known, and, on the whole, did not go beyond him, except for his work on behalf of Mannheim, in whom his interest was largely confined to the epistemological question.

The one writer who knew all of European sociology was Professor Pitirim Sorokin, one of the most erudite of men. In his *Systematic Source Book of Rural-Urban Sociology,* he brought more concrete European sociology to America than any writer, but it passed unnoticed by the general run of sociologists, even in the field of rural sociology. His *Social Mobility* was a pioneering inventory; it was duly noted but it was uninfluential in its own time and on the later generation which turned to the study of social stratification and mobility. His *Sociology of Revolution* was disregarded by his contemporaries of the twenties because very few of them were interested in revolution, and it was contemned by the oncoming generation of the thirties to whom revolution was of greater value. In general, except in the cases of Robert Merton and Arnold Anderson, Professor Sorokin's erudition and acumen failed to transmit itself to the generation which was trained in the thirties and forties. The failure was partly a matter of an idiosyncratic rhetoric and a disputatious and rivalrous temperament partly a matter of the misfortune of being a "premature refugee." Cast too soon out of his motherland into a world not yet ready, his idiom was never harmonized with the idiom of his contemporaries. The importance of his work remains for the future to discover.

V

The Great Depression was the most important event in American sociology of the 1930s. It changed the field of attention of the student generation by the experiences to which it made these students witnesses, and it had a deep impact on the more open-minded of the older generation.

By the middle of the 1930s a new spirit was abroad. The Great Depression animated the radicalism which was latent in the reformative traditions of American social scientists. Robert Lynd, whose work on *Middletown* had been so impressive a decade earlier, became one of the leaders in this change. *Middletown in Transition* was a new beginning. Conceived as a comparison of the more recent Muncie with the earlier one, it was in fact a different kind of sociological study. It turned into an analysis of class structure and the power of a wealthy dynasty—features of the life of the community which had been accorded no prominence in the earlier study, although they must have in fact been as important then as they were later. American sociologists had been dealing with the poor and the neglected, and they had dealt with mobility of occupation and residence, which was mobility of status. They had been well aware of the differences in life made by occupation and income. They were aware of the differences in the mode of life of the different classes; Harvey Zorbaugh's *Gold Coast and the Slum* bears witness to that. Nonetheless Robert Lynd's *Middletown in Transition* seemed to many younger sociologists to be playing a new theme. Certainly the moral tone was different. There was an air of accusation. There was also something more—namely, the image of a society dominated and manipulated by the powerful. This had been absent before from American sociology. Even Albion Small, who was very critical of the inequalities of capitalistic society, did not think that society was controlled and manipulated by its beneficiaries.

The implicit radicalism of the American sociologists had been in hibernation together with muckraking, municipal reform, and the Wilsonian liberalism. It is not that sociologists had become mere yea-sayers to their society. They had continued to be aware of its shortcomings, but the growing scientific aspiration of sociology, as well as the retraction of radical sentiment and action throughout the country, had dampened the once flaming passion for reform. The visibility of unemployment and poverty in America and the growth of the power of National Socialism in Germany brought the sleeping tradition into a state of hyper-wakefulness. The New Deal attracted many sociologists; rural sociologists and demographers found employment. Those who remained in the universities welcomed the idea of national planning. With it came a greater sensitivity to inequalities in income, status, and power. A more than academic interest in Marxism in the youngest generation of social scientists, mainly in New York, was a response to the Depression. Intellectually the contact with Marxism was not very pronounced but it was more pronounced than it had been earlier. Albion Small's sympathy with Marxism had more to do with Marxism as one among other movements towards the realization of the democratic ideal. William Ogburn felt some affinity with that aspect of it which could be called "the technological interpretation of history." The one avowedly Marxist sociologist in the country did not hold an academic appointment; he was Arthur W. Calhoun, the author of a learned work on *The Social History of the American Family*.

The Marxism of the 1930s in American sociology was more animated than that now forgotten work but it was still rather subdued. The second major European influence of the 1930s was the coming of the refugees, who brought to America a touch of the excitement of a faltering Central Europe. The refugees in the social sciences brought the awareness of the possibilities of decay of a social order, of the possibilities of disruption of what once seemed so stable. They brought the exhilaration of intellectual melodrama—they brought Freud and Marx and a respect for the name of Max Weber. But they had little contact with the larger academic world of the United States. They were concentrated in two emigré institutions.

I do not think that American social science of the 1930s would have continued to be what it had been even if the refugees had not come. The subject had been making progress both academically and intellectually. Its acceptance as a respectable academic discipline had reduced the urgency of self-justification. It was getting on with the job of meticulous documentation. The decline in European immigration as a result of the First World War and the xenophobic legislation which followed it had made the study of immigrants and their vicissitudes in America—one of the standard themes of the earlier generations—less interesting. The growing sophistication and specialization of intellectual life in the country at large would have, in any case, made academic social scientists less ready to associate themselves on a plane of intellectual equality with social workers, probation officers, and municipal reformers; they were trying to become more scientific. They were, out of their own intellectual development, already seeking a deeper understanding of "the subjective side of culture." The translation of Durkheim and Max Weber had already begun. The external events of the Great Depression, and the European intellectual immigration, brought closer to them catastrophic social events, political violence, and the idiom of bitter conflicts carried on in the name of "class." Neither the older nor the younger generation went overboard. Nonetheless a change in sensitivity did occur at this time.

Not that the achievements of the twenties and early thirties were eradicated without a trace from the memory and practice of social scientists. The depth and vividness of *The Polish Peasant* and the Americanization studies of Park et al., the scholarly documentation and broad scope of *Middletown,* the intimacy and understanding of *The Gang, The Ghetto, The Gold Coast and the Slum,* and the rigorous quantitative scholarship of *Recent Social Trends* were not lost. Furthermore, the newly emergent movements, which were generated in newly established or newly creative centers did not sweep the field. The older interests and points of view in human ecology, ethnic relations, family disorganization, and juvenile delinquency continued to engage most sociologists, in the backwaters of the country and the subject. Nonetheless, *Middletown in Transition,* Alfred Winston Jones' *Life, Liberty and Property,* Lloyd Warner's *Social System of an American Community,* and John Dollard's *Caste and Class in a Southern Town* did represent this modified sensitivity.

One of the important participants in this change was Lloyd Warner, whose anthropological experience and desire to apply this experience to the understanding of a modern community brought the study of social status and class stratification explicitly into American sociology in an idiom appropriate to the empirical temper of the times. It had not been absent before but he gave it greater prominence. Lloyd Warner came to the subject of social stratification not by the usual more or less Marxist course, nor through any contact with that current of German sociology which had sought to understand the significance of the unequal distributions of income, authority, deference, and opportunity. He came, rather, partly through an anthropological theme which had not been greatly featured in social anthropology, and partly as a counsel of desperation, when the inherited analytical scheme of social anthropology proved helpless in the face of even a small modern community. He was the pioneer of this subject; and whatever the shortcomings of his accomplishment, the fact will always remain that Professor Warner was the first social scientist ever to attempt, by relatively systematic and relatively rigorous procedures of fieldwork to confront the fact of inequality of deference in a modern community. He did not reach very far into the heart of the subject, but the fact that it was done at all was notable.

Once he had done it, the way was clear for a treatment which touched more deeply on the costs of indignity and the gains of ascendancy. John Dollard's *Caste and Class in a Southern Town* followed the line of Professor Warner, with the additional complication of a more or less psychoanalytic interpretation which, though simplified, was a serious approach to the misery of human beings. He extended the Chicago and Columbia studies of the American Negro by connecting social stratification with ethnic relationships. The connections have still not been adequately elucidated but Warner and Dollard did move the matter forward. At about the same time, Everett Hughes, one of the closest protégés of Robert Park, did the same thing for Drummondville in Quebec in his *French Canada in Transition*. With these studies, a new foundation was laid for the extension of American sociology. These three authors, by placing ethnic relationships into the setting of the system of stratification of the larger society took a step toward the construction of a macrosociology, which had only been implicit in the work done at Chicago between 1910 and 1930.

A similar macrosociological sensitivity was expressed in the new field of industrial sociology. Industrial psychology had been given a great impetus by its incorporation into industrial management. The inquiries into the conditions affecting industrial output at the Hawthorne Works of the Western Electric Company were conceived in this tradition. The inquiries themselves were ingeniously but cumbersomely designed and they showed little awareness of the social setting or the social structure of industrial work. While the research was in progress, Elton Mayo, who was the moving spirit behind the Hawthorne investigation, was groping towards a view of the nature of industrial society and the sources of conflict within it which corresponded fairly closely with the already established view of modern society. A selective compound of the views of Tönnies, Durkheim, Weber, Simmel, Marx, Park, and Sorokin already contained the ingredients of a picture of society quite far from one in which disorganization and reorganization were adequate concepts. It was a picture of modern society without moral unity, where personal ties had broken down and where conflicts of classes and restless individual ambitions coexisted with apathy. Force and money held this atomized society together. This was the conclusion with which Elton Mayo had been struggling. He was not satisfied with it.

This Hobbesian conception of modern, and particularly contemporary American, society received considerable reinforcement from the second entry of psychoanalysis into the social sciences in the last part of the thirties and in the beginning of the forties. Karen Horney's *The Neurotic Personality of Our Time* had presented a less intricate psychoanalytic interpretation which fitted well with the increasingly antibourgeois temper of some members of the younger generation of sociologists of the second half of the 1930s. Horney was no Marxist, but her analysis was concerned with the "neurotic" components of competitive striving. Nothing could have been more congenial to the critical attitude toward the capitalistic order. Then, too, Margaret Mead's writings made an adroit use of a scheme derived from psychoanalysis, and it too "relativized" and "explained" the bourgeois character. The mood of the times, and, above all, the decay and discrediting of puritanism among the younger generation, fostered a more sympathetic attitude toward the general inclinations of Freudian psychoanalysis. The sometimes unwilling and unwitting shift toward psychoanalysis in clinical psychology and its increasing, even if fragmentary, acceptance in psychiatry, moved in the same line and gave encouragement to the pioneers to persist. Then, at the end of the decade, Erich Fromm, who had already about ten years earlier essayed an amalgamation of Marxism and psychoanalysis, came upon the scene with an interpretation of the sources of National Socialism. *Escape from Freedom* presented, without the dogmatism of a political party, a plausible conception of a cataclysmic event of modern history, and it was, moreover, one which was harmonious with the enhanced and widened political sensitivity of the new generation of sociologists. It, too, was a critique of the social order of capitalism, and it seemed applicable to the situation of the United States as well as Germany. It brought into the center of analysis the class system, the motivations which impelled its acceptance and rejection, and the political consequences of such motivations in a period of large-scale unemployment.

Some words should be said here about the Institut für Sozialforschung which, after leaving Frankfurt shortly after the coming of the Nazis to power, and then after a short sojourn in Paris, settled in New York under the name of the Institute for Social Research. It had little influence in the remainder of the period which culminated in the entry of the United States into the Second World War. Its only link with American sociology at that time was through Paul Lazarsfeld, who himself was an impecunious refugee without a proper academic appointment. Nonetheless, connections were being formed and ideas were being developed which after 1945 played an important part, at least for a time, in American sociology.

More penetrating was the influence of the technique of surveys of opinion. In the eight years between the publication of *Recent Social Trends* and the American entry into the Second World War, the sample survey of public opinion gave a new appearance to American sociology. As a result of this innovation, sociology acquired a greater authority within the sociological profession and in the larger public. It became more technical and its conduct became more highly organized. Sociological research done primarily by individuals as a part-time activity or in fulfillment of the necessity of a doctoral dissertation, yielded to a concentration of the efforts of many cooperating hands.

The public opinion survey was the creation of a psychologist who had entered market research. Sociologists proper had played a negligible role in its earliest development, but few techniques have had a profounder impact on sociology. It has caused sociologists to think of whole national populations. It has greatly enhanced the statistical sensitivity and rigor of sociologists, thus continuing the process which had been advanced by *Recent Social Trends*. It set such a relatively high standard of precision in the description of the present that the disregard for history, so common among sociologists in America, was reinforced. (It was only later, when public opinion surveys had become part of the national culture, that historians began to see the possibility of procedures in historical research which would meet some of the standards of studies of present-day political opinion.) As the scientifically most advanced part of the subject, public opinion— and electoral—studies also defined the image of sociology, both within and outside the academic world.

Of these features, it was the development of the interview which was most representative. The technique of interviewing began to receive much more attention than it had in the previous decade. The larger number of interviewers who had to be trained, their lack of previous sociological experience, and the need to treat the records of their interviews statistically rather than impressionistically accentuated the pressure to standardize interviewing procedures. Participant-observation and the study of "life-history" documents, which had been among the finest contributions of the generation which ruled the twenties, fell aside from the major run of sociological interest in favor of the more superficial and more simplifying, but more rigorous, methods of the survey. Another consequence was a greater focus on individuals and less attention to the communal setting of the behavior of individuals.

Much of the responsibility for this turning within the academic community rested with Paul Lazarsfeld. His interests, as a psychologist who was one of the early market research workers in Europe, his enthusiasm, and his technical virtuosity gave him a crucial position at this stage of American sociology. Towards the end of the 1930s, he had been the prime mover of the Office of Radio Research. With the support of the Rockefeller Foundation, he vigorously prosecuted investigations into the content of mass communications. He initiated an inquiry into voting in a presidential election in Sandusky, Ohio, in which he interviewed recurrently a panel of fixed membership. His collaboration in the ensuing decades with Professor Robert Merton, who was the heir of most of what academic sociology had hitherto presented, transformed the social as well as the intellectual structure of American sociology and with it the other social sciences which were capable of becoming sociological.

Columbia University had long been among the respected centers of sociological study and teaching. It had on its staff men who were learned and productive, and Robert MacIver and Robert Lynd were among the most distinguished in the country. Interesting dissertations emanated from the Department of Sociology as well as from a major research project on Negro migration to New York City. But it represented no distinctive current of thought or practice; its graduates did not colonize the country sociologically in the way in which gradautes of the department of sociology of the University of Chicago had done for a long time. When sociology was mainly a middle western subject, Chicago had enjoyed an almost unchallenged hegemony. The Great Depression, the growth of the mass communications and publicity branches of American economy and culture, and Paul Lazarsfeld helped to change that.

The restless, curious, and ingenious mind of Paul Lazarsfeld found a congenial context in and around New York. Having to make his way in a new setting, he put aside the socialist beliefs which he had brought with him from Vienna and he entered with enthusiasm into his new environment. When he settled in the United States in the first half of the thirties, market research was just beginning to soar; it rose with radio broadcasting advertising and the profligate pictorial weeklies. New York City was the major center of commerce and the ''communications industry'' of the country. It was inevitable, therefore, that the sociologists of one of the universities in New York City should respond to the new possibilities of research into the outlook and responses of listeners and buyers and thus become the locus of the new type of research. New York City, Columbia University, and Paul Lazarsfeld were the optimal combination of place, institution, and man.

Within a relatively short time, the most prominent part of sociological research changed, from a subject individually cultivated by university teachers as one part of their general academic responsibility and by postgraduate students doing research on dissertations for which they almost alone were responsible, into a more highly organized activity with a differentiated division of labor carried out by a large staff under central direction. There had, of course, been collaborative research before—the collaboration of equals, or of teachers and their advanced students, or of a teacher and one or two research assistants who were usually also graduate students submitting some part of the collaborative research in the form of a dissertation. There had been team research ever since the first great urban surveys; and *Middletown* and *Yankee City* each employed a temporary staff, established for the particular inquiry. But none of this type of team research has assumed a stable institutional form, with continuous administration and staff employed on a long-term basis without regard to particular research schemes.

Many sociologists still work in the traditional mode, with the cooperation of a few students or student-assistants. Even at the center of the stage, this pattern of organization still obtains to some extent. Nonetheless, this large-scale, institutionally planned and executed research has become increasingly important. The sample survey has become the genre with the greatest expansiveness. It was able to do so because it was more "scientific" than the other techniques. Furthermore, because so much of it was done under the auspices of commercial enterprises, it was able to obtain financial support on a scale which only some years later began to become available from the private philanthropic foundations and then the federal government.

In a sense, the vague and misformulated aspiration of forty years ago, the desire to become a science, seemed to be coming closer to realization—but the realization was rather different from the aspiration. In the course of this transformation, the intellectual skills which sociologists had thought worthy of cultivation, the ends ideally to be striven for, changed. Sociology became a discipline demanding more exact procedures, more self-consciously and more reliably applied than in the past. Techniques of sampling, interviewing, and statistical analysis became much more rigorous in the course of this development. Training and experience were rendered more specialized, and with this specialization came a considerable increase in the number of technically proficient sociologists with a sense of membership in a profession. The general standard of technical competence rose, and, with it, a sense of self-sufficiency and even complacency. In certain centers, institutionalization and specialization were accompanied by an indifference to "deeper" variables and to problems of a more general, more theoretical significance. At Columbia, the close collaboration of Professor Merton with Lazarsfeld kept a closer relationship between sample surveys and sociological theory. At the University of Michigan, where the Institute of Social Research became a major national center for the conduct of surveys, the interest was more exclusively descriptive than it was at the Bureau of Applied Social Research, at Columbia. But there too the use of the data gathered in the surveys by sociologists contributed to the growth of political sociology. This field which dealt mainly with the grounds and stability of attachments to political parties was one which had heretofore been very little cultivated by sociologists. Other new fields of substantive interest were laid open by the powerful new technique of the sample survey, and others were in consequence neglected.

VI

Sociological theory as it was taught in universities for the first third of the century was mainly a review of what had been said about the subject-matter and major concepts by Comte, Spencer, Gumplowicz, Schäffle, Ratzenhofer, et al.

Until well into the 1930s, much of what was called sociological theory was classificatory and definitional; real events served mainly to provide illustrations. Not that this classificatory function was useless. It was valuable in the ordering of reality; it gave names to events and processes; and it enabled those who drew on it to see certain similarities in otherwise apparently very disparate particular occurrences. One of the functions of theory—the reduction of the heterogeneity of concrete experience to a smaller number of "principles"—was performed by this kind of theory.

There was, of course, also a more explanatory kind of theory but it was only implicit in certain kinds of concrete research, particularly that which took place mainly in Chicago, under the inspiration of William Thomas and Robert Park. It was, however, largely inarticulate and it was not easily made explicit. Thomas' ideas about the tendencies of institutions, groups, and societies in crisis to set in movement processes of reorganization in which the "four wishes" come into play, his perception that the processes of disorganization and reorganization are constantly going on in all institutions, groups, and societies are illustrative of that kind of unsystematized theory which is effective through its pervasive influence in observation and analysis rather than through explicit adduction. Parks' ideas about the ceaseless sifting which locates, shifts, and relocates institutions and groups in space, and about the interpenetration, intensification, and attenuation of the four major processes of competition, conflict, accommodation, and assimilation was a differentiation of Thomas' ideas about disorganization and reorganization. These theoretical ideas were not sharply formulated, they were not explicit or systematic, and they were used in an ad hoc fashion. They were not put into a form in which they could be confirmed or disconfirmed.

A pronounced change in the situation began in the middle 1930s. The change has largely been the work of Professor Talcott Parsons. His theoretical efforts began quite apart from contact with American social research or from the effort to understand American life. They arose, rather, from a strenuous effort to understand, locate, and correct the utilitarian tradition of economic theory. This led him into the most fundamental problems of social order and change. He drew upon the greatest classics of German and French sociology to aid him in this task, and, in doing so, also was able to make explicit its postulates. *The Structure of Social Action* was not only an original work of interpretation of the fundamental ideas of Max Weber, Vilfredo Pareto, Alfred Marshall, and Emile Durkheim, it was also the beginning of an independent interpretation of the basic elements and conditions of human action. He worked at a deep level and with a great generality. In the thirties he had still worked mainly on the great theorists, and this isolated him somewhat from the empirical side of sociology. At that time, he was still clearing the way by demonstrating the untenability of biological, psychological, economic, and cultural reductionism. Yet unlike Durkheim, he did not think that everything could be explained sociologically. Aside from his monumental treatise, he also interested himself in a study of the medical profession in the light of the conceptions which he had elaborated in that work. Only a few of his students of that decade, such as Robert Merton and Kingsley David, bore witness to his powers, while among his coevals in sociology his work was powerless. His influence on American sociological thought became more effective only with the beginning of the second half of the century.

The other original sociological theorist of the 1930s was Harold Lasswell. Academically, he was a political scientist but his exceptionally wide range of knowledge and interests brought him into the territory of sociology at many points. In learning from Europe large ideas which he developed in his own way and sought to apply to substantive problems, he was a rare bird among the American-born political scientists who became fertile in the 1930s. His interests lay in the great macrosociological questions of political and social order, and in their connection with the interior life of the individual. In a way which bewildered many of his contemporaries, but which has since become commonplace, he pioneered in the adaptation of psychoanalytic interpretation to the study of fundamental attitudes towards authority. He was interested in the distribution of things which are valued in society and in the revolutions in these distributions. He was interested in the processes of diffusion of ideas and institutions from major centers of innovation. This brought him face to face with the problems involved in the generation and spread of the great political ideals, in the composition and transformation of elites, in the hunger for power and in its rejections and in the readiness for submission. The sources for the consideration of these problems he searched out in the writings of Freud, Weber, Pareto, Mosca, and Michels. He was a forerunner in the breaking of the boundaries of the social sciences. He was one of the most influential teachers of the decade; his influence may be seen in the wide range of work associated with the names of Almond, Rosten, Leites, George, Brodie, Pool, and Janowitz. The interpretation of political events according to the categories and surmises of sociology—which is now taken for granted in sociology and in political science—owes much to the intellectual atmosphere which he helped to create.

By the end of the interwar period, the sociological sciences had established themselves as academic disciplines. They had found an adequate subject-matter and extended it. They had developed techniques of observation, and they had found an appreciative if narrow public outside the academic world. It was not that they had any demonstrated scientific propositions to offer to the world. But, in a world which values information about itself, sociological research seemed to offer a more acceptable sort of information than casual experience and random and occasional reflection. For circles which thought that they must manipulate their fellow men and which believed in science as the instrument of manipulation, social research appeared to be an appropriate handmaiden. The results of social research, uncertain as they were, began to exercise and to gratify that fascination which psychoanalysis met earlier in the century. Sociology had actually come to be about human beings and their society, in an age curious about and sensitive to the nuances of motive and conduct and eager to know what went on behind the face of reason and respectability. The Second World War drew all these impulses together and intensified them.

VII

The muses may be silent in wartime, but the muse of the social sciences was not silent during the Second World War. Whereas the First World War helped to raise the confidence of psychologists, the Second World War enhanced the confidence of the sociologists and those who shared the culture of sociology. Sociologists and their like were nearly everywhere in the national exertion. In the Information and Education Branch of the Office of the Adjutant General sociologists and social psychologists under the guidance of Samuel Stouffer studied an immense range of the sentiments and attitudes of soldiers—from their feelings about service conditions to experiences in combat. In other sections of the army, sociologists and social psychologists studied the attitudes and backgrounds of prisoners of war, and even in these disorderly conditions the apparatus of the public opinion survey was brought into play. In the air force, psychiatrists conducted sociological studies of bomber crews. In the Special War Policies Unit of the Department of Justice, sociologists studied ethnic minorities and "nativist" fanatics, their social and political organizations and their possible relations with the enemy. In the Federal Communications Commission (Foreign Broadcast Intelligence Service), sociologists labored with and without the aid of systematic content analyses to divine the enemy's view of things from his broadcasts and from his newspapers, while others studied the state of sentiment and opinion within the territories ruled by the enemy as sovereign or as conqueror. In the Office of Strategic Services and in the Office of War Information, similar activities were carried on. In the Department of Agriculture, the sample survey experienced an unprecedented prosperity.

The end of the war did not mean the end of this extraordinary range and diversity of activities. Some of them continued within the government. Most of the social scientists who had been in the government went home to their universities. Some went into business as employees or as enterprisers, and a small group went into the RAND Corporation. All of them carried with them the high confidence and enthusiasm which had been generated in wartime in government service. Sociology and its growing body of subsidiaries flourished now as never before.

The deeper causes of the exceptional prosperity of the social sciences after the Second World War are manifold. The change in fundamental attitudes towards one's own and others' experience seems to have enabled sociology to catch on. The subject would have remained meager and amateurish if it had not been for the great productivity of the American economy, the traditions of the private philanthropic foundations, with their great resources and their confidence in the potentiality of social science as science and as a means "to solve the problems of society." The generosity of the three great foundations, Rockefeller, Ford, and Carnegie, and of many lesser endowments, as well as the much enlarged munificence of the federal government, has furthered among sociologists and their fellow travelers in cognate fields the sense of being vaguely at the center of things in national life. After the exciting work of the war, which all too often was disregarded by the officers and officials charged with responsibility for actual operations, this was reassuring.

This self-confident readiness for large undertakings, ample resources, and a more potent technical preparation have all contributed to bring into being what was scarcely more than prefigured before the war. Within universities, the research undertakings of individual staff members have become more complex in technique, requiring larger bodies of assistants, and their financial provision and administration have developed accordingly. The Russian Research Center and the Laboratory of Social Relations at Harvard, the National Opinion Research Center at Chicago, the Institute of Industrial Relations at Berkeley were all extensions of the research of the teaching staff members. They are adaptations of the traditional university structure to the new scale and complexity of social research. More sociologists and greater prolificness, more sociological books and journals filled the space around sociologists.

The establishment of sample survey institutions, such as the Survey Research Center at Michigan, the National Opinion Research Center at Chicago, and the Bureau of Applied Social Research at Columbia, affiliated to universities and supported by income from market research, government contracts, and contracts with private and civic bodies, has also helped to change further the face of sociological research. It has led to a narrowing of the conception of the right procedure of research; and it has probably also narrowed the imagination of some of its younger practitioners. While it raised the level of technical proficiency of the average young sociologist, it also tended to reduce sociological research to a routine in which difficult problems could be passed over in the interests of precision and "operational" practicability.

This increase in the appreciation of sociology is not just a function of the greater precision of its procedures and the amplitude of its factual findings, nor is it primarily a consequence of presumedly greater economic and institutional utility and, more indisputably, of its greater prosperity.

It is the product of a number of developments, some as wide as American society, some more individual. The promotion of the belief that higher education must be available to all brought about the expansion of the universities and with that the expansion of students studying sociology out of genuine interest and the absence of equally satisfying alternatives. This meant more posts for sociologists, and more postgraduate students hoping to become academic sociologists. More young persons became committed to the teaching of sociology as a career—with its attendant obligation of research. Sociology is all they know and it appears to them to be, in one or another of its variants, the only way in which to understand the world. Having invested their years in it, they have a "vested interest" in it. The fact too that so much public attention is devoted to contemporaneous affairs and that sociology is largely about contemporaneous affairs— sometimes the same ones—gives sociologists and their public the conviction that sociology is about important things, things which are worth knowing about. Sociology has become an auxiliary device of the passion to know about the present.

Another factor is pertinent when we attempt to account for the appreciation of sociology in the decades which followed the end of the Second World War. It was the coming-of-age during the later 1940s and the 1950s of a new generation, European in its intellectual attachments through nativity, as in the case of Professor Reinhard Bendix, or through a sense of affinity, as in the case of the young Jews who received a form of worldly education in the radical political movements of the late 1930s. The latter were offspring of the Eastern European Jewish immigrants who had come to America between the 1880s and the First World War, and they had a quite different outlook from the generation of social scientists which had preceded them. They were youths who thought easily and familiarly of a Europe where they had never been. It was a Europe of autocracy and of revolutionary movements, of a consciousness of struggle for power, of class consciousness, of political sects and conventicles—a Europe where theory was respected, where learning touched all that was deep and vital. The Russian Revolution, Marxism, and the trade union and socialist movements meant very much to these young men, many of whom spent their late adolescence and youth on the edges of such movements in the United States. They were internationalists in their sympathies and in their curiosity. Professors Lipset, Selznick, Bell, Gouldner, and Janowitz came from such immigrant families.

VIII

The movements which came to the surface in the years just before the war continued in a denser way after it. Social stratification and mobility, industrial sociology, the study of organizations, mass communications, and political sociology throve. There was much interest in sociological theory. The major fields of sociological activity of the period before the Depression—ecology, urban sociology, and ethnic relations—became less prominent. Rural sociology, which had been an important part and a formative influence, diminished and became isolated. Of course, in a profession spread over so many universities and colleges, the changes were not uniform. In many institutions, things remained as they had been; in others, the older interests continued with the newer ones being added through the appointment of a practitioner of the new dispensation. At other institutions the newer subjects took the central position.

With the newer subjects there entered a second contact between American and European sociology. The first contact occurred when young Americans went to German universities in the last quarter of the nineteenth century. They did not obtain much in the way of substantive sociological ideas. They did acquire ideas about academic disciplines, the conduct of seminars, the importance of research, and the contributions of social scientists to the formation of public policies. Except for Simmel, there was probably no European sociologist who had a positive influence on that older generation. Even Tönnies had little direct influence and such influence as he had was an extension and elaboration of Simmel's ideas about the impersonality of urban and commercial life and the contrasts between the specialization, separation, and impersonality of the city and the closed, relatively undifferentiated, and consensual character of life in a small town or village. Gumplowicz had some influence on Park, but it is likely that the Danish plant and animal ecologist Warming had much more.

The European sociology which the generation of the 1940s and 1950s knew—the generation now between the ages of thirty and fifty—was one which, with the exception of Harold Lasswell and

Talcott Parsons, had been unknown before to most indigenous American sociologists. Most of it derived from Max Weber, with additional contributions from Tocqueville, Mannheim, Simmel, Durkheim, Michels, and Marx. (It is only since the late 1960s that Karl Marx has been retroactively promoted to the status of a founder of sociology.) It was a sociology concerned with bureaucracy and the "bureaucratization" of modern society; it was a sociology concerned with power and authority, with the individual, solitary and defenseless unless he became a member of a powerful organization which in any case was dominated by an oligarchy. There was a mixture of deep and sober understanding and melodramatic exaggeration in this importation. The fundamental lines of this more sober side were to a large extent the achievement of Professor Talcott Parsons, whose book, *The Structure of Social Action,* was published in 1937. Its influence began to be felt as a guide to European sociological thought only when, after the Second World War, ethnic relations, urban sociology, human ecology, and social disorganization, which had been the first subject-matters of American sociology, ceased to be so, and, in their stead, the new subject-matters came forward. Then the sociology hitherto hidden in the European classics was discovered.

In so many of these things, Harold Lasswell had been a portent. Yet, when, after the Second World War, the new generation of social scientists who had not worked with this pioneering teacher at Chicago, or with his former pupils, turned toward a social science formed out of elements offered by Freud, Marx, and Weber, Lasswell was not the object of their turning. Margaret Mead and Ruth Benedict, Erich Fromm, Harry Stack Sullivan were taken as guides to a psychoanalytic sociology. Talcott Parsons had a similar pioneering role with respect to Weber and Durkheim. Unlike Lasswell, he continued for several decades to be a major force in the development of a sociological outlook which assimilated much of the best European substance and gave it a new existence.

The refugees did not have any significant influence until they had been in the United States for about a decade. Their substantive contribution was to the melodramatic portrayal of modern society.

IX

It was at the very end of the 1930s and then, after a wartime suspension of political thought, in the postwar years that the consequences of European ideas and events began to make themselves felt in American sociology. The refugees brought the insistent disposition to contemplate power; they brought the image of a society which had done as Hobbes had said societies would do. They came from a society which had suffered a relapse toward a state of nature, and which had responded to the relapse by a self-subjugation into an absolutism more ironclad than any tyrannical regime had ever been.

As the sociological disciplines in America grew in worldliness, the experience of the disorder of the last years of the Weimar republic and the order of the Nazi regime took a prominent position in the imagery of some American sociologists. The intellectual precipitate of this experience was the idea of "mass society."

Emil Lederer, the dean of the Graduate Faculty of Political and Social Science—the "University in Exile"—wrote *The State of the Masses;* Max Horkheimer, the director of the Institute of Social Research, had depicted the horrors of modern society in a series of essays; his protégé and colleague Fromm had added his mite to the portrait of human beings as irrational and defenseless in the face of authority. Although the two institutions held themselves aloof from each other, and one was definitely more radical than the other, their contributions to American sociology were quite congruent. The idea of "mass society" was an amalgam of the construction of the last phase of the Weimar republic as the prototypical modern society, compounded with a melodramatic view of modern industry, Kafkaesque conceptions of administration, and a sublimated Marxism. The idea of "mass society" was one of the least salubrious achievements of the German refugees and of those sociologists who in their adolescence and youth in the 1930s had dreamt the great dream of socialism.

Another product of the European influence was the study of elites, to which Harold Lasswell had drawn attention in *World Politics and Personal Insecurity* and *Politics: Who Gets What, When and How.* The subject had been sporadically cultivated in Europe by Harold Laski and Fritz Giese; it had a distinguished founder in Francis Galton. In the United States, Pitirim Sorokin's *Social Mobility* and a number of papers by George Counts had contained a similar interest. For some reason the subject lay dormant until after the Second World War. Then it expanded rapidly. Lasswell himself initiated a series of studies of elites at the Hoover Library; the study of local elites formed the subject of a new field: "the study of community power." C. Wright Mills, who combined the influence of Veblen and that of the melodramatic current among the refugees, wrote *The Power Elite.*

Older American writers such as Arthur Bentley have been reinstated to give legitimacy to this new attention to the characteristics and conduct of elites. Unlike the theory of "mass society," which was never reduced to the terms in which it could be investigated by current sociological techniques of research, the study of elites was in a short time transformed to the point where its relationship to its original European models could scarcely be recognized. Once the subject was laid open to investigation it expanded far beyond the framework of its European point of departure.

X

Sociologists who studied the city sometimes referred to it as a laboratory. They did not mean that they conducted experiments on it or in it. They meant rather that what they studied in it was representative of something larger than what was studied. It was representative not only of other instances of the same class of phenomena, e.g., a ghetto or a wealthy residential quarter or a slum; it was respresentative in the sense that it was part of the larger society—the particular urban society, the regional society, and the national society. Some subject-matters, such as immigrants, had to be understood in the setting of a rudimentary international society. The first interest of American sociologists was in the formation and character of modern society. The city was studied because it was the epitome of the most characteristic features of the then-emergent modern society.

The first generation of American sociologists of this century had a definitive macrosociological bent. Cooley was concerned about the characteristics of the large national society which had emerged in the framework of the national state and from the elements of local societies. Thomas in fact went so far as to describe the structure of a whole society as the background from which to view the migration of Poles to the United States. Park's continuous curiosity in the press and in the flow of information was part of this macrosociological interest in the functioning of the national society. The process of "Americanization" to which Thomas and Park devoted *Old World Traits Transplanted* was conducted with a macrosociological assumption.

Be that as it may, this macrosociological interest did not grow in Chicago, Michigan, or Columbia, nor did it appear in Harvard when sociology was established there. Despite the emergence of the study of social stratification and the increased interest in industrial sociology, sociologists tended to treat the local objects of their study as if they were largely self-contained; at best they treated them as microcosmic illustrations rather than as microcosmic parts of a macrocosm. A change took place after the late 1930s. The interest in "mass society" was nurtured by the conjunction of the arrival of the central European intellectual refugees, the study of "mass communications," the discovery of political apathy in the course of political-sociological investigations and the experience of the disorders of the Depression. The urban sociological studies of the first third of the century provided a fertile soil of tradition from which the new seeds could grow.

By the middle of the century, macrosociological study received a new impetus, and, in response to it, a whole range of new problems was elicited. The establishment of Max Weber's sociology was perhaps the most important single intellectual factor. Another, extraneous factor, as important in its way as the urban immigration and the Depression had been in their time, was the appearance of the new states of Asia and Africa.

The political emergence of Asia and Africa—previously the concern of students of mandates, trusteeships, and colonial administration, of anthropologists seeking real existence in villages and small societies, of students of primitive art, etc.—led to a dramatic turning point. The problems involved in understanding the movement towards the formation of a society from separate tribes and kinship groups made social scientists reflect to a greater extent than they had hitherto on the nature of a society and not just on the functioning of its parts. The contact with social anthropology was very beneficial for both sociologists and anthropologists. The latter learned some of the quantitative techniques which sociologists had been developing; the sociologists who had pioneered in community studies were reminded of what they had forgotten by the anthropologists' study of the interdependence of the different spheres of life in a community observed at firsthand.

The Ford and the Rockefeller Foundations and the Carnegie Corporation helped this change by their generous provision in direct and indirect forms. The Committee on Comparative Politics of the Social Science Research Council, the Committee for the Comparative Study of New Nations of the University of Chicago, and South Asian Studies committees at Chicago and Berkeley furthered this macrosociological interest and accomplishment. Their funds made a large difference to young scholars with a new curiosity to go far off to observe and interview from morning to midnight, to learn languages outside the traditions of American erudition, to live in the midst of demonstrations, guerilla skirmishes, and civil wars, to meet chiefs, cabinet ministers, and senior civil servants, and to come to know the society and its elites far more vividly and comprehensively than they could ever know American or European societies and than their academic disciplines would have hitherto allowed. New problems: the relationships within elites, the relationships of ruling elites and those they ruled, the relations between centers and peripheries, between national cultures and regional and local cultures and societies came to the attention of sociologists. In dealing with these problems, the sociologists reanimated parts of their own tradition which they had forgotten and gave these parts a prominence which they had never had in their own time.

Within a decade, sociologists and sociologically sympathetic an-

thropologists like Lloyd Fallers and Clifford Geertz, and political scientists like David Apter, created a body of literature of a new type.
In the nineteenth and early twentieth centuries, scholars, travelers,
and journalists had written comprehensive books on particular
societies. Alexis de Tocqueville's *De la Démocratie en Amérique,*
W. H. Dawson's *Germany and the Germans,* T. H. Escott's *Social
Transformations of the Victorian Age,* and Wilhelm Dibelius' *England* are illustrations of this genre.

In social sciences, however, this tradition did not become established. It appeared to be too superficial, too unscientific. Only the
anthropologists studied total societies, but their societies were small
and special in the sense that kinship and locality were their major
integrative bonds. Sociology and political science had become
specialized in a set of segregated fields. After the discovery of the
potentialities of macrosociology overseas, sociologists turned to the
United States. Lipset's *America: The First New Nation* marked a
transition to a more realistic picture of the working of American national society. The growth in the powers of the federal government
reinforced the impetus to a macrosociological view. The works of
Morris Janowitz, particularly *Social Control in the Welfare State,*
have consolidated the macrosociological view. The traditions on
which this new and more emphatic macrosociology drew were in the
first instance those which had been formed from the orientations
contained explicitly and implicitly in the writings of Max Weber. Parsons and Lasswell had been the mediators of this tradition, into which
were drawn elements from Park, Thomas, and Redfield.

The broadening of the sociological horizon has not been confined to
present-day American society or to the new states of Asia and Africa.
The contemplation of whole societies in relation to the fundamental
elements of social life has gone backward in history. In the former
movement, comparative analysis has reappeared without the encumbrance of evolutionist prejudice. American social scientists, who were
for so long "historyless" and who, outside contemporary America,
were familiar only with the recent history of Western Europe and a
few primitive societies, have in a few outstanding instances greatly
extended their reach into the past of human experience. George Homans was the first sociologist who interested himself in the domains
outside the Western present and the then ostensibly timeless primitive; and he was the first to do original research up to the level of
proficiency of the technically trained historian. He was followed in
time by others, like Charles Tilly and Neil Smelser. The tradition of
Weber, mediated by Parsons, is visible in the work of the latter, less
so in the case of the former. Homans himself was probably more
influenced by Pareto and Henderson. Sociologists like the forgotten
James Mickel Williams had studied the history of their communities;

the neglected Arthur Calhoun had written on the history of the family in America. The more recent historical interest of sociologists like Kai Erikson and the sociological interest of historians like Stephen Thernstrom seem to be new growths and have little to do with the flickering tradition of the earlier historical sociology.

Although specifically historical research by sociologists continues to be rare, there has been an increase in the historical sensitivity of sociologists and in their historical learning. Reinhard Bendix has led the way in this regard and many more have followed after him. It is much more common nowadays for an American sociologist to work on a topic which requires the knowledge gained from historical monographs than it used to be. This contrasts markedly with the situation of the years between the two great wars. Occasionally sociologists—as in the case of the contributors to *Recent Social Trends*—took a long historical perspective. For the most part, however, sociologists were content to accept the potted version of modern history contained in Comte's "law of the three stages." The specialization of sociological instruction as well as research cut sociology off from historical studies. The effort to construct a general sociological theory also washed out the temporal element. It is true that Albion Small in analyzing the *Origins of Sociology* dealt with great German historical writers like Niebuhr and Savigny. This however had nothing to do with the substance of sociology as it developed over the ensuing decades. Generally speaking, the more scientific sociology became, the less historical it became at the same time. This too is now changing, at least to a modest degree.

The scope of these movements in sociology is significant but it should not be overestimated. The mass of American sociologists continue to work in their special fields, using increasingly refined techniques and drawing on theory in an *ad hoc* and fragmentary manner. But the fragments are taken from major traditions as exemplified in the work of leading contemporaries such as Parsons, Merton, Coleman, Janowitz, and Duncan. The theory seeps into their work and it is mainly one or another variant of the theory which has now been dominant for about two-thirds of a century.

XI

Thus it was that sociology gradually changed in the United States. The changes originated from the unfolding of the tradition which had got under way in Chicago and from its interaction with the traditions which had grown up in Columbia and later at Harvard. The changes came about too through fusion with certain European traditions which had been brought into the United States by a few Americans through the study and translation of certain European classics. Other European traditions were brought to the United States by European refugees. There were certain changes in institutions which fostered the changes in traditions. For example, the formation of the Department of Sociology and then the Department of Social Relations at Harvard fostered the development of a sociological tradition which was relatively independent of the Chicago and Columbia traditions. (These traditions were never wholly self-contained; Ogburn brought a certain way of looking at society from Columbia to Chicago, where it had not flourished previously; Stouffer brought to Harvard a way of doing research which had developed at Chicago.) Institutions that were created to conduct of sample surveys and that were closely linked with universities, gave sociologists opportunities to do a new kind of research—and this in turn affected the substance of the tradition.

The institutions of publication also affected the vicissitudes of the sociological tradition. After the publication of W. E. B. DuBois' *The Philadelphia Negro* as a monograph of the Academy of Social and Political Science, most American sociological publications for nearly five decades took the form of papers in learned journals or of textbooks. The journals were published by university departments and presses; the books were published by commercial publishers. The latter preferred books which could be sold in fairly large numbers. Textbooks fitted this policy very well. They also fitted the tradition of sociological theory which consisted of systematically ordered definitions of the main institutional structures and the main processes. Like DuBois' *The Philadelphia Negro*, monographs which reported on studies of particular communities or institutions were published by university presses. The University of Chicago Press was much in the lead; Columbia University Press also published such monographs.

The few sociologists who were ready to embark on an extended treatment of a large theme or topic were induced by this convention of publishing to deform it into the style of a textbook, so that it could be "adopted" as the required book of a course. Even Talcott Parsons' *The Structure of Social Action*, which was as far from a textbook as a learned treatise could be, was published by McGraw-Hill in its series of sociological textbooks. There seemed to be no other form. In the 1920s and early 1930s, the two main American "theoretical" treatises were *An Introduction to the Science of Sociology* by Robert Park and Ernest Burgess and Robert MacIver's *Society: Its Structure and Changes*. Both of these were intended to be textbooks and theoretical treatises. The major translation of German sociological theory in the early 1930s was made from Von Wiese's *Allgemeine Beziehungslehre*, which was published as part of a series of sociological textbooks. This was not solely the fault of the publishers. It was also a convention which had grown up among sociologists; their nourishment of their students on the pap of textbooks was reinforced by the belief, among publishers, that there was no market for sociological books other than as textbooks for students or as community studies like *Middletown*. A few commercial or university presses would occasionally publish books like John Mecklin's *The Decline of the Saint* or James Mickel Williams' *The Expansion of Rural Life* and *Our Rural Heritage* or would even reprint Thomas and Znaniecki's *The Polish Peasant in Europe and America*.

The development of sociology led to a situation in which books on broad topics, and investigations which were not community studies or studies of particular institutions, were being written. Eisenstadt's *From Generation to Generation*, Janowitz's *The Professional Soldier*, Lazarsfeld and Thelen's *The Academic Mind* were in a different genre from the sociological books produced before the Second World War. They were the products of the greater density and intensity of research and of the fusion of theoretical interest and realistic and detailed scholarship. This new direction was greatly fostered by the activities of the Free Press, a small publishing enterprise conducted by Mr. Jeremiah Kaplan, a young man of Russian Jewish origin, who came from the same milieu as Professors Lipset, Selznik, Bell, et al., and he was of the same generation. The Free Press began by reprinting books which were out of print and in demand in colleges and universities; the translation of Durkheim's *Division of Labor* which had become out of print was one of the first. The republication of *The Structure of Social Action*, out of print for a decade and unappreciated during that decade except for its potted versions of the European classics, was a major event in the development of American sociology. The Free Press also published new translations from the German, the works of Max Weber, above all, and then of Simmel, and new publications by living authors. It also published collections of essays, particularly those of Robert Merton and Talcott Parsons, which were very influential through the provision of instances of studies of particular topics, such as kinship, bureaucracy, and anomie in the framework of a general sociological theory. It was also a pioneer in the publication of anthologies of major papers on topics like public opinion and propaganda, bureaucracy, urban sociology, and political behavior.

The Free Press focused the minds of the younger generation of American sociologists on the kind of sociology which was then emerging—a fusion of the tradition of Chicago sociology (itself a development of an older European tradition)—with a new tradition deriving much of its direction from Max Weber's and to a lesser extent Durkheim's ideas. Its existence encouraged further work in the new genres and in the newer forms of the older traditions.

In the 1960s the Free Press went into decline when it moved from the environs of the University of Chicago and became part of a large commercial firm. Its role was assumed in a different form by the Heritage of Sociology, a series of the selected works of major sociologists of the past two centuries. The series is edited by Professor Morris Janowitz and is published by the University of Chicago Press which thus renews the role which it had played earlier as a concentrator of attention through the Chicago Sociological Series.

XII

There was no complete consensus in the sociology which was taught and created in the two decades after the end of the Second World War. Generally there was a considerable agreement about the most important topics and about the urgency of stringent research procedures. There was agreement about the necessity of theory. There was also agreement about the fundamental categories of analysis of individual and institutional action. The ideas of the active, end-seeking human organism, drawn from Dewey, and of the value-oriented, norm-oriented, interest-oriented actor capable of rational thought and decision, drawn from Weber, came together. Strictly behavioristic interpretations of human action were not favored. Psychological and sociological reductionism were also not favored. The cultural component in action was generally although vaguely and residually acknowledged. There was a general acceptance of the idea that society is integrated—to the extent that it is integrated—by "common values," authority, power, and the concert of interests.

Aside from the approximate consensus on these general orientations, there was less agreement. There was disagreement about the merits of a general theory as against a theory of middle principles—although much that was fundamental was held in common by both of these two positions. There was a wide diversity of interests in particular subject-matters. Sociology had never been so specialized as it became in this period. There were sociologists of the family, sociologists of formal organizations, sociologists of mass communications, specialists in the experimental study of small groups, studies of voting behavior, of "community power," of industrial relations, ethnic relations, religious bodies, the military. Some of these topics were more studied than others: on the whole, those who studied one did not study the other, although they all knew that all of the institutions existed within a larger setting or, as it came to be called, a larger system. Talcott Parsons attempted to unify these diverse fields by treating many of them in particular essays in which he applied and differentiated his general orientation. No sociologist went further than he did in attempting to apply his general theory over such a wide and concrete range of topics. His theory in its differentiated formulation was not widely accepted but it left a deep impact and many parts of it were repeatedly applied by many sociologists who did not regard themselves as adherents of his general theory. In that sense there was a considerable degree of consensus about the way to view society or particular institutions and relationships. The consensus was a precipitate of the ideas of Thomas, Park, Weber, Durkheim, and Parsons. The consensus was a loose and ambiguous one and Professor Parsons' effort to make it explicit and systematic like the less systematic and more ambiguous ideas of the other eminent sociologists was only used in a piecemeal fashion.

Quite apart from the segregation of specialities which was partly bridged by the common tradition there was emerging a set of disagreements which came from divergent interpretations of the common tradition and from the adduction of a deviant tradition. Some sociologists contended that there were no common values, no common affirmation of symbols of the society as a whole. They insisted that, to the extent that society was integrated at all, it was integrated by potentially coercive power and by manipulation; they saw the mass of the society as the pawn of manipulation. Sentiments of loyalty and attachment to the central institutions of the society were regarded as evidence of "false consensus." These views were put by sociologists who wrote about "mass society" and above all by C. Wright Mills. These sociologists criticized those who did not share their views; they charged them with being politically conservative, as "serving the interests"; they called them "functionalists." There was little explicit examination of the substantive observations and interpretations made by the sociologists with whom they disagreed. It should not be thought that this disagreement came primarily from a difference in the traditions of sociology. The major tradition of modern sociology shared by almost all the important writers from the beginning of the nineteenth century to the present emphasized that modern society, i.e., urban society, was individualistic, rationalistic, oriented towards the material advantages of the individual. This tradition asserted that moral beliefs and the sense of identity with the collectivity—whether it be a village, a rural community, a congregation, or a country—had become enfeebled. The loosening of the attachments of the individual to other individuals in families, neighborhoods, work places was generally thought to have declined. Some writers took this to be a unilinear process although the leading exponents of this sociological tradition did not think so. Thomas' ideas about social disorganization and reorganization, Park's ideas about the incessant processes of accommodation and assimilation going on concurrently with competition and conflict, Max Weber's ideas about the resurgence of the charismatic in conditions of crisis were certainly not unilinear interpretations of the features of modern, urban societies.

The introduction of Marxism, which itself was one current within the larger tradition which has gone into sociology but which is one with its own history, accentuated this dissension. The dissension became more pronounced in the 1960s. A spirit of discontent with the hitherto prevalent sociology found a more open expression. Yet the substantive traditions of sociology remain as strong as ever. The critics have not been able to break out of them any more than have their more affirmative adherents.

The current of sociology which calls itself "phenomenological sociology" claims the ideas of Alfred Schutz as its foundation. But these ideas, much like those of Talcott Parsons' construction of the paradigm of interaction and of the fundamental components of action, have their origins in Max Weber's definition of action which in turn was an attempt to put into systematic analytical form the elements of action which were basic to Tönnies' distinction between *Gemeinschaft* and *Gesellshaft*. And this in turn goes back to Hegel, Hobbes, Locke, and Aristotle.

The recent dissension in sociology cannot be gainsaid. But sociology, like any other intellectual activity which is carried on by many persons over generations, can never be wholly consensual. Even sciences far more rigorous and precise than sociology are witnesses to a perpetual dissensus. If they did not, they would come to an end as actively growing bodies of knowledge. Sociology is a much more loosely jointed body of knowledge and dissensus must exist within it all the more. Its ambiguities alone would guarantee that. This observation must not, however, be allowed to obscure the rather large measure of consensus which exists around the fundamental traditions of sociology.

3   The Confluence of
Sociological Traditions

I

Was it only a coincidence that the two most noticed philosophers of the nineteenth century, even in the circles of qualified philosophers—Auguste Comte and Herbert Spencer—were also thought of as sociologists? The nineteenth century is often regarded as the age of historicism and as the age of belief in science. But it was also the age of sociology. It was an age when it began to be believed that all of man's misfortunes were the product of his environment, meaning by that, the social conditions under which he lived. It was an age which began to devalue beliefs—religious, philosophical, and all others, except scientific ones—by showing that they "arose from social conditions." It was an age which began itself to believe in the value and efficacy of the investigation of "social conditions." But all this was as nothing to what happens in the ensuing century.

The third quarter of the twentieth century has been the time of the "sociological explosion," in which the vast numbers of sociologists who have had specialized training in sociology are employed to teach sociology and to engage in the conduct of sociological research. In the United States, Great Britain, France, the Scandinavian and the Low countries, Germany (East and West), Poland, Italy, and in many other countries in all the continents, almost all universities have departments of sociology; in many technological institutes, medical schools, pedagogical training colleges, and schools of business administration, there are either departments of sociology or sociologists employed in various departments such as those of industrial management, marketing, business organization, etc. The multiplication of sociological research institutes, within and outside universities, conducting research on contract with governments and private bodies or from funds supplied by governments and philanthropic foundations, bears witness to this belief in the value of sociology; so does the employment of sociologists by governments, by private business firms, by hospitals, welfare associations, and civic organizations. Of course, these employments are more common in the United States than elsewhere, but they are growing throughout the world. It is not just in North America and Europe with their experience of scientific research and their belief in the efficacy of science in every sphere of life that sociology has been given such prominence and has had so much potentiality attributed to it. In countries with very different traditions such as

India, Japan, Turkey, and many Latin American countries it has been taken up. It has emerged in black Africa among indigenous sociologists, and it has reemerged in the Soviet Union after active beginnings and a long period of suspension. It has reappeared in Spain.

There has been a general acceptance of the legitimacy of sociology as an instrument of policy-making and administration, and as an intellectual and academic undertaking. Governments, political parties, armies, private firms, and public enterprises and institutions employ sociologists to survey the opinions about them held by the public at large, to investigate their internal administrative problems, and even to advise on the solution to these problems. Even where little or no attention is paid to the results of the research which has been commissioned, it is still felt that it was necessary to commission it.

Sociologists are no longer preoccupied by questions concerning the intellectual legitimacy of their subject; they take that for granted. They have ceased to fret about the status of their subject in the academic world. In the few universities where sociology has not become fully established as a subject equal in status to any other academic subject, sociologists no longer doubt that this is the fault of the university and not the fault of their subject.

There are many reasons why this has happened. Throughout the educated and influential sections of the population in most contemporary societies, there is a greater general preoccupation with one's own society and one's fellow man, a preoccupation which sometimes appears obsessive. There is a more widely diffused curiosity about what goes on in one's society. There is a curiosity to penetrate into the lives of others; there is a restless urge to pass judgment on one's own society and on one's own civilization, to take its temperature at frequent intervals. There is a greater concern on the part of authorities to know the desires and feelings of those over whom their authority is exercised and to enjoy their approbation. It has become self-evident that one should act on the basis of knowledge gained by ostensibly scientific methods, and sociology has been a beneficiary of that belief. For these reasons, the study of contemporary society, the techniques and theories it employs, and its vocabulary, too, have all found acceptance among the educated and the powerful as well as among the academic.

The data of sociology have enjoyed a similar elevation. Three-quarters of a century ago, the data of sociology seemed to be lacking in dignity. They referred to the working classes, the lower classes; they seemed to deal with outcasts, failures, broken families, delinquent children, unmarried mothers, and prostitutes. The old quip that "a sociologist is a person who at the cost of $50,000 can locate a bordello" pointed to the grossness of the subject-matter of sociology as well as to its cumbersome and costly ways of rediscovering the obvious. Professors of humanistic subjects, of history and literature in those days had to occupy themselves with human greatness. University teachers of that time formed something like a patrician class and they expected their subject-matters and their results to be of corresponding dignity. This has ceased to be the case; the humble, the base, and the degraded have become as fit subjects for intellectual contemplation as more elevated ones. There was another reason for the problematic status of sociology: it dealt with the contemporaneous at a time when universities did not concern themselves directly with current events. Traditionally, universities had dealt with the timeless and the completed part. That was where significance was to be discovered. The contemporaneous, the meanness of the subject-matter, and the particular, in combination, did not fit into the academic scheme of things. Changes were already discernible in Max Weber's time and country. The emphasis of the historical school on social policy and concrete and particular studies paved the way. New conceptions of the task of universities also opened the way to the admission of the contemporaneous as a fit subject for academic study. By being a sort of anonymous history of present-day life, sociology came into its own. But some of the causes for the change in the status of sociology lie in the changes which have taken place within sociology itself. The increased density and structure of the sociological profession itself is one of these new factors. This diminished anxiety about the status of sociology in the hierarchy of the sciences is a function of the multiplication of sociologists to the point where they can associate exclusively with sociologists and can thus heighten each other's self-confidence. They need no longer dwell in the presence of their contemners in other faculties. (The fact is that the other faculties have come to accept sociology's legitimacy as nearly everyone else in the world does nowadays, regardless of their disciplines, their professions, their politics, or their *Weltanschauung.*) Numbers alone, however, do not account for this increased self-confidence.

The most important changes have occurred within the substance of sociology itself. The stratification of sociologists into theoretical sociologists and empirical sociologists, the old distinction between *Sinnhuber* and *Stoffhuber,* has begun to fade away. There is still a distinction between theory and research, and some division of labor, but it is no longer a hierarchy the upper and lower strata of which do not mingle with each other. They have found a common task and a common ancestry. For the early generation of empirical research workers, the great theorists from Montesquieu and Comte to Gumplowicz, Hobhouse, and Durkheim were silent or irrelevant. The acknowledged ancestors of the early generation of empirical sociologists were Quetelet, Engel, Booth, Eden, von Thünen, and not

Marx or Hegel or Montesquieu or Tocqueville or Comte. It is true that Max Weber and Durkheim, Park and Thomas did not share this view. To most of Max Weber's European contemporaries, empirical research did not appear to be a dignified part of sociology. For the most part, it was not done by persons who were admitted to be sociologists. It was done by government officials, philanthropists, and economists.

When Max Weber died in 1920, sociology in the United States was beginning to develop in the direction which has now become a broad, worldwide roadway. In the early 1920s, Chicago was the main center of empirical research, and there it was guided by the ideas of William I. Thomas and Robert E. Park. It was not a very elaborate theory and the research was not very technical or differentiated by present-day standards. The theory was not done from an "armchair"; it was not done exclusively from books and there was no sense of cleavage between theory and research. But the distinction did not die away. For a long time, there was a persistent defiance on the part of research workers towards "theorists," and a readiness to dismiss empirical research for its "triviality," for its blindness in matters in which it was thought theory conferred vision. The situation was not improved as the participant-observer technique declined in the frequency of its practice and as quantitative and survey research methods grew in importance and power. "American empiricism" became pejorative in sociology, applied to a random enthusiasm for collecting facts in any subject whatever, without regard to their "meaning." In the 1920s and 1930s, certain sociologists who regarded themselves as the custodians of theory conducted a desultory campaign, largely a retreat, in the face of the steady increase in the magnitude and prestige of empirical research. It is now a little difficult to see what was the issue. There was probably no intellectual issue at all; it was largely a matter of temperament. It was not all-pervasive. Numerous inquiries of considerable implication were conducted—mainly in the 1930s—Dollard's *Caste and Class in a Southern Town,* Roethlisberger and Dickson's *Workers and Management,* Lazarsfeld and Berelson's *The People's Choice,* Halbwachs' *Les Causes du suicide,* Jahoda and Zeisl's *Die Arbeitslosen von Marienthal,* Hughes' *French Canada in Transition,* etc. These were all studies of particular communities or classes of phenomena, using officially gathered statistics or observations made directly by the investigator or through interviewers. Dollard's and Halbwach's researches were exceptional in that they had a fairly explicit theory; the others were guided by theoretical conceptions which were not articulated. But despite this fusion of theoretical analysis and research, the tension continued. Each side was on the defensive vis-à-vis the other.

Sociology made progress during these two decades. It extended the scope of its substantive activities tremendously. From a relatively sparse collection of studies of villages and neighborhoods, of broken families, juvenile delinquents and boys' gangs, immigrants and Negroes, it moved in the 1930s into the study of occupational mobility, status stratification, the relations of ethnic groups, the organization of industrial work, political campaigns, radio-listening practices and tastes, the internal structures of families (and not merely broken ones); it studied the effects of unemployment on family structure and moral outlook; it made a more subtle analysis of the consequences of membership in deprived ethnic minorities. The social structure of new housing estates, leisure-time activities, social reform movements, the occupational aspirations of young persons were added to the list of subjects it investigated.

Certain subjects which were seldom if ever treated before by sociologists have come to be conventional subjects of investigation. Hospitals, research laboratories, student halls of residence, boarding schools, grammar schools, military units large and small, trade union locals, religious sects and churches, philanthropic and civic associations, local branches of political parties, government offices, industrial firms, gambling casinos, prisons have been added to the list of objects of firsthand research. So have the professions: lawyers, physicians, university professors, scientists, army officers, artists and writers, social workers. So have social stratification—occupational mobility, styles of life, aspirations and motivations, images of one's own position in society and of the society within which one has that position, attitudes towards one's own and other classes, beliefs in the justice and injustice of the prevailing legal and social systems, and political choices or decisions at the level of the voter, the legislator, and the administrator. All these new subjects, and the old ones like the broken family, the adolescent gang, criminality, suicide, and recruitment to occupations and professions have engaged the sociological research worker. Each of them has developed its own tradition, following on from and referring to earlier work on the subject, much of the earlier work having been done by persons who, like M. Jourdain, as an unwitting speaker of prose, did not know that they were being sociologists.

Every sociological study began with some other sociological study as its antecedent; many studies broke new ground by dealing more intimately with a topic. These studies continued a previously existent interest and enriched it; they did not usually express their increments to knowledge in articulate, explicit fashion. Each continued an earlier line of inquiry or interest and made more differentiated the understanding of its particular subject-matter. They were not closely articulated with their predecessors; categories were differently defined and the variables studied were different from one investigation to the next. But there was a continuing current below the surface of the particular inquiries carrying them forward. Being studied by amateurs in different fields, these various subject-matters of, let us say, criminality and occupational selection had little connection with each other. There were a few clusters of topics such as the studies of the broken families, delinquency, and criminality which were related to each other by their investigations.

Such unity as existed among all these diverse inquiries into so many different sociological subject-matters came from an implicitly accepted common view of motivation, of the compelling effect of institutions and social situations on the behavior of those acting in them. These changes have been accompanied by a distinct change in the ethos of sociological work. The sociologists' conception of their undertaking has changed in an important respect. There was a long period when sociologists regarded their productions in the way in which artists or administrators regard their accomplishments. Artists think of each work as of intrinsic value, administrators regard each action as meeting the exigency of the moment. Sociologists with theoretical ambitions thought of constructing a comprehensive and definitive synthesis from which nothing would be omitted and to which, therefore, nothing could be added; they now see that their subject is a perpetually open one. Early investigators, before the institutional establishment of sociology, regarded the investigation as having a definite end, such as reporting on a state of affairs at a given time or informing the public about a social condition the amelioration of which was desired. The intention is now more complicated. Such a practical ending may be sought but there is also a belief that a particular piece of research should also result in a proposition—however vaguely formulated—which will be more general than the description of the particular "facts" reported. From a time when the disclosure of "facts" which would arouse public opinion or serve the needs of civic or governmental bodies were among the motives of empirical research, the discovery of a meaning "deeper" or more general than the "facts" themselves has become the ambition of sociologists. Of course, these trends were in process over a longer period than the first three-quarters of the present century. The attitudes which they displaced never had the field entirely to themselves. Now that sociologists think of themselves as sociologists, their self-image carries with it some sense of obligation to be like scientists and scholars who are engaged in a continuously unfolding task. Sociologists have acquired a different conception of the intellectual cosmos in which they operate.

Sociology is not a science—at least not yet—but it has now passed to the stage where it has acquired one of the major social features of science. This is the sense of being involved in a joint undertaking, of collaboration with predecessors and those who follow after. In this view, the individual's results are not exclusively his own accomplishment which will stand by itself and be appreciated for its well-rounded coherence and finality. Sociologists have come at last to the condition described by Max Weber in *Wissenschaft als Beruf*:

> In science, we all know that whatever we accomplish will become out-of-date in ten, twenty or fifty years. This is the fate to which scientific work is subject; it is inherent in the very nature of scientific work.... Every scientific "solution" raises new "problems"; it demands its own transcendence and obsolescence. Whoever undertakes to serve the ideal of science must accept this.... Scientific works...will be surpassed scientifically.... This is our common fate: it is in fact our intention. We cannot do scientific work without hoping that others will advance further than we have. In principle, this progress will go on without ever ending.

The process of successive replacement is not the replacement of one self-sufficient system by another self-sufficient system which negates its predecessor; nor of one body of definitively reported facts by another body of definitively reported facts. It is a dialectical process of affirmation and denial, of acceptance and revision.

Sociologists nowadays regard it as their first obligation to assimilate into their work the concepts and the orientation, the data and the hypotheses based on that data, produced by other sociologists. They regard it as their first task to improve what they receive by their own thought and observation, knowing at the same time how much it stands in need of improvement. Their aspiration now must be that their own work will enter into the stream of the work of their contemporaries and successors, to be assimilated and improved by them in turn.

As it became a more empirical discipline, sociology became highly diversified and fragmentary. Although the diverse subject-matters of sociology had a common point of departure in certain elementary views about motives and institutions, the links between the subject-matters were neglected. There was no systematic theory of society which could locate them and enable each to be seen in relation to the other and at the same time adhere to a fundamental conception of motivation, institution, and social situation. Theory in the sense of general propositions dealing with the interrelations of different sectors of society was almost entirely lacking. The general systematic theoretical treatises of the 1920s and early 1930s such as von Wiese's *Allgemeine Beziehungslehre,* Znaniecki's *Social Actions,* Sander's *Allgemeine Gesellschaftslehre,* etc., tended to be primarily definitional and classificatory; because they were also very abstract, they were difficult to apply to the situations which sociological research dealt with. Much of what was called theory was the study and interpretation of the great figures of sociology—Simmel, Durkheim, Comte, Spencer, Hobhouse, Tönnies, Weber, Pareto. There was little attempt to use what they had said about the nature of modern society in the direct, firsthand study of modern society. The macrosociological views of the famous figures of sociology did not enter into the daily idiom of sociological discourse which investigated what could be investigated with relatively rigorous methods.

There were a few exceptions—Mannheim and Merton, at the end of the 1930s, drew on Weber's ideas of bureaucracy and the "Protestant ethic" to account for the phenomena which concerned them. Mannheim was perhaps the first sociologist who attempted on a few transient occasions to draw into a wider frame of macrosociological interpretation, derived from Weber, Marx, and Freud, the results of particular pieces of empirical investigation by other sociologists. Merton's work on the history of seventeenth-century science in England in the light of Max Weber's ideas was one of the very few instances of an original, firsthand investigation conducted in general, theoretical categories. The Institut für Sozialforschung drew on Marx and Freud to interpret family structure macrosociologically, but such firsthand materials as they gathered bore little relationship to their theory. (It was only in the late 1940s that their theory and research became more intimate.) But the chief monuments of empirical research of this period, *Recent Social Trends,* above all, and *Middletown* and *New Survey of the Life and Labour of the People of London,* were unaffected by these incipient trends. (*The Negro in America,* which actually appeared in the 1940s but belongs intellectually to the tradition of the 1920s and 1930s, was a synthesis of numerous researches on the American Negro, many of them inspired ultimately by Robert Park, and it placed the Negro squarely within the framework of American society. It could be seen as evidence of the macrosociological sensibility of Park's kind of sociology but it did not go any further itself.

Aside from the traditions and tasks left behind by the sociological research of the 1930s, there was a more important inheritance. Until that time, a theorist was a person who wrote or taught about sociology. There was no obligation that he or his protégés should be engaged in fieldwork in a community, interviewing or studying unpublished documents, governmental statistics. Theory was accepted as being discourse about society, not research into details such as can be found only by industrious application. Books like Leopold's *Prestige,* rare enough in this time, have become even rarer. A sociologist like Simmel, quite apart from his great talents, has become an unallowable category. Nowadays most sociologists regard it as natural that evidence should be provided for whatever a sociologist says and that that evidence should be quantitative and statistically reliable; that, even if it is not quantitative, it should be based on interviews and observation or, if not on these, then on primary documentary sources. Sociology has come to mean research, firsthand research or "re-analysis" of firsthand data. At the same time, research has become more "theory-conscious." It is not that research workers like the "theory" which they have, but they think they need it. They might bridle against any particular sociological theory—as the late Samuel Stouffer, one of the most refined investigators in the recent history of sociology did—but they believe it obligatory to proceed with the benefit of theory.

In the course of these developments, the duality of "research" and "theory" and the hostility which the practitioners of each had towards each other and which endured for many years has to some extent faded away. It is not that there are no longer any theorists in sociology who do relatively little firsthand research; there still are and there will undoubtedly continue to be such theorists. But no theorist, however abstract and however preoccupied with fundamental concepts of variables and relationships of variables, can any longer carry on his work without feeling that the empirical sociologists are looking over his shoulder and that sooner or later he must answer to them. He knows now that his work can no longer be self-sustaining but that it must justify itself by what it contributes to research.

This situation did not exist fifty years ago. There were many writers, especially in Germany but also in the United States, who were sociological theorists in the minimal sense that they wrote about society without concerning themselves with any connection between what they were doing and concentrated and persistent research. They regarded definition and classification as their main tasks. Von Wiese was one of the most eminent of these. Theodore Geiger in *Die Gestaltung der Gesellung,* Joseph Pieper in *Die Grundformen der sozialen Spielregeln* were representative of this mode of proceeding. G. L. Duprat and Haserot wrote "systems of sociology" which were supposed to be exhaustive. Vierkandt's *Gesellschaftslehre* fell into this category. Then there were writers like Park and Thomas who were very acutely absorbed by "empirical" research but who saw everything theoretically while introducing their theory into their research largely in the form of aphoristic observations. They wrote little which would have been called theory and what they wrote was vague, superficial, and inchoate in comparison with the implications of their remarks made in passing.

There has been another kind of theory produced in the past three decades. It is the kind of general theory written by Talcott Parsons and his collaborators and followers. There has never been any theory so elaborate and at the same time so fundamental—going down to the basic elements of the structure of human action, of institutions and social situations, and so differentiated in its application to so many parts of society. It goes far beyond the most detailed and refined classification although it contains many classifications. It is a theory which is ambitious to explain why things happen.

It cannot be said that this general theory has thus far been a resounding success, if success is measured by the extent to which it has been integrally assimilated into research. There is still not much contact along a broad front between general systematic theory and concrete research. One reason is that general systematic theory, differentiated though it is, is not differentiated or particular enough in its categories for the requirements of empirical research in its present state. It does not reach down far enough toward concreteness, it does not come close enough to the events seen by the research worker, and, because it does not do so, it is unable to bring the results of the analysis of the data back into itself. At present the fullest contact of the general systematic theory is with very abstract research such as that performed experimentally in contrived situations or with macrosociology which uses comprehensive and relatively undifferentiated categories, and which is also not subjected to the discipline of documented historical accounts in the way in which the run of sociological research is disciplined by the "facts" as apprehended in conventional categories. There does not appear to be any incompatibility between the "theory" which is implicit in so much current sociological research and the general systematic theory. The difference seems to be in the greater undifferentiatedness of the former which allows for adaptation, improvisation, and unconstrainedness in interpretation while systematic general theory is not only abstract and explicit but also seems to entail so much that the freedom of the research worker to improvise his interpretations is inhibited.

Perhaps general systematic theory should not expect to provide more than a "general orientation"; perhaps it should be content with the provision of certain pregnant concepts, enigmatic and capable of extension—e.g., social system, integration, boundary. Yet it should also be said that general theory is a failure only if the criterion of success requires its complete adoption in such a way that all subsequent research is guided by its conceptualization of variables and its formulation of relationships among those variables. There are however successes short of this, and general sociological theory can claim some of these. Sociological theories on the grand scale have been like the buildings of antiquity which were used by ensuing generations not to live in, in the style of their original owners, but to be rebuilt or occupied in accordance with the tastes and resources of later times or as quarries for the materials from which new buildings, more congenial to the tastes and resources of a new generation, could be built.

This is what has been happening in the relations between sociological theory and research. There has been a partial assimilation of the general theory. Categories like particularistic and universalistic, specific and diffuse obligations, and boundary-maintenance are now widely used; they were not used before the coming into prominence of the general theory. In the same way as concepts like charisma, bureaucratization, and anomie, which were not accompanied by such comprehensively systematic aspirations, have been assimilated into sociological research over the past thirty years, a comparable assimilation of elements of the general theory has been occurring.

The ambition of sociological theorists to construct systems which are definitively and cosmically comprehensive and which admit new knowledge only as illustration has practically disappeared. Theory is more open and tentative now than it used to be, but it has not yet found the idiom and style most appropriate to a more integral relationship with research. Theories are still extremely cumbersome to apply; they tend to be too general. The theory which is analytically constructed and which claims to be closer to research is also usually too vague and too undifferentiated for "close" application to the particular events on which research is done. Sometimes it is arbitrary in its constructions, especially when it purports to be constructed for purposes of research; the relationship between indicators and variables is much too arbitrary, the variables are often carelessly delineated. The theory which grows out or which purports to grow out of research often bears the birthmarks of the particular events for which it was constructed. The greatest success of theory lies in the "tacit theory," the theory which the investigator has accepted more or less unspokenly, which he "applies" in the interpretation of his specific observations, and which he adduces to justify the interpretation of his results. This is a very inchoate sort of theory, but it has the merit of not claiming more for itself that it can deliver. It moves fitfully; it probably illuminates the results of research more often than it receives from the research. The lines separating the different kinds of theory are vague and one type slips over into the other. What is fruitful in the general type of theory becomes assimilated into the "unspoken" type of theory. The use of some of the pattern variables in an *ad hoc* manner is one instance of the way in which the older tradition of ad hoc theory and the newer one of systematic theory came together and became fused with the tradition of empirical research. The bridge between research and theory, i.e., between the results of research and the explicit general concepts and propositions in sociology, has not been closed. There is, however, throughout the serious parts of the sociological profession a conviction that it should be done, although there is less conviction about the achievement of closure thus far.

The techniques of description are now more rigorous; they are less impressionistic and are very seldom satisfied with anything less than an adequate sample of the universe they study. They are less content with assessments of magnitude which rest only on the clinical skill of the individual investigator. Furthermore, these "objectivized" modes of assessment of particular variables have become more subtle. That is, they have begun to deal with less grossly observable variables. They are trying to cope with those variables which have hitherto been discerned by "insight."

This greater rigor and artfulness in description has begun to be employed to study events which are thought to be "theoretically significant." Events which were previously investigated because they were "interesting" in themselves or because they were of practical concern to reformers, politicians, and administrators are now being "theorized." (One may cite the history of American sociology in the 1960s, when the federal government was beginning to be attentive to juvenile delinquency. Its officials insisted that the research it commissioned and the policies it sponsored be conducted in conformity with "sociological theory"—in this case Professor Merton's reformulation of the concept of anomie.) Research on the subject is being subsumed under general, "theoretical" categories—or at least that is the purported end. Thus, the study of satisfaction and dissatisfaction in work is not a new interest for sociologists. Nor is the study of criminality and delinquency. Far from it. But to study these phenomena as particular embodiments of anomie has been one of the turning points in the history of the subject. (Of course it should be added that the results remain ambiguous.) To take another example: voting preferences had been studied by sociologists since before the First World War, and the correlation, for example, between voting for the Democratic party in the United States and being Roman Catholic, urban, and working-class, on the one side, and voting for the Republican party and being Protestant, small town, and middle class, on the other, was a considerable accomplishment of contemporary political sociology. But it took the process one step further to go behind the correlation and to analyze the primary-group links through which these factors operated. The perception of the importance of primary groups in fields of activity as diverse as industrial work, the adjustment of immigrants, the conduct of soldiers, and consumer behavior, is a typical manifestation of this "theoretical" interpretation of diverse concrete phenomena in the light of a more "fundamental" conception of the primary group. To see apathy in nonvoting and to see apathy as a phenomenon generated by the conditions of "mass society" might be wrong or even intellectually perverse, but it indicates the tendency towards reducing the fragmentary and unconnected character of the results of particular investigations. It means that a more general variable is sought in the concrete or particular event studied. It is not just that the latter is put into a general class, e.g., delinquency—that is inevitable—but that the class is somehow connected with the variables which were treated by the classics of theoretical sociology. Research reaches out towards theory more deliberately than it used to. The result of the reaching outward towards theory is often neither illuminating nor persuasive in its more explicit formulations; below the surface of explicitness, the result is not infrequently a more differentiated and more intimate picture of the phenomenon under investigation.

The "tacit" theory does not stand still. It assimilates increments from the systematic general theory. A few illustrations may be in order. The most important of all these selective assimilations is the adoption of the concept of system. I think that one could look for a long time in the literature of empirical research before the late 1940s to find institutions, organizations, and relations conceived as systems. Thanks, however, to Pareto and then Parsons, many investigators now conceive of the objects of their inquiry as systems. This is not merely a terminological adornment; it marks a substantive change in the way of thinking about any institution or situation or about a whole society. A new sensitivity to interdependences has been generated by this systemic orientation. Again, practically no one uses, to take another example from the work of Parsons, the whole scheme of the pattern variables, but a considerable number of sociologists have found a freely adapted use, in their research, for the pair called ascription-achievement, or that of specificity-diffuseness. Max Weber's threefold classification of the types of legitimate authority certainly has not been explicitly accepted for purposes of research, but his conception of rational-legal—bureaucratic—authority has become one of the chief sources of contemporary research on organizations; one variant of traditional authority combined with the bureaucratic variant has become the basis of Eisenstadt's great work on *The Political Systems of Empires*. Blau's work has its point of departure directly and indirectly in the writings of Weber on bureaucracy— indirectly through Merton. The study of organization, for example, although it is one of the newer fields of sociological study, being in its present form not much more than about thirty years old, has more of a theoretical content and a closer relationship between theory and research than most other fields of sociology. One of the reasons is that the field came into existence when there already existed several bodies of literature in a variety of previously separate fields all of which bore on organization and which were simultaneously theoretical and yet fairly particular in their reference. I refer to the writings of Chester Barnard and Herbert Simon, of Max Weber, of Elton Mayo, of T. N. Whitehead, of Roethlisberger and Dickson, and finally to

Robert Merton's essay on "Bureaucratic Structure and Personality." The appearance of cybernetics also made a difference here. Most of these sources were part of or were otherwise connected with the major theoretical orientations of present-day sociology, i.e., Max Weber and Emile Durkheim, and they helped to give research in this field a focus and direction practically from the very beginning. The common views regarding motivation and institutional structure also permitted the study of bureaucratic institutions to be more coherent withe the rest of sociology; it had a wider interest and accessibility to other sociologists because of this.

The study of corporate organizations did not have the background of a large body of empirical research; the study of occupational mobility and of the family did have a considerable body of research but it had relatively little even of "tacit" theory underlying it. As a result, much information accumulated in such fields in a theoretical vacuum. The study of organizations, having come later into sociology, after a theoretical orientation had become patently available, was in a more fortunate position than the sections of sociology which had been objects of empirical research for a longer time. Mannheim's ideas about ideology likewise have been adopted by no one in the form in which he put them, but the direction of thought set off by them has certainly had considerable influence; it has even been influential in the analysis of the data of sample surveys of political opinion—a field of research once thought to be among the most "empiricist" and therefore the most impervious to theory. Similarly, Pareto's ideas about elites have never been accepted in the form he gave them, but in reformulation, first by Lasswell and then by Hunter, Guttsman, Dahl, Janowitz, and Mills, they have markedly changed the character of community studies, of national political institutions, and the studies of certain occupations. The conception of legitimacy was scarcely known among sociologists before it entered sociology from Max Weber's writings; now it has become a commonplace.

Within the field of political sociology, the study of party organizations and party systems has perhaps been more "theorized" than the study of voting behavior. The reason again lies in the state of the theory of the particular field when it became an object of sociological investigation. Roberto Michels' *Political Parties* contained a basic proposition about the structure of political organization based on his own observations in the German Social-Democratic party and on Ostrogorski's earlier work (*Democracy and the Organization of Political Parties*). The theoretical content of political sociology also became more clearly articulated through its relations with Max Weber's ideas of bureaucracy in political organizations; certain of Schumpeter's propositions about democracy as the competition of parties also helped to create the theoretical point of departure for this field.

In contrast with this, voting behavior studies did not have a similarly theorized point of departure. Before the application of the opinion survey technique and the earlier and simpler ecological analyses, voting studies had no aspiration other than the correlation of voting choice or abstention with certain conventionally conceived variables such as class, occupation, age, and sex. The effort to go beyond this point, as we have recently witnessed in studies of consensus and cleavage, had little in the way of already existing theory to help it.

Yet despite these movements towards the unity of theory and research, the disunity is still very considerable. Even the study of social stratification and of social mobility, despite the considerable number of informative works—e.g., works by Glass et al., Halsey, Floud, Lipset and Bendix, Geiger, Karlsson, Svastaloga, Blau, Duncan, Hodge, Lockwood, Runciman, Rossi, Inkeles, Reiss, and numerous others, and the traditions of Marx and Weber—has not been satisfactorily penetrated by theory. It is indeed one of the fields of sociology in which there is much discontent with the theory which is available for it—and this despite the fact that two of the most famous figures in the history of sociology are at the sources of its traditions.

One of the difficulties is that, as techniques of collection and processing of data become more and more sophisticated, existing general theory becomes less adequate because of its vagueness and abstraction. The research on the subject has become stuck in the mire of a complex called "social-economic status," or in a classification of occupations which corresponds to that ill-defined complex. "Social-economic status" obviously refers to something which is real and which is relatively highly correlated with other features of conduct. It is therefore very convenient to use it in research but its composition has never been satisfactorily unraveled by the theorists of social stratification. They speak of deference and power and "class position"—themselves all vague enough. There is not a very good "fit" between the theorists' talk about it and the research workers' study. Research on this subject multiplies but the criteria by which the population is classified into strata remain unclarified by the theory of the theorists and the theory of the investigators.

Because of the deficiencies in the applicability of existing systematic theory, or even of fragments of it and because of the belief that "theory" is necessary to "research," some sociologists are pressed to create their own theory to guide their research and to explain its results. Such a theory is not likely to go much beyond the existing framework, despite the investigators' efforts.

The picture of the relations between theory and research is thus very variegated but the effort of research to reach outward toward theory seems to be irreversible. The theoretical impulse in research runs in all directions. It aims at times to place its problems and results on the same foundation of the theory of motivation, institution, and situation which is accepted in the investigation of very different subject-matters. It also tries to extend and elaborate the theory which seems most appropriate for dealing with the patterns internal to the subject-matter under study. Finally, there is a desire for a theory which will place the particular subject-matter studied, e.g., voting behavior or familial solidarity, within the context of the larger society.

Sociology remains a disunified field, but the lines which separate the various sections of the field have become broken through the research conducted by sociologists and their desire for theories which will ''make sense,'' in a variety of ways, of what they are doing. The separate sectors are now less separate than they used to be. They do show signs of some connection. Certain subfields of sociology have been incorporated into the central territory of sociology; these subfields at one time had a quite independent existence in relation to the theoretical interests of sociology. Family studies, criminological studies, educational-sociological studies—the studies of classrooms, of differential participation in the educational system, etc.—have increasingly come into some modicum of intellectual community with other parts of sociology. The idea that prisons and schools are social systems has carried with it the idea that, as such, they have certain common properties and certain common problems, and as a result the interchange among the studies of these substantively disparate subject-matters has helped to create a fundamentally unified subfield: the study of organizations. This is another way in which the fragmentation of sociology, despite the increased output of literature, with its consequent pressure for the specialization and confinement of the range of attention, is to some extent being offset.

The extent to which sociology has become substantively unified should not be overestimated. There are still pockets of sociological research which have remained relatively immune to any of the newer sociological theory. Rural sociology is one of these fields, but this too is changing. Demography, which is one of the most important fields of sociology, has still not been effectively assimilated into the rest of sociology.

The danger in discussing such matters is that the present situation will be judged by a false ideal. No theory can ever be wholly adequate to original research; its originality is evidence that it is not provided for in the theory. There are bound to be difficulties in sociology which are not so insistent in the natural sciences. Sociologists deal with phenomena of the sort which they also know in the round of everyday life. Yet theory always and necessarily is more abstract than the particular events which it is employed to understand. In physics the traditions of the subject do not have to contend with the traditions of ordinary social life; in sociology they do and there is bound to be some conflict. It is in any case difficult to view in abstract categories what we experience concretely: there is bound to be some dissatisfaction with the discrepancy.

Nonetheless progress has been made. The progress of the past half-century lies both in what has been accomplished in this process of unification and in the general affirmation of the rightfulness and necessity of mutual penetration. The mutual distrust of the earlier generation has decreased because sociologists who are largely taken up with research and those who do sociology while not doing much or any empirical research recognize that they are engaged in a common enterprise, despite the difficulties of bringing that community fully into being. The task, however, becomes more difficult as more and more data pile up and the machinery for their processing becomes more capable of elaborate operations, and as sociologists themselves become ramified in more and more differentiated practical activities which pull them away from the center of sociology.

Yet, in the face of all these adverse circumstances which do not become more favorable, the fact remains that there is a richer measure of unification than there was when our period began. A common language and a common set of expectations have been growing. The narrowing of the gap between theory and research has also created bridges which unite the increasingly numerous and ramifying specialities. It is extremely hard to describe the common language and expectations in which these tendencies towards unification are to be seen. They lie mainly at the level of "tacit" theory, the theory which sociologists have assimilated from the "atmosphere" of sociology, from reading and talking about the concrete things of sociology with their colleagues and pupils. They are the postulates and the overtones of the specific hypotheses the "testing" of which by research are reported in sociological journals.

II

This halting, heavily obstructed, but nevertheless real growth of a common language, and a common way of looking at society, has been going on within most of the countries in which sociology is practiced on a substantial scale. It has been going on in Poland as well as in the United States, in England as well as in Sweden, in the Federal German Republic as well as in India. Almost every country in which sociology has long been practiced has an indigenous tradition the beginning of which goes back at least to the end of the last century and, in Britain and France, well before then. The history of sociology in the present century has seen a very uneven fusion of some of these national traditions. A fusion has been going on across national boundaries. Sociology is beginning to become a single discipline—perhaps a

The Confluence of Sociological Traditions 151

single set of subdisciplines—despite its cleavages; a common understanding of sociologists in many countries is emerging.
Sociology was never, nationally, a wholly parochial subject. Because sociology moved in the wake of major intellectual movements—e.g., Comtean positivism and Spencerian evolutionism—
from the time of its preacademic existence in the middle of the
nineteenth century, the leading writers of sociology became known
and appreciated outside their homelands. The German influence
on the American universities in the last third of the nineteenth
century brought across the ocean some knowledge of Simmel,
Ratzenhofer, Gumplowicz, and Tönnies, and of German ethnology. They had significant influence there. Durkheim was known
in Great Britain and the United States although he had little influence
in either of them. Tarde was known in the United States where his
ideas did have some acceptance. Sighele was known in France and the
United States; he had some influence in the latter. The British surveys
became known in the United States, where they had a very pronounced influence. French sociology drew much from German and
British ethnography. German sociology was almost wholly self-
contained, although part of Tönnies' inspiration came from Great
Britain through his study of Hobbes and Maine. University teachers
and administrators were very aware of the international character of
learning and of the affinity of universities across their national frontiers. Sociologists were part of the larger world of learning and they
participated therefore, although modestly, in the lightly attended international concourse.

When sociology became a more empirical discipline after the First
World War, the cultivation of international links became much thin-
ner, although what had been absorbed from foreign sociologists in
earlier years remained part of the tradition of each national sociology.
The great figures who had been known previously had been theorists.
They were builders of systems of thought which were as much their
own creations as any comprehensive intellectual synthesis can be.
These individual creations, however idiosyncratic and however
steeped in their own national traditions, were regarded by their
creators as universally valid and hence entitled to universal interest.
This was, to some extent, the basis of such internationality as they
possessed.

In Max Weber's lifetime, sociologies which claimed universal validity were really parts of nationally parochial traditions which bore
the imprint of a few great innovating figures in the intellectual histories of the countries of the creators and of their national academic
and cultural traditions. Such sociology as existed in England continued the tradition of concern with social evolution, ethnographic
data, and surveys of poverty problems; sociology in France had

transcended its evolutionary preoccupation and was focused largely on intensive studies based on ethnographic and statistical materials of certain fundamental social processes and structures.[1] In Germany, empirical sociology, of which Weber himself was perhaps the only significant and generally unknown practitioner, scarcely existed; theory—i.e., classifications of types of groups and relationships, greatly influenced by Tönnies' distinction between *Gemeinschaft* and *Gesellschaft*, the phenomenological analysis of particular concepts, and the scholarly treatment of macrosociological problems—held the field. In Weber's lifetime, American sociology, which, via Park, Thomas, Giddings, Ross, and Sumner had taken over elements of French, German, and British sociology, was developing its own unique properties and direct fieldwork, the technique of participant-observation, the study of personal documents.

Much of what would be called empirical sociological research was done in connection with welfare administration or on problems which social reformers thought should become objects of welfare policy, such as the standard of living and family life of the poor, education, immigration, juvenile delinquency, criminality, and penal administration. Much of it was done by civic and philanthropic organizations and governmental bodies. This occurred at a time when the bearers of the name of sociology, eager to see their subject become a science and academically respectable, were deliberately attenuating their relations with social policy. Then too, much of this unacademic research was very particular and often very amateurish. Even when it could be found and read, it was often designed in very concrete and *ad hoc* categories, without regard for the categories used by other investigators working on similar subjects elsewhere—in the same and other countries. Little of it found circulation beyond the national frontiers in which it had been carried out; it often was not widely circulated within those frontiers.

Not all of empirical sociological research was extraacademic or carried on in universities outside departments of sociology. In the United States, a large amount was produced in the universities, mainly by Ph.D. candidates but also by teachers. Poland, Great Britain, and France had a good deal, according to the then prevailing standard. Outside the United States, however, a substantial proportion of what we would now call empirical sociological research went on in academic departments of education, demography, psychology,

---

1. It is true that the French style of sociology was unique to France but it was not parochial in its interests. The great figures of the French school collected information about their subjects from the records of all countries and, in the bibliographical pages of *L'Année sociologique*, they directed their eyes outward beyond the boundaries of France in a way in which no other sociological publication has ever done. Perhaps this exceptional transcendence of parochiality was connected with the fact that they did not do fieldwork.

and geography. This too removed it from international sociological circulation. Much of this research was practically lost to sociology even within the country of its origin; internationally, the parochiality of the preoccupation of the investigators further assured its exclusion from international attention; linguistic ignorance and obscurity of place and form of publication also contributed to this outcome.

As sociology in the 1920s became both more empirical and more productive and more sustained by its own national tradition and less by the contemporaneous importance of sociological knowledge produced in other countries, it became more preoccupied with its own society. If we look at some of the representative pieces of established sociological research of the 1920s and early 1930s—Thrasher's *The Gang*, Zorbaugh's *Gold Coast and the Slum*, Lynd's *Middletown*, the *New Survey of the People of London*, Dreyfuss' *Beruf und Ideologie der Angestellten*, Nothaas' *Sozialer Auf- und Abstieg im deutschen Volk*, Geiger's *Die soziale Schichtung des deutschen Volkes*, or Lederer and Marschak's "Das neue Mittelstand," Halbwachs' *Les Causes du suicide*, the numerous studies of Roumanian villages by Gusti—we see that, in each case, a sociologist was studying his own country in the traditional style of research of his own country.

It is obvious that, as sociologists began to study society at first hand or from unpublished sources, they would naturally turn to their own countries as objects of study. Quite apart from prior knowledge and interest, economic considerations would dictate that they study situations and sources near at hand.

There was also a tendency for sociologists to disregard the literature of their subject produced in countries other than their own. Not that the generation before the First World War outside the United States ever showed much interest in the sociological works written abroad.[2] But in the 1920s the situation seemed to get worse. Robert Park still kept up irregularly with foreign literature. Morris Ginsberg and Maurice Halbwachs both read widely on an international scale. Louis Wirth and Howard Becker in the United States, Chalasiński in Poland knew the foreign literature well. Pitirim Sorokin was however exceptional in his intimacy with the research and theoretical literature in the English-speaking countries, France, Germany, Italy, Russia, and Poland. Generally, more empirical workers knew little about other countries or the work of their foreign colleagues on subject-matters similar to their own.

Since empirical research was on "national" subject-matters and since it had not so much overt relationship to "theory," which remained more international, the very development of sociology as a discipline for research rather than speculation accentuated the sepa-

2. Max Weber himself, despite his great erudition, seems to have known very little of the sociological work done in other countries.

rateness of the "national" sociologies from each other. There was some change in the 1930s when the exile of so many Jewish liberal and socialist scientists and scholars from Germany brought some German sociology to France, the Netherlands, Denmark, Great Britain, and the United States. It had little impact on any sociologists except those who were already interested in German sociology and on a small number of students.

Sociology became a genuinely international subject after the Second World War. The productivity and high prestige of American sociology, coinciding with the "sociological explosion" throughout the world, promoted the emergence of a sociological consensus. The consensus was an agreement about the methods of sociology, and about the literature which sociologists should know. The fact that sociologists in various countries were to some extent reading the same books and papers, citing similar authors, resulted also in an increased uniformity of outlook. National traditions persisted but they became interwoven with a common international tradition.

The number of academically trained sociologists increased at a time when, because of the still persisting dearth of literature, much which the students had to read and which the teachers had to teach was American in origin. Of course, much in the national traditions survived but these traditions were forced to make some place for the American literature. The pressure of the American literature increased as empirical research methods and reports were given more prominence in teaching. As a result, after about 1955, the proportion of persons trained in American sociology and doing sociological research increased very markedly. Amateurism almost disappeared from sociology so that, unlike in the prewar period when many persons doing sociological research and even teaching in the subject had no academic training in sociology, most persons who now conduct sociological research have received an academic training in the subject. It was not necessarily the superior truthfulness of American empirical sociology which led to its enshrinement in the common culture of sociology internationally; it was available, its large stock was imposing, and the appreciation of empirical research made it welcome.

This multiplication of sociologists and sociological research, the institutional establishment of sociology, and the growth of a common sociological culture within each country could not in itself have furthered the internationality of sociology without the simultaneous change in the substance of sociology which made for a greater community of problems and subject-matters across national boundaries. One need only look at the pages of the *Revue française de sociologie*, the *Kölnische Zeitschrift für Soziologie*, the *Zeitschrift für Soziologie*, the *British Journal of Sociology*, *Sociology*, *The Sociological Review*, the *Sociologische Gids*, *Polish Sociological Bulletin*, and the *Ameri-*

can Journal of Sociology to see that social stratification and mobility, mass communications, "youth culture," the situation of the aged and voting behavior are now internationally cultivated, using the same techniques and referring to the same international corpus of research and theoretical literature. The establishment of institutions for the survey of public opinion and for market research in so many countries has greatly aided this formation of a common sociological culture. Many of the practitioners of opinion surveys have been trained in sociology and they, no less than university teachers of sociology, have become organized internationally. They meet at intervals and they are aware of each other's activities. The more intimate relations between university sociology and extraacademic sociology within each country have also helped to make the common sociological culture more widely shared internationally.

The closer approximation of theory and research and the increased sophistication of techniques of research and analysis within the major countries have made more visible the peaks of accomplishment. Academic disciplines have always had elites who were regarded as representing the highest standards. The formation of such elites in the major countries in which sociology is done has created an international sociological elite. In consequence of this, the major figures in past and current sociological accomplishment stand out above the multitude of sociologists; there is more awareness of this international sociological elite. Certain individuals, living and dead, and certain institutions where such traditions and persons are or have been relatively concentrated, become more central in the field of attention of sociologists in each country and throughout the world. The new life of Max Weber's and Emile Durkheim's ideas throughout the whole world of sociology and the assimilation of some of Karl Marx's concerns into sociology have helped to give sociology a common universe of discourse on a worldwide scale. Harvard, Chicago, Columbia, Berkeley, Ann Arbor, London, Paris, Oslo, Lund, Copenhagen, Tübingen, Cologne, Warsaw, Cracow, Leiden, Gröningen, Amsterdam, Zurich, Tokyo, Delhi—among others—have become nodes of an international network. As a result, there has been a tendency toward a greater concentration of minds on a relatively restricted number of ways of conducting research and ways of conceiving of society and its parts.

The increased size of departments of sociology, with a much larger number of students and teachers doing research, meant that the major centers of radiation of sociological work had a larger body of recipients, continuators, and developers of major themes and subject-matters. There have been far more contacts of the students and teachers, especially the younger teachers of the subject, across national lines. Programs for the promotion of "international understanding'' and national cultural propaganda as well as the more disinterested activities of the private philanthropic foundations, especially the American ones, have sent teachers and students in many directions across the boundaries of their countries. This has left a lasting impact in all directions and at all levels of the academic hierarchy. The establishment of the International Sociological Association, with its quadrennial meetings and its numerous research committees also did a lot for some years to support this movement towards the formation of an international community of sociologists with a common sociological culture.

This process has been aided, of course, by institutional developments which have heightened the mutual awareness of sociologists of different countries, widened their horizons, and brought them into an unprecedentedly effective collaboration. The speed of travel, and the greater availability of financial resources, have increased the frequency and scale of international conferences, of special international commissions and study groups, of visiting professorships and traveling fellowships, of refresher courses, of long visits for research and teaching or for simply becoming acquainted with persons and work, and all of these things have contributed to this growth of the sociological sector of the international intellectual community. The awareness of one's fellow sociologist as a person, gained from seeing him and corresponding with him, opens sensitivity to his works and to the works of his students. It leads to the exchange of offprints and mimeographed preliminary reports on a wider territorial scale, it puts one "on the lookout" for the work of the persons one has met, however briefly. It assimilates them into one's mind.

Important though mimeographed "preprints" have become in sociological communication, journals still retain great importance among the institutions for the communication of the results of sociological work. The change here is very marked. Before the Second World War, non-Dutch sociologists who wished to know what sociologists in the Netherlands were doing had to read *Mens en Matschappij;* if non-Polish sociologists wished to know the work of Polish sociologists, they had to read *Przyglond Socjologiczga;* if they were not Scandinavian and wished to know what Scandinavian sociologists were doing they had no Scandinavian sociological journal to read at all. Now, even if they can read only English, they can consult *Sociologica Nederlandica, The Polish Sociological Bulletin,* and *Acta Sociologica.* Genuinely international journals like the *Archives européennes de la sociologie* and the *International Social Science Journal* and *Social Science Information* testify to the transnational character of contemporary sociology.

The community within which sociologists work still tends, in the first instance, to be mainly national. Quite apart from the self-enclosing function of a common language, of a common educational experience, and the much greater probability of individual encounter and interaction with sociologists of their own nationality within their own universities and countries, sociologists tend to study local situations and national institutions within their own countries. All this notwithstanding, sociologists are no longer able to confine their concerns to the parochially located and significant. The larger world of the other centers of sociology impinges on their consciousness, either through the research which they produce on closely related subjects or on the theory which is either separately presented or embodied in their research.

The "theorization" of empirical research has made sociologists in each country more conscious than they used to be of the affinities of their own local subjects and the local subjects of their fellow sociologists in other countries. The sociologists of other countries, working on their subject-matters and problems, have become parts of their "internal population"; they are coming increasingly to live in the midst of what other sociologists in other countries are thinking and investigating. Studies of occupational mobility or self-identification in terms of class in London seem to bear on studies of similar phenomena in California; studies of juvenile delinquency in Liverpool bear more readily on studies of the same subject in Detroit; studies of reading habits in Bordeaux have to be put alongside of studies of reading habits in Baltimore. The writings of Srinivas and Beteille on social change, on social stratification and mobility in India are read by sociologists in France, Great Britain, Germany, and the United States and not only by sociologists who specialize in the study of India. The "fit" is very far from perfect but there is a conviction that the effort is necessary. So much for the empirical side.

On the theoretical side too a process of international integration has moved apace. The implantation of Max Weber's ideas in the United States, his later penetration into France, and his return to Germany in consequence of his elaboration and deciphering in America, the reassessment of Durkheim, the renewal of interest in Michels in the United States (following the republication there of the translation of *Political Parties* made in 1915 by two British translators) have all made for a multilateral and crisscrossing movement of theoretical ideas which have contributed to the incipient formation of a common sociological culture on a world scale.

Like the process of "theorization" and the unity emerging from it within each country, the internationalization of sociology is a slow and irregular process in which the entire world population of sociologists participates very unequally and intermittently. Only a minority of all sociologists participate in it directly through their own research and teaching or through their organizational activities. I think here in the first instance of Professors Aron, Lipset, Janowitz, Eisenstadt, Boudon, Coleman, Bourricaud, Parsons, Lazarsfeld, Szczepański, Ben-David, Wiatr, Dahrendorf, König, Glass, Bottomore, Marshall, Rokkan—among others; they are also among the most influential sociologists in their respective countries and they thereby radiate some of this international sociological culture to those who participate in it less intensively. A great many more participate in the internationalization of sociology indirectly through their response to research and analyses performed by the "international elite" and by their opposite members in other countries.

The internationalization of sociology is not a unilinear movement which is carrying all before it. Some of the obstacles to a total internationalization arise from one important characteristic of empirical sociology, which is its documentary function. Much sociological research is conducted and supported because it is intended to illuminate a local or national situation and it is bound thereby to be of greater interest to other sociologists' investigations of the same local or national situation. It will in any case be more attended to by them. The amount of comparative, trans-national research is bound to be limited by capacity and interest. The amount of research by sociologists of one country into societies other than their own national society is also bound to be limited by capacity, interest, and resources. There are not only national subject-matters, there are also national traditions, not all of them very old, of sociological study, of procedures and outlook, which will persist, not only because of the power of traditions to reproduce themselves in successive generations but also because in every country where sociology has become institutionally established in universities, some universities will be more eminent than others and will hence diffuse their influence throughout their national sociological community. This can further the internationality of sociology, but it will also, either concurrently or in opposition, sustain as national traditions their own institutional traditions.

In addition to these limits, there are also political and ideological resistances to the internationality of sociology. In the Soviet Union, for example, the freedom of sociologists to accept the sociological outlook of sociologists in Western Europe and North America is very confined by the reigning political authorities. The same occurs in the German Democratic Republic. The institutionally more powerful sociologists affirm this attitude. There are also sociologists in Middle Eastern Arab countries, and others in Asia, Africa, and Latin America who assert that the dominant type of sociological thought is a part of an "imperialistic, exploitative ideology" which must be resisted. Some of these critics are not sociologists at all but are cultural politicians; they have nonetheless acquired a voice and even influence in international sociological bodies. In Western countries too there are sociologists who make the same charge, often from the standpoint of some variant of Marxism. Nationalistic sentiments too have some effect here. Some sociologists in Asia—and in the United States, France, and Western Germany—assert that the prevailing sociology is only "Western sociology" and is not appropriate to the study of non-Western societies.

III

The strengthened sense of trans-local and trans-national affinities among sociologists has been accompanied by an extension of the territorial radius of sociological research such as scarcely existed before the Second World War. Until very recently, most empirical research was local; and it was mostly the locale of the investigator which was studied. Few sociologists studied anything outside their own countries; those who did firsthand empirical research did so even less frequently than those who did their research in libraries. (The great works of Durkheim and his followers had a more extensive territorial radius than did those of any other group of sociologists in the first quarter of the twentieth century, but their studies did not involve fieldwork.) When data about foreign countries were employed, they were used to test or exemplify a proposition about a specific phenomenon like the elementary forms of religious life, or primitive forms of classification, or the gift. There was little interest in the foreign society as such. There were few exceptions, such as Professor van den Hollander in his works on the poor whites of the American South and on the society of the Hungarian plains, Thomas and Znaniecki in their work on the Polish peasant in Poland and the United States, Bakke on the unemployed of Greenwich, Heberle on internal migration in the United States, Myrdal on the American Negro, and Dorothy Thomas on internal migration in Sweden.

The costs of doing research in a foreign country are considerably greater than doing it in one's own country and financial support for such research is less readily available than is support for domestic research. Linguistic differences add another obstacle. Nonetheless those who do research outside their own countries are now more numerous and they deal with more subject-matters in more countries. Almond's and Verba's studies in Italy, Mexico, England, and Germany; Dore's and Abbeglen's on Japan; Geertz's and Palmier's on Indonesia; Ashford's, Gellner's, Waterbury's, and Geertz's on Morocco; Bailey's and Wiener's on Indian politics; Ross' on the Indian family; Janowitz's on German social mobility; Berger's on Egyptian bureaucracy; Bourricaud's on Peruvian society; Dahrendorf's on the skilled worker in Great Britian; Rose's on voluntary associations in France; Kantowski's on Indian villages; Bastide's on

Brazil; Banton's on Sierra Leone; Trow's on British universities; Singer's on businessmen in Madras; Ben-David's on academic freedom in America and Europe; Foster's on Ghanaian education; Pitts' on the French family; Chalasiński's on African intellectuals; Fallers' on Uganda and Turkey—these are only a few chosen at random. The instances could be multiplied several times over.

This transcendence of parochialism in the selection of subjects of research means, among many other things, that sociology is becoming more universal in the range of its sympathy and interests. It is becoming more comparative. Of course, general sociological theory has always aspired to embrace all human societies within its scheme of analysis, but on the whole it has done so with insufficient differentiation. But the new movement toward comparative sociology is not comparative in the sense that Herbert Spencer or the German ethnologists of the nineteenth century were comparative. It is not an attempt to assign societies to their respective places on an evolutionary scale. It does not involve the application of a rigid classification or typology of societies. It is more tentative, more exploratory. It is more empirical; it is usually based on fieldwork or on the use of primary archival sources in the country studied. Yet it is also theoretical in the way in which latter-day empirical sociology has become theoretical; it makes what use it can of those elements of existing theory, explicit and implicit, which will help it to explain the events which it observes.

More than the empirical work which sociologists do in their own countries, comparative sociology is also either directly or indirectly macrosociological, and, as we have indicated earlier, it is easier to be theoretical in macrosociological than in microsociological analyses. The reason is that many of the classical figures of sociological theory—e.g., Weber above all, Marx, Tocqueville, Pareto, Thomas—had a very strong macrosociological bent. Thus, the new comparative sociology aims rather at the understanding of a part of a society in the context of a whole society, and of a whole society within the context, implicit or explicit, constituted by other whole societies. A sociologist who studies a problem in a country other than his own is almost compelled, by virtue of the fact that his original concepts were formed with reference to problems in his own society and his own culture, to compare the situation he is studying in the foreign society with the situation in his own whole society. This could, of course, result simply in an ethnocentric distortion of his perception of the foreign situation. That, however, is something judicious sociologists try to guard against, and if they are successful in doing so, then the outcome is an enrichment of the sociologist's awareness of the range of variety among societies and of the macrosocial setting of microsocial situations.

The outcome, incipiently visible at present, is a new kind of comparative sociology which sees different societies and institutions within those societies as variants of a single species. There might be evolutionary overtones, but on the whole the intellectual core is sound and unaffected. The new sociological analysis has grown up in an atmosphere of relatively high detachment, and its practitioners are determined to resist any inclination towards cognitive ethnocentrism.

The new comparative sociology which acknowledges the differences among societies breaks away from the historicism which stressed the incomparable uniqueness of whole societies. It recognizes the identities of societies by seeing, behind the factual differences, an identity of fundamental potentialities, an identity of the fundamental problems faced by all human societies.

A comparative sociology is a sociology which is the study of all human societies and not just of the industrial societies of modern times. Comparative sociology can, therefore, be a study of particular societies within a general theoretical framework like most of the studies mentioned earlier; or the study of types of societies within such a framework, like Eisenstadt's study of bureaucratic empires; or it might be the general theory differentiated enough in its concepts and proportions to cover the whole range of societies and the particular societies within the range, like Parsons' *Societies*. In all these variants it strives to overcome parochialism and moves toward universalism.

The present interest in comparative sociology has been facilitated by the improvements in statistical sources (e.g., national census data, survey data, and the compilations of statistical series by the organizations of the United Nations). It has been impelled, too, by the widening of the horizon of sociologists and the extension of their intellectual curiosity and moral sympathy. But it would not have been possible without the development of general sociological theory. Much of the recent comparative work by political sociologists owes a great deal to such theorists as Parsons, Aron, Levy, Eisenstadt, and Almond—all directly influenced by Weber and to a lesser extent, directly and indirectly, by Marx.

It is too early to say what the impact of these studies of foreign societies will have on the mass of sociological studies which will continue to be about the national societies to which sociologists are native. It is possible that they will be read and pondered only by "area specialists." It is more likely that being conceived and carried out in terms of the general and "tacit" sociological theories, they will be assimilated into the sociological outlook of sociologists who stay closer to home. If that occurs, the result should be a better understanding of the uniqueness of societies within a framework which places them as members of a single family of societies. There will be, in short, another step towards the confluence of the diverse strands of the sociological tradition.

Another consequence of these studies of societies which are foreign to the sociologist who studies them is an accentuation of the tendency towards a macrosociological perspective. This has already been underway for some time. In the writings of the forerunners of sociology such as Montesquieu, Comte, Spencer, Tocqueville, and Marx, this perspective first became available to sociologists. It was very prominent in Max Weber's writings, and it was very close to the level of explicitness in Park's and Thomas' writings, as well as in Cooley's and Ross'. But in the period when sociology began to develop the techniques of investigation which established its reputation for intellectual solidity, the macrosociological interest faded. It lived on, in the 1920s, in Sorokin's writings on revolution and social mobility, and in Edwards' *The Natural History of Revolution* which was stimulated and sponsored by Park. It began to revive in the 1930s under the influence of a new interest in Marxism, the second phase of Karl Mannheim's career, in which he began to write about "mass society," and in the writings of Horkheimer. The growing interest in Max Weber's ideas was perhaps the most decisive force. The otherwise sterile discussion of "mass society" also drew attention to the macrosociological issues; political sociology and the discussion of democratic and totalitarian societies in the 1950s had a similar effect, which was heightened by the emergence of the idea of "political development." The idea itself was not very fruitful and it led to much confusion but it did shape attention towards the formation of national societies and national politics.

The studies of the new states, concerned as these studies were with the development of political society, could not, even when they confined themselves to local politics, adhere to the microsociological tradition of social anthropology from which, nonetheless, they learned a great deal. It became obvious that it was necessary to go beyond the village in order to understand the village as a site of change. The village or region had to be seen against the background of national politics and the ambitions of the ruling elite. Inquiries like Apter's *Gold Coast in Transition* and Coleman's *Nigeria: Background to Nationalism* began with an interest in the exercise of power over the territory of a sovereign state. These studies did not, however, disregard the more parochial collectivities, village, caste, tribe, lineage and family, etc. In consequence, for the first time in the recent history of sociology, studies which combined microsociological observations in a macrosociological framework began to appear in sufficient numbers to mark a new genre of sociological study. Dahrendorf, Srinivas, Bendix, Porter, Janowitz, Lipset, Austin, Levine, Fallers, Eisenstadt, Geertz, Wriggins, and Zolberg, in their general theoretical works and in their monographic works on Germany, India, Ghana, the United States, Canada, Ethiopia, Israel, Indonesia, Uganda, Ceylon, Turkey, and the Ivory Coast, integrated the results of many particular inquiries and observations on communities, parties, business firms, kinship groups, and social classes into analyses of the working of total societies.

Macrosociology brought sociologists closer to historical studies, from which the development of empirical studies had isolated sociology for some time. The techniques of empirical study, of firsthand observation and of survey analysis, had seemed at one time antithetical to historical perspective. Macrosociology—but not macrosociology alone—showed that this presumed antithesis was spurious. Changes cannot be studied without going into the depth of history. As a result, historical background had to be borne in mind in the way in which the classical empirical investigations of the period up to the Second World War had seldom done, or done only to provide "background" to the aspect of the study which was of primary interest. This situation has changed very perceptibly. The reconciliation of sociology and historiography is still a process which engages only a minority of sociologists and a minority of historians. Nonetheless a fusion of separable traditions and the elicitation of hitherto dormant traditions in each of the two disciplines has begun to come about. The movement has come from both sides of the line hitherto and still largely separating the two disciplines. Historians discovered that some of the techniques and concepts of sociologists could be adapted to their purposes; sociologists discovered the availability of data from the past in which they could use techniques and concepts hitherto reserved for dealing with the present.

In illustration, we may mention here historical voting studies of Lazarsfeld and his school, such as are also carried out independently and in a different way by John Vincent and other Cambridge historians; the work in historical demography of Laslett and Wrigley; the work of LeRoy Ladurie and Chevalier proceeding from the great French school which has developed from the work of Marc Bloch, Lucien Febvre, and Fernand Braudel; the historical sociology of religion initiated by Gabriel LeBras; the studies of nineteenth-century German society instigated by Conze; the still unexhausted riches of the Indonesian studies of Schrieke and van Leur; the prosopographical studies of Namier and Syme; the joining of classical studies and social anthropology by Momigliano and Humphreys; and the historical studies of the structure and fate of particular classes, such as Stone's on the English aristocracy of the seventeenth century, Hobsbawm's and Thompson's on the English working classes of the nineteenth century, and Fogel's studies of American slavery. The number of such studies which are helping to undo the temporal superficiality of sociology is large and growing.

This movement is now only in its beginnings. It undoubtedly has limits in the nature of the records of past epochs, but these limits have certainly not been even remotely approximated. Certainly the major resource of sociologists—the creation of their own data by interviews, surveys, and direct observation—is not available to historian-sociologists. But even if, "in the end," the data of the historians do not meet all the requirements of empirical sociologists—just as the theories of the sociologists will not meet the requirements of the historians—the undertaking itself is beginning to make a deep imprint on the course of sociology. The outcome might be a sociology which is not confined in its scope to concepts and propositions which are valid only for still existing societies. An understanding of the wide variety of human possibilities disclosed by history, which cannot be disclosed by concentration on the study of contemporaneous societies, is a full requirement of a comprehensive sociological theory. It will be almost as important for microsociology as it will be for macrosociology.

IV

The import of this cursory survey of the growth and confluence of certain traditions of sociology and adjacent disciplines over the past half-century—as full of gaps and injustices as it is—is that sociology, under circumstances which have demanded incessant specialization, has also experienced a process of unification. Even though the results leave much to be desired, theory and research, within nearly every country where sociology is carried on, are in a more active interaction and reciprocal assimilation than they have been before. Despite numerous resistances, some passive, others more active, sociologists are forming, more than they have ever done before, a worldwide intellectual community which cultivates a very loosely but also commonly shared intellectual undertaking. The world's societies are beginning to be seen as members of a single family in which variations and changes occur within a framework of shared attributes and potentialities.

The realization of all these tendencies which are scarcely more than incipient is not imminent. There are numerous obstacles in the path. The sheer intellectual difficulty of doing what has not been done before is, as it is in all sciences, the greatest obstacle to progress. Then there are other obstacles—language, ignorance, national and cultural pride, and political and ideological passion.

Still, the fact of confluence remains. It has brought sociology and its related disciplines closer to the ideal of a *science humaine*.

4 Tradition, Ecology, and Institution in the History of Sociology

Sociology at present is a heterogeneous aggregate of topics, related to each other by a common name, by more or less common techniques, by a community of key words and conceptions, by a more or less commonly held aggregate of major interpretative ideas and schemes. It is held together too by a more or less common tradition—a heterogeneous one in which certain currents stand out—linked to common monuments or classical figures and works. It is also held together by the knowledge which its practitioners possess that they have in common—their location in universities, a common set of journals, and a group of publishers who produce their works.

The tradition, more or less commonly shared, lives in a self-image which links those now calling themselves sociologists with a sequence of famous authors running back into the nineteenth century. Although in fact the lines of the main ideas which live on in contemporary sociology have a much older history, sociologists do not generally see themselves as having an ancestry originating any earlier than the nineteenth century. All see themselves immersed in much shorter traditions, but they are recurrently reminded of the longer past.

Most of sociology is not scientific in the sense in which this term is used in English-speaking countries. It contains little of generality of scope and little of fundamental importance which is rigorously demonstrated by commonly accepted procedures for making relatively reproducible observations of important things. Its theories are not ineluctably bound to its observations. The standards of proof are not stringent. Despite valiant efforts, its main concepts are not precisely defined; its most interesting interpretative propositions are not unambiguously articulated.

There are differences, of course, among the various substantive fields of sociology, some being more scientific in certain respects than others, but on the whole the standard of scientific accomplishment is low. This does not mean that in those parts which are not very scientific there is not some very substantial learning or that there is not an accumulated wisdom which merits regard and consideration. Nor does it mean that some of it even in its present intellectual state is incapable of contributing, if it were taken to heart, to the improvement of policy, administration, and to civility in a broad sense. It only

This is a revised version of an essay that originally appeared in *Daedalus*. Reprinted by permission from *Daedalus*, Journal of the American Academy of Arts and Sciences, Boston, Mass., vol. 99, no. 4 (Fall 1970).

means what it says, namely, that much of contemporary social science is not very scientific in the sense in which the term has come to be understood.

Nonetheless, sociology does exist. It has a large institutional embodiment in departments of sociology in universities and in many research institutions, some affiliated to universities and some independent. It has a history which present-day sociologists regard as their history—although of course the image of this history varies somewhat from country to country and among sociologists within particular countries. It has a contemporaneous existence constituted by its vast and rapidly expanding stock of works, a large and also rapidly expanding personnel working in and forming academic institutions given over to sociological research, teaching, training and consultation; these include governmental institutions for sociological research and consultation and private, nongovernmental, nonacademic institutions in which sociologists perform some of the same activities as they perform when they are employed in governmental institutions. The stock of works, heterogeneous though it is in its particular subject-matters, in its techniques of observation and analysis, and in its particular interpretations is also characterized by a few widely pervasive major ideas or beliefs about society, by a few major concepts or delineations of significant variables. It is characterized above all by the sociological approach which believes that human actions and, at least in part, social actions are affected in varying degrees by the social setting in which they are carried on. The sociological approach is as simple as that; it is an approach of far-reaching implications. It is the faith of sociologists and it gives them their self-confidence.

Its characteristic concepts include those of social system, of society and its constituent institutions, of primary groups, of social stratification and social mobility, of power and legitimate authority, of elites and ruling classes, of law and freedom, of social status, of occupational roles, of bureaucracy and corporate organization, of kinship and local community, of history and tradition, of intellectuals and ideology, of consensus and conflict, of solidarity and alienation, conformity and deviance, charisma and routine, of reverence before the sacred and rebellion against institutions. These various concepts have been grouped into a conception of modern society or *Gesellschaft* (and its variant of mass society) which is further defined by contrast with a conceptual construction variously designated as folk society, traditional society, or *Gemeinschaft*.

How has all this come about? Why has the intellectual stock of sociology come to be what it is and why has it taken that form in particular places? Why have certain ideas which are now thought to be constitutive of sociology come to dominate the subject?

One of the older answers was that sociology could not emerge until men were capable of sufficient detachment from involvement in their own affairs and in their beliefs about these affairs; a corollary of this was that sociology could arise only when authority had lost some of its sanctity, when traditional beliefs became somewhat discredited, and when a secularized attitude had come to prevail in the educated parts of society. This view has been put forward by a number of writers, most notably Durkheim and Sombart. There is something in this view—but not enough. The heavens belonged to the gods and religious beliefs and to those who took those beliefs in their charge on behalf of the gods, but that did not prevent the emergence of astronomy. It might have impeded the emergence of astronomy but it did not prevent it. Man's body in the West was God's creation, but that too did not prevent the study of anatomy or the understanding of the circulation of the blood. In Greece and in Rome and in medieval Islam, in the writings of Aristotle, Polybius, Thucydides, and Ibn Khaldun ideas were put forth which have reappeared in modern sociology, but the subject never became precipitated in the way in which physics or mathematics became established in the seventeenth and eighteenth centuries. Ancient Greece and Rome and medieval Islam were not secularized societies, they were not traditionless societies in which authority and custom had receded from earlier strength. So the hypothesis that sociology requires for its existence a secularized society is not quite satisfactory. There is however something in the hypothesis that sociology requires a cultural matrix or setting which is not so exigent in its demands on substantive belief that it stifles detachment. There is something in the hypothesis that sociology requires a loosening of the belief that divine or magical powers intervene at will in human affairs. It is also true that sociology as a body of generalized knowledge about society requires freedom from a jealous and pervasive ecclesiastical or secular authority which is apprehensive about the potential dangers of the formation of beliefs which are not necessarily identical with those it holds about itself and its society. These conditions, however, are the conditions of any intellectual activity which is not wholly committed in advance to agreement with the views held by ecclesiastical and earthly authorities in matters which those authorities believe are vital.

What I wish to say here is that the recession of earthly and ecclesiastical authority, and a loosening of the grip of traditional beliefs which consecrate that authority, are only very general preconditions. They tell very little about the intellectual direction and the territorial location of the growth of sociology.

Sociology, even if it is not very scientific, is, in its better manifestations, an intellectual accomplishment. The practice of sociology—i.e., sociological teaching, sociological investigation, and sociological reflection—is an intellectual activity. As an intellectual activity, it operates within the pattern of thought contained in intellectual traditions; each sociological action takes place within the framework of the traditions which it in turn affects and, in some important instances, modifies markedly. The traditions of sociology are even now not rigorously coherent and authoritative in their presentation and they were less so in their earlier states in the nineteenth and twentieth centuries. These traditions have offered to their recipients a variety of possibilities. There has been a process of selection by individuals confronting the traditions. The selection has been limited by intellectual givenness or self-evidentness (which is characteristic of any tradition), and opportunity for exposure of individuals to particular streams of tradition; this exposure is disciplined when it takes place through institutions which both consciously and unthinkingly determine which constituents of the traditional stock should be presented to the individuals who expose themselves. Institutions have not created sociology; it has been created by individual sociologists exercising their powers of observation and analysis on social situations apprehended within the focusing framework of sociological traditions. Observation includes second- and third-hand observation through informants, documents, and printed works which report observations by others. Each of these sources is a precipitate of observations made within the framework of traditions. It is the task of the sociologist to interpret these precipitates of other traditions in the light of his own sociological traditions. These sociological traditions can be acquired by individuals who seek them out in the books and persons in which they are embodied. Institutions reduce the task of seeking; they make it easier and they reduce the freedom of a somewhat more random, autodidactic search. Institutions concentrate attention on particular elements of a tradition; they reinforce certain selected ways of perceiving and interpreting experience. Institutions foster the production of works, and the works, with what they contain in the way of interpretation of social reality, become part of the focusing tradition. Institutions present a resonant and echoing intellectual environment to those within them and they make what is produced under their influence more visible in the public realm outside the institution. The sociological ideas which undergo institutionalization are thereby given a greater weight in the competition of interpretations of social reality.

Institutionalization

By institutionalization of an intellectual activity I mean the relatively dense interaction of persons who conduct that activity within a social arrangement which has boundaries, endurance, and a name. The interaction has a structure. The more intense the interaction, the more its structure makes place for authority which makes decisions regarding assessment, admission, promotion, allocation; the authority also sets the criteria for the selection of those particular traditions which are to be cultivated in teaching and inquiry. There need not be a formal stipulation of the criteria; they can and usually are simply embodied in the practice of the authorities—in this case, those who are most imposing intellectually. The high degree of institutionalization of an intellectual activity entails its teaching and investigation within the regulated, scheduled, and systematically administered organization. The organization regulates access through a scrutiny of qualification, and it provides for the organized assessment of performance; it allocates facilities, opportunities, and rewards for performance, e.g., study, teaching, investigation, publication, appointment, etc. It also entails the acquisition of the resources—monetary or material—needed to support the activity from outside the particular institutions. It entails too, provision for the diffusion of the results of the activity beyond the boundaries of the institution through publication in the most general sense of making the results available to the public, lay or specialized, outside the boundaries of the particular institution. (Marginal exceptions exist with regard to this last feature: an institution for the cultivation of a hermetic science or philosophy, or an institution doing "secret" research with the results of the research being transmitted to the privileged "user.") An intellectual activity need not be equally institutionalized in all the indicated respects. It should also be remembered that an intellectual activity can be carried on fruitfully with only a very rudimentary degree of institutionalization. Indeed, some of the greatest periods of intellectual production in the sciences and philosophy have been marked by relatively rudimentary institutional organization. There must be some institutional organization for the acquisition of elementary instruction and for the transmission of the results of inquiry in printed or manuscript form. Institutional organization is not necessarily good. All I contend here is that its presence and form make a difference to the fate of traditions.

Sociology is more institutionalized where it can be studied in a university than where it has to be the object of private study; where it can be studied in a university as a major subject than where it can only be studied as an adjunct subject; and where it has a specialized teaching staff of its own rather than teachers who do it only as a marginal obligation while their main obligation is the teaching of economics or philosophy. Sociology is more institutionalized where there are opportunities for the publication of sociological works in specifically sociological journals rather than in journals devoted primarily to other subjects; where there is financial, administrative, and logistic provision for sociological investigation through established institutions rather than from the private resources of the investigator; where there are established and remunerated opportunities for the practice of sociology in teaching and research; and where there is a "demand" for the results of sociological research.

Sociology today is a relatively highly institutionalized branch of study in the countries of Western Europe and of North America—more recently in the former than in the latter. The social sciences became established as academic subjects later than most of the other major academic disciplines, e.g., mathematics, physics, chemistry, zoology, botany, classics, oriental studies, the national language and literature, which are now to be found in university courses of study. Sociology was the last of the social sciences to attain this status. The social sciences have, however, now made up the distance. Degrees, undergraduate and postgraduate, are now awarded for the completion of organized courses of study in these subjects; research training under qualified teachers is provided, often in research teams whose work is organized by the teachers, supervised, and reported preliminarily in seminars where the work is criticized. Journals with professionally and academically qualified referees and often supported by learned societies and sometimes by commercial publishers are available for the publication of the results of research in each field and often for quite specialized subfields. In addition to more routine and periodic meetings of learned societies, there is, for practitioners and apprentices in each field and in many subfields and even in the informally circumscribed domain of a problem, an elaborate network of communication through the circulation of offprints, memoranda, and preliminary versions of research reports. Practically all of these activities are firmly incorporated into the structure of universities and professional societies which have a momentum of their own.

In the first half of the nineteenth century, sociology did not exist as an academic subject anywhere, although of course it had academic forerunners in the *Staatswissenschaften*, in the juridical sciences, in the occasional teaching of economics, especially historical economics, and in moral philosophy. Its academic establishment which began slowly and unevenly in the last years of the nineteenth century was however made possible by a loosely articulated set of intellectual traditions of study which extend back of Western antiquity and which acquired focus and delineation in the course of the nineteenth century. The successful intellectual development of economics in England and its relative failure in Germany show that institutionalization is neither a necessary nor sufficient condition of intellectual achievement. Economics was only very faintly institutionalized in the former and it was quite well institutionalized in Germany. To be well institutionalized is in a certain sense to be a success, but this is not the same as intellectual success.

The chief figures of the tradition of economic analysis in Great Britain were not generally university teachers; often they were not even university graduates. Indeed, not even in economics which became an intellectually orderly discipline—relatively speaking—much earlier than sociology and political science did the academic element have the field to itself. Adam Smith stands out as the first great important academic contributor to the subject, although political economy was only one of the four subjects for which he was responsible within his rather short tenure as professor, first of logic and then of moral philosophy. He had been out of academic life for thirteen years when *The Wealth of Nations* was published in 1776. Ricardo was never an academic, nor was James Mill, and the Reverend William Paley's teaching at Haileybury could not be regarded as strictly academic since that body was closer to a secondary school than a university. The synthesist of economic theory of the middle of the century, John Stuart Mill, had only the most marginal academic connections; he was rector of St. Andrews, a wholly honorific position and a very transient one; he never attended a university or taught at one. Cairnes, Senior, Fawcett, Sidgwick, and Jevons were university teachers, and beginning no later than with Alfred Marshall's first academic steps, serious students could obtain at a few places in Great Britain disciplined training in economic analysis. Empirical economic research was another matter, being largely in the hands of government officials, private amateurs, and voluntary bodies; it was largely avocational and minimally institutionalized. Even in this field, however, the possibility of acquiring guidance in the techniques of research existed within the academic frame. Thorold Rogers as professor at Oxford and Archdeacon Cunningham at Cambridge and King's College, London, could help a young man to learn to do economic research with a quantitative accent. If we compare the situation with that prevailing in France where economics was taught seriously only in the Conservatoire des arts et métiers, at the École des ponts et chaussées, and at other technical institutions where young men were being prepared for technological careers, or at the Collège de France where there were no students in economics, or at the Faculté de droit in Paris where economics was established in the 1870s and was suffocated under the legal lumber, we see one of the reasons why British economics led the world in the nineteenth and early twentieth centuries. British economics first established a sound intellectual tradition and became institutionalized only after it had done so.

It must be repeatedly emphasized that reference to institutionalization does not by any means wholly account for the great ascendancy of British economic analysis in this period. The British economists had a better idea of the problems to be studied, and this was partly a function of the high level of the organs of public opinion in Great Britain; the contacts of economists with the worldly affairs of parliament, investigative commissions, governmental departments, and leading politicians and businessmen also gave them experience on which they could exercise their analytical powers. The British economists had a more fruitful point of departure because they analyzed the equilibrium of an economic system and not the budgetary economic necessities of govenments. It was preoccupation with the latter which held back the development of economics in the German universities since it obstructed the understanding of the autonomy of the market. The discovery of the market was not a function of the academic institutionalization of economics; but once the discovery was made institutionalization did help to clarify, correct, and differentiate the original insight and to make it more widely available.

Sociology is little different in age from economics, and its institutional establishment in universities in the United States follows the institutional establishment of economics by only a few decades. Economics, however, had two clearly defined traditions—British economic theory and German historical economics—and it had one great figure who presided over the institutional establishment of economics in Great Britain; this was Alfred Marshall. Sociology had no such distinguished figure who was present at its academic establishment, and this caused the subject to lead a motley intellectual life, even up to the present.

Sociology had several important figures who established the name of the subject—itself a significant step—and who studied its subject-matter. Auguste Comte and Herbert Spencer were the greatest of these forerunners.

Each had many admirers and critics who regarded themselves as sociologists. When sociology was being established in universities both of them had fallen from the height of their reputations and there was no authoritative body of knowledge and theory to replace their doctrines. Tocqueville and Marx can certainly be regarded with legitimacy as forerunners of sociology but they were not recognized as sociologists at the beginning of the present century; it is only recently that they have been nominated for retroactive membership in the tradition. They were neither more nor less academic than Comte or Spencer, they had no students, no assistants, no monographic series or seminars; no dissertations were written under them to work out their ideas and to apply them to situations with which they had not dealt.[1] Comte and Spencer installed themselves at the beginning of the tradition by giving a name and a vague set of boundaries to the subject

---

1. Spencer's *Descriptive Sociology* played no part whatsoever in his entry into the tradition of sociology—which in substance departed very far from his ideas and has only recently showed a partial turn towards them.

still to be born. But when the time came for sociology to be admitted into universities, they became part of the unused tradition.

Other originators, German historians and British and French statisticians, who in effect generated and impelled forward the tradition from which sociology as we know it emerged, have also not been equally acknowledged as the forerunners of sociology. The techniques which these scholars used and the subject-matters which they chose left an enduring imprint on the sociology which developed, but the substance of their ideas was not equally regarded. They merely added to the heterogeneity of sociology as it moved towards institutional establishment.

The European Founders: Academic Cultivation without Institutionalized Establishment

The distance between the universities and sociology during the first three-quarters of the nineteenth century was reduced when founders replaced forerunners. Sociologists taught in the universities but sociology could not be studied. The five European founders who stand between the forerunners and the academically established generations of the present century were all academics. Only one of them, however, was academically responsible for teaching and training in sociology. Ferdinand Tönnies was *Privatdozent* in philosophy and later for several years professor of economics and statistics; he taught sociology only after his retirement. Vilfredo Pareto never taught sociology; he was a professor of economics for about five years in his late forties. Max Weber during his short academic career was professor of economics; he apparently taught sociology only after his brief return to university teaching in 1918. Georg Simmel taught philosophy as *Privatdozent* and *ausserordentlicher Professor* for most of his career—he occasionally lectured on sociological topics—and became *ordentlicher Professor* (but not for sociology) only a few years before his death. Emile Durkheim was the only one of the generation of founders who made a full academic career with an official responsibility for sociology. He was professor of sociology and education at Bordeaux from 1887 to 1902 and from then until his death in 1917 professor of the same subjects under various titles at the Sorbonne.

France. Of all the founders of sociology, only Durkheim was successful in establishing his subject during his lifetime. Only he had pupils and collaborators, regularly, over a long period. Sociology acquired an academic institutional form only around Durkheim and that was less through provision by the university than from Durkheim's own organizational initiative and skill in the formation of the *Année sociologique*.

Durkheim followed the German pattern: the professor of the subject covered the whole field himself, trained younger collaborators through intensive discussions, and published the results of their individual and joint work in the organ of the institute which was reserved primarily for contributors from his personal circle. One difference was that in Germany the university provided funds for the "institute" which was attached to the chair; in France there was no such provision for university professors.

Another important difference between Germany and France was that in German universities those who worked with a professor in his institute were specializing in his discipline, were writing dissertations on it, and would depend on his sponsorship for *Habilitation* and subsequent academic appointment. There was provision for training in research at an advanced level in Germany from the early part of the century; in France it was only when the École pratique des hautes études was founded in 1868 that there was provision for training in research. But neither in Germany nor in France were these opportunities available to sociologists at the beginning of the twentieth century. Sociology as part of the "human sciences" came into the EPHE only when the *sixième section* was formed after the Second World War. There were furthermore few opportunities under the French educational and administrative systems for persons who had experience in sociological research. Those who studied sociology did it because they were genuinely interested rather than because they expected to make a career out of it, since very few could. This meant that Durkheim's entourage consisted of intellectually deeply interested persons whose professional possibilities and aspirations lay outside sociology. While they were active members of his circle they produced important sociological works, but once they became active in their own careers, which entailed research and teaching in specialized fields such as sinology, ethnography, comparative religion, and philosophy, they produced little which belonged to the core of sociology. Their reproductive capacity as sociologists was slight since very few of them became teachers of sociologists. They became sinologists, linguists, administrators, etc. They did not train sociologists because there were very few students of sociology; there were very few students of sociology because there were practically no posts in sociology to which they could hope to be appointed later in their careers.

In France, therefore, the institutionalization and the resultant expansion and continuity of production was generated almost entirely by the personal force of the individual professor. He was helped, of course, by the existence of the EPHE and the section on *sciences réligieuses,* which was not dominated by professors.[2]

2. Because the EPHE was not dominated by professors, it was possible for Durkheim to attract to his circle young men who were preparing to enter other disciplines. This would have been impossible in Germany. A professor would

The sociological ideas of Durkheim largely died away in France not very long after Durkheim himself died, as far as their application to modern society was concerned. Davy, who published an important Durkheimian treatise in the early 1920s, taught in a provincial university, entered educational administration first in a provincial university and then in the government, and became a professor of sociology only in 1944. Bouglé too became an administrator and ceased to concern himself primarily with sociology. Simiand worked as a government official and only later in his life became a professor—of labor history. Granet continued to be a faithful and creative Durkheimian and a great sociologist but his teaching was entirely sinological and he had no students of sociology. Mauss became professor of "primitive religion" early on and later became director of the Institut d'ethnologie at the Sorbonne as well as professor at the Collège de France; in none of these capacities did he have students of sociology, understood either as a general theory of society or as the study of modern societies. The *Année sociologique* came upon hard times and appeared with increasing infrequency during the 1920s; no other French sociological journal replaced it.

Durkheim left behind a wonderful band of disciples in specialized fields which were at the periphery of sociology; but since sociology was not institutionalized at the center, their accomplishments remained dispersed. There was no consolidation and no sociological succession. Only Maurice Halbwachs continued the Durkheimian tradition as a sociologist studying modern societies, but, aside from his own work, there was little extension. Halbwachs was a man of exceptional intellectual power and great erudition and he was also a very productive author. He was faithful to Durkheim's tradition but he was not paralyzed by it; he approached new topics and he had original ideas. Yet he was unable to reestablish the school by extending and deepening the traditions flowing from Durkheim. His work and that from which it drew the main lines of its outlook was not taken up by younger French sociologists and did not enter into the course of the sociological development.

A tentative explanation does not seem too difficult. Halbwachs was a professor at Strasbourg, a distinguished university, but not one to which the best students flocked from all over France. It had recently

not hold commerce with a research student who did not give promise of becoming a disciple, and a student would not dare to risk his career by serving a professor outside his own subject, the subject in which he wished to make his career. French professors were jealous and students depended on them for patronage. Nonetheless, Durkheim did attract young men who could not make a career in sociology and who would ultimately have to make a career in some other academic discipline. Perhaps this is to be accounted for by the power of Durkheim's intellectual personality and by the fact that in the fields from which Durkheim drew his adherents there were so few opportunities that even subservience to the incumbent professor was usually professionally fruitless.

been converted from being a German university. At Strasbourg, Halbwachs as a sociologist was alone. He did not, as far as I know, supervise dissertations, this privilege being reserved by convention and prudence for Parisian professors. He had no younger colleagues to associate themselves with him. Thus, this powerfully and sensitively intelligent man who carried forward the Durkheimian tradition, but in no uncritically submissive way, had no juniors of sufficient quality and in sufficient numbers on whom to leave a mark. The intellectual population around him was not dense enough; the necessary complement of institutions—specializing students, postgraduate training, research projects, and research assistants and journals—were not available to him.

Durkheim's ideas were of course available in a "free-floating" form, as Max Weber's were in Germany in the 1920s. Not all intellectual filiations need to be transmitted by an apostolic succession within the framework of a corporate body. Influences certainly need not be transmitted only through institutional establishment and impressed by reenactment in research and publication under supervision and in collaboration. This situation requires the existence of a lay public interested in the subject and ready to support it financially and intellectually. This was lacking in France. The heart had gone out of the quest for a new secular morality which was one of the driving forces of Durkheim's sociology. The teaching of sociology in the lycées which was intended to realize this goal did not compensate for its evaporation.[3] It is sometimes said that the death in battle of some of the most distinguished of the younger collaborators of the Année sociologique was the cause of the cessation of the Durkheimian outlook in French sociology, and there is some truth in this. More important, however, was the fact that the institutional structure built by Durkheim rested only on him and was not integrated into the institutional structure of the French academic system or into the opportunities for professional careers outside the universities.

Germany. The fate of sociology in Germany supports this interpretation. Since the three great founders of sociology in Germany were not professors of the subject, they had no research institutes such as German professors ordinarily had for their subjects. They had no ongoing seminars for training students in research and for bringing their dissertations to the point where they could be published as

3. The one form in which Durkheimian tradition was institutionalized in France after his death was in the teaching and the textbooks of civic morals used in the lycées. But rather than recruit sociologists, it alienated persons who might have become sociologists. Raymond Aron was one of those who was alienated from Durkheim's tradition by this mode of presentation. He was recovered only by encountering Max Weber when he went to Germany at the beginning of the 1930s.

monographs. Also there was no place for them to go as professional sociologists once they finished their training—had such training been available in Germany. There were before the First World War no professorships of sociology in universities, in technical or teacher-training colleges. There were no junior posts in sociology in the universities, just as there were no senior posts. There was practically no employment for sociologists as sociologists outside universities.

Max Weber was located in Heidelberg from 1896 to 1918. It was in Heidelberg that he developed his most significant sociological ideas. He did not teach during most of this time, and his audience was confined to personal friends and his "circle"; not many of them did much to develop his ideas further. There was no established academic except Ernst Troeltsch who worked out any of Max Weber's ideas. Ernst Troeltsch was professor in Heidelberg from 1894 to 1914 and it was while he was professor there that he published his *Die Bedeutung des Protestantismus für die Entstehung der modernen Welt* and *Die Soziallehren der christlichen Kirchen und Sekten,* which Max Weber in his turn helped to amplify and more widely distribute.

Weber had close relations with Heinrich Rickert and Karl Jaspers in Heidelberg but they were only marginally interested in sociological work. Eberhard Gothein was a little closer to Max Weber's sociological interests. Among younger scholars Georg Lukàcs and Paul Honigsheim were the closest to sociology; the former became a Marxist during the war, then a communist, and spent the rest of his life as a Marxist literary critic and philosopher with little understanding for sociology; Honigsheim never succeeded in making an academic career in Germany. There was no chair of sociology in Heidelberg and hence no seriously interested students. The *Archiv für Sozialwissenschaft und Sozialpolitik* covered all the social sciences and could not give sociology the dignity which a journal of equal quality concentrated on the subject could confer. Weber shared the editorship of the *Archiv* with other distinguished scholars whose interests were not primarily in sociology. His intellectual-convivial life was spent in a diverse company which included philosophers, jurists, and literary critics, and Weber neither gave it a sociological focus nor shaped its output in the manner in which Durkheim had done with his entourage.

In the next generation, Alexander von Schelting and Karl Mannheim were Weber's main sociological continuators. Alexander von Schelting understood Max Weber's methodological ideas with a precision and elaborateness which was unique. He was not, however, *habilitated* until after the end of the Weimar republic. He went into exile and taught briefly at Columbia before the renaissance created by Merton and Lazarsfeld. Then after years of severe poverty in Switzerland he died without influence and with the sociological part of his study of the Russian intelligentsia unfinished. His *Max Weber's Wis-*

senschaftslehre remains the most thorough analysis of the subject. It was drawn on by Parsons in his analysis of Max Weber's methodological ideas but it remained without influence in Germany. Mannheim was in Heidelberg through the 1920s. He was a protégé and devotee of Alfred Weber; from him he adopted the idea of *frei-schwebende Intelligenz.* He attended Marianne Weber's colloquia. Max Weber's ideas were a living presence but only a very general one at Heidelberg at that time. Except for Mannheim, none of the numerous professors and *Privatdozenten* who professed sympathy and admiration for Max Weber's ideas undertook to apply them. It was Max Weber's ideas on bureaucracy which Mannheim absorbed and which he tried to elaborate in his essay on *Erfolgsstreben;* Max Weber's ideas about rationalization were at the bases of *Mensch und Gesellschaft im Zeitalter des Umbaus,* which he wrote and published while in exile. It was also an idea of Max Weber, the idea of a charismatic revolutionary directly inspired by a believed contact with ultimate things, which Mannheim adapted in his essay on the utopian mentality in *Ideologie und Utopie* and which he took up again towards the end of his life in his development of the notion of "paradigmatic experiences" in the *The Diagnosis of Our Time.*

Mannheim's relations with Max Weber's ideas were affected by the fact that he came to Heidelberg only after Weber had died, and his mind was confused by his subjection to certain fundamental categories of Marxism at the same time that he was aware of its untenability; he was also affected by working in Heidelberg in a situation in which there was no systematic analysis or discriminating application of Weber's substantive sociological ideas. It should also be said that the failure of the imprint of Weber's ideas was fostered not just by the absence of any sustaining intellectual-institutional structure around Mannheim, but also by Mannheim's hidden and ambivalent struggle to establish a distinctive line of his own different from Scheler's, different from Marx's, and different from that of German idealism.

When Mannheim went to Frankfurt, he replaced Franz Oppenheimer, who had been a *Privatdozent* and finally a professor after nearly twenty years in private medical practice and whose immense eight-volume treatise, written in the service of his ideas on the monopoly of landed property owners, had no intellectual afterlife at all. Mannheim brought Max Weber's ideas to Frankfurt. He was an attractive teacher and had enthusiastic students but his tenure was too brief and there were few opportunities for employment for those who took their degrees under him. In any case, they were soon scattered by exile or silenced by National Socialism. This was the end of Mannheim's influence in Germany. It was also the end of such influence as Max Weber's ideas had had through Mannheim's interpretation of them.

During the Weimar republic there were many professors of sociology or of sociology and a related discipline. They were poorly equiped to do research in the light of their own ideas and they were not disposed towards the acceptance of Weber's ideas either. Some of the work on white-collar employees owed something to the stimulus of Weber's writing on bureaucracy, although I think that only Hans Speier's work is clear-cut in this respect. The professors of sociology in Germany in the Weimar period—Vierkandt, Rumpf, von Wiese, Geiger, Freyer, Meusel, Walther, Dunckmann, et al.—were proper German professors in the sense that each one wanted to have a system of his own which he wanted his students to carry on. Most of them wrote books of "principles" which were largely variations on the theme of *Gemeinschaft* and *Gesellschaft*. They had few ideas of their own; they had little interest in research which would do other than reiterate some part of their conceptual scheme. They certainly had no interest in Max Weber's substantive sociology. They were, however, unlike the classical type of German professor in that they created nothing important of their own and they trained no *Nachwuchs*. Albert Salomon, who was a professor in a normal school for training teachers, was a devotee of Max Weber but he had no products and no heirs. Hans Speier, who was a pupil of Mannheim and a protégé of Emil Lederer, was one of the very few who did interesting research on social stratification much influenced by Max Weber's ideas.

In any case, it all ended with the virtual obliteration of sociology by the Nazi regime.

Max Weber faded out of German sociology in the decade when a number of professorships in sociology were created in universities and technical and pedagogical colleges. It was an outsider to Heidelberg and Germany who did more for the animation of Max Weber's sociological ideas than anyone else. Talcott Parsons came to Heidelberg in the middle of the 1920s. He did more to bring Max Weber's sociological ideas into the heart of the subject than anyone else. But that is another chapter.

Until the 1920s, when the *Kölner Vierteljahreshefte für Soziologie* was founded, German sociologists had no journal of their own in which they could publish their works and thereby define their identity as sociologists. In consequence of this, there was no concentration of minds on the ideas of great potentiality which came from the three or four great German figures to whom the sociological world now looks back as founders. The ideas of Max Weber, Georg Simmel, and Ferdinand Tönnies—and possibly Max Scheler—did not undergo the process of reinterpretation, partial assimilation, and elaboration which is the characteristic course of development of intellectual products. The failure to do this reinforced the causes of the failure. At the University of Cologne there was, it is true, one active professor of philosophy and sociology, and one professor of sociology. Leopold von Wiese was the professor of sociology; he had students, a research institute, and a journal, those three important constituents of the institutionalization of an academic subject. Unfortunately for German sociology, von Wiese's ideas were incapable of development. He was concerned primarily with nomenclature and taxonomy and led his students to no other tasks. Institutionalization could only have consolidated intellectual sterility.[4] Max Scheler, who was professor of philosophy and sociology, was an extremely fertile scholar who worked in the area between philosophy and sociology. He was full of interesting ideas and for a time gathered about himself a number of younger scholars but he left the field after five years and returned to philosophy.

Great Britain. Another "founder" of sociology was L. T. Hobhouse, who was professor of sociology at the London School of Economics from 1907 until 1929. Hobhouse had a widely ranging comparative interest. The breadth of his knowledge and his interest in the trends of social changes were in some ways comparable to Weber's, and he organized one major piece of research which was unique until recently for its use of quantitative methods in comparative study. In his time, he was the only professor of sociology in the United Kingdom devoting all his time to his subject. The subject was not taught in other universities. There was no employment for graduates in sociology, no undergraduate specialization in sociology, and very few postgraduate students. The one sociological journal, *The Sociological Review,* in Hobhouse's lifetime was under the dominion of geographers and amateur followers of Le Play. *The New Survey of London Life and Labour* seems to have been planned and executed without Hobhouse's participation. He lacked an interest in the concrete details of modern societies. His power of inspiration was not great enough to offset the institutional obstacles. Today Hobhouse is almost entirely disregarded by sociologists.[5] Part of the explanation for the oblivion into which Hobhouse has fallen lies partly in the fact that his interpretation of modern society was not vivid enough to arouse the interest of the students of the London School of Economics so

4. Von Wiese's pupils did do a small amount of fieldwork (see *Das Dorf als soziales Gebilde* [*Kölner Vierteljahreshefte für Soziologie,* Beiheft I, 1928]). The result was simply the discovery of illustrations of the concepts of *allgemeine Beziehungslehre.* Dr. Willy Gierlichs, a pupil of von Wiese, taught in a police training college; again this first step in the institutionalization of sociology in an applied form led to nothing because von Wiese chose the most sterile part of Simmel's sociology to try to develop. Neither the conceptions of formal sociology nor of *Zu- und Auseinander* were very fertile points of departure and von Wiese did not have the imaginative powers to draw out of them what little they contained.

5. In the index of the *International Encyclopaedia of the Social Sciences,* there are two references to Hobhouse, fifty-eight to Durkheim, and sixty-four to Max Weber.

that they would risk their careers in order to benefit from his guidance. This was a major difference between him and Durkheim. Hobhouse had a colleague, Edward Westermarck,[6] who taught part of each session; they were the sole incumbents of professorial chairs of sociology in the United Kingdom. Furthermore, despite the sympathetic support of R. H. Tawney, there was no informal consensus among the more esteemed academic personalities regarding the value of the sociological approach to social matters. (Such a consensus began to appear only after the Second World War.)

The great tradition of empirical sociological inquiry in Great Britain which had developed independently of the universities remained so until well after the First World War; it had been the work of government officials and public-spirited private citizens of means without the help of the universities. Officially, the situation was not too different from that in France, but the strength of Durkheim's personality, the persuasiveness of his convictions, and the superior prestige of the Sorbonne in the French university system—which the London School of Economics did not at that time possess—made a great difference. More important than the relatively low prestige of the London School of Economics in British academic life during Hobhouse's career there from 1907 to 1929 was that the type of young collaborators available to Durkheim at the Sorbonne were not available to Hobhouse at the London School of Economics. Whereas Durkheim was able to draw to himself young scholars who were specialists in folklore, oriental studies, and linguistics, these subjects did not exist at the London School of Economics. Such studies were pursued at University College, London, and at the School of Oriental and African Studies, where they had practically no contact with sociology. There were few postgraduate students and young lecturers at these other institutions and they had to make their careers by meeting the specialized requirements of their own departments. Young Oxford and Cambridge dons in classics and oriental studies in the first quarter of the present century were unlikely to be drawn to a professor at the London School of Economics. The fact that the latter was not an imperious personality like Durkheim and lacked his organizing enterprise and the fact that evolutionism, even of the more cautious type espoused by Hobhouse, enjoyed little intellectual esteem at the time in British academic circles, tightened the limitations on any influence which Hobhouse might have exerted. Hobhouse's one distinguished protégés was Professor Morris Ginsberg, who succeeded him, but Ginsberg was a shy and self-critical person and not a vigorous organizer like Durkheim. The result was that the French sociology of Durkheim's

6. Westermarck, whose own work was in the tradition of German *Völkerkunde*, had one pupil who transformed his subject; that was Malinowski, and what he did was for a long time coterminous with social anthropology.

circle left behind a massive deposit. British academic sociology—
Hobhouse's variant of sociological evolutionism—left behind only the
one work on the material culture of simpler peoples.[7]

The eugenics movement, which was not academically institutionalized, came in a roundabout way to have a more powerful
impact on British sociology. It did so through its connection with the
development of sophisticated statistical techniques by Galton, Pear-
son, and Fisher and through the short-lived Department of Social
Biology at the London School of Economics under the leadership of
Lancelot Hogben in the 1930s and the Population Investigation Committee, which has had a longer life. Important British studies in social
selection and mobility belong to this tradition rather than to
Hobhouse's. The greatest British survey was *The Life and Labour of
the People of London* in seventeen volumes. This work was a culmination of a tradition of the *Reports* of the poor law commissioners and
of the work of the great officials interested in public health, housing,
and "sanitary conditions." Practically none of this work was done
under academic auspices. The surveys of the middle of the century
were done by government officials. Mayhew's *London Labour and
the London Poor* was the work of a journalist; Booth was a wealthy
shipping merchant who financed and directed his survey as a private
inquiry. Rowntree, who conducted the survey of York called *Poverty:
A Study of Town Life* at the beginning of the century, was also a
wealthy businessman without university connections.

When in the 1920s a *New Survey of London Life and Labour* was
undertaken, it was directed from the London School of Economics,
but it had no connection with the Department of Sociology at the
school. Furthermore, it was a transient enterprise. When the survey
was finished, the organization through which it had been conducted
was disbanded. While the Population Investigation Committee
functioned at the London School of Economics and produced important works in demography and social selection, it worked wholly in-

7. Professor Talcott Parsons spent one year at the London School of
Economics before going to Heidelberg where he also spent a year. Hobhouse,
whose seminar he attended, made no intellectual impact on him—all he could
say of it years later was, quoting Crane Brinton, "Who now reads Herbert
Spencer?" Weber, who had been dead for about five years when Parsons came
to Heidelberg, made a profound impression of lifelong duration. Here again it
is obvious that institutionalization is not the only factor which determines
intellectual impact—in both Germany and in England, in their different ways,
sociology was very slightly institutionalized academically. The power of their
intellectual penetration, the pregnancy of the problem, the scope of its
ramifications, the persuasiveness of the argument (insight, logic, evidence),
and the magnetism of the rhetoric and the responsiveness and intellectual
power of the student are surely of the first importance. Yet, the fact that Weber
had no impact in Germany despite his greatness and his ubiquitous fame shows
that the factor of institutionalization is an independent variable of some
importance.

dependently of the department of sociology. It did not serve to train and recruit professional sociologists, except for Professor David Glass who was at that time a geographer and who came into the department of sociology only after the end of the Second World War. A department of research techniques was created after the war; it was also entirely separate from the department of sociology but it at least represented the institutionalization of social research. By this time, opportunities for employment in social research had begun to increase as a result of the use of survey techniques by government and private business.

American Founders: The Beginnings of Institutional Establishment in the Universities

Sociology had a different fate in the American universities. It became institutionalized earlier in the United States than anywhere else in the world; it became institutionalized earlier at the University of Chicago than elsewhere. Provision for teaching sociology at Columbia and Yale universities also occurred at about the time it did at Chicago, but by the turn of the century provision for training and research began at Chicago—hesitantly but encouragingly. There was not much to show at first. Research was occasional and discontinuous. In its first decade Chicago had little to show apart from very minor and scattered pieces of research. The University of Pennsylvania, which sponsored W. E. B. Du Bois' *The Negro in Philadelphia*, and Columbia University, where James Mickel Williams did a pioneering community study, *An American Town*, as his doctoral dissertation, did not lag markedly behind Chicago at this time. The youth of the latter, the first president's determination to make it into a university in which research was as important as teaching—Gilman had already taken the lead in this direction at Johns Hopkins University—the large number of vigorous young professors wishing to install in Chicago the research-centered seminars which they had known in German universities, created a propitious atmosphere for research from the very start. Furthermore all the departments being new, there was no "old guard" to hamper the immediate establishment of a department of sociology. There was also a "demand" for sociology in the city of Chicago. Movements to improve the condition of the poor and to improve the quality of public institutions were also very active and from the first they drew to themselves the professors of the new university, above all Professors G. R. Henderson and G. H. Mead. It was perhaps the first time that academic sociologists as a class were welcomed by reformers with much practical experience. There were so many propitious signs.

Nonetheless, the movement of sociology was slow and there was little to show for it. Albion Small was steeped in German historical scholarship; indeed, it was there that he had found the origins of sociology. But scholar and idealist that he was, his confidence in the future of the subject with which he had been entrusted by the president of the university rested on its capacity for direct, firsthand observation of the contemporary scene.

Small believed in what later came to be called "empirical research"; he believed in seminars and postgraduate studies where such research would be treated. But for the time being, there were none. Henderson, who was primarily concerned with urban welfare problems, also appreciated the desirability of descriptions and analyses of urban life, particularly the life of the poor, the immigrants, the working classes, etc., but he did not do research either. He also believed that it should be done, that it should be based on firsthand observation, and that its results would be helpful in the improvement of society. The Germanic respect for learning, intellectual curiosity, a belief that what had been inherited was not enough and that the welfare of society had need of it, all made for the conviction that a new type of research was needed. It did not come straightaway. Even W. I. Thomas, who received the third Ph.D. granted by the Department of Sociology and who became in a sense the first American sociologist of the new dispensation continued to work at first from printed scientific literature in physical anthropology and from the published literature of ethnography.[8] Participant-observational studies and the use of human documents came forward only gradually.

W. I. Thomas was more than any other person responsible for this development. He developed further a new type of study which had been created in Germany—the *Volkskunde* of living German rural society, based on field observation and interviewing—but which had never found a place in German university studies in the social sciences.[9] Thomas' readiness to observe directly, to collect the "human documents" of living persons was welcomed by Small and Henderson. They did not think that it was undignified for a professor or for the professor's pupils to wander about the streets or to interest themselves in "low life." This was very different from the German academic situation where even those senior academic figures who were members of the *Verein für Sozialpolitik* and thus very concerned about the condition of the working classes thought that information about them had to be obtained through *Sachverständige*, i.e., from middle-class persons who in a professional capacity—as magistrates,

8. As did William Graham Sumner at Yale. Sumner never went beyond this, and since his students were in the vast majority undergraduates who had no interest in pursuing sociology further Yale did not become an important center of sociology.
9. Thomas spent the academic session of 1888–89 at the universities of Berlin and Göttingen. This was before he enrolled as a Ph.D. student at the University of Chicago which was, in fact, nonexistent during Thomas' German years.

clergymen, municipal administrators, physicians, etc.—were in contact with the lower classes. Even Max Weber in his studies of the East Elban agricultural workers used that device.

This accomplishment of the Chicago Department of Sociology in the first decades of the century hardly seems to be a great intellectual accomplishment. Yet it marked the beginning of a specific and vital feature of modern sociology. It was a change from the concern with abstractly formulated laws, from cut-and-dried pronouncements about statistical regularities; it was an introduction of vividness and immediacy. It linked sociology with journalism and literature. It opened it to a wider audience. It gave it a new strength and added another weakness. This distinctive development went further when, at the beginning of the second decade of the century, W. I. Thomas, succeeded in persuading Robert Park, who until then had led a somewhat errant existence as a newspaperman, an organizer of the American Congo Society, a student in Germany, an assistant in philosophy at Harvard, an amanuensis to Booker T. Washington at Tuskegee Institute, and a man of omnivorous intellectual curiosity and of a capacious and variegated learning, to join the Department of Sociology at Chicago. Park brought with him several things which were already present at Chicago but which he reinforced to the point where they made a great difference. As a newspaperman interested in urban life and as a detached observer of the humanitarian and civic movements, he was already acquainted with the surveys by which civically concerned bodies and individuals had attempted to arouse public opinion regarding the condition of the poor in the great cities. These surveys were an intellectual inheritance from the American promoters of social improvement of the second half of the nineteenth century and the muckrakers at the turn of the century; they were of course greatly influenced by the British surveys of the preceding century.[10]

The surveys which attracted Park's attention had been conceived and carried out without benefit of academic sociology and without any connection with universities; when they were finished, the organization which had been created to carry them out disbanded. There was no provision for training a new generation of "surveyors" or for studious criticism of the techniques with a view to their improvement. The Chicago Department of Sociology changed this. Although the department itself never conducted surveys of the types conducted in Pittsburgh, Cleveland, and Springfield, it assimilated their techniques of direct observation and interviewing and the quantitative treatment—albeit elementary—of results into the training of postgraduate students. It pondered the technique of field study, reflected on interviewing, on the dangers of bias, and on the need to combine

10. See Abrams, Philip, *Origins of British Sociology* (Chicago: University of Chicago Press, 1968).

detachment and intimate understanding. I do not know whether Park had reflected much on these technical matters before he came to Chicago but he certainly thought a lot about them once he settled down to become a professional socioiogist.

Park also brought to Chicago a fresh and vivid sense of the essential themes of German analytical sociology. Park had attended Simmel's lectures at Berlin, he read his works, and he absorbed his views about certain features of modern society,[11] such as the limited character and impersonality of relationships and the rationalizing, calculating attitude. He brought too an awareness of American society outside the large cities of the North and the small towns of the Middle West; Africa, Asia, and Europe were already on his mind. The movements of peoples and the mixing and conflicts of ethnic groups, the restless expansiveness of nationality and the integration of societies through the flow of information were among his interests; they were not identical with Thomas' interests but they were close enough for the two men to precipitate an enduring sociological outlook. They were together only for less than a decade but during that short period each one reinforced the other. Without collaboration on any particular piece of research, they developed a basic consensus. Thomas alone, standing somewhat apart from the piety, humanitarianism, and civic agitation of the other members of the department, might not have had the impact on sociology in the 1920s which he did in fact have. Park, for his part, had never before been constrained by the presence of a powerful intellectual equal in close daily contact. Thomas' presence imposed some discipline on the intellectually wilful Park; and Park tried to formulate some general themes in a more orderly way than he had done before. His essentially ruminative mind was forced into a greater orderliness by the conventions of academic discourse. The combination of Park and Thomas and the intellectual virtues each evoked in the other showed the value of the American departmental mode of organization. The German chair placed the professor in a position of a supreme being whom only professors of the same subject in other universities could criticize—often acrimoniously. Colleagueship is the heart of the department as an institution; it brought valuable results to sociology.

This combination came to fruition just after the end of the First World War—just as Thomas was forced to leave the University of Chicago. Privately financed, nonacademic bodies concerned with the relations of ethnic groups provided *debouchés* for sociologists. Among these

11. He undoubtedly encountered the ideas of Tönnies about *Gemeinschaft* and *Gesellschaft,* but there is no reference to Tönnies in his dissertation, *Masse und Publikum,* or in his autobiographical reminiscences. He did reproduce a section from Tönnies *Die Sitte* (1913) in the *Introduction to the Science of Sociology* (Chicago: The University of Chicago Press, 1921), pp. 103–5.

were the Carnegie Corporation's studies of "Americanization" which enlisted the collaboration of Park and Thomas·and a number of former students at Chicago; the report on *The Negro in Chicago* supported by the Commission on Race Relations, guided by Park, and conducted by Charles Johnson, then a graduate student in the Department of Sociology; and the Chicago Crime Commission, which employed John Landesco. Civic and municipal organizations concerned with juvenile delinquency likewise provided support and employment opportunities as well as willingness to open their records to sociologists. The establishment of the Institute of Juvenile Research provided employment for a number of graduate students, some of whom later became quite eminent sociologists. The institutional framework for a department of sociology which had been provided by Harper, Small, and Henderson before there was an intellectual content to put into it had such a content put into it by Thomas and Park. Without that framework, the content might not even been as well precipitated as it was; certainly this was so in the case of Park. The presence of Thomas, and then, after the latter's departure, the presence of energetic graduate students put Park on his mettle but it also kept him in the discipline of attempting to work out his ideas through teaching and guiding research.

The decade of the 1920s was the time when sociology became well-established institutionally. The teaching of sociology centered on "Park and Burgess," which promulgated the main principles of analysis. Ernest Burgess, whom Park chose as a collaborator, was a younger colleague; he carried on the tradition after Park withdrew. This tradition entailed undergraduate courses, postgraduate courses of lectures, seminars, examinations, individual supervision of small pieces of field research to be submitted as course and seminar papers and dissertations done under close supervision fitting into the scheme of analysis developed by Thomas, Park, and Burgess. It was sustained by the publication of some of the best dissertations in the Chicago Sociological Series published by the University of Chicago Press, which was also the publisher of other works by Chicago social scientists, and by the transformation of the *American Journal of Sociology* from an organ of aspirations and programs into an organ for the publication of the best research being done in the country. It was a means for keeping the graduates who had gone out to teach sociology in other universities and colleges within the intellectual community which had its most intense form in the department. It was reinforced by public authorities and civic groups which offered sponsorship and access to the records needed for research and by financial support from the university and from the Rockefeller Foundation. It was fortified by the proximity of the Department of Political Science in which Charles Merriam, Harold Lasswell, Leonard White, and

Harold Gosnell complemented the work of the Department of Sociology. Merriam had a stock of knowledge on Chicago which was as intense and intimate as Park's, Thomas', and Burgess'.[12] The Local Community Research Committee which he initiated, with funds supplied by the Laura Spelman Rockefeller Memorial fund, brought together all those interested in working on Chicago. Lasswell, who was much younger, had interests as wide as the world; he spent many hours with Park, acknowledging a "long-standing indebtedness" to the older man for "his sagacious insight" and expressing admiration for Park's "creative interplay between hours of high abstraction and days of patient contact with humble detail."[13] Leonard White studied *The Prestige Value of Public Employment in Chicago*[14] and Gosnell studied voting and abstention from voting, and Negro political leaders in Chicago.[15]

> *An International Illustration of the Difference Made by Institutionalization: The Diverse Fates of Horkheimer and Mannheim*

The significance of the institutional setting of sociology even in the limited measure in which it was possible in sociology in Germany in the 1920s and the early 1930s may be seen in the divergent destinies of the ideas of Karl Mannheim on the one side and of Max Horkheimer on the other. The differences in impact of the ideas of Mannheim and Horkheimer after they left Germany also attest to the consequences of the differences between Great Britain and the United States with respect to the institutionalization of sociology.

Mannheim was the more original and many-sided of the two. He had a richer theoretical imagination, a more differentiated perception of contemporary society, a more vivid grasp of particular details than Horkheimer and at least the same breadth of interest in macrosociological anaylsis. His knowledge of contemporary empirical research was greater than Horkheimer's and some of his ideas could more easily have been translated into concrete research problems than Horkheimer's. He wrote more and on more particular topics than Horkheimer. Mannheim raised important problems; he dealt with many issues of which only a few may be mentioned for illustrative purposes: the conditions of political detachment and partisanship

12. Charles E. Merriam, *Chicago: A More Intimate View of Urban Politics* (New York: Macmillan, 1929), and Charles E. Merriam and Harold F. Gosnell, *Non-voting: Causes and Methods of Control* (Chicago: The University of Chicago Press, 1924).

13. Harold D. Lasswell, *World Politics and Personal Insecurity* (New York and London: McGraw-Hill, 1935), pp. v–vi.

14. Chicago: The University of Chicago Press, 1929.

15. *Getting Out the Vote* (Chicago: The University of Chicago Press, 1924), and *Negro Politicians* (Chicago: The University of Chicago Press, 1935).

among intellectuals, the patterns and functions of beliefs in society, the conditions of different forms of conflict and consensus among generations, the influence of different types of political partisanship on conceptions of historical time. He touched on important epistemological questions and had vivid insight. His problems involved matters of great contemporary interest, and some of them were capable of being empirically investigated in the current sociological style. Yet Mannheim has had little influence, and Horkheimer is in certain respects one of the most influential of modern intellectuals. Mannheim was, according to some of his former students, a scintillating teacher, but in Germany he was a professor for only four years before he was forced into exile. Although several very interesting dissertations[16] and other works were produced under his inspiration, the output of his pupils during his Frankfurt period was neither massive nor concentrated enough to provide a focus of attention and to create a far-reaching consensus as to what ought to be done and how to go about it; several of them had in fact to be submitted after the Nazis had come to power and their authors were scattered over the earth. In 1933, Mannheim left Germany and went to the London School of Economics where, as in the time of Hobhouse and Westermarck, there were still very few postgraduate students of sociology, where there was little institutional provision for the organization, support, and supervision of research in sociology, where there was no organ of publication, and where there were no opportunities for the employment of those who had been trained in the subject. The years of the depression blocked numerous potential academic careers in Britain in well-established subjects while the labor market for students of a fledgling subject like sociology remained at a standstill. The war years brought further attrition of what was already meager. Mannheim left the London School of Economics in the middle forties and became professor of the sociology of education at the Institute of Education in London. He died in January 1947. He had, it is true, succeeded in establishing the International Library of Sociology and Social Reconstruction, an eclectic series which became a popular organ of sociological ideas after his death, although few of the works published in the series developed Mannheim's own line of thought.

The fortunes of Horkheimer's ideas were very different. Hork-

16. Hans Gerth, *Die sozialgeschichtliche Lage der bürgerlichen Intelligenz in Deutschland um die Wende des 18ten Jahrhunderts;* Wilhelm Carlé, *Weltanschauung und Presse;* Jakob Katz, *Die Entstehung der Judenassimilation in Deutschland und deren Ideologie.* (These three works were printed only as dissertations.) Norbert Elias, *Uber den Prozess der Zivilisation,* 2 vols. (Basel: Vorlag zum Falken, 1938); Hans Weil, *Die Entstehung des dentichen Bildungsprinzips* (Bonn: F. C. Cohen, 1930), E. Kohn Bramstedt, *Aristocracy and Middle Classes in German Literature in the Nineteenth Century* (London: P. S. King, 1937).

heimer's ideas themselves were relatively simple: all thought is embedded in the historical-social context in which it is conceived; modern society has become increasingly destructive of individuality as authority has become more concentrated and as organization has become more inclusive and more impersonal; man has become a pawn manipulated by the powerful; the capacity for and the use of reason have declined. They were the basic ideas of the "theory of mass society."

In many respects Horkheimer's ideas were like Mannheim's although they were simpler and exhibited a slighter intimacy with the facts of contemporary societies. Horkheimer became in the course of several decades one of the most influential sociological writers of his time. He has certainly had a much greater impact on sociological work than Mannheim. Why was this so?

Horkheimer had the advantage of taking over the professorship of Professor Carl Grünberg, a historian of the emancipation of the peasantry in Central Europe and of the labor and socialist movements. Since before the First World War, Grünberg had produced an admirable scholarly journal, the *Archiv für die Geschichte des Sozialismus und der Arbeiterbewegung*. In the middle 1920s Grünberg began to publish a series of *Beihefte* which contained monographs on the subjects which came within the terms of reference of his chair—terms of reference which were becoming broader throughout the 1920s. An institute of social research was under Grünberg's direction. The same wealthy patrons who supported Grünberg's activities took over the responsibilities for the activities associated with the chair when Horkheimer succeeded to it. When Horkheimer was appointed to succeed Grünberg, the title of the chair was changed from "the history of socialism" to "social philosophy"; the *Archiv für die Geschichte des Sozialismus* was wound up and it was replaced by the *Zeitschrift für Sozialforschung*. The *Zeitschrift für Sozialforschung* and the Institut für Sozialforschung provided Horkheimer with two important institutional conditions for the expansion of his influence. Friedrich Pollock was the editor of the *Zeitschrift* but Horkheimer was obviously the leading spirit intellectually in the determination of editorial policy. The Institute already had to its credit a number of large monographic publications, one of which was a major work of sinological scholarship by the then Marxist scholar, K. A. Wittfogel (*Wirtschaft und Gesellschaft Chinas*), and another, under commission, was a Marxist study of European thought by Franz Borkenau (*Der Übergang von feudalen zum burgerlichen Weltbild*). No additional volumes of the series appeared during the remainder of Horkheimer's direction of the Institute in Germany. The journal was changed in content from the history of socialism and the labor movement to Marxist macrosociology and social psychology which combined

Marxism and psychoanalysis. Only a few issues appeared before the Nazis forced the Institute to cease its activities in Germany and to emigrate. It went first to Paris, where it was given transient hospitality at the Centre de documentation sociale which Charles Bouglé had created and attached to the École normale supérieure. In Paris, the *Zeitschrift* was taken up again and the large collaborative work on *Autorität und Familie* was published. This volume which combined psychoanalysis and Marxism—called "critical philosophy" by Horkheimer and his colleagues—was an impressive undertaking. It brought together the work of numerous collaborators and it testified to Horkheimer's outstanding skill as an organizer.

Since his patrons apparently had much of their wealth abroad, it was possible for Horkheimer to emigrate to the United States, together with his most devoted collaborators, and reassemble the group once he got here. Thanks to Horkheimer's enterprise, the Institute became affiliated to Columbia University. Horkheimer was granted a special status as a member of the staff of Columbia University and close ties were cultivated with certain members of the university. A collective institutional life was maintained and the journal was again produced, this time under the title of *Studies in Philosophy and Social Science*. When the United States entered the war, several of its members found employment in the Office of Strategic Services. Meanwhile, other members were making their way as authors and as scholars. As the war came towards its end, Horkheimer became research director of the American Jewish Committee which granted him a sum of money, which for that time was very large, to conduct a widely ranging study of anti-Semitism. This afforded financial support for a number of the stipendaries and associates of the Institute and it also brought the Institute into closer connection with American academics who were qualified in these techniques of social-psychological research. On the intellectual side, this arrangement permitted the Institute to fuse its "critical" point of view—an amalgam of Marxism, psychoanalysis, and patrician contempt for "mass society," i.e., American society—with the techniques of American social psychology and with the idiom then prevailing in American sociology. The outcome was a weighty, quite technical work on *The Authoritarian Personality* and a number of monographs on anti-Semitism and ethnic prejudices. The former work aroused a great deal of attention and has had a considerable influence on subsequent research. Franz Neumann and Otto Kircheimer, who did not belong to the inner nucleus of the Institute, after their service in the Office of Strategic Services became members of the Department of Government of Columbia University in the postwar expansion of the social sciences. They exercised much influence over younger staff members and postgraduate students. Both were notable scholars in their own right. Leo Löwenthal became professor at the University of California in Berkeley in the School of Speech and in the Department of Sociology. He became a leading writer on "mass culture" and on the sociology of literature. Herbert Marcuse, after having worked in the Office of Strategic Services and having then played a minor role as a "Sovietologist" at the Columbia University Institute of Russian Studies, became a professor at Brandeis and then in California and by the cunning of history, if not of reason, became an intellectual idol of the "new left." After establishing his reputation by warning against the dangers of freedom, Erich Fromm became the apostle of a society to be constituted by love and the sage of "socialist humanism." Karl Wittfogel became a leading anti-Communist student of Chinese history, after having been a crude and aggressive Communist polemicist as a young man in Weimar Germany. He became an eminent member of the University of Washington in Seattle.

The Institute then returned to Germany, carrying with it what it had learned of American sociological and social psychological techniques, and its own "critical philosophy" and its theory of mass society. It began at once a monograph series—not at all like the historical-sociological studies of the pre-Nazi period, but based to some extent on fieldwork, on interviews, sample surveys, group discussions, etc. Horkheimer and Adorno came to rank with the leading intellectual figures of the German Federal Republic.

In Germany, Jürgen Habermas, the leading protégé of Horkheimer and Adorno, became the main exponent of "critical sociology" and for a time one of the main intellectual inspirations of the Sozialistsche Deutsche Studentenbund. One of its younger associates, Ludwig von Friedenburg, became minister of education in the government of Hesse in which capacity he promoted the "emancipationist" doctrine of the Institute in the reform of primary and secondary education until he was forced to resign.

But the history of the Institut für Sozialforschung in Weimar Germany, the United States, and the Federal German Republic is not just the story of the cat which landed on its feet. It is a testimonial to the skill of a shrewd academic administrator, who by good luck and foresight inherited a favorable institutional situation and developed its connections within the various universities in which it was located, maintained its internal structure, and extended its external connections outside the university. As a result it became the mechanism by which some of the most influential ideas of present-day sociology developed. The doctrine of "mass society," which asserts the dehumanizing effects of subjugation by authority and which analyzes "mass culture" as a result of this dehumanization owes a great deal to the Institut für Sozialforschung. The allegations about the potentialities for fascism in liberal-democratic societies, and the delineation of the "power elite" are likewise in debt to the Institute. It has not only provided current ideas of the "new left," it has influenced and called forth a large amount of research among sociologists who had no direct connection with that political belief. In contrast with this, Karl Mannheim, who lacked the institutional setting which might have helped to create an orderly following, has found none since his death, despite the repeated calls for a sociology of knowledge.

This digression about the Institut für Sozialforschung has been intended only to show the significance of institutional establishment for the propagation of a set of ideas. Institutionalization is not a guarantee of truthfulness: it only renders more probable the consolidation, elaboration, and diffusion of the set of ideas which possess an appropriate institutional counterpart. It is not the sole determinant of the acceptance of diffusion of ideas. Intellectual persuasiveness, appropriateness to "interesting" problems, affinity with certain prior dispositions and patterns of thought of the potential recipient are also very significant. Institutionalization serves however to make the ideas so affected more available to potential recipients, it increases attention to them and renders concentration of effort on them more likely. In so far as it offers the possibility of a professional career in the cultivation of the particular intellectual activity, it both makes more likely the continuity and concentration and it adds a further motive for further exertion on their behalf. The existence of practical-intellectual professions which require the study of a particular body of knowledge as a qualification and as a constituent of professional practice provides a student body and teaching opportunities—and therewith research opportunities which develop in the interstices of teaching. In these ways, institutional establishment has made a difference in determining which currents of the heterogeneous tradition of sociology have become dominant.

The Institution of Sociology and Academic Systems

The practice of sociology may be seen as a constellation of centers and a set of overlapping and concentric circles formed by institutions and individuals. In Durkheim's case we saw the creation by an outstanding individual of a rudimentary institution of sociological work, which did not attain, however, an elaborated corporate structure in the production of the works themselves. Durkheim did not conduct seminars; he held informal discussions with his protégés. A corporate form was achieved in the organization and production of the *Année sociologique* and the *Travaux de l'Année sociologique*. The circle which Durkheim formed was a rudimentary institutionalization. It had various *ad hoc* connections with other institutions, e.g., the École pratique des hautes études, the École des langues orientales, etc., where the informally adherent members of the circle had their employment, and with Félix Alcan, the publisher of their works. Durkheim himself held a professorship at the Sorbonne and he himself therefore was an incorporated member of an academic institution: it was not, however, in that capacity that he organized the work of his circle. He created a protoinstitution with only peripheral and fragmentary institutional connections.

Max Weber's activity as a sociologist was much less institutionalized. He was not a professor of the subject; he supervised for a limited period several research projects for the Verein für Sozialpolitik, he tried—and failed—to institutionalize two research projects on the press and on voluntary associations through the Deutsche Gesellschaft für Soziologie; he wrote *Wirtschaft und Gesellschaft* as one section of a comprehensive series of handbooks on economics, organized by the publisher Siebeck; he edited a great journal of social science and social policy, very little of which was devoted to sociology. The connections of his sociological activities with institutions were peripheral, fragmentary, and transient.

Thomas and Park were more institutionalized in their practice of sociology—they taught the subject regularly within the framework of a systematic course of study, organized toward the granting of an undergraduate degree; they taught courses, conducted seminars, and supervised the research of students who were working towards postgraduate degrees. They themselves conducted organized research projects, employing assistants or collaborators, supported by university or externally granted funds. Many of the students whom they trained went on towards sociological careers as teachers and research workers. They occupied a constitutionally provided position in the structure of the university. They were linked relatively densely with civic, municipal, and private bodies which were interested in the results of their research and which encouraged them by their interest and occasionally by their financial support as well as by accommodating research workers in their midst or under their auspices. In the 1920s, private philanthropic foundations established the grant of funds for sociology, the Social Science Research Council established predoctoral and, later, postdoctoral fellowships for the promotion of sociology; some of these fellowships were granted for study in Chicago. In the decade of the depression, Chicago sociologists found employment as social statisticians in a number of governmental departments and agencies. Thus Chicago sociology, i.e., the sociology of Thomas and Park, was institutionally established at its center and in a fairly dense network of connected institutions removed at various degrees from their main activities in education and research.

The primary institutional system of sociology is thus affected by its linkages with the environing institutional context—the university itself, foundations, civic bodies, government, occupational careers, publishing enterprises, etc. The availability of the external institutions was of some consequence for the internal, primary institutional establishment of sociology, by the provision of legitimacy through the sponsorship of established institutions and through the provision of resources and opportunities for employment of students who had been awarded degrees in the subject.

The study of the establishment and diffusion of sociology and the influence of this process of institutionalization on the substantive composition of the sociological traditions cannot be confined to the study of primary institutionalization. It is necessary to ask why sociology was able to become institutionalized at a particular time in the United States when it did not become equally institutionalized in Europe, although at the same time the intellectual accomplishments of European sociology were greater in certain respects than those of American sociology.

To account for this we must go beyond the tradition of sociology and beyond the primary institutionalization of sociology. We must consider the wider social structures which permitted it, or inhibited it, or fostered it. The academic systems first of all: In Germany the creation of a new chair depended on the consensual decision of other professors in the same faculty (rivals for resources and prestige), of the university senate, and of the state minister of education. A new subject might be created by a *Privatdozent* but it could not by virtue of that become established in the university. An old university had an established allocation of resources, the beneficiaries of which would not readily allow it to be changed in favor of a subject lacking the legitimacy of age and accomplishment. New universities were more likely to allow new subjects to be taught than longer-established universities—thus sociology was first given the dignity of a professorial chair in Cologne which was founded—for the second time—in 1919 and in the University of Frankfurt which was founded as a private university in 1914. It became established as a teaching subject more easily in technical colleges than in universities. It was more sympathetically viewed by ministers of culture after the republican regime was established at the end of the First World War.

In France as in Germany, universities were rigid. The oligarchy of established professors of a faculty and the high degree of centralization of the control over the total university system in the hands of the national ministry of education hindered the creation of new chairs for new subjects. In British universities, although a chair was created at the London School of Economics in 1902—on a private endowment—no additional chair was created until after the Second World War.[17] At Oxford and Cambridge, the matter was not even canvassed until after the Second World War and then the democratic

17. Westermarck's chair was occupied only during the Easter term of each year from 1907 to 1930.

oligarchy of the representatives of established subjects in those universities prevented the diversion of resources to a subject of questionable legitimacy.

In the United States, in contrast with the academic systems of Europe, the universities were independent of central control and professors of established subjects did not rule the universities. Sociology first became institutionalized in the era of the autocratic university president. Such a president could create a new department if he desired to do so and if he could persuade the board of trustees to agree and raise the financial resources to pay for it. The availability of private financial support and the practice of its active solicitation gave a flexibility to university budgets which the European universities did not have. This too helped.

It was not, however, only the structure of government of the universities which facilitated the earlier academic establishment of sociology in the United States. There were in the middle-western American culture of the period of the establishment of sociology a number of features which made a notable difference. It was in the Middle West that sociology first became academically established—in Chicago, Wisconsin, and Michigan primarily but also in Indiana, Iowa, Nebraska, and Illinois. The intellectual leaders of the universities of the Middle West were in a relationship of rivalry with the hegemony of the older Eastern universities; they were distrustful of what they thought was the excessive respect for the past of those universities. They thought that knowledge was not degraded by being about contemporary and practical things. There was, in short, no hard, thick incrustation of genteel, traditional, humanistic, Christian, patrician culture such as prevailed in the older universities in the East. The hierarchy of deference was weaker in the Middle West, there was more egalitarianism and a greater sympathy with the common life, more understanding for ordinary people and therefore more readiness to be intellectually and socially concerned about them.

Among middle-western intellectuals—publicistic and academic social science intellectuals—there was a more critical attitude towards the activities of the business class—industrialists, railway magnates, and bankers of the Eastern seaboard—and a greater skepticism about the adequacy of the classical economic theory which was adduced to explain their actions. It was in the Middle West that "institutional economics" was developed, most notably by John R. Commons, who emphasized that there was more to society than what was accounted for by classical economic theory.[18] Sociological jurisprudence was

18. Walton Hamilton, prior to going to Amherst where his pupils included Talcott Parsons, was at the University of Texas—away from the pressure of conventional economics. It should however be acknowledged that Johns Hopkins University in Baltimore played an early part in this introduction of Ger-

part of the same atmosphere; in the United States it was largely the work of Roscoe Pound from Nebraska and Brandeis, an outsider by origin to the dominant culture of the educated classes of the northeastern part of the country. Pound, despite his sociological interest, did not succeed in having a department of sociology established at Harvard University. At the University of Chicago, the most eminent professor of law, Ernst Freund, collaborated with sociologists and political scientists in numerous civic enterprises.

Quite apart from the cultural relations of the Middle West and the Eastern seaboard, it should be pointed out that the middle-western universities, even those which were founded before the Civil War, became intellectually expansive at that time. Harvard, Princeton, Columbia, Yale, Pennsylvania had developed strong cultures of their own before the Civil War and they were, therefore, somewhat more resistant to the German academic culture which was being brought back into the United States by an increasing number of young men with scientific and scholarly ambitions in the post–Civil War period. German historicism, which was one of the main sources of sociology, and the conception of the university as a scene of teaching and research were more readily received in the Middle West—at Chicago, Wisconsin, and Michigan especially, than in the older universities of the East. Johns Hopkins University, which was only a little older than the University of Chicago and which was the first university in the country to receive and adapt the German model of research and research training, did not establish a department of sociology for many years.

Sociology and the Larger Intellectual Tradition

In Great Britain the empirical tradition of sociology grew up in a setting of a tradition of the discussion of the control of authority. Authority was to be scrutinized and held to account; it had to justify itself by its actions. From Bacon to Bentham, there developed also a related tradition of belief which asserted that systematically gathered empirical knowledge—scientific knowledge—could be an instrument for the improvement of man's estate. The great civil servants who encouraged the system of social reporting which accompanied the legislation enacted under Benthamite inspiration were themselves the heirs of this tradition. Knowledge acquired through field surveys, the acquisition of information from experts and experienced persons through questionnaires and through depositions before commissions of inquiry were intended to be assimilated into the process of enacting

---

man historicism into the United States. But Johns Hopkins was the new university of the country until the University of Chicago was founded. (Simon N. Patten was an exception who does not fit into this picture; his most eminent pupil was Rexford Tugwell, who did not take any interest in sociology.)

laws and verifying their efficacy. The ancient English universities and the Scottish universities did not share this attitude towards knowledge, and public opinion outside the universities did not share it sufficiently to pervade the universities and cause them to change their minds. This belief was confined to limited circles of politicians, publicists, businessmen, and administrators.

The situation was otherwise in the United States. There was a fairly widespread belief in the superior value of a life illuminated by knowledge of nature and of man. There was also a widespread belief in the value of knowledge as an integral part of ameliorative action. The federal establishment of the land grant colleges and the generous support by middle western state legislatures was impelled by this belief which was best realized in the state of Wisconsin. There, academic social scientists, perhaps earlier than anywhere else, were summoned by politicians to aid them in the drafting and execution of legislation. Even sociologists like Robert Park, who was not very sanguine about the efficacy of movements for reform, thought that the results of social research would enter into public opinion and thus affect the state of society. There is no evidence that Park ever read the writings of Jeremy Bentham, but he believed that social surveys which disclosed an existing condition of society enlightened public opinion and brought moral judgment into play and were therefore integral to the movement of society. In his analysis of "collective behavior" he used to point to the role of the "survey movement" as a stage in the mobilization of belief about what had to be done to improve social conditions. The view of the matter held by sociologists was shared by many other persons in civic organizations, in business, and in the learned professions. However censorious traditional historians, economic theorists, and physicists within the universities might have been about the capacities of sociology, there were at the same time other quite estimable persons who had higher hopes for what sociological knowledge could offer to what they thought was a rational program of the improvement of society. The willingness of wealthy individuals and organizations to support sociological research gave this research a ground for self-respect at a time when its intellectual achievements were still insufficient for that purpose.

This is not to say that the intellectual content of the sociology which was taking form within the support of this extra-academic attitude was determined by it. It does mean, however, that the prevailing culture outside the universities contributed to the institutional establishment of sociology in the United States. The particular subject-matters of sociology in the United States—and in Great Britain—were also in part selected by the direction of interest of its sympathizers, admirers, and patrons. The principles of interpretation—the intellectual substance of the central tradition—derived, however, from more strictly intellectual sources, and increasingly so as the years passed.

The Ecology of Sociology

An intellectual field or discipline has an ecological pattern as well as an institutional structure. Intellectual activities have, of course, a spatial location but ecology is not just about position in space; it is also about hierarchy, about domination and subordination, and about the movements to and fro, upward and downward. Institutional establishment occurs within a bounded space. Ecological processes are about the relationships between the institutions within their bounded spaces. To illustrate: we would say that sociology became institutionally established at Chicago, Wisconsin, and Columbia; the positions of Chicago, Wisconsin, and Columbia in the cosmos of American sociology would fall into what I call here the ecological sphere. Institutionalization and ecological position are closely related to each other; there is no clear definitional boundary between them—at least thus far—but they can nonetheless be distinguished from one another, as they are in this paper.

The construction of a relatively new idea in a tradition always occurs in space, and so does its acceptance. A successful idea is one which is true and which finds acceptance by someone other than its creator. This always involves some movements in space. Obviously the rational pervasiveness of an idea is one of the major determinants of the extent of its movement, but it is not the only one. Institutionalization is one of the factors which affects the directions of the spatial movement of an intellectual activity and its substantive results, just as it is a mechanism of elaboration, promotion, or utilization of ideas. Ideas are likely to move with more momentum if they are institutionalized at their place of origin; just as they are more likely to be taken up, elaborated and "used"—at least up to a certain point—the more institutionalized they are at their place of reception.[19]

The movements are both national and international.

International

From Germany. Before the First World War Max Weber seems to have been quite unknown in the rest of Europe and in the United

19. Science in the heroic age might be reexamined in the light of the approach taken in this paper. Aside from the genius of its main actors, it owes some of its growth to its informal organization as a society of correspondence among individual scientists who worked in relatively dense centers of scientific activity. It is plausible to say that before the existence of scientific periodicals a more important role was filled by communication directly addressed to particular scientists. This gave individual scientists more control over where their ideas went in their own lifetime. Nonetheless, the directly addressed audience of known persons remains an important feature of contemporary science. The publication of books and papers apparently addressed to an almost entirely anonymous audience does not mean that their contents move in all directions randomly and indifferently to their authors' intentions.

States despite his journey to the exposition in St. Louis and the publication of one paper in English in the proceedings of the conference held there. Hugo Munsterberg, a German philosopher and psychologist then teaching at Harvard University, arranged for Weber's invitation to the exposition but he did nothing else which made Weber's ideas known in America. No American sociologist referred to Max Weber before the First World War. Even Albion Small, who knew a lot of German sociological literature, did not refer to him in his writings; there is no evidence that he dealt with him in his teaching. Troeltsch's *Die Bedeutung des Protestantismus,* with numerous references to Weber, was translated into English in the Crown Theological Library, yet this too passed unnoticed by American sociologists.

After the First World War, the situation did not change much. Frank Knight of Chicago, who was always interested in the limits of neoclassical, analytical economic theory, while himself being one of the most eminent economic theorists of the interbellum period, translated the *Wirtschaftsgeschichte,* the book made up from the lectures which Weber delivered at Munich in the last year of his life. It was not noticed by sociologists. The appearance of Parsons' translation of the first part of the *Religionssoziologie* likewise made no stir among sociologists. Theodore Abel's doctoral dissertation at Columbia, W. J. Warner's doctoral dissertation at the London School of Economics, Heinrich Maurer's writings in the *American Journal of Sociology,* Parsons' Heidelberg dissertation on Weber and Sombart, and L. J. Benniou's dissertation on Weber's methodology were the first writings by American sociologists in the 1920s to deal with Weber. It is interesting that three of them were done as doctoral dissertations outside the United States; only one of them was done in a leading department of sociology.

There was more attention to Max Weber in the United States in the 1930s. The Graduate Faculty of Social and Political Science at the New School of Social Research presented Weber's ideas in their courses and in their journal, *Social Research.* Knight gave a seminar on *Wirtschaft und Gesellschaft* at Chicago in 1935; von Schelting lectured and held seminars on Weber at Columbia in the second half of the 1930s; the appearance in 1936 of the English translation of Mannheim's *Ideologie und Utopie* brought some of Weber's ideas before a wider audience. Taylor Cole's dissertation at Harvard on the Swiss civil service was part of the thickening atmosphere of awareness of Weber's ideas. The most decisive event however was the publication in 1937 of Talcott Parsons' *The Structure of Social Action.* It was a work of fundamental theoretical importance in its own right; it was a clarification, elaboration, and extension of some of Weber's own fundamental ideas and it was also a rich restatement of certain principal themes of Weber's work. It was a memorable movement in the ecology of sociology.

In France Weber seems to have caused not even a ripple. Durkheim reviewed Marianne Weber's book on the legal status of women—rather slightingly—but he did not discuss Max Weber. I do not know of any reference to Max Weber in France before the First World War aside from those contained in the French translation of Sombart's *Der Bourgeois*. The two leading Germanists in France at this time were Charles Andler and Lucien Herr. Neither of them seems to have paid any attention to Weber. In the numerous denunciations of German professors by French professors during the war, Max Weber's existence and his criticism of imperial policy passed unnoticed.

The situation did not change significantly after the end of the war. French sociology itself was in a process of dissolution after the death of Durkheim. Only Maurice Halbwachs, at Strasbourg in that period, knew of Weber and in fact wrote in an obscure Strasbourg journal one of the most understanding of any of the secondary treatments of Weber's ideas on the Protestant ethic and the growth of capitalism and then, in 1929, a more comprehensive essay on Weber in the *Annales de l'histoire économique et sociale*. Then there was silence until Raymond Aron wrote a well-rounded, thoroughly informed chapter on Weber in his little book on *Sociologie française contemporaine*. Then there was silence again until after the Second World War, when under Aron's auspices translations of some of Weber's work began to appear in French and Aron himself lectured at the Sorbonne on him and then published a full treatment of Weber's ideas in *les Étapes de la pensée sociologique*. Since that time, Max Weber's ideas, although not absorbed, have been present in France as much as those of any serious foreign writer of the present century.

In Italy too, Weber was unknown.[20] Pareto never referred to him, nor did Mondolfo or Antonio Labriola. Only his protégé, Roberto Michels, who in 1907 had become a *Privatdozent* (*libero docento*) in Turin, referred to his writings steadily; but there was no echo. The situation did not change significantly until after the Second World War and the end of the Fascist regime. Then many books began to treat Weber's ideas, e.g., those of Carlo Antoni, Paolo Rossi, and Franco Ferrarotti. *Wirtschaft und Gesellschaft* was translated into Italian.

There were a number of references to Max Weber in British publications before the First World War. The translation of Troeltsch's *Die Bedeutung des Protestantismus* in English under the title of *Protestantism and Progress* was the first appearance of Weber's name in

20. It appears that his "Agrarverhältnisse im Altertum," and *Zur Geschichte der Handelsgesellschaften im Mittelalter* were unknown to Italian classical historians and medievalists of his time.

Great Britain. Not long after that an essay by an Anglican clergyman, H. G. Wood, in an anthology on the rights and duties of the owners of property referred again to the Protestant ethic. By the 1920s there were many references to Weber in the British literature; George O'Brien's *The Economic Effects of the Reformation* and, above all, R. H. Tawney's *Religion and the Rise of Capitalism* brought the "Weber-thesis" to public attention. It became sufficiently known for John Clapham at Cambridge to prompt his pupil H. M. Robertson to write a doctoral dissertation which denied Weber's argument; it was published under the name of *The Rise of Economic Individualism*. In sociology proper, Morris Ginsberg was quite well acquainted with Max Weber's writings but did not regard them sympathetically.

The situation changed in 1933 with the coming of Karl Mannheim and a considerable number of refugees, one of whom, Franz Neumann, was for a time a postgraduate student at the London School of Economics. Mannheim presented Weber's ideas in his teaching and by references in his writings. T. H. Marshall and Morris Ginsberg did the same. This was a time when, despite the limited existence of sociology in Great Britain, Max Weber's ideas became accepted as part of the subject—and not just as an ingenious thesis bearing on a much-discussed problem of economic history. I think that this was to a large extent a result of Mannheim's propaganda for his own kind of sociology, which included much that was derived from Weber's ideas.

After the Second World War, partly as a result of the assimilation of Max Weber into American sociology, Weber became more or less naturalized in British sociology. His writings became as much a part of the British academic syllabus in sociology as they were of the academic syllabus in the United States.

At the beginning of the century Simmel was better known abroad than Max Weber. In France the *Année sociologique* published a translation of one of his works. Durkheim's early approval changed markedly: both *Soziologie* and *Die Philosophie des Geldes* were censured by Durkheim, and that was the end of Simmel as far as French sociology was concerned. In the United States various essays of Simmel appeared in English translation in the *American Journal of Sociology;* translations were published before the appearance in Chicago of Robert Park. It was undoubtedly Small who was responsible, but there was no trace of Simmel's ideas in Small's work. Only when Robert Park came to Chicago did Simmel's ideas take up residence in Chicago sociological research. Simmel's influence received its definitive expression in Louis Wirth's "Urbanism as a Way of Life," whence it became a common possession of American sociology, but this took place very much later.

Simmel was also taken up in the United States by Arthur Bentley, who attended Simmel's lectures in Berlin in the academic session of 1893–94. Simmel's ideas about groups overlapping in membership and the common ground of parties in antagonism appeared in Bentley's writings. But Bentley was not a university teacher, he was a journalist and then a private scholar and it was only after many years that his ideas began to exercise influence in political science through their assimilation in an already existing interest in "pressure groups." As far as sociology is concerned, Bentley seems to have had little influence although he taught for one year as a "docent" in the department of sociology at the University of Chicago. Despite the intellectual congeniality of Albion Small, who shared Bentley's interest in Simmel and Gumplowicz, Bentley departed for journalism and farming without leaving a mark on sociology.

Tönnies, despite his sojourn in Great Britain, his major contribution to Hobbesian studies, his close affinity to Henry Sumner Maine, and his great emphasis on quantitative work, found no response in British sociology. Durkheim knew *Gemeinschaft und Gesellschaft* but despite a certain community of outlook, criticized it sharply, and his adherents made no use of Tönnies' ideas. In the United States on the other hand, these ideas were resonant in Park's writing and teaching. Tönnies' main categories and theories, like those of Simmel, entered into American sociology through Robert Park's and Robert MacIver's writings.

The Austrian sociologists whose names were once famous may be mentioned here. They are Gustav Ratzenhofer and Ludwig Gumplowicz. The former was a professional soldier whose sociological work was avocational; the latter was professor of law at the University of Graz, and his sociology too was avocational. Their works were widely read in Europe but their effective contribution to sociology came about as a result of their being read by Albion Small. Unlike German sociologists of his time, Small was in a position in which what he read and accepted could make a difference to the generation which followed him. There have been writers of great influence whose work was not carried on and diffused in the setting of institutional establishment: Charles Darwin was the greatest of these but many other instances could be given. Nonetheless, under modern conditions, when so much of intellectual activity is institutionally established, those authors whose work is not produced and diffused in such a setting are handicapped. Both Gumplowicz and Ratzenhofer were victims of this situation. Only the intervention of Small into the path of their writings permitted them to have a longer afterlife in sociology. This seems to have come about in obscure and indirect ways. I do not know whether Small encountered their writings while he was studying in Germany or whether he encountered them by reading reviews and following up clues given by other writers. He did however give their ideas a prominent place in his own sociological theory. W. I. Thomas, who was less interested in the theories of other sociologists, must have found the views of the two men congruent with his own interests in the conflicts of national groups in German Poland. They were certainly attractive to Robert Park. Park did not show much interest in Gumplowicz and Ratzenhofer before he came to Chicago and he did not cite them frequently in the 1920s or after. But I have the impression that during the First World War, when he was attempting to develop his conception of the four processes of competition, conflict, accommodation, and assimilation, he was rather affected by their view about the conflicts of ethnic and national groups. Thus although their names are no longer seriously considered when the forerunners and founders of sociology are enumerated, they have anonymously entered into the substantive tradition of sociology. They have been enabled to do so because their ideas were taken up by scholars in an academic institution and were incorporated there into a widely used textbook and into the syllabus of instruction.

From France. For founding ideas to travel across national boundaries in subjects which have no universally intelligible symbolism such as that provided by mathematics, language barriers must be absent or there must be many translations. There must also be, as in the case of the Weber-Parsons relationship, a strong intellectual personality who has immersed himself deeply in the founding ideas and who can sustain the newly acquired ideas either with the aid of institutions in the new setting or through sheer force of intellectual character.

Durkheim's ideas traveled little out of France because there was no one to carry them. Ziya Gökalp took them to Turkey, but that was a dead end because Gökalp, although he taught sociology at Salonika and became professor of the subject in Istanbul, was not a strong intellectual personality: he was more interested in legitimating Turkish nationalism and secularism than in sociological theory and research. Nor did he have research students. One of the reasons why he had none was that there would have been no careers for them. There was nothing in British sociology of the period before the Second World War which bore marks of Durkheim's influence. *Les formes elémentaires de la vie réligieuse* was first translated and published in Great Britain in 1912. It did not create much of an impression, certainly not in the very restricted circles which were interested in sociology. Although students of religion such as Clement Webb—who was negative—and anthropologists like Radcliffe-Brown—who was positive—were interested, it did not gain the serious consideration of Hobhouse or Westermarck. Durkheim visited England once, at the beginning of the century, and delivered a lecture before the Sociological Society justifying the existence of sociology. The brevity of the visit, the inconsequentiality of the subject, and the absence of receiving institutions formed no bridge over which Durkheim's ideas could travel. Sociology did not yet exist as a university subject in England at the time of Durkheim's visit. Sociology was a subject of the laity which was interested in eugenics, in evolution, and in the condition of the poor. There was nothing in Durkheim which made an immediate sympathetic connection with any of these.[21]

Germans took no interest in those ideas of Durkheim which were available in the original, in German translation, or in the surveys of the sociological theories of Squillace and Sorokin and in the dissertation of a Roumanian named Georges Marica. There was an extended treatment of Durkheim and his followers in *Philosophische Strömungen der Gegenwart im Frankreich,* a work written in German by a Swiss, Isaac Benrubi. I cannot recall its having ever been cited by a German sociologist nor do I recall Durkheim ever being mentioned in the 1920s by Ernst Robert Curtius, who was the chief German connoiseur of French intellectual life.

Max Weber never referred to Durkheim. Tönnies had some interest in Durkheim but his views were not affected by him. Max Scheler was the only important sociologist who took seriously some of Durkheim's ideas as they bore on his own effort to construct a sociology of knowledge. Franz Jerusalem was also aware that Durkheim had something to say about that subject. Karl Mannheim studiously avoided reference to Durkheim in his essay on the sociology of knowledge in the *Handwörterbuch der Soziologie.* The other German sociologists who were interested primarily in classificatory schemes had no occasion to bring Durkheim into their work.

Durkheim fared only a little better in his first contacts with American sociology. In the United States before 1914, sociology was either under the inspiration of Germanic ethnographic erudition, e.g., William Graham Sumner, or it was conscientiously making its first contacts with the poor of the big cities—an effort unprecedented in academic life but carrying on a civic tradition which had been cultivated by philanthropists and administrators in France, Great Britain, and the United States over about three-quarters of a century. Theoretically, it was struggling with the idea of "social forces" and the facts of social conflict, disorder, and change. It too was critical of the inherited evolutionary theory of Herbert Spencer but it did not quite find an acceptable answer in *De la Division du travail social.* Perhaps American sociologists thought that their intellectual guidance could best come from Germany. Durkheim's existence was certainly

---

21. Durkheim did exert through Radcliffe-Brown a marked influence on British social anthropology, but until very recently the social anthropology deriving from Radcliffe-Brown and Malinowski had very little connection with British sociology.

known to Small but he did not assimilate any of his ideas into his own writings or teachings. There were only two American sociologists who had the theoretical sensibility to learn from Durkheim before the First World War, because they were both deep and learned enough to have been able to accommodate his ideas. One was William I. Thomas, whose study of the European sociological literature ceased as he immersed himself in his great inquiry into the Polish immigrant in America.[22] As far as I know, Thomas was quite ignorant of Durkheim; he certainly did not regard him as a source of his ideas, although as a matter of fact his views in many matters were very close to Durkheim's.[23]

The other was Robert Park, who had studied in Strasbourg, Heidelberg, and Berlin with Windelband and Simmel, but whose knowledge of Durkheim—and of Max Weber for that matter—was slight but appreciative. Park was pleased to have Durkheim's idea of *représentations collectives* since that fitted so harmoniously into his own ideas about the mechanisms of public opinion and collective behavior. Later in his life, he was much drawn to the idea of anomie as a description of certain aspects of urban society, but I have the impression that it was his reading of Elton Mayo more than his reading of Durkheim which commended it to him.[24]

Charles Gehlke, who later became professor of sociology at Ohio State University, wrote a doctoral dissertation at Columbia University on Durkheim. It was nominally about Durkheim's "contribution to sociological theory" but it was in the main about his definition of a social fact. Gehlke apparently never wrote anything in subsequent years in which Durkheim's ideas were applied. Nonetheless, Park did read the dissertation, and some of his knowledge of *représentations collectives* came from it.

At Chicago, under the inspiration of Park and Burgess, Mrs. Ruth Shonle Cavan wrote a book, *Suicide,* in which Durkheim was not

22. It may be noted in passing that not many years earlier Max Weber had studied the German side of the same problem—the impact of the immigration of Polish agricultural laborers into the East Elban landed estates—while Thomas was studying the consequences for the Polish immigrants of their movement into the United States. There is no evidence that Thomas was aware of Max Weber's work on the subject.

23. Thomas' *Source Book for Social Origins* contains nothing written by Durkheim and there are only two references to articles by Durkheim in a bibliography of forty-two pages.

24. I knew him well in the period just after his retirement from the University of Chicago and used often to talk with him, or rather listen to him, but he never mentioned Durkheim or Weber, even though he knew I was more or less conversant with European sociology. I attended his last lectures at the University of Chicago in the spring of 1934, and, although Bagehot, Tarde, and Sighele and all sorts of books including Theodore Geiger's *Die Masse und ihre Aktion* were mentioned, Durkheim was passed over without a word. There were, however, two excerpts from Durkheim in *An Introduction to the Science of Sociology.*

more than mentioned. Ellsworth Faris never did more than refer to the "exteriority of the social fact." The important research in *Mental Disorder in Urban Areas* by Robert Faris and Warren Dunham—a very "Durkheimian" problem—also did not consider Durkheim's ideas about social and personal disorganization. Herbert Blumer at the beginning of the 1930s knew the writings of Durkheim and his followers and heirs very well, but I do not think that he ever wrote anything about it. His various critical essays about certain trends in American sociology were made from an anti-individualistic, anti-psychologistic standpoint which showed the influence of his Durkheimian studies. Durkheim had been given a bad name by Alexander Goldenweiser in 1916 and it took a long time for his reputation in the United States to recover.

The implantation of Durkheim's ideas in the United States was largely the work of Elton Mayo and Talcott Parsons. I am not certain how Elton Mayo came to be interested in Durkheim. Perhaps it was through Radcliffe-Brown. Nonetheless it was through Mayo that the idea of anomie, which he applied in the interpretation of the results of the studies of the Western Electric plant at Hawthorne, Illinois, became better known to American sociologists. Professor Parsons' interest in Durkheim grew in the atmosphere generated by Elton Mayo and Lawrence Henderson in the late 1920s and early 1930s. At a time when there was little interest in Durkheim in France, and not much more in the United States, it was Professor Parsons whose imaginative reinterpretation of Durkheim placed him into a position in sociological thought which he scarcely occupied even in his own lifetime in France. As a result of the prominence conferred by Parsons' treatment in *The Structure of Social Action* and the subsequent translation or republication of the old translations of Durkheim's books, American sociologists began to study Durkheim seriously for the first time. Parsons' assimilation of Durkheim to Weber's themes and categories helped in this, as did the facts that *Suicide* was a statistical study and *De la Division du travail social* was so systematically and even schematically formulated that it seemed to lend itself to the construction of scientific hypotheses. Robert Merton, who first studied Durkheim under Parsons and Sorokin, and Lloyd Warner, who was guided by Elton Mayo, also gave strong impetus to the installation of Durkheim in American sociology. Merton's systematic reformulation of the concept of anomie made it into a common possession of sociologists. It has entered from his essay on the subject, reproduced in *Social Theory and Social Structure*, into the studies of criminality and delinquency and of what is now called "deviancy," poverty, rebellion, and "counter-culture." It has given new life to the older study of "social disorganization" and "social pathology." Lloyd Warner's success was smaller, but, for his invocation of Durkheim in the last volume of his voluminous work on "Yankee City," Warner must be given some of the credit for the growth of appreciation of Durkheim among social anthropologists and hence for the establishment of many bridges between sociology and social anthropology which is one of the overdue accomplishments of recent years.

From Great Britain. The relatively uninstitutionalized structure of British sociology up to 1914 permitted a great miscellany of sociological tendencies to have an erratic existence. Some of them, such as the interest in genetics and eugenics, came subsequently to have a very great impact on American sociology and then on sociology all over the world through the development of refined statistical measures of general application and of less weighty but still considerable influence on the study of social mobility. Francis Galton was in both cases the great progenitor. Sorokin's *Social Mobility,* which summarized the great body of this literature, was a significant transmitter of this influence. Taussig and Joslyn's *American Business Leaders,* Bendix and Lipset's *Social Mobility in Industrial Society,* Blau and Duncan's *Occupational Mobility in the United States,* to mention a few of the high points, owe much to the stimulus and techniques which arose from this current of British sociology. (Two important intermediaries of this influence were Hogben's *Political Arithmetic* and Glass' *Social Mobility in Britain.*)

No less important was the related field of the social survey of the condition of the urban working classes. This is one of the oldest traditions of British sociology, and the surveys in London and York at the turn of the century had a marked influence on American urban sociology. Robert Park assimilated their lessons and adapted them to the financial position of doctoral research at the University of Chicago. The study of *Middletown* was the first major American survey of an entire community, and it too bears the marks of the British influence—although it was much influenced by the original work of Galpin and his colleagues and the social anthropology being developed by Franz Boas at Columbia. The technique received a tremendous impetus from the development of sample surveys of opinion which began to flourish in the 1930s.

The evolutionary sociology deriving in part from Spencer did not find much response in the United States, except marginally in the work of Sumner, in the early works of Thomas, and in the unimportant textbooks now rightly forgotten.

These great influences on sociology in the United States and elsewhere came mainly from those parts of British sociology which were not institutionally established. The institutionalized parts of British sociology were for the most part rather incapable of expansion beyond the classroom or the seminar—although these are, under the appropriate circumstances, the very heart of institutional establishment of a field of intellectual activity. L. T. Hobhouse had no influence outside other than that exercised by *The Material Culture and Social Institutions of the Simpler Peoples* on Lloyd Warner's *The Social System of a Modern Community*. Family studies, which in the United States were mainly the study of family disorganization, were not influenced by Westermarck. In so far as they were subjected to influences from Great Britain they derived rather from the British social survey tradition with its interest in the conditions of life of the poor. (They were also to some extent influenced by the German studies of standards of living which had been initiated by Le Play and Engel and applied in the United States by Carroll D. Wright, the commissioner of the Bureau of Labor Statistics.) Morris Ginsberg's several studies of social mobility were assimilated into American work in that field but his theoretical concerns were without issue. Carr-Saunders and Wilson's study of the professions became a standard work referred to by American sociologists more perhaps than any single investigation, even though American studies used quite different techniques. T. H. Marshall's *Citizenship and Social Class* has entered as an ingredient into much recent work on social stratification and the development of the welfare state. The interchange between British and American sociology has become very active. British sociological journals are the most read by American sociologists after their own, and British sociological works are frequently published in the United States as well as in Great Britain. Since the British output is very much smaller than the American sociological output, except for the case of Marshall's ideas on the development of citizenship, it tends to be assimilated without a significantly identifiable influence.

From the United States. American sociology had practically no echo in Europe before the Second World War. A few American sociological works were translated into European languages. The translation of Charles Ellwood's textbook into French is hard to account for because even though Ellwood was once considered a sociologist of note, not even at the height of his fame was he regarded as a scholar of the first rank. It is possible that René Worms found his ideas about instincts attractive; in any case there is no evidence that Ellwood's writing ever influenced sociological theory or research in France. Durkheim was utterly uninterested in American sociology (although he did make considerable use of British ethnography in *Les Formes élémentaires de la religion*). Halbwachs, who visited the University of Chicago in the late 1920s, wrote an extremely intelligent and well-informed paper on urban sociology in Chicago in the *Annales de l'histoire économique et sociale.* This occurred while he was working on "social morphology," and he saw an affinity between what he was doing and what the urban sociologists were doing. It did not however go much further than that. Except through Halbwachs, American sociology in France was nearly unknown in the 1930s. While the *Nouvelle encyclopédie scientifique,* which was published by Alcan, did include the solid little book by Raymond Aron on German sociology and a quite good one by Bouglé on *Sociologie française contemporaine,* there was never even the announcement of any parallel title on American sociology. It probably would have been difficult to find anyone who could have written it except perhaps Halbwachs.

In Germany, nearly complete ignorance of American sociology existed before the First World War. Simmel never indicated the slightest awareness of American sociology but he must have had some inkling of its existence. He did after all agree to serve as a member of the editorial board of the *American Journal of Sociology* when it was founded and he probably gave his permission for the translation of parts of *Soziologie* for publication in that journal. Max Weber on his visit to the United States came to Chicago and would appear to have gone out to the University of Chicago, but there is no record of his having met any of the teaching staff. He never referred to any American sociological work although there is an obscure passage in *Wissenschaft als Beruf* where he refers to "the Americans having developed technical sociological concepts" to describe the success of the second or third candidates in a contest over the originally favored candidates. No names were mentioned. He met W. E. B. Du Bois and invited him to contribute to the *Archiv für Sozialwissenschaft und Sozialpolitik,* which he did; Small attended the exposition in St. Louis at which Weber delivered a paper but there is no record of their contact. In any case, Max Weber carried nothing of American sociology away from his visit. He read a goodly amount of American religious history and he was much interested in American politics, but American sociology did not attract his attention.

Tönnies was a little more informed. He was appreciative of Walter Lippmann's *Public Opinion* and he reviewed a few American sociological works. Nonetheless, his views were formed long before he ever read any American sociology and they were not affected by the little that he read.

With von Wiese, we come to a different condition. He definitely was attracted by E. A. Ross' *Principles of Sociology* and it was translated into German under his aegis. He did in fact regard himself as a mediator between American and German sociology. Perhaps because of his liberalism and perhaps too because he had an American disciple—Howard Becker, who was translating the *System der allgemeinen Soziologie* and adapting it by adding American material to it—he had a sense of affinity with American sociologists. He was also in touch with Louis Wirth, who had begun to translate the *Beziehungslehre* independently of Becker and who renounced the task once he learned of Becker's undertaking. When the Nazis seized power in German, von Wiese came for a time to the University of Wisconsin and Harvard University and furthered his knowledge of American sociology. This appeared more fully represented—to the extent that this could be done in a tiny volume of the *Sammlung Goschen*—in a postwar edition of *Soziologie, Geschichte und Hauptprobleme*.

Max Scheler was acquainted with Ross' sociological work and with a few other writers who were less interesting than Ross.

There was one general book on American sociology written by Andreas Walther of Hamburg at the end of the 1920s. It was a poor book since the author, not knowing enough to discriminate the better from the poorer work, treated it all indiscriminately. In the style of much of German sociology of that time, it dealt with definitions of groups, instincts, attitudes, processes and relatively little with the results of sociological study. Nonetheless it did indicate a greater openness to American sociology than was present in other countries at that time, where indifference or disdain were common among the few who knew of its existence.

A change was presaged when Louis Wirth visited Mannheim in Frankfurt in 1931 or 1932. Mannheim was much more open to American sociology than any other German sociologist had ever been. On Wirth's recommendation, he read Thomas and Znaniecki's *The Polish Peasant in Europe and America*. By arrangement with Wirth, he wrote a long review of the "casebook" entitled *Methods in Social Sciences* which had been edited by Stuart Rice on behalf of the Social Science Research Council; it appeared in the *American Journal of Sociology* in 1932, not long before Mannheim went into exile. His response was not too different from the conventional defense of "theory" against "empiricism," of large perspectives—of what would now be called macrosociology—against small, precisely defined investigations. Still it left an imprint when in the following year Mannheim published a plan for the organization of sociological teaching in Germany; the reading of Rice's "casebook" and of some American sociological literature was evident.

After going into exile, Mannheim's interest in American sociological literature increased steadily. The shift in attention from the sociology of knowledge to the study of social structure was not attributable to this interest but the shift did make it easier for him to assimilate a certain amount of American material in so far as it fitted into his desire to show the feasibility and desirability of democratic planning. In his years in Britain, he was surely the sociologist most interested in learning about the achievements, such as they were, of American sociology.

Shifting Centers and Peripheries

After the passing of Comte and Spencer from dominance over what was called sociology in the second half of the nineteenth century, the subject became much more national. Comte and Spencer receded even in their own countries; they certainly lost their international dominance. In so far as they were still treated it was to refute their views, not to affirm them. Durkheim used Spencer as a foil, Scheler used Comte for the same purpose. As the literature of sociology increased in volume and diversity in each country, so each country increasingly lived from its own sociological products. The spread of sociology into the Netherlands and the Scandanavian countries accentuated this tendency which never came to complete fulfillment. When Spencer and Comte were dethroned, French sociology became nearly self-sufficient.[25] So did German sociology; Dutch sociology too moved in the same direction as did Swedish sociology (which was very sparse); Polish sociology seemed to move in a similar fashion. American sociology which almost from the beginning became better established institutionally than the sociology of other countries soon built up a large body of literature and its own distinct concerns. But it also kept to the path which it had laid out for itself when it first became committed to the ideas about urban society which it drew from Germany as well as from its own experience. Nonetheless, through the interwar period American sociology in its most productive centers was also becoming self-sufficient. It was only the belated appreciation of Weber's and Durkheim's ideas which created an anachronistic dependence of certain creative centers of American sociology on centers which had in fact disappeared. German sociology and French sociology of the time of the resurrection of Weber and Durkheim in the United States had declined to a rather low point.

The Second World War in so far as it did not suspend the practice of sociology in universities accentuated the self-sufficiency of the various "national sociologies." It was really only in the United States that sociology continued to be practiced throughout the years of the war. Many sociologists were taken into governmental service as sociologists, but more remained in universities, even though there were very few students. American sociology also had the advantage that the United States became engaged in the war more than two years later than

25. Although Durkheim disregarded foreign writers who called themselves sociologists, just as he disregarded French *soi-disant* sociologists, he did make much use of ethnographic work from Germany and Great Britain and, to some extent, the United States. Spencer and Gillen's writings on Australia provided much of the factual foundation of *Les Formes élémentaires de la religion*.

France, Great Britain, and Germany. (I omit the Soviet Union, which also entered the war considerably later than the Western European states, because sociology had virtually ceased to exist there since the 1920s.)

The far greater degree of institutionalization of sociology in the United States, the large scale of its output before the war, the continued activity in American sociology throughout the war, the postwar ascent of the United States to a condition of academic centrality in many subjects (as well as the greater power and prominence of the United States outside the intellectual sphere), and the formation, to some extent, of an international sociological culture all contributed to change the direction of the ecological process. The United States became the chief center of sociology and Europe and the rest of the world went to sociological school there.

This process has been much aided by the increased institutionalization of sociology in teaching and research in Europe. It has also been aided by the increase in institutional and individual communication in sociology across national boundaries. Institutionalization increases receptive power just as it increases radiative power between countries as well as within countries. Institutional establishment reduces random movement and it also reduces the freedom of the individual sociologist to do whatever he wishes. If syllabuses and reading lists prescribe more American sociological literature, the European student's freedom is restricted. The sheer quantity of American sociological literature and its interestingness imposed itself on Europe after the long sociological drought in that part of the world.

The greatly increased facility in the reading of English in almost all sections of the population in the European continent, institutions like the Salzburg Seminar, and the availability of grants and stipends for study in American universities affected many subjects and sociology not least. The opportunities offered by institutions would not have been sought had not American sociology become so attractive. The preponderance of the American center diminished after several decades. European sociologists became more numerous and more productive than they had ever been before. They created new journals, new monographic series; new publishing houses embraced sociology, new universities offered more appointments to sociologists, and more students chose to study sociology. This has been happening in every Western European country. From having been largely peripheral for about a decade European sociology began to take the form of a network of national sub-centers: American sociology still continued in its central position but the distance between center and periphery has been greatly diminished.

After the Second World War, sociology in Germany had almost to begin again. Practically no sociologists had been trained in the twelve years of the National Socialist regime. A few very old sociologists such as Alfred Weber and Leopold von Wiese were called back into service. The refugees Horkheimer and Adorno returned from the United States. Von Wiese in a more appreciative way, Horkheimer and Adorno more grudgingly brought American sociological literature into their syllabuses. At first, there was too little German sociological literature for pedagogical purposes. American literature had to be turned to. Not long after the war, I encountered German students who had read Max Weber only in English because they could not obtain German editions.

As the demand for sociology in the universities increased, the demand for books also increased. The result was a rapid growth in the publication of sociological books.

The expansion of sociological publication in Germany has been accompanied by the publication of translations of American sociological works on an unprecedented scale. The teaching of sociology in German universities has been extended with many more chairs, assistant professorships, and assistantships. Sociological research has not had a similar institutional expansion. Survey research institutes are independent of universities, and as a result the proportion of empirical research in the total body of academic sociological publications is fairly small. For several decades the very considerable German knowledge of American research and theory and the frequency of citation from the published literature contrasted sharply with the small amount of research done in Germany. This has begun to change. German sociological monographic series, e.g., Göttinger Abhandlungen zur Soziologie, Frankfurter Beiträge, Bonner Beiträge zur Soziologie, Soziologische Gegenwartsfragen, increasingly give place to reports on field research although there still remains the practice of publishing summaries and assessments of the work of leading theorists.

Similarly, although the proportion of papers devoted to research in the *Volnische Zeitschrift für Soziologie* is very much greater than it was when the journal was first revived and than it was in its earlier form, reviews of the literature and general papers still predominate. The new *Zeitschrift für Soziologie* has moved further away from the older tradition.

The academic establishment of sociology has increased in France as it has in Germany; there are many new universities and many chairs of sociology as well as numerous posts of lower rank. France too has moved towards the reassertion of an autonomous production, although not perhaps to an autonomous tradition. New periodicals accord a large proportion of their space to reports of the results of research. The deficiencies of the French universities with respect to their provision for research and advanced training are compensated institutionally—to some extent at least—by the generous policies of the Conseil national de la recherche scientifique (CNRS). The establishment of the Maison des sciences de l'homme, of the sixth section of the École pratique des hautes études, and of the Centre européenne de la recherche sociologique at the initiative of Raymond Aron have greatly enhanced the institutional provision for the conduct of, and training in, research. In France, however, as well as in Germany, the point of reference is still largely the American literature of theory and research.

The situation is not greatly different in Britain. There too the increased number of universities and the increased interest in and appreciation of sociology have led to a pronounced increase in the number of students of sociology and of teachers of sociology in universities, institutes of education, and technical colleges. The creation of the Social Science Research Council has increased the funds available for sociological research. There are now three journals of sociology devoted to publication of papers by professional sociologists, in contrast with one journal before the war that had relatively few papers contributed by professionally qualified sociologists. The market for sociological books among the laity has increased. The traditional British study of social stratification has persisted, the study of the poor has persisted; professional sociology has shown recognizable continuity with amateur or avocational sociology. British sociology is more continuous with its past than German or French sociology. Nonetheless there too the presence of American sociology has become very tangible; it is perhaps most acknowledged where it is most criticized.

Thus the international ecological pattern of sociology has changed and changed again since the beginning of the present century. There have been concurrent changes within national societies and nowhere more than in the United States.

Ecology: Within National Sociological Communities

I shall confine my observations on the ecology of sociology within a national society to the United States and more particularly to the relations between dominance and institutionalization. From about the outbreak of the First World War to the end of the Second, the Department of Sociology of the University of Chicago was the center par excellence of sociological studies in the United States and in the world, although in the last decade of its dominance it was living from the momentum of the preceding two decades. As the leading institution for postgraduate studies in sociology, it had continuously present a group of mature and concentrated students, each of whom was engaged in a piece of research—almost always field research—under the inspiration and often the direction of two men who were in a close and assymetrical consensus—Professors Park and Burgess. What they taught had been in principle codified—rather primitively by present-day standards—in "Park and Burgess," their *Introduction to the Science of Sociology.* Intensive instruction was amply provided in seminars and informal lectures as well as in numerous individual consultations between teachers and students. The teachers lived near the university and were in their offices much of the time; the students had ready access to them. "Term papers" and the "seminar papers" were obligatory, and they had to be based on research in the library and in the field. Each student accepted it as an ineluctable obligation to produce such a paper, and the teachers regarded it as theirs to supervise their production and scrutinize their results. The good relations which the Department of Sociology had built up with civic, local, and manicipal groups in the first twenty years of the existence of the department made it easier for the students to gain entry into the field for direct observation, interviewing, and the collection and examination of documents. There were certain adjunct institutions to which students could be attached for their research (and sometimes employment) such as the Institute for Juvenile Research, the Chicago Crime Commission, the Juvenile Protective Association, etc. For the most successful there were the rewards of publication in the journal conducted by the department, the *American Journal of Sociology* or, even higher, inclusion of a finished work in the Chicago Sociological Series. The journal, although owned by the University of Chicago and edited by the Department of Sociology of the university, was the official organ of the American Sociological Society and it was the only important national journal on the subject. Relatively few students attained the dignity of publication in the *Journal,* but its existence near at hand made them aware that publication is the end which any scholar should seek. The existence of the Chicago Sociological Series exemplified the standards of the department in visible form and it added to the awareness of membership in an institution at the center of the world of sociological activities. For many years the seat of the American Sociological Society was at the University of Chicago. In nearly every important state university of the Middle and Far West, sociology was taught by graduates of the department. Even in famous universities like the University of Michigan, much older than the University of Chicago and with at least one sociologist as distinguished as those at Chicago, there were Chicago graduates. Departments of sociology at state universities like those of Washington, Iowa, and Illinois were headed by Chicago graduates. It was to Chicago that they turned most frequently for new members and it was to Chicago that they sent their best graduates for further study. There were other departments of sociology in the country, most notably at Columbia, Michigan, North Carolina, Brown, Pennsylvania, Yale; each had its distinctions and each had its small areas of hegemony to which its graduates were appointed. There were eminent sociologists at some of these institutions. Ward had spent his last years at Brown, Sumner had been professor at Yale, Odum at North Carolina, Ogburn, Lynd, and MacIver had at one time or another taught at Columbia, Cooley at Michigan; and valuable monographs based on dissertations were produced. But all these lesser centers were different from Chicago. None had the common standpoint of Chicago's sociologists, its continuity of effort, or the liveliness and intensity of its intellectual community.

It succeeded in rising to ascendancy not only because of the intellectual power of some of its staff members, but because, in addition to that intellectual power, it was more institutionalized; it produced more work with a common stamp, and the quantity as well as the quality aroused attention and respect. This in turn enabled it to draw outstanding graduate students whom it trained and then sent out to maintain the dominance of Chicago's sociology and sociology department.

Although the sociology which Chicago practiced was embedded in a more ramified corporate network, one important feature of its institutional establishment was like that of Durkheim's school. It depended very much on one major intellectual personality at a time. For a while, between about 1912 and 1919, there were two, but when Thomas' academic career came to an inglorious end there was only one. When Robert Park withdrew from Chicago towards the end of his life, preferring to spend his last years at Fisk University with his old pupil, Charles Johnson, then president of the university, Chicago sociology began to falter. None of the other members of the department had such wide interests and concerned himself so much with every aspect of the subject as Park had done. A spurious conflict between quantitative methods represented by Ogburn and Stouffer and some other method represented by Blumer and Wirth, and later Hughes, infected the department. Students came to think that they had to be partisans. Members of the department began to think that the central administration was hostile to their subject. The early years of the depression also produced a feeling of despondency. The work of the department lost its focus on urban and ethnic studies; new persons, changes of interest, and a diminution of intellectual authority within the institution in consequence of intellectual and then personal disagreements all contributed to weaken the sense of centrality in the subject.

Perhaps more important was the fact that the fundamental ideas of Chicago sociology were coming to a standstill and were not being extended and deepened. With Park's departure, the analysis of ecological processes diminished and so did the use of the "ecological technique." Park's going coincided with the appearance of the sample survey. The use of the survey of samples of individuals permitted correlations of the characteristics of individuals instead of the characteristics of aggregates such as census tracts. "Spot-maps" lost their heuristic value. As a result, the spatial aspect of social events became less visible; the ecological problems of the causal and symbolic significance of spatial position and of the relationship between spatial and social positions faded away. The problems had never been sharply or systematically formulated—that was not Park's way—and when they lost the immediacy which cartographic representation gave them, they practically disappeared. The studies of small and local communities also declined so that there was no development of the concepts which would have permitted more refined studies of the type which had once been so productive. Burgess' predictive studies of the adjustment of engaged and married couples, Ogburn's statistical time series of various social phenomena, Stouffer's subtle studies of internal migration were all outstanding intellectual accomplishments. But they all seemed to be separate from each other. None of them had the perspective which Park's unlimited curiosity and his incessant movement between microcosm and macrocosm conferred on even the narrowest and most specialized study. The radiative and attractive power of Chicago as a center was reduced. Ogburn's interest in the quantitative description of long-term trends and his simplistic and undifferentiated concept of "cultural-lag" were never articulated with microsociological analyses of situations which could be studied by methods of participant-observation. The inchoate, global, macrosociological interests of Park found no steady, persistent, and compelling formulation. The individual who best represented Park's view of society was Everett Hughes, but in the situation in which he found himself in the department he could not take over the intellectual leadership. There had always been a heterogeneity of interests and talents in the department at Chicago but they had also been congenial to each other. This ceased to be the case.

There was no successor to Park at Chicago strong and expansive enough intellectually and temperamentally to continue the Chicago tradition and to assimilate into it the new problems and modes of thought and inquiry which began to emerge in the years just before the outbreak of World War II. No one at Chicago at that time was ready to move onto the problem of the integration of the national society, which in a very fragmentary and disordered way was emerging as the main problem after the war. Not that other departments were successful in grappling with the problem, but the department at Chicago did not undertake to do it. Under Burgess' and Ogburn's chairmanships, Blumer and Stouffer departed for California and Harvard respectively. Wirth's death and Faris' retirement weakened the current of the older tradition. The loss of a center within the department accompanied the loss of centrality in the national sociological system. The relationship was a circular one.

It was not only internal developments which reduced the centrality of Chicago. New centers were emerging at universities in the East which had never been subcenters of Chicago. Columbia and Harvard came forward into prominence. Columbia by the early 1950s markedly surpassed Chicago as a center. There were several major factors. One of the most obvious is that Columbia possessed two major intellectual personalities, Robert Merton and Paul Lazarsfeld, who combined what was most "needed" in sociology: ingeniously contrived techniques of survey research with interesting, quite specific substantive hypotheses. The second factor, closely connected with the first, was the formation of a superior form of institutionalization at Columbia in the Bureau of Applied Social Research. The scale of operation, the interests of Lazarsfeld, who was its moving spirit, and the stage of development of sociology at the time required and permitted a higher degree of formalization of procedures—intellectual and organizational—than temperament, capacity, the more primitive state of the subject, and the small scale of operations had fostered at Chicago in earlier decades. The routinization of training facilitated the routinization of research organization and research procedures, at the very moment when new techniques of observation—sample surveys of opinion— and new techniques of analyzing data were brought into sociology from market research and statistics. The research for which Columbia graduate students were trained could be done without personal inspiration; it was made easily capable of reproduction and multiplication. This brought the Columbia center to a relatively high level of technical competence and diffused its procedures and mode of thought into many nonacademic institutions that had not been penetrated by sociology before. It also made Columbia sociology into a national and international center.

Another reason for the emergence of Columbia as a center was the intellectual style of Robert Merton. A product of Harvard, where he had studied under Parsons and Sorokin, Merton had a very wide sociological culture. Unlike Parsons, who possessed a profound vision of sociey which he struggled unceasingly to articulate in a systematic manner, Merton's view of society was less comprehensive or less unitary but it was more adequately articulated and it had the expository advantage of being less abstract. Merton's espousal of "middle range theories" was perhaps less profound than Parson's efforts at a "general theory," but they were easier to apprehend and therefore more effectively taught. Easier to formulate in a testable way, they seemed to involve no *weltanschauliche* commitment, and they were more congenial to institutionalized routines. Merton himself became directly interested in the improvement of the techniques of research and this rendered easier his collaboration with Lazarsfeld. All these factors together resulted in a larger production of works bearing a common stamp and of persons capable of producing more such works in the future. This led to a wide diffusion of Columbia sociology and it generated—more on the level of procedure than of substance—a mode of work in sociology which was capable of endurance.

Harvard before 1945 in Comparison with Chicago

The development of sociology at Harvard University suggests some instructive observations on the significance of institutional arrangements and of the traditions which are fostered by them.

The teaching of sociology began at Harvard University at about the same time that it began at the University of Chicago. In 1893, Edward Cummings began to teach Economics 3 as an assistant professor. This course covered more or less the same subjects as the sociological teaching of Charles Henderson at Chicago. It was centered on "the social problem," i.e., the conditions of the urban poor. It treated housing conditions, child labor, women's labor, sweatshops, desertion and divorce, orphans, the organization of charities, and similar topics. Like Henderson, Cummings desired his students to observe the phenomena at first hand, and he arranged for them to visit institutions. He was also interested in objective, scientifically disciplined methods of investigation. Like Henderson, he believed that the knowledge which could be provided by scientific social investigation was a necessary condition for ameliorative action. Admission to the course was restricted to undergraduates.

Cummings like Henderson was a clergyman; unlike Henderson, he had not studied in Germany. Also unlike Henderson, he seems to have known about contemporary European sociological interests. All in all, in their individual intellectual qualifications the two men matched each other fairly closely. Yet Henderson, in a diffuse way, was rather influential in the development of sociology at Chicago while Cummings left no mark at Harvard.

At the beginning of the twentieth century, Cummings' appointment was discontinued. He was replaced by Thomas Nixon Carver in 1901; Carver taught theoretical sociology mainly along the lines laid down by Herbert Spencer. He had little interest in empirical investigation nor did he follow the more recent development of sociological works by Durkheim, Tarde, and others as Cummings had done. Alongside of Carver, William Z. Ripley gave a course on "labor problems," and he wrote a large book on the races of Europe. Edward Cummings' brother, John, taught "statistics in relation to social investigation" and wrote critically on physical anthropology in relation to society.

These were, then, the rudiments of a potential development of sociology at Harvard; yet nothing came of them. The most important reason for this failure was that the sociologists were neither independent nor enabled to concentrate their activities on being sociologists or thinking of themselves as sociologists.

Teaching of a rather similar sort was offered in the Divinity School at Harvard by Professor Francis Greenwood Peabody. From 1883 on, he had taught a course on "ethics and theology and moral reform" in which he dealt with temperance, charity, labor, prison discipline, and divorce. From 1906 onward, this course became Social Ethics 2. (It too was confined to undergraduates.) Peabody himself was less interested in scientific investigation than Cummings but much of the course dealt with particular social conditions. Undergraduates used to refer to Peabody's course as, "Peabo on drains, drunkenness, and divorce." In 1906, as the result of a gift of $50,000 by Alfred Treadway White, a department of social ethics was created and was assured of space in the newly built Emerson Hall, one floor of which was to be devoted by the terms of the gift to the new department. Two subsequent gifts of $100,000 each from the same source assured the position of the Department of Social Ethics. Within the department, a course on "practical problems of charities, public aid and correction" was taught, as well as one on "criminology and penology." The training of social workers was provided for in conjunction with Simmons College. After Peabody's retirement in 1913, his professorship was left vacant until 1920 when Richard Clarke Cabot, then professor of clinical medicine at Harvard Medical School, was appointed. Cabot had little interest in empirical social investigation and none in sociological theory. A variety of younger colleagues who later became moderately well known as sociologists at other universities were members of the department.

This was the position at Harvard just after the First World War. By this time there had been an independent Department of Sociology at Chicago for more than a quarter of a century. Its head, although he had written little of substance in sociology, was a tireless champion of its possibilities. He was eclectic in his ideas about sociology, he knew the large body of sociological literature and was sympathetic with a variety of possibilities. He had moreover the German ideal of *Wissenschaftlichkeit;* he wanted sociology to become an intellectual discipline and his position and influence in the University of Chicago enabled him to keep this ideal alive while waiting for the time when it could be realized. His second in command did no sociological research of his own but he helped to focus the minds of the students on the life of the lower classes in the city of Chicago. The department had graduate students, which was another advantage over Harvard; one of the graduate students of the Department of Sociology in the University of Chicago was W. I. Thomas. Thomas developed slowly as a sociologist and began to produce significant sociological works only after being a member of the department for more than ten years. Park had joined the department in a marginal capacity before the First World War and taught about one course per year. Like Small, Park was well educated in the literature of sociology; unlike Small, he was also acquainted at first hand with urban life and the world in general. He had also studied the empirical research done by British and American sociologists. He was ready to do the kind of work which later defined the character of sociology. The availability of graduate students to receive his ideas and to carry them out in their doctoral dissertations was decisive; he himself did little research of a sustained sort but he could give direction and inspiration to others to do research. Graduate students had for more than ten years increasingly been coming to take advanced degrees and were being set on problems of empirical investigation conducted mainly within the city of Chicago. Here again Chicago's departmental organization of sociology gave it an advantage over Harvard. Chicago had still another advantage over Harvard. This was the *American Journal of Sociology;* there was not yet anything like enough solid material to publish in such a journal but its existence helped to consolidate the goal of a professional, scholarly sociology producing works of intellectual substance like any other dignified academic discipline. There were other advantages. There was a large number of well-established and reputable persons in the city of Chicago who looked to the Department of Sociology for investigations of "social problems" and for cooperation in the guidance of reforming activities. Finally, the city of Chicago itself was the most rapidly and energetically growing city in the United States. It pressed on the attention of socially sensitive academics problems which startled and horrified persons of conventional middle-class experience; the mind could not be averted from them. Boston too had problems which were not wholly dissimilar but Boston was not growing so rapidly, and Harvard had in a sense surrendered Boston to the immigrants and their politicians. The University of Chicago had no such self-enclosed culture as Harvard with its long history and traditions possessed at this time; it was more exposed to the outside community. Although it was located in an outlying area, Hyde Park itself was not as self-contained vis-à-vis Chicago as Cambridge was vis-à-vis Boston.

The representation of sociology in the Departments of Social Ethics and of Economics at Harvard by no means exhausts the sociology which existed at Harvard in the 1920s. Indeed, the activities of those two departments gives very little sense of what important things began to go on there from the middle of that decade onward. For one thing, there was Lawrence J. Henderson, whose enthusiasm had been aroused by Pareto's *Trattato di sociologia generale* (Henderson probably read it in the French translation). Disregarding the sociology which was going on elsewhere at Harvard and the sociology being done elsewhere in the United States, Henderson became a passionate partisan of sociology as he understood it from his reading of the *Trattato*. In the early thirties he organized a seminar which had a large attendance of senior and junior members of the university, including such eminent scholars as A. D. Nock and such promising younger ones as Crane Brinton. There was also Talcott Parsons, who, having returned from Heidelberg in 1927, had been appointed to an instructorship in the economics department, where presumably he taught economics with a sociological bent.

By 1927 there was growing discontent at Harvard about the standing of sociology as a subject for studies and research. In that year a Committee on Sociology and Social Ethics was appointed under the chairmanship of Ralph Barton Perry which recommended that something more fully corresponding to sociology as generally known at the time should be established at Harvard.

At the same time, under the inspiring pressure of Henderson, there had been established an industrial fatigue laboratory for studying the physiological factors affecting the productivity of industrial workers. Elton Mayo was in charge of this and was working under the guidance—or domination—of Henderson. The work was proving to be less fruitful than anticipated. In order to explain differences in the output of individual workers, Mayo and Henderson began to consider "larger systems." Mayo had studied Radcliffe-Brown and Durkheim and was moving closer and closer to a sociological interpretation of industrial productivity. He gathered around himself Dickson and Roethlisberger, T. N. Whitehead, and finally Lloyd Warner. The latter was encouraged to undertake a study of an entire "larger system," namely, the town of Newburyport. Also in the 1930s, George Homans, an unemployed graduate from a well-connected Harvard family, came under the influence of Henderson and was persuaded that he should become a sociologist in the Paretian manner. Homans wrote a small book on Pareto with George Curtis. Then he began an investigation into English history following the instruction of Henderson, who ordered him to immerse himself in the facts of some particular subject. Homans, having studied Anglo-Saxon as an undergraduate in English at Harvard, began to work on English medieval economic history and, having read Seebohm's book on the English rural community, began the investigation which led to his *English Villagers in the Thirteenth Century*.

Meanwhile the Committee on Sociology and Social Ethics had moved to recommend the establishment of a full department of sociology. The university invited Pitirim Sorokin to become the professor of sociology and chairman of the department. The department of social ethics was pushed to the wall and ceased to function, although officially it was to be incorporated into the Department of

Sociology. Sorokin brought with him Carle Zimmermann, a rural sociologist from the University of Minnesota, where Sorokin had been professor after he came to the United States as a refugee from the Russian Revolution.

By the middle of the 1930s, then, the department consisted of Sorokin, Zimmermann, and Parsons. It had acquired, largely in response to Parsons' teaching, an outstanding group of graduate students, the most eminent of whom were Robert Merton, Kingsley Davis, Logan Wilson, and Robin Williams. Henderson continued to teach and promote his own brand of sociology. Towards the end of the 1930s he gave his Sociology 23, which was attended by a number of young men later to become eminent sociologists; Homans was put to work by Henderson on the "wirebank" experiment at the Western Electric plant. In short, sociology at Harvard was launched. With outstanding teachers, outstanding students, and an independent department, the work in sociology began to produce some important results. In 1937 *The Structure of Social Action* appeared. Robert Merton's doctoral dissertation on seventeenth-century science, which showed the influence of both Parsons and Sorokin, was produced towards the end of the decade.

Harvard after 1945

Harvard's later centrality, based on traditions transplanted from Heidelberg (Max Weber), and Vienna (Freud), was attributable to a new pattern of institutionalization which emerged in the second half of the 1940s. At Harvard, under the leadership of Talcott Parsons, Henry Murray, and Clyde Kluckhohn, a deliberate attempt was made to integrate the theories of social structure, culture, and personality. The teaching program was adapted to this conception of the subject, but the research training program did not keep up with it. The Laboratory of Social Relations never became the intellectual factory and drill ground which the Bureau of Applied Social Research became shortly after the end of the Second World War. It became the administrative sponsor and the home of a variety of investigations which, to a greater extent than at Columbia, were small-scale projects which required neither an intricate division of labor nor a thorough-going routinization and stereotyping of procedure. It never became the solidary collectivity with an identity of its own which the Columbia bureau succeeded in becoming and, even before the death of the gifted Samuel Stouffer who had come there from Chicago via the War Department, it became more of an administrative name and rather less of a corporate intellectual reality. Although valiant efforts were made to create it, Harvard lacked the high degree of consensus among its central personalities which was possessed to such a degree at Columbia. As long as the center at Harvard was a triumvirate with an outward appearance of unity, it presented a powerful force to the outer world of sociology. Nonetheless, it was in fact a center consisting internally of several relatively noncommunicating segments—and this reduced its capacity to impose itself effectively on the subject as a whole. Each of the major segments was a powerful intellectual personality—Parsons, Murray, Kluckhohn, Bruner, Stouffer, and Homans, each of them was in one way or another a forceful generator of ideas and works, but there was no fundamental agreement among them. It did not have what Chicago possessed at its height, namely, a pervasive agreement underlying a wide diversity of substantive interests. A higher degree of consensus among them might have swept the field. (They did very well as it was!) It also lacked what Chicago in the 1920s and early 1930s possessed, namely, its own distinctive organs of publication and stable extra-academic institutional links with the local community for research and training purposes.

On the other hand, it had in Professor Parsons a motive force of great power; his continuous and pervasive productivity spread his influence over the country into the by this time numerous subcenters with highly institutionalized training provision for postgraduate students. The role of one particular publishing enterprise—the Free Press—which became the main source of sociological nutriment for the growing number of graduate students and young teachers from the end of the Second World War until about 1960—provided Professor Parsons with a surrogate for a journal of his own. His numerous, widely scattered essays were concentrated into a few easily available volumes. These essays enabled a new generation to acquire the underlying disposition of Parsons' theory as it was manifested in confrontation with a wide variety of particular problems. The enhancement of the prestige of Harvard University as a whole coincided chronologically with the prestige of the department of social relations which was largely the prestige of Talcott Parsons—although not exclusively so. This attracted to Harvard a succession of gifted students.

Other centers

The sociology department of the University of California in Berkeley also should be mentioned in these observations about the emergence of new centers in American sociology. The University of California in Berkeley was the last great American university to establish a department of sociology. It came into existence after Chicago, Harvard, and Columbia were well-established with dominant traditions of their own. Berkeley could not recruit its staff from within except at the level of its youngest members; it had to recruit its staff from other universities, e.g., Lipset trained at Columbia under Merton and Lazarsfeld, Blumer under Mead and Faris at Chicago, Bendix under Wirth at Chicago, Selznick at Columbia, Kornhauser at Chicago,

Kingsley Davis at Harvard, Löwenthal at Frankfurt. The size of the staff of the department and the size of the student body as well as the amplitude of resources all made for centrifugality. The high degree of institutionalization coexisted with a diversity of standpoints so that, despite the eminence of the department as an aggregation of outstanding and productive sociologists whose works drew the attention of the country and the world, it lacked the coherence which Durkheim, Park, and Parsons gave to their respective circles of colleagues, collaborators, and pupils.

Sociology at the University of Michigan had been gently influential through the writings of Charles Cooley ever since the turn of the century. Both Thomas and Park had assimilated Cooley's ideas about the primary group into their own dominant traditions. There had not, however, been an independent department of sociology at Michigan until 1930, when Roderick McKenzie, a Chicago product and a close collaborator of Park, came there from the University of Washington. The Department of Sociology at the University of Michigan became one of the major departments of the country, partly through the extension of ecological studies and partly through the establishment of the Survey Research Center there. The latter was an important step in the institutionalization of training and research at Michigan; in its ecological and related studies, Michigan continued and developed the Chicago tradition with the aid of many recruits from Chicago.

From Chicago in its earlier years and from Harvard and Columbia in the several decades after the end of the Second World War, we know how effective is a unitary center created by one dominant or two strong consensual figures. A pluralistic assemblage of eminent figures is not likely to be equally effective. Berkeley did not show a capacity to create a *Nachwuchs* which could renew the department while unifying it or to produce a body of graduates who would diffuse its "line" more widely in the United States.

The functions of a center are performed, nationally and internationally, through the channels of communication which are integral to institutionalization; namely, learned journals, monograph series, and books. But one essential organ of institutionalization is the face-to-face encounter of teachers with students. It is through these encounters that the *Nachwuchs* is formed and that ideas are generated, tried out, and selected from among a variety of alternatives.

The absence of a systematically trained *Nachwuchs* does not mean that an intellectual subject cannot develop: it did so in the heroic age of science prior to the formation of the modern university. The absence of a systematically trained *Nachwuchs* means that the pressure of tradition is lightened. The development of an intellectual subject under such circumstances is more a matter of individual genius than it has become since the transformation of universities into institutions of research and training.

The questions which then follow are: would the proliferation of centers damage the subject intellectually, would it disorder sociology by making its work less coherent and more scrappy? Is a unified center possible under present circumstances in the world of learning? The proliferation of sociologists and of sociological works in the past quarter of a century has resulted in great specialization; in a subject still as deficient in fundamental theory as is sociology this might mean that it will disintegrate, losing whatever coherence it has gained over the preceding three-quarters of a century. Sociology might break up into the specialisms like those which exist now in the physical and biological sciences, without being able to draw on a basic or fundamental science like physics, chemistry, or genetics.

The constituent elements of the traditions of present-day sociology have been in a process of selection and coalescence through the work of Weber, Durkheim, Parsons, et al. This coalescence is still very imperfect. (It can never be perfect, and, if it did become perfect, the subject would come to a complete halt.) Greater coalescence than it possesses at present is, however, a necessary condition not just for aesthetic or architectonic reasons, but because, until there is such a coalescence, the interrelations of the different phenomena in society will be too poorly understood. The multiplication of sociological persons and works and the high degree of specialization might render more difficult the ascendancy of a more complex and comprehensive theory because it would render more difficult the ascendancy of a theorist whose mastery of the results of specialized study would be great enough to call forth the respect and adherence of the practitioners of the diverse and numerous specialisms.

Sociological Traditions: Selection, Rejection, Coalescence

If one takes up the compendious work by Sorokin, *Contemporary Sociological Theories,* which presented the stock of sociology of the fifty years which lay across the turn of the century, one is struck with how few of the names which are cited are known today by any but sociological antiquarians. Weber, Durkheim, Pareto, Park, and Thomas are there, so are Floyd Allport, Otto Ammon, Emory Bogardus, Stuart Chapin, Filipo Carli, E. de Roberty, Charles Ellwood, Franklin Giddings, Maxim Kovalevsky, E. A. Ross, Gabriel Tarde, William Graham Sumner, Alfred Vierkandt, Leopold von Wiese, L. Winiarsky, and Sorokin himself, who is cited more than any other two authors. What has become of these authors and of the ideas they espoused? They have fallen by the wayside.

Some of them were weak intellectually, and their ideas did not recommend themselves to critical contemporaries. Some of them were in the wrong places, their books were the only ways in which they spoke to their contemporaries, they had no students or no students who had the ability, received the inspiration, and learned how to press further with what they had received. They might have been in the "wrong" countries and written in the "wrong" language. Some of them were known and respected figures, contemporary with Durkheim, Weber, and Park, but the world turned away from them. There were many ideas floating about in sociology in the latter part of the nineteenth century. Practically all of them were influenced in one way or another by Hegel, Comte, and Darwin. Evolutionary and biological ideas were common. The major idea was one of historical stages of human society from simple to differentiated, from traditional to rational, from unenlightened to enlightened, from societies with tool-based technology to societies with a machine-based technology using artificially generated power, from loosely integrated societies to closely integrated societies. The Darwinian evolutionary viewpoint fitted into and rendered more plausible this theory of stages of development; the prestige of Darwinism also activated a tendency to analyze social structures and their functions in society in the categories appropriate to the study of biological organisms. (This type of sociological analysis was submerged rather early and left little trace.) The Darwinian influence was also present among those sociologists who, impressed by the competition of species, stressed the importance of the competition and the conflict of races as a central phenomenon in society. Others, also impressed by the idea of natural selection, were concerned with social selection and hence with the social origins and the presumed biological heredity of the members of various strata, above all, the leading strata in contemporary Western societies. Many studies were intended to demonstrate the biological transmission of socially relevant characteristics. Much of the substance of these traditions no longer has any place in the currently effective traditions of sociology. Certain variables in this set of beliefs have survived, for example the study of the social origins of elites and the social origins of particular professions, but the matrix of propositions has fallen away. And what has survived has not been comfortably assimilated into the traditions of sociology now prevailing.[26]

A few words should be said at this point about Marxian sociology which has so many self-alleged proponents at present. "Marxian sociology," such as it is, is an amalgam of Hegelian evolutionism into which has been inserted a conception of conflict drawn from Darwinism[27] and from the studies of the "poor." It includes also a con-

26. I refer here to the awkwardness of present "elite studies" which are sometimes legitimated by associating them with the study of power and authority—very unconvincingly—at other times with the "circulation of elites" which likewise has not found a comfortable home in contemporary sociology.

27. One variant of the Darwinian tradition elaborated by Ratzenhofer and Gumplowicz had an enduring afterlife via Albion Small, W. I. Thomas, and

ception of "interest" which has been generalized from the conservative conception of the "landed interest" which was developed in the seventeenth and eighteenth centuries in England. This results in something different from the mere substitution of "class" for ethnic, national, and territorial "groups," which had been stressed by Ratzenhofer and Gumplowicz, and it is also something different from that type of conflict which arises from contention for the possession of scarce objects. The prevailing conception of society derived from Weber and Durkheim allows, despite the assertions of the critics of the "consensus-model,"[28] ample place for conflict but it can make no place for "real" interests which are independent of what is desired by actual human beings in situations of scarcity. This historical metaphysics of "real" interests could obviously not find a place in a tradition which received one of its possible promulgations in *Towards a General Theory of Action*. The same may be said about the distinction between the superstructure and the substructure and about the causal primacy of the latter. The distinction derives from a conception of human action which is alien to the more realistic, synthetic tradition which is contained in much of contemporary sociology.

Thus a considerable amount of the Darwinian or biologistic and the metaphysical evolutionary conceptions could not be fused with the traditions which prevail in contemporary sociology. They have either become extinct or they lead a restless, uncomfortable existence recurring intermittently at the margins of sociological culture, functioning to criticize but incapable of positive development in a culture which is committed to empirical research—however theoretical.

Of the Comtean and the Hegelian concepts of social evolution, certain very important elements have survived. The conception of society as a moral order in which discrete individuals are bound together in collective actions of various sorts by common images of themselves as parts of that order and by common beliefs defining themselves and their obligations to the collectivity is one of the chief precipitates of the coalescence of the various intellectual traditions of the eighteenth and nineteenth centuries. From Rousseau's conception of the collective will, from Hegel and the German theorists of the Volksgeist, from Comte's portrayal of the morally disintegrated condition of the then contemporary society in its "critical," skeptical state, and from Marx's conception of the dissolution of the moral bonds in modern bourgeois society emerged a variety of conceptions

---

Robert Park. The affinity of this conception of conflict to competition in the animal and plant worlds had a powerful effect on Chicago sociology. It also had a pronounced influence on Arthur Bentley and through him on American political sociology.

28. A characteristic allegation of this sort appears in an essay by Professor Ralf Dahrendorf: "Out of Utopia," *American Journal of Sociology* 64, no. 2 (1958).

of the significance of beliefs (about the ultimately valuable) in the regulation of individual conduct and in the determination of the degree of integration of society. Max Weber's typology of legitimate authority was developed from the presupposition of the significance of beliefs and of a consensus of beliefs about ultimate things; the moral state of society which engaged Durkheim's interest, the conception of *Gemeinschaft* and *Gesellschaft* in Tönnies, the conception of the moral order in Park—all these beliefs about the scale and significance of a consensus of moral beliefs in the working of society have been the products of a confluence of traditions to which Hobbes, Rousseau, Hegel, Marx, Lazarus, Steinthal, and H. S. Maine have contributed. The Marxian concept of bourgeois society unbridgeably divided into competing and conflicting classes; the Simmelian conception of urban society, differentiated by division of labor, sectional interests, and individuation; Tönnies' conception of modern bourgeois society—*Gesellschaft*—which resembled Hobbes' picture of the state of nature where a relationship of *homo homini lupus* prevailed; all implied a great concern with the extent and the significance of a consensus of moral beliefs. The problem was: to what extent do individual men act on the basis of conceptions of themselves, their rights and obligations, in ways which minimize or aggravate the conflicts between themselves as individuals and as members of groups, with other individuals and groups. Consensus became the main variable of analytical or theoretical sociology. Even those authors who claimed that modern societies were atomized had their point of departure in an image of a consensual society: they regarded the dissensual character of modern societies as the phenomenon to be accounted for. The very definition of modern society involved placing the variable of consensus in the center of attention.

The struggle for existence which was one variable of the sociological Darwinism and the basic theorem of the sociological theory of the *Rassenkampf* could be assimilated into the emerging sociological tradition because it constantly raised the problem of "defective consensus." In Ratzenhofer and Gumplowicz, the conflict of races was given; it was not problematic. In the analytical sociology which became ascendant in the work of the European and American founders, conflict was not a given; it became a variable to be accounted for. Its converse—consensus—was likewise not given. It too had to be explained. Research on the adjustment of immigrants or on family disorganization, on ethnic conflict, on segregation, suicide, anomie, on the formation of sects, on the role of charismatic authority and of rational-legal authority were all attempts to cope with this fundamental problem. Features of other ideas which could not be assimilated were discarded.

Certain other important ideas of contemporary sociology were possible only within the context of a concern about the moral beliefs of a society. The idea of the charismatic or the sacred was an extension of this conception. The delineation of the properties of bureaucratic authority and the assessment of the role of bureaucracy in modern societies were elaborations of the conceptions of *Gesellschaft* in Tönnies and of capitalistic society in Marx. The same obtains for the conceptions of "mass society," "modernization," and "organizations" which assumed such prominence in subsequent sociological studies; they were developed out of the fundamental conceptions of the sociology formed by the continental founders of the subject.

Even before it became anywhere nearly as institutionalized as it had been for the past thirty years, this tradition was in the process of gaining ascendancy. It was, as Talcott Parsons pointed out in *The Structure of Social Action*, contained implicitly in the three main European traditions of idealism, positivism, and utilitarianism and it was elicited from potentiality by the powerful intelligences of the major European theorists. The American theorists of the founding generation were not of equally powerful theoretical intelligence, but they too—Thomas and Park—came upon the essential. In neither the case of Thomas nor of Park did they ever succeed—nor did they try in any large-scale effort—in discarding the elements of incompatible traditions. In Park's case, fragments of Darwinism remained in his ecological ideas. Thomas, indeed, after his exclusion from the University of Chicago, turned away not only from his sociological work but also from the framework which he had developed in it and which brought him near to Weber and Durkheim; he was attracted by an eclectic behavioristic psychology which was alien to what he had believed previously. (There is some reason to believe however that, after this digression, he began to find his way back again, but no published work ever announced his arrival.)

Somehow, despite its very scanty institutionalization in Germany, despite its submergence in France, despite its numerous competitors in Great Britain, the now dominant tradition grew and ramified. With institutionalization and the emergence of new centers in which a more stringent formulation of the tradition was presented, it finally triumphed over competitors—not totally—in the United States. Once the United States became the center, however, the reinterpreted and modified tradition then spread back to Europe, where, despite resistances, it established itself in all the main European countries in a way in which it had never done before when Europe was itself the center from which the tradition emanated.

To what extent is its wide diffusion and dominance attributable to institutionalization?[29]

---

29. It must be remembered that what is institutionalized is an intellectual process and that an account of the process is not exhausted by an account of the institutional setting in which it occurs. There is the sheer power of intelligence in confrontation with problems. The problems can be perceived through

The turning of direction of a tradition, the amalgamation of elements of several traditions, is a creative action. It is not an institutional action. It is the work of an individual mind and it can and has been done under conditions of very rudimentary institutionalization. As a matter of fact it might even be said that institutionalization, as important as it is for consolidation, multiplication, and diffusion, can be something of a hindrance to the turning and amalgamation of traditions. Max Weber had the advantage of an uninstitutionalized sociology in his time. He had studied law and economics, he came on the study of religion without institutional supervision. Durkheim had not studied sociology as an academic subject. Park studied it under conditions of very scanty institutionalization and Thomas studied it in Chicago when the subject still scarcely existed intellectually, although an institutional structure had been created for it.

A tradition can give birth to a product at one stage of its existence which it could not produce at an earlier time. Its potentialities might be presumed to have an inherent sequentiality and it is quite possible that this stage had been reached at the end of the nineteenth century so that, in a number of countries, persons who had assimilated positivism, utilitarianism, and idealism began to produce results which had marked affinities with each other. Those who produced these results entered into practically no contact with each other. It was for the next generation of those born after the beginning of the new century, with Parsons in the forefront, to draw together into a more explicit and coherent pattern these separately generated approximations to a tradition. The subsequent history of the consolidation and diffusion of the tradition is very much a history in which the institutional system of sociology has played a crucial role.

Endogenous Traditions, Exogenous Traditions, and Exogenous Stimuli

An intellectual discipline exists when a number of persons believe themselves to possess an identity defined by the common subject of their intellectual activity, when many or all of the problems which

---

a number of mechanisms. They can be contained in the intellectual works which a searching, questing intelligence has discovered—either by its own curiosity or by moving along paths which it has made for itself in only very lightly charted territory. Intellectual works themselves are linked with other intellectual works contained in them by references to other books and authors. Even without the aid of the contemporary institutional elaboration of teaching, of bibliographical services, libraries, learned societies, a seeking intelligence with the sensitivity of an Indian tracker could find like-minded persons across the stretches of a relatively unorganized Europe. Nonetheless, the task was more difficult before institutionalization through universities and learned journals.

they study are raised by or derived from the tradition, i.e., the body of literature and oral interpretation produced by those who regard themselves as practitioners of the discipline. An intellectual discipline is an academic discipline when it is taught, discussed, and investigated in academic institutions which bear the name of the discipline or something akin to it, and when its members publish works in organs bearing the name of the discipline. A discipline has an intellectual and social structure.

In the early years of sociology, while its proponents were still struggling to establish their intellectual and academic dignity, a relatively common activity of sociologists in Germany, France, Great Britain, and the United States was the delineation of the field of sociology, its demarcation from other already existing academic disciplines, and the laying out of its internal subdivisions. Sociologists at that time had no social structure for their discipline in most instances and so they sought to define it by its intellectual properties. This was extremely difficult to do since the ancestry to which they laid claim was not universally acknowledged by nonsociologists and because there was little intellectual substance which they could invoke in self-legitimation. This was why they argued in principle and made claims for the future. This activity has now practically ceased, mainly because most sociologists have come to accept a vaguely delineated body of problems, ideas, and procedures as sociological, despite the unclarity of boundaries and the heterogeneity of subject matters, problems, and "approaches." The large body of literature which contains these problems, ideas, and procedures, which appears in sociological journals, which is reviewed there, and which is produced by persons called sociologists, fortifies this sense of sociological identity. Sociology is also now recognized as a subject by the educated public inside and outside the universities, and this too helps to define the boundaries of the subject and of the profession which cultivates it or at least to allay apprehensions about its legitimacy.

The definition of sociology by the social structure of sociology and by its corpus of works has a retroactive effect on the construction of the sociological tradition. While traditions work forward in time, the construction of a legitimatory, inspirational tradition is a movement through time in the reverse direction. Tradition is not, however, a mythological construction, although it has some of the functions of mythology. The works and ideas which have been admitted to a tradition, i.e., which are regarded as part of it, help to set the problems. They can set problems in a situation in which the ostensibly valid part of the tradition is the work which has most recently been published, although the problems of the recently published works were set earlier by a major work which might have been written many years in the past. Alternatively—although it is not so different—current work might constantly refer explicitly to a major work done many years earlier. Sociology is at present a mixture of these two relationships to "its own past." The significant fact is that sociology now has a number of less dominant traditions. Some of these less dominant traditions are in a sense "counter-traditions." These counter-traditions are mainly polemical rather than substantive. Behaviorism as exemplified in the work of George Lundberg was one of these; the self-designated "critical sociology"—an evasive name for highbrow Marxism—is another. Both of these counter-traditions, when their adherents produce substantive works, turn out to have little nutritive value intellectually; their adherents are in fact dominated by the prevailing central tradition in their selection of problems and in their selection of the major variables with which they operate. Even allowing for the ambiguity and lack of rigor of practically all sociological work and the large degree of freedom of interpretation permitted by the poor data and the disjunctiveness of detailed empirical research, even the interpretations offered by adherents of the counter-traditions turn out to be little different from the interpretations offered by the adherents of the dominant tradition.

Some of the less dominant traditions are subsidiary traditions which are not polemical. They have a more positive relationship to the dominant traditions. They are viewed sympathetically by adherents of the dominant traditions. They have become tributaries which flow into the dominant traditions even though they arose outside them. Comparative religious studies are of this sort. Thanks to the work of Weber and Durkheim, the results of comparative studies in religion have found a place in the dominant traditions, although comparative religious studies still constitute an autonomous field of work with a great central tradition of its own, with a vast literature and many very distinguished contributers. Modern economic analysis is another. At one time, in the writings of the European founders, economics up to the time of Mill and Senior found its way into sociology. Talcott Parsons succeeded in bringing in Marshallian economics too (his later efforts to assimilate the Keynesian development from neoclassical economics has apparently been less successful). More recently economists like Becker, Arrow, Nerlove, and Schultz have applied economic analysis to subjects like the family, ethnic relations, and education, ordinarily treated by sociologists, and the results of these enquiries are likely to be assimilated into sociology.

Animal and plant ecology and the economic theory of location also coalesced with the central sociological traditions as Chicago was emerging into dominance, but they fell away as the center shifted from Chicago. Since these subsidiary traditions were never persuasively and explicitly integrated in an authoritative work by Park or his associates and protégés, they became submerged or disassociated as far as sociology was concerned.

The psychoanalytic theory of personality is another tradition which partly coalesced with the central sociological tradition. The particular propositions of psychoanalysis might not be true; the mechanism of the Oedipus complex might not be as psychoanalysis has described it; the same can be said about the genesis and mechanisms of aggression, conscience, anxiety, repression, etc. Nonetheless, these variables in the coherent pattern which psychoanalysis set forth have been assimilated into the sociological tradition. The naming and description of these phenomena has made sociologists more aware of them, more realistic in their perception of them, in the assessment of their magnitude, and in the estimate of the probability of their occurrence under determinate conditions.

The traditions of social anthropology are similarly subsidiary traditions with respect to the main traditions of sociology. Social anthropology developed quite independently of sociology. There was a time when they were both independently established within the same academic department, but even then they were separate. They each had a distinctive subject matter; one studied modern Western urban societies, the other studied "primitive" agrarian societies in Asia, Africa, and the Americas. They used techniques of research which were quite different from each other. They sometimes overlapped when sociologists studied illiterate peasants or aboriginals within their own societies, as they did in South Eastern Europe or when social anthropologists studied the urbanization of African tribesmen in East or South Africa. By and large however each kept to its own jurisdiction and cultivated its own theories. When Radcliffe-Brown drew on Durkheim, a step was taken towards the fusion of the two sets of traditions by the adduction of a strand of tradition which was common to both. Robert Redfield's adaptation of Park's ideas to the study of villages in Mexico and Guatemala was another such step. Still another step was taken when Lloyd Warner, who had studied Australian aborigines, undertook to study sectors of contemporary American society. Bit by bit, the two traditions began to come closer to each other. When after the Second World War, anthropologists, sociologists, political scientists began to study the problems of the new states of Asia and Africa, the sociologists among them had to read the literature of social anthropology, even though they were studying institutions of a type which had not existed earlier in the societies studied by social anthropologists. Thus the two traditions came closer to each other. The two subjects are not amalgamated; they remain institutionally separate from each other albeit within the same universities. Nonetheless, in certain respects, the subsidiary tradition of social anthropology is becoming incorporated into the sociological tradition; the same is true in reverse. Each remains an integral and distinctive tradition but each has incorporated a considerable amount of the substance of the other.

There have been other coalescences of the sociological traditions and the intellectual traditions external to sociology. Traditions from various currents of philosophy, e.g., from phenomenology, from legal studies, from literary and linguistic studies, have flowed into the sociological traditions, sometimes becoming conceptually well integrated, sometimes less so.

Sometimes the traditions which reach towards sociology are contemporaneously active. Sometimes they have been relatively dormant outside of sociology for a long time. The most striking instance of the latter is the revival of Tocqueville's ideas about the consequences of equality and the delineation of the structure of an equalitarian society. The revival of Tocqueville occurred first in political science after the Second World War and it moved into sociology with the increased attention to the structure of "mass society." The account of Tocqueville as a sociologist in Raymond Aron's *Etapes de la pensée sociologique* has now made Tocqueville's ideas retroactively into a constitutive element in the contemporaneously effective traditions of sociology.

Sociology and comparative religious studies, sociology and economics, sociology and ecology, sociology and psychoanalysis, sociology and social anthropology, sociology and cybernetics, sociology and the theory of administration—all these coalescences with their simultaneous modifications of the content of sociology today and of the image which sociologists have of their own past are coalescences of substantive traditions, of traditions which have grown out of the sociological tradition endogenously and of intellectual traditions which have developed outside of sociology. But they are all substantive traditions. Sociology is not merely a body of substantive assertions: it purports to be a science, and as such it exists within the more broadly embracing tradition of discourse which requires systematic confirmation of its assertions. In consequence of this sense of intellectual obligation, the substantive traditions of sociology have increasingly, although unequally, become affiliated to traditions of observational, analytical, and statistical techniques. The entire conception of sociology as a science is of this character.

There is a long and many-streamed tradition of sociological procedure which has become more and more coalescent, in practice and in retrospect, with the substantive traditions. Albion Small looked back to Niebuhr and Savigny; Paul Lazarsfeld drew a retrospective map which went back to William Petty and the English demographers of the seventeenth century. Later, he established Quetelet as a precursor. Philip Abrams more recently presented a coherent account of the course of the "statistical" tradition and Keith Baker has reinstated Condorcet as a precursor of the science of society. Every new step in sociology towards a more rigorous procedure of empirical research adds a new set of ancestral deities to the pantheon of the sociological tradition. These in turn add their force to the movement of coalescence. These newly acknowledged traditions are not fictions. It is true that, in some instances, they were not effective until they were proclaimed to be traditions. The fact that Park and Thomas and Durkheim and Weber did not incorporate Tocqueville into their work does not deny that, for later generations, he has become a part of their effective tradition.

The initiatives for the coalescence of endogenous and exogenous intellectual traditions have in most cases come from within sociology. In that sense sociology has been a realm of its own with its own center of gravity, its own discriminatory powers. This has been tantamount to a continuing expansion of sociology in its subject-matters, in the differentiation of its analytical schemes and its corresponding interpretative hypotheses; it has entailed the increasing stringency of its procedural standards.

The tradition which is regarded as sociological is heterogeneous; it is really more proper to speak of sociological traditions within a sociological tradition. It is heterogeneous because of the imperfections in the assimilation or integration of the many coalescent subsidiary or tributary traditions, and it is heterogeneous because very few sociologists accept or even know all of it. The various strands of the sociological tradition are not shared equally by all sociologists. Not only are there the limitations imposed by the specialization of knowledge, but there are also differences in interest and esteem which mean that any particular sociologist will be more sympathetic to one strand or family of traditions and more hostile towards certain others.

Sociology does not however live from an intellectual inheritance alone. Its exertions are not confined to the refinement and enrichment of that inheritance by the study of the problems which that inheritance offers and by the incorporation of new elements from exogenous intellectual traditions. Sociology does not just live within its primary institutional system however dense and absorbing that is. It also belongs to the larger world. Its subject-matter is that larger world. Those who profess it are parts of the larger world. Sociologists are members of social classes, nationalities, ethnic groups, religious communities, political organizations, and they share to some extent the culture of these parts of society. They belong to their society and their generation and they share to some extent in the cognitive beliefs and evaluative attitudes of their society and generation. Sociologists are citizens in their own societies and they respond to the problems of their societies. The institutional establishment of sociology proceeded partly on an assumption that sociological knowledge would be "used" to improve societies; it has entailed training students for roles in their societies. The institutionalization itself has been greatly furthered by the belief of those in positions of authority and influence in that larger world that sociology "has something to contribute" beyond its contribution to the intellectual improvement of the sociological tradition. Part of the institutionalization of sociology in recent decades has involved both the financial support—by grants and contracts—of research by university research workers on particular subjects designated by the patron and the conduct of research within the corporate framework of public or private bodies concerned in a practical way with certain problems which sociological knowledge would presumably help to solve.

It has been claimed that sociology often chooses its problems and its subject-matters according to criteria of value-relevance and not just in terms of the pattern of problems presented by the intellectual tradition. For example, the study of the Negro, as developed by the Chicago sociologists, has been asserted to be a "response" to the problems of urbanization and migration. It was that but it was at least as importantly a study of the processes of competition, conflict, accommodation, and assimilation and of the conditions of their increase and decrease. These categories had been developed by Park from his study of Simmel, Kistiakowski, and Gumplowicz, from his study of the work of Warming, and from his own observations, both direct and historical, in the United States and in other countries. These seem to me to be still more or less the right categories in which to study the relations between groups, including those between whites and blacks in the United States. Before the Second World War, the study of the Negro in America was further enriched by the introduction of certain variables of psychoanalytic origin, and a number of valuable monographs were produced along these lines. There was nothing in the world of practical affairs which "required" this reaching out from sociology towards psychoanalysis. It simply appeared to John Dollard, who was a collaborator of Ogburn and connected with Lasswell, to be reasonable to interpret certain actions and attitudes in psychoanalytic terms. But at a time when the Negro question was not less urgent than it had been before, and for no good reason other than the fact that the newly emergent sociological theory did not deal with ethnic groups and their relations with each other as a particular concrete subject-matter, the Negro receded as an object of sociological study in the United States. This occurred very little after the time when Myrdal's vast synthesis of American, to a large extent Chicago, research appeared. Why? Had the analytical problems involving competition, conflict, accommodation, and assimilation been so exhaustively solved that the subject no longer had anything interesting to offer? Or did the Negroes themselves cease to be a "value-problem" in the United States? Neither of these answers is acceptable.

The decline in intellectual interest in the Negroes in the United

States was a result of several factors. The first is that the new centers of sociological study—Harvard and Columbia in particular—had their own substantive intellectual traditions which did not include in substance the study of the Negro. In Max Weber, primordial things received little explicit attention—in *Wirtschaft und Gesellschaft* only one small chapter eleven pages in length is given to "ethnische Gemeinschaften," and in the writings of Talcott Parsons they received no attention until the 1960s, when the Negro problem became very urgent in the United States. I think that until relatively recently not more than two Harvard Ph.D. dissertations were written on Negroes. At Columbia, where several interesting dissertations had been written on Negroes, e.g., Kiser's *Sea Island to City*, in the 1930s, the period in which Paul Lazarsfeld and Robert Merton ruled, the subject nearly disappeared. It did not recommend itself theoretically and there was little interest in supporting research on it. The eclectic analytical outlook of Professor Merton could certainly have been accommodated to almost any subject matter and the technical virtuosity of Professor Lazarsfeld was likewise as applicable to the study of race relations and to the study of Negro society as it was to mass communications, housing estates, etc. Yet practically no work was done at Columbia on the Negro, although the Negro quarter of New York was immediately adjacent to Columbia University. In Chicago, in the disorientation referred to earlier and under the impact of the Harvard and Columbia styles of sociological theory and research, the interest in the Negro was allowed to lapse. The old center lost its confidence in its own substantive tradition.

In the 1960s, when the "Negro problem" came to the forefront of American political and public opinion with an unprecedented urgency, the study of the Negro was revived, but within a rather narrower framework and in any case a different one from that which guided the earlier studies. New methods of measurement of occupational discrimination, of the share of the Negro population in the national income, etc., have been undertaken, but the social structure of Negro communities and of Negro-white relationships as developed in the tradition of W. I. Thomas, Park, and Burgess by Charles Johnson, Franklin Frazier, Bertram Doyle, Harold Gosnell, Edward Thompson, and Everett Hughes has not been taken up again. The "Negro subject-matter" of sociology might have survived the period from 1940 to 1960 if the Chicago tradition had received an authoritative theoretical formulation capable of demanding explicit incorporation into a new analytical scheme equal in attractiveness to that which was developing at Harvard. Since, however, it had not gone beyond fragmentary, only implicitly coherent statements, its competitive power was not sufficient. Thus, despite the analytical affinity of the Chicago tradition with the newer developments in the sociological tradition, its idiom was submerged and, with that, its particular subject-matter. Had its idiom survived in the new analytical scheme, its associated subject-matter would likewise have survived.

The vicissitudes of the study of the Negro in the United States would indicate that the substantive analytical or theoretical tradition is not primarily a product of exogenous, nonintellectual occurrences. The change in the tradition of studying a particular subject-matter was, in my view, to a large extent a result of the adhesion of particular subject-matters to particular analytical traditions and of changes in the institutional system of sociology (e.g., the relocation of the center from Chicago). It was not wholly so; the absence of patronage for research on Negroes was probably another factor as was the fact that in the 1950s many white sociologists were giving their attention to other problems of American life such as "McCarthyism," "mass culture," "underdeveloped countries," etc. The reemergence of the Negro as a subject-matter of sociological research has indeed been a consequence of exogenous events, which occur outside of the intellectual sphere as well as outside sociology. The migration of Negroes to northern cities in response to opportunities for employment and the greater measure of freedom, and the determination of the federal government to assure the civil rights of the Negroes, were events which might be called demographic, economic, and political. They belonged to a category of things different from sociology but they drew the attention of sociologists and induced the sociologists to study these events. But the scheme of analysis was not much affected by these demographic, economic, and political events. Rather it remained very much a product of the sociological tradition; in its emphasis on the anomic element in the black section of American society it drew more and more on the Durkheimian element of the sociological tradition, mediated by Merton's reformulation.

The study of "popular" or "mass culture" is another illustration of the interplay of endogenous and exogenous intellectual traditions and exogenous nonintellectual events. Tönnies, Simmel, and Weber created the tradition, but it was the sociologists'—especially Mannheim's and Horkheimer's—response to the National Socialist movement and its triumph in Germany and the great expansion of the study of the content of and "exposure" to mass communications which led to the expansion of attention to "mass society" in American sociology in the 1950s. Changes in the outlook of certain literary and publicistic intellectuals in the United States—I think particularly of their disillusionment with Marxism attendant on the identification of Marxism and Stalinism and the simultaneous disillusionment with the "working classes" for their failure to act as agents of revolution and as the "heirs of German classical philosophy"—made for the animation of certain elements already contained in the central tradition of sociology. The nonintellectual events—the successes of the

National Socialists and the increased prominence of "mass culture"—did not divert the tradition of sociology. The tradition of sociology elaborated what it already contained in order to treat these events.

The career of industrial sociology and the sociology of work is another instance of a subject which was developed in the framework of the central tradition of sociology—much influenced by Durkheim's ideas about anomie and Max Weber's ideas about bureaucracy—and supported by private business management. In the United States, after about twenty-five years of fairly fruitful work by Mayo, Whyte, and Hughes, the subject lost its glamour—although obviously not its intellectual or practical significance. American sociologists left the subject.[30]

They went on to organizational analyses—under the inspiration of Chester Barnard, Max Weber, and Herbert Simon—and on to studies of the professions of medicine, law, and science. The theoretical or analytical scheme remains what is offered by the older tradition, enriched and differentiated by the new data. The change in particular subject-matters is perhaps more a product of the availability of financial support for the study of these subjects, the much greater prominence in public opinion of the learned professions and especially of the scientific profession, and the decline among intellectuals of the prestige of the working classes. Following this, sociologists in the United States returned to the lower classes—not so much to the employed "respectable" proletariat as to the unemployed, the "poor," or what was called by Marx the *Lumpenproletariat.* This change is partly a function of changes in the focus of attention in public opinion and in intellectual circles and of the opportunities afforded by the availability of financial support for such research. The relocation of subject-matter interest is relatively recent but thus far there is no evidence that it has affected the intellectual pattern of the central tradition.

These successions of subject-matters are never disjunctive. When a subject-matter ceases to be cultivated at a center, the cessation does not simultaneously occur at the peripheries or at secondary centers. A subject-matter tends to persist longer at the periphery than at the center. Indeed sometimes an institution in the periphery or a sub-center may persist in dealing with a certain subject-matter over a long period during which a center can pass through several fashions in subject-matter.

In Great Britain, a large proportion of the much increased volume of sociological research in the quarter of a century following the war

30. During the years of the depression of the 1930s, interesting investigations were made into the effects of unemployment on individual morale, family life, etc. Such studies were dropped from the agenda of sociological research when nearly full employment replaced massive unemployment.

was concerned with the working classes and the poor. This showed the strength of the British intellectual tradition—largely pre-academic—deriving from the statistical surveys of poverty of the nineteenth and early twentieth centuries, as well as of the availability of financial support for inquiries into such subject-matters. The power of this tradition in Great Britain has been so great that the analytical tradition such as has been preponderant on the Continent and in the United States has not made its way easily. The chief analytical achievement of British sociology, T. H. Marshall's *Citizenship and Social Class,* is very much an elaboration of the British tradition, formulated in more general terms than ever before. Yet this tradition has been brought into fusion with the American and Continental variants of the sociological tradition in the work of Michael Young. W. G. Runciman, and David Lockwood.

What we see from these few sketchily presented illustrations is that exogenous nonintellectual conditions or situations have indeed played a significant part in bringing subject-matters into the center of attention of sociological research. This happens because sociologists are citizens of their societies and are concerned with what they think are its practical problems; it also happens because governments and philanthropic bodies are more inclined to support sociological research when it deals with a "practical problem," i.e., studies a condition with which government and public opinion are concerned, than they are to support research which does not appear to be practical. Nonetheless, these variations in the choice of subject-matters do not impose parallel variations in the analytical framework of sociology which is contained in the central tradition. This traditional framework of sociology has extraordinary continuity and stability. At the same time, this framework remains vague and ambiguous in its major categories; this gives it flexibility and assimilative capacity. That is why it has been able to incorporate into itself certain exogenous intellectual traditions. These exogenous traditions when they are incorporated sometimes only involve making more explicit elements in the central tradition itself, as in the case of the incorporation of some elements of the "science of religion" into sociology. In other instances, as in the case of the elaboration of the "theory of culture," they are compelling the jettisoning of the Darwinian, Deweyan-Freudian tradition that cultural works are the products of the efforts of the individual organism to survive in a dangerous environment.

The Form of a Sociological Work

The strength of a dominant tradition of sociology vis-à-vis exogenous intellectual traditions and practical situations is evident also in the character of its influence on contemporary research.

A tradition can be influential in an academic discipline in several ways. In one way, the most recent period's output of works provides the immediate point of departure for the next stage of research; the works produced in that most recent period were produced from a point of departure constituted by a body of works produced still earlier. The works of the relatively remote past—the past of the middle distance—are influential either through having served in their own time as a point of departure for the step which followed or through the constitution of a framework of concepts or variables and fundamental problems within which the works which constitute a sequence of successive points of departure are produced. The latter are the monuments of the subject, not merely honorific monuments, but effective ones. It is conceivable that these monuments are unknown by name to those who work within the framework to which the monuments have contributed. There is nothing especially damaging about this except for the shamefulness of ignorance and disregard of intellectual ancestry and indebtedness. It is often said that what is relevant for the development of knowledge in a given field is after all contained in the latest stage of the tradition, that is, in the detailed research or the detailed analytical paper which provides the immediate point of departure for the next stage of the subject. But nutriment is also to be obtained from constant recourse to the monument.

There are thus two patterns in the relationship of present work in a field to the tradition of that field. These two patterns correspond to the patterns prevailing in the natural sciences and in sociology respectively.

The most common form of scientific work is the short journal article which states the problem, which formulates and locates the hypothesis in relation to what has been established and what has been left open by previous research, which describes the arrangements of research or experimental procedure, reports the observations or experimental results, and proposes the modification of previous hypotheses or beliefs required by the results of the reported investigation. There are also synthetic, compendious summaries of existing theoretical and experimental work which intend not to establish new knowledge but to consolidate and order what is known in a broad field. These might be monographs with an element of originality of interpretation of what has been demonstrated by research or they might be textbooks which summarize what students and research workers at a certain level of their scientific development are expected to know.

In sociology, parallel to the differences in the procedures and intellectual structure of the subject in comparison with the sciences, works tend to take the following forms: monographic treatises describing a particular subject-matter, e.g., a territorially delineated sector of society, a group or a stratum or a profession. They sometimes take the physical form of the monograph of twenty thousand words or more frequently a full-length book of one hundred thousand words. (The latter is often only an expansion of the former.) They contain much descriptive data with analytical remarks and usually, at the end, a general interpretation of the phenomenon in relation to its larger setting. These monographs or monographs-within-books are usually directed at a problem—relationships between variables—although their ostensible point of departure is a particular subject-matter, e.g., the medical profession in a given city or country, or a particular process, e.g., social mobility within a given country. There are also monographs which seek to deal with problems: these begin with an attempt to explain a major phenomenon, e.g., specifically capitalistic acquisitive behavior as in Max Weber's *Protestant Ethic,* the causes of various kinds of suicide as in Durkheim's *Suicide,* the effect of political campaigns on voting choice as in Lazarsfeld's *The People's Choice,* or the influence on the educational accomplishment of school children of the intellectual composition of their school class as in Coleman's *Equality of Educational Opportunity.*

There is also the journal article—corresponding to the scientific paper—which summarizes the existing state of knowledge on a particular problem, formulates a hypothesis, presents the data which report observations made by the author or by others—and then attempts to harmonize the resultant interpretation of the data with previous interpretations.

There are also essays which clarify, refine, and differentiate particular ideas—concepts, categories, processes, variables, etc.— without close reference to observations except for illustrative purposes, and which put forward hypotheses about the relationships among variables only incidentally or illustratively.

There are also comprehensive theoretical treatises which present "all" the major concepts or variables which the author believes relevant to sociology as a whole as well as some hypotheses about the behavior of these variables under different conditions. One might mention here works as various as Weber's *Wirtschaft und Gesellschaft,* Parsons' *The Social System,* and Homan's *Social Behavior.*

These theoretical treatises verge at their lower levels into textbooks which cover all the concepts of variables and present illustrative data and some hypotheses. Such works as Kingsley Davis and Wilbert Moore's *Society: An Analysis,* H. M. Johnson's *Sociology,* or Park and Burgess' *Introduction to the Science of Sociology* are representative. Sociological textbooks usually contain much descriptive material from monographs and articles but very little rigorously established, widely accepted knowledge—unlike textbooks in the natural sciences.

Finally, there are collections of essays of single authors; this form has become relatively widespread since the end of the Second World War. Indeed collections of essays by Parsons and Merton have been among the most influential books of the past two decades. The essays have usually been analyses of concepts, elaborations of themes, rather than scientific papers.[31] Such collections are also found in the sciences, but for the most part they are monumental in intention, being the works of very distinguished figures, living or dead, and many of the papers published in these collections have already played a great part in the development of these subjects and have outlived their immediate usefulness. They have a different function from the collection of papers in sociology because of the longer life of the sociological paper.

The function of the books composed of sociological essays discloses a major difference between the characteristic patterns of the growth of the knowledge in sociology and in the sciences. In the latter, the most important means of speedy, non-oral communication are journal papers and, more recently, preprints. The journal paper in its original form is important in the production of scientific research; when reprinted in book form, it is likely only to have historical interest. The "preprint" in science is the very opposite of the reprinting of sociological essays in book form. The scientific "preprint" is a product of the speed with which the tradition of a scientific field is being modified or supplemented; the reprint of a sociological essay is a function of the continued dominance of the tradition, particularly the dominance of the monuments.

The essay can be reprinted in a sociological book because it has a long life, whereas a scientific paper must perform its function within a relatively short time after its moment of publication.[32] The difference

31. The collection of essays is different from the "reader" which in sociology is a more "scientific" type of textbook than the conventional compendium of discursive expositions of concepts and illustrative data. The "reader" as a textbook is usually a collection of research reports which have appeared as articles in journals. The editors, unlike the authors of textbooks in scientific subjects, do not consolidate existing knowledge as it bears on particular problems; they simply present the sources—journal articles—from which in scientific textbooks interpretative consolidation is made.

32. The tendency, now widespread among social scientists, to distribute their writings in mimeographed, dittoed, or xeroxed form before publication is not an effort to inform the rest of the social science community of results achieved and verified, but rather the opposite. The distributed paper is a preliminary version, and the distribution is an effort to elicit criticisms; it is an acknowledgment of the tentative and uncertain status of what is presented in the paper circulated. It is also a product of the affluence of university departments and of the generosity of research grants which could offer the financial means for such reproduction and distribution of preliminary results. There is little fear in sociology of "anticipation" by other workers engaged in research on similar problems; this is one of the considerations underlying the production and circulation of "preprints" in the natural sciences.

might be accounted for by the much sharper focus of research in the sciences, by the more consensual perception and interpretation of the results of any particular piece of research, and by the more immediate response in the form of further investigation of the problems which that particular piece of research raises.

The completion of a piece of research in science entails its publication. Scientific knowledge is a collective possession; the results of research become accredited as scientific knowledge when they are affirmed by other qualified scientists. Discovery, therefore, integrally entails publication. To launch on a campaign of discovery is to launch on a course which requires publication as the temporary end-state of the act of discovery. A work of research which does not contribute to the pool of knowledge is a wasted effort and failure to publish results which might be right is as much of a waste as wrong results. If the delay in publication is long, then the results of research will usually be rendered out-of-date. They will have been superseded by the results of the research of someone else. This high probability of supersession is a function of the greater precision of the formulation of problems in the sciences and of the greater specificity of formulation and the greater concentration of effort on particular problems in the natural sciences.

There are relatively few instances of the very specific articulation of successive research papers in sociology in comparison with any field of comparable scope in the natural sciences. This is partly a function of the much lower degree of specialization and the much less differentiated division of labor in sociology than in the sciences. The less differentiated division of labor in sociology is in turn a function of the much greater quantity of literature produced in any field of the sciences and of the closely related phenomenon, the larger number of persons working in any special field in the sciences. But without the specificity of focus and the greater consensus about the crucial problem which is characteristic of the natural sciences, the number of workers and the volume of literature on a given problem would not be decisive in abbreviating the life span of a scientific paper.

This greater concentration of minds on particular, specifically delineated problems results in a more rapid obsolescence of works in the natural sciences than in sociology. That is why the book made up of essays published over a period of twenty years can be an esteemed sociological work, as it has been in the case of the collections of Parsons' and Merton's essays, while its counterpart would make rather little sense in the natural sciences.

It would be wrong to describe the movement of any specialized branch of the natural sciences as linear. Nonetheless, movement in those fields is more linear than it is in sociology. In sociology, the function of a classic is not to be assimilated, surpassed, and rendered out-of-date as in the natural sciences, but to be elaborated, adapted, put into a new idiom, applied to a new situation. The results of research support an illustration and confirm the plausibility of a general theme; there are very few instances of a demonstration or confirmation of a general proposition. There is little linear movement in sociology: there is an intensification of intimacy. That is why the monuments, the classic works of sociology, continue to intrigue sociologists. I do not know whether it must necessarily be so for all times in the future. That, however, is the way it has been.

There are many reasons for this persisting value of the classics of sociology. In the first place, the greatest sociologists are plainly much better than most sociologists. Sociologists, despite the disparagement to whch they are often subjected, do have a sense of quality and they appreciate broad perspective and the deeply penetrating insight. This is not the whole story. These broad perspectives and penetrating insights are into social situations which interest sociologists. They are directed towards relatively contemporary situations. After all, sociological theory has mainly been about modern Western society; other societies have been treated for purposes of a clearer delineation of the features of modern society, and modern Western society despite marked changes over the course of the past century still has sufficient identity with what it was a century or three-quarters of a century ago for observations made then to be pertinent to the understanding of present-day society. Furthermore, because of the disjunctiveness of particular investigations, the results of any single investigation, not being articulated with other investigations, the same subjects have no coercive influence over theoretical interpretation. Sociological theory has been relatively free from domination by the results of research. Theory has not been rendered out-of-date by research because research is not consulted by theory, partly because of the discreteness of many investigations into the same subject-matters.

Indeed it is because of the chaos of the results of research that the famous theorists are clung to; they are sources of intellectual order in the midst of intellectual disorder. Such sense as can be made of the variegated results of so many disjunctive inquiries can only be made with the aid of the leading theorists. Their ideas, however they might be judged *sub specie aeternitatis*, are the best ideas available to sociologists and they are in fact often very helpful for the task to which they are summoned. The movement is not circular. Theory might help in the interpretation of the results of particular investigations or in synthesizing those results, but the theory is not correspondingly enriched or made more precise. The continuing independence of theory from research or at least the very loose relations between them explains to some extent why the classics of sociological theory do not become absolute in the way in which great works of natural science do.

The Profession of Sociology

Whereas at the turn of the century there were very few persons who called themselves sociologists anywhere in the world and even fewer who made a livelihood from it, there are now many thousands who teach what is called sociology in lists of courses offered in universities and thousands who are employed by governmental bodies, independent research institutions, market research organizations, public opinion surveying organizations, industrial firms, hospitals, military organizations, to do research which is generally classified as sociological. Most of the colleges and universities in the Western world now provide teaching in sociology and so do many in Latin America, the Far East, South Asia, and Africa south of the Sahara. Most of them permit sociology to serve alone or in one combination or another as a qualification for a degree. There are at least twenty-five journals in the major languages which have the word "sociology" or "sociological" in their titles or subtitles. There are about thirty national professional sociological societies, and in some countries there are also more specialized professional associations which regard themselves as covering a section of sociology. There is an international association with affiliated societies in every continent. Sociology has become a subject of a profession formed around a rather loosely delineated body of learning and a more or less common intellectual interest.

One consequence of the formation of this profession is a movement towards homogeneity. National differences still exist among the dominant types of sociology—differences in theoretical inclinations, preferred subjects of research, favored techniques, etc.—but there has also formed a large common sociological culture—just as there is such a culture, despite specialization, within each country with many sociologists.

This common culture is the result of the fusion of productions of major writers from different countries into a common pool and of the ascendancy of the sociologists of a particular country—in the last three decades, those of the United States. It is true that sociology written in the English language enjoys the advantages of an assymetrically greater accessibility. Sociologists everywhere read what is written by sociologists in English, but sociologists in the English-speaking world read less of what is written in most other countries. Efforts are made to overcome this by publication in English, e.g., the *Acta Sociologica* of the Scandinavian countries and *Sociologica Nederlandica* which brings representative works of Dutch sociologists before those sociologists who cannot read Dutch. It is probably true that on average the sociologists of the English-speaking world are less capable of reading French and German than their predecessors were seventy-five years ago. Nonetheless they probably have more of

European sociology more easily available to them through translations and personal meetings than did their predecessors.

The professional cultivation of sociology has not made sociology self-sufficient. It has continued to draw upon other intellectual traditions, both academic and nonacademic. In each country sociology has also found an audience outside of professional sociologists. Before sociology became institutionally established, the audience of sociological writings was inevitably lay to a very large extent. Comte and Spencer wrote for all educated and earnest persons. In the early years of sociology at Chicago, the intended audience was both lay and professional, although not always in the same writings. This bifurcation became more pronounced through the 1920s. *Middletown* was written for both lay and professional audiences; so were the books in the Carnegie Corporation's series on "Americanization" by Park, Thomas, and others. Nonetheless, most writings by sociologists were intended for study by other sociologists. In the 1930s *Recent Social Trends* was intended for the two audiences simultaneously; so was *The American Dilemma* which although written by a Swede was very much an American sociological work. While more and more sociology was being written exclusively for a professional audience, books like *The Lonely Crowd* were obviously intended as much for a lay as a professional audience. The writings of Horkheimer, Adorno, Habermas, Schelsky, and Dahrendorf in Germany certainly have not been intended only for a professional audience. Much of the work of Raymond Aron is likewise intended for an audience wider than students of sociology and their teachers.

Despite the fact that sociology in the English language has shown a potentiality of isolating itself through its ponderous and inexact language and stylistic barbarism the isolation has not in fact occurred. The curiosity of the educated classes outside of sociology has grown as their stylistic intolerance has diminished. Perhaps they no longer know any better, perhaps they do not mind—the rest of the academic profession now writes in a style not too different from that of sociology at its worst. In any case, sociology has not been rendered inaccessible to nonsociologists by reason of its astonishing literary qualities. It is not even likely that the mathematization of sociology which is in prospect—in some measure at least—will isolate sociology from the increasingly mathematically educated classes. As the years pass, with the proportion of the population which has attended university still increasing, the proportion which has studied some sociology at university is still increasing. This creates a lay audience with a smattering of the knowledge possessed by professional sociologists.

The earlier generations of sociologists in the present century were for the most part a fairly optimistic lot of men. Max Weber was rather exceptional. They assumed that knowledge itself was a good, they assumed that sociology was on the right path towards the development of a better knowledge of society, and they thought that society would be correspondingly improved as it guided itself through taking into consideration knowledge created and provided by sociologists. The institutional establishment of sociology was intended to further the realization of all three of these desirable ends.

Institutional establishment has certainly occurred in nearly all its aspects and probably beyond the capacities of the sociologists attracted to the profession and hence beyond the knowledge which they have been able to create. There are dangers to a society the expectations of which are greater than its resources, economic and cognitive. Truths are expected of sociology which sociology has not yet produced and which it might not produce in the near future. A society places itself at risk when it entrusts itself—even if only in small measure—to lightly attained opinions which pass as knowledge. Institutional establishment only strengthens the position of such opinions; it does not necessarily correct them.

The Dominance of Tradition and the Growth of Sociology

As sociology has become more institutionalized, it has become more prolific. The institutionalization of training has produced a human product with a mastery of some techniques of research, a modicum of a sociological culture, and an ethos which prizes research. The institutionalization of research—the institutional provision of opportunities, funds, and employment, of facilities for research and publication, the standardization of research procedures, and the general approbation of research within intellectual institutions and the larger society all contribute to an increased volume of research. This is true in the United States above all but it is also true of numerous countries where the contemporary type of research is a much newer growth, whether it is either a new implantation or a renewed practice of an older tradition.

This change has taken place under the auspices of "science." Sociologists increasingly believe that their work falls under the tradition of science and that it is one member of the family of sciences. The old discussions regarding the differences between the natural and the social sciences have evaporated with the arguments which demonstrated that sociology had a rightful place in "the classification of the sciences." The discussion as to whether sociology is a "natural science" is cold mutton. Part of the conception which sociologists have of themselves is expressed in their preferred form of publication, namely, the paper published in a professional journal. The bibliography of sociology is increasingly made up of papers in journals in which the state of the problem and its literature are reviewed, a hypothesis formulated, data presented, and an interpretation made. With the multiplication of the literature, the size of the subcommunity of sociologists becoming larger in almost every subfield of sociology, a sociologist can now spend most of his sociological career as a specialist on juvenile delinquents, military organization, the aged, the mass media, penal institutions, urbanization, the police, narcotics addicts, etc. Many of the specialized fields acquire and establish an identity of their own with their own elites and counter-elites, their own culture, sometimes their own journals. The literature of the other specialized fields becomes more and more remote from them. As sociologists become "professionals," as so many proudly aver, specialization is accepted, sometimes with the melancholy resignation counseled in *Wissenschaft als Beruf*, sometimes with an air of self-congratulation. The new professionals of sociology are a tough-minded lot, they shun armchairs, they speak of questionnaires as "instruments," they speak of "research technology," they are conversant with the language of computers, they are condescending towards "grand theory," negotiations for grants for research projects are frequently on their minds and lips. They are doggedly optimistic about building a science of sociology and, as a science under present-day conditions, it must in their view be specialized and it must be cumulative.

There are limits to specialization in sociology as there are in the natural sciences; as a result of these limits, specialization which is necessary is not likely to be injurious. The limits are not those which would arise from the sterility of an uninhibited narrowing of the focus of attention—of "knowing more and more about less and less." They are limits engendered by the institutionalization which has made specialization possible within sociology. This specialization is not likely to disintegrate the community of sociologists.

There has formed within each country—and increasingly between countries—an intellectual community, the members of which read each other's works, some of them even before publication. To some extent they read more or less the same body of literature; they exist within departments which are diverse in the specialized interests of their members, but as teachers jointly responsible for the students' education in sociology they have to look beyond their own specialized research.

It is of course true that the large number of sociologists within a large national sociological community, and internationally, does permit the formation of relatively self-centered subcommunities of specialists in such fields as educational sociology, gerontological sociology, etc.

These specialized fields do not however wholly isolate their members from those of other specialized fields. No field fails to impinge on another equally specialized field. Thus, for example, a sociologist studying the aged cannot avoid the necessity for studying the literature on the family, on urbanization and demography, on geriatric medicine and medical sociology, etc.; and the same holds for every other field of sociological specialization. As a result, the consensus as regards techniques of research, findings, and lines of interpretation extends beyond the boundaries of any subcommunity of specialists into adjacent subcommunities of specialists. In this way a series of overlaps links the entire profession of sociology. Specialization of sociology has not yet progressed to the point, nor is it likely to do so in the foreseeable future, where one field cuts itself off entirely from its intellectual neighbors or from the sociological family as a whole.

There are, furthermore, limits in specialization imposed by the dominance within the institutional system of the tradition which is constantly reexhibited in the sociological essay, which is common, and in the less frequent sociological treatise. After all, the institutionalization has occurred in universities, and in universities abstract ideas have a pride of place, however hard pressed they are by the demands of specialization. If a postgraduate student has done sociology as an undergraduate, he has acquired a sociological culture which is common to sociologists; even if he has done a different subject as an undergraduate and begins his sociological studies in a situation committed to specialized research, he must nonetheless absorb a certain amount of the common sociological culture which is made up of the dominant traditions and some of the subsidiary traditions.

Sociological training is much less specialized than sociological research. A student must cover a much wider body of literature than that directly pertinent to the field in which he will do his research. Sociology now being an academic subject, the leading research workers are also teachers of sociology: and this means that they have often to teach subjects which are somewhat outside their specialized field of research. This, too, has a unifying effect, although it does not create or maintain a completely common sociological culture. The fact that sociology is no longer the work of amateurs but is taught and largely practiced within universities in which "theory" has prestige despite the criticism directed against particular theories, means that the prestige-conferring "classics" are taught in practically all universities. For better or for worse, there is a *tronc commun* from which sociologists derive some of their intellectual dignity. Durkheim, Weber, Parsons, Merton, and lesser lights are repeatedly quoted and invoked over a very wide range of specialized fields of research.

These famous sociologists are so generally recurred to, not just because those who have recourse to them wish to avoid the appearance of being no better than intellectual hewers of wood and drawers of water. They are brought in because there is a deeply felt need among sociologists to be part of an ongoing intellectual tradition which has among its other merits that of helping to explain one's particular findings in the light of certain major variables, such as solidarity and conflict, equality and inequality, deference and presumption, authority and rejection, charisma and rational and traditional routine, bureaucracy, etc., and the vague, unarticulated interpretations which are associated with them. Contemporary sociologists are less the creators of their tradition than they are its beneficiaries and prisoners.[33] They cannot escape from their traditions. This might hold sociology back from making marked scientific progress but at the same time it enables it to cope with otherwise bewildering results of empirical research and from the loss of perspective which specialization would otherwise engender.

It might be said that the unifying classics of sociology are so important to its contemporary practitioners because sociology is not at present a real science. If sociology were a science, its masterworks would have become so assimilated into the flow of sociological work that their accomplishment would have been taken for granted. The classics of sociology remain important because sociological analysis is so much devoted to the elucidation of certain major themes which continue to dominate the attention of sociologists, partly because the great figures drew attention to them, and partly because experience and the concern which they have molded have shown them to be the proper subjects of study.

An effective intellectual tradition is not merely a timeless gallery of works nor is it merely a sequence in time of works arranged by later scholars. An effective intellectual tradition is a linkage of works through influence exercised over time. This is the kind of tradition which obtains in the real sciences and it also obtains in sociology. In the real sciences, intellectual influence is usually fairly immediate—there are exceptions—and the works which are enduringly constitutive of tradition function through entering anonymously into the continuing flow; they lose their identity in so doing. Such tradition-setting works provide a framework of concepts which sets research tasks—and they provide the next stage of research, particular hypotheses to be revised, rejected, or confirmed, and observations which may be accepted as given or which require reinterpretation. In sociology the situation is both similar and different.

33. One of the difficulties is that we cannot imagine anything beyond variations on the themes set by the great figures of nineteenth- and twentieth-century sociology. The fact that the conception of "postindustrial society" is an amalgam of what St. Simon, Comte, Tocqueville, and Weber furnished to our imaginations is evidence that we are confined to an ambiguously defined circle which is more impermeable than it ought to be.

It is similar in the sense that major works provide a framework of concepts which set tasks for research. It is different in that particular investigations are only loosely and vaguely linked with their guiding and legitimating ideas and are also only very loosely linked with other particular investigations of the same subject-matter which have gone just before.

Sociological theory does not quite stand still, but such progress as it makes is not the result of revisions in the light of accumulated observations, rigorously conducted and analyzed.

Many years ago I wrote about the "discontinuity" of sociological development; I had in mind among other things the flightiness of sociologists who take up a subject, cultivate it for a time, and then drop it before the subject has been brought to intellectual fruition. I had in mind as instances the study of human ecology and of primary groups. I also had in mind the more specific unconnectedness of exact investigations of ostensibly identical subject-matters or problems. This latter type of discontinuity between specialized investigations of what are alleged to be the same variables persists relatively undiminished, despite the greatly increased "scientificness" of sociology.

It is at just this point that one of the chief difficulties of present-day sociology lies. To take up where one predecessor left off entails the acceptance of the delineation of the variables studied by the predecessor in exactly the form in which they were put by the predecessor. The point of leaving off in sociology is difficult to locate because of the vagueness in the definition of variables and the vagueness of interpretations of data. The categories involved in interpretation, i.e., the theoretical categories, are always broader and vaguer than the categories in which the data were collected or the observations made. The latter vary much from one investigator to another, even though they believe themselves to be working on the same problem. When, for good reasons or for poor ones, each subsequent investigator "improves" on his predecessor's working delineation of the relevant variables, by asking different questions or using different indicators, then articulation, comparison, and accumulation become difficult. What does in fact happen is that a somewhat different variable replaces the one previously studied; they are both presumed to represent the same thing when such is not actually the case; careful attempts to collate them and to make the results coherent are often frustrated. There are many other causes for this disarticulation: different populations studied; different criteria of classification, etc. One additional source of this difficulty lies in the "great ideas" of sociology; they obviously refer to very important things—otherwise they would not hold the attention of sociologists as they have for so many decades—but they are extremely ambiguous and they are resistant to authoritative clarification.

The unity which transcends the passage of time and the growing specialization in sociology rests on this common preoccupation with a relatively small number of "key words." The "key words" and the ideas which they evoke have become indelibly imprinted on the sociological tradition—so much so that they can never be merely an honorific decoration. They have become constitutive of sociological analysis. They have formed the sociological mind. Theory is recognized as such by the presence of those "key words" in all their misty and simple grandeur. Their adduction in dealing with the results of empirical investigations into particular contemporary situations is an essential phase of interpretation.

It would be better if sociology had a much more differentiated set of categories, a much more differentiated set of names for distinguishable things. It would be better if it could name many more things and name them in agreed and recognizable ways. Above all, it would be a great improvement if the general terms of theories could become more intimately and more rigorously linked with the particular things which are observed. But this will involve moving from research to theory as well as from theory to research and from theory to theory.

There is no necessary reason why this should be impossible. It is simply difficult. It has not been done before and the deficiencies of institutional establishment cannot be adduced to explain the failure. For a time, at the height of their collaboration, Merton and Lazarsfeld at Columbia seemed to be moving in the right direction. But this moment has passed and the prospect seems less bright than it was.

Now this does not mean that all sociology is prattle or that even if it never becomes truly scientific that it is not a very worthy activity as an understanding, intimate type of history. Its theories are not superfluous just because they have not been scientifically confirmed. Some of them—or at least parts of them—do render events more intelligible, they do illuminate the associations which research discovers among particular facts. They are not arbitrary; sometimes they contain exceptionally wise insight into human affairs. Some of the theories make more sense out of the diversity of events than others, but even then much is left in a blurred condition.

Institutional establishment has not been able to overcome this difficulty although it has provided conditions for the amelioration of a situation which was once worse in this respect than it is at present.

The benefits of institutional establishment are real but there are vices which it cannot cure and errors which it cannot prevent. It cannot make wise men and women out of fools; it has not been able to prevent the outcropping of antinomian ideology which puts itself forward as serious sociology. Just as fruitful theoretical interpretation requires good judgment and much learning so does institutional establishment. Without persons committed to the traditional ethos of learning, institutional establishment is powerless. At its best, institutional establishment can foster the mutual criticism which is needed for the improvement of the present situation: it can by its support of continuous teaching and research keep the challenge and demand alive. It can keep the stage set for the closer approximation to what now appears to be the desirable next steps. But these steps cannot be set in motion by the design or the by-products of institutions. For that, imagination on the order of genius is required, proceeding from the tradition which we now have. This tradition might be an encumbrance but it must also be the point of departure for the next steps which are urgently needed for the improvement of sociology.

Part Three

Sociology and Society

5   Social Science and Social Policy

The problem of the right relationship between thought and knowledge on the one side and will and action on the other has been present from antiquity. The terms in which the problem has been discussed have varied with the changes in the types of knowledge most pursued and esteemed, but the problem has remained.

It has remained because it is given in the nature of action and because thought cannot renounce preoccupation with action—although thought deals with many other things than action. It has remained because thinkers cannot renounce their conviction that action would be improved by the assimilation into it of the results of thought and because those whose main concern is practical action are always beset by contingencies in which they think that they need the aid of thought. It has remained because thinkers and those who act in positions of authority are never satisfied with each other. Thinkers believe that they know things which would bring benefits to those who take practical action. The latter often disregard what the former would have them believe.

The efflorescence of the social sciences over the past two centuries has brought new aspects to the perennial problem. It cannot be said however that the problem is any closer to solution. The following reflections do not pretend to solve the problem. They are no more than reflections on a variety of aspects of the problem as it has been raised through the prominence of the social sciences—meaning thereby sociology, social anthropology, psychology, and political science—in the program and production of intellectual works, and by the heightened efforts of rulers to control and direct their respective societies.

I

The line of thought from which contemporary social science has come forth was occupied with problems of the right ordering of society in ways which have since become very much less prominent in the work of social scientists of the present century. The classic figures of social thought—Aristotle, Plato, Adam Smith, Montesquieu, Jeremy Bentham, James and John Stuart Mill, Ricardo, Hobbes, Locke, Burke, Machiavelli, and Hegel—accepted as their task the definition of the

This is a revised version of an essay that originally appeared in *Philosophy of Science* 16 (July 1949): 219–42, © 1949, The Williams and Wilkins Co., Baltimore.

proper ends of society and the derivation therefrom of the obligations of rulers and citizens. This activity was accompanied by many observations about the conditions and consequences which would affect or flow from the effort to do what is right or to omit to do so. The task of a politician, be he a prince or an elected legislator, was to create and maintain order, a right order. The philosopher's task was to counsel him by teaching him when he was young, by advising him when he was in office, and by instructing public opinion and politicians through writings setting forth the right principles which embraced both ends and means and which considered conditions.

In a gradual process which ran over several centuries of the modern epoch, a change took place. The change was concurrent with the emergence of aspirations to construct a social science—one that would be scientific like physics or astronomy, dealing strictly with observed things.

The great ancestor of modern empirical social research, Sir William Petty, who regarded his intellectual task as the quantitative, matter-of-fact description of what existed, accepted, as the setting of his problem, the prince's need to safeguard and maximize his power. Early economic theory accepted the same setting for its problems; it accepted given ends and analyzed causes and consequences. When mercantilism gave way to liberalism, economic theory was still intended to demonstrate what was the right order of things in society but it was also concerned with conditions, costs, and consequences.

The analysis of conditions, costs, and consequences became more prominent; and the definition of ends receded. Sir William Petty was a forerunner of the view that science was to be built by the observation of empirically ascertainable events. The knowledge gained by this new empirical science would disclose to a ruler the resources available to him, the procedures to make these resources useful to him.

Philosophers who wrote about society and government and the economy had also on occasion been tutors and counselors of princes, members of the entourage of royal courts. In the role of tutor or counselor a philosopher could help to make a ruler wise, as philosophers are wise. The wisdom which the philosopher could infuse into the prince was the knowledge of the right ends of society and government. The prince would thereby be made to approximate the philosopher.

In the course of the great change of modern times, the relationship changed. Intellectual specialization caused philosophers to concentrate on metaphysics, epistemology, the nature of mind, logic, and ethics. The scattered emergence of the social sciences from the interstices of mathematics and astronomy, police statistics, travelers' memoirs, philanthropy, journalism, economics, legal and historical studies was more or less contemporaneous with the scientific belief that religion and philosophy as the guides of human life had failed, and only science could put the human race onto the right path. There was consequently no need for philosophical reflection on the ends of social life or on the right ordering of society. The ends were either self-evident or they would be discovered by scientific research into actually existing situations.

A paradoxical situation came into being. On the one side, social scientists of the nineteenth century studied what they thought were "important social problems," i.e., they studied conditions and activities which they thought needed to be and could be improved or eliminated or which were immovable and which would have to be taken into account by anyone seeking improvement. Improvement, the approximation to or the realization of an ideal, was a common justification for their efforts to describe and understand society. On the other side they had ceased to believe in the possibility of defining the proper aims of policy except by scientific or historical research.

One consequence of this was that social scientists became less "political," in that sense that they attributed less efficacy to the desires and will of governments and the politicians who were in charge of them. They did not think that the decisions of rulers, princes, prime ministers, presidents, and legislators could be decisive; such power to change or to maintain existing social arrangements, in so far as it lay with human beings at all, lay in the "deeper social forces" and in public opinion. It was therefore to the latter that social scientists addressed their work as well as to the more restricted circles of their like-minded professional colleagues. Only by a better understanding of the "deeper forces" at work in the processes and structures of society could the course of society be affected. The main task therefore was to create a scientific social science.

The social sciences became "de-politicized"; the study of politics turned to the production of specific recipes for administrative practice and the description of governmental processes. The other social sciences—economics and the slowly growing sociology and anthropology—were substantively and methodologically apolitical. The desire to establish their disciplines as rigorously scientific and their belief that political preconceptions and passions would hinder this drew them away from politics and politicians.

If the results of the social sciences were to be "useful"—so it came increasingly to be believed—they would be "useful" because they described accurately the situations to be dealt with, the preconditions which would be necessary for the attainment of ends, and the consequences, including those which would not be foreseen except by social scientists, of the actions taken to attain the ends the politician sought.

Many of these considerations came together in Max Weber's essay on the "evaluative neutrality" of the social sciences. Max Weber explicitly denied the older view that ends or ideals could be discerned through the study of society. The social sciences could state the conditions which had to be present if a given set of actions were to achieve a specific end; they could say whether the end in question could be attained by the means employed under the conditions in which the action was undertaken; they could say what consequences would follow from the actions undertaken, given the obtaining conditions. Social science could tell nothing about what ends ought to be pursued, unless those ends were no more than means to some ulterior ends.

A social scientist who became a politician or who became a political partisan would in those capacities not be the same as a social scientist. He would be performing a different kind of activity. Politics and social science were separated from each other in one very important and ineluctable respect, namely, the social sciences could logically assert nothing about the ends of policy or of political decisions. They were, as far as political decisions are concerned, confined to the provision of the knowledge needed for social technology. The social scientist could therefore never be a counselor or princes in the classical sense which had prevailed until the beginning of modern times. He could in addition to being a scientist—or scholar—be a technical advisor to politicians or civil servants or he could be a publicist who illuminated public opinion about the condition of its society and about the possibilities, costs, and limits of changing it or maintaining it.

The development of economics as a self-contained science in the nineteenth century was probably encouraged by the liberal principle of the "separation of spheres," of separating church from state, of church and state from the economy, of the actions of individuals and voluntary associations from the state. The relative autonomy of the spheres, towards which Western societies moved in the nineteenth century, made plausible a belief in the self-containedness of the subject-matters of the different social sciences. The nature of the ideal economy, "prescribed" by the liberal economic theory, which was the most striking product of this intellectual division of labor, minimized the importance of large decisions. Economics studied and appreciated a system of dispersed decisions into a great multitude of actors and institutions in free and mutual adaptation to each other. The intellectual preponderance of economic theory among the social sciences in the English-speaking world thus reinforced this tendency of each social science to rid itself of any political traces in its content and especially in its conception of its calling. (The academic separation of political science, sociology, and economics from one another in departments of their own in the United States was rather extreme; it never went as far in Germany where the system of faculties and the beliefs of the *Kathedersozialisten* hindered the separation of politics and the academic social sciences.)

Germanic political science—which in Germany at least had some connection with the theory of the state as the embodiment of the highest values—was introduced into the American universities by men who had had their training in Germany in the 1870s and 1880s. In the United States the German theory of the state found only a faint echo while the institutional recipes which formed a large part of the remainder of the syllabus of the *Staatswissenschaften* were accepted as useful by teachers who thought that the main problems of public policy could be resolved by the reform of the civil service. Generally, American politicians in those important decades did not enjoy the esteem of American academics, despite the fact that there were many like Woodrow Wilson, Robert La Follette, and Theodore Roosevelt who had great admirers in the universities. They were thought to be the exceptions and the hope, but for the time being the ordinary professional politician was abhorred. In the meantime, hope lay in the improvement of the civil service and it was to the civil service as well as to public opinion that social scientists addressed their discourse. The belief in the efficacy of the civil service fitted into the ascending aim of making the social sciences scientific and of reducing the importance of "politics." An effective civil service would be able to "make use" of the results of the new science.

In the early part of the twentieth century, "scientific management" was in the air. From Frederick Taylor's application of scientific methods to the study of "time and motion," the idea was extended to the organization of industry and government. The science to make management scientific would be social science. This was what the social scientists could offer to the improvement of their society. Civil servants and businessmen would have the ends, social scientists could tell them about the most efficient and economical means.

In the period before the First World War much of the activity of academic political scientists was given over to the study of ways of circumventing politicians by such means as the "initiative," the "referendum," the "recall," and the "city manager plan." They wished to reduce politics to a minimum.

American sociology, which set out, or at least claimed, to make up for the limitations of political science and economics, did nothing to compensate for this somewhat negative attitude towards politics and politicians. In order to prove their right to existence, sociologists sought to find a sphere of events left untouched by the older social sciences. The distinction between the state and civil society was ready to hand in a liberal society, and sociologists welcomed it. Even though they found a justification for their independent existence in the numerous "social problems" which had arisen in connection with urbanization and immigration, they seldom expected them to be solved by the actions of politicians; they counted on public opinion, on voluntary action, and on civil servants. They were inclined to look upon politics as epiphenomenal; they looked upon politicians as morally problematic. These views were also found in the "new history" which was being propagated in the United States. The "new history" was a historiographical revolt against political history which was the history of rulers, i.e., of politicians. The "new history" intended to be the history of what was really important—the life of the people, of the family, social classes, technology, science, beliefs—in short, of all the deeper forces in contrast with the superficial events of politics.

The years between 1875 and 1925 saw all over the Western world the growing prestige of the natural sciences with their apparent expulsion of all questions of metaphysics, morals, politics. This model aroused the admiration and the emulation of the social scientists who were newcomers in the university environment and who had to make their way against the distrust of the humanists on the one side and the natural scientists on the other; they sought to legitimate their status as scientists and as searchers for truth in the same way as the already established branches of university life. The humanistic tradition did not seem to offer sufficiently immediate sustenance, and a misunderstood pattern of natural science procedure and outlook came to dominate the minds of social scientists. Political ideas and ethical judgments were regarded as alien to science; a social scientist was thought in some circles to endanger the integrity of his scholarly work if he did not hold his partisanship in check. It was believed almost universally that academic disciplines would have more chance to become scientific if they ceased to render evaluations. The expulsion of value judgments went so far that some sociologists thought that it was improper to express political or moral preferences until sociology had progressed much more towards its objective of becoming a science. This latter attitude was not the most common; most social scientists thought that they could be objective in their studies and in their civil roles, could act in concert with movements for the improvement of society—but not through politics.

Social scientists served on and testified before governmental commissions and some of them had close relationships to legislators and politicians, but on the whole they were very exceptional among the leading figures of their time. Woodrow Wilson as professor of political science and president of the United States was a great exception to the American academic social scientists who rejected politics as unclean. American social scientists thus set themselves into a position in which they could exercise their civility in cramped forms. In so far as they were not "oppositional" publicists, they had the alternative of offering their knowledge, skills, and judgment as technologists to the civil service. The intellectual development of their disciplines, the tradition of the relations between intellectuals and politicians, the change in the metaphysical postulates of political knowledge all disqualified them as counselors of princes. They were qualified to be technologists to the ruler's subordinates. They could also act as public critics of the ruler and his actions. The former function they could perform by giving "expert" advice—which later came to include doing research—or by accepting employment in an executive capacity, i.e., by becoming civil servants in roles in which they could use their expertise as social scientists. Yet the desire for a variant of the traditional role as the prince's counselor did not die out.

II

It was the First World War which showed, particularly in the United States, that academic social scientists could be employed by governments and by all organizations interested in controlling and modifying human behavior. The work of psychologists in testing the intelligence of the recruits to the United States Army during the First World War was the use of a scientific technique to assess capacities instead of doing this through the exercise of discriminatory powers developed in practical experience. Immediate uses in political propaganda, and in the formulation of the terms of peace, were also found for the presumably "expert" scholarly knowledge possessed by political scientists, historians, and geographers. Economists too were employed as administrators and as statisticians—performing quasi-research—in various bodies established to aid in the conduct of the war. After the war, psychologists immediately found many practical applications for their skills in testing, and many organizations, educational, industrial, and commercial, found their classificatory skills apparently worthy of employment. The great extension of advertising after the First World War offered employment to psychologists and encouraged the belief that the systematic scientific study of human behavior could produce knowledge which described the conditions of action in particular detail or which offered generalizations which could be applied in concrete cases. Psychologists could be employed as "staff officers" to provide "intelligence" or they could be employed to use their knowledge in executive tasks. Psychology of the type which was brought into service during and after the First World War was only marginally a social science but its employment was later regarded as evidence of the capacity of social science to be "useful."

Today governments and private, civic, and economic organizations are approximating universities and endowed research institutes as employers of social scientists. A cognitive appetite has developed among those who exercise authority; they wish to have more information about their own institutions and those towards whom they have to act. They wish to know the major magnitudes of the things with which they have to deal; they wish to know why certain events have occurred; they wish to know what will happen. These are the things which they like social scientists to tell them. Even if they do not pay any attention to the information and interpretations which they are given by social scientists, there is nonetheless a belief that such information and interpretation should be provided. The more governments extend their sphere of action, the more they call upon social scientists to provide factual descriptions and explanations through research, to offer advice ostensibly based on their "expertise," and to perform executive actions which entail the knowledge which being a social scientist brings with it.

The inadequacy of the conventional decennial population censuses for the comprehensive and intricate purposes of contemporary government has led Western liberal-democratic governments to establish, or purchase the services on contract, of special social research organizations to conduct sample surveys of opinions and actions. In the United States the widespread conduct, by government departments, of sample social surveys, is evidence of a desire for the more precise description of a field or situation, such as social scientists are able to render. Here the social scientist is employed to provide intelligence, i.e., information. Sometimes the intelligence is analytical as well as merely descriptive; it tries to explain configurations and not only to describe them. In British and American industry after the Second World War, social scientists—not merely industrial psychologists but also sociologists and anthropologists and clinical and social psychologists—were called upon as consultants or as regular employees to conduct descriptive investigations, to supply generalized interpretations and advice about costs and consequences of certain proposed or already adopted policies.

In an unprecedented extension of its activities in these fields the British government after 1948 granted considerable sums to psychologists, psychiatrists, anthropologists, etc., to promote the discovery of the nontechnological determinants of industrial productivity and the invention of techniques for the stimulation of greater productivity. Anthropologists were taken into the employ of colonial governments and were given funds to conduct research, the results of which were expected to be useful—in some indeterminate ways—for the formulation or execution of policies concerning primitive peoples. Demographers and sociologists were employed to carry out descriptive investigations and to advise, drawing on their previously accumulated knowledge and understanding, on the best arrangements needed to achieve certain vaguely defined ends in town-planning projects and policies.

Since those early years of the postwar period, there has been a huge multiplication of such activities. Out of a very general belief that the "social sciences" are indispensable to the "solution of social problems," social research has been supported on a scale which was never imaged fifty years earlier when the same faith in the efficacy of social science was expressed. Governments make grants and let contracts for social research, they maintain social scientists within their staffs to aid in the placement of such grants and contracts and to organize and direct "in-house" social research. Social scientists are invited to participate in the planning of programs to "solve" social problems; they are invited to serve as members of "working parties" and commissions of inquiry, they are brought in as occasional and regular teachers in academies for the training of civil servants, diplomats, and officers of the armed forces. There are few major sectors of modern governments in which social scientists are not active in one way or another.

Within governments, social scientists work in consultative and advisory roles, they perform "intelligence functions." The "intelligence function"—by which I do not mean espionage or counter-espionage—engages the vast majority of the social scientists in the service of government. Social scientists are not drawn upon for their wisdom as counselors to lay out the right path of action or to delineate fundamental alternatives or to give guidance in the choice from among these alternatives once discovered. Neither in the main are they looked to for summarizing some basic truths about human behavior derived either from rigorous scientific research or from gradually accumulated wisdom. Although innumerable references are made on every side about how important it is that the social sciences be developed in order to "solve our social problems," in actuality many social scientists are employed mainly as instruments for producing descriptive data about particular and concrete situations and actions. Much of their work consists in the quantitative estimation of the magnitude of different variables such as the numbers of persons who are "poor" or who live in particular types of housing accommodation or who are illiterate, etc. They report on the frequency of alleged intentions to perform particular actions, such as changing residence, sowing a certain number of acres, etc. The precise statistics about such events are of less interest than the general order of magnitude to the politicians and civil servants, whose arguments are fortified by the authority of statistical evidence prepared by persons of recognized and esteemed qualifications. What the politician or civil servant wants is only the major magnitudes of the situation about which they might wish to take action. Precision lends authority but otherwise it is not useful; it has to be turned into general magnitudes to be assimilated first into the mind and then into rather general predictions of what will occur if they act this way or that or if they make the decision not to act at all.

The social scientists are not often successful in making predictions and interpretations in an authoritative way. Even if their predictions and interpretations were better than they usually are, politicians and civil servants who have some experience and who have developed a certain amount of "practical wisdom"—which is not invariably true—would not accept the predictions of the social scientists unless they incline that way already. Social scientists have, however, been accepted as able to conduct surveys of things already existing probably more reliably than the general impressionistic assessment made by any but the very best officials or politicians; their surveys may not be subtle or deep but they are, as far as they go, fairly sound and are accepted as such. Nonetheless those who have to make decisions retain their freedom of interpretation. Even where they accept what is offered to them as truthful, it is usually open to multiple interpretations. The surveys almost always deal with the relatively recent past which is even further past by the time the results of the research come before the officials or politicians. The interpretative and analytical sides of social science do not appear directly in these surveys; when they do appear they are not usually considered seriously unless their results conform with what the makers of policy already believe or prefer to believe. The social scientist may indeed accompany his inventory or survey with his own interpretations of the way in which these magnitudes will be affected by the various intended policies, but in the majority of cases at present the interpretations are not rigorously demonstrated. This does not, of course, completely exhaust the type of intelligence functions carried out by social scientists for the makers of policy.

Social scientists also execute what is called "policy-research."[1] In

1. It is neither in the logical structure of the propositions with which an investigation concludes, in their subject-matter, nor even in the aims of the investigator that the significant differences between applied social research or "policy-oriented" research and other types of social research can be found. The term "applied research" in the social sciences may be understood to refer to investigations performed for policy-makers who ostensibly wish to "use" the resulting propositions as elements in their decisions. It is simply research, the results of which are to be applied in some way to practice by those who are charged with responsibility for decisions about practical affairs. It is not "applied research" in the sense of the application of scientifically tested general principles obtained in "basic" or "pure" research to the explanation of concrete and particular situations or to the management or construction of concrete and particular constellations of actions. Applied social research of the latter type might indeed develop in the social sciences in the course of time if the body of basic propositions rigorously tested by systematic empirical procedures were to grow. Since there are practically no such propositions in social science today, this type of applied social research cannot exist, at least for the time being.

"policy-research," the social scientist determines not merely isolated magnitudes such as the gross national output for the preceding year or even for the ensuing year or years, or the number of illiterates or of children below a certain age in fatherless families, but rather analyzes the structure of the situation in terms of the causal relations among those variables. In this latter type of applied research the concrete inventory or description of the situation remains central to the research, while the causal explanation is a separable part of it. Because of the looseness of the demonstration of causal connections in most present-day social research, this phase of the research report is usually not compelling in its effect on the officials responsible for making the decisions. Moreover, such causal interpretations are most often ambiguous enough to permit alternative interpretations. This is why the description of what happened is more likely to be accepted than the explanation of why it happened. Insofar as this is true, the social scientist is still largely regarded as the producer of inventory-like surveys, even though he himself conceives his aim to be otherwise. The explanations are not usually irrefutably persuasive to those who are not already inclined to agree with them.

At a time when social scientists were not so fastidious about the difference between being a "scientist" and an "expert," professors of social science contributed to the drafting of legislation from their knowledge of similar legislation in other countries or states and from what they knew, on an impressionistic basis, of the efficacy of the legislation in bringing about the desired ends. In Max Weber's sense, they advised about the most efficient means of attaining an end set by a governor or a legislator, about means which would best realize the ends sought while avoiding the negative consequences which had occurred in other countries. (It is possible that they also helped to define the ends which the legislation sought to achieve.) A further step in the study of the efficacy of a given policy as a means to an end was reached when the consequences of the legislation themselves were directly studied. This is now done by social scientists under the name of "evaluation studies."

"Evaluation studies," which have recently become highly regarded parts of "policy-analysis," are the realization of the fourth stage of the Benthamite recipe: "Investigate, agitate, legislate, inspect." They are efforts to inspect the extent to which particular policies have been successful. They have illustrious precedents and they have added to the inspectorial techniques of modern social science. Their inventory of the situation which has come after the execution of a particular policy tends to be regarded as reliable, while their interpretation suffers from the same measure of uncertainty as most interpretations in the social sciences. They rest on *ad hoc* insights which are frequently very penetrating and plausible, and on the adductions of theories which are ambiguous and sometimes arbitrary. The procedures employed in surveys often result in descriptive conclusions which are open to interpretations which are quite contrary to the interpretations not unreasonably made by the authors of the particular reports. The assessments which their authors make are often plausible, but given the state of the data and the state of social science theories, other no less plausible interpretations may be made. If the "evaluation-studies" persuade their readers, it is often because the readers share the same outlook as the social scientists. The claim that systematic empirical research can demonstrate that a particular policy has been successful is tenuous in the extreme; it is rarely justified.[2]

When social scientists become "advisors," either by being appointed as such or by giving testimony, invited or volunteered, before a legislative committee, their "advice" which recommends one particular policy in preference to others usually goes beyond the function of providing intelligence. Nor is it generally confined to explaining that the present situation will develop in a certain way or that each alternative policy will have certain corresponding consequences. They do not simply present the results of research—either in the form of a descriptive survey or a prediction. They recommend one policy and argue against other policies. The social scientists cease to be scientists and become the partisans of particular policies. They often disagree with the same intensity of passion as partisans who are not social scientists; and they invariably go beyond what is soundly or scientifically established and make assertions which are very suppositious.

They are disregarded where they recommend a policy which is not already regarded as politically feasible or desirable by legislators or civil servants. Their own authority as scientists is too slight and they

2. In recent years, since the growth of expenditures on scientific research and the increase in size of the scientific profession, there have grown up two derivative intellectual activities. One is the theory of science policy, which is the effort to define the criteria by which particular fields and projects should be selected for support; the other activity is the study of the social structure of scientific work, e.g., the patterns of communication among scientists, the hierarchy of the scientific profession, the institutional mechanisms for the assessment, diffusion, and acknowledgment of scientific discoveries, etc. According to the propagandists of the latter field of work, which has variously been called "the science of science," social studies of science, or "the sociology of science," such research contributes to the practical work of science policy. In fact however no connection has been shown and there is no likelihood that a connection will appear in the next few decades. In so far as a connection will appear it will be between practical decisions in science policy and the inventories of recent expenditures on different fields of science. There is no theoretical "sociology of science" or a theoretical "political science of science"; even if there were, an experienced administrator of science who had once been a scientist himself would probably not find any practical guidance in it.

are sometimes treated like any other propagandists by politicians. Civil servants might treat this advice most respectfully, especially when the social scientists espouse policies which would go more in a direction in which they themselves are already inclined. In general, however, the treatment accorded to social scientists as proponents of a policy by civil servants is like that accorded to them by politicians. This is true even in the case of scientists from fields like physics, systems analysis, and economics, which have attained higher degrees of precision than sociology and related social sciences.

Social scientists are listened to more attentively, and their proposals are more likely to be accepted, if they are taken into the inner circle around the peak of authority in a governmental organization. There are not, however, very many cases where social scientists—excluding economists (as we are doing throughout these observations)—are brought into such situations. The "working parties" which were created in the executive office of the president during the administration of President Lyndon Johnson included social scientists and it seems reasonable to believe that they did have some influence in the choice of the policies which went into the making of the program of the "war on poverty." In an earlier period of American history, the state of Wisconsin, during the time when that state led all others in "social legislation," important bills were drafted by professors of the state university. The civil service law of 1905, the public utility law of 1907, the law of 1911 establishing the industrial commission, and the child labor law of 1907 were all drafted with the close collaboration of John Commons—but he was an "institutional economist." Edward A. Ross, the sociologist, was a member of the Saturday Lunch Club which met regularly with Governor La Follette and his highest officials, but his contribution did not match those of the professors of economics and law.

The highest executive roles, such as the presidency, the prime ministry, or cabinet offices, have seldom had social scientists—again specifically excluding economists—as incumbents. Aside from Woodrow Wilson as president of the United States and Thomas Masaryk as president of Czechoslovakia and Eduard Benes as his successor, and Jomo Kenyatta in Kenya and K. A. Busia in Ghana, no former social scientists have ever been heads of government or state. There have been economists in the present century in such offices. Apart from economists, I think of John Gardner, Daniel Patrick Moynihan, Robert Wood, and Mancur Olson, who had been professional social scientists and then occupied high office in the federal government of the United States in recent years; and Fraga Ibarne in Spain is another exception. It is difficult to discern any trace of their expertise in the social sciences of their time in their political activities. Their knowledge drawn from social sciences seems to have been as remote from their political activities as was Chaim Weizmann's knowledge of chemistry.

The achievements of social science with respect to practical action are not to be underestimated despite these qualifications and strictures. On the descriptive side, the social sciences have established their credentials.

They have moved into one particular part of the realm of the making of policy where scattered impressions and improvised assessments formerly prevailed and they have shown that, although their surveys may lack subtlety in detail, the broad outlines of the picture they present are good enough to be taken seriously. Sometimes indeed their surveys are taken so seriously that politicians regard them as having implications which are incontestable.

At the other extreme, the social sciences have a pervasive influence on the state of opinion, particularly the opinion of the educated classes and those who are responsive to it. This pervasive influence on opinion is very difficult to asses; it occurs in attenuated form and over considerable stretches of time. Some of these beliefs, generated in or given additional force by the social sciences are: deprivation leads to aggressiveness; the discipline required by obedience to authority inhibits creative powers; "egalitarian" groups work more efficiently than "authoritarian" groups; there is a "lag" between technological innovations and social institutions (which should be adapted to reduce the "lag,"); all human beings are fundamentally equal in their capacities and differences in performance are consequences of differences in immediate social situations; immediate social situations are primarily consequences of the structure of the larger society and particularly of the distribution of income, wealth, and deference; school children must have "role models" of their own ethnic groups if they are to succeed in their studies. Such "theories" are not the result of rigorous research and rigorous theoretical analysis. They are or were part of the prevailing opinion of the profession of teaching and research in the social sciences. Some of them have long been part of the stock in trade of the social sciences, e.g., belief in the formative power of the "social environment," others have been taken up more recently. None of them is utterly outlandish intellectually and plausible arguments have been made for them. However that may be, they have been widely accepted by many social scientists and through their teaching and writing these beliefs have passed into the minds of their students and readers. Certain other intellectual products of the social sciences, such as the image of the distribution of income and the proportion of the population to be classified as "poor" have also passed into public opinion. It is not that there were no beliefs on these topics in public opinion before the recent ascent of social science; there certainly were. They were not, however, asserted with the authority given by their allegedly "scientific" character. Traditional beliefs, religious beliefs, beliefs based on experience and derived from the study of the classics made up the deeper strata of the public opinion of the much smaller educated class of the earlier centuries of the modern age. These were complemented and to some extent displaced in the nineteenth century by natural–scientific beliefs and by political economy and the social philosophy which was associated with it. In the most recent decades of the present century, the recession of articulated religious beliefs among the educated, the decline of classical education, and an intensified scientism have left a considerable vacancy into which the social sciences have been drawn as a replacement for the beliefs which have lost their persuasiveness. The social sciences are for better or for worse the unintentional beneficiaries of this conjuncture.

III

In a vague way, the present role of the social sciences was on the agenda of the founders of the empirical social sciences in the nineteenth century. That role was adumbrated in the image of the future envisaged by Francis Bacon in *The New Atlantis*. Still, in one very important respect the situation is different from that anticipated. The social sciences have moved into their present eminence without having become sciences of the type which was then envisaged. They have developed many differentiated ideas and they have developed a capacity for gross description of social situations. Their imagination regarding society has become more elaborate; they have stimulated and stored many penetrating insights. They are more amply provided with renumerative and esteemed employment in universities, governments, and private bodies. They have very large sums of money allocated to them for research and they have many institutional arrangements through which their research can be carried on.

Much of this prosperity is attributable to the belief in public opinion that the social sciences are needed for the "solution of social problems." This is one of the reasons why governments support research in the social sciences on such an unprecedented scale and why they support the teaching of the social sciences in universities. Behind them is a public opinion which also believes in the "solution" of social problems through the application of scientific knowledge in the ways in which medicine and agriculture both benefited from the application of scientific knowledge.

This munificent support is given out of the belief that the social sciences are already of practical and cultural value and that they will become more so as they become more scientific. It is thought that they will become more scientific the more amply they are supported.

This is not entirely misconceived. A single sociologist could not interview a national sample, do all the coding and tabulation himself unless he spent a very long time in doing it. The value of his survey would be reduced by the long lapse of time between the conduct of the early and the later interviews; the situation prevailing at the beginning of the survey would have passed by the time it was completed. If speed of completion and national coverage are required, then many collaborators are required. If the processing of the data is not to be done impressionistically then much clerical labor is required for coding. If elaborate calculations are to be made, computers have to be used. All these require large sums. The new type of research which has developed with the sample survey and elaborate statistical analysis can no longer be done by a university teacher working in the time which he has free from teaching and administration, and having the help of a part-time graduate assistant. The earlier type of institutional case study which could be done by a single doctoral candidate as a dissertation has been pushed to the side. Research in the social sciences has become "big science"—not of the proportions of high-energy physics but in comparison with what social science research was forty to fifty years ago.

It has acquired such a scale because of the belief that the social sciences are "useful" and that a provident government, wishing to "solve social problems," must make the social sciences sufficiently scientific to help them become capable of that; and it also must draw on their help at present. This is beneficial to the social sciences. It has enabled them to improve their techniques of gathering data and of analyzing them statistically.

There can be no doubt about the intellectual benefits which have come to the social sciences through involvement in practical affairs. The development of techniques of research, which has been one of the most notable developments in the empirical social sciences since the Second World War, has, to a very large extent, been fostered by the interest of government, business, and the private philanthropic foundations interested in promoting a social science which would aid in the cure of society's ills. The development of surveys with the support of government and commerce has certainly advanced the techniques of sampling and interviewing. Progress in sampling technique certainly owes very much to the needs of governments for frequent assessments of a wide range of variables which the traditional type of census was too costly and cumbersome to provide. The "open-ended" interview was helped by its use in the work of the United States Department of Agriculture (Division of Program Planning and Surveys). The technique of content-analysis—although first adumbrated in a purely academic atmosphere—underwent considerable elaboration when applied in the service of the government in the Library of Congress Project on Wartime Communications and the Federal Communications Commission. Since that time it has become, in a variety of forms, a common feature of empirical research. The technique for the scaling of attitudes underwent very notable improvement in the course of the studies conducted by the Research Branch of the Adjutant General's Office of the Department of War. The study of the structure of small groups, especially of the techniques of discovering the underlying dispositions of interpersonal relations in small groups, was advanced by the leaderless-group technique which was first used in officer selection and in psychiatric rehabilitation in the British Army and was then furthered by its use in American veterans' hospitals. The recent advancement of many high-powered statistical procedures could not have been possible without the financial support from a whole range of governmental bodies.

The situation is however somewhat equivocal. Speed, largeness of scale, the need for simplified operations which can be performed by persons of less than the highest quality sometimes endanger the intellectual substance of the inquiry. Questions which are adequate to the complexity of the phenomena studied are excluded because of the pressure of time, the incapacity of the interviewer, and the sheer difficulty involved in formulating them.

Of course, even if there were no expectations that the research should be relevant to policy, the same conditions might result from the nature of large-scale research and from the temporal restraints imposed by governmental budgetary practices and, in some cases, the deadlines imposed by the necessities of practical decisions. Governmental expectations of relevance to policy in itself need not have deleterious consequences on the intellectual quality of research. In the present state of the empirical social sciences there are really few significant differences between "applied research" or "policy research" and "pure" or academic research. Both tend to be concretely descriptive, both deal with recent events. Research which is "relevant to policy" does tend to be less interested in deeper interpretation, less interested in theory. This is not inherent in "policy-relevant" research. Given the technical and descriptive interests of social sciences, most social research tends to shirk such interpretation. There is however no necessity inherent in its relevance to policy which requires that it do so. The awareness that the research is expected to contribute to the delineation of the tasks and consequences of policy only strengthens a previously existent disposition.

There is a tendency towards superficiality in the definition of the objects of study in large-scale social research. This is partly because of the sheer recalcitrance of social phenomena to rigorous empirical study but it is also a consequence of the desires of government. Governments are not generally interested in the more fundamental forces, they are interested in getting through the term's work. When they award contracts for particular pieces of research, they are more interested in information than in deeper understanding. They would not object if the research results in the understanding of societies but that is not what interests them.

The specificity and concreteness of their interests can also maintain a dispersion of interests into numerous discrete subjects. Social research in the present century has already been characterized by an extraordinary scattering of attention over a great variety of uncoordinated problems which were investigated on a very concrete level. This was true before the support of social science by government began on anything approximating its present scale. Although our knowledge of contemporary society has been greatly increased in consequence of these numerous investigations carried out by university teachers and postgraduate students, our understanding has grown largely in the interstices. Survey research which is sounder in technique is also more superficial.

It should be emphasized that the choice of topics or problems for research in accordance with "relevance to policy" is not a new thing in the history of the social sciences. The most important works in the modern history of social science such as Weber's *Gesammelte Aufsätze zur Religionssoziologie,* Durkheim's *Le Suicide* and *De la Division du travail social,* Booth's *Life and Labour of the People of London,* and Thomas and Znaniecki's *The Polish Peasant in Europe and America* were also undertaken with a view to deepening understanding of situations which were of "practical" relevance—practical being very broadly understood. Such general understanding as we have in the social sciences owes a very great deal to these works. It is clear that concern with matters of "practical" importance is therefore not a barrier to enriched understanding. "Applied social science" which is applied in the sense that it studies types of activities or situations about which governmental or civic action is thought necessary should not in itself be regarded as a hindrance to intellectual progress in the social sciences. Concern with policy, assuming that investigators are not seeking by subtle or gross means to produce descriptions which will be interpreted in ways favorable to their own political and social program, is no handicap to scholarly achievement in the social sciences.

Nonetheless, there are some cautions which should be expressed in view of the inevitable dependence of empirical social research of the more recent sort on governmental financial support. The first of these is that much governmentally supported research is so supported because it is believed to be of prospective use to the government in connection with a particular "program." Governmental programs vary, depending on the tides of political and public opinion, and, with them, the subjects of research change. This does not mean necessarily that subjects studied earlier disappear entirely from the horizon of social scientists. Still, the discontinuity of effort which has been a bane of social science throughout its history as a set of empirical disciplines may be reinforced.

There is another caution which should be borne in mind. The most tangible demonstrable progress of the social sciences in recent decades has been made in the techniques of gathering information and in its statistical analysis. Less progress has been made in the clarification of the character of the actions or beliefs which are studied and in the analysis of their interconnections. This has nothing to do with preoccupation with policy. It is a result of doing those things which can be most readily and effectively done and leaving aside those which are more resistant at the time to fruitful treatment. This situation is likely to be maintained if not aggravated by the interest of the governmental patrons of empirical social science in reliable descriptions.

Finally the attachment of social science to the problems of contemporary policy carries with it the likelihood that social science will be preoccupied with that which is morally and socially problematic. It has often been said that sociology in its origins was an "oppositional science"; it focused its attention on those features of its contemporary society which were reprehensible and which, according to advanced opinion, should be changed. The outcome has been a concentration of effort on injustice, dissensus, corruption, frustration, and misery. This has been a valuable service of modern social science, even though from a more radical or revolutionary point of view, it has been accused of being interested only in "patching up" society rather than making a whole new garment. But it has also had the effect that a powerful tradition has been established from which few social scientists have escaped. It is the tradition of looking upon contemporary society as a machine which damages human beings, maltreats them, exploits them, degrades them, and all the rest of the bill of charges. It becomes even more difficult thereby to understand how that society manages to go on reproducing itself, maintaining some continuity of character. The explanations are as distorted as the picture of the situation which they seek to explain. This fact, coupled with the high degree of contemporaneity of empirical research and the ineluctable tendency, even for the historically ignorant, to pass judgments of epochal comparison, leads to the currency of wrong ideas about modern societies.

Just as the craft of dentistry is concerned with cavities and malformations and pays little attention to sound teeth, so social science disregards that which is not morally "problematic." When attempts are made to account for those things which are not "problematic," they reinterpret the unproblematic in such a way that it too is made morally problematic. The preponderance of "policy-oriented" research strengthens this tendency. Research has to be on "problems," which ought to be resolved by "change." The agenda for the support of social research gives a high place to that which is concerned with "national needs" and they are invariably unsatisfied "needs." This is quite a reasonable procedure for government which wishes to repair deficiencies but it does have a distorting effect on the image of modern society which the social science of the present-day offers.

None of these cautions point to consequences which are inherent in the governmental support of social science. The consequences to which reference has been made are just as much the outcome of certain deeply rooted traditions of the social sciences, traditions which were flourishing long before governments took to the support of social science on the scale recently reached. Governmental science policy with respect to the social sciences has aggravated the tendencies of these traditions.

IV

Under present conditions it appears to be quite certain that governments will provide a very preponderant share of the total budget of the social sciences. This necessary condition for the practice of social science, i.e., munificent financial support, might not be forthcoming from governments if public opinion, politicians, and civil servants do not continue to believe that the social sciences are necessary for the "solution of social problems." This is one of the arguments social scientists have used in justification of their disciplines long before governmental funds became available for empirical social research. They themselves acted on this assumption. They thought that their expertise as social scientists gave them the right to lay their opinions before governments, public opinion, and civic bodies. When, after the Second World War, the natural sciences began to receive very large sums of money, social scientists claimed that they should be provided for with equal generosity. The argument was that they too would be useful—as useful in their own way as the natural sciences had proved themselves to be. A condition of this usefulness was that they must become scientific and for that they would require financial resources, not as great as for the natural sciences but far larger than they had ever had before. In the course of several decades, they were successful. First in the United States, then in France, Great Britain, Western Germany, the Netherlands, the Scandanavian countries, Belgium, Switzerland, and Japan, governments heeded the call.

All this while, the "problems" which the social sciences have been expected to have "solved" have not diminished in scale or intensity. Indeed, since the first large appropriations for the social sciences were made, the problems seem to have become aggravated. Now this might be a result of the actual aggravation of the problems; it might also be a result of the increased prominence given to the phenomena which constitute the "problem" by the increase in the amount of research which has been done on them and by the increased publicity which the work of social scientists receives in the press and on television—itself a result of the enhanced attention to the social sciences and the enhanced faith in them.

The problems remain and perhaps grow worse. The social sciences can show nothing like the advances in medical sciences, physics, or agricultural research. They cannot point to nuclear weapons, or to electricity produced by nuclear energy, or artificial joints, plastic aortas, or new types of strains of wheat or rice, or transplantation of hearts and kidneys. In fact, they cannot point to any technological improvements which have been made on the basis of their research. Nor can they point to purely cognitive accomplishments such as those which have distinguished astrophysics or archeology or molecular biology or other sciences in recent years.

In the past decade, there has been a certain amount of disenchantment with science. Expenditures for science have not only not grown at the rate of the two preceding decades, they have even been reduced to some extent. Nonetheless it seems unlikely that disenchantment with the natural sciences will go on to the point where governmental support will recede to the low waterline of the decades between the two world wars. The natural sciences have produced too many great discoveries of which educated laymen have heard and they have produced directly or indirectly too many technological devices which have affected the lives and the imaginations—in most cases gratifyingly—of the less well educated laity for them to turn against the support of training and research in the natural sciences. It is true that there has been a resurgence of an "anti-scientific" attitude as a part of the diffuse antinomianism of a visible and audible but small part of the educated class but it does not seem to be likely to grow greatly in strength or to affect markedly the policy of governments to support the natural sciences.

The social sciences are on far less secure ground. The things the social sciences work on are more "political." Public opinion has assimilated the secularistic views of modern science; most influential churches have accepted almost all of the claims of modern science within a generally respected boundary line which separates the sacred and the secular. Social scientists have not observed a similar boundary between the "political" and the scientific. It would have been difficult to do so because the "political" and the "politically affected" make up a very considerable part of the subject-matter of the social sciences. Laymen have beliefs about the activities and the situations about which social scientists make assertions which are ostensibly based on their research. Even the descriptive surveys of social scientists are about the condition of society, and laymen too have images of these conditions. Still descriptive surveys have attained a measure of authoritativeness which explanatory interpretations have not attained. This not only restricts the esteem in which the social sciences are held by the laity; it also encourages contention against their explanations. The explanatory drift of the social sciences often runs against the drift of traditional moral beliefs; nowhere is this more true than with respect to the interpretation of criminal and delinquent—now, significantly, called "deviant"—conduct.

It is not merely the moral overtones of the explanations insisted on by social scientists which occasionally give umbrage to politically significant sections of the laity. Social scientists do not discipline themselves to adhere to the strict separation of "statements of fact" from "statements of value." Many of them nowadays condemn the distinction, and they do not refrain from the emphatic espousal of their own preferences for one policy rather than another. They can be as insistent as any politician in their arguments on behalf of one particular policy and in their opposition to alternative policies.

Such is their right as citizens. The situation is complicated however by the fact that in their partisanship they adduce their professional authority as social scientists and that is in fact why they are often invited to render their opinions. In matters of policy, many social scientists have for a long time been progressivistic in their ideas about the right direction of society. They have usually favored governmental programs which increase the provision of goods, services, and opportunities for the poorer classes of society, they have been sympathetic with criminals and delinquents, critical of the police and other agents of order, they have been critical of traditional morality in familial and sexual matters.

All this means that the social sciences, which as yet have few tangible scientific or technological accomplishments—according to the standards by which the natural sciences are judged—also have the further handicap of from time to time running contrarily to prevailing cognitive and moral beliefs and of sometimes being drawn into contention because of the partisanship of social scientists.

These difficulties all existed before the governmental patronage of research on a large scale began. Social scientists not infrequently aroused the antipathy of the laity when they took up partisan positions, outside the university. Edward Ross at Stanford and Wisconsin, Werner Sombart at Breslau, Charles Beard at Columbia University, Harold Laski at the University of London were sometimes severely criticized by laymen for the particular positions which they espoused and they were sometimes dismissed from their academic posts. The civil liberty of academics was involved, and in these and numerous other cases it was infringed on. There was, however, no question of reducing the funds supplied by governments for research in the social sciences. There was no question because governments contributed negligibly; the withholding of funds was not a sanction when no funds had previously been supplied.

Conditions are now different. The social scientists are now more intricately connected with policy; they not only study the situation with which it deals, they pass judgment on and espouse policies and they receive support for their studies from governments. They have in the course of these activities become much more prominent publicly. Their studies and beliefs have become political facts.

In all these filiations with the political and public sphere, social scientists enjoy one advantage over natural scientists. Their knowledge not being in a stated form in which it can be applied technologically in the way in which knowledge of nuclear fission could be applied in the making of nuclear weapons or in the construction of nuclear power plants or in the way in which the knowledge of deoxyribonucleic acid could be used to insert alien genes into viruses, they cannot be charged by laymen or by scientists with having allowed their knowledge to be misused. They are not held responsible for the use of their knowledge in the way in which certain publicists and agitators concerned with the natural sciences have declared that natural scientists should be held. Nonetheless, the furious attacks both from within the academic world and from outside it against Professors Jensen and Herrnstein are indications of the possibilities in situations in which the actual or prospective results—scientific and technological—of research appear to affect practical affairs.

Interestingly enough, although academic social scientists have been abused by radical academic ideologists for being subservient to the powerful in the government and in the economy, and empirical social scientists have been derogated as "spies" on "the poor" on behalf of government, neither group has been especially insulted for receiving financial support from government for their research. Indeed, Professor Gouldner, who has been a leading critic of the fallacies of a social science which does no more than serve the interests of the powerful in the United States, has expressed himself very explicitly on the desirability of increased financial support by government for the social sciences.

Yet these inconsistencies might be only transient; radical ideologists who regard cooperation with government as contaminating and those who are protective of traditional moral beliefs might come together in their belief that the social sciences should not be supported by government on anything like the present scale.

Thus far, at least, the curtailment of intellectual or academic freedom by government in consequence of its power of the purse seems to have been very small. In commissioning research, of course the choice of subject-matter has lain with governmental officials. As regards techniques and "theoretical approaches," governmental officials have deferred to professional social scientists. They have not intruded into these crucial zones.

The freedom of publication of research done on governmental commission or with governmental support is to be answered less unequivocally. It is obvious that much of the research falling under these headings is not published in journals available to the public, learned and lay. Much of it is perhaps not good enough to be published. It might be too trivial or too incompetent or its analytical importance might be so slight that the editor of a learned journal might justifiably refuse to accept it for publication. Some of the reports in social research into matters like the armed forces might be considered as "confidential" or "secret" but the proportion of such research is probably rather small. The authors know in advance whether their results will be "classified" and the restriction of freedom of publication in such instances is different from what it would be where a decision to withhold the report from publication was made after the results had been obtained. There is little evidence of such suppression.

Research which is not specifically commissioned by governmental officials but which is supported by grants made on the basis of proposals submitted by academic or otherwise private social scientists has not been restrained from publication in any cases known to me. I do not see any prospect of change in this policy of freedom of publication. In this respect, it must be acknowledged that the orientation of the social sciences to problems of practical social importance and the dependence of social sciences for the support of government in order to do research has not diminished the freedom of social science as an intellectual activity.

Nor for that matter, despite the accusations of radical ideologists, has dependence on governmental support for "policy-oriented" research made social scientists subservient to government. The explicit criticism of government and the espousal of policies which imply a radical attitude towards existing society were not more widespread among social scientists when governments did not provide financial support for research than they have been in the years since "policy-oriented" research, done with governmental support, has become common. In fact, the contrary is the case.

V

It would be good to have a detailed investigation into the actual accomplishments of the social sciences as here understood in the formation of policy and an evaluation of those policies which have been in one way or another guided or affected by social science. It would be good to have a detailed analysis of the type of social science which has emerged from its connection with policy, i.e., from having been undertaken with the intention of serving or influencing policy. Such investigations have not yet been done.

Still it is not too premature to venture some general views about the impact of social science on the making and execution of policy. To begin with, a distinction should be made between the sympathetic patronage of social science by legislators and civil servants and the incorporation of the results of social science—both the results of empirical research and the theories—into the practical action of making laws and carrying them out. It is clear that there is much sympathetic patronage. There would not have been so much financial support given to the social sciences had there not been a belief among administrators and legislators that the social sciences have, in some still unthought-out way, important knowledge to offer, knowledge which will enable governments to deal effectively with the problems which they and the electorate wish to have dealt with. This sympathy is a reflection of experience with the physical and biological sciences; it is a faith that "it stands to reason" that better, i.e., more scientific, knowledge will enable society, through its elected representatives and its appointed officials, to eliminate certain morally undesirable features of society or at least to reduce them and to help forward the movement of society toward the realization of certain ideals. It is often suggested that the advancement of the social sciences will provide those in authority with "techniques" which will bring about these desired ends. The "techniques" are nothing less than certain institutional arrangements, such as "community participation" or "integration" of ethnically heterogeneous groups in school classes, which once established by the compulsory or permissive power of laws—including judicial decisions—will lead to the desired results. It is a matter of "applying" certain "scientifically" established propositions in a situation. Legislators and administrators order or provide the resources or do both so that certain arrangements will be brought into existence. Those arrangements will then have certain presumably predictable consequences. In other words, the "use of social science" presupposes that there are scientific propositions which can be used. This was what Max Weber must have had in mind when he said that, logically considered, it lay within the possible capacities of social science to assert what were the conditions under which certain ends could be attained and what would be the repercussions and costs, i.e., undesired consequences, of the attainment of those ends. This presupposed, and presupposes, the existence of these predictive propositions and the employment of the legitimate coercive powers of government and its ability to provide the financial incentives and means necessary for bringing about the preconditional arrangements. Max Weber asserted too that social scientists could not, at least within the logical framework of the knowledge provided by the social sciences, define the ends for the attainment of which social science could specify the causally necessary conditions, or means.

To what extent have these stipulations of Max Weber been observed? In the first place, the social sciences today are not in a position to offer to the practicing politician or administrator scientifically established propositions which permit reliable predictions of intended consequences and undesired repercussions or costs, which will flow from specific conditions. The social sciences have many plausible ideas, reasonable guesses, based on observation and reflection and deduced from general theories which are not scientific in the sense that the natural and biological sciences are scientific. It might well be, however, that these interesting, imaginative, and plausible guesses or "hunches" are no better, no deeper, or no more differentiated than the predictions which politicians and civil servants would make without drawing on the counsel of social scientists. Humility and respect for truth require that this be recognized.

It has often been pointed out that legislators and civil servants who accept the social scientists' plausible guesses, predictions, or interpretations of causal connections and of consequences which will flow from certain legislated or decreed arrangements, do so ordinarily when these interpretations are in agreement with their own beliefs; they disregard them when they do not agree with their previously held views or when they would support a decision which is unappealing to them on political grounds. This might be regarded as evidence of irrationality of politicians and civil servants, but it is also evidence that their esteem for the rational persuasiveness of the propositions of social science is not very high.

Be that as it may, the situation might conceivably change in the future. Politicians might become as susceptible to the plausible guesses, explanations and theories of social scientists in the future as they are now to the results of opinion polls and the constructions which their polling experts place upon them. This might occur in consequence of the enhanced prestige of the social sciences in a scientific age, just as the authority of public opinion polls over the conduct of politicians is dependent on the populistic beliefs of politicians and their deficient self-confidence. It might also be a consequence of the improvement of the intellectual quality of the social sciences; the social sciences might become more scientific. It is not unreasonable to think that they might become so; certain branches of psychology, those parts which are closer to neurology and physiology, have become more scientific in the past century and similar success might well await the social sciences in the future.

Let us assume that this will occur. What then? What will the social scientists have let themselves in for? Will they become the providers of predictive scientific propositions to government so that it may more effectively manipulate, through the broadly legitimate coercive power of the law and of administrative specifications under the law, the conduct of the citizenry? Thus far, it may be noted, much of the application of the scientifically problematic social science of the present day—disregarding the descriptive surveys—is directed towards children, criminals, delinquents, and addicts of narcotics. They have traditionally been regarded as fit objects for authoritative manipulation by parents, teachers, penal officials, and police and physicians. John Stuart Mill thought that the manipulation of children and of primitive peoples was acceptable because they were not capable of rational use of individual freedom. The status of law-abiding, normal adults was thought to be different from that of children, criminals, and others who could not or would not use their freedom rationally.

Many social scientists nowadays do not look with favor on the role of social scientists in market research, especially in the devising of advertising "campaigns" in order to promote the sale of particular commercial products, despite the fact that many social scientists gain their livelihood by market research. (The late Paul Lazarsfeld in the last years of his life was discomfited by having done so much market research for commercial enterprises.) Now some of this aversion is to be attributed to the hostility of many social scientists to private business enterprise, but at least some of them have an attitude of aversion towards the manipulation of adults. They are not happy about the use of the knowledge which they have acquired to elicit actions from human beings by means of which they are unaware or do not understand. If this attitude is extended from market research on behalf of private businessmen to social research which produces scientific results to be used by government, they will be placed in a dilemma. On the one side, they will be parties to a relationship of adult human beings to governmental authorities like that of the ill with their physicians. This might be a benevolent relationship but it is not the same egalitarian one to which so many social scientists are committed.

Is there an alternative to this?

One way out, taken by many social scientists who have not worried much about the problems of manipulation, is for them to refuse to be confined to the supplying of descriptive information of predictive propositions. They aspire instead to be the creators of policies, to prescribe ends to be sought as well as the means to attain those ends. They wish to exercise power without having had to go through the turmoil of seeking elective office or to be confined by the routines of the civil service. They wish to have the prerogatives of the powerful without the constraints and sacrifices. The more "activistic" they are, the more insistent they are in promulgating and promoting "innovative programs'' which will lead to the egalitarian ends they seek. They exploit the prestige of the social sciences for being scientific but they do not wish to confine themselves to being advisors who have been summoned because they possess scientific knowledge.

This does not change the manipulative situation. It means only that such social scientists do not serve the legitimate manipulation of politicians and civil servants but become manipulators who do not have quite the same degree of legitimacy as elected politicians or appointed civil servants.

There is nothing in the nature of the social sciences which puts a moral prohibition on a social scientist changing his occupation to become a civil servant or a politician. But when he performs the activities which are appropriate to the politician's or the civil servant's role, he is not a social scientist. An elected politician or an appointed civil servant is in a very vague way legitimated by the process through which he accedes to his role. A social scientist who is brought into the service of government as a scientific expert performs the role of a scientific expert legitimately when he puts forward an interpretation in explanation of a given state of affairs or asserts that a particular policy will have certain consequences. Having been invoked as a social scientist, he is acting within the limits of his powers as a social scientist when he performs any one of those activities.

When he goes further and becomes an exponent of a particular policy and an opponent of others because their views are contrary to his own ethical and political ideals he exceeds the limits which are implicit in the role of the scientific expert.

It so happens that civil servants often do not make such fine distinctions and do not draw such limits on the jurisdiction of the social scientists whom they commission to conduct research for them or to advise them. The social scientist in this role may be acting beyond the capacities of social science but he cannot be accused of manipulation any more than a politician or a civil servant is to be accused of it. The social scientist avoids the manipulative role by becoming one of the exercisers of power, however partially and however indirectly. Is there any way out of this intertwinement with the exercise of authority? I do not think that there is as long as social scientists are not content to understand society but wish to pass judgment on it and to have their judgments taken seriously by those who make policies which affect society.

Social scientists cannot avoid doing research which is relevant to policy because their disciplines deal with facts about which policies are made, and they cannot avoid this as long as they interest themselves in society. There are differences in degrees of ''relevance to policy.'' Some work in the social sciences deal directly with those facts and factors with which politicians and civil servants are immediately concerned. Other work, if it is intellectually significant and does not deal directly with the things in which politicians and civil servants are interested at the moment, surely deals with things which should be taken into account by anyone who wishes to arrive at a serious and responsible judgment. In that sense all social science is potentially relevant to policy, however empirical or theoretical it might be.

The realization of this possibility is not confined to the performance of descriptive research, the provision of explanations and predictions, and the recommendation of and contention for particular policies. The enlightenment of public opinion outside government is the method which was used by the great figures of social science at the end of the last century. Max Weber's and Emile Durkheim's researches on agricultural labor and on suicide were not intended to be advice to the makers of policy, and they were not only intended to advance the scientific understanding of society. Robert Park and Charles Cooley also intended that their works should enter into the "larger mind" of public opinion. They thought that better understanding, resting on a more scientific study of society, would beneficially affect the decisions of those who acquired that understanding. These persons would bring that understanding into their own decisions as philanthropists, social workers, judges, newspaper publishers and employers, and they would also communicate to politicians and civil servants their practical proposals for policy, improved by the understanding conveyed by social science. The illumination of opinion thus turns out in the end to be the illumination of the opinion of those in positions of authority or influence. The enlightenment of opinion is not disjunctively separated from the technological application of social science.

Must the public opinion to which social science is addressed be only the opinion of those in positions of authority or influence? What about those who have relatively little influence or authority, being ordinary citizens who go about their business, look after their families, are concerned about their neighborhoods, and who are not active in discussing or trying to influence the longer course of affairs? What about the "poor" or the "lumpenproletariat" about whom there has been so much solicitude shown in recent years? And what about children, mentally backward persons, the infirm, the aged, et al. who have been the traditional concern of philanthropists and reformers? Could they be brought to share in the understanding which the social sciences might provide?

As things stand now—quite apart from the limited value of what the social sciences can convey—there are limits imposed by intelligence or the capacity to comprehend what the social scientists disclose. There are limits imposed by interest too and limits imposed by lack of confidence in the reliability of the knowledge conveyed by the social sciences. And there are the limits imposed by the cognitive deficiencies of the social sciences. It might be that these limits will not be relaxed in the foreseeable future.

Let us, however, suppose that these limits of cognitive deficiency, uninterestedness, lack of confidence, and incapacity to comprehend were relaxed. What would a society of this "scientific" culture be like, in which everything became transparent to everyone, in which there were no secrets, no areas of indifference or willing ignorance, in which everyone understood whatever was known about society in general and his own society in particular? This society would be the realization of the ideal which has been increasingly espoused since Bacon. It is the scientistic, progressivistic ideal. It is however an ideal which has never been thought out. Each particular improvement or change intended to be an improvement attributable to the increase in knowledge and its rational application seemed to be a very good thing. The desired effect was a small increment to the already existent knowledge, and it was relatively easily assimilated into the accepted picture of society. The ideal was to move unceasingly towards the application of expanding knowledge with foreseeable improvements in social arrangements resulting therefrom. It is not clear that the great figures of the Enlightenment really thought out what they were recommending. Sometimes they seemed to be thinking of a scientifically enlightened despotism. At other times, they, or their successors in the optimistic social science of the present century, seemed to be thinking of a society in which the illumination generated by a scientific social science would be available to and even possessed by all; but they never told us what such a society would be like.

6   Learning and Liberalism

I

The center of American society has settled in the federal government. Private business enterprises and other private institutions exist in very large numbers. Municipal and state governments still exist but the sphere of initiative and influence which they once had have been narrowed by the expansion of the powers of central government. The intellectuals, the learned professions, and those occupations which are not quite learned professions but which deal in knowledge are more attentive to central government than they once were and are also more affected by its actions. Universities have become dependent on the federal government; the medical profession and scientific research come increasingly under the dominion of the federal government. The federal government is now intervening into certain affairs which the legal profession once reserved for itself.

For many years socialism and communism were abhorred because they wished to establish a type of society which gave much importance to the state; they were cherished only by very small minorities. "States' rights" were invoked in justification of the restriction of the powers of central government. Nowadays however the belief that most of what needs to be done in society must be done by the government is as widespread as was the relatively recent aversion against that type of society in which the state, dominated by a single party, is deemed by its admirers as capable of monopolizing all initiative, of controlling the actions of all its citizens, and of accomplishing any end which it sets for itself.

The movement towards a ubiquitously intrusive, allegedly omnicompetent central government has had its main impulse in the desire to improve society. Legislators, the judiciary, and the civil service press onward in this direction on the grounds that the improvement of society is possible only through their own action. They are distrustful of initiative which originates outside their own boundaries. The original impulsion of the welfare state lay in the belief that the welfare of the poor should be promoted and that the wealthy and strong be kept in check to prevent their harming the poor and the weak. This expansion of governmental activities in the promotion of the common welfare—in a far more comprehensive and penetrating sense than was conceived in earlier times—is now accepted as right. The new view has replaced the older view that the necessary progress of society would be taken care of by the free activity of individuals and by that of private organizations, while the state filled in the interstices of failure and eased the severity of collisions among private persons and groups. There is however much discontent in the educated classes and especially in that part which is publicly articulate. Much of the discontent is not at all about the arrogation of such large powers and such great resources by the government; the point of dissatisfaction is that the state does not go far enough in the use of its potential power for the public benefit. The government has been much criticized in intellectual circles, especially among social scientists, for not doing more than it does. It is blamed for lack of strong convictions, for divided counsel, and for heeding self-interest instead of exercising the powers of which it is capable. Any end could, according to this view, be accomplished if the will is there. There are no "problems" which government with the right intentions could not solve. Its capacity to confer benefits is regarded as limited only by the total resources of the society, if it would only use them, and its actions are thought capable of increasing the resources as well. It is no new thing for groups to demand subsidies for themselves. But now the groups demanding subsidies are far more numerous than they have been and they demand more. It is not only, however, the subsidies which are demanded. The subsidies are to accomplish new, hitherto unaccomplished ends. Many scientists criticize the government for not providing enough support for scientific research. Some economists criticize it for not pressing ahead vigorously enough towards the equalization of income. Artists have even begun to criticize it for not giving them the patronage which other parts of the intellectual classes receive. Educationists criticize it for not acting with sufficient munificence to overcome the deficiencies of "ghetto schools." Penologists demand more money for the rehabilitation of criminals. Trade unionists criticize it for not spending enough to eliminate industrial accidents and occupational illness. The government is expected to redress not only recent but long past wrongs. It is pressed to establish the equality of sexes, races, classes, and generations, and it does not deny that these things are beyond its powers. However much it undertakes, it is still criticized for not doing enough.

Nonetheless, the state with all its pretensions to omnicompetence and all its unprecedently large activity is not appreciated by those in society who believe in the rightful omnicompetence of the state to redeem all wrong and to solve all "problems." Politicians are disesteemed; bureaucrats are distrusted. "Confidence" in governmental institutions declines. Yet more and more is demanded of them. The welfare state as the guarantor of a minimal level of material well-being for the poor and weak is thought not to be enough. The welfare state has arrived too late on the scene. Its arrival was met by expectations which had already gone further. By the time it came into existence in the United States, the welfare state, in the sense in which progressive social reformers understood it, was no longer regarded as adequate. More than an animal level of welfare was demanded. The inadequacy which is charged against it lies, it is thought, in its failure to realize the ideal of equality.

The intervention of the state to control and limit the excesses of private action was coupled with the older idea of the welfare state. The interventions of the state, according to this older view, were not intended to replace private initiative but rather to restrict its excesses. The new idea is that the state should be a positive and initiatory force in the construction of a society which will conform with "human needs."

At the same time that so much positive action is demanded, there is also a contradictory current of thought which has equally widespread adherence. This is that the government should act to emancipate human beings from restraint and to relieve them from the responsibility for the consequences of their actions. This demand for emancipation is expressive of a general disapproval of authority and of a desire to be free of it. It contradicts the simultaneously expressed desire that government should be the dominant power in society. The demand for "emancipation" is consistent with the demand for an omniprovident government, however, in the primacy which both demands give to "needs." To "meet human needs" is the task set for a comprehensively and positively active government. There is a long and profound tradition for this demand which has now come into fuller flowering. The demand for the emancipation of human impulses springs from a hostility towards authority which also has a long tradition, no less profound. The release of the individual from the control of institutions and from the pervasive dominance of the prevailing culture was not in the past conceived of as something to be achieved through government. Those who espoused this antinomian or "emancipatory" program had no expectations that government could be anything but repressive. For them, the ideal would be realized with "the withering away of the state." These two tendencies of thought have now become part of a single outlook.

The previously reigning puritanical individualism, that flourished particularly at the center of American society, had little place in its imagination and sympathies for the unsuccessful in the struggle for existence. The first sharp turn took place with the New Deal when the social security system was established and a variety of programs were improvised to aid the unemployed. Subsidized housing, under the auspices of the federal government, appeared then for the first time. The penetration of government into agricultural production also occurred at this time. The idea of "planning" came into American thought and government simultaneously. It has all gone forward since then, and has changed markedly in the course of its persistence.

II

In the 1920s, there were a few progressive states in the United States in which the governments had enacted legislation to protect women and children in industry and in the family, to help those who were injured in industrial accidents, and to diminish the danger of industrial accidents. Compensation in periods of unemployment was provided. The range of actions and scale of benefits were small. The federal government and the Supreme Court afforded little support to the efforts of the reformers.

Nowadays, however, social services of sorts undreamed of in the times when the welfare state was being conceived and established on the European continent and in the United Kingdom are being supplied in the United States by successive federal administrations. Old-age pensions and payments to relieve the hardships of those who had been employed and had been dismissed through no fault of their own came first; they were the achievement of President Franklin Roosevelt's administration. The beginning of large programs of federally subsidized housing of families with low incomes took root under President Truman. The "integration" of blacks in the armed forces also belongs to this phase. Under President Eisenhower, who was regarded by many as a "reactionary" Republican, the groundwork of the welfare state was consolidated. President Johnson's administration, seeking the "Great Society," released a cascade of social programs in addition to the expansion of older ones like governmentally subsidized housing. These included occupational and training provisions for sections of the population which previously had little, energetic action against employment policies which left blacks and females at a disadvantage, free lunches in schools for children, food stamps, programs for the cure of drug addiction, legal services for the poor, the reconstruction of blighted cities, innovations in penal procedures which are less constraining of the prisoner, and, more generally, a powerful movement against the repressive powers which had been claimed to be necessary for the maintenance of public order. Under President Nixon, despite his numerous hostile gestures, the movement from the welfare state to the omnicompetent state did not cease. Provision for the satisfaction of the aggrieved took a forward step.

The list of features of the omnicompetent and omniprovident state is a very long one and it includes a range of actions which earlier ideas of the welfare state, conceived in less affluent times, did not incorporate. The ideas of "busing" school children to achieve a particular ratio in classrooms of children of different ethnic characteristics and thereby to improve the scholastic performance of those whose performance would otherwise be poor; of the assignment of teachers to schools on the basis of their ethnic characteristics; of "remedial education" for children of uneducated and culturally backward parents; of actions to dissolve the differences of social classes by enforcing the mixing of social classes within residential districts; of "universal" higher education are illustrations of these innovations. The aspirations of the omnicompetent and omniprovident state have been made possible by the productivity of the economy, and it has postulated a high standard of amenity; the "poverty line" defined not by moral conventions but by governmentally employed statisticians has been moved upward. The omnicompetent state no longer confines its attentions to the marginal classes or its restraints to the injurious and predatory. The middle classes, who were once proud of their self-sufficiency, have become involved as beneficiaries. Except for a national medical service, the new policy in the United States covers nearly everything which the European states introduced within the past century, and much more; and even in the provision of medical service, a very considerable advance beyond the older idea of the welfare state has been made.

President Nixon nominally called for the "reform of the welfare system." This, presumably, meant reducing its scale and munificence, making more stringent the procedures and criteria for admission to its benefits. Yet he did not succeed. In his first term he denounced it and repeatedly announced his intention to reform it, but he did little more than that. His second administration was cut short without any accomplishment in this regard. His resignation and his succession by his vice-president made little difference. The repeatedly announced need to reduce the federal budget has not concluded in reductions in governmental expenditures. President Carter announced that he would reform the welfare system; his first proposals were estimated to cost six billion dollars more than the "unreformed" welfare system.

The principle of the state as the provider for welfare is now accepted. At least, there is no assertion or argument of a contrary principle. The responsibility of the state to maintain a condition of full employment is likewise unchallenged. In the working and middle classes, there is discontent with the new dispensation because the government takes so much of the national product and employs so many persons in occupations which, to the classes still living in the earlier tradition, are of inferior dignity; it is disliked because it is so "bossy," so slovenly, so intrusive, and so imperious. It is also disliked because it seems to support actions which are contrary to traditional puritanical morality. Nonetheless, those who disapprove of the new policies offer no arguments of principle against them; they dislike the taxes which are levied to pay for them. Many also find various elements of the welfare policy morally repugnant but they lack either the intellectual skill or the courage to deny the moral postulates of the new state and the type of society it is engendering. The arguments which are made against the universal action of the state are almost never arguments of principle, they are criticisms of particular inefficiencies and ineptitude, instances of corruption and anomalies, but they seldom raise any question as to whether it is right in principle that the government should act so comprehensively and penetratingly. Nor do the propagandists of the welfare state promulgate the postulates of their policy. A pervasive and unspoken outlook has prevailed. Put in its simplest terms, it is that whatever is amiss in society can and should by put right through the actions of the state. At the same time, it is expected that all individuals and groups should be free to act as they wish, that they should be free of the constraints of tradition and institutional authority, and that the state should be the guarantor of this freedom. In the demand for these guarantees the legitimacy of the state is denied. In a more extreme form, the program aims at substantive equality and the emancipation of impulse and sentiment from restraints. Of course the program is not executed. There are many restraints imposed by the resistance of the party of traditional outlook, some of which runs through the outlook of those committed to the progressivist view. There are inefficiencies in execution and repeated conclusions in failure.

There are also internal contradictions in the program. The attainment of equality entails inegalitarianism as a means; to render the ethnic groups of the lowest achievements and status equal to others, it is thought necessary to discriminate against these others, to deny to them opportunities which are opened to those of lower status. Furthermore the bloc of traditionality has many votes, and legislators are influenced by this as well as their own inner resistance to the trend of opinion to which they are drawn and against which they have no explicit arguments of principled conviction.

The demand for the American welfare state, the extension of this demand into the demand for the omnicompetent and omniprovident state, and the simultaneous denial of the state; accomplishments of behalf of equality and "emancipation" have their origin in a very complicated unfolding of the potentialities of several major traditions. In this process a large part was played by the anti-capitalistic reformatory intentions of American academics in the years between about 1875 and the Second World War, supplemented and amplified by a combination of the traditions of antinomianism and the belief that an all-powerful state could be an instrument to achieve an ethical ideal.

The first stage of this development owed much to the academic profession, in cooperation with politicians and publicists. In the second phase, too, the academic profession has taken a major part but it has been acting in a tradition which is new to it.

III

Before the First World War, in the United States, progressivist intellectuals, who were in a minority in the academic world, in the learned professions, and in journalism, thought that America's face was disfigured by the rampant pursuit of wealth. They regarded "big business" as the source of evil. Others who were not progressivist in their outlook also regretted the preoccupation with the pursuit of wealth which they thought was characteristic of American society. Overlapping with both of these attitudes was a quite different one; this was a skeptical discomfiture going as far as refusal to accept the prevailing puritanical rules regarding sexual conduct and the gratification of impulse.

Laissez-faire, as a policy in which the government acted to sustain the freedom of private business enterprise and to protect the sacred right of private property, was unsympathetically contrasted by the progressivist minority with the practice of European countries where governments took more positive measures on behalf of the lower classes, or those classes which were thought incapable of protecting themselves from the ravages of life in general and of industrial and urban life in particular.

Europe, in the first quarter of the present century, was thought to be morally and politically superior to the United States, just as those who were aesthetically interested and sensitive thought it was culturally superior. Progressivistic American academic intellectuals were aware of the social hierarchies in Europe with their emblems and beliefs about social superiority and inferiority, and they regarded that as a flaw; the fragmentary egalitarianism of the United States affected the attitudes of American academics—especially in the social sciences—towards Europe just as it affected their attitudes towards their own society. This did not prevent them from thinking that Europe was superior to the United States in important respects, such as in the strength of socialist parties and of the labor movement, in the proliferation of social legislation which had been enacted in response to the demands of working classes, or as a means of forestalling them, in the probity and efficiency of civil servants, and in the apparent influence of academics in public affairs.

In the universities, the spokesmen for the idea of the welfare state were mainly in departments of economics, which in the beginning of the century was a heterogeneous and unintegrated subject with far-flung boundaries. They had allies in departments of sociology, history, and political science. Very few of them were of European birth and upbringing. Most of them were native Americans of northwestern European stock who had studied abroad or who, if they had not done so, were impressed by the social sciences and social developments there. Some of them were sympathetic observers of socialist and labor movements in Europe, although very few were overtly socialistic in their views about the United States. Working-class immigrants were their main concern—as, latterly, blacks, Puerto Ricans, and Mexicans have been the concern of academic social workers and social scientists. (There was no educated social service bureaucracy then, as there is now, to act as a powerful force in its own right.)

American academic economists were divided into "institutional" and "classical" economists. The "institutionalists" were primarily of Germanic inspiration, although they were also inspired by the few British writers like Cliffe-Leslie and Arnold Toynbee who had supported the rejection of classical economic theory. Many of them had studied in Germany in the time of the supremacy of Gustav Schmoller, Karl Knies, Gustav Schönberg, and, above all, Adolf Wagner. A strong state which educated efficient and honest civil servants, a strict regulation of private economic enterprise, governmentally operated railways and municipal transportation, governmental operation of the supply of water, illuminating gas, and electricity, and unemployment and sickness insurance formed a whole which stood in a contrast of light with dark alongside the state of affairs in the United States. In social legislation, Europe presented a map of the destination towards which the United States should be propelled. The investigations of the institutional economists were descriptive; they described the machinery of regulation of public utilities, labor legislation and industrial regulation, the statistics of wages, hours, and conditions of work and standards of living, the working of the banking system, schemes of taxation—all in very concrete terms. They did not aspire to the heights of theory and they were generally very critical of what they thought were the excesses of abstract economic theory and the policy of laissez-faire which was associated with it. They were generally more quiet than the muckrakers, whose dramatic style was not in accordance with the usually maintained academic decorum, but they shared many of the views of the muckrakers. They supported Theodore Roosevelt when he promised to call the "trusts" to order and they welcomed Woodrow Wilson's "promise of American politics."

Political science was not then the independent "scientific" discipline which it is now; it was more closely linked to legal and historical studies. Johns Hopkins University and Columbia University were the first seats of this new field of learning in the United States. At Johns Hopkins it grew from the historical work of Herbert Baxter Adams, who had studied at Heidelberg and Berlin, where Treitschke had been one of his main teachers. Like his colleague Richard Ely, Adams gained his doctorate at Heidelberg; Bluntschli was his supervisor and Knies one of his examiners. At Johns Hopkins, in addition to specialized teaching and research on local institutions and very energetic editorial accomplishment, he also gave thought to "the application of historical and political science to American politics." He wished to create in Washington a "civil academy" which would be like the École libre des sciences politiques and which would train higher civil servants and diplomats. Like many of his German-trained American coevals, he hoped for an educated and hence honest and competent civil service. Great Britain stood alongside of Germany in presenting a model of a civil service which would be immune to the temptations of corruption. The corruptors were presumed to be the businessmen who stood to gain by making civil servants and politicians subservient to their desires; civil servants appointed by and dependent on politicians were in no position to resist their venal superiors.

They were less weary of politicians than they were of businessmen; they had some allies and heroes among the former. Their faith reposed primarily in civil servants since they could be carefully trained in universities and selected by impartial examination which discriminated in accordance with intellectual merit. The academic critics also thought that politicians could be made more civil by direct democracy and by an active and alert public opinion. Businessmen could not be appealed to on moral grounds. They could not be trained or selected by examination; they could only be controlled by the exercise of governmental power.

Although many of the political scientists thought of "popular government" as a way of preventing the improper exercise of influence by industrialists, bankers, and municipal traction and railway magnates over the federal, state, and local governments, they had no great qualms about conferring great powers of regulation and expenditure on a reformed government as long as it had an educated civil service selected on the basis of educational qualifications and supported by educated persons in the legislatures. In the pursuit of this program, political science was directed, first, towards the promulgation of a theory of the state which legitimated the exercise of power to keep the society together and to protect and promote the public good; second, toward the construction of the administrative machinery which would enable the state to attain its proper ends; and third, toward the training of the educated administrators who were to work the machine towards those ends.

This intellectual plant, imported from Germany and intended as a specific for the deficiencies of American public life, was most zealously cultivated at Johns Hopkins University, the first university in the country to become an institution of the higher learning in the German style. The chief gardener was Richard T. Ely. Ely had gone to the University of Halle in 1877 to study philosophy; there he met Simon N. Patten, who in later years was his companion-in-arms and who led him into economics. Patten too was one of the progenitors of things to come. As a result of Patten's arguments, Ely left philosophy at Halle and began to study under Johannes Conrad, an exponent of "historical economics." From there he went to Heidelberg when he imbibed the pure milk of historical doctrine from Karl Knies; after completing the doctorate there, he went to Berlin where he was guided by the lectures of Adolf Wagner. At the suggestion of the acting American minister in Berlin, he studied the municipal administration of Berlin and the Prussian purchase of the railways from their private owners. He was won over to belief in the superiority of German bureaucracy. In 1881 he began to teach at Johns Hopkins. Among his pupils were John R. Commons, Albion Small, Edward A. Ross, Woodrow Wilson, Amos Warner, Frederick C. Howe, William Willoughby, Albert Shaw, and Thorstein Veblen. Only Veblen did not feel at home under his teaching. All of them became leading participants in the movement to reorganize American society in ways which would confine and restrain the influence of wealthy and powerful businessmen. They were all inspired by Ely's creation of a "new school" of economics which would play the same part in the United States which "historical economics" had played in Germany. The main intellectual target of his criticism was classical economic theory, the main practical target of his criticism was the free market. In 1885 he initiated, with the help of Patten, the American Economic Association to spread his beliefs and to frustrate the classical economists who had organized a Political Economy Club in 1884. In the declaration which justified his new association, Ely wrote "We regard the state as an educational and ethical agency whose positive aid is an indispensable condition of human progress. While we recognize the necessity of individual initiative in industrial life, we hold that the doctrine of *laissez-faire* is unsafe in politics and unsound in morals . . . . We hold that the conflict of labor and capital has brought to the front a vast number of social problems whose solution is impossible without the united efforts of Church, State and Science."[1]

Ely's pupils made a profound mark on American life. Commons was one of the creators of the welfare state in Wisconsin under the government of Robert LaFollette. Albion Small became the head of the Department of Sociology and dean of graduate studies at the University of Chicago; he acted on his belief that sociology must become

1. Quoted from Benjamin G. Rader, The *Academic Mind and Reform: The Influence of Richard T. Ely on American Life* (Louisville, Ky.: University of Kentucky Press, 1966), p. 35.

a science which would then serve as an instrument for social reform. Edward Ross, after a turbulent career at Leland Stanford University and a brief period at the University of Nebraska, became the head of the Department of Sociology at the University of Wisconsin, where in season and out he denounced "predatory" businessmen and contributed towards the realization of "the Wisconsin idea." Veblen's unsteady career took him through several universities; but the unsteadiness of his career did not shake the firmness of his criticism of the irrationality and predatoriness of private business enterprise. All of them were stern critics of the mores of American capitalism, all regarded the state—a regenerated state—as the power to domesticate private business and to reconcile social conflicts.

For the economists, the railways were the most immediate problem; they saw the railway magnates as vultures tearing the flesh of the body politic. Bankers were an unceasing concern. The corruption of government and the exploitation of working men and farmers were their constant charges against the industrialists, bankers, and railway owners. Practically none thought of socialism as a solution to the problems of American society. What was needed was an aroused public, using the devices of a more democratic democracy and a more powerful and more virtuous government. The economists took upon themselves the task of educating the public about the realities of American economic life and of devising laws and institutions for bringing the "captains of industry" under control. Publication in popular magazines and addresses to laymen were among the major activities of academic economists.

The sociologists came out of backgrounds rather similar to those of the economists and political scientists and they faced similar situations. Many of them came from clerical or religiously observant farming families; some came from business families. All seem to have been reared in a puritanical environment; none were of Eastern or Southern European derivation. Many had studied for the clergy in an age of liberal Protestantism and the "social interpretation of Christianity." They had been troubled intellectually by the pious identification of God's will and plan with the order of private property and capitalistic enterprise. Practically all of the leading figures of the first generation of American academic sociology had studied in Germany: Small, Thomas, Ross, Park, Sumner—Cooley and Giddings were perhaps the only exceptions and Cooley spent some time in Germany, although he did not actually pursue a course of studies there. None of them studied sociology, as we now know it, in Germany—it did not exist as an academic subject—but they all studied subjects closely akin to sociology. Park came closest, attending Simmel's lectures, and in any case a sort of proto-sociology was in the German academic air. They had not been especially preoccupied with social problems when they went to Germany but they were well aware of the gap between the theological-economic teachings they had received in college and the turbulence of American society after the Civil War. They were all Protestants by origin, feeling the first stirrings of liberal Protestantism as well as a diminishing interest in the main theological trends of Protestant Christianity. In Germany, they imbibed not only German learning, but something of the German academic ethos, its respect for the authority of government, and its postulate that government should be honest and should care for those whom misfortune had befallen. The concern of the German social sciences for "the social problem" was transferrable to the United States where "the social problem" was attracting more and more of public attention. On their return from Germany their aroused—and increasingly secularized—Christian humanitarianism, their knowledge of German institutions, and the objects of their disciplines as defined by their German teachers were still with them when they came face-to-face with the life of the great cities, swollen by the immigrant working classes; the problems were those of poverty, broken families, alcoholism, juvenile delinquency, poor housing accommodations, and prostitution. They believed that their tasks as academic social scientists should be the investigation of "social problems," the disclosure of their results to a public of responsible citizens, and the consequent generation of an opinion insistent on improvement. Their civil action tended to be more confined to local institutions; they continued the older British and American traditions of "scientific philanthropy." They were concerned to gain the cooperation of municipal institutions, courts, prisons, and the police, which they hoped to arouse and guide by their investigations.

The lines were not sharply drawn between the sociologists, the institutional economists who envisaged the constitution of the regulatory welfare state, the political scientists who wished to render government impregnable to corruption by businessmen, and the social workers and businessmen reformers who sat on the governing bodies of civic and philanthropic associations. The sociologists were the liberals; they did not see the state as capable of remaking society. Few went as far as William Graham Sumner, who even disparaged ameliorative activity, but the many among them who were reformers by inclination or professional convention counted more on lay voluntary and local activity rather than on the power of the central government to provide, protect, regulate, initiate, and tax.

Professors of law also tended to be liberals in the older sense. Despite their professional involvement in the state, they were on the whole on the side of private institutions and privately made arrangements. They believed in the rights and obligations of contracts and in the rights conferred by the ownership of private property. They were usually against the expansion of the powers of the state. Roscoe Pound's sociological jurisprudence was exceptional in its time. Its stress on the need to know the detailed facts of the current situation declared its kinship with the similarly intended empirical interests of sociology and political science. It also meant that the norms inherent in the statutes and judicial precedents were not enough. To say that judges should, in general terms, make law in the light of "social forces" and "social needs" and thus compensate for the ethical insufficiency of existing legislation was also to acknowledge the failure of the executive and legislative branches of government to act up to their responsibilities to society. But it also showed sensitivity to the moral shortcomings of the existing social order and a belief in the capacity of a government, properly redirected, to remedy those shortcomings.

The teachers of social science and a few teachers of law saw much in American society which they did not like, and for the most part they believed that government was the right instrument for eliminating the morally repugnant features of that society. Most of the vices of American society were thought by its critics to flow from the free operation of the market and the unrestrained action of businessmen. Crime and delinquency, broken families, illegitimacy and prostitution were offensive in themselves and needed to be eliminated or reduced, but they were regarded as symptoms of something deeper and not as self-generating. It was common to interpret them as incidents of "greed" or the "profit motive." The institutional economists and political scientists were optimistic about what government could do, especially under the pressure of an informed and active public. They took for granted that the expert, the scholar who had specialized in the study of economics, social legislation, and administration would play a vital part in the process of purifying and strengthening of the state. The "classical economists," the adherents of the principle of the "night-watchman" state, were regarded in the academic profession as a group apart, and complaisantly inhumane. The sociologists were in the main reformers; William Graham Sumner stood alone in his refusal to approve "welfare." Some of the sociologists looked forward to a society in which reason illuminated by scientific knowledge would prevail and injustice and hardship would cease; they thought that the change would come through the "organs of society," of which government was one. They anticipated an animated democracy, in which the growth of the "social mind" or the "larger mind" ran parallel with the release of man's imaginative, moral, and rational powers. From the theoretical, even doctrinaire, Lester Ward, through the perceptive and hopeful Cooley to the experimental John Dewey, there was belief in the power of opinion enlightened and made rational by the development of the social sciences and the diffusion of their results. Most of them thought of democratic government as the organ of rational action in an institutional form. They were critical of those European governments which were in the hands of monarchs and aristocracies but they also admired the efficacy and probity of their civil servants. American government, once it was made an instrument of an enlightened and rational popular opinion, seemed obviously capable of avoiding the defects and acquiring the best qualities of the European governments. Some empirical sociologists, who were chiefly at the University of Chicago, were less sanguine about the powers of social self-transformation, particularly through the state. Nonetheless they were almost all reformers who thought that their knowledge should and would contribute to the amelioration of "social conditions." Even Robert Park and W. I. Thomas, who had absorbed less of the zeal of liberal Protestantism and who were more skeptical about the efficacy of the reformers' agitation, could not stand wholly apart. Even though they were more detached, they studied the same subject-matters and had the same external institutional connections as their more sanguine colleagues.

The members of the humanistic disciplines in the universities did not in general share the views of their colleagues in the social sciences who were interested in reform. There were exceptions like Robert Morss Lovett at Chicago and Joel Elias Spingarn at Columbia. They too were not entirely at ease in American society; they did not at all approve of the "materialism" of the decades after the Civil War and they were distressed by the corruption of governments, municipal, state, and federal. They thought that utilitarian and "business" ideals were eroding the traditional idealism of the American society and its higher intellectual pursuits. They were conservative in their political bent although they accepted democracy, the republican form of government, and the idea of moral progress. They were the custodians of an elevated and serious cultural tradition, puritanical, idealistic, patriotic, and vaguely Christian, to which most leading politicians, businessmen, publicists, and even literary men gave allegiance, even though many did not act in accordance with it. The consequences of the immigration from Eastern, Central, and Southern Europe were on their minds and they had some of the same apprehensions and preoccupations about it as their colleagues in the social sciences. They were anxious about the consequences of the Eastern and Southern European immigration for the cultural traditions which they had drawn from England; they still looked to England as the center of their culture although they valued highly American writers who were working in those traditions. They took an affirmative attitude towards tradition. The literary productions of the present were not within their jurisdiction. Classical studies, which were more prominent and more esteemed then and now, were of course excluded from treatment of contemporary works. Literary and historical studies also stopped short of the present, which, it was thought, could not be objectively assessed when it was still so near. This professional refusal to deal with the present was supported by abhorrence towards the unpleasant amalgam of vulgarity, democracy, politics, and materialism which characterized the present.

The natural scientists seem to have accepted the social and political order without much cavil. They were not particularly interested in the external political world, they seem not to have followed it in the detail which many of their heirs do nowadays. Like most American intellectuals of that time and since, they had an aversion especially to local politicians, political bosses, and political machines. Even when they were also averse to the genteel tradition, they shared its distaste and low esteem for professional politicians. But politics did not worry them; they thought it was only a passing phase in the history of the human race and some of them exerted themselves to influence federal legislators so that they would give governmental patronage to scientific research. On ceremonial occasions they praised the progress of American society and the contribution which research made to it. They did not expect their research to be guided by government; they did not think that government could become the major factor in the progress of the country except by leaving the field open to the initiative of private business and of science, which did not in fact depend on or serve government. They believed in progress; they believed in science as a surrogate for a lost or waned religious faith and as the motor of social and cultural progress. In so far as they were attentive to "social problems" and believed them soluble, they placed their confidence in scientific knowledge and the scientific outlook.

The teachers in the professional schools of medicine and engineering probably did not give much thought to the political "system" or to "social problems." There were some medical men who were concerned to improve the quality of medical education and hence of medical practice but there was not much thought given to the "delivery" of medical treatment. Generally they were satisfied to be borne along on the stream of progress. They gave their faith to research from which progress would continue to flow. There was a general confidence in the capacity of science and the scientific approach to carry mankind forward. They subscribed to the moral code of progressive individualistic Protestantism. Science and independent initiative were what society needed; the state was not regarded by them as the engine of progress.

Taken as a whole, the academic profession in the United States before the First World War did not care for politicians. There were exceptions to this general distaste. Theodore Roosevelt, William Howard Taft, and Woodrow Wilson were the exceptions in national politics; La Follette in Wisconsin was a similar exception in state politics. This does not mean that there was not considerable attention given to politics or that there was indifference to the moral quality of political activity and the condition of American society. There was much disquiet along the whole academic frontier, although only a minority—mainly economists and a smaller number of teachers of law and political science—thought that the government was the best instrument for righting wrongs and improving society. Except among the scholars in humanistic subjects, scientism had taken over the field. In the humanistic fields, there was less confidence in science and there was also a feeling that events were moving on the wrong track. For the others, scientific knowledge, gained by scientific methods and research, and the "scientific approach" to the problems of society would provide for progress.

Very widespread in the academic world, even among those who believed in the ideal and reality of progress, was the belief that things as they were in American society were unsatisfactory. Those who wished the state to be more active and those who wished it to be less so were equally discontented. Religious doubts and misgivings about those who were powerful economically and politically lay in quiet readiness for agitation against the transcendent and earthly centers. The closer an academic discipline or field was to technology, the less sense there was of being disconnected from the earthly centers of man's existence. The disconnection was greatest, in quite different ways, for the humanistic disciplines and the social sciences. The former experienced the disconnection between the prevailing central value-system and the serious spiritual ideal of Judeo-Christian, Graeco-Roman tradition, still mediated through the high culture of modern Britain; the latter—the social sciences—experienced the disconnection between a civic and political ideal and the economic and social order which was emerging in the United States in the period between the Civil War and the First World War.

IV

Before the entry of the United States into the First World War, there were no prominent American academic intellectuals who were revolutionaries in the sense of being members of any revolutionary bodies or of subscribing to the principle of the rightness and necessity of revolution. Daniel De Leon, who taught in a junior post for about four years at Columbia University, was obscure as an academic and his Socialist Labor party was known only to connoisseurs of political microscopy. Scott Nearing was certainly no revolutionary when he was summarily dismissed from the University of Pennsylvania in 1915; Thorstein Veblen was certainly critical of American society and government, but he was not a revolutionary and probably did not even have much respect for revolutionaries before the Russian Revolution of 1917. Louis Levine—later Lorwin—was no more than sympathetic with the desire of the copper miners to organize into a trade union when he was dismissed from the University of Montana. Max Eastman was a bohemian socialist who taught philosophy for a short time at Columbia University, but, until the war, he had only vague aspirations for revolution. Arthur Calhoun had a brief and undistinguished academic career before he was diverted to radical sympathies and a career in an educational institution intended to serve the radical wing of the trade union movement. There were a few—like Veblen himself and Carleton Parker—who were not unsympathetic with the Industrial Workers of the World. The famous "academic freedom cases" of Edward A. Ross at Leland Stanford University and of Leon Fraser, H. W. L. Dana, and J. McKeen Cattell at Columbia University did not touch on socialistic or revolutionary beliefs; in the case of Ross it was criticism of the importation of Chinese coolie labor; in the latter cases it was a critical attitude towards American foreign policy regarding the war in Europe. There were some—but still relatively few compared with later years—who were critical of the social-economic order of the United States from a socialistic standpoint. The Intercollegiate Socialist Society had a small number of university and college teachers among its members; it had been founded by Jack London and Upton Sinclair, who were not academic figures. Its members were mainly students and they were not numerous either. Jesse Holmes, who taught philosophy at Swarthmore, was proclaimed as a socialist; Robert Morss Lovett, who taught English at the University of Chicago, was another; Vida Scudder, who taught at Smith College, was a "Christian socialist." There was no academic intellectual of any weight or reputation who took the view that a revolutionary transformation of American society was necessary and feasible. The Marxian view that governmental provision was a deception of those classes of the population which otherwise would pursue their true interests, which, in turn, entailed nothing less than the abolition of the capitalistic system, had no audible echo among them. The political radicals and their bohemian literary and artistic sympathizers called welfare measures "palliatives," "sops to the workers"; but such epithets were not used in the universities, where many social scientists desired exactly such welfare measures. The absence of such radical views in the universities was in fact one of the reasons why radical intellectuals like Upton Sinclair regarded the universities as "tools of the capitalists."

The Russian Revolution of 1917 intensified and broadened the espousal of revolution among literary men and women and artists but it did not, at first, cause much of a ripple among academics. In the

United States in the 1920s, as before the war, most of the intellectuals who vaguely or definitely espoused the cause of revolution were to be found in literary circles. John Dos Passos was perhaps the most eminent among these. For the rest they were rather minor figures. The same was true among artists, although communism did attract a number of talented cartoonists, of whom Art Young was the best known. Radical or revolutionary publications led an exiguous existence through the 1920s. Whereas many of the contributors to the collectivist, liberal *Nation* and *New Republic* were academics, the *New Masses* had very few indeed. John Dewey, Rexford Tugwell, Zachariah Chaffee, Robert Morss Lovett, and Paul Douglas were frequent contributors to the reformist weeklies. There were no academics of any significance at all on the *New Masses*. A good deal of what was left of the reforming zeal of the progressive era had found refuge in the universities. Sympathetic interest in the Soviet Union gradually became part of their outlook; this was later to be a bridge between radicalism and reformism, but this had not yet happened in the 1920s.

The University of Wisconsin continued to be the center of collectivistic liberal thought. John R. Commons, now supported by Selig Perlman, steadily maintained the ideals of social reform; they were in favor of a trade unionism which stopped far short of socialism. They wanted social legislation to protect the marginal sections of the population, not governmental action which would replace voluntary collective action. Edward Ross, no longer as truculent as he had been in his youthful years at Stanford and Nebraska universities was still a populist although his eugenic ideas did not go well with the newer brand of reformism. At Johns Hopkins, Broadus Mitchell continued, in the vein of descriptive economics, the social concerns which had been implanted there by Richard Ely. At Amherst, Walton Hamilton taught institutional economics which made no bones about its critical intentions. At the University of Chicago, Paul Douglas, on a higher theoretical level, carried on the older tradition of interest in the condition of the working class, e.g., wages and hours of work; he was closely associated with the League for Industrial Democracy, which had replaced the Intercollegiate Socialist Society. Frank Knight, first at the University of Iowa and then at the University of Chicago, subjected the system of the market to the most severe ethical analysis—no socialist was as deep or subtle—but he always remained a liberal extremely suspicious of the collectivistic variant. "Institutional economics" still flourished, with its distrust of the "market" and its confidence in intervention and regulation; it had vigorous proponents in Clarence Ayres at Texas and Rexford Tugwell at Columbia. There was much concern with the problems raised by tariffs and monopolies but both of these subjects were part of the agenda of traditional liberal economics. In the main, economics departments in the universities taught neoclassical economics, but there was much eclecticism. Almost every department of economics of fairly large size had at least one person responsible for teaching about household budgets, wages and working conditions, labor legislation, and the trade union movement. This work was seldom incorporated into economic theory and it was often critical of it. Like its predecessor, the institutional economics of the 1920s was critical also of many features of American society and it looked to legislation to repair these defects. It thought of these defects as marginal and hence of governmental intervention as marginal and corrective. The "poverty line" was defined on a more ascetic standard and governmental activity was not thought of as being under egalitarian obligation. Rexford Tugwell's symposium on the *Trend of Economics* was a manifesto of the latter-day version of the "historical school" brought up-to-date and Americanized; there were still distinguished academic figures who were called "institutionalists" but the trend of academic economics was against them.

In the academic social sciences, the tone of the 1920s was against collectivist liberalism. The great private foundations, particularly those which grew out of Rockefeller philanthropy, acted in ways which applied the benefits of the earlier investments over a wide range of subjects. The general intention was to improve society through the application of scientific knowledge. A scientistic confidence prevailed; there was a general assumption that there were many things about contemporary American society which needed improvement, and a "scientific approach" seemed to provide the best assurance that these improvements could be brought about. Little was said about how and by whom the scientific knowledge which was in prospect would be applied.

In sociology, the reformative zeal had slackened; emphasis was now laid on the improvement of the reliability and precision of sociological knowledge so that it could return in time to the improvement of society. The "ordering and forbidding" techniques which had from time immemorial characterized the exercise of authority would, according to the sociologists who were seeking to make their subject into a science, be replaced by the application of social scientific knowledge. Some warned against unseemly haste in attempting to apply knowledge which was not quite scientific. Government was not conceived as the "user" of the knowledge to be gained by scientific research. The study of public administration was accorded a prominent place in the interests of political science—a continuation of the older reformative impulse which had pushed for the "merit" system in the reform of the civil service and the "city manager" plan in municipal government—but this time it was more detached, more scholarly study. Charles Merriam, Leonard White, and Louis Brownlow at Chicago and Luther Gulick at Columbia continued the tradition which had been established by Woodrow Wilson and carried further by Frank Goodnow at Columbia in the study of public administration. Quantitative studies of electoral behavior and studies of the psychological factors in political activity were beginning but they were still poorly represented in comparison with the study of public administration. The idea of "scientific management" which had taken hold in industry was extended by political scientists to their study of government. "Good government" meant scientifically managed government but this did not entail a vast extension of the powers of government; it was intended primarily to improve the exercise of its existing powers.

The greatest monument to the belief in the power of social science, scientifically conducted, to discern the insufficiencies of society, to formulate its "problems" and to aid in their solution by the provision of the requisite "scientific" knowledge was *Recent Social Trends*. Although published only in 1933, it was a work of the 1920s. Four of the leading social scientists of the country, Charles Merriam, trained at Columbia and then professor at Chicago; Wesley Mitchell, trained at Chicago and then professor at Columbia; Howard Odum, trained at Columbia and then professor at the University of North Carolina; and William Ogburn, previously at Columbia and then at Chicago, were the planners and directors of this work of social science done at the behest of Herbert Hoover. It took a broader view of "social problems" than its forerunners but it was equally concerned with improvement.

Psychology, passing beyond psychophysics and physiological psychology, entered more intensively into the study of intelligence, skills, aptitudes, and the selection of personnel for particular industrial occupations and tasks. "Behaviorism," with its pervasive popularization of the concept of "conditioned reflexes," lent more plausibility to the view that scientific psychology would contribute to the better management of society. The studies of Margaret Mead, originating in Boasian anthropology and Freudian psychoanalysis, seemed to show the variability of human society and cultural ideals and its dependence on the mode of "child-rearing." Its implications were relativistic and scientific. It was a period of great optimism about the scientific potentiality of the social sciences and of their consequent contribution to the more rational arrangement of human society.

Social science was seeping into the law schools. At Harvard, Roscoe Pound was at the height of his fame as the pioneer of "sociological jurisprudence." Walton Hamilton was appointed to the Yale Law School in 1928, having gone there from the Brookings Institution which he had joined four years earlier; he had left Amherst College four years before that in protest against the conservatism of the trustees of that college. At Yale, he began to exercise a profound influence in the direction of collectivistic liberalism but this was only at the end of the decade. The main themes of the new jurisprudence were that the judiciary must use "sociological" knowledge of the conditions of society to arrive at decisions which would increase governmental intervention and regulation. Institutional economics thereby gained a powerful ally in its pursuit of the program which Richard Ely had set for it some decades earlier.

The Social Science Research Council, supported by the philanthropic and financial resources of the Rockefeller Foundation, was a notable influence in the better ordering of the social sciences and in the encouragement of the hope that the self-mastery of society would be achieved through the application of the understanding gained through the social sciences. It was hoped that the development of the social sciences would in the course of time come abreast with the mastery of nature through scientific technology, itself based on the scientific understanding. All this rested on the traditional perception of the curable imperfections of human society but was carried on without the fervor and anguished sense of urgency of the reforming social sciences of the earlier period, when the "social gospel" was at the flood tide of its powers. In so far as an answer to an unasked question can be inferred, it was thought that government or an enlightened public opinion working on government would be the means through which the scientific knowledge to be gained would find its practical effects.

The outcome would be a more just, more orderly, more rational, more effectively democratic society. The ideal was as it had been, but it drew less on the imagery and inspiration of Protestant Christianity and more on the scientism which had gradually taken over its vocation. The decade of the 1920s was a period of less agitated academic social science, but in this last phase of serenity in the universities, the older ideal of a more beneficently active government was making steady and quiet progress. It was not explictly conceived in these terms. Nonetheless, with the coming of the Great Depression in 1929, the implications of the campaign for making the study of society more scientific, for making management and administration more scientific, and for increasing the powers of the central government to deal with the infinitely numerous problems of an industrial society were ready to be drawn.

V

Rather fundamental changes in the beliefs of academics about their place in society and of the type of society which they wished for occurred in the 1930s. These changes continued certain strands of the older tradition and they also added new ones.

In the 1930s, there was a great increase in the numbers and visibility of those who needed succor and protection. Measures to provide that succor and protection enjoyed a great support among American academics in that period. This support was generally undoctrinaire. Ordinary humanitarian sympathy counseled approval or demand for measures which would have helped the unemployed urban workers and coal miners, the dispossessed and impoverished farmers, and the severely afflicted aged no longer able to work. Classes of which only a few "social economists" and social workers had known before—such as the southern Negro sharecroppers, the itinerant agricultural laborers, the "Okies," the "hillbillies"—came into prominence. Skillful photographers, gifted documentary filmmakers, and novelists and journalists made the country more aware of the poor and of the devastation caused by the depression among those respectable strata which had recently been cast downward in society.

The years which made the economic hardships and the wounded pride of many ordinary Americans visible to the academics were also the years in which many of them were grazed by such hardships themselves. Many of the American academics of that generation came from rural families and small towns which had been painfully affected by the depression. The revenues of the state governments in the Middle West, where most of the great state universities were located, declined with the depression in agriculture. There were reduced funds for salaries and equipment. Few new appointments were made and graduate students had to lower their sights and to take employment different from that which they had anticipated. Many changed their subjects in the hope of obtaining employment. Most of them had hoped to become teachers and to devote themselves to research; they were diverted into the civil service where many stayed even when conditions became more favorable to their earlier aspirations.

Much of the 1930s was a time of exhilaration and despondency, of excitement and alarm, among literary, artistic, and journalistic intellectuals outside the universities; within the universities, the excitement and alarm were missing. Research went on steadily in almost every field and progress was made on many fronts—in the physical and biological sciences and in all the social sciences. Nonetheless, many academics, who previously had confined themselves to their subjects and not questioned what they would contribute to the well-being of their fellow countrymen and mankind in the long run, began to believe, on the periphery of consciousness, that it was not just politicians and big businessmen who were unsatisfactory, not just the social program of secularized Protestant Christianity which was inadequate. They felt that there was something fundamentally wrong.

The younger generation was especially prone to this feeling. Their careers were derailed. This was shattering enough, but the alternatives which they took up—temporarily at first—also shook them. The increased opportunity for employment in social work—in the service of local and state agencies for the distribution of "relief"—spread into sections of the educated class which might otherwise have been oblivious to its awareness of poverty and of the failure of the economy to provide employment. The growth of the various federal agencies which made up the New Deal drew into government service university graduates who had not thought of making careers in government and who had not hitherto concerned themselves with government or society. A generation of graduate students who had hoped to make academic careers disappeared into the federal civil service. Many of them were never to reappear. They became uncritical devotees of collectivistic liberalism, being its lesser agents. Those whom they left behind in graduate school and who persisted into academic careers acquired a very similar outlook.

Something else important happened. University teachers began to enter the service of the federal government at quite high levels on an unprecedented scale. "Institutional economists" such as Rexford Tugwell had taken a very prominent position ever since the beginning of Franklin Roosevelt's first presidential campaign. Raymond Moley was another one. Eminent professors of law and graduates from the law schools of Harvard and Yale universities, where the sociological jurisprudence of Roscoe Pound and "institutional" economics of Walton Hamilton were influential, took up important positions in President Roosevelt's immediate entourage, in his administrative creations, and in the federal judiciary. The social security system was designed by a university professor; the reform of the banking system was also a professorial invention. The huge increase in the quantity and quality of statistical information which was gathered and published by the government and which several decades later was so important in facilitating the "discovery of the poor" was to a large extent the work of academic sociologists and economists called to Washington by the government to cope with the depression. The espousal of an adapted Keynesian economics among academic economists, finding its epitome in the role of Alvin Hansen as special economic advisor to the Federal Reserve System, the participation of academic sociologists and political scientists in the work of the National Resources Planning Board, the work of political scientists to promote a more effective administration to deal with the new tasks being assumed by government (represented above all by Louis Brownlow's and Charles Merriam's role in the commission on governmental reorganization) were particular manifestations of the belief that the responsibilities of the federal government for the economic and social well-being of American society must be expanded. Although it had taken many steps in that direction, the United States was still only incipiently and fragmentally a welfare state by the end of the 1930s. Nonetheless the idea of a welfare state was generally affirmed in the politically concerned parts of the academic profession.

The dreams of the admirers of the *Verein für Sozialpolitik* were beginning to be realized, more elaborately than they had dared to hope. The aspirations of the "institutional economists" to subject the market to governmental control were being brought into reality. The hope of sociologists that sociological knowledge would be made to bear in a rational way on the "social problem" so as to ameliorate the conditions of the poor seemed to be moving towards realization; the interest of other sociologists in government on the basis of a statistically sound knowledge was likewise being met. The "merit" system urged year in and year out by academic political scientists made steady progress in the civil service; the machinery of government was being prepared for the great advance.

It would be an exaggeration to say that the welfare state as it took form at the end of the Second World War was the work of academic social scientists or that it was exclusively a product of the intellectual traditions of the social sciences. Their efforts to promote humanitarian and progressivist reforms of existing arrangements were always exerted in collaboration with social workers, amateur and professional, businessmen, journalists, politicians, clergymen, and lawyers many of whom had never attended a university and whose knowledge of the literature of the social sciences was scant. The legislative enactment of the diverse welfare measures required, of course, the active participation of politicians who had never either been university teachers or readers of the literature of the social sciences. It would be no less mistaken to insist that the establishment of the welfare state was simply the outcome of "pragmatic" or "practical" considerations of tough-minded persons facing certain social situations which could be "dealt" with only through the measures which constitute the welfare state. The "solutions" which were found to the crisis of industrial society were, it is true, "adaptations" to new conditions but they were "adaptations" which occurred within a tradition. The tradition was one of ideas, of ideas which had begun to take this specific form and direction early in the nineteenth century before universities became so important in the promulgation of the ideas which engaged public opinion and before the social sciences acquired their cast of mind which has been distinctive of them for nearly a century.

Nor should it be thought that the academic social sciences were confronting a wholly uncongenial block of opinion. Christian and allegedly secular humanitarianism, the interests of some of the leaders of the trade union movement, and diluted socialistic ideas were current in the public to which academic social scientists addressed themselves when they spoke and acted outside their specifically academic roles as teachers and scholars. Certain currents of public opinion were moving along the same lines as academic opinion but they were usually not so clearly worked out and they did not carry the authority of "factuality" which the academic social scientists and their published works possessed. Working and thinking within a tradition, academic social scientists gave it greater specificity and force. They did more than give a voice to the tradition of reform; they elaborated it and made it more definite and articulate. In so doing, they formed and guided it. They were, as Shelley said of poets, "the unacknowledged legislators of the world"—the world as it was coming to be in the early years of the administration of President Franklin Roosevelt.

VI

The academic social scientists were changing in response to events outside the universities. The humanitarian attitude grew in more of them; more of them began to believe that reforms were urgent. The growth in the popularity of the Soviet Union and of the increased influence of the Communist party in American universities and colleges coincided with this extension of awareness and sympathy of the academics.

There had hardly been any sympathetic curiosity about the Soviet Union among university and college teachers in the 1920s. Russian history and the political and economic systems of the Soviet Union were very little studied and taught in American universities and colleges at this time. Very few works by American academics on the Soviet Union were published. Books on this subject were mainly by journalists or by European writers, and there were not so many of either of these. Perhaps there was some fear among those who would have liked to study the Soviet Union, but the main cause was a plain uninterestedness. Paul Douglas had accompanied a trade union party which visited the Soviet Union in about 1928; a small student association also visited the Soviet Union at about the same time. (A very junior teacher of philosophy at the University of Pennsylvania who accompanied the latter, was dismissed after he delivered a public address about his visit to the Soviet Union.) Such interest was very unusual.

In the 1930s, interest became more widespread and quite sympathetic. The Soviet Union was presented as the "land without employment"—at about the time when more than a million persons there died of hunger or of diseases which flourished in bodies weakened by hunger.[2]

The social services, especially the medical and pediatric services of the Soviet Union, were repeatedly presented for universal admiration, and they succeeded in gaining a very great deal of it. Henry Segerist, the distinguished Swiss-American historian of medicine, who was professor at Johns Hopkins, diverted himself from his history of medicine to write an enthusiastic account of the accomplishments of the Soviet Union in the provision of medical service. It was claimed by Frankwood Williams, an American propagandist of mental health, that there were hardly any mental disorders in the Soviet Union thanks to the introduction of a just economic system which provided security for everyone (at a time when hundreds of thousands of persons were being imprisoned on no reasonable grounds at all). This was allegedly made possible by the revolution of October 1917 and by the existence of a socialist society.

A popularized version of psychoanalysis as applied to modern society supported these false ideas about the Soviet Union and sustained a comparison between American and Soviet societies which was entirely unfavorable to the former. Karen Horney asserted that neurosis was engendered by competition and the stress laid on achievement in contemporary American society. Neither Karen Horney nor Frankwood Williams were academic social scientists, but, as interest in a sociological version of psychoanalysis grew among academics, their ideas and others like them drew forth an academic echo.

The Institute for Social Research, first at the University of Frankfurt and in the 1930s and 1940s loosely attached to Columbia University (it later became a fountain of a new variant of radicalism), was spreading through the writings of Erich Fromm and Max Horkheimer the idea that "bourgeois individualism" and the repressiveness of bourgeois familial morality caused aggressiveness which found release in the support of totalitarian movements and governments. Such interpretations were of a piece with Frankwood Williams' observations. The Institute for Social Research was never Stalinist, and its Marxism was artfully disguised. Nonetheless, its publications conveyed a tone of hostility towards bourgeois society

---

2. I recall reading a letter of a then well-known fellow-traveling teacher of political science specializing in, of all things, international relations, national socialism, and communism. It was written during a visit to the Soviet Union sometime in 1933 or 1934; he wrote mockingly of seeing "thousands of corpses piled up along the railway tracks" while he was going through the Ukraine. He regarded the accounts of some Western journalists describing the famine as a fit subject for elephantine humor. In fact, the journalists were right and the professor of political science was a compliant dupe.

and an intimation that under socialism a "truly human life" would come into existence.

The younger generation of social psychologists—who later became organized into the Society for the Psychological Study of Social Issues—were much less sophisticated intellectually; their simple political convictions were similar in spirit to those suggested by Karen Horney and the exiles of the Frankfurt school. Kurt Lewin's famous investigations at the University of Iowa into the consequences of "authoritarian" and "democratic group atmospheres" were generalized into a condemnation of authority. These social psychologists were not Stalinists either, but their ideals added arguments to those which were already being made on behalf of the merits of communism, in which "democratic planning" rendered authority redundant. The message was the same as that of the refined Marxists: authority is pernicious.

The improved fortunes of Stalinism could be remarked by the appearance in 1936 of *Science and Society*, a quarterly journal produced under Stalinist inspiration. The appearance in its pages of scholarly papers and long erudite reviews by a small number of young and obscure American academics and by leading European scholars of Stalinist outlook was evidence of an emergence of a new group of sympathizers with communism, still small but larger than had existed heretofore.

From 1935 onward—i.e., from the Seventh Congress of the Communist International—the policy of the "people's front" and of the grudging support, at least in public, for reforms within the capitalistic system made for an easier transition to a more radical position; the new position contained the previously separate movements of revolutionary radicalism and reformism. Those who received their political education as fellow-travelers and participants in this movement in the 1930s and 1940s thus received at the same time an ambivalent attitude towards the reforms leading to the establishment of the welfare state. The fusion of radicalism and reformism in the period of the "people's front" was a historically necessary step in the unfolding of the egalitarian critique of the welfare state from within the ranks of those who supported and executed it.

The Communist party spread this outlook through cells established within universities and colleges. They did best in institutions with a tradition of liberality and sympathy for reform movements and where there were brilliant young teachers and graduate students who were "progressive." The communists and their fellow-travelers were probably very few in number in the colleges and universities of the country as a whole; they were relatively strongest at City College of New York, and even there they did not have great influence either in the teaching staff or among graduate students. At Harvard University, at the University of California at Berkeley, and at the University of Wisconsin, with its great tradition of progressivism and the attraction of Alexander Meiklejohn, some progress was made in attracting young teachers and graduate students. Some of them later became quite eminent; some received much unpleasant publicity during the time of Senator Joseph McCarthy's campaigns, long after most of them had divested themselves completely of sympathy with the Communist party. The line separating persons who were in fact members of the Communist party and those who were sympathizers cannot be drawn precisely; it is in fact not a line but a broad obscure band. Falling within this band were persons like J. Robert Oppenheimer, Dirk Struik, Paul Sweezy, Granville Hicks, Newton Arvin, Abraham Edel, F. O. Matthiessen, Kirtley Mather, and V. J. McGill, some of whom were already well known in their respective fields of scientific and scholarly study. Despite the vigorous efforts of such men to convert their colleagues and pupils, the Communist party obtained very few academic adherents. This contrasts markedly with the party's success among literary men and women, artists, and screen writers.

One characteristic of these small groups in the universities and colleges was their pertinacity in seeking new adherents and in harassing those who disagreed with them. They harassed particularly those who were not far removed from them in outlook but who were not to be persuaded by them. They harassed liberals and Trotskyites especially; they hated "Mensheviks." Conservatives and Republicans were left alone since they were thought incorrigible. The communists were organized into cells within organizations of "fellow-travelers" and in bodies which had no sympathy with communism. The aim was the propagation of the prevailing communist "line."

There was however no effort to change the system of authority in the university or college or to change the syllabus or courses of study. The entire focus was on the outer world, not on the university or college, and the aim was to gain support for the Soviet Union and to support those groups in American public and political life which supported the policy of the Soviet Union, whatever it was at the time. Despite the failure of the handful of communist academics to win adherents to their organization, they did succeed in imparting a tincture to the progressivist outlook. The tincture was a strengthening of the praise of socialism and of the disparagement of capitalism, liberalism, and bourgeois democracy. Those who did not go so far as to think that liberal democracy was wrong in itself or wholly illusory were made a little more skeptical by the communist arguments. The hypocritical, skeptical support of the communists for the policies of the Roosevelt administration in general fostered a shift in the postulates of progressivism. The shift was toward a belief in the rightfulness of a universally active government. The model of the Soviet Union, with many qualifications and explicit disavowals, slipped into the conception of the right order of society.

In the atmosphere of the 1930s, the coincidence of the heightened visibility of "need," the persistence of the tradition, only transiently submerged, of the ameliorative obligations of academic social scientists, and the experience and opportunity "to do something about it" through government introduced a subtle change into the outlook of American social scientists. Although American academic social scientists had not in the past held themselves entirely aloof from government, the administration of President Roosevelt with its call for their services gave them a greater self-confidence and a greater sense of the own importance. There was a change from the earlier morally and theologically enjoined sense of obligation to care for the weak and defenseless members of the flock and to do so with other morally sensitive members of the congregation or community. The new attitude contained the older spiritual sense of calling but to it was added a new type of spiritual arrogance, a sense of power which lay within oneself, through one's own cognitive qualifications and through the now more evident availability of a powerful and usable instrument, namely, the state. The tincture of Stalinist fellow-traveling added its own tone to this enhanced confidence in the power of government as an instrument and to this increased disapproval of one's own society and its businessmen and politicians.

VII

A change was also taking place on the humanistic side of the university. There was a shift towards contemporaneity of interest. Hitherto humanistic studies in the universities interested themselves in the past. The classics still held a relatively central position although there had been a steady displacement from the time of the introduction of the elective system. Modern literary and linguistic studies—English, French, German, Italian, and Spanish—scarcely touched the twentieth century and, in any case, did not deal with contemporary literature. The proper objects of these studies were those great authors and works which the passage of time had tested and assigned to their place on the higher reaches of the slopes of Parnassus. It was not that professors of humanistic subjects were entirely ignorant of contemporary works. Some of them did indeed write reviews in the weeklies and monthlies and pass judgments on contemporary authors, but that was usually an auxiliary interest which was not given a large place in their academic work. The present and its works were not yet accepted as fit academic subjects. This situation began to change towards the end of the period between the two great wars. A bridge was being thrown up between the universities and the world of living writers. Although it is said that the American literary intellectuals of the 1920s were apolitical, this was not so. They had for a long time been pained by what they saw was the philistine culture of their country, the uncouth character of its political leaders, and the grossness of its great businessmen. There was an implicit political attitude, close to the surface, in their uneasiness with American society. This they had in common with the academic heirs of the genteel tradition.

H. L. Mencken was an interesting deviant from this pattern; he was not an aesthete of quivering sensibility and he had no sympathy for American radicals, except in so far as they were persecuted by brutal businessmen, busybodies, and politicians. But in his antipolitical attitudes, in his contempt for politics and politicians, for their corruption and boorishness, he appeared to be an ally of the literary intellectuals; in certain matters, such as censorship, he shared their repugnance against puritanism. Mencken did not draw the conclusions of these beliefs which some of his coevals and many of his juniors did in the years of the depression. Whereas he withdrew to philology and autobiography, they went on from bohemian radicalism to the support of the Soviet style of socialism—even where they diverged from the Stalinist view of things—as the ideal solution to the deficiencies of American society and politics. There was a certain justness in the adaptation by the communists of the name of *The Masses* to their own journal, *The New Masses*. They claimed to be the heirs of that bohemian-radical literary tradition and they were not entirely wrong in doing so. Of course, not many of these heirs of Greenwich Village were members of the Communist party or deliberate and closely allied fellow-travelers. Much more common was a loose approximation to the "line." Those who separated themselves from the Communist party and its organizational "fronts" to become Trotskyists still held to the belief that a socialistic organization of society was the only acceptable one.

The "line," despite its ostensible patriotism, was hostile to nearly every aspect of American society. It conformed with the advice which Lenin gave in *What Is to Be Done?* which was to support every grievance and to turn it in a revolutionary direction. In this view, contemporary American society had no substantial merits, only shortcomings. Only "progressives," as they were called, had merit; the "progressive" program required governmental action to remedy all the deficiencies to which the grievances called attention and which were extensive and pervasive and deep-seated. Yet the remedy always lay in the hands of the government. The resolution of these problems entailed the omnipotent state.

Such views were as far as they could be from the traditional beliefs of American academic humanists. Nonetheless, the opening towards the present, the greater feeling of the importance of contemporaneity, taken together with a quickening of the "social conscience" in the face of unemployment as well as the sense of being brushed oneself by the wings of the angel of unemployment and penury caused many American academic humanists to loiter near the bridge or even to cross over it. The *Partisan Review,* after it ceased to be Stalinist, became an important link between the younger academic generation of humanists and a radical political interpretation of "modernist" literature. The bohemian aesthetic outlook of the first thirty years of the century thus came into parts of the universities to which it had previously been strange. With it came some of the potential for political radicalism which had lain close to the surface and which was now cropping out.

The academic social scientists had no bohemian radical counterparts. Very few academic social scientists mixed in those circles. Alexander Goldenweiser and Paul Radin had such connections but they were exceptional. It has been said that William I. Thomas had bohemian connections in Chicago, but they must have come to an end when he left Chicago shortly after the end of the First World War.

VIII

The coming of the Second World War caused a suspension of concern with domestic affairs. Perhaps even to a greater measure than in the First World War, American academics entered into the war in spirit and in action. Far more numerous were the opportunities for academic participation in the tremendous variety of activities connected with it. Economists simply continued in increased numbers the activities which had engaged them previously; the economy became much more subject to regulation than it had been in the first two administrations of Franklin Roosevelt. Anthropologists and sociologists found employment in various types of intelligence work which, perhaps under their influence, came to include aspects of the enemy societies with which intelligence had dealt only very slightly in earlier wars. Political scientists were trained for the administration of conquered territories. Thousands of graduate students and young teachers were trained in foreign languages by the Army Specialist Training Program, and most of their teachers were academic linguists and anthropologists. The natural scientists had even more opportunities. The largest of these was the Manhattan Project but there were many more in the Radiation Project, in research in the detection of submarines, in medical research, etc.

The zest of participation was joined by the impressive experience of the efficacy of governmental action. The extraordinary achievements of the government in recruitment, assignment, provisioning, and transportation of soldiers and sailors as well as the tremendous feats of production of weapons, ships, planes, and munitions were extremely persuasive. The organization of research on chain reactions and the production of the atomic bomb and much else seemed to show that government had infinite capacities.

Once, however, the war was over, the expanded role of government was not allowed to contract. The government accepted the responsibility for maintaining full employment; it continued to support scientific research on a scale unimagined before the war and in a way which brought much satisfaction to academic scientists and administrators. This belief in the enlarged powers of government was the presupposition of the later idea of the omnicompetent, omniprovident state as a regime of equality.

Nonetheless, for more than a decade after the end of the Second World War, there ceased to be great deal of concern among American academics for the welfare state, apart from the interest in full employment, and certainly not for its egalitarian extension. The belief that social science could be more effective after it became genuinely scientific meant that much effort was put into the improvement of techniques of research and into the construction of theories. For a decade, at least, the poor were not much thought of in academic circles. Sociologists turned away from the older topics, and explicitly from the "social problem." In the universities, "race relations" and the study of ethnic groups—mostly of the working classes—after having been one of the most engrossing subjects of sociological investigation for about a third of a century, fell away from the center of sociological attention. Industrial sociology, which had flourished before the war—particularly since the Western Electric studies—also declined. The study of criminal behavior became more theoretical too. Some sociologists became more concerned with government as an object of sociological study.

Sociologists benefited much less from the extension of governmental support for academic science than did the natural scientists. A small number were employed or consulted by the Rand Corporation, which did research for the United States Air Force. Others served on advisory committees. The multidisciplinary study of Soviet society was supported to some extent by the government. Nonetheless, sociologists were relatively separate from central government. They did not however go back to the preoccupation with local social problems and to collaboration with voluntary social-work associations. What concern they had with government tended to be with the central government, at least to a greater extent than in the two decades between the wars.

Whereas before the Second World War, Max Weber's ideas had been taken up mainly at Harvard and Chicago, during this period they became rather well known among American sociologists. In Max Weber's work, there are variant strands of analysis which are kept in a subtle and complex balance. One of these postulates the limits of human powers, the ineluctability and the ultimate insolubility of certain fundamental problems of human existence. Another closely related theme of Max Weber's is the tense relationship between the growth of power of bureaucratic authority and the difficulty of effective control of it and even of resistance to it. Another theme is the frailty of all types of authority and their dependence on beliefs about their legitimacy. A further, overlapping theme is the tension between the "ethics of responsibility" and the "ethics of conscience." Max Weber was far from a utopian, but his disenchanted analysis of modern Western society can, by selective reading, be made to bear witness to a radical condemnation of that society on behalf of a utopian aspiration. This is what happened.

Both from Max Weber and their own observations, American sociologists were impressed by the concentration of governmental authority and the bureaucratization of modern society, but they accepted these processes with equanimity partly because they were put into the service of policies which the sociologists affirmed. As long as the processes served the provision of welfare and the regulation of private action, the sociologists did not see much wrong with them. Michels' analysis of the "oligarchical tendencies of modern democracy" was also accepted as an unalterable fact of nature which could be held in check only under very special conditions. C. Wright Mills diverged from this view of things; he accepted the emergent view of the concentration of power and he exaggerated it even further. The difference between his view and that of other sociologists lay largely in his very hostile attitude towards those in whose hands power was said to be concentrated. Mills was not a humanitarian and he despised the reformist attitudes of the older generation of sociologists. He was perhaps the only sociologist of eminence in the 1950s who used the rhetoric of radicalism—a mixture of Veblen's ideas and American populistic and Marxian images and idioms. Although he denounced this concentration of power and the concomitant bureaucratization, the alternative ideal which he implied and occasionally proposed entailed an even greater concentration of power. He did not until near the end of the 1950s and the end of his life espouse what later came to be calle   participatory democracy." But whatever he desired for the future, he saw for the present an unrestricted power manipulating, without resistance, an utterly malleable "mass society." He was much esteemed by the younger generation of sociologists and, although very few sought to emulate him, many accepted his account of American society. His account was only one of several slightly variant accounts with similar content.

One of these was the "theory of mass society" which many of the new generation of sophisticated sociologists espoused under the Germanic influence exercised by Karl Mannheim, Hannah Arendt, and Max Horkheimer. It supported an image of society in which the powerful few can manipulate the powerless many; it stressed the potentiality of modern Western societies to grow into totalitarianism. Bohemian radicalism, a highbrow disparagement of democracy, and certain strands of Max Weber's sociology were mingled in Dwight MacDonald's *Politics,* a magazine much appreciated by some of the advanced younger social scientists in the years just following the end of the war.

The more old-fashioned political scientists were still concerned with the improvement of administration; the concern with urban "machine politics" and the once strong interest in municipal reform declined. The study of "community power structure" replaced it. The techniques and the terminology of these studies might have been novel but the underlying ideas were not. There was however a new tone. A preoccupation with and an implied condemnation of "elites," and a suspicion of self-aggrandizement compounding the injustice of inequality in the distribution of wealth and power, became more prominent features of American sociology and political science. Power as such was beginning to appear to be a bad thing. Yet it was generally accepted that government was the sole resort if American society was to be improved. The cure for the excessive concentration of power was thought to be in an increased governmental power. Those who censured modern American society for the high degree of bureaucratization saw nothing contradictory in reposing their confidence in increased governmental power as a means of compensating for the imperfections of the market, the injustices of capitalism, and the misfortunes of human existence.

Academic economists also underwent a great change. Already before the Second World War "institutional economics" had lost its intellectual position. Whatever the success of "institutional economists" in the administration of President Roosevelt, descriptive studies of poverty and estimates of the numbers of families below the "poverty line" nearly vanished from the leading universities as did quantitative descriptions of wages and hours of work. Economics became more oriented towards policy and in that sense more "practical," but, at the same time, it became much more theoretical. Economic theory—neoclassical and Keynesian—extended its jurisdiction, and as it did so "poverty" disappeared from view. Unemployment replaced poverty as a concern of economists. Keynesian economics enhanced the belief that it was government on which the prevention of unemployment depended. Economic growth, the increase of the gross national product also helped to push poverty into the background, but these new foci of interest did not lead most economists to give less prominence to the positive role of government than had the "institutional economics" which their theory had supplanted.

Psychology was a very different sort of subject with very different traditions. In its earlier years it scarcely touched on matters which were connected with social policy. It was only when it was applied to the "selection of personnel" in industrial, commercial, and military organizations that it began to be regarded as a means of improving society through making it more efficient. Just as the First World War had given a stimulus to psychology, so did the Second World War. Psychology reinforced its position as one of the subjects which could help man to become more rational and more effective in his collective self-government. It seemed to offer a better alternative to the irrationality and traditions of existing authority. It gave a prospect of a more scientific mode of government. Clinical psychology and the study of personality, both deeply influenced by an emancipatory interpretation of psychoanalysis, attracted many students and large financial support. These studies offered to free human beings from the compulsive inhibitions imposed by authority and cultural tradition. So did experimental social psychology and the study of group dynamics; in both, a combination of manipulation and the release of repressed impulses were vigorously espoused. The more progressive social psychologists, grouped in the Society for the Psychological Study of Social Issues, were all for the emancipation of the individual and an increase in governmental powers. Individuals would be freed from crippling prejudices and inhibition, increased governmental powers would render obsolete competition among individuals; governmental policies would be rendered more scientific and effective through the employment of psychologists as advisors and their support as scientific investigators of the processes to be controlled.

A huge study of *The Authoritarian Personality,* done under the guidance of the quasi-Marxist, quasi-psychoanalytic doctrine of the Institute for Social Research, before it reassumed its old name as the Institut für Sozialforschung, gained much attention and esteem. It was part of a larger project supported by the American Jewish Committee to acquire the knowledge needed for the prevention and obliteration of anti-Semitism. The main theme of *The Authoritarian Personality* was very simple: the traditional outlook was "proto-fascist"; liberalism of a progressivistic, collectivist tendency was the right outlook of a personality free from paralyzing inhibitions and a crippling submissiveness to authority. The political outlook of this allegedly free personality corresponded very closely to the program of the Progressive party, which had Henry Wallace as its standard-bearer and numerous fellow-travelers as its supporters. Those who were not hostile to American society were put into a very uncomplimentary light by this investigation. The first postwar decade was a euphoric and distracted decade in the academic world as it was in American society. The universities burgeoned with students; staffs and resources multiplied. The natural sciences scarcely lost the momentum which the war had added to their forceful forward movement continuing from the prewar decades. Collectivistic liberals were demanding and optimistic about the expansion of governmental powers. The "cold war" and the McCarthyite harassment of scientists, academics, and civil servants, who were accused of communistic affiliations and sympathies, distracted minds from the criticism of "social conditions"; radicals were intimidated. The welfare state as an ideal of care for those in marginal conditions was nearly forgotten. Full employment, economic growth, the new scientific technology, and a high standard of living which resulted from them, were accepted as a solution to whatever problems the welfare state had in principle been intended to resolve. Yet, underneath all of this lay the new assumption of policy, namely, the capacity and obligation of the federal government to deal effectively with any problem which might arise in society. This and the belief in the sterility of traditional social institutions were the postulates of the new version of the welfare state—the omnicompetent, omniprovident, selectively egalitarian state—which was to take hold of the minds of a majority of American academic intellectuals in the ensuing two decades.

IX

The discovery of the "poor" was an accomplishment of the beginning of the 1960s. The civil rights movement was not at first a part of it. The civil rights movement did not seek to remake American society, only to give to Negroes the places in it to which they were entitled as citizens of the United States. It could be looked upon as a demand that the state continue in an older role of the "night-watchman" state, a role which entailed the protection of the integrity of weights and measures, the maintenance of highways, respect for private property, the security of the public peace, but also, and above all, the guarantee of the rules of the competitive game. What the Negroes active in and supporting the civil rights movement wanted was that the rules of the competitive game of a liberal society be guaranteed for them as for everyone else. They wanted the same competitive freedom and opportunity as the liberal legal order guaranteed for others. They wanted to enter professions and occupations for which they were qualified; they wanted to be able to attend schools, colleges, and universities for which residence and intellect qualified them; they wanted to shop in retail establishments where their purchasing power could pay for the same goods that others with similar purchasing power could buy; they wanted to live wherever they could afford to pay the same rentals or purchase charges which white persons paid. They did not seek special subsidies from the state or quotas, or "targets," imposed by the state. They wanted to be judged in courts in accordance with the rules of evidence and by the laws which applied to them as they applied to white persons. They wanted to vote freely as did other citizens. They did not wish to be maltreated by the police or treated discourteously by municipal officials. The civil rights movement stood clearly in the tradition of the liberal order in which human beings were evaluated in accordance with their achievements and judged by laws. The civil rights movement sought what radical and revolutionary detractors of the liberal order have called "merely formal rights." Predominantly, the demands of the civil rights movement had as much to do with the "welfare state" as the law of contract or the principle of *nulla peona sine lege* had to do with it. The early years of the civil rights movement accepted the structure of American society as it was, except for its exclusion of Negroes from the opportunities and freedoms engaged by whites.

The contribution of the American academic profession to the civil rights movement was only indirect, and it began many years earlier. The immediate events involved the actions of black undergraduates from black colleges in Southern states. They were guided and encouraged by black clergymen and civic leaders in organizations in which a few white academics had once played a part of some importance. Professors Joel Elias Spingarn and James Harvey Robinson, both of Columbia University, had been important figures in the early history of the National Association for the Advancement of Colored People; Robert Park of Chicago in the National Urban League. White academics had no part in the civil rights movement, which included peaceful civil disobedience, although white university students did. The main contribution of white academics to the civil rights movement was the long series of sociological studies of Negroes, inspired and guided by Robert Park and carried out by numerous protégés at the University of Chicago and Fisk and Howard universities, most notably by E. Franklin Frazier and Charles S. Johnson, and by Howard Odum, Guy B. Johnson, and Rupert Vance at the University of North Carolina. Investigations by these scholars and their pupils over a period of twenty-five years were brought into synthesis by Gunnar Myrdal, with the aid of a Swedish statistician and Arnold Rose, a young sociologist of the University of Chicago and later of the University of Minnesota. Myrdal had been advised by Louis Wirth at the University of Chicago; Wirth had been a protégé of Albion Small and Robert Park.

An important shift in intellectual opinion had taken place in the years between Park's work and Myrdal's; it was a shift in the direction of a belief that governmental initiative and power were indispensable to the improvement of American society. Park, who had spent a number of years as an amanuensis of Booker Washington at Tuskegee Institute, was a liberal who detested discrimination on ethical grounds but did not think that it could be eliminated by the exercise of governmental power. It was in his view a phase in the movement, to and fro, of the processes of competition, conflict, accommodation, and assimilation. Myrdal was a European socialist and a convinced exponent of economic planning; his advisor, Louis Wirth, had been a pupil of Small, who combined sociological scientism and the "social gospel." Wirth himself had been a sympathizer with communism as a youth and in the 1930s he became a devotee of "planning." Myrdal's synthesis brought together the knowledge which had been produced by the liberal reforming sociologists and his own and Wirth's conviction that government had the capacity to re-order society. The book which summarized all these investigations and reflections—*The American Dilemma: The Negro in America*—had a permeative influence on American opinion, and it reached into the documentation and deliberations of the United States Supreme Court in one of its most monumental decisions. It was a point in the movement from liberal "reformism" through the welfare state to the omnicompetent, omniprovident egalitarian state.

The uncontested ascendancy of the civil rights movement among its black adherents and white supporters was relatively brief. Its aspirations were not realized sufficiently to satisfy its adherents and its supporters, at least those who were more articulate and vigorous. There was harsh resistance from many whites who were attached to the older patterns of discrimination, particularly in the South. Furthermore, its civil procedures could not contain the passions of parts of the black population. Nor did it satisfy the white intellectuals who had been erstwhile well-wishers of the movement. It was too bourgeois, it was too content with American society as it existed in the years between the end of the war and the assassination of President Kennedy.

White academics played no significant role in the yielding of the civil rights movement to the slogans of "black power" and to the fame of the Black Panthers. Nor did black academics participate centrally in this movement. The "black power" movement did receive much applause from some white, and most of the small number of black, academics. The movement was a denial of the legitimacy of the authority in American society and a disavowal of its culture, and it coincided with and drew support from the increased numbers of white academic intellectuals who regarded themselves as liberals. However he might have displeased the alumni of Yale University, President

Kingman Brewster was in fact expressing a view held by quite a few American academics at that time when he said that a Black Panther could not expect fair treatment in the courts of the United States. It was a denial of the moral legitimacy of governmental authority.

The outbreaks of violence in black districts of large cities in the United States found their academic apologists in sociology and political science, who argued that the riots were "natural," "expedient," or "rational." This was the time when "black studies" made their appearance. Some academics yielded to the demand for such spurious courses of study because they wanted to avoid an altercation with radical students; others did so because they had so renounced belief in the validity of traditional Western literary and scientific cultural achievements that they thought black students should not have to study "white subjects" at a university. It became common for teachers in departments of education which had long been carriers of progressivist beliefs to assert that the culture of the black *lumpen-proletariat* was "as valid" as the culture which schools had traditionally inculcated. The fact that they were at the periphery of society allegedly conferred validity on their culture. The blacks, according to this view, were entitled to exemption from the obligations of law-abidingness and of assimilation of the higher culture of American and Western society. They gained merit from the fact that they lived in slums, in wretched dwellings; virtues were imputed to them because they were unemployed, were the "last hired, the first fired," because their children attended schools where teachers were prejudiced against them, and because they and their offspring were the victims of police brutality. All these things give dignity to their "black experience," a dignity which, it was said, was denied and distorted in "white" intellectual works. Of course these views were not held to any great extent by any except literary and academic intellectuals, social workers, and school teachers—white and black; it is not likely that they led many ordinary blacks to accept them. Still, such an attitude did find some proponents among social scientists, particularly in sociology and anthropology, and among some teachers in departments of English literature. It watered the old plant of populism and gave it a new bent.[3]

X

The United States has been a populistic country practically since its origin. Alongside of a pseudo-Darwinian belief in the superiority of the "Anglo-Saxon races" and an anglophilic hankering after the com-

3. I think that "elitism" was first used by political scientists in the 1950s and early 1960s, perhaps first by Professor Peter Bacharach, to refer to the theories of Pareto and Mosca about the inevitability of elites in society, their vicissitudes and functions. It seems to have acquired its pejorative sense only later.

pany of "lords and gentlemen," there was also a resentful ambivalence about "Society" and an outright denial of the superiority of those in high positions of wealth, power, and deference. This was part of the roughhanded but selective egalitarianism of the Middle West. It asserted the greater virtue of the humble and laborious classes of society over those with more refined manners and pretences to superiority. It affirmed the superiority of the experience of everyday life over "book-learning." In the United States, populism was also committed to success in achievement and to the rewards of such success. Populists opposed inherited wealth and "social position"; they admired those who came from "humble" circumstances. The "reputation of success" was unblemished. Despite ambivalence, differences in accomplishment were acknowledged and the reality of accomplishment was not denied. This was even before the coinage in sociological and anthropological theory of the concepts of "achieved status" and "ascribed status," or of "achievement" and "ascription" as criteria of the assessment of virtue or merit. All this was connected with distrust of the motives of those who exercised authority. American social scientists inclined in this direction. The academic establishment of social science in the Middle West—transplanted from Johns Hopkins University—coincided with the swelling of populistic sentiment. Richard Ely and Edward Ross were among its most active spokesmen. There was a very strong current of populism in Veblen's thought. The interests of empirical sociologists, where they were not focused on the poor, on criminals, and on the immigrants were directed towards village life and the farming population. Rural sociology, stimulated by governmental support for the agricultural experiment stations, explored the life of the ordinary citizen in the countryside. The gentle Cooley was always concerned with the ordinary citizen, and the improvement of society was constituted by the attainment of more influence for the ordinary citizen and the diminution of the influence of the wealthy and powerful. His "Genius, Fame, and the Comparison of Races" stressed the creative powers of those who were not well-born. Some of these ideas were drawn from the early German work in "folk psychology," and the populistic mood of the Middle West reinforced them. Where populism did appear in academic circles, it was placed in the setting of a much more widely held attitude. There was distaste among American academics for the materialism of American life in the latter part of the nineteenth century, and not only among humanists of the genteel tradition. The latter and the populist tradition together left a residue of hostility towards businessmen throughout the 1920s. It was common among sociologists to believe that familial advantages, the advantages of birth, or of "marrying the boss's daughter" gave some wealthy businessmen a position in front of the starting line in the race for success. The collusion of corrupted politicians and corrupting businessmen was generally regarded as a feature of American urban life. Yet, not all successful businessmen were condemned by social scientists. Those who had experience of municipal reform movements often had loyal collaborators among businessmen; sociologists concerned with crime, delinquency, and broken families drew support from businessmen-philanthropists. Denunciation of railway and municipal traction magnates, of "malfactors of great wealth," did not mean that American social scientists were unqualifiedly hostile to the very wealthy and powerful. Nevertheless, the fulfillment of "the promise of American life"—an aspiration which in one way or another was very much on the minds of American social scientists before the First World War—did not entail either the establishment of a socialistic order of society or a thoroughgoing egalitarianism. Puritanical respectability, respect for achievement, and populism went hand in hand. They formed a fundamental moral attitude even though its components were not entirely consistent with each other.

It was moreover universally accepted within the academic profession that there was such a thing as "leadership" and that it was inevitable and even desirable that this should be so. It was not regarded in academic circles as contrary to nature or morality that "white Anglo-Saxon Protestants" should fill most of the leading posts in the executive, legislative, and judiciary of the federal government, that they should be the presidents of universities and the most prominent publicists, publishers, and businessmen.

Most academics until the Second World War were in fact "white Anglo-Saxon Protestants." There were practically no Negroes teaching in white universities and Jews had not yet acquired the prominence in the academic life of the country which they have since attained. Roman Catholics were sealed off into a separate sector of American society; there were very few in academic life.

Pronounced changes occurred during the depression and especially after the Second World War. Puritanism had been much weakened between the wars. The prestige of the wealthy had been damaged by the Great Depression of the 1930s. The offspring of the Eastern European Jewish immigrants who had come to the United States between 1885 and 1912 and who had married in the first decade of the century, reached intellectual adulthood in the 1930s. Had it not been for the depression, they would have made their talents manifest earlier. Many of that generation were lost in the civil service since academic opportunities were few. The next crop had better fortune. The years of the war saw them come to maturity, and the expansion of the scientific institutions and the universities after the war gave them new opportunities.

The entry of the intellectuals of Eastern European Jewish origin into the learned world was a unique event. They had a sense of affinity with Europe. Socialism seemed to them to be a "natural" thing. Many of them were repelled by capitalism. They came up in a scene on which there already existed a very visible leftist anti-Stalinist intellectual movement; the remnants of bohemian radicalism still survived. During the "cold war," their hostility against Stalinist communists and fellow travelers gave them an appearance of patriotism and of individualistic liberalism. The appearance was transient and most of these opponents of Stalinist communism slipped back into an attitude composed of an appreciation of literary and artistic modernism and a vague sympathy for socialism.

Their successors, who were by this time becoming more numerous in the universities, had not experienced the deceptions of the Stalinists as either victims or antagonists, and came into the radical inheritance with fewer codicils and qualifications. Populism, anti-capitalism, bohemian radicalism, and contempt for patriotism came more easily to the generation which came of age after 1956. It was then that I heard the epithet "Wasp" for the first time. The pain of injured self-esteem of years past seemed to be poured into the resentful utterance of the term. It then overflowed into the denunciation of all ascendency. Socialism and "anti-elitism" gained ascendancy in the younger and middle generation of academic social scientists.

There had not been a "ruling class" in the United States; there had been only a small number of families which continued in eminence over the generations. The size of the United States and its rapid growth meant that most positions of power, wealth, and fame were occupied at any one time by persons whose ancestors had not been of similar prominence. Nonetheless, until the 1930s most of them were white, of northern and western European ethnic stocks, of Protestant religious beliefs or at least origins. It was bound to be that way because that is what the majority of the population was until the great immigration which began in the 1880s. Most of the professional classes and the academics had been of such origin, and, however widely different in their sympathies, they did not regard it as a misfortune or a moral deficiency to be of such an origin. The academic social scientists, with all their readiness to regard the "trusts" as the causes of deficiency in social life, did not attribute any significance to the ethnic or religious origins of the malefactors. If anything, they thought that the Catholic immigrant from Ireland and eastern and southern Europe and the Jews—immigrants and the "poor"—were the problems which had to be solved. They thought these groups had to be "Americanized," that the process of assimilation had to occur, and that it was right that it should occur. All this changed, at least on the surface, from the second half of the 1950s onward. The culture and society of white

Anglo-Saxon Protestants came under general attack from literary intellectuals; there was little new in this but now they were joined by academics in the humanities and the social sciences. The "Wasps" themselves in the universities took the assault very compliantly. They too thought "elitism" was a bad thing.

At the same time, academic social scientists and generally the academically educated classes, were beginning to subscribe, at least in principle, to "cultural relativism." Cultural relativism was an inheritance from the Enlightenment: it was a way of deflating the pretensions of Christian theologians and naive moralists. It was part of the intellectual apparatus of the theory of progress, although it was also contradictory to it. Indeed the more progressive the person, the more insistent he was on his acceptance of the "relativity" of ethical and cultural judgments. In the Enlightenment and in the course of the nineteenth century, this relativity was thought to apply only in judgments which compared Western societies with oriental and pagan societies; it did not apply within Western societies. William Graham Sumner insisted that "the mores can make anything right," but he had no doubts about what the right order of things was as far as American society was concerned.

It was generally accepted, not only in practice, but in principle as well, that there were real and appreciable differences in achievement and that they should be rewarded differently. It was also thought that there was a standard which distinguishes superior merit and achievement from inferior merit and achievement. On the whole, American academic social reformers did not busy themselves with the expansion of educational opportunity; they were much impressed by the extent to which it was already being provided for in the American educational system. They approved of it; they approved of the goals. They accepted that one of its objectives was the formation of the "larger mind"; i.e., a more comprehensive moral and cultural consensus. At the same time they accepted that American society would be stratified.

XI

Academics in the United States generally believed that "life is real, life is earnest." Up until the end of the 1920s American social scientists knew little about Max Weber's ideas of the "Protestant ethic" and the proposition that the striving for success was connected with a particular body of religious beliefs. The Protestant beliefs were decreasingly accepted by social scientists in the major universities, but the idea of success as a reward for individual amibition or, in other words, the rightfulness of an eqivalence of achievement and reward was simply taken for granted.

The reward of exertion was thought to be earthly well-being, the prosperity of one's affairs in business and in domestic life. For the puritanical businessman portrayed by Max Weber, this prosperity was a sign of God's grace. For those who differed from this theological outlook, as was the case with most social scientists, success was a good in itself, a self-evident earthly object of striving. For those who were very successful, a sense of having done something useful and right, a luxurious domestic life, and the respect of one's contemporaries were the appropriate rewards; for their heirs it was a life of unearned leisure and ease. There was, however, some ambivalence about this. A life of unearned leisure devoted to the pursuit of pleasure—marginal though it was—was not esteemed. On the other side, there was no ambivalence at all among social scientists about material well-being.

Traditional European radicalism had attacked the "leisure classes." A standard object of radical caricature was the bloated plutocrat, gorging himself; champagne was a symbol of this immoral luxury. Veblen's *Theory of the Leisure Class* gave a sardonic academic expression to this attitude. Nonetheless this concern did not make much headway in academic circles because social scientists did not interest themselves in this class. The hope of confining the worst ravages of poverty and of the attainment of a respectable standard of living was present in many minds. Scientific technology was praised by many economists and a few sociologists as the instrument of a rising standard of living, particularly after the First World War. Severe academic moralists like Irving Babbitt at Harvard and his latter-day followers, the "New Humanists," denounced the materialistic outlook and the striving for worldly success which they thought were pervasive in American life, but this attitude did not have any proponents among social scientists. Those who frowned most on a life based on the productivity of modern industry, such as Ralph Adams Cram, were scarcely to be found among academic social scientists. The forerunners of the "Southern Agrarians" who in the 1930s called on the country to disavow its commitment to an industrial economy, were not yet in evidence in the southern universities. When the movement did gain a small following, it contained no social scientists; it was made up of academic humanists and literary men.

Natural scientists justified their research, at least to some extent, by the "material benefits" it would bring in the long run. Certainly the patrons of scientific research and the leaders of the scientific profession did so. In the social sciences in the 1920s there was no criticism of the life of material well-being. William Ogburn was beginning to make his name in sociology as the analyst and admirer of technological progress. At the same time, sociologists of the 1920s ceased to be as concerned as they had been from 1890 onward about "poverty."

Extreme poverty ceased to interest them partly because they were determined to become more scientific and partly because the problem ceased to appear so urgent to them.

In the years of the Great Depression it would have been preposterous to criticize the aspiration for a high standard of living when so many persons could not even have a livelihood such as they had enjoyed while they had been employed. The notion of "two cars in every garage" was mocked by publicists and academics in the 1930s, but that was because the prediction made by one who was charged with responsibility for the Depression was so far from realization rather than because it was a contemptible aspiration. Still, not very many returned to the older concern about poverty. After the Second World War, the prevailing attitude in the universities was much the same. American society almost ceased to be criticized for its materialism; the rise in the standard of living was regarded by most academics, even in the humanities, as a great accomplishment and a worthy objective of individual striving and public policy. Those who were concerned about inequality were concerned with inequality in the distribution of power, not with poverty.

A turn occurred at the end of the sixth decade with the appearance of Michael Harrington's writings on poverty. Alongside of the newly awakened consciousness of poverty, there emerged a new hostility in academic circles towards "the affluent society." American society was criticized by the younger social scientists because it was "affluent" and vulgar. This coincided with the criticism of "mass society." The affluent mass society was castigated for selfishness, materialism, indifference to the public good, triviality, and vulgarity. The critical attitude towards contemporary American society partook to some extent of the older radical criticism of the "leisure classes," with a strong injection of the dislike of mechanical technology of which John Ruskin and William Morris had been the main sources of inspiration. The criticism of the affluent society was a criticism of private business enterprise and of the incapacity of private business to provide the conditions of a good society; the criticism of the mass society was a criticism of the lower and middle classes for preoccupation with trivial material and spiritual satisfactions.

The idea was given its most eloquent and influential expression by Professor J. K. Galbraith. His book on *The Affluent Society* became one of the authoritative texts of the egalitarian radicalism of the 1960s. It was not at all taken up by economists; economics, after all, was still in effect the "science of wealth," as some of its earlier practitioners had long ago defined it. Nor did any of the already well-established sociologists, political scientists, or anthropologists espouse Professor Galbraith's ideas. Nonetheless, by the latter part of the 1960s, it was taken for granted by the new generation of the radical social scientists that one of the vices of modern American society was its concern for increased consumption. Their argument that the desire for consumer goods was a result of advertising and was impelled by the industrialists' desire to increase the market for their otherwise unvendible and unnecessary products was neither very original nor very convincing. The belief in the effectiveness of advertising had been expressed by academic psychologists since the 1920s; it had been taken up again with the reinforcement of sociologists who were engaged in market research. It had already appeared in the "theory of the mass society." The second half of the interpretation of the "affluent society" had a major affinity with Marxism, which was beginning to be stylish among teachers and graduate students in sociology. At some points, it was confluent with the aesthetic bohemian contempt for the bourgeois mode of life which had become increasingly assimilated into the outlook of many academics in the 1960s. Its view that all could be put right by the activity of government was an extension of the older ideas of the institutional economists of the early decades of American academic social science. In all this the concern for the "poor" was minimal. It took several extra-academic events to arouse again the interest of academic social scientists in poverty. Michael Harrington's book was of great significance; Lyndon Johnson's "war on poverty," which sociologists helped to design, the riots in Negro districts of the larger cities, and the generalization of the objects of student agitation in the second half of the 1960s brought the "poor" back to the consciousness of academic social scientists.

XII

In the 1930s, one occasionally heard young academics, more or less informed about European intellectual affairs and more or less turning towards radicalism, express regret that the United States did not have any connoisseurs and friends of Marxism in the universities such as there were in Europe. They were more or less right. The United States had nothing to show in its universities in comparison with the learning of Carl Grünberg, Werner Sombart, Gustav Mayer, Charles Andler, Arthur Rosenberg, Rodolfo Mondolfo, G. D. H. Cole, and Maurice Dobb, who were masters of the intricacies of Marxist theories and of the history of socialism. Between the wars, there were some published dissertations on Marxism in the United States, e.g., by Morton Bober and Sherman Shang at Harvard and Pennsylvania respectively. Before the First World War there was a book on *The Economic Interpretation of History* by E. R. A. Seligman of Columbia University; it was published in 1902. At Columbia too, Louis Levine—later Lorwin—wrote a dissertation on French syndicalism. Paul Brissendon wrote on the Industrial Workers of the World, also at

Columbia. All these taken together did not provide much of a tradition of American Marxism for a young American academic in the 1930s seeking some intellectual forebears in his own environment. Until the 1930s, most of the small number of Americans who wrote about Marxism or from a Marxian standpoint, such as Louis Boudin, Ernest Untermann, Harry Laidler, A. M. Simons, and Moissaye Olgin, were not academics.

In the 1930s, some outstanding scholars and scientists showed themselves amenable to the charms of the "popular front" but there were no Marxian scholars among them. In the city colleges of New York, there were a few young men such as Samuel Bernstein who knew a lot about the history of socialism in the nineteenth century. There were a few younger scholars like Moses Finkelstein and Charles Trinkaus whose research on ancient Greece and Renaissance Italy was influenced by Marxian ideas. Paul Sweezy had not yet become the erudite Marxist economist whose work on *The Theory of Capitalist Development* appeared during the war. At Wisconsin, Professor Albin Winspear was said to be a Marxist in his approach to the study of Greek culture. The one scholar who had made a thorough study of Marxism and its intellectual antecedents was Professor Sidney Hook, whose learning gave little pleasure to the growing body of fellow-traveling academics because he was so critical of communism. *Science and Society,* a Marxian quarterly, had relatively few American academics among its contributors. Such acceptance as there was of Marxian ideas in the American academic profession occurred more in the humanities and the natural sciences than it did among social scientists.

The situation did not change much after the Second World War. Paul Sweezy, his appointment not renewed at Harvard, departed from academic life and became editor of a communist periodical, *The Monthly Review.* Some of the pre-war Marxists had ceased to be Marxists but their earlier experience raised the level of scholarly knowledge of Marxism; this knowledge was not, however, accompanied by conviction of the correctness of the theories studied. So the situation remained until the last years of the 1960s.

The Students for a Democractic Society and the *New University Review,* which was published originally by some graduate students at the University of Chicago, were singularly free of the ornamentation of Marxist doctrine. "Participatory democracy," which had no place in traditional Marxist doctrine, was their chief contribution to contemporary radical belief in the academic world. *Studies on the Left,* published from the University of Wisconsin, was more clearly determined to promote the scholarly study and exposition of Marxism. Both of these journals were forerunners of radicalism within the universities.

The student agitation against the universities, against the war in Indochina, against conscription, against the president of the United States, against the "system," left behind it not only the stains of bad conscience, rancor, and a self-justifying radicalism of the disappointed older patrons of the "student revolution." It left behind a sediment of novel academic radicalism as well, which has continued to accumulate. Within each of the social sciences in the American academic left, there is now an articulate and organized block of Marxists.

For the most part, the publications of academic radicalism consist mainly of denunciations of non-Marxist colleagues and their work and of programmatic declarations of intention. The Conference of Socialist Scholars, the Group for a New Political Science, and the newer type of "reflexive" or "critical" sociologists have as yet no serious scholarly work to which they can give their auspices; "unmasking" of what others do has been their main activity. "Radical philosophy" seems on the whole not to be "dialectical materialism" but a politically polemical criticism of the works of philosophers who are not radicals. In the humanistic disciplines, too, programmatic declarations and denunications of hitherto prevailing practice seem to dominate. The achievement in historical studies seems more substantial although not very original. In the sciences, there is naturally nothing distinctive in substance but again much denunciation of the "scientific establishment" and of "elitist science" and praise of "people's science" and of "critical science"; there are occasional shyly flirtatious glances towards astrology and alchemy. This has all been accompanied by much more study of the writings of "the young Marx" and the "humanistic Marx." "Marx-philology" has not yet taken root, although acquaintance with Marxian works is now far more widespread than it has ever been in the American academic world.

Whatever the consequences for science and scholarship, radicalism is now firmly implanted in the younger academic generation. It is populistic, egalitarian, antinomian, emancipationist, and utopian in its hopes for a socialism which would be planned, egalitarian, and participatorily democratic. The Soviet Union is no longer the exclusive or even primary bearer of its hopes—although no criticism of it except by radicals is tolerated and the foreign policies of the Soviet Union are generally supported, particularly towards the United States; China, Cuba, Yugoslavia, Vietnam, Tanzania, Angola, and the Chile of Allende have variously been the favorites. It is sympathetic with the "urban guerilla" and with *jacqueries* in the countryside. "Multinational corporations" and "neo-colonialism" are roundly scored; the "third world" is a special object of its solicitude. It desires a total transformation of the order of society obtaining in the West. It is not against the omniprovident state but it has no respect for its present form. It is against any restraints or inhibitions on individual conduct, especially in the erotic sphere. Marx, Engels, and Lenin have had to make room for Frantz Fanon, Régis Debray, Louis Althusser, Lucio Coletti, Antonio Gramsci, Ché Guevara, and Jürgen Habermas. Its intellectual standard-bearers were not confined to those who call themselves Marxists. They go beyond this to Wilhelm Reich, Jacques Lacan, and Michel Foucault, to a freely interpreted Freud, and beyond that to William Blake. Herbert Marcuse, Norman Brown, and Theodore Roszak have been among the most attractive and attended to of the academics who speak in behalf of the radical breaking of traditional patterns of conduct and imagination. Since they have no name and no orthodoxy like the Stalinist Marxists had, they are free to pick and choose and to emphasize what they wish from the constellation of beliefs which form the repertory of egalitarian, "anti-elitist" emancipationist radicalism. The older concerns of the reformers who helped to create the welfare state are no more to them than the "merely formal freedoms" of association, assembly, representation, and the expression of political and religious opinions were to their Marxist-Leninist ancestors. The arrangements of the welfare state are honored only when they are infringed on and these shortcomings are utilized primarily as a stick with which to beat their adversaries, as a means of aggravating and propagating grievances and of spreading their own beliefs.

The various beliefs of present-day quasi-Marxist academic social sciences have not yet coalesced into an articulated doctrine. The idea of participatory democracy has still not found its theorist. Egalitarianism of the newer sort has only recently acquired a rigorously systematic exposition in Professor John Rawls' *The Theory of Justice*. "Anti-elitism" is still without its theoretical promulgation. Emancipationist beliefs drawing on Schiller, Marx, and Freud have been formulated by Herbert Marcuse, professor first at Brandeis University and then at the University of California, and by Norman Brown of Wesleyan University. Whatever the shortcomings of their theoretical formulation, the various elements of the resurgent radicalism have in their own way become as coherent as the more dogmatic Marxist orthodoxy. But whatever its state of promulgation, this amalgam of bohemianism, traditional socialistic radicalism, and Stalinist communism, with incidental seasonings such as Maoism, Trotskyism, environmentalism, primitivism, psychotherapy, guild socialism, anarchism, and hostility towards science in various combination now has considerable following in American universities. Like the editors of and contributors to the "little magazines" who were originally very antagonistic towards the "genteel tradition" which was transmitted in the universities, intellectual radicalism has now found its chief locus within the universities.

This is all a far cry from the situations of fifty and seventy-five years ago. Seventy-five years ago the critics of the existing order of society within the universities were as "respectable" as those they criticized. The postulates of their criticism were the widely accepted Christian injunction of charity and the Christian strictures on greed. Fifty years ago, these criticisms had become assimilated into the range of acceptable academic beliefs; the radical critics—mainly communist sympathizers—were more surreptitious in their proceedings. At present the most recent type of radical criticism works in a far more propitious and prosperous setting. Radical critics are far more numerous; they are not apprehensive of sanctions; they have more organs of communication at their disposal; and they make no appeal to an illustrious tradition of academic learning in their support. Fifty years ago the center of radical criticism of existing society was outside the universities; now it is within them.

The recent academic exponents of radicalism have been successful in imposing their views and proceedings on some of their older colleagues. This has happened osmotically among those numerous academics who hold fast to the collectivistic liberalism of the type prevalent before the newer type of radicalism appeared. The infiltration of the radical outlook was concurrent with the student agitation against the second administration of Lyndon Johnson and the entire presidency of Richard Nixon; to some extent it occurred simply from weakness of character and inability to make pertinent distinctions. The inchoate but turbulent student radicalism has affected beliefs about the tasks of universities, the standards of academic assessment, and the substance and pattern of courses of study.

The new radicalism enjoys the legitimacy of appointments on the teaching staffs of universities and colleges—public as well as private. Sometimes on grounds of "methodological pluralism," sometimes on grounds of an unthinking interpretation of "academic freedom," radicals have been appointed, reappointed, and promoted to permanent tenure. They are not organized in "cells" as the few academic members of the Communist party used to be before the Second World War. Instead they form "caucuses," "blocs," "platforms," "galleries," and other informal groups. They have become a legitimate presence, small but deferred to and taken in account, and expanding themselves by concerted action. They are a loosely knit fraternity, quick to come to each other's aid, helpful in promoting the appointment of their political and moral affines. Criticism of their political activities within the universities is denounced as infringement of academic freedom.

They have established themselves in sociology and political science departments, in English and modern languages, and in history departments and in schools of divinity. They are to be found in philosophy, mathematics, theoretical physics, and evolutionary biology. They are to be found in great universities and in small colleges, especially but not only those which have prided themselves on their liberalism. They are to be found in Protestant and Roman Catholic colleges, many of which have been eager or at least compliant in divesting themselves of their own traditions.

It would be too much to say that they have exercised an influence on governmental policy and public opinion comparable in scope and penetration to the influence on governmental policy and public opinion comparable in scope and penetration to the influence exercised by the collectivistic liberal reformers who began to assemble their forces in the last decades of the preceding century. They have not been at it long enough. But in comparison with their forerunners who contributed so much to the intellectual precipitation of the omnicompetent, omniprovident state, they have certain advantages. For one thing, student bodies are very much larger and a larger proportion study the social sciences in which the new academic radicals are so active. For another, journalism and the electronic media of communication provide employment for university graduates to a greater extent than did the daily newspaper press fifty years ago. As a result the ideas which are current in social science can now move more readily into public opinion than was the case in earlier times. The ideas of the social sciences also move more easily into politics, now that more legislators are university graduates, and the same is true of the civil service. Indeed the "activism," i.e., radicalism, which has in the past decade become part of the experience of many younger social scientists as well as one of their prerogatives has now become a property of the federal bureaucracy too. The relationship appears to be more than parallelism.

The tradition of collectivistic liberalism which eight decades ago was largely an academic possession has taken root and flowered. In the course of the changes in its environment and the grafting onto it of certain strains of Marxian and bohemian emancipationist belief, it has evolved into something quite different from what it once was.

XIII

Before the Great Depression of 1929, there were four realms in American culture: the serious academic culture, the traditional literary culture, the advanced or "modernist" literary and artistic culture, and frivolous culture. They did not mix with each other, they had little contact. The serious academic and the traditional literary cultures did not concern themselves at all with the frivolous culture and they did not approve of the advanced literary culture. The world of vaudeville, circus and carnival, sporting and athletic events, pornography, "low life," and slang was a world apart from serious culture and particularly from academic culture. Even those academics whose professional tasks or reforming interests brought them into contact with sections of society in which frivolous culture was common did not take note of it, and they certainly did not become assimilated into it. There was also a clear separation of academic society from bohemian society; the separation was marked largely by differences in sexual morals and family life but there were other objects too which separated them. Respectability and bohemianism differed in their attitudes towards work and saving, towards tradition and authority; respectability was puritanical, bohemianism was hedonistic. Bohemianism preferred present pleasures and emphasized the gratification of the senses. It was disrespectful of authority and of practices and beliefs which were associated with pastness. Bohemia was not regarded as having any place in universities or colleges. In the larger and urban universities, a certain amount might be tolerated among students but it was frowned upon by senior members. Literarily inclined undergraduates at Harvard in the years before the First World War were attracted by the bohemian style of life. John Reed and John Dos Passos made gestures in that direction but this did not affect their teachers, who did not join in that type of life. There was a literary bohemia at the edge of the district in which the University of Chicago was located but there were practically no connections between it and the teachers of the university. Veblen's difficulties in his various universities were connected with his bohemian mode of life. Harry Thurston Peck, professor of classics at Columbia, had to leave his post because of a "scandal." One of the leading American sociologists, William Thomas, was summarily dismissed from his post at the University of Chicago in 1919 after it was reported in a newspaper that he had had sexual intercourse with a woman who was not his wife. Alexander Goldenweiser and Paul Radin were alleged to have suffered in their academic careers because of infringements on the prevailing standards of sexual propriety. Radicalism and bohemianism were coupled with each other in the press—they were both supposed to practice "free love"; the same belief appeared occasionally in universities and colleges and endangered the careers of the few known radicals.

From their own side, the bohemian literary and artistic circles shunned the universities, which they regarded as insufferably philistine in their tastes and reactionary in their political and social attitudes. Before the First World War, it was still common for novelists not to have been at university; F. Scott Fitzgerald and John Dos Passos were the first important American novelists of the century who had been to university. Journalism was more often the path of the novelist, particularly if he worked in the naturalistic mode. There were several minor novelists who were also university teachers but they were rare—a situation very different from the present one in which the most esteemed novelist of the country is a professor at a university and numerous colleges and universities have "writers-in-residence," "poets-in-residence," "artists-in-residence," etc.

The battle against the "genteel tradition," which was not wholly but still very largely the intellectual tradition of the humanistic departments of the universities and colleges, and very dominant in the pattern of conduct of most of their senior members, was joined with vigor by H. L. Mencken. He made the "school-marms," the "*Gelehrte,*" into his enemies and did so by covering them with obloquy. He included among his targets Thorstein Veblen, who was himself an enemy of the genteel tradition and an opponent of much that Mencken also opposed.

The "modernist" movement in literature which traced its origins to Baudelaire and at a later stage to Rimbaud and Verlaine in poetry, and to Flaubert, de Maupassant, and Zola in prose and which in the twentieth century was formed around the writings of Yeats, Joyce, Eliot, Pound, etc., followed a very different path from the spirit which still prevailed in the 1920s in American universities. The new literature was pessimistic about the prospects of the human race, it was hostile to the hedonism and the scientific secularism of the academic profession, it was not humanitarian, it cared very little for improving the material conditions of life, it was not sympathetic with democracy and had no interest in the improvement of the machinery of government. Except for Eliot and Yeats it had no sympathy with religious belief, and even in Yeats that sympathy was eccentric.

Eliot apart, the chief figures of the new tendency in literature and in art had in the main no feeling of affinity with the sense of propriety, the conviction of philanthropic obligation, the respect for traditional high culture, or the certainty that there was order in the universe which moved toward the good of the human race, either through divine redemption or scientistic progress. Puritanism, which was the epitome of these qualities, had already been assaulted for some years in the United States. The First World War and its aftermath made the academic profession aware that a new spirit was on the loose and that it was moreover a spirit which bore no reverence for the values cultivated in the universities.

After the end of the First World War, the universities stood fast for more than a decade against this great antinomian aestheticism. The natural scientists were having a very good run. The patronage of the Rockefeller Foundation and the optimism of great American business enterprisers together helped the scientists to respond to the new stimuli in many fields of physical and biological sciences. The exhilarating and absorbing tasks which they set themselves, the availability of an increasing number of exigent and productive colleagues in their

342 Sociology and Society

own universities, in the country at large, and in the recovered German, British, French, Italian, Dutch, Belgian, and Scandinavian universities left little time for attention to the doings of "unscientific" *littérateurs*. The social scientists also had little interest in these literary and artistic developments; they were too busy improving the social sciences so as to make them more useful to society and acting in various civic and consultative capacities to bother themselves with such unserious matters. The academics of the 1920s had become specialists who were proud of specialization. Specialization seemed to have no drawbacks. Breadth was dilettantism, specialization was a precondition of scientific—and hence of social—progress. The departments of English and modern languages were the first to feel the pressure of "modernism" and to respond to it. The most powerful and fundamental resistance came from Irving Babbitt, Paul Elmer More, Norman Foerster, and the other "new humanists." They went to the roots of the new current by attacking "romanticism"; it is interesting that the humanist declarations called out no response from natural or social scientists in the universities although they were just as much under criticism as literary and artistic romanticism. The custodians of the new spirit did reply.

In any case, most of the departments of English and modern languages continued on their way, yielding gradually by new appointments, by head-shaking, and by wearily accepting the "necessity" of being "up-to-date." The triumph of the adversary was made easier by the depression.

Puritanism, already put on the defensive after the First World War, was severely shaken by the depression. Hard work and saving lost their compellingness through unemployment, the failures of the banks, and the foreclosures of mortgages. The delay of marriage by ambitious young men until the time when they could support a family was also rendered questionable. Ambition itself was discredited because it seemed so unavailing. The decline of puritanism was part of the diminution in the legitimacy of a pattern of moral life and of the political, economic, and social orders.

The displacement towards political radicalism among academic social scientists was blocked by their incorporation into the institutions of the New Deal. At lower levels, their graduate students had a parallel experience. The humanistic faculties did not have similar opportunities and benefits. The depression was harder on them; they did not moreover have the tradition of reforming activity which kept the social scientists on course.

Despite this, most academics held firmly to what they had believed previously. There were some of them who were drawn towards radicalism; the new view seemed only to be an extension of the earlier belief in the necessity of philanthropy and civic reform. The New Deal appeared to be little other than the application in a more through-going form and on a national scale of the older ideals promulgated in institutional economics and the social gospel. Those who accepted the radicalism of the 1930s saw that too as a more thoroughgoing, more "root and branch" fulfillment of the older aspirations. It was however something different and more than what they thought it was. It was an opening into a quite different tradition which had led a separate life for more than a century.

The tradition of romanticism in literature and in art had always given a large place to dissatisfaction with existing institutions and their authorities. Shelley and Byron, the young Wordsworth and Cole-ridge and Heine made available an ancestry which could be proudly claimed. Since before 1848, literary intellectuals in France had criticized the bourgeois regime, sometimes from an aristocratic standpoint, sometimes from a socialistic one. Beyle felt that life, after the inspiring times of Napoleon, was simply boring. Baudelaire, who had been on the side of the revolutionaries in 1848, soon gave up his revolutionary zeal but not for attachment to French society. Victor Hugo was at odds with the Second Empire. Zola had to his honor conducted a courageous campaign against the government of the Third Republic, and a large number of literary intellectuals and humanistic academics had joined him.

The whole trend of the modern literary movement was in one way or another against the existing political, economic, and social orders. The great literary heroes of the modern movement in literature had all in one way or another denied the moral legitimacy of those orders. Ibsen left Norway for many years because he felt that he would be stifled there. Turgenev had portrayed revolutionaries with the warm-est sympathy. Tolstoy in the later decades of his long life was re-garded as a dangerous radical by the Tsarist regime. Chekhov had, in a gentle way, shown the moral weakness of the old order of society. Gorki, who began life was an outcast and who became a socialist and a Bolshevik, was known as a friend and regarded as the heir of the great Russian writers of the Tsarist regime. Oscar Wilde presented himself as a socialist. George Bernard Shaw was indeed a Fabian socialist and he remained a socialist after he had ceased to be a Fabian. H. G. Wells was many things but he had been a Fabian socialist. Anatole France, now almost forgotten, was a Dreyfusard and a socialist. Gerhart Hauptmann had taken the side of the rebel workers in the textile industry in one of his early plays. Convention, authority, and wealth were all under the unceasing fire of nineteenth-century literature.

The literary scene was extremely variegated in the first third of the twentieth century, but nearly all the great writers were in one way or another dissatisfied with their own societies, and with European and American civilization. American literary men shared in this culture of dissatisfaction. Henry James found America wanting and took refuge in England. The two best young poets, Eliot and Pound, did the same. Mark Twain was interpreted to have been profoundly at odds with American society.

When the Great Depression came on with its evidence of the insufficiencies of contemporary economic and governmental institutions and the failures of business and political leaders to restore employment, many of the literary men of already established distinction, such as Theodore Dreiser, Sinclair Lewis, Ernest Hemingway, and Sherwood Anderson, found an economic and political focus for their moral and cultural dissatisfactions. Among the younger writers, politics began to be taken very seriously, while the Communist party, with all its distrust of intellectuals, made increasing efforts, through a variety of ostensibly independent organizations, to attract writers, artists, scholars, and scientists and to claim the merits implied by their support of the party and the Soviet Union. The party was successful but not completely so. There were many backsliders among their converts and the fissile tendencies in all radical movements, both religious and secular, came into play in the middle of the 1930s. One of the most important conversions and diversions was the transformation of the *Partisan Review* from a Stalinist domain into a Trotskyist one with very indeterminate boundaries. One major consequence of this transformation was the release of literary judgment from the narrow-minded application of criteria of political orthodoxy. *The Partisan Review* soon came to the forefront as the patron of the modern movement in literature in fusion with general radicalism inspired by Marxism. It became the favored periodical of the younger generation of academic students of literature.

The American yearning for the European cultural center, fed and guided many years earlier by William Dean Howells and William Lyon Phelps, Hjalmar Boyessen, and the young publishers Stone and Kimball, and later Alfred Knopf, Albert and Charles Boni, Horace Liveright and the Modern Library, now had in the *Partisan Review* a journal of its own to gratify it. "Modern literature," freed finally from Victorian constraints, now was at home in the United States under radical political auspices. The "new spirit" had been knocking at the American door for nearly a half-century. It had from the beginning been proposed and recommended as a departure from American naiveté, provincialism, puritanism, materialism, and optimism.

A small number of American writers had become politically radical after the Russian Revolution of 1917 but they were not among the more eminent—John Dos Passos was perhaps the one marginal exception. The radical sympathies of Greenwich Village and the much smaller bohemias of Chicago and San Francisco had no echo outside themselves. They were conducting a "holding operation." The establishment of the *Partisan Review* in its Trotskyist phase was an opening into a wider world. A few eminent university teachers like Meyer Schapiro, Sidney Hook, Lionel Trilling, and Jacques Barzun soon began to write for it. It had been a practice of long standing for well-known university teachers to write for the liberal weeklies like *The New Republic* and *The Nation;* avant-garde literary magazines were a different thing. They had hitherto kept themselves aloof from the universities, and academics had returned the compliment. In the 1930s, when the world appeared to be turned upside down, academic humanists moved from an apolitical indifference and moral discomfort towards a more far-reaching, more assertive distaste for the political and economic order of the country. They did not move towards the actively improving attitude of the institutional economists and their heirs. They passed beyond it to a radically critical attitude towards American society and culture. The *Partisan Review* provided the organ through which this attitude could be expressed and received.

The barrier which had separated bohemian culture from the universities began to go down. The enfeeblement of the domain of puritanism opened the way to a more reactive aesthetic sensibility in sections of the population which had previously been insensate or hostile towards nonrepresentational art. Hitherto, when the philistines had any sympathy at all with works of art, it was only those works which were formed in traditional modes which appealed to them. Already before the war, the authoritative center of society began to show, in fragmentary fashion, a quite novel sympathy with artists and writers who departed from the conventions of the "old masters" and from Victorian artistic representation. Schemes were set in motion to provide employment for writers and artists; unconventional artists and writers were among the beneficiaries of these schemes. Public buildings began to be decorated with murals by painters of "advanced" views and styles. The Writers' Project of the Works Progress Administration was a remarkable step for the federal government; in the past it had been rather disapproving of the artists and their works who went beyond the most traditional styles. Although the universities were very impecunious in the 1930s, they too began to grant official recognition to the new styles of literary and artistic production.

The opening of the mind in larger sections of the society to the experience of expressive works and to the superiority of expression over representation also made for a greater readiness to appreciate the bohemian radical overtones which had for a long time been associated with avant-garde artistic production. The conception of the artist as a genius hampered in the free expression of his genius by institutions devoted to the routine affairs of society and spurned by an insensitive public opinion has had a long life. This belief always had political implications which began to be more emphatically drawn in the 1930s. To be avant-garde in art, i.e., to be "expressive," meant being avant-garde in politics. The artistic beliefs of the avant-garde were part of a more comprehensive outlook which regarded the untrammeled expression of freely moving sentiment as the ultimate criterion of what is right and good. The boundaries between "advanced art" which was consecrated to "expression" and bourgeois society were overrun. This came to be especially the case in the humanistic faculties of the universities, where "modernism" supplanted the genteel contemplation of the great works of the past and the philological scholarship with which it had shared the platform.

The universities now exist in a culture which has accepted the rightfulness of spontaneous expression and which does not defer to tradition. The narrowly specialized education which had been given to the generation of academics trained just after the Second World War left them intellectually disarmed before the culture of expressiveness when it appeared in their midst. All they had with which to resist it was their conventional upbringing—already weakened by depression and war—and their own passionate devotion to their scholarly subjects. These defenses sustained those who had the benefit of them. But many did not have such benefits. Many of these went over to the other side. They were full of talk about the exhaustion of the older humanistic tradition and of the supremacy of "modernism." The rush to the universities in the years after the war made for a receptive state of mind; many of those who rushed in unthinkingly discovered that academic learning was not to their taste, but by the 1960s they had gone too far to withdraw. They had invested too many years and they could moreover not think of anything better to do. Nonetheless they did not like the traditional subject-matter of their humanistic disciplines—this appeared also in other parts of the universities as well. Many members of this generation, who had been brought up in a period in which expressiveness was beginning to be regarded more widely as a virtue and in which the restraints imposed by traditions and institutional authorities were irksome, found themselves in academic careers which imposed tiresome demands and constraints on them. The burden of learning was an uncomfortable one. All this distress over a wrongly chosen career coincided with the partial abdication and failure of authority in national life of the 1960s. This was the breach in the wall through which bohemian radicalism poured into the study of modern literature and languages and philosophy.

The great artists of the Renaissance had sought to improve their status by denying that they were craftsmen like shoemakers and blacksmiths and asserting instead that they were scientists who applied such sciences as geometry and anatomy. This was the beginning of the academies of art; they were intended to replace the guilds which municipal ordinances had sometimes forced the artists to join. The conception of artistic creation as a science did not survive long in competition with the alternative idea that artists were geniuses and that the laws of genius are incompatible with the laws of society. This idea drove deep roots into very fertile soil. As a result there was maintained a wall between universities and the production of art. This wall has now been cast down. The idea of the artistic genius at war with traditions and institutions carried through the eighteenth and nineteenth centuries by generations of bohemian artists—free souls—has now passed over into the territory on the other side of the wall. At the time when this invasion was occurring, the modernist outlook in art and literature also extended itself more openly into the political sphere. The revolt against the constraints of representational art and grammatical construction was manifested in a cognate denial of the legitimacy of the conventional rules of society and of the authorities who spoke for them and tried to carry them out.

At this point the radicalized heirs of the reforming critics of modern Western industrial societies came abreast, in the same line of march, with the exponents of literary and artistic modernisms. Bohemia and the social gospel were now in the same party; modernism and institutional economics were now comrades-in-arms.

XIV

From the very beginnings of the American university in its modern form after the Civil War, the belief in the idea of progress was very prominent in providing the justification both for the claim of the university to be supported and for the granting of that support by public and private patrons. The natural sciences were of course foremost in this. They were the standard-bearers in the replacement of false by true beliefs, the replacement of what was superstitious in religious beliefs by scientifically demonstrated, realistic knowledge. The sciences represented and impelled the progress being made by the human race.

The contribution of scientific research to material well-being was no less praised. In the course of the next four or five decades, scientists themselves lost the idiom of the somewhat secularized evolutionary Christianity which saw history as the "education of man by God," and replaced it by the proud argument that the path of evolution was laid out by the course of scientific discovery as the engine of progress in health and in material well-being through the improvement of technology. Many scientists had looked with contempt upon their colleagues in the social sciences who were interested in the reforming of society; these scientists thought the social reforms sought were either trivial and superficial or ineffectual, and they believed that they were making possible a more genuine, deeper, and long-lasting improvement in the lot of their fellow countrymen and of humanity in general.

The social scientists, both those interested in immediate social reforms and those who were less active, believed that as their subjects became more scientific they too would come abreast of their colleagues in the natural sciences in their capacity to improve in a fundamental way the condition of the human race at large, and, more particularly, of their own fellow countrymen. This was the argument used to solicit support for the social sciences after the First World War, when the first large financial grants began to be made for social science by the private philanthropic foundations.

The practitioners of the humanistic disciplines also believed in progress towards the ideal, even though they were dismayed by American "materialism." Many of them were patriotic in their belief that the original ideals of the American republic had been temporarily relegated to ineffectiveness and that the forward cause would be resumed once more.

In the United States, the first breaking of the front of progress was not primarily the work of academics. Some of the early skeptics were, it is true, university graduates or teachers. The brothers Adams, Charles Eliot Norton, and Irving Babbitt were among the most severe critics of the idea of progress. George Santayana was perhaps the most famous professor at a famous university who did not share the hitherto prevailing view (he was not an American by origin and he resigned his post at Harvard around the end of the first decade of the century in order to return to Europe). The "revolt" against optimistic humanitarianism and the powers of science to understand, explain, and master the problems faced by human beings was not however an academic revolt.

Literary men and publicists outside the universities denounced the narrowness of vision of the belief in progress and of the quasi-Christian optimism which looked on science as the instrument of earthly redemption. Optimism became the mark of a fool; this was the main theme of H. L. Mencken and of many others who did not share his hedonism. Optimism and materialism were regarded as the twin vices of the American bourgeoisie. This was a common view in literary circles. Within the universities these views had few adherents. Even those academics who were skeptical of the prevailing American optimism were nonetheless believers in progress. William Graham Sumner, although skeptical of progress through scientific research and philanthropic provision, was a believer in progress through conflict. In the social sciences, with all their conviction of the need to reform contemporary American society, there was still optimism about the outcome in the long run. Indeed, commitment to social science was in part derived from belief that an improved social science would be an instrument of the progress of society. The beneficent contribution of the natural sciences was generally accepted. Thorstein Veblen, who was the most radical academic critic of American society, was nonetheless a believer in progress through scientific discovery and also through the diffusion of scientific ways of thought in society. William Ogburn, who was not so cynical about the present, was confident that the advancement of scientific research and technological invention guaranteed the superiority of the future to the past.

When the slight turn towards communist and "fellow-traveling" radicalism occurred in the 1930s and 1940s, the progressivist faith in scientific discovery as the instrument of the forward movement was unabated. The "left" shared the postulate of progress through science. The failure of capitalistic society could be seen, according to some of the academic fellow-travelers, in its "frustration of science." According to the intellectuals of the "left" a planned socialistic society would be scientific in its procedures and in its use of scientific knowledge; capitalistic society, obsessed with profitability, prevented the use of inventions which would lower the price of material goods or make them fit for longer use. The merit of Marxian socialism was said by its zealots to consist in its being an application in practice of a scientific theory. In this respect, there was little difference between Marxism and collectivistic liberalism; they both drew on the same traditions of the Enlightenment and beyond that on the Christian tradition of the idea of redemption which formed the foundation of the idea of progress.

There had been criticism of science in the humanistic part of the universities but by the end of the Second World War, most of the humanists had given up the struggle. The entry into the academic world of the beliefs of bohemian radicalism opened the way for the entry of an anti-scientistic outlook, inimical to science as a body of knowledge, as a mode of thought, and as a calling. The turn against science in the universities in the 1960s was alien to the dominant traditions of progressivism in the universities. Whereas in the past academic progressivistic liberalism had been faithfully devoted to science, a break in the front now occurred. It did not come directly from the progressivistic tradition. It came from the radical extension of progressivism in alliance with bohemian radicalism. From the former it drew the criticism that science is contaminated by its association with government and business and the view that existing scientific knowledge is an imposition by authority without an objectively justified foundation; from the latter it drew the criticism of the oppressively dehumanized environment by scientific technology. From both it drew the criticism of science as the work and possession of an elite and hence as something to be repudiated. Professors Theodore Roszak's and Barry Commner's specific strictures on science do not have many proponents. Nonetheless, their mood has been widely appreciated and shared. The use of napalm in the war in Indochina, the pollution of air and water, the damage to "ecological balance" through the use of insecticides and through industrial wastes, the potential dangers in the use of nuclear energy through accidents, the difficulties of disposing of radioactive waste, and the possibility of illicit diversion of plutonium from industrial reactors have set loose many tremors of apprehension; they have put scientists on the defensive. So have dangers which lie in research into "recombinant DNA." Some, although not all, of these problems are attributable to academic science, but they are nonetheless fused into a single blanket accusation against science, scientists, the scientific establishment, and the universities which are the loci of fundamental research.

The new critics of science are mainly in the universities. For the most part, they are younger scientists. Very few of these scientist-critics of science are as opposed to science as Professor Roszak and his adherents. They oppose the institutional authority which is the setting of science; they are opposed to methods of selecting proposals to be supported by the National Science Foundation and other patrons of science; they oppose the application of science; they oppose the honors given to eminent scientists; they criticize the system of assessment of scientific papers submitted for publication; they oppose the collaboration of scientists with government; they oppose the dependence of scientists on government; they allege that scientific knowledge is an "elitist" convention and has no objective grounds; and they say that science is dominated by white males and gives no opportunities to "minorities" and women. They are extremely critical of the organization of scientific advice to government which they say is no more than mutual arrangement for support among politicians, the federal bureaucracy, and the "scientific establishment." In its place they variously propose "adversarial science," "advocacy science," or "critical science." But all the same, they were very much opposed to the failure of the federal government for some time to have a chief scientific advisor and they are opposed to any diminution in the financial support provided by government for scientific research.

These criticisms of science are nearly always associated with other parts of the program of radicalism. They are extensions of certain of the traditions of collectivistic liberalism, which by extension has turned upon itself. The distrust of authority has now come home to science itself. The freedom of the individual from the impositions of conventions, traditions, and institutions has been extended so as to become the emancipation of impulses from inhibition.

Whereas the substance of the social sciences and the humanistic subjects has begun to show the results of the movement towards radicalism, the sciences have been immune. Even though some academic scientists espouse these hostile attitudes towards science, the work of science goes on without being affected substantively. This is, of course, compatible with an influence of such a radical outlook on public opinion, on legislation, and on the governmental support of science. The "environmentalist" movement has certainly influenced governmental action, and much of the leadership of this movement has come from academic scientists. The greater stringency of the governmental efforts to control the pollution by industries of water and air, the greater governmental concern for "occupational safety and health," the staying of the construction of plants for the production of nuclear power are some of the results of the "environmentalist" movement in which academic scientists have played an influential part. The attitudes expressed in the environmentalist movement would appear to be innovations in the beliefs of academic and in their influence on public policy. Yet, in looking back at the slow growth of the influence of the academic institutional economists and the early reforming sociologists of three-quarters of a century ago, one sees certain very striking identities. In fact the main themes of these different periods remain very much the same. They are a demand for increased activity on the part of government and an attitude of hostility towards a demand for the restriction of private business enterprise.

XV

The long history of the American universities shows that they were never, as it is often charged, "ivory towers." The American universities were never intended to be monasteries in which learning would be cultivated to be exclusion of every other consideration. Learning was appreciated as an activity ultimately of benefit to society. In the long run the dignity of the entire society would be elevated by the cultivation of learning; in the long run too even the most recondite academic investigations were thought of as building stones in a pattern of knowledge which would benefit humanity by improving its mind and which would also improve its material condition through the transformation of knowledge into technology. All this was apart from the assigned and accepted role of universities in the training of persons who would participate intelligently and hence beneficently in the daily affairs of society; such was the notion which underlay the acceptance of the tradition of training civil servants, lawyers, divines, and physicians. In the twentieth century universities have also been expected to train engineers, businessmen, accountants, and statisticians; and later still social workers and journalists and, more recently, television producers, nurses, and the practitioners of the other "service professions." For about a century the universities have also been concerned with the improvement of the understanding of members of the educated public, whatever their occupations and professions, just as educators before the Civil War attended to the formation of the moral character of their students regardless of their subsequent occupations.

Thus there has always been a centrifugal force in American higher education. Academics have been concerned to instruct young persons with a view to forming their minds so that later in their lives they would affect what was done in their society. They have also been concerned to affect their society more directly by instructing members of the public who were not their pupils. The Chautauqua and the extra-mural services of the universities both came within this class of action by academics to improve the cultural and moral level of their fellow-countrymen beyond the corporate boundaries of their universities. To these functions, in the state universities, were added direct service to agricultural enterprises, research undertaken on problems raised by individual farmers or by representatives of the agricultural interest. Alongside these, there developed at the University of Wisconsin, first of all and almost at the same time, the intermittent or detached service of governments, state and federal. Finally, members of the academic profession engaged in publicistic or representational activities, individually or as members of civic and philanthropic organizations intended to persuade the politically active public and the government to modify particular social or economic or administrative arrangements through legislation.

All of these activities were carried on simultaneously. The direct performance of services was carried on mainly by the state universities but some of the lesser private, urban universities have also performed such services for business enterprise or municipal governments. All these intellectually peripheral activities were carried on with great vigor without interfering very much or at all with the central tasks of teaching and investigation. The large budget of activities was made possible by strong moral convictions on the part of the academic staffs of the universities and by large departments which gave a reasonable amount of freedom to their members, especially to the senior ones.

The universities, corporately, and university teachers, individually, were much concerned with their society. Unlike monks, they did not just think of the next world and their own monastic life. Some, by the subject-matter of their studies, others, by their peripheral activities, were in contact with the society outside the universities and eager to contribute to its well-being and improvement.

These activities did not proceed frictionlessly. There were disagreements within the universities between some colleagues who engaged in such activities and others who disapproved either of the particular bent of these peripheral activities or of the class of activities as a whole. Those who were more concerned with learning regarded these activities as distractions and derogations of the right standard of academic activities; the more conservative disapproved of the reformers. There were also conflicts between teachers and university presidents and governing bodies both lay and academic, some of which disapproved of activities that were—as many were—hostile to some particular arrangement in society. And of course there were persons, organizations, and institutions outside the universities which did not like being criticized by university teachers and which did not want to change those arrangements which univerity teachers wished to change or discontinue. It was in this setting that the famous cases of "academic freedom" arose, cases which were not uncommon a half-century ago and which have not disappeared even now.

The public outside the universities always took a lively and ordinarily a very deferential attitude towards the universities. It tended to appreciate the spectacular accomplishments of natural scientists and the contributions to medicine which came from the universities, but there was also admiration for the more quiet and "impractical" achievements in erudition and in theory. Even though academics, engaging in civic and publicistic activities of a sort which caused offense to those criticized, were accused of being "theorists," theory was not regarded disparagingly within its proper sphere.

There was then a somewhat ambivalent attitude in the interested public. It was not desired that universities should be aloof from the practical interests of their societies but there was at the same time a sense of discomfort about the critical publicistic and representative activities of university teachers. The American Association of University Professors was established to protect from sanctions by the governing authorities of universities those academics whose civic and publicistic activities had aroused such disapproval.

Censure and sanctions by governing bodies and high administrators, and by parts of the public acting through these, did not deter American academics from regarding civic and publicistic activities as an obligation which was laid upon them by the tradition out of which they had grown. This was especially so among the social scientists.

All of this time the universities were growing both in the size of their student bodies and in the size and variety of their staffs. After the Second World War, the system of financial support for research in science which had been developed by the philanthropic foundations between the wars was greatly extended as a result of the interest of the federal government in the cultivation of scientific and technological research. A process of disaggregation of the universities was accelerated by this munificent support of "projects" and by the increase in intermittent or detached services to governments and private institutions by academics in the natural and social sciences. These activities were undertaken with enthusiasm and sometimes with intellectually valuable results. They were moreover carried on without any sense that the traditional obligations of the academic professions were being infringed. In point of fact, these traditions as they have developed in the United States were not infringed by this intensification of research and publicistic, civic, and advisory activities. They were, however, put under strain.

Like all traditions under strain, they were undergoing unnoticed changes. A break came with the outcropping of radicalism in the universities. Then, among other things, it was demanded, briefly, that the universities as corporate bodies issue pronouncements on matters of public policy. The radicals also insisted that the university teachers break their ties of service and consultation to external bodies. The radicals and many who were not radicals but who did not wish to be behind the times demanded that the universities accept as one of their major functions the "criticism of society"; by this was meant that university teachers should take as a major task the censure of the activities of government and private business from a radical standpoint.

Less stress was placed on the obligation of detachment, of concern for wider temporal perspectives, etc. The universities were given responsibility, from the radical standpoint, for furtherance of the egalitarian ideals of openness to all sorts of students, those unqualified as well as those qualified by prior educational achievements and previously attested capacities, and of elimination of discriminating assessment of the achievements of students. For a time, radicals within the universities dreamed of revolution and went so far as to believe that revolution was imminent; students replaced the working classes in the adulterated Marxian theory of the "new left" within the universities. The universities, making use of one side of their otherwise so disparaged autonomy, were to become the fortresses and arsenals from which the rest of society would be conquered.

Of course, these were baseless fantasies from the very beginning and most of them were, in their details, soon dissipated. There are few academics among those who formerly were possessed by these fantasies who still attribute any reality to the aspiration they contained. The image of American society and of the world and of the value of learning which this radical upsurge delineated has however survived. American universities have long been under criticism from within; Irving Babbitt, Abraham Flexner, and Robert Hutchins are only a few of the stringent critics of American universities for their excessive concern with affairs outside learning itself. Clark Kerr by his affirmation of these concerns seemed to confirm the criticisms. These critics, whatever their distortions and the rejections, at least affirmed the central activities of the transmission of the tradition of learning by interpretation in teaching and by its extension in research. The radical criticism went very much further; it disparaged the outward concerns of the universities as wrong not because of their outgoingness but because they were concerns about substantively wrong values. Indeed, the radical criticism wanted the universities to be concerned only with external things, such as a fully egalitarian society, revolution, and the like. With regard to the central concerns of universities, the radical criticism would have disposed of them by requiring that teaching be addressed to the task of "raising revolutionary consciousness" and that research be aimed at serving "people," frustrating government, discrediting authority, and promoting revolution. The acquisition of valid knowledge was despised as a "reactionary" act of deception, irrelevant to serious values, and in any case unrealizable in general and, most certainly, under conditions of modern bourgeois society.

The radical criticism is now disarmed in the sense that radicals no longer agitate so vehemently and no longer attempt to lead their adherents to insurgency by disruption of the regular activities of universities. But, disarmed, it is not inert. It still maintains in a condition of "half-life" many radical attitudes towards learning. University administrators, partly because they are more sensitive to external nonacademic demands on the universities, have become the carriers of some of these radical demands, even though they are far from radical in their aspirations. The acceptance of the requirements of "affirmative action" is an instance of the way in which the external demands of the governmental egalitarian policy has been taken up by administrators. Universities as institutions of learning are a relatively new phenomenon in the world and above all in the United States. The tradition of devotion to learning as their primary obligation has never been unchallenged either inside the universities or outside them. For a long time this tension was kept in balance by the idea that the efficacy of practical action in society rested on a basis of scientific and scholarly knowledge. In this pattern, those who were concerned primarily or solely with science and scholarship could coexist in harmony with those who regarded learning as instrumental to the attainment of the ideals of a collectivistic liberalism. This equilibrium has latterly been menaced by the radical extension of the ideals of collectivistic liberalism. As a result of this extension, there has been a turning against science and scholarship by those whose responsibility it is to care for it. They have however not been wholly successful, although the federal government, the enlarged powers of which are in part attributable to the works of their intellectual academic ancestors, has, in some respects, been on their side. The battle is still joined.

7 The Pursuit of Knowledge and the Concern for the Common Good

I

When the social sciences were at the height of their glory from the late 1930s to the middle of the 1960s, they were even then not without critics. There were some dissentient voices. Denunciations from outside the universities were few; an occasional radical criticized them for evading "fundamental problems." From within the American universities, there were occasional denunciations and warnings against an overreaching pride. Historians criticized them for superficiality and for too much reliance on statistics and on abstract categories. The denunciations were generally unheeded; those who uttered them were regarded as echoes of a dead past. Then came the radical change in intellectual opinion, the turbulence of students and the unprecedented establishment of Marxism in the universities and colleges of the United States. Social science departments were among the main scenes of these developments. From the ranks of students and teachers came a series of rancorous charges against the social sciences and the social scientists. They were accused of triviality of concern. They had long been accused of triviality by literary historians and critics and by philosophers who compared the great works with which they dealt with the humble facts and inconsequential conclusions of social scientists; historians had criticized them because they generalized without the meticulous regard for facts which was the historian's pride. Now the charges went beyond the boundaries of the cognitive sphere.

The newer criticism of the social sciences asserted that there was a morally base and deceptive intention underlying their triviality. They were not just misguided by intellectual error, according to these critics; they had corrupt motives. Social sciences were said to be trivial in their choice of objects of study because they did not wish to throw a discrediting light on their contemporary society; they studied the trivial to avoid the important. They were accused of being in collusion with the powerful against the weak; they were charged with serving the interests of the powerful in order to maintain and improve their own situation. Their latter-day critics said that they avoided the study of important problems primarily in order to gain favor for themselves with the powerful. The triviality of their studies was part of a larger

This is a revised version of an essay that originally appeared in *Controversies and Decisions,* ed. Charles Frankel, © 1976, Russell Sage Foundation, New York.

political intention to maintain the existing distribution of wealth and power in contemporary society by diverting attention from what was important. They were corrupted by their connection with government and private foundations. They were charged with being interested in their own advancement, in higher status for themselves, better financial rewards and more power. Worse yet, the baseness of the social scientists was not simply misconduct, which good will could correct. Their categories of thought, their canons of truth were such as inevitably served the interests of the powerful. Their corruption infected the core of the intellect. They used categories which were ethnocentric; they accepted the postulates of a program aimed to preserve capitalistic society.

The social scientists' image of themselves as scientists and scholars engaged in the disinterested pursuit of an attainable objective truth about society was dismissed with a knowing contempt. The social scientists' belief that the knowledge which they acquired through their studies possessed cognitive dignity was rejected out of hand. Even their belief that the truths which they allegedly sought could contribute to the improvement of society was scorned by the resentful current of criticism which refused to admit the possibility of a compellingly truthful knowledge of society and its beneficent application in a liberal capitalistic society.

These critics have not thus far attained eminence in their respective disciplines although they form a block to be reckoned with in the learned societies and in many departments of the social sciences, especially in sociology. What they lack in intellectual accomplishment they make up in a self-confidently accusatory air. In its extreme forms, their criticism has often been abusive; at its worst it has been coupled with outlandish assertions to the effect that social scientists were like police spies, jailers, colonial soldiers, exploiters of that part of the working class formed by the university student body, etc. Their criticisms are directed against their colleagues as well as against the leaders of their disciplines. Any criticism of them is rebuffed as "McCarthyism" and "repression."

Not all of the recent critics of the social sciences have gone so far. There are some who believe that the social sciences have not been wholly trivial or false; they do not believe that the public and private sources of funds are necessarily corrupting or that social scientists are the witting or unwitting servants of the prevailing powers.

Among these critics who are not so far-reaching in their criticisms, there is some belief that social scientists have gone too far in their scramble for funds for research, that they have unwisely propagated their subject beyond its present intellectual and practical capacity and that they have not fulfilled the claims they have made about its scientific validity and its practical value. There are also critics who think that the social sciences, although capable of being truthful, have failed to be so because of the partisanship of social scientists, particularly their uncritical partisanship on behalf of or against the impoverished and the degraded.

There are critics who think that the effort to create a body of scientific knowledge of society was a misguided enterprise from the beginning. They deny that dispassionate, reliable knowledge of human society is at all possible. For them it is a mistake to think that objective knowledge which does not contain ethical judgment is possible. Since value judgments entered into the very definitions of terms and categories, the idea of scientific objectivity was simply erroneous. This attitude shades into another which asserts that the individuality of human beings and the uniqueness of historical events render impossible anything like scientific knowledge. Few of these last criticisms are new. Many of the more serious ones long predate the present century and were not originally applied to the social sciences, which did not yet exist. Some of them belong to the long accepted body of cautions to all who wish to do scientific or scholarly work; others delimit the range of applicability of the categories and methods of the physical sciences. Social scientists have become used to these criticisms and they have for the most part paid little attention to them, going their own way and trying to be as scientific as possible. Their forebears were impervious to these epistemological criticisms and they remain impervious to them.

It is rather different with the criticisms of the motives of social scientists and the functions of social science. Asserted without evidence and with aggressive rhetoric, these criticisms have had a startling, even bewildering effect, and many of the criticized have accepted some of the criticism, even though it has not changed their conduct.

Until the recent outburst of criticism from within, social scientists, especially those of the first few generations of university teachers of the subject in the United States were confident that they were doing the right thing. They had often been criticized on the ground that they were propagating radical doctrines or that they were destroying old beliefs. They had not been troubled by these accusations because they were confident that they were doing the right thing. They had no justification in their own minds if they believed what they were doing was incapable of ever reaching the level of science and if the science which they were trying to create was not going to improve the lot of mankind. They were, after all, converts to their subjects. They came to the social sciences from other fields of study with which they had been dissatisfied because they thought that in the particular social science to which they were drawn, there was a vital new beginning.

Whatever the discipline from which they came and whatever the discipline which they entered, they were certain that objectivity was attainable in the study of society. It required scrupulous respect for "the facts" and hence for the techniques of collecting them. They had not doubt that society had an existence independently of the imagination of the investigator. The task of the investigator was to discern that reality; the obstacles were prejudice, sustained by emotional attachments and animosity, carelessness and inattention to the facts, whether they were the facts directly observed or elicited by interviews or studied in documents, printed and unprinted. The other article of faith which they all shared was that such objective knowledge was a good thing. They had no doubt that human life would be enriched by the truth about itself, they thought that individuals are improved by the sheer possession of knowledge, and a society of many such individuals was a better society simply by virtue of that fact. They thought too that society would be improved by the application of that knowledge although they did not have clear ideas about just how the application and improvement would occur.

A combination of skeptical criticism and faith in the attainability of more reliable and more fundamental truth than we have at present is one of the oldest traditions of Western civilization. The Platonic epistemology, the Socratic dialectic, and Aristotelian metaphysics were aimed at the dissipation of error in the apprehension of the fundamental reality. They sought the truth through a critical attitude which went beyond the face value of generally accepted evidence. This is what Socrates did when he asked his contemporaries so many questions, which showed them that what they had hitherto believed was not sufficiently well-founded. Philosophy was no more and no less than a matter of getting at the truth. The technique and the necessity of rising above error were the concerns of philosophers.

The coming of the revealed truth of Christianity did not change this. The task of discerning and ordering the true meaning of the Christian revelation made much of the pagan philosophy acceptable. Underlying all this was the assumption that the hitherto accepted interpretation was susceptible of improvement and that it had to be improved by critical scrutiny always with the assumption that a better apprehension of the truth was attainable. That is why the Christian philosophy of the eternally true underwent an unceasing revision and reformulation.

In the sixteenth century, natural scientists sought to demonstrate the superiority of the "new" methods of natural science to the speculative and ratiocinative procedures which accepted revelation and tradition and which had been prevalent up to and in their own time. The effort to found a "science of man" by irrefragable observations logically analyzed and independent of recourse to traditional philosophical and religious beliefs was as evident in the writings of Hobbes as it was in those of Sir William Petty. The various efforts to found a science of "social physics" were an effort to construct a more truthful picture of society; they were also efforts to vindicate a certain way of going about it which would be superior to previously employed methods. Hobbes believed that society would be better ordered through the possession and appreciation of the truth at which he arrived by elementary observation of man's nature and by his analysis of the conditions of the maintenance of order in society.

By the eighteenth century it was already assumed that knowledge of the nature of society was possible and that it would be beneficial to society once it was created. A courageous attempt to establish a theoretical social science was undertaken by Condorcet, who, taking his point of departure in the theory of probability, contended that a science of society based on postulates and analytical procedures similar to those of the natural sciences could be no less scientific than the natural sciences and no less contributory to the progress of mankind. The great accumulation of social statistics, which was a by-product of the machinery of control maintained by the absolutist state, seemed to offer the empirical or observational data from which such a science could be constructed. Both in Prussia and in France, the early stirrings of a scientific social science were linked with the model of the natural sciences on the one hand and the working of the machinery of state on the other. The very names of the subjects—*Statistik, Staatswissenschaft, Kameralwissenschaft*—expressed the conviction that the "science of society" would serve the state, which was the highest organ of society. The subsequent development of quantitative social science in the nineteenth century was exemplified in Quetelet, whose work was carried further by official statisticians in various European countries. It was a part of the great movement to create a knowledge of human society which would avoid the pitfalls of mythology, traditional beliefs, prejudices, and impressions, biased by interests and desires. This aspiration was accompanied by the belief that the knowledge thus created would be of practical value to society as well as being of intrinsic value.

The mighty effort of the German historians of the nineteenth century to create a scientific history based on a rational criticism of sources was a parallel movement in another closely related field and in another intellectual tradition. It had been preceded by the work of classical scholars from the sixteenth century onward, of whom Scaliger was the greatest, to reestablish the "true" texts from which the inherited texts had departed and of the medievalists of the preceding century and a half, most notably Mabillon, Maffei, and Muratori. The aim of the latter was to "purify" the sources so that really true history could be written. Here too there was a conviction that historical events possessed an objective existence separate from the observational powers, the imagination, and the analytical capacity which sought to grasp it by successive approximation.

The growing self-consciousness of the anthropologists which resulted in the *Notes and Queries* of the Royal Anthropological Institute was likewise an effort to overcome the distortions imposed by observers in observing "primitive" societies. Guides to confine the observations of travelers so that they should observe what was of fundamental importance had already been prepared in the first half of the nineteenth century. They were like scientific instruments which replaced the vagaries of the observational powers of the unaided senses of individuals by a uniform set of units and a mode of measurement which did not vary arbitrarily among individuals. James Mill provided such a "schedule" for Henry Crabb Robinson to guide his observations in Germany in the 1820s; Harriet Martineau produced a similar set of questions which travelers, who wished to report on what they saw, should attempt to answer. Even Karl Marx designed an *equête*. These social surveys were undertakings which accepted the rigor and impersonality of science as the standard to which social science must adhere if its results were to be as persuasive to rational and dispassionate persons as were the results of research in the natural sciences.

Auguste Comte, who was also interested in establishing the mode of analysis appropriate to sociology as a discipline which would gain scientific knowledge of society, thought that sociology would reach maturity as a "positive science." He thought that society would benefit from the application of the knowledge comprised in sociology, indeed that the attainment of a good order of society could only be established on the basis of a scientific knowledge of society. Windelband's, Dilthey's, and Rickert's attempts to formulate the epistemological foundations of the *Kulturwissenschaften* and the *Geisteswissenschaften* by distinguishing them from the *Naturwissenschaften* may be seen as likewise positing the knowability of cultural and historical objects as entities with an independent existence. Although they thought that there were different modes of apprehension of the external world, they did not doubt that it was knowable and that the knowledge of the cultural and historical objects could be communicated and tested. Unlike the French, British, and American authors who wrote in the social sciences, they did not interest themselves in the practical use of that knowledge. The German movement reached its culmination and its greatest achievement in Max Weber's essays on "objectivity" and on "evaluative neutrality." Weber had no doubt about the possibility of establishing the truth about social phenomena by the methods of science and scholarship. He asserted that *Wertbezogenheit* was a property of the selection of problems; he also insisted that, once the problem was chosen, it was possible to establish the truth of factual propositions about human conduct. The validity of such propositions would be compelling to all who had the intellectual capacities and skills to perform the needed observations and analyses. Max Weber knew that social scientists could distort the image of reality if they did not discipline their political, ethnic, national, religious, and class attachments and sentiments; he believed this self-discipline could be achieved. He knew that there was a manifold reality outside the individual, the coherence of which could be grasped by the mind, disciplined by the intellectual tradition of rules, categories, and canons of understanding. He also believed that the knowledge gained by the social sciences could be applied. He thought that this knowledge could, if applied, make policies more realistic, more consistent, and less self-defeating. He saw no conflict between the cognitive end and the practical ends of those who wished to ''face the facts'' and to act rationally.

An evolution of nearly three centuries culminated in a widespread conviction of the attainability of truthful knowledge about the conduct of individuals in society and of their formation into institutions, strata, corporate bodies, and whole societies. However critical social scientists have been of any particular work or of the particular observations in it, they have believed that, with discipline and deliberation in observation and analysis, it is possible to describe and explain social events in a way which meets the canons of veracity. The pursuit of knowledge could be conducted in a way which would withstand the distractions, diversions, and temptations presented by passionate desire, vanity, attachment to institutions, received beliefs, and the prospect of material advantage.

In all these reflections, which extend over two millennia, there has been a recognition, sometimes at the center of attention, sometimes at the periphery, that the particular intellectual activity involved in the understanding of society exists in a matrix of other human concerns. Intellectual activity coexists and overlaps with the spheres of religious experience and reflection, of political action and espousal, of attachment to the family, nation, state, tribe, locality, and social stratum in which the individuals seeking to understand society are enmeshed. The acquisition and formation of knowledge about society have occurred in the matrix of all these concerns. One element of that development has been the attempt to fix the procedures through which the distracting influence of these extra-intellectual attachments and aspirations on the intellectual activity of knowing society could be held in check. The establishment of an autonomous mode of striving for the knowledge which generally falls under the heading of social science has had to resist the possible influence of the beliefs which were integral to these other institutions and to the demands for loyalty made by these other institutions. As individuals and members of academies supported by or patronized by the rulers of the state, as members of universities supported by the state or the church or by wealthy private persons and princes, as officials of governments, as wealthy businessmen, and as citizens with private means, social scientists attempted to find a way of carrying out their obligations to truth while meeting their other obligations. The affirmation of the ideals of freedom of thought and inquiry, of academic freedom and university autonomy was intended, and did in fact serve, to sustain the exclusion of the noncognitive concerns and attachment from the sphere of cognitive activities. They were intended to preserve the integrity of cognitive activity so that it could attend to the attainment and promulgation of truth without the deformative consequences of fear.

Much of the effort to improve the intellectual standard and standing of social science has in fact been devoted to affirming the possibility and desirability of keeping moral—or political and otherwise practical—evaluation apart from the interior of cognitive activities. Social scientists proceeded on the assumption of the possibility of acquiring knowledge which could stand up to the test of validity, regardless of the ethical or political desires of the social scientists who discovered it—as long as they themselves abided by the rules of observation and analysis.

The ethical and, particularly, the political beliefs of many social scientists have in fact often been discernible in their writings; in many cases these beliefs have had a distorting effect on what they observed or on their theories. These conditions have not been regarded as evidence—as indeed they were not evidence—of the logical or empirical impossibility of discovering truths about societies and society which would be true regardless of the social scientist's political or ethical standpoint. On the contrary they made the urgency of such ethical neutrality all the greater.

Of course, there have been and still are many other impediments to the intellectual growth of the social sciences. Even if the intrusion of the practical into the cognitive, the bending by practical concerns of cognitive capacities away from the path they were committed by their own principles to follow were averted, there would still remain the gigantic and primary task of learning the truth about reality. The incursion of the social scientist's noncognitive concerns into his cognitive sphere is only one of the hindrances to the social sciences.

This view argues that there is a disjunction between knowledge of what "is"—on whatever stratum of immediacy or of remoteness from immediate experience—and knowledge of what "should be." It argues that the knowledge of what "is" can proceed independently of the knowledge of what "should be." It argues that criteria of truth are independent of the criteria of goodness or justice.

II

The view that the cognitive sphere is and should be held analytically separate from the practical sphere is a relatively new idea. The idea that there is a stratum of being which in itself conveys no immediate ethical instruction and which should be apprehended by the exercise of mental powers and functions which are not by their nature practical actions or ethical judgments was not part of the dominant intellectual tradition which came down from antiquity to early modern times. According to this view, our knowledge of reality is a knowledge of the functions and natures of entities. The nature and function of an object or an action or an institution entails a normal or proper state. The knowledge of the nature of an object is knowledge of the function of that object. The function entails a norm to which the object must adhere if it is to be what it is. If one acquires truthful knowledge of any object such as an action or an institution, one, by virtue of possessing that knowledge, also knows how the acting person or member of the institution should behave. The knowledge of what "should be" is integral to the understanding of the fundamental properties of any existing object, process, action, or institution.

In antiquity, the relationship appeared to be self-evident, and it was diametrically opposite to what it is now believed to be. It was the task of philosophers to discern and analyze the nature of things, and the understanding reached in this process entailed the answer to the question of what is good and worthy of pursuit. Once one succeeded in laying bare the nature of an action, an occupation, an institution, there was no remaining normative problem. The discovery of the nature of an activity simultaneously disclosed the ethical standing of that activity. There were counter-currents of skepticism and sophistry which denied this but they made little headway against the overwhelming metaphysical self-evidence of the identity of what really "is" and what "ought" to be.

The knowledge of the nature and function of a thing could be attained only by breaking through the superficial crust of events which obstructed the way to truthful knowledge. There was, however, no question of separating cognitive activities from normative or practical judgments. They were inevitably conducted simultaneously and identically.

The ethical silence of the infinite spaces has now spread to the most immediately proximate objects of our efforts to understand nature and society, and it is difficult to comprehend the classical view. Nonetheless, it lasted well into modern times and it has not yet been completely dissipated.

After the revolution wrought by Hume and Kant in our fundamental conceptions of "is" and "ought," the idea of the normative imperativeness inherent in the stratum of reality laid bare by cognitive processes took refuge in history. God and nature, having lost the imperative power resident in their timeless unchangingness, found a new home and a new form in history. It was no longer the permanent nature or the essential quality of things which provided imperatives for action; it was the "true nature" of the stage of development which came to provide those imperatives. Whether it was the stage in the unfolding of the spirit through time, or the stage in the consequence of types of "relationships to the instruments of production" or to the state in the evolutionary process, man's ethical obligations were cut out for him. Historicism has many variants; it may be seen not only in Marxism but in the efforts of evolutionary humanists like Julian Huxley and Conrad Waddington to construct ethical principles from a "scientific" analysis of the "evolutionary imperative." Each stage of development—of the "world spirit," of the mind, of the economy, of the species—prescribes, according to this view, the tasks and ethical obligations inherent in its nature. There was no room for disagreement once the nature of the stage of development was "correctly" discerned. The philosophy of history, idealistic or Marxian, and the science of evolution were the intellectual means of eliciting ethical imperatives from the study of reality.

The historicist conception of the ethical or normative—or, as it is now called, "policy"—imperative inherent in each historical epoch still had a strong link with the classical outlook. It simply confined the duration of the "really real" to a stage in a historical or evolutionary sequence. It was a peculiar combination of a belief in the timeless uniformity of nature and a belief in the disjunctive sequence of epochs, each of which was *unmittelbar zu Gott.* Each stage had its own nature and, once that was discerned by philosophers, economists, or evolutionary biologists, there were certain ethical— "policy"—imperatives which followed. (One epoch could not criticize another ethically since the ethical standards of each epoch are peculiar to and appropriate to itself alone. In this respect this view bore a close resemblance to ethical relativism, except for the fact that there was not a meaningless variety but rather a meaningful sequence of unfoldings and realizations). The classical position would deny the pertinence of the task undertaken here, namely, the task of discerning the ethical imperatives inherent in each stage of history. The nature of things is indifferent to superficial historical variations.

Historicism was an odd heir of the classical tradition but it did retain the classical belief in the discernibility of the norms of action from the systematic study of what is or has been. It too therefore asserted the constitutive position of normative judgment within the cognitive judgment. The very categories of observation and analysis were determined by the evaluative context and derivation of cognitive activity. Historicism made all cognitive activities and achievements dependent on the character—or structure—of the epoch or stage of social development in which they were carried on. Each epoch being distinctive and having its own ethical imperatives, also had its own cognitive procedures, criteria, etc., which were not universally applicable. The power of the mind, benefiting by specifically intellectual traditions, to discern the truth was implicitly disparaged by making that power wholly dependent on the main features of the stage in which it was exercised. The "new philosophy" initiated by Frances Bacon was in many respects antithetical to the classical position of the Aristotelian and scholastic philosophy. It is in the tradition of that "new philosophy" that the social sciences have been carried forward. The empirical side of the social sciences in France and Great Britain, and then the United States, was not significantly affected by the classical metaphysical conceptions of "nature" and "function." Its practitioners did not, at least in their research, pay heed to the classical tradition. The more theoretical strand of the social sciences too separated itself from that tradition. The "naturalistic," "scientific," interest in seeing things as they really are, even though accompanied by judgments of what was "good" and what was "evil," was regarded as having no necessary or inherent connection with these judgments. In the course of time, the distinctiveness and logical separateness of the two types of intellectual activity—the cognitive on the one side and the ethical, political, or evaluative on the other—acquired the status of self-evidence; the task then came to be the inhibition of the latter when the former was at work. Ethical judgments had to be kept out when cognitive activity was being carried on.

The relationship of the social sciences to the historicist modification of the classical position is rather different. Historicism arose more or less contemporaneously with some of the main currents of the social sciences. The historical interest was in the concreteness and particularity of historical events; in Germany especially, there was both affinity and overlap between historicism and the social sciences.

In historicism the normative implications of the "factual" could be read out from the "factual" account. The Marxian sociological outlook was especially impregnated with historicism. As Karl Mannheim and other writers influenced by Marxism began to make their voices heard in sociology and the other social sciences as well, the relations between the cognitive and the normative were given a different accent. In the idealistic variant of historicism the crisis of the cognitive powers was not so radical. If the evolution of the spirit or mind from epoch to epoch and within one epoch was an evolution in the direction of an increasingly comprehensive consciousness, then the powers of the mind to reach further into reality were not really deformed or distracted by their inherent normativeness; they were, on the contrary, extended. When however, as in Marxism, the structure of "the relations of production" and the conflicting "interests" integral to the different (class) positions in the relations of production were the characteristic and determining features of an epoch, then "interests" became decisive in the determination of what could be perceived. Cognitive activities and achievements were accordingly shaped and warped by "class interests."

The derivability of the "normative" from the "factual" had been accepted by traditional Marxism, with the innovation that the "normative" element was replaced by "interests." Thus the working class would, according to this doctrine, become socialistic and revolutionary as it became "class-conscious"; it would become socialistic and revolutionary as it gained realistic understanding of its actual position and its "real interests." At the same time that traditional Marxism encompassed this modification of the classical and the idealistic historical views, it was also impregnated with the modern positivistic view of the cognitive powers which were active in scientific discovery. It had an ambivalent view of these. On the one side it accredited them; and on the other side it sacrificed them to its historicist conceptions. It did the latter by declaring scientific knowledge to be part of ideology.

The wheel had turned by one hundred and eighty degrees. Instead of ethical norms being discovered concomitantly with the discovery of reality, now ethical beliefs, which were really transfigurations of "interests," determined what was perceived and these beliefs led to error. "Interests"—except for the "interest" of the working classes—prevented the truthful perception of reality. Ascendant classes could perceive more than descending classes; but, except for the working class, the interests of which were identical with the interests of all of society, no class could ever see reality.

III

The type of social science which developed in the twentieth century lived under the aegis of the scientific movement and the philosophical revolution brought about by Hume and Kant. The reality to which the social scientist could penetrate was ethically silent. It was acknowledged that the social scientist would have ethical, political, and normative beliefs but they were logically of a different order from his cognitive beliefs. He could not derive the latter from the former but the former could impinge upon the latter, to the disadvantage of the latter. Hence it was important that the social scientist should free himself from the distorting influence which ethical and political judgments might have on his perception and understanding of society. The understanding of this ethically silent reality became a good in itself; the experience of understanding, the cognitive experience, was a sufficient and autonomously valuable end. It stood alongside the sphere of ethical judgment as an autonomous sphere of at least equal intrinsic dignity. The classical relationship between the two spheres was thus profoundly altered. The idealistic historicist position was denied for the same reason. The pursuit of an ethical ideal through the effort to understand what society "really is" came to be seen not only as a vain pursuit but as dangerous to understanding. Understanding required the effective suspension of the exercise of ethical judgment of what was studied. It was feared that rendering ethical judgment or aspiring to discover what the right ethical judgment should be might cloud the mind's eye and cause the observer to fall into observational error. The active presence of ethical belief concurrently with the cognitive action of the observer was a mixing of alien things which, it was thought, could lead him to see only what he wished to see and to obscure from his eye that which he did not wish to see.

Bacon at the beginning of the modern age had warned against the "idola." Herbert Spencer in *The Study of Sociology* called them "biases." Passions, desires, loyalties, ethical aspirations, and ideals were put into the same class. No distinction was made between good and bad ones; they could all upset the mind and lead it astray. They were a danger to the scientific study of society. Spencer was of course far from indifferent to questions of the well-being of society, and he thought that the truths of sociology would show the vanity of policies such as state intervention, which he abominated. He thought nonetheless that the clarity of perception, the weighing of evidence and analytical thought would be darkened by the intrusion of evaluative preoccupations. There was no remedy for this except by scrupulous adherence to rigorous canons of scientific procedures.

The early figures of American social sciences intended to evaluate society, to render ethical judgments about it, and to contribute, in one way or another, to its improvement. At the same time, they intended that their observations should be increasingly scientific; to have their observations attain the status of science was their ambition. They thought that the more closely they approximated to their scientific ideal, the better would be the prospect for the improvement of society. They saw no incompatibility between the search for truth by the most reliable methods available and their intention to improve the life of man by action directed towards events which were scientifically understood. Ward, Thomas, Park, Cooley, Small, Giddings, and Sumner did not need to discover their ethical ideals through sociological research. They already had ideals or ethical standards derived from Protestant Christianity, British liberalism, and American liberal democracy. They did not claim that these ideals had been discovered through scientific research; they did claim that they could be better realized through a more scientific understanding of society and through a greater readiness on the part of the public and of government to accept that understanding. They were not apprehensive lest their sobriety in the assessment of events be diminished and the accuracy of their perception blurred by their practical interest. They were not apprehensive because they thought that the disciplined methods of science and their own self-discipline in the pursuit of the scientific ideal would protect them from the temptation to see only what they wished to see in their study of society.

Although the social sciences became well established in most of the major American universities by the end of the First World War, and perhaps because they had few notable successes to show for their pains, these men were very conscious of the pitfalls which lay in the path of their progress. That is why they laid so much emphasis on "methods." William Ogburn, who was one of the social scientists who led in the campaign to make the social sciences more scientific by the use of quantitative procedures, was very sensitive to the pitfalls into which bias might lead the investigator. In an essay entitled "Bias, Social Science, and Psychoanalysis,"[1] he called attention to the possibly deleterious effects of unconscious bias. Albert B. Wolfe likewise pointed out the deformative potentiality of extra-scientific interests.[2] Graham Wallas[3] and John A. Hobson[4] also showed an awareness, following Herbert Spencer, that extra-intellectual interests could mislead the mind in its quest for truth.

It was considerations of this sort—among others—which led many American sociologists in the 1920s to press for the dissociation of sociology from social work and from reform movements. It was not that they were unsympathetic with the aspirations of social workers and reformers; rather they feared that close association between these and the proper scientific interests would make sociologists "sentimental," i.e., too ready to yield to the influence of moral sentiments and therefore too inclined to allow these sentiments to affect the detachment of mind needed to see things as they really were. Before the First World War, men who contributed much to the improvement of sociology in the United States were very actively engaged in movements of social reform. Neither Small nor Henderson were themselves engaged in the type of research which later became typical in sociology but they repeatedly emphasized how much the improvement of society depended on the availability of reliable scientific knowledge about society. Richard Ely, Franklin Giddings, and Wesley Mitchell all laid great emphasis on the scientific knowledge of soci-

1. Reprinted in Otis D. Duncan, ed., *William F. Ogburn on Culture an Social Change* (Chicago: University of Chicago Press, 1964), pp. 289–301.
2. Albert B. Wolfe, *Conservatism, Radicalism, and Scientific Method* (New York: Macmillan, 1923).
3. *Human Nature and Politics* (London: Constable, 1908) and *The Art of Thought* (New York: Harcourt Brace, 1926).
4. *Free Thought in the Social Sciences* (London: Allen and Unwin, 1926).

ety as a precondition for the effective and beneficent guidance of the affairs of society.

Many of the American social scientists of the period between the two great wars were liberals in the American sense. They favored governmental regulatory and ameliorative action; they were progressivists as far as technological innovation was concerned; they were against tradition and prejudice, which they assimilated to each other. They placed their hopes for the progress of society on the progress of social science through the use of scientific methods, which entailed disinterestedness and self-divestment of bias. There was already enough evidence of the benefits conferred by scientific research on the technology used in the practice of medicine and agriculture to convince social scientists and their supporters that the development of a scientific knowledge of society would bring similar benefits to the "solution of social problems."

This purification of social science from the diversions of passionate engagement in practical affairs was impelled jointly by genuine conviction about the right way to do intellectual work and by conviction about the rational and scientific foundations of any valuable and lasting social improvement. It was also in part impelled by the desire to raise the standing of social science by being as objective as the natural sciences and as free as the natural sciences from derogatory association with quackery and nostrum-peddling. It was probably also aimed at making the social sciences like the natural sciences, which having set aside superstition, prejudice, tradition, and suppressed personal passions other than the passion for knowledge, had made such great progress. If the social scientists could be like the natural scientists in this regard they would make greater intellectual progress and they would raise their status in the universities and in public opinion and increase their influence for the good.

In recent years some historians of social science have asserted that this concern for objectivity was not a genuinely intellectual concern. These observers from a distance of fifty and a hundred years assert that the social scientists of those times alleged their devotion to the ideal of objectively valid knowledge in order to allay the suspicions of their patrons and the otherwise powerful about their actually radical convictions. In short, the quest of objective and valid knowledge and the praise of objectivity were only rhetorical devices to divert suspicion and to protect academic appointments from unsympathetic and politically conservative deans, presidents, trustees, businessmen, politicians, and journalists. It is possible that such protestations of devotion to the ideal of scientific objectivity might have had such protective consequences; they certainly were not impelled by such motives in most cases.

The accomplishments of social scientists in the study of business cycles, ethnic attitudes, urban communities, the conditions of work in industry, rural sociology, American-Indian societies, elections, and social trends were attended by a growing conception of the social-scientific role. The social scientists who were developing an idea of themselves as scientists in the conduct of their work tried to resist the pressure of sentiments and the commands of beliefs other than those which made up the body of social science knowledge. This conception of themselves was sometimes associated with a belief that the social scientist *qua* citizen had no moral obligations other than objectivity. Social science appeared to some social scientists as a way of life which entailed a form of asceticism and required the avoidance of any ethical or political judgment or attachment; social scientists were conceived as a priesthood of factuality. This was the image which certain social scientists in the 1920s had of themselves—especially the propagandists of the new type of quantitative sociology. The latter included George Lundberg and Read Bain and, with many qualifications, Wesley Mitchell, William Ogburn, Ernest Burgess, Stuart Rice, and Stuart Chapin. They also believed that there were right-thinking citizens and officials who would learn from the results of the research of social scientists and who would use that knowledge for the benefit of society. Mitchell, Ogburn, and Burgess certainly did not disavow their political and social sympathies but they thought that such sympathies should and could be stilled when they engaged in scientific research. Otherwise, truth would escape them and the social sciences would fail to live up to the ideal of academic science and scholarship. The hard-won academic citizenship of the social sciences would be endangered by failure to maintain the standard of detached, dispassionate, impersonal procedure and bearing which had been achieved in the natural sciences. In some respects the program was successful. It had its most fervent devotees among the social scientists who espoused the use of quantitative technique as the scientific method par excellence. It was scarcely less attractive to those like Park, MacIver, Sorokin, Sutherland, et al., who were unwilling to take such an exclusive view about scientific procedure.

In general, belief in the need to subject oneself to the discipline of scientific methods and the concomitant desire that the scientific knowledge of society should be "used" for the benefit of society was not part of a more general "scientistic" outlook. The scientistic belief that the scientific knowledge of society could provide the norms for the guidance of society did not have so many followers. William Ogburn was perhaps the most important one; he never swerved from his commitment to the ideal of scientific objectivity, but he also thought that by scientific studies one could discover "cultural lag," i.e., the "lag" of culture and institutions behind the possibilities offered by technology. The very observation of "cultural lag" contained the normative requirement of its elimination. The theory of "cultural lag" treated the state of technology as the norm to which belief, actions, and institutions should be "adapted." This was nothing but "technological historicism," which postulated the normative imperative that all institutions and beliefs should be made harmonious with the potentialities of technological innovation. The discovery of "cultural lag" by the techniques of social science imposed an obligation, incumbent on all members of society, to accept the "consequences" of technological innovation and to devise new institutional arrangements which would give free scope to the technology to realize its potentialities. I do not think that any other social scientist of the 1920s and 1930s went as far as Ogburn, but there was a drift of belief in this direction.

There were few American social scientists of the 1920s and the early 1930s who knew Max Weber's writings on "objectivity" and "evaluative neutrality." Nonetheless, in a fairly unsophisticated, positivistic manner, some of these social scientists occupied a position not very different from that represented by Weber's conclusions regarding the relations between social science and practical action.

They thought that one had to learn to "face the facts," indeed, one had to seek them out. Once discovered, the facts could give instruction regarding the condition of the attainment of particular goals, the consequences of such attainment, and the "costs" of attainment. Rationalistic and enlightened as these social scientists were, most of them did not believe that scientific knowledge could provide the goals of action.

Increasing methodological self-consciousness was characteristic of this period. The more frequent use of quantitative methods, the development of the technique of quantitative content-analysis, the measurement of attitudes, the stabilization of techniques of interviewing, the improvement of sampling methods and of techniques of factor analysis and other types of correlation were all aimed at overcoming the dangers of impressionistic assessment which normatively or passionately impelled desires might too easily dominate, with resultant distortion of observation and analysis. "Bias" was the enemy and it could be best expelled by means of systematic, rigorously controlled methods of observation and analysis.

Up to the 1930s, American social scientists knew little about Marx aside from some version of the "economic interpretation of history." And even those who were not entirely out of sympathy with the Marxian approach, as a principle of substantive interpretation, did not think that it held any implications for their own "scientific approach." The Marxian theories about ideology and about the determinative influence of "interests" on ideas were hardly discussed. They were certainly not discussed with reference to the standing of knowledge in the social sciences. There were very few Marxists among American social scientists, and those who were, e.g., Bernhard Stern, were positivists; they made Marxian interpretations of society but not of their own analysis of it. Stern, who was a protégé of Ogburn, certainly did not diverge from the prevailing belief in the possibility of objective knowledge, free from the intrusion of influence of ethical beliefs or political references.

Most American social scientists of the 1930s—and of the ensuing decades up to the present—continued to espouse the ideal of objectivity and to avoid the explicit assertion of evaluative or ethical statements in their reports on research and in their theoretical treatises. They often were very self-conscious in their separation of "value judgments" and scientific statements. This did not inhibit them from the espousal of political views. Many of them were enthusiastic supporters of the New Deal, not only because it corresponded to their own progressivistic views but also because it seemed to promise the application of the results of scientific social research in the pursuit of its ends. The fact that they offered "a lot of jobs for de resoich ahtists," as Alfred E. Smith is reported to have said of the agencies created by President Roosevelt, did not affect the methodological beliefs of the social scientists, regardless of whether they were employed by government. All through the decade of the 1930s, strenuous efforts were made to render the techniques of social science more scientific. The National Bureau of Economic Research made great strides forward; the coming of sample surveys of public opinion was also a step in the same direction. The quality of governmental statistics was also improved under the care of social scientists like Robert Nathan and Stuart Rice.

IV

There were however two rifts in this fabric in the 1930s. One of these was connected with Karl Mannheim's assertion of the pervasive domination of the ethical, political, or normative beliefs of the analyst over all analysis, however empirical, of social phenomena; in almost the same breadth, Mannheim tried to escape from the relativistic consequences of his argument.[5] Brought into the context of American sociology, this ambiguous undertaking was adapted by Louis Wirth to fit into the earlier preoccupation with the expulsion of "bias." In

5. Mannheim himself silently withdrew from his embarrassing position in the course of the fourteen years between his arrival in the United Kingdom and his death in 1947. As he become more interested in substantive problems than in methodology, the relativistic element in his work receded. He began to cite empirical research studies as evidence in his studies without ever discounting their bias or referring to their "categorical apparatus." He did not refer their results back to the *Denkstruktur* from which they were made and he did not

this undertaking, Wirth was influenced by John Dewey's ideas about the instrumental origins of knowledge and by Charles Beard—himself encouraged in this regard by his reading of Mannheim's *Ideologie und Utopie*. Beard had taken a leading part in the commission on the place of social and historical studies in the secondary school curriculum. In this commission there was much talk about "indoctrination" and whether it could or should be avoided. Some educationists came out strongly for the view that the schools should "dare to build a new social order," presumably influencing schoolchildren in a collec-tivistic-progressivistic direction; others argued that the teachers should seek to avoid imposing their own normative beliefs on the children. Beard's view, for which he adduced Mannheim's support, was that, willy-nilly, normative beliefs could not be evaded since they were inherent in the "structure" of knowledge about society.

Earlier writers like Ogburn and Wolfe had accepted that bias could be eliminated by conscious self-discipline. When Wirth first began to think about bias, his view was not unlike that of his elders. Bias was acknowledged to be undesirable and unnecessary, and it could be eliminated by becoming more scientific. Earlier in his career, Wirth had thought that by self-scrutiny and the will to purify one's own mind, the bias could be expelled and the mind opened for objective knowledge. After his contact with Mannheim's ideas in the first half of the 1930s, Wirth began to think that bias was inexpungible. He found Mannheim's "relationism" to be a solution to the dilemma. As the decade advanced he became more explicit in the assertion that bias entered into the categorical structure of thought and could, therefore, not be eliminated. All that could be done was to make these biases explicit so that the audience to which the social science works were addressed could "discount them" and "make allowances for them." This view implied that through the "discounting" of bias and "making allowance for" bias, its distorting effects could be eliminated and what remained would be objective knowledge.

This line of argument did not escape from the assumption of the possibility of objective knowledge. Wirth did not press his analysis very far, and he did not apply it to his own work. In his sociological writings in the last years of his life and his contributions to the reports of the National Resources Planning Board, the same objectivist at-titude prevailed as had been expressed in the writings of his intellec-tual ancestors and patrons, Small, Thomas, and Park. Like Small, Wirth was a sympathizer with and even active in reform movements, at first local and later on the national stage. Yet, when he put forward

---

attempt to strengthen their validity by interpreting them in their "relation" to the situation in which they were made. He cited the results as plainly, simply, and obviously true. He came to think that reality could be discovered, and that it had an existence independently of the "social position" of those who made assertions about it.

a factual analysis, he argued that it was disclosure of some really existent situation, a disclosure made possible by empirical research. His statements about bias were superimposed on the more traditional attitude which combined the belief in the attainability of objectively valid knowledge of society through "scientific procedure" with a desire to improve society through the "application" of that objectively valid knowledge. Wirth's acceptance of the inexpungibility of bias coexisted in his mind with the program of removing bias by the self-discipline of scientific method.[6]

Wirth's views reached a wider audience through their incorporation by Gunnar Myrdal into the "methodological appendix" of his *The American Dilemma*. Myrdal, more than a decade earlier, had exposed "the political element in economic theory." Now, as a result of his intensive discussions with Wirth in connection with the large-scale survey of the situation of the Negro in the United States, Myrdal formulated a solution which accepted the possibility of objective knowledge but which placed it beyond the reach of the social scientist; paradoxically, it was left to the reader of the social scientist's work to realize this possibility of objective knowledge. According to Myrdal—and his mentor, Wirth—the work of social science, given the universal inexpungibility of bias, could not be taken at its face value. What it offered had to be purified into objective truth by the reader, whose correction of the biased account was made possible by the investigator's avowal of his bias. It is important to point out that Myrdal in the text of his important works on the American Negro and on South and Southeast Asia, as did Wirth in the essays which he published in the last decade of his life, wrote as if what he said about society was true and did not need to be "discounted" by corrections which compensated for his bias.

In the then prevailing atmosphere of positivism in social science, Mannheim's idea, through Wirth and Myrdal, did not have a significant influence. The objectivity of knowledge was preserved as an attainable ideal. Throughout the decade, led by Ogburn, Burgess, Chapin, and Stouffer, joined in the second part of the decade by Lazarsfeld, sociologists were continuously active in trying to improve their scientific procedures so that the program of objective knowledge could be safeguarded and guaranteed. The more intensive and more sophisticated study of statistics by students of sociology and political science was one manifestation of this effort. The efforts devoted to the construction of attitude-scales, and the attention to techniques of interviewing, bore a similar witness.

Robert Lynd's *Knowledge for What?* which appeared shortly be-

6. Wirth wrote very little on this subject. His main publication on it was the introduction to the English translation of *Ideologie und Utopie*. Most of what I assert above is based on my recollection of my conversations with Wirth, and on his lectures and statements in seminars. I give so much space to him here because of his influence on Myrdal's "methodological appendix."

fore the Second World War, was the second rift in the culture of the social sciences of the 1930s. It had more influence than Mannheim's ideas. It was both a foreshadowing of what was to come more than a decade later as well as an echo of a past voice. Robert Lynd, like some of his predecessors in sociology, had been trained for the clergy and, like them, he believed that social science should be "used" for the improvement of society. He first appeared in sociology under the patronage of the Institute of Social and Religious Research. *Middletown* did not reveal his evangelical zeal. The tradition of the rural sociological studies of Charles Galpin which the Institute of Social and Religious Research continued and the factual anti-evolutionary anthropology of Franz Boas and Clark Wissler were the first influences on his outlook. *Middletown* was the product of that confluence. In the 1930s, he moved with the times; his second study of Muncie, Indiana—*Middletown in Transition*—saw a renascent evangelical attitude expressed in an idiom akin to the Marxism of the years of the depression. Class structure and the concentration of power through the concentration of wealth were emphasized in a way in which they had not been in *Middletown* itself. In accordance with the spirit of the times, Lynd's "social Christianity," which had been an ingredient of the reformatory interests of the preceding generation of sociologists became a radical, loosely Marxist, loosely populistic attitude. Nonetheless, Lynd did not challenge the possibility of attaining more reliable knowledge of society by the methods of social science. *Knowledge for What?* was not a criticism of objectivity; Lynd did not go in for epistemological refinements and he did not doubt that it was feasible to arrive at objectively valid knowledge of society. He criticized the American social sciences not for presenting a false account of what they actually studied but rather for contributing to a distorted picture of American society as a whole by the avoidance of certain problems of central importance. He charged them above all with failing to study the distribution of power in the United States and the consequences which followed from that.

Lynd's criticism of the American social sciences of the 1930s was that by their failure to study certain features of American society they did not serve the right cause, i.e., that they served ends which were injurious to the long-term interests of society as a whole; they served the parochial interests of the powerful. This attack came as a shock to many social scientists who had regarded Lynd as one of themselves; by virtue of *Middletown,* his professorship of sociology at Columbia University, and his contribution to *Recent Social Trends,* he was an important figure of professional sociology.[7] Sociologists had not been

7. At the Atlantic City meeting of the Sociological Research Association in 1937, Lynd, under the guidance of Paul Lazarsfeld, presented a devastating critique of Mannheim's *Ideology and Utopia.* He showed no sympathy for Mannheim's epistemological questioning of the prevailing belief in the possibility of an objective social science.

criticized from within the profession for studying trivial things nor had they been charged with avoiding more important subjects because of fear of facing the facts about their own societies. When Robert Park laid out an agenda for urban sociological research in his essay on "The City as a Spatial Pattern and a Moral Order" in 1915, he did not impugn the motives of sociologists who had not studied the subjects which he thought important. The Social Science Research Council initiated a series of monographs recommending research thought desirable on the social effects of the depression. The monographs were written by the leading figures in the various special fields of sociology of the 1930s. There was no implication that those who failed to investigate the recommended topics were morally reprehensible. This was an implication of Lynd's criticism. Lynd's criticism caused a ripple among sociologists because he suggested that they had been subservient to those who wished to preserve the main features of the existing order of society.

This criticism of academic social science in the United States had in fact been foreshadowed by Mannheim in a long review of *Methods in Social Science: A Case Book* (edited by Stuart Rice on behalf of the Social Science Research Council).[8] In that review Mannheim made the point that American sociologists did not study the deeper issues of conflicts about power but had been preoccupied with the smaller problems of the internal adjustments of the various ethnic groups which he, like Lynd at a later time, thought trivial in comparison with class conflict, revolutionary movements, the power of the very wealthy classes, and the like. Mannheim's observations fell on deaf ears; perhaps he was not well enough known at that time, perhaps a long book review was not an effective organ. Lynd's criticism about seven years later gained more attention but it did not have any effect on the character of sociological research.

V

Sociologists had in the past studied what interested them and, after research in the social sciences began to become expensive, they studied those subjects for which they could obtain financial support. Large grants were few and far between and those who received them and those who failed to do so saw no danger to the intellectual integrity of the social sciences in these grants. The interest of foundation officials in the promotion of scientific social sciences was accredited by all. The fact that the foundations legitimated their support of social science by the belief that the study of socially important problems

8. Karl Mannheim, "American Sociology," in *Essays on Sociology and Social Psychology* (London: Routledge and Kegan Paul, 1953), pp. 185–94; originally published in *The American Journal of Sociology* 38, no. 2 (September 1932): 273–82.

would contribute to the improvement of society was of a piece with the social scientists' own convictions. Both the patrons of social research and the social scientists were equally convinced that nothing less than scientific knowledge should be their first objective. Only if the social sciences were built up in that way could the science be used for social improvement.

When research was an activity undertaken by academic social scientists single-handedly or with an assistant—often a graduate student who was paid a meagre stipend—or through graduate students working on dissertations, social scientists studied what interested them. They might be interested in a particular subject-matter, e.g., juvenile gangs in Chicago, or they might be interested in a general problem, e.g., the cultural effects of "social marginality," or they might be interested in a phenomenon such as juvenile delinquency. They often conducted such studies in the belief that it would be of practical value to their society to know the mechanisms of operation of the phenomena which they studied. There were not many cases in which social scientists studied a subject in which they were not interested but which they studied nevertheless because someone or some institution paid them to do it. Even when they did study a subject proposed to them by an external body or by the concerns of the public opinion, they followed their own intellectual bent in procedure and interpretation. The studies of the Americanization of immigrants which the Carnegie Foundation sponsored at the end of the First World War and for which the collaboration of Robert Park and William I. Thomas was enlisted were on a straight line from their previous work on ethnic groups, which they had initiated entirely on the basis of their own intellectual curiosity. Charles Johnson's work on *The Negro in Chicago,* done under Park's supervision, was commissioned and subsidized by the Commission on Race Relations but the work itself was a characteristic piece of work of the Chicago sociology of that time.

The greatest commissioned, collaborative inquiry of the period was *Recent Social Trends.* It was guided intellectually by William Ogburn, Wesley Mitchell, Howard Odum, and Charles Merriam; its financial support was provided privately but the initiative which led to it owed much to President Herbert Hoover. Hoover took a great interest in the work and had high hopes for its contribution to governmental policy, but he did not affect the procedure or the interpretation. It was a grandiose work, unprecedented in its time and probably unequalled since then. It drew on the labors of many of the leading social scientists of the country. Procedurally, it attained a high point in the tradition of quantitative description, the chief exponent of which was Ogburn; theoretically it showed the influence of the theory of "cultural lag" which was also Ogburn's creation. It did not study every aspect of American society. Since the available data did not cover all phases of the many subjects studied, it was often impossible to answer questions of deep interest. It would certainly be very difficult to demonstrate any bias in the work other than that contained in Ogburn's own determination to assert what he thought could be scientifically demonstrated and his beliefs about "cultural lag." "[A]ccuracy and reliability are more important in such an undertaking than the zeal to do good."[9] Certainly neither the federal government's nor the foundations' political beliefs were in evidence, and no social scientist of the time believed that the sponsorship and source of financial support had intruded substantively or conceptually into the work itself.

To refuse to deal with a problem out of the conviction that the existing body of data and the accumulated understanding of the problem do not permit scientifically authoritative conclusions is one thing. To avoid dealing with it because one does not wish to incur the disfavor of wealthy persons, university administrators, or powerful politicians or because one is apprehensive about the censure one might incur through the disclosure of unpalatable truths is another. Recent critics of American social science have amalgamated these motives so as to make it appear that the assertion of the first reason was really a mask to hide the second. This procedure has nothing but polemical rhetoric to recommend it. It makes it appear that the proponents and practitioners of the social sciences up to the coming of the Second World War did not actually believe what they said about their desire to contribute to the advancement of a scientific study of society or about their belief in its feasibility. It suggests that they were aware that what they studied was trivial but that they feared to study subjects they knew were important because they knew that they would suffer for it.

These imputations, for which there is no evidence, imply that the academic social scientists really knew better than they said; they knew what the "important problems" really were but they did not study them because they did not dare to do so, given the probability of sanctions against them if they did. According to this view, the social scientists of the half century which ended in about 1940 knew what was what in society, i.e., they shared the beliefs about society of contemporary and subsequent radicals but, for reasons of self-advancement or of self-protection, they deliberately refrained from conducting investigations which would confirm their suppressed radical beliefs.

Even those critics who do not make these insinuations of cowardice and hypocrisy are unwilling to take at their face value the reforming intentions of the social scientists or their belief that a scientific body of knowledge about society could be created by systematic investigation

9. Introduction to *Monographs on Recent Social Trends*.

and analysis. The critics do not appreciate that if Charles Henderson, for instance, wished to reduce alcoholism in the working classes, the study of the consumption of alcohol in the working classes in Chicago in 1905 was to him an important problem. Problems are important to those to whom they are important! Scientifically, macrosociological problems are not more important than microsociological problems. Yet it has been a recurrent refrain of radical critics of academic social science that it has been "avoiding" macrosociological problems out of considerations of personal and professional prudence.

The fact is that the social scientists were for the most part progressive liberals and they studied those subjects which needed to be better understood and more widely known if ameliorative action was to be taken. It is probably true that, if they had been revolutionary radicals, they would not have been appointed in the first place and promoted thereafter. But they were not revolutionary radicals. The revolutionary, radical, Marxist view of society did not attract them intellectually because with all their limitations of intellect and culture they did not find it adequate. They were, unless very strong evidence to the contrary is produced, honest scholars and compassionate patriots. They were optimists about the potentialities of their subject to become scientific and they were also optimistic regarding the improvability of their society, particularly if it drew on the scientific knowledge which was still to be created.

Lynd's criticism of sociologists for a timorous and hypocritical avoidance of "important problems" came just at the moment when the country and its social scientists were about to become preoccupied with the war and when social science was entering into the height of its glory. Although Lynd was one of the most respected American sociologists of his time and was well liked personally as well, his polemic against the prevailing sociology and his accusation of subservience to patrons and powers did not arouse an observable response. Social scientists took for granted, as their predecessors had, that they and their colleagues would be concerned with the practical problems of their society. Even the most scientistic social scientists had never claimed to be totally indifferent to the well-being of society and its improvement; they had only insisted that men must not meddle ignorantly in complex affairs but should intervene, if at all, only on the basis of scientifically valid knowledge.

Sociology was, in its first establishment in American universities, predominantly a middle-western subject; the academic profession of sociology, moreover, drew to itself many persons who had been brought up in strict Christian households; a fairly large minority had been trained to be Christian clergymen. It grew up in an atmosphere of moral seriousness, populism, the social gospel, and municipal reform. Except for Lester Ward, who had been a federal civil servant for most of his life, and Charles Cooley, who was a federal civil servant for a short time, sociologists before 1914 had little contact with government, least of all with the federal government. A few of them, most notably Ogburn, served in the federal government during the First World War. The first large-scale contact of sociologists with the federal government was the interest and sponsorship which Herbert Hoover provided for the *Recent Social Trends* inquiry. Rural sociologists had a good deal of contact with state governments, particularly with state departments of agriculture. Urban sociologists had little contact with governments; they were more intimately connected with private civic and welfare associations, sometimes sponsoring their causes, usually drawing on them to gain access to the data which they needed for their research.

Economists and political scientists had much more contact with the federal government. Political scientists in the three decades which ended in the early 1920s, were less directly influenced by vaguely religious concerns, but they too were reformist. Government was their subject-matter, and they were critical of the achievements of American governmental institutions of the decades just before and after the turn of the century. Much of the literature of political science was concerned with populistic reforms such as initiative, referendum and recall, the cleansing of the civil service, the improvement of legislative organization and procedure, and the washing away of the shame of the cities.

But even though the political scientists were more at home with the affairs of government, they were not very confident of it in its existing form. Charles Merriam, who had been an alderman and a candidate for the mayoralty of Chicago, was an unremitting critic of municipal government as it was practiced before the First World War. If political scientists were more inclined to look upon the federal government to serve as an organ of the public interest, it was largely for negative reasons. They thought it was less corrupt than municipal government and local politics and less immovable for the ends of reform than the state governments. Progressivism before the First World War and the New Deal before the Second World War and Presidents Theodore Roosevelt, Woodrow Wilson, and Franklin Roosevelt helped to attach the political scientists to the federal government as a means of realizing improvement in society. Their own contribution to this improvement was to lie in providing the realistic knowledge acquired by scientific means, as a basis for the action of the people's representatives.

Political science, despite its name, had less pretensions to the status of a science than sociology, perhaps because its academic standing was older and more secure, and because, claiming Aristotle, Plato, Cicero, Locke, and Rousseau as its ancestors and subject-matter, it had good connections with established academic disciplines and a special relationship to the intellectual traditions of the founders of the Republic. The political scientists lived more in the tradition of modern historical scholarship than did sociologists but they too were reformers and they did not see any incompatibility between being at the same time reformers and scrupulously dispassionate scholars. They regarded cooperation with government, particularly the federal government, as desirable because it appeared to them to heighten the probability of their influence for the public good. They did not see a judicious proximity to government as a threat to their intellectual integrity.

Anthropology was academically and numerically a fledgling subject. Under the inspiration of Franz Boas it had, on behalf of a meticulous factuality, renounced far-flung evolutionary theories. Its objectivity could not be placed in doubt; nor did it object to its marginal relationships with the federal government. The federal government was one of the greatest patrons of anthropology; the *Reports* of the Bureau of Ethnology were an essential part of the tradition of American anthropology. Anthropologists saw no reason to avoid contact with the federal government, as long as they were allowed to study the problems which seemed to them to be scientifically important. The mastery of the techniques of ethnography seemed to them to provide the protection they needed against the inroads of political and moral bias.

The academic economists were at the other extreme from the anthropologists. They were involved in government intellectually and increasingly in practice. The liberal or "laissez-faire" economists had to face and argue against the growing trend in public opinion for governmental intervention into the economic sphere. They engaged in public contention about tariffs and monetary policy. They did not approve of governmental action but they did not worry about any corrupting effects of governmental service on the practice of economic research and analysis. They had confidence in the intellectual tradition of their discipline and in the good intellectual character of their colleagues.

The other kind of economic analysts, namely, the "institutional" economists, were perfectly confident of the powers and capacities of a properly conducted government. They knew that the American governmental system needed improvement; otherwise it could not meet the requirement of the far-reaching and penetrating intervention and regulation which they thought vital to a well-conducted society. They too thought of this improved government as basing itself upon the scientific knowledge which economic research would provide. They welcomed close connections between economists and government. They saw only the improving effects of the former on the latter; they had no anxiety that economists might be "corrupted" by being drawn into government as officials or as advisors.

Thus, reform, the advancement of the public good through cooperation with private bodies or government, the acceptance of sponsorship and even financial support from such sources, and scrupulous objectivity in observation and in the analysis of data gathered through careful observation, all seemed perfectly compatible with each other. The criticisms that they were avoiding social responsibility by studying problems of less than primary importance would not have impressed most social scientists of the period up to the Second World War. They were studying the phenomena which they thought important in the light of their own—widely shared—ethical and political convictions and they were studying them by means of techniques, concepts, and theories which they and their scholar-ancestors had devised according to their best lights.

That is why Lynd's *Knowledge for What?* seemed an oddity in his time. Veblen had said much the same in *The Higher Learning in America* but his views had not been taken seriously. But at Columbia University, the message by Veblen and Lynd did find a vigorous continuation in C. Wright Mills, whose *The Sociological Imagination* appeared in 1959. This time the message was not passed over. It received much more sympathetic response, especially by the younger generation of social scientists. Mills, when he wrote *The Sociological Imagination*, [10] was already a very well established sociologist. In this respect he was in the same position as Lynd, whose *Middletown* had placed him in the front rank of American sociologists. There was, however, a difference. Lynd, despite the Marxist-populistic tinge of *Middletown in Transition,* was regarded by others and himself as a proper sociologist. Mills was in a different position. He was critical of the prevailing sociology from a position which was first formed under Veblen's influence and later came to be guided by Marx and Trotsky. He deliberately cultivated the role of an "outsider." At a time when the fortunes of the "left" were at low ebb in the United States, Mills declared himself a "leftist"—although in fact much of his sociology was part of the stock in trade of the prevailing variants of sociology. He was interested in macrosociology, he was interested in the sociology of knowledge, he was against quantification, and he was critical of the theories of Professor Parsons. All of these elements existed in American sociology. He joined them together into a rhetorically distinctive position. By putting it into radical rhetoric and by espousing radical political positions, he began to draw to himself a following of the younger social scientists who were not at ease in the sociological Zion of the time.

The flush of the first great victories of the social sciences of the period after the war had already begun to fade. Senator McCarthy was dead and had no powerful successors. Students and teachers of radi-

10. New York: Oxford University Press, 1959.

cal inclinations were no longer so intimidated as they had been. "Poverty" had just been discovered. Enormous numbers of students were enrolled in social science departments and many of them were being taught by young teachers of low academic status with uncompleted qualifications. Many graduate students and young and middle-aged teachers were cynical about the research which they were expected to do as doctoral dissertations or as part of the struggle for academic existence. In the larger universities where most of these persons worked, dissertations were often chips off the huge blocks of data assembled on large-scale research projects. The prosperity of the sample surveys, which were such an achievement in the movement of the social sciences towards scientific objectivity, also bred discontent.

Mills' critique of sociological research was written at Columbia University, where the tradition of Robert Lynd's earlier critique seemed more pertinent than ever since it was there that sample surveys were being conducted on a larger scale than ever before and where the systematic training of graduate students of sociology in the new methods of scientific research was most advanced. The training in survey technique there was the most demanding in the country and therefore a more tangible source of discomfort and a more visible target for criticism. The enlarged scale of research required a corresponding enlargement of financial resources; these came for the most part from government, private business, and private foundations. The warnings of Veblen and Lynd now seemed more pertinent than they had hitherto appeared to be.

Mills' criticism of empirical research referred to a common experience; it had an audience ready to hand. The charge of serving the "interests" of the powerful, of lulling the conscience by the guaranteed objectivity of scientific procedures and of obscuring the "realities" of society by technical concerns appeared to have a more evident foundation. His animadversions against the techniques of survey research as practiced and taught by Professor Lazarsfeld and Merton were made more resonant by his recasting of Lynd's argument concerning the avoidance of the study of power and inequality. He accused the reigning sociology of being preoccupied with trivial "milieux," by which he meant what is now called "microsociology," instead of concentrating its efforts on what is now called "macrosociology." He alleged—incorrectly—that American sociology failed to deal with "social change," either because it wished to prevent it or because its conservative desires made it impossible for it to acknowledge "social change" and because its favorite theory theory blinded it to such central events.

Lynd had not denied the objectivity of the traditional method of research to which he himself had been a major contributor. Mills went a little further to castigate the use of quantitative survey methods, but in an appendix to *The Sociological Imagination* he set forth the main lines of the technique of research which he regarded as most conducive to truthful results. It was more favorable to impressionistic research than the quantitative emphasis of recent years had recommended, but, except for that, it accepted the prevailing positivism.

After Mills, the criticism of sociology began to cover a wider range, extending the positions of Mannheim, Lynd, and Mills into new accusations. Mannheim's epistemological relativism was revived by a graduate of Columbia University, Professor Alvin Gouldner, who made all sociological knowledge a function of "background assumptions"—a beclouded amalgam of desires, attachments, and beliefs. Interpretations of the ideas of Professor Thomas Kuhn about "scientific revolutions," which stressed the cognitive arbitrariness of the "paradigms" instituted by "scientific revolutions," gave additional rhetorical force to Professor Gouldner's relativism. (Like all other relativists, Professor Gouldner put forward his arguments as though they were entitled to acceptance on grounds other than the "background assumptions" of those to whom they were addressed.)

Professor Gouldner's sociologistic epistemology was complemented and elaborated by the reiteration of the arguments made by his masters at Columbia, Lynd and Mills. They charged sociologists with preoccupation with trivial problems and intimated that it was because of pusillanimous prudence and the dominance of the patrons of research. Professor Gouldner went further by adding that sociology in the United States had been reduced to the status of being an instrument of the powerful in American society, for whom it provided a useful device of effective control. He added insult to injury to assert that American sociology had become like sociology in the Soviet Union. The convergence in the substance and function of sociology as practiced in these two countries was a consequence of the convergence of the two societies themselves. Thus Professor Gouldner brought together into a single book the epistemological and political criticisms.

There was also another implication of Professor Gouldner's view. This was that sociology had been reduced to a branch of the technology of subjugation. Numerous lesser mirrors reflected this smoky light to the accompaniment of loud cries. The charge that sociology had been turned by its practitioners and patrons into an instrument of "internal colonialism" was an accompaniment of the "student revolution" and it has not, at least up to the present, received a serious exposition.

Meanwhile the mass of the sociological profession has gone its way. The criticisms have been noted and passed over. At the margins of the profession, some sociologists reiterate the accusations and then continue much as before. Sociologists still study "social problems"; they study the patterns of urban settlement; the family, drug addiction, social stratification and mobility (now called "structured inequality"), delinquency and criminality, large organizations, ethnic groups, professions, and almost all the subjects which they studied a half-century ago; and they study quite a few relatively new ones which are variants of the older ones. Corresponding to their greater numbers, they produce a larger body of literature on each of these subjects, so large, indeed, that it can barely be read by those who do not specialize in the subject in question. Despite some shifts in public and academic opinion as to what constitutes a "significant problem," the guiding interpretative ideas have a striking continuity. Some older writers are revived, and other older writers maintain a continuing vitality. The newer writers, even those who denounce the tradition of "meliorism" and what they vaguely call "value-free" research, do not escape from the tradition of sociology. The addition of Karl Marx to the ancestry of sociology scarcely changes the substance of sociology. It does change its rhetoric, and even then much of the profession of sociology remains obdurate.

The "establishment" of sociology—so much inveighed against by radical sociologists—is genuine. The possibilities of careers in the profession of sociology, which became numerous and attractive to many young persons, and the pressure of expectations and the qualifications for advancement as well as the ethos of the profession itself and the lack of fundamental originality among most of its members, including those who bridle against it, all exercise a compelling force for continuation along certain lines of inquiry and on certain substantive themes.

But with all this continuity of the heterogenous and variously linked traditions of sociology, there have also been large changes in its situation which merit examination. They merit examination because they do raise issues, issues which, in a distorted and almost deranged form, have been raised by some of the more or less radical critics of sociology. They deserve more serious discussion than they have received. The change in the scale of financial support and the source of such support is one of these issues.

Since funds for sociological research are limited, decisions must be made as to who is to receive them. Those who decide the allocations are not those who will do the proposed research. It is not unreasonable to think that the direction of sociology could be much influenced by the deciding bodies which are not themselves made up of sociologists. And even if they were, the direction of sociology might be influenced by the criteria preferred by the deciding sociologists. The hypersensitivity of radical academics to the improper influence of government and private business in their own capitalistic society—the problem is never considered for socialistic countries—has prompted accusations against the arrogance of patrons and the subservience of sociologists and the resulting deformation of sociology.

When research first became so expensive that those who could not afford to pay the costs of their research from their own private or academic incomes could not do research, and when research became almost mandatory for academic social scientists, the situation was not seen to raise any ethical problems. For one thing, patronage was scant and its distribution ad hoc. Before the First World War, a sociologist who needed funds for his research sought out an individual patron whom he thought to be sympathetic. The patron would seldom have definite ideas of what research should be about, and the personal connection could be counted upon to assure the freedom of the investigator to go his own way. Thomas and Znaniecki's *Polish Peasant in Europe and America* was supported by a wealthy lady in Chicago. No questions were ever raised about the propriety of this patronage and no one ever suggested that Thomas and Znaniecki's views about the Polish peasants in Poland and the United States were in any way affected by the source of the financial support for their inquiry.

After the First World War, private foundations (particularly the Carnegie Corporation and the Laura Spelman Rockefeller Fund) began to make substantial grants for social research. Their role increased greatly in the 1930s, and after the Second World War the Rockefeller and the Ford Foundations and the Carnegie Corporation became the chief supporters of significant social science research in the United States. The federal government has more recently become an unprecedented patron of sociological research. The National Science Foundation, the Department of Health, Education and Welfare, the National Institute of Mental Health, and other parts of the government are now the major supporters of large-scale research and they are increasingly coming to support even the research which in the past would have been done from the investigator's own resources.

The suggestion that the system of authority obtaining in the United States today is utilizing sociological research and its results to strengthen its "oppressive control," in any sense in which that term has traditionally been used, cannot stand a moment's scrutiny. It is not however unreasonable to inquire into the question whether the support of sociological research by private foundations or the federal government has affected the intellectual integrity of the social sciences. By intellectual integrity I mean the strict observance of intellectual criteria in the conduct of an investigation, i.e., in the collection of data, in the analysis and interpretation of the data, and in the formulation of the conclusions of the investigation. This entails, at the very beginning, strict adherence to intellectual criteria in the selection of the variables to be examined, given the problem at hand.

The great social scientists of the nineteenth and early twentieth centuries, long before the appearance of the great private foundations as patrons of social science, always chose their problems and subject-matters of investigation entirely according to their own lights. They were guided by what they regarded as intellectually important; they regarded intellectually important results as throwing light on problems of fundamental importance to society, namely, the problems concerning the maintenance and change of social order. All of these eminent figures dealt with problems which they thought were relevant to the understanding of their own societies and this entailed a concern for events and conditions which were morally problematic in the view of intelligent public opinion in their societies. They took their point of departure in their own societies; they attempted to enhance the understanding of the situation or condition of their own societies—as wholes or in their parts. When they were interested in a particular situation or condition of their respective societies, they simultaneously had a deeper interest in the natures of the societies in which they lived. This more general, more fundamental analysis is what makes them still interesting to us. The interest which subsequent generations have taken in their works is evidence of the persuasive power of their analyses which transcended the immediate situations or conditions of their own times. They contributed to the formation of the intellectual tradition of subsequent generations. Their interest in the particular details of their societies was the occasion for the coming into play of their analytical powers and it is the product of those analytical powers which constitutes their merit. Neither Auguste Comte, David Ricardo, John Stuart Mill, Herbert Spencer, Henry Sumner Maine, Karl Marx, Ferdinand Tönnies, Max Weber, George Simmel, W. I. Thomas, Frederic Le Play, Emile Durkheim, nor Gabriel Tarde received subsidies from large foundations or from governments for their books. Nor did Freud receive any subsidy from a foundation or from a government.

It is not likely that Marx or Weber or Freud or Durkheim would have adulterated his fundamental interpretation of society or man because an official of a foundation or a governmental official who paid his salary or provided him with funds to cover the costs of his research would have affected his lines of interpretation. I have never heard or seen any allegation that Marx tempered his interpretations to please Engels, who contributed to his financial support, or that Max Weber's ideas about religion were deformed from what they would have been otherwise because he received a salary from a ministry of education. The great founders of sociological analysis are credited with intellectual character strong enough to resist the desire to please the powerful by offering them works which would flatter their prejudices and conform with their wishes.

The lesser but still outstanding figures in the history of sociology who have flourished since then—Robert Park, Ernest Burgess, Samuel Stouffer, William Ogburn, Karl Mannheim, Robert Merton, Maurice Halbwachs, and Raymond Aron—have carried on the intellectual traditions of the founders of present-day sociological analysis. These social scientists have invariably faced the facts discovered through their inquiries, regardless of whether they were supported by governments and private foundations, in the light of their inherited standards of scientific objectivity and the substantive traditions of their subjects. The substantive traditions of sociological analysis are extraordinarily powerful and it is difficult to go beyond them or to break away from them. Their influence is far more powerful than that of patronage on the course of sociological studies. Changes in these traditions are the products of the exertions of original minds capable of strenuous and original intellectual exertion. Such minds are not affected in their fundamental propensities and convictions by the sources of the financial support of their research or by the wishes of those who allocate this support.

It is true that officials of private foundations and officials of governmental bodies who allocate funds for sociological research do have a preference for research on subjects which they think are important for an understanding of situations which they think are problematic and which should be better described and understood. The officials of the Laura Spelman Rockefeller Fund thought that urban life needed to be better understood, just as the officials of the Carnegie Corporation wanted to have "the Negro problem" better understood and the Adjutant General's Office wished to have a better understanding of the characteristics and behavior of American soldiers. The officials of the Department of Health, Education, and Welfare and of the National Institute of Mental Health wish to have a better understanding of juvenile delinquency and narcotics addiction. The fact that they then agree to allocate funds for the study of these subjects is not the same as stipulating what sociologists should say on these subjects, apart from demanding that the best techniques and theories of sociology should be applied in the conduct of these studies, from their formulation to their conclusion. In arriving at their decisions these officials, who in many cases have themselves been well-qualified students of the subjects under consideration, draw on the advisory assessments of leading scholars active in each particular field.

Nonetheless, it is probably true that the decisions of officials do have an effect on the attention to or disregard for certain particular subject-matters. This however is a very different thing from the proposition that the fundamental theoretical lines of interpretation are guided by these decisions about particular subject-matters. Robert Park formulated his scheme for the study of urban society in 1915, some years before the Laura Spelman Rockefeller Fund made money available to the Local Community Research Council which aided the numerous sociological studies of Chicago; these were done entirely in the spirit of, i.e., in accordance with the lines of interpretation and the techniques developed by, Robert Park and Ernest Burgess. The sponsorship by Herbert Hoover and the financial support by the Rockefeller Foundation certainly did not determine either the mode of collection of data or its analyses which appeared in *Recent Social Trends* and the monographs produced in connection with it. An examination of Ogburn's *Social Change* and a knowledge of his commitment to quantitative description ever since the second decade of the century would surely disabuse anyone who believed that. The Carnegie Corporation supplied the funds for the study of *The Negro in America* but no one acquainted with the studies of the Negro guided by Robert Park and by his disciples from the time he first joined the University of Chicago before the First World War, and with Myrdal's work as an economist in Sweden, would insist that it was the views of the officials of the Carnegie Corporation which provided the lines of interpretation and the resultant account of the situation of Negroes in the United States.

Critics of these investigations might still think that the investigators were wrong in their interpretations or that they studied insignificant problems. They might insist that Park and Ogburn and later Stouffer and others failed to see important problems. There are legitimate differences, however, in the estimation of important problems. I myself think that Wright Mills did deal with important problems in some of his works, but he certainly did not deal with all the important problems, and in any case the validity of his conclusions was even more open to rational denial than the more meticulous and more circumspect conclusions arrived at by Ogburn, by Park's followers, including Myrdal, and by Stouffer.

To reject the criticisms of Lynd, Mills, and Gouldner is not the same as to regard the views of the dominant figures of sociology of the earlier decades of the present century about the potentialities of their subject in its relations to the society they studied as unqualifiedly acceptable. It seems to me that those earlier figures who were interested in the "application" of sociological knowledge were far too uncritical about how the knowledge which they hoped would be produced by sociologists would be translated into the action of society. They took for granted that once the knowledge pertinent to action regarding a problematic feature of society was discovered or created and was made available to "society," it was bound to be acted upon and with beneficial effects. Quite apart from their confidence in the openness of public opinion to the results of sociological research, they gave little or no thought to the institutional arrangements for the transmission of that knowledge. When Robert Park was a young man, he was drawn to the project for a journal which was to be called *Thought-News,* but this was before he was a sociologist. As far as I know, he did not recur to the problems of the diffusion of sociological knowledge and its incorporation into action. But then he was no reformer. Small, Henderson, Burgess, Ogburn, Mannheim, and the others who believed that sociological knowledge should be assimilated into the practical improvement of society did not give any thought to these matters. (The Marxist ideas on these subjects were a little more explicit but even more crudely technological. According to Lenin in *What Is to Be Done?,* professional revolutionaries would persuade aggrieved workingmen of the correctness of scientific socialism, whereupon they would become revolutionaries and establish a dictatorship of the revolutionary party which would impose on the rest of the society a pattern derived from the scientific study of the laws of motion of society!)

In the 1920s and 1930s, when the philanthropic enterprises of the Rockefeller family supported the advancement of sociological research, the trustees and administrators gave this support in the belief that there were important "social problems" which had to be "solved" and that a scientific social science would play the same part in this undertaking as the biological and physical sciences had played in the improvement of medical treatment and agricultural production.

Both Charles Merriam and William Ogburn, particularly the latter, were essentially "technocratic" in their ideas regarding the "application" of social science. The conflicts between Merriam and Ogburn regarding the relationship which should be allowed between President Hoover and the investigators during the course of the work in *Recent Social Trends* indicates that Ogburn had no hesitations about the technological status of social science. Merriam, who had much more political experience than Ogburn and who was also more confident of the power of the electorate and its representatives, spoke very nebulously about "democratic planning" and the role which social science could play in that. Yet the National Resources Planning Board was attached to the executive office of the president and was as "technocratic" as an arrangement could be where the concurrence of the legislature was required.

VI

In the nineteenth century, in those countries which inherited the traditions of the Enlightenment, the ethical value of the knowledge of society was unproblematic. The scientific knowledge of society did not occupy the high status of the knowledge of the cosmos of physical nature and of reflection on the good order of society and on the nature of man. Most thinkers of the Enlightenment did not conceive of the possibility of a science of society. Much of what we would now consider social science came under political and moral philosophy and universal history. Nevertheless what there was of the knowledge of society was regarded as a contribution to the *progrès des lumiéres.* Truth was one of the highest goods, man's self-knowledge was a moral obligation. There was confidence that the exercise of the observational and rational analytical powers could only be good. Only obscurantists, whose position in society and whose self-esteem rested on the prejudice, ignorance, and error of the mass of the population could fear the continuing growth of truth. What was needed was to free the mind from the hindrance which impeded its continuous expansion into all corners of the universe. Man's pursuit of knowledge of himself, his society, and the universe was a morally elevating activity to those who did it, and the diffusion of its accomplishments could bring nothing but benefit to mankind.

These traditions, which still govern the minds of social scientists, had their origin in a time of very restricted literacy. Although philosophy in antiquity was not ordinarily confined to hermetic circles, much of its communication occurred in face-to-face situations between like-minded persons of high and more or less equal degrees of intellectual sophistication. When philosophers sought an audience beyond the circle of the philosophically minded, they addressed themselves to tyrants, princes, and the great of the earth. They sought to convert their auditors into philosophers. They anticipated that the beneficiaries of this philosophical self-transformation would then rule more wisely and justly than they would have done without the enrichment of their spirits by philosophy. They certainly did not look upon themselves as technologists who offered factual knowledge which could be "used" by the person who received it as a means to the attainment of his pre-existent ends.

In the Enlightenment, philosophical—now extended to include scientific—knowledge was presumed to be appropriate to a public broader than the stratum of princes and their immediate counselors and servants. Again knowledge was not conceived primarily as instrumental knowledge, as means for the attainment of ends which were logically disjunctive from the knowledge gained scientifically, although that conception had been gaining the ascendancy over the classical conception. Philosophical knowledge—including political and social philosophy—was envisaged as having effect through the clarification of the mind, the elimination of superstitious and traditionally founded beliefs which had no rational or empirical basis. As a result, conduct would be more reasonable, more tolerant, and more benevolent. Again, the effects of the diffusion of this proto-social scientific knowledge would be in the nature of the self-transformation of the person. First his mind and then his conduct would be improved. It did not envisage the improvement of conduct by any means other than the extended diffusion of knowledge. Since social science was not technological, there was little concern with the possibility of manipulation. The problem was raised by Condorcet's conception of social science, but he did not acknowledge the problem nor did any one else.

By the latter part of the nineteenth century, social science had acquired many enemies among those who were attached to the traditional hierarchical order of society and who affirmed the truth and value of religious belief. This was not so much because of the cognitive substance of the social sciences but because of the more general outlook which pervaded them. There were overtones of moral relativism in the social sciences, especially in the ethnographic evolutionary kind of sociology which suggested the principle of *autre temps, autre moeurs*. Comparative sociological studies in embryonic form and ethnography often bore an overtone of criticism of the incumbent authorities of the writer's own age and country. Comtean sociology and in consequence other kinds of sociology proceeded quite forcefully on the postulate that the old order was finished and its disappearance awaited only a sufficient spread of enlightenment. Sociology and socialism were often confused by those who knew little of either, but the amalgamation was not utterly unjustified. Many sociologists of the empirical sort were acutely interested in social reforms, and those who out of skepticism about the eradicability of evil or out of "vested interest" had no high regard for reform saw sociology as a foolish and possibly pernicious affair. These attitudes gradually faded and by the 1920s social science was being looked to, particularly in the United States, as a solvent of the difficulties of society. Nothing but good could come of it; so at least it was thought at that time, and this view gathered adherents as the decades passed. This was so in the United States where it was part of a thriving scientistic outlook; it became increasingly so in Western Europe too. As a good in itself and as a good in its consequences, the advancement of social science seemed to raise no problems. All that it had to do was to become more scientific. In doing so it would be fulfilling its own inherent destiny and it would make itself fit to deal with the practical tasks which were expected of it.

Reflective and erudite observations about the mind and society were formed through the study of books and from the experience of life in society. Except for cases of ethnographic observation, this kind of knowledge did not involve direct, deliberate, firsthand observation in which knowledge of the persons observed was the primary end. The procedures for acquiring knowledge of man's life in society have changed profoundly since the Enlightenment. The social scientist's relationships outside the circle of those who are identical with himself have in consequence acquired a new dimension.

The expansion of fieldwork in social anthropology, carrying on from the traditions of inquisitive travelers, ships' physicians, missionaries, and colonial administrators, likewise did not give any explicit consideration to the ethical problem of the relations of the investigator to those he investigates. Such consideration was perhaps not necessary when the investigator dwelt for an extended period in a village, because he could not attain a position in which he would gain the villagers' confidences about their society unless he rendered himself acceptable to them by his amiability, courtesy, and friendliness. There was not much point in explaining the observer's scholarly and scientific interests to those who had not sufficient education of a sort to enable them to appreciate the intentions of social-anthropological investigation. Furthermore, the indigenous poeples accepted the investigator as a person connected with their colonial rulers, and they usually submitted to his inquiries accordingly. What he ultimately published about them was most unlikely to come to their attention; it would be read only by a narrow circle of colleagues and perhaps a handful of officials. Its effectiveness would expire before it ever reached those who were the objects of inquiry.

The large-scale social surveys of the conditions of the poor in the latter part of the nineteenth and in the early twentieth centuries had sufficient moral justification in the minds of the investigators—they were seeking means of improving the conditions of the poor as a class—for few questions to be raised in their minds. The Springfield Survey was regarded by those who carried it on, and by those who admired it, as a communal undertaking—as an enterprise of the "entire community"—which would provide the intellectual basis for an effort of collective self-improvement.

Thus, social scientists generally had a good conscience; they were serving the interests of the advancement of knowledge. They were gathering information which would be of value to the efforts to improve society, and it seemed reasonable to expect that those whose lives were studied would be willing to cooperate by allowing themselves to be observed. What is more, no harm could come from knowledge disinterestedly sought by means of procedures which were accredited through the acknowledged achievements of past scientific research.

This situation began to change with the development of a new technology of observation. The use of "one-way" screens, of undeclared transmitting, amplifying, and recording devices, of hidden cameras, and of the extension to social psychology of the experimental procedures of psychophysics and the other more scientific parts of psychology were stages in this change. These technical innovations brought with them opportunities and temptations; these created new responsibilities of withholding information from the subjects of research, of giving them false information, and, in a variety of other ways, of treating them as objects to whom the investigators had none of the ordinary obligations of social life.

When certain of the new observational devices were employed in the study of infants and children, there was not only a transference of the "scientific" attitude from psychophysics and the other scientific branches of psychology, but there was also no challenge from the subjects themselves. Early social psychological experiments were often carried out on school children and on undergraduates enrolled in social psychology courses; in a deferential age, they did as they were instructed. Even if they were not under the authority of their teachers, they entered into the spirit of the thing and raised no questions. Frightening them, embarrassing them, observing aspects of their behavior, which they had not been told were to be observed—all these seemed to fall within the rights of "scientists" whose ascendancy was reinforced by their pedagogical authority.

In recent years there has been a rather extended discussion of the ethical problems raised by experimentation on human beings. Quite recently there has been some rather critical attention paid to an experiment on black prisoners in which certain methods of treatment of venereal diseases were investigated. The fact that the prisoners were black made the criticism even more pointed. A rising wave of distrust of scientists and of the medical profession and the sensitivity of prominent blacks to affronts to the dignity of black men and women were important in bringing the affair to public attention. Yet, at the same time, social scientists, sociologists, students of public administration, and economists have been urging that more large-scale social experiments should be carried out.

The increased resources available for social research, the increased technical imaginativeness of social scientists and their greater concern for affairs closer to the center of society than the poor, the immigrants, the ethnic minorities, the children, and the criminals on whom they used to concentrate their inquiries have all contributed to bringing the social sciences onto a collision course. Their greater aspirations for more rigorous, more intensive, and more comprehensive studies have had the same effect. And finally the availability of a powerful technology of research and a more effective organization works in the same direction.

The movement towards the establishment of data banks stored in computers brings all these factors together. When data banks were first discussed by social scientists, they had no concern for the protection of the privacy of the persons they studied; data about these persons would be consolidated, stored, and made available without their approval. The gradualness of the evolution from the use of governmental statistics and the observations of "experts" like clergymen, probation officers, governmental inspectors, and magistrates to direct observation by sociologists and then to participant-observation obscured the issue. Nevertheless, much sociological research does entail an intrusion into the private sphere of the individuals studied. There should be a more ample exploration of the implications of this intrusion and the justifications for it.

Another ethical problem of sociological research is raised by the possibility of "social experiments." It has not been in the tradition of sociology to conduct experiments. For many years one of the reasons adduced for the scientific backwardness of sociology was the impossibility of experimentation on society. Experimentation appeared ethically unthinkable and politically and socially impracticable. Even though the situation of sociology has changed, very little sociological research is experimental. Hence the ethical questions of manipulation which arise in connection with research which entails experiments on human beings do not apply. The use of "control groups" for comparison of the effect of certain conditions on conduct or performance of individuals or organizations raises no ethical questions for sociologists as long as they themselves have not participated in creating the differences between the "control" and the "experimental" groups.

The approximation to the centers of authority in society changes the situation of sociology, at least potentially. Whereas, in the past, one obstacle to experimentation in society was the political unfeasibility—it simply would not have been tolerated by politicians and the leaders of public opinion—the situation has now altered. The "scientific outlook" has now advanced even in this time when skeptical questions are being raised about it. Governmental officials are now more sympathetic with sociological research. They have a practical interest in having it done on the subject for which they are constitutionally responsible; they are desirous of knowing about the efficacy of particular measures of policy before they have been introduced on a country-wide scale. Experiments would enable them to obtain this knowledge and they are consequently more willing than they formerly were to provide the financial support for such experiments. This is a situation which sociologists in the past did not have to face. It is one which they might have to face more frequently in the future.

In addition to the ethical problems of intrusion into privacy and of manipulation which might arise in the conduct of research, there are also problems which arise from the completion of research, which includes publication. The diffusion of the results of sociological inquiry has always been regarded as essential to the conduct of such inquiry. For one thing, a contribution to scientific knowledge is such only when it has been accepted by scientists other than the would-be contributor as valid in accordance with the criteria of scientific truth. Many sociologists also desire that the intellectual result of their research should influence the state of affairs in society, not only through its incorporation into their own action as citizens together with other citizens or as consultants to governmental and civic bodies, but also through the reading of their work, directly or indirectly, by a larger nonacademic public.

To influence a state of affairs involves influencing the situation of human beings who are parts of that state of affairs. To affect the working conditions of "sweated" factory or domestic workers in the garment trade to the benefit of the workers necessarily entails affecting employers in ways which are not beneficial to them. To publish a report on research into a municipal civil service might well call forth in readers a low opinion of municipal officials and the politicians who appointed them; it might result in a wave of indignation in sectors of the public, which could in turn lead to the dismissal of many of the civil servants and to the injury of the power and status of the politicians who appointed them. Such consequences were inherent in efforts to reform an existing situation, and they often were unquestioningly accepted—that is, in so far as any notice was taken of the losses to the persons whose actions were to be restrained and whose advantages were to be diminished or eliminated in consequence of the reforms.

This pattern has a long history. Sociology is in many respects a part of the tradition of the Enlightenment. The spread of enlightenment was expected to eliminate superstition and the fear of nonexistent spirits. It was taken for granted that the dissipation of the shadows on the mind caused by religious belief would be of benefit to those who had hitherto accepted them. This view was passionately contested by articulate believers in the views to be dissipated. But even for those who were not adherents of those threatened beliefs, the matter was not as simple as it appeared to the great figures of the Enlightenment. The same may be said of the diffusion of the results of sociological research. The founders and the best representatives of sociology have never wanted their observations and analysis to be a hermetic body of knowledge valued and understood only by the duly initiated. Further thought about the consequences of its diffusion seem to me to be called for. Increased literacy and hypersensitivity on the part of individuals to imagined affronts against the dignity of the groups with which they identify themselves are likely to increase hostility against sociology. The abuse against the monograph on the family life of American blacks by Daniel Moynihan is one instance of what may be in store. Sociologists themselves, and not merely the black ones among them, might find in this denunciation without reflection that they are sawing off the branch on which they are sitting.

In the past three decades the responsibility of natural sciences for the practical uses which had been made of their discoveries has been vigorously recommended. Much less thought has been given to how such responsibility could be exercised. If no scientist published any of his discoveries, this would be practicable, but then science without publication dissolves into a body of learning like the secret magical techniques of civilizations very different from our own. If scientific works are published, how can their reading be prevented? Again, such a prohibition of the reading of scientific works by any one who is intellectually capable of doing so would be contrary to the ethos of science. When such an "embargo" was placed on research in nuclear physics during the Second World War by the militarily administered Manhattan Project, a rumbling resentment was generated among scientists.

The position of sociology and of sociologists with respect to publicity about their much less scientific results is the same. Publicity is part of the ethos of sociology as an intellectual discipline and as a part of the program of the improvement of life through enlightenment. The publication of the results of research in learned journals is also integral to the academic career.

Now it is easy enough to decide that it is unqualifiedly wrong for social scientists to do research which entails evil actions on the part of the social scientists themselves. But the matter is not so simple. Although some actions are clearly evil, it is not so easy to locate the boundary which separates the evil from the good. But this is an easy task compared to predicting the consequences of any piece of research if it were applied. The consequences of application, assuming that they are susceptible to accurate investigation, even if they bring about some evil consequences, might also bring about some beneficial ones. Furthermore, how can it be foreseen whether the results of a research project, itself morally unexceptionable, will be used for evil ends at some time in the future? The mere evidence that an investigation has been supported financially by a particular body such as those castigated by radical sociologists is not evidence of the evil character or consequences of the investigation.

Most of the discussion about this matter has been academic in the most pejorative sense; it does not deal with real cases. First of all there are relatively few cases in which the specific results of social science research have been applied. To be applied they have to be taken seriously, and up until now the results of sociological research are taken seriously primarily by sociologists. On the whole, the empirical research of sociologists is still not taken very seriously by those who make decisions, except for sample surveys, which more than any other sociological research are indeed taken into account by politicians and administrators. Politicians pursuing their political ends take these surveys into account in estimating their chances of success in electoral campaigns, and this probably does influence their procedures and discourse. Politicians in office might be affected by the popular view of their performance, as disclosed by public opinion surveys. They might be intimidated by the menace of disapproval. (This is a far cry from the morally transforming effect on princes of the counsel given to them by philosophers; but it is closer to the Benthamite view.)

The other parts of sociology which go beyond descriptive and particular propositions and which make assertions about causal connections, which make generalizations, usually have very little demonstrable effect on the behavior of politicians and administrators. The lesser effectiveness of explanatory sociological propositions probably results from the fact that they compete with common sense and reflection on experience and, of course, prejudice. Whereas DDT might be prohibited by a government department or a legislative body when it is shown that it enters into foodstuffs with demonstrably deleterious effects on health, research which shows that variations in the composition of school classes affects learning by children in those classes would probably not have been acted upon by persons in positions of authority unless it confirmed what they already wished to believe and legitimated what they already wished to do.

Still, the diffusion of sociological ideas into the larger society does occur, and it occurs in forms quite different from the manipulative or technological mode which some sociologists would prefer and which their critics abhor.

The image of a society which its members have of it can, in an educated and literate society, be much affected by the productions of intellectuals. Their interpretation of their institutions, their picture of what they are and how they function, might well affect the conduct of those who come to accept those interpretations. Professor David Riesman's *The Lonely Crowd* is one instance of a sociological work which has been widely read and has perhaps had some direct and indirect influence on the attitude of American citizens towards their own society. C. Wright Mills' *The Power Elite* is another. Through their popularity as textbooks in undergraduate courses and their wide circulation in the educated public, they have, in amorphously pervasive ways, probably had some influence on the conception of American society held by many Americans. As such, these works and others like them have acquired social consequences. In my own view, they have probably had a greater impact than the many pieces of technological sociology.[11]

There is an evaluative bias in sociology which has not been wholly expunged despite the valiant and watchful efforts of many sociologists

11. Professor Riesman has written a thoughtful assessment of the impact of *The Lonely Crowd* on American opinion in the two decades which followed the publication of his book. He says there, among many interesting observations:

over many years to attain a higher standard of objectivity. It is a bias deriving from the progressivistic, liberal beliefs of many contemporary sociologists in a paradoxical admixture with the traditionalist conservative beliefs of some of the founders of sociology. Sociology has been called an "oppositional science." In the decades of its foundation, it focussed its attention—and often with some truthfulness—on those aspects of modern society which were repugnant to a traditional conservative outlook. It focused on the breakup of the old order and on certain features of the new order—the liberal bourgeois society which succeeded it. These included the impersonality and individualism of the new regime and the larger place held in it by instrumental rationality. These very features of modern society came to occupy a prominent place in the sociological outlook and, at the same time, they were singled out by radical and progressivistist critics of modern society as that which ought to be overcome through revolution or reform. There are now very few conservatives among sociologists—most of them are progressivists—but the substantive tradition of social science in which they have been formed remains as strong as ever.

The reforming interest of sociologists and their desire to contribute their scientific knowledge to the effective improvement of their society led them to do their early empirical studies on those situations which were in need of improvement and which there seemed to be some practical probability of improving. Those features of society which did not appear to them urgently to need improvement were not brought into the center of the scientific attention. This accentuated the peculiar conservative, even traditionalistic, theme which sociology acquired in varying ways from Comte, Maine, Le Play, and Tönnies. The radicals no less than those they criticize are the heirs and the prisoners of this tradition. Their accusations against liberal democratic society as dehumanizing, unintegrated, and bureaucratized is exactly what they have learned from the sociology which they so fervently denounce.

It is not that sociologists have falsified their observations, or that they observed wrongly. The bias has resided in the selection of problems and in the image of the context of the situations which they have investigated so meticulously. This does not hold equally for all sociological works but it does for many, including some of the best and the most interesting. The interpretive theory into which this bias has been incorporated has changed considerably and to some extent it has been expunged. Nonetheless it is still present in a large amount of

---

"the book has contributed to the climate of criticism of our society and helped to create or reaffirm a nihilistic outlook among a great many people" (" 'The Lonely Crowd' 20 Years After," *Encounter* 33, no. 9 [October 1969]: 36).

sociological work. It is more present in the macrosociological part of sociology than it is in the microsociological part and even in the former it is far from universally present. It is moreover very respectable intellectually and it is not a product of a deliberate effort to discredit modern society. It is not propaganda in any crude sense of the term.

The rancorous attacks on sociology for "mystifying" the image of society transmitted to those who study it are as unjustifiable on intellectual grounds as the assertion that sociologists are the equivalent of a police and intelligence service working on behalf of an "internal colonial" power. But in so far as sociology ceases to be of interest only to professional sociologists and reaches into the outer society through the writings, teachings, and political and consultative action of sociologists, they must think simultaneously of their two traditional ideals: the improvement of society and the objectivity of their knowledge.

VII

The institutional arrangements available to social scientists for the clarification and "enforcement" of their old and their newly acquired ethical obligations are very rudimentary. Indeed they scarcely exist. They are much scantier than the arrangements for the sustenance of the ideal of objectivity. In recent years, there has been some discussion among social scientists of the ethical obligations which should be observed in the conduct of their disciplines. There has been a certain amount of attention given to the avoidance of the performance of research the results of which are to be "classified," i.e., to be kept secret. There has also been considerable attention paid to the sources of financial support. The need for strictness about experimentation on human subjects and for their "informed consent" has been discussed but not very deeply.

The consequences of the diffusion of sociological knowledge have been less pondered. Here and there, apprehension has been expressed about research the results of which might be injurious to the reputation of "minorities," but nothing like the agitation about research in the genetic transmission of intelligence which has taken place in neighboring disciplines has occurred in sociology. By and large sociologists still adhere faithfully to their old tradition which regards the understanding of society as a good in itself and as a benefit to the society in which it is produced and diffused.

The concern about the sources of financial support is quite beside the point. It is not entirely irrelevant but it is marginal. Deception or mendacity about the source of financial support of sociological investigations is reprehensible no less than the deception of persons interviewed or lying in general, whether in connection with research or in any other sphere of life. The truth of a sociological proposition—particular or general—rests on the evidence presented and on the probity of the investigator; neither of these has any inherent connection with the source of the funds supporting the investigation. The contention that support from certain institutions should be disallowed by sociologists is really little more than political propaganda. If sociologists are worried about what will be done with the results of their research that is a matter for them to settle with their own consciences as a private matter. If they fear the "misuse" of knowledge which they produce, the solution is to withhold it from publication—both from limited publication in classified form and from the more conventional form of publication in learned journals. Sociological knowledge diffused through the latter means is just as subject to "misuse" as that diffused in restricted "classified" form. After all, the wicked can "misuse" what they read in a learned journal as well as they can that which they read in classified reports of research commissioned by themselves and reserved to circulation only within the boundaries of their own wicked organization!

Of course much of the apprehension about "misuse" is misapprehension. Most sociological knowledge, even that produced under the sponsorship of a body which ostensibly intends to "use" it, is in fact not "used" at all. Much of what is now called "evaluation research" is stillborn; it might be read in the research division of the department or ministry under the budget of which the appropropriation falls, but that is usually as far as it goes. Sociologists, even though they would function as "technologists" and would make sociological knowledge into part of "social technology" are preserved from the consequences and risks of their own desires by the inattention of politicians and administrators.

If sociology is not entirely an affair contained within its own boundaries, if only professional sociologists read the writings of professional sociologists and their ideas are not diffused at all beyond those boundaries, then there would be no problem about the influence—about the "use" or "misuse"—of sociology. This is not what sociologists desire and it is certainly contrary to the tradition of the founders of sociology, a tradition which is still generally honored. It is sociology as a part of public opinion rather than sociology as technology which constitutes the moral problem, and it is a subtle and difficult one too.

If sociologists are concerned about the use or the misuse of their ideas, then they should be even more concerned with the intellectual quality of those ideas. Sociological knowledge which is addressed not to colleagues of equal expertise but to laymen such as undergraduate students and the larger public is addressed to those who are not as qualified to protect themselves by informed and discriminating judgment as professional sociologists should be. They want sociological ideas partly because they attribute to sociologists the authority of the disinterested pursuit of knowledge as truthful as the sociologists can make it, or they want those ideas because they conform with their existing beliefs, whatever these might be. Sociologists who reflect on the matter for a moment will draw back from the latter as a justification for the diffusion of the results of their observations and analyses. Even those who enjoy popular acclaim will quite understandably not wish to acknowledge this as a justification. The only acceptable argument for the diffusion of sociological knowledge to the public is that the public will come to possess a cognitively better understanding of society by virtue of that knowledge. This brings us back to the value of the objectivity of knowledge.

The objectivity of knowledge presupposes that there is something outside the observing subject which can be known in a way which can be confirmed by other observing subjects. It presupposes that evidence can be assembled which is persuasive to others who have scrutinized it and who have found it acceptable in the sense that it corresponds to what they conclude on the basis of their own previous studies and their examination of the pertinent evidence. It says nothing against the objectivity of knowledge to assert that the knowing subjects have been born in "the same social class" or that they make certain "background assumptions" regarding the right order of society. The objectivity of a statement is not impugned by an assertion that the persons who put it forward and accept it share a common political ideal, whatever that might be. The question is whether other persons than the one asserting a particular proposition find it acceptable on the basis of the best evidence. The quality of the evidence is constituted by its conformity with rules of observation and interpretation and with observations made previously in accordance with those rules and conforming with fitting theories. The constant improvement of knowledge by subsequent new discoveries does not impugn the objectivity of the knowledge possessed at an earlier stage.

This schematic and simplified account of the objectivity of knowledge does not bear much resemblance to the knowledge which sociologists offer today. Some of the assertions in current sociology are closer to this standard than others but practically none meets the standard to a very high degree. But the standard represents the ideal which must be sought and respected. If it is not, then sociology must be justified like a purely expressive literary work; and even literary works are assessed with respect to their veracity, but in a deeper and yet less exacting way than is expected of sociological works.

The objectivity of sociological work can be fostered by scruples in observation, rigor in analysis, and meticulousness in bearing in mind what is already known about the subject by other workers who have given evidence of the merit of their published work. Even then, most sociological work is far from watertight.

Yet it is on the presumption of its reliability as knowledge, of its conformity with the best canons of sociological knowledge, that sociologists present their work to their colleagues in the discipline, to those in adjacent disciplines, and to the wider public. Some sociologists address only the first or the first two of these publics. Some address all three simultaneously. Works which are presented to the first of these publics have increasingly in the last decades adhered to a more demanding standard of scrupulousness, rigor, and meticulousness. Those which are to a greater extent addressed to the third public have usually subscribed to less exigent standards. This is not solely because sociologists are inevitably less honest in dealing with an inexpert public than they are with one which is more expert. It is also, perhaps primarily, because very particular and narrowly circumscribed subjects can be brought under the control of these exigent standards more easily than larger and "deeper" subjects can.

There are probably some sociologists who are preponderantly concerned with the acclamation of the wider public or with advancing certain political ends. There are probably very few to whom these ends are the only ones. They too contend that what they say about society is true. They claim the attention and affirmation of the wider public on the ground of the truth of their assertions. They do not say that "my assertions are a product of my background assumptions" or "of my values" or "of my bias." They allow it to be believed and they encourage the belief in the wider public that what they say is "true," as true as they can make it, that they are speaking about a reality which exists outside themselves and which the wider public must acknowledge because it is true. When Myrdal published a great number of statements about the condition of the Negroes in the United States he did not for each statement assert that this statement was true only for a person who shared his "bias" or "values." His declarations in his "methodological appendix" were not applied to his own substantive statements throughout the book. There he based himself on the material provided to him by the scholars who had established reputations as scrupulous observers, by his assistants who scoured the available official and unofficial statistics according to the generally accepted rules for the assessment of the reliability of such material, and by his own observations. His assertions about bias were simply a decoration to show how detached he actually was; they also showed that he respected the right of the public to objective truth as distinct from his own biased account which, because of that bias, was less truthful than it should have been.

It would have been more consistent for Myrdal to have said that, being aware of the possibility that his socialistic and egalitarian desires might have led him to distort the picture which should have been presented, he had, bearing those desires in mind, scrutinized his account as carefully as possible in order to make it more truthful. That would have been a better procedure than simply to clear his conscience in an appendix.

Still he was aware, albeit very crudely, of the problem. Much more than Karl Mannheim, he opened the way to an improvement of the sociological knowledge which he presented to the larger public domain. He came up to but did not quite cross the line which separates scrupulousness in the scholarly correction of error from self-indulgence in the form of general statements about the incorrigibility of error.

VIII

For the earlier generation of sociologists, the attainability of an objective knowledge of society, of a true and reliable knowledge, was the point from which they took their departure. Their whole enterprise would have made no sense had they not believed in the possibility of objective knowledge. Albion Small, when he wrote about *The Origins of Sociology,* paid particular attention to the development of the critical assessment of the reliability of the documentary sources for historiography as an early stage in the striving of sociologists to establish a scientific knowledge of society. Franklin Giddings also believed that the study of society could be made more scientific in its procedures, and that is why he promoted the study of statistics within the Department of Sociology at Columbia University. Statistics were intended to assure the objectivity of sociological knowledge just as the training in "methods of fieldwork" at the University of Chicago was intended to do. The intention of these kinds of training was to overcome or discipline the waywardness and obduracy of individual judgment; to control passion and prejudice so as to prevent them from infringing on the rules of scientific procedure. The task set in the training of sociologists has been to render impotent those contrary forces which interfere with the attainment of objective knowledge. "Background assumption," "bias," *"Aspektstruktur," "Seinsverbundenheit des Denkens"* were to be attenuated or overcome by the modes of thought conducive to the attainment of objective knowledge. Until the establishment of sociological training at Chicago and Columbia, the pursuit of the ideal of objectivity was dependent on the accidents of the confluence of tradition and character. When sociology was an amateur activity, it benefited from the attraction of powerful personalities seriously devoted to the truth and scrupulous in their efforts to meet the high standards which had been set in Western intellectual history in philosophy, science, and humanistic scholarship. The availability of governmental statistics was the foundation stone of the construction of objective knowledge. The emergence of scientific journals and societies in the field of sociology and related disciplines gave some support to the aspiration towards objectivity. They opened sociological work to the scrutiny of competent persons who examined evidence and arguments. In the second and third quarters of the twentieth century, when sociology became well institutionalized and offered professional careers for large numbers, it probably also ceased to draw into itself such a large proportion of persons of such deep inner propensity to seek a truthful understanding of society. But this change in the composition of its practitioners was compensated by the pressure of institutional control of selection, training, promotion, and assessment. Self-selection into academic sociology still continues to operate; it has been greatly reinforced by life in an academic environment with its admissions and promotions, its examinations and seminars, and the discipline of preparing a dissertation under the close supervision of a more experienced sociologist. These have helped to guarantee the assimilation and the maintenance of the ethos in which objective truth is the major value. To this was joined the growing literature of the methods of sociological knowledge and analysis, most of which has been focused on the problems of enhancing the reliability of observation and analysis. The machinery of "refereeing" papers submitted to learned journals and criticism in staff seminars has reinforced the internalized controls.[12] The arrangements for appointments and promotions have worked generally in the same direction.

On the whole these various institutions of the community of sociologists have not been without effect. They have suffered somewhat from the vagueness and instability of the concepts which are current in sociology and from the imprecision and incomparability of the results of empirical investigations. The rigorously articulated analysis and verification which in the natural sciences comes from the continuous assimilation of prior investigations into their successors have been lacking for the most part in sociology. Minute and meticulous analysis of what has just gone before as the basis of the next stage

12. Social scientists seem to have a lower standard of intellectual accomplishment than their colleagues in the natural sciences. They submit more papers which are not up to standard than do natural scientists. Professors Harriet Zuckerman and Robert Merton state that, in 1967, 84 percent of the articles submitted to two political sciences journals, 78 percent of the articles submitted to fourteen sociological journals, 70 percent of the articles submitted to seven psychological journals (excluding those in physiological and experimental psychology), 69 percent of those submitted to four economics journals, and 40 percent of those submitted to two anthropological journals were rejected. (Harriet Zuckerman and Robert Merton: "Patterns of Evaluation in Science: Institutionalisation, Structure, and Functions of the Referee System," *Minerva* 9, no. 1 [January 1971]: 76.)

in research is still very difficult in sociology because of the incomparability of categories. Successive writers on the same subject or problem usually bear in mind what their recent predecessors have written. Where it supports the results of their own studies, they use it in support of their own conclusions, but it is hard to form a coherent picture of the phenomena which they purport to describe. Assessments of accomplishments in reviews of literature and in appointments and promotion tend to be loose; it would be difficult to make them otherwise. Yet the criteria of scholarship, the respect for truth, and scientific integrity, are certainly present in most decisions and those who aspire to make their careers through this course are aware of it. It helps to compose their minds to know that they will not "get away with" playing lightly where truth is concerned.

Book reviews in sociological journals are less important in the process than they could be. They tend to be brief and fragmentary in their discussions of the merits of the work being assessed. They are generally recommendations that the works they review should be accepted into or, more infrequently, rejected from the corpus of sociological knowledge. There is rarely close-grained and stringent analysis of a particular work. Exceptions to this are relatively rare, but the careful scrutiny given to Kinsey et al., *The Sexual Behavior of the American Male,* and to the studies of *The American Soldier, The Authoritarian Personality,* and *Equality of Educational Opportunity* may be mentioned.

It is primarily at the stage of the doctoral dissertation that research is scrutinized with great care and that detailed criticisms are regularly made. This same service is sometimes performed by the referees of articles submitted to journals. There is also a considerable amount of reading by colleagues of manuscripts before publication. The learned societies in their meetings do not contribute greatly to this process of criticism. There is little close discussion of the papers presented in the public meetings. Departmental staff seminars vary in the intensity and rigor of their analyses of the work of colleagues presented there. It is my impression that the criticism in these seminars is much less detailed and exigent than that made in graduate seminars.

So it comes out that, by and large, the ethos of the search for objective truth is largely dependent on the conscience of each individual sociologist and on his belief that, if he falls short, sooner or later the assessment of his achievements will disclose his shortcomings and result in damage to his reputation and career.

The fact that this ethos works as well as it does rests in part on the belief of sociologists that they are writing for an audience of their colleagues in "the profession." Their belief that some of their qualified colleagues will read their writings has a constraining and improving effect. If they were to write solely for the general public or for an audience of "users" who were technically unqualified, the results might be different. Very few since the end of the Second World War have written works which are "classified" and which the writers in question were content to leave classified. They want their works to appear before their professional colleagues and to be judged by them. The standards of academic publishers of sociological works are generally very similar to those of the professional journals. Since the audience is ultimately an audience of sociologists, editors and referees apply the usual standards of competence, objectivity, and importance. In this process of acceptance and rejection, nonintellectual criteria play only a small, probably negligible part. Where this standard is departed from, there is nonetheless little evidence that political considerations and solicitude for the interests and sensibilities of the "establishment" are of any importance at all. Political criteria, in so far as they play any part in the assessment of works for publication, are more often applied by the social scientists with radical sympathies than by any other sector of the profession. In none of the cases known to me has the adduction of political criteria in determining whether a work should be published been successful in preventing publication.

Three Cases in Point

The first one I shall mention had to do with my paper on "Authoritarianism: 'Left' and 'Right'" which was written for the collection edited by Professors Richard Christie and Maria Jahoda entitled *Continuities in Social Research: Further Studies in the Authoritarian Personality* (Glencoe, Illinois: The Free Press, 1954).

I need not enter into the content of this essay except to say that it was a very detailed criticism of the procedures used in the investigation of *The Authoritarian Personality;* it pointed out that the "instrument" which was used precluded the investigators from detecting authoritarian traits among "leftists." I also sought to show that the postulates which underlay the choice of questions used in the "instrument" were those which are also found in Marxist and quasi-Marxist views of the structure of political attitudes. When the essay was received by the editors, a great commotion began. First I received a letter requesting that I make a number of changes which would make less explicit my contention that the selection of items which went into the interview schedule was affected in a demonstrable way by the political conceptions of the guiding spirits of the inquiry. There has never been any question about the validity of my criticism. One of these editors wrote me that in view of the atmosphere which then prevailed in the United States—it was the early 1950s and Senator Joseph McCarthy was at about the height of his rampage—it would be imprudent to publish the paper as it stood; the opinion of my friend Professor Harold Lasswell was invoked in support of the view that it was "dangerous" to give sustenance in this way to McCarthyite allegations. I was not much impressed by the force of these arguments and refused to make major changes which would have blurred my main argument. Then, according to Mr. Jeremiah Kaplan, who was at that time the publisher of The Free Press, under the imprint of which the book was to appear, there followed a series of long, long-distance telephone calls from Professor Else Frankel-Brunswick objecting to the essay on grounds of political prudence and from another eminent professor in a pertinent subject at the University of Michigan solicitously expressing apprehension about the damage which might be done to my career if I persisted in my intention to have it published. It was also intimated to him that the American Jewish Committee, the sponsors of the research, would take legal action against The Free Press if the book were published with my paper in it. It was suggested that Mr. Kaplan try to persuade me to withdraw the article or that he should refuse to publish it. He did neither of these. After about one month, the furor died down. The article was published without the proofs having ever been sent to me and with a number of modifications which I had never approved nor even seen.

The second instance I shall mention is probably not political, although an eminently political academic was involved; it certainly represents an intrusion of nonintellectual consideration into the process of assessment.

It involves the late Professor C. Wright Mills, Professor Charles Page, and myself. On the invitation of the then book review editor of *The American Sociological Review*, the late Michael Olmstead, I wrote a review of about 10,000 words of *The Sociological Imagination*. After I wrote it, the editor of *Encounter*, having learned that I was writing a long review, asked me to let him have a brief review of the same book. I wrote this shorter review and sent it to him. A few days later as I was on the verge of departure from the United States, I telephoned Professor Page, who was then the editor of *The American Sociological Review*, to determine whether my recently posted review had arrived safely. He said it had and that he was delighted to have it for his journal; he said that it was a little long—although I had been assured by the book review editor who had died meanwhile that I could make the review as long as I wished. I told him that he might reduce it by about 1,000 words; I also told him about the brief review which I had recently sent to *Encounter* and which was still not published. He raised no question about this. When I was in London about two weeks later, there arrived the typescript of my review accompanied by a long letter from Professor Page telling me that he would have to reject my review because it was the policy of *The American*

Sociological Review never to use a review by someone who had published a review of the same book elsewhere. Professor Page was ingenuous enough to say that this rule had practically never been invoked before and to explain that this decision was taken after a telephone conversation with Professor Mills. It is not possible for me to give a precise account of what went on between Professor Mills and Professor Page, but the main outlines of the affair are clear. The review had been solicited. It was appreciatively accepted by the editor and it was then returned to me by the editor with a letter of rejection asserting that the change in his decision was taken after a telephone conversation with Professor Mills. The fact that Professor Page in invoking the hitherto uninvoked rule did not give me the choice of withdrawing my still unpublished review from *Encounter* was nothing more than finding a way out of the embarrassment caused him by Professor Mills' remonstrance. I suppose that had I pressed Professor Page and also withdrawn my review from *Encounter*, where it had not yet been published, I could have saved him from the bad conscience of yielding to the pressure of Professor Mills. But I did not wish to do that since I was compensated by obtaining evidence of the devotion of a major figure of the "left" to the freedom of publication. Furthermore, shortly afterwards, I published the text without abridgment in *World Politics* (12, no. 4 [July 1961]).

The third case of attempted interference was described to me by the late Dr. Bernhard J. Stern, who showed me all the documents on it. It involved the late Professor William Ogburn, Dr. Stern, and a leading industrialist. Professor Ogburn was the research director of the Committee on Technological Trends and National Policy of the United States National Resources Planning Board. In that capacity, he commissioned a number of studies of technological innovation in its various aspects. One of them was to deal with resistance to technological innovation. The study of this subject was assigned to Dr. Stern, who had written his dissertation on resistance to medical innovations. In his report, Dr. Stern asserted that a large American corporation had refused to develop certain inventions out of considerations of commercial profitability. The president of the corporation, who was also associated with the National Resources Planning Board, protested to the chairman of the board, who transmitted the complaint to Professor Ogburn. The complaint cast aspersions on the intellectual and scholarly qualifications of Dr. Stern, who was at that time a sympathizer with the Soviet Union and connected in various Stalinist enterprises, such as *Science and Society*. Professor Ogburn unqualifiedly and in very sharp terms rejected the complaint against Dr. Stern, whose work he had known intimately for many years, and reaffirmed his complete confidence in Dr. Stern's intellectual integrity. Dr. Stern's contribution to *Technology: A National Resource* was published, unaffected by the industrialist's complaint. In this case, one conservative layman attempted to intrude into the process of assessment: Professor Ogburn, who was thought to be a Republican, rebuffed this intrusion and vindicated the primacy of intellectual criteria.

I should add that when, at the end of the 1930s, I conducted a survey of the freedom of expression in the social sciences, I did not encounter any cases in which it was contended that some work of social science had been refused publication on account of political considerations. The survey covered a period when "academic freedom cases" were not uncommon.

It is my impression that sociologists have been as faithful to the ethos of objective truth in their assessment of the works of their colleagues and in their readiness to grant them printed access to the community of sociologists as they have been in their commitment to that ethos in their own pursuit of objective truth.

Whether they would have been so scrupulous had they not believed that the objectivity of knowledge was an ideal to which they were under obligation is of course difficult to say. If there were no ideal of objectivity and if "background assumptions" and other such standards which are nowadays put forward as superior to the denounced and despised "evaluatively neutral science" become the criteria for assessing sociological works and sociologists, sociology would be affected not only by its intellectual shortcomings but by an arbitrariness of intellectual judgment and by political considerations which are alien and even hostile towards intellectual achievement.

It is not that sociologists should not have political views or that they should not render political and moral judgments of what goes on in their society. It is not that they should not be active partisans in the political sphere. They may even be as passionate in their political beliefs, attachments, and antagonisms as Max Weber was during the First World War. While he was writing impassioned polemics against imperial policy and the conduct of the war (the essay on *Wertfreiheit* was published during the year), Weber was at the same time writing some of his greatest works. *Hinduismus und Buddhismus, Das antike Judentum,* and sections of *Wirtschaft und Gesellschaft* dealing with the sociology of religion were written during this time of fervent political activity. The systematic, conceptual part of *Wirtschaft und Gesellschaft* was written under similar circumstances. The highest standards of macrosociological analysis and of the construction of an analytical framework were observed during a time of similarly passionate concern about the state of Germany and its future. Max Weber was a genius, the like of whom has never existed in sociology before or since. He showed what was possible in the striving for objective knowledge.

IX

Despite their long history, sociologists and social scientists taken as a group have most of the road before them. The difficulty of the road is attested by the very limited rigor and reliability of the results of sociological research. The road has recently become additionally difficult because of the newer involvements of sociology and the other social sciences in the life of the larger society. These involvements are connected with the greater prominence of sociology and of the social sciences more generally in higher education, the greatly increased numbers of social scientists and of students of social sciences, the greater sums of money required and provided for social research, the greater "use" of social sciences in governmental and other organizations, the greater readiness of public opinion to look with favor or tolerance on these disciplines and to assimilate them into the general culture of the society.

Tasks and temptations result from these involvements. The recent radical criticisms of the social sciences are intellectually insubstantial. They are by-products of the enormous changes in the situation of the social sciences, they are results of the intellectual immaturity and frivolity which the ambiguous standards of assessment in the social sciences have allowed to flourish.

The central fact which must be acknowledged is that the state of objective knowledge in the social sciences is far from satisfactory. It is not just that the state of our generalized knowledge is unsatisfactory—ambiguous, excessively abstract to the point of in-applicability to empirical observations and therefore extremely difficult to confirm or disconfirm—but that the condition of our empirical findings is also not satisfactory.

Research which is based on intimate understanding and direct observation over an extended period by one or a few persons is inevitably bound to be impressionistic. Even when some efforts are made to control observations through sampling procedures, precise recording, etc., the amount of labor involved in such procedures is beyond the powers of one or a very small number of persons who must complete their work within a relatively short time. As a result, the statistically disciplined part of such investigations are usually only a small part of the whole. There are many open places in such investigations for impressionistic judgments, and these offer more opportunities for arbitrariness than quanitatively controlled observations—which are also subject to such deficiencies.

Investigations which entail a great number of observations to be made over a very extended territory, and which must be brought to completion in a short time and which must be treated statistically, are inevitably beyond the power of a small number of investigators. They require a considerable number of collaborators and a division of labor among them and they require that the categories of observation—questions for interviewers—be so simplified that they can be utilized in brief interviews and so stereotyped that many persons, many of whom are of very modest ability, can be instructed in a short time to apply them in a way which will not vary from interviewer to interviewer. The work in these investigations is usually so differentiated and internally specialized that no one on the project has an intimate relationship with the events studied. This being so, the "sense of realilty" which is a product of prolonged and intimate contact with the persons investigated, does not develop and the questions asked are often not adapted to the subtlety and complexity of the events—beliefs or actions—being investigated. Interpretative constructions which do not conform to the "shape" of the events studied are the result. Despite the intention of concreteness and particularity, the accounts arising from empirical research are often as abstract—in relation to the events studied—as the sociological theory which is so unmanageable for purposes of realistic study. Both of them allow a very large amount of discretion in interpretation. Where discretion is permitted arbitrariness can easily enter. The arbitrariness of judgment might be the product of political or ethnic or class attachments or sheer idiosyncracy and the beliefs connected with them; some of them might be simply the result of poverty of knowledge, insufficient experience, weak reasoning powers, lack of sympathy, or deficient imagination. There is a very thin line separating imaginative from arbitrary interpretation.

There is nothing new about these difficulties of ascertaining the truth in an objective manner. Ever since men began to be critical of the sources of their knowledge, i.e., ever since classical philosophy and the emergence of hermeneutics as a means of establishing the meaning of texts, sacred or profane, this problem has bedeviled the human mind intent on understanding.

The physical and biological sciences were able to escape from it by the use of instruments—real instruments and not the factitious questionnaires which scientifically ambitious social scientists sometimes call "instruments"—which standardize observations. They were greatly aided by the use of purified substances with reliably determinate properties and by the use of experimental methods as well as by quantitative and mathematical methods which enhance precision and rigor. The social sciences have moved unevenly and haltingly in these directions; the progress of these methods moves them away from particular situations and events and the awareness growing out of direct experience and thereby simultaneously impairs the beneficence of these procedures.

No science, no intellectual discipline, however rigorous its methods, however reliable its instruments, however unambiguous its theory, can dispense with imagination. By its very nature, the imagination operates in the area of the unknown; it takes no imagination to learn the already known except in the cases of those isolated geniuses who rediscover the already known. How can the imagination be disciplined without suppressing it and reducing science and scholarship to an arid "factuality"?

One element in the discipline of the imagination is the belief that there is something outside itself to which it owes an obligation; not just a moral obligation—although that is of great importance—but a cognitive obligation. For the scientist there are the facts of his observation, for a scholar there are the facts of the texts, inscriptions, and monuments. They are the fragments of the external, objectively existing world to which the cognitive obligation is due, and between and behind those fragments is the external objectively existing world into which the fragments must be fitted.

Truth cannot be discovered unless its discovery is believed to be possible. This is the *sine qua non* of the quest for objective truth. The "politicization" of the social sciences, the view that our intellectual beliefs and assertions are inescapable functions of our "class interests" or of some other nonintellectual determinants, is an impossible barrier to the attainment of truths, however trivial or important. Fortunately despite the clamorous assertion of these views, not many persons believe them, including those who assert them. Even they believe that what they say is true and should be accepted by their auditors or readers, even those with other "interests," "background assumptions," or "biases." Those who allege that "all thought is ideological" are only engaging in polemics, and they then go through involved contortions to rescue their own assertions from the long-established absurdity of propositions of the sort that "all men are liars." Those who engage in such polemics overlook furthermore one of the most obvious and integral features of intellectual activity in science and scholarship, namely, its sheer difficulty.

The hard fact of existence is that any serious truth is terribly difficult to discover. It requires an exceptional curiosity, capacious memory, powerful intelligence, and great imagination as well as stamina and self-discipline beyond the ordinary allotment to human beings. It requires the discipline of a tradition; it requires the acceptance of an inheritance of knowledge; the reception and assimilation require strenuous exertion. To extend and to differentiate it require much more. All this is easier if the tradition of a scientific and scholarly discipline is precise in content and hence more indicative of where to begin on the paths which ought to be pursued. Except for economics, the social sciences, despite the greatness of some of their monumental works, still do not have such a tradition. This is a great handicap and it puts a tremendous burden on the intellectual and moral integrity of the investigator.[13]

Most of the events with which social sciences deal and about which it is worth having well-founded beliefs do not at present show themselves wholly amenable to the treatments which permit rigorously founded beliefs. The things which it is important—for both practical and fundamental intellectual purposes—to know about are at present very inadequately known. Yet we must have beliefs about them; practical action and the need for a coherent picture of society require them equally. How is this picture to be composed when we have only fragments of factual evidence? We have, in addition to these fragments of factual evidence which are susceptible to diverse interpretation, our own sense of reality arising from our experiences, refined by reflection and study, and we have our theories. There must be tentativeness in whatever we assert and we must scrutinize ourselves as well as the data.

This brings us back to the solutions suggested by Wirth and Myrdal. They came near to useful truth but it eluded them. It is necessary to be aware of our "biases," not only our political, religious and ethnic and cultural "biases," but also the biases arising from personal vanity. But being aware of them and telling our audience that we have them—while continuing to affirm them—and persisting in the interpretation to which they have led is a poor substitute for attempting to nullify these "biases" and to tell the truth to the best of our ability. The truth on any topic on which the data are fragmentary is bound to be uncertain, but some interpretations of the data are more plausible on intellectual grounds than other interpretations. It is necessary and possible to make a choice among these interpretations. It is more important to avow the uncertainty of our choice of a particular interpretation while giving the cognitive ground for it than to leave the matter with a conscience eased by the avowal of "bias."

The gaps in our knowledge of society are enormous and numerous, and the necessity of estimating what might be contained in those gaps is not less great. The gaps are in fact filled in by social scientists. They are too often filled in from a reservoir of cognitive beliefs associated with political, ethical, and religious beliefs. The scrutiny of the cognitive grounds for a cognitive assertion entails the separation of these grounds from the extra-cognitive ones. It does not entail the renunciation of those political, ethical, or religious beliefs; it does entail their separation from cognitive beliefs.

---

13. The obstinate, rebarbative moralist Georges Sorel was once asked his opinion about the best method for sociology. His reply was, "Honesty."

X

Is there a way out of the present disorder of minds in the social sciences? Several remedies suggest themselves. The first and most important is hard intellectual work in the improvement of theories and techniques of observation and analysis. More exigent programs of training for the profession of social science, an unremitting vigilance in the assessment of accomplished works. "Refereeing," book-reviewing, the examination of dissertations should become more demanding. In other words, the professional institutions of the social sciences must be tightened.

The legal and the medical professions have the power to deprive certain of their members from the right to practice if they transgress on certain standards of "professional conduct." They have juridical procedures and the legal power to act on the basis of the conclusions reached by such procedures. Social scientists have no such procedures. Nor do they enjoy the relationship with the state which permits them to exercise the authority of exclusion which is necessary for such procedures. I doubt whether those social scientists who have recently been most vehement about these issues would be willing to cooperate with the state to establish such a system of authoritative professional licensing. And what would exclusion from the American Political Science Association or the American Sociological Association or the American Anthropological Association amount to? Who would care about that? Membership in such associations is not necessary for appointment to universities or for receipt of grants from governmental bodies or foundations.

Given the state of the social sciences and the standing and standards of the professional associations of the social scientists, it would be contrary to the principles of academic appointment and of university autonomy if universities were to accept their criteria of appointment from these professional associations. There is at present no institutional machinery capable of exercising such authority. Nor should there be, certainly not until the social sciences become much more scientific and until social scientists have shown themselves to be much more reflective about such questions than they have been hitherto.

There has been much agitation within some of the professional associations of social scientists in recent years but it has been political agitation. Most of it has been initiated by radical or "left-wing" social scientists and it has been directed towards the censure of other social scientists for their allegedly conservative or "right-wing" attitudes or affiliations. This is as reprehensible as would be efforts by the latter to censure the former. These efforts to censure certain individual social scientists, certain types of political attitudes, or certain relationships with bodies which support research are not concerned with scientific or scholarly standards; they are not concerned with the ethical problems of the creation and diffusion of the knowledge gained by social scientists. This does not mean that the professional associations of social scientists should not at all pay attention to ethical problems or that social scientists should be indifferent to ethical problems or that social scientists as individuals should eschew the espousal of political programs. It does mean that they should not introduce political criteria into the assessment of the scientific or scholarly work of their colleagues and that they should use their associations for the promotion of the intellectual quality of the social sciences and for the promotion and diffusion of objectively valid knowledge. These two ends were the impulsions which underlay the birth and development of the social sciences. They are the best inheritance of the Enlightenment and they were the inspiration of the founders of the social sciences in all countries. These two ends were very generally conceived and often they were not explicitly formulated. They are in need of clarification in the light of the intellectual development of the social sciences and of the unforeseen complexity of their relationships to the society which the earlier generation of social scientists wished to improve. Nevertheless the ends remain valid. The achievement of objectively valid knowledge of society remains the justification for the cultivation of the social sciences; unless that end is affirmed, the other end—the improvement of society through the diffusion and ''use'' of that knowledge—makes no sense at all. The improvement of the human race through the growth of scientific knowledge is in many respects a problematical ideal, but it is not a meaningless ideal if objective scientific knowledge is possible.

Some words in conclusion. The social sciences have entered upon a new situation. One of the causes of this entry is a vast overestimation of the intellectual accomplishments thus far of the social sciences; the social scientists have been the beneficiaries and the accomplices of this overestimation. This overestimation has led to a degree of intertwinement with the larger society, an involvement which at present is neither necessary nor beneficial to the social sciences and to society. More modesty and greater realism are called for. The new ethical problems of the social sciences must be appreciated but they must be seen in a perspective which does not falsify their terms or exaggerate their incidence. This will not be done unless at the same time there is more sobriety about the intellectual quality of the social sciences themselves.

Part Four

The Ethics of Sociology

8 Social Inquiry and the Autonomy of the Private Sphere

I

Humanistic reflection on man from antiquity to the nineteenth century was traditionally based on observations gathered in the course of the daily business of life and on the study of literary works, philosophical treatises, essays, and historical writings. Having its point of departure in living human beings, it sought no vantage points other than those of ordinary intercourse and of works in which earlier writers had reflected on their objects, drawing on similar sources for their knowledge. Humanistic scholarship confined itself to the analysis of the lives and works of men and women no longer living. Classical historians like Thucydides and Tacitus dealt with relatively contemporary events; they often wrote on the basis of their own experience of participation in these events, their study of books written by other authors, and hearsay. Travelers wrote descriptions of societies which they visited, sometimes simply as curious travelers, sometimes in the course of military service or diplomatic missions. The observations of living human beings which the authors of these works made were not done for the primary purpose of scholarly or scientific study. When universities became the loci of humanistic research, the consideration of contemporary events did not occupy a prominent place. The scholarly study of literary works dealt with those of the past; academic historians did not deal with contemporaneous events; legal scholarship was not based in the study of living individuals.

So it continued well into the present century. Historical studies dealt with "history," which meant the "past"; academic literary studies dealt with works which had "withstood the test of time." No faculty or department of a university at the beginning of the present century in Europe was pledged to the direct observation of the conduct of living human beings. Economists who were becoming established, in so far as they were not theorists, studied documents produced by governments; geographers and ethnographers—who were very few—did some "fieldwork" but they relied for the most part on reports written by missionaries, explorers, soldiers, administrators, and other persons who had "business" in these places they wrote about. Some interest in "disinterested" firsthand investigation developed in the course of the nineteenth century. Schedules of ques-

This is a revised and expanded version of an essay that originally appeared in H. D. Lasswell and D. Lerner, eds., *The Human Meaning of the Social Sciences* (World Publishing, Meridian Books, 1957), pp. 114–57.

tions to which answers were to be obtained by travelers and officials were prepared by curious persons. James Mill prepared such a questionnaire for Henry Crabb Robinson when the latter was to go to Germany. Harriet Martineau wrote a little book with a similar end in view. The *Notes and Queries* of the Royal Anthropological Institute was intended for the same purpose. Inspectors of sanitary conditions and police agents made firsthand observations and directly interrogated those from whom they sought information. Their results entered into social science, but these persons were not collecting the information in a scholarly capacity, they were executive officials.

It was the establishment of society as an academic subject in the United States which changed the situation. Ever since its first modern stumblings, sociology has inclined towards immediate contact with the sentiments and actions of living human beings. It is true that there are still substantial parts of the social sciences today to which this does not apply, for example, economic theory, much of sociological theory, "historical" or comparative sociology, the analysis of economic growth, political philosophy, large parts of comparative religion, and numerous other parts which use printed and written official documents, officially gathered statistics (published or unpublished), written records of organizations, legal and administrative documents, published books and periodicals, unpublished manuscripts, etc. The trend, however, has been towards the diminution of the proportion of effort devoted to the study of such sources and to increase greatly the effort to study living human beings, observing them directly and above all by asking them questions which have no intended function other than to obtain information about the interrogated persons' beliefs, sentiments, and actions. The study of man has shifted increasingly towards the assembly of data by direct, deliberate, and orderly observation and by interviewing, which enters in growing measure into spheres of sentiments and intimate personal relations which have traditionally been studied only by retrospection, reflection, and the analysis of works with an objective existence of their own. It is not primarily the novelty of the subject-matters which has brought about the change. Essays and maxims on friendship and love, biographies of the dead, editions of the personal correspondence and journals of persons whose lives were over, historical reconstructions of the motives and intrigues of politicians and ecclesiastical dignitaries were by no means uncommon, but they were as far as traditional humanistic scholarship went in this sphere. The events studied were either definitely in the past or, if they were contemporaneous—which was rare—were usually studied at a distance from the principals, and above all from their private sphere.

Where, as in British social science at the end of the last century, the direct approach was developed in the study of living aborigines or of the lower social and economic classes of the social scientist's own society, there did not seem to be any serious ethical issues. Parallel intellectual movements in France, Germany, and the United States did not give rise to any different responses. In the first place, these inquiries did not enter very deeply into the private sphere of their subjects; the inquiries mainly confined themselves to economic matters and to publicly observable actions. There was some restraint on curiosity, deriving from the puritanical ethos of the culture from which the investigators came. There was, furthermore, no obvious problem in intruding on the privacy of savages or workingmen, particularly those at or near the poverty level, because, at bottom, the investigators did not quite regard those they observed or interrogated as being subject to the standards which the investigator regarded as fitting to observe in his relations with his equals. These subjects possessed no secrets which were sacred to the investigators; they possessed no secrets penetration into which could be expected to arouse discomfiture among the investigators or the circles in which they moved. Had any moral qualms arisen, they could have been allayed by the thought that the investigations were being undertaken with a view to the improvement of the welfare of their society.

In the United States, the first large-scale inquiries based on interviewing dealt with slum dwellers, Negroes, immigrants, persons with dubious moral standards such as "fallen women," "unadjusted girls," "jackrollers," et al. Such persons were not regarded as possessing the sensibilities which demand privacy or the moral dignity which requires respect for privacy. Moreover, the investigators were inhibited in their curiosity by the wider culture and by the traditions of the discipline under whose aegis they were working. Of course, it was always accepted that individuals would be rendered anonymous in the reports of the investigation. There was furthermore no coercion involving those who did not wish to be interrogated and simply did not reply to questions.

The shift to the study of the "respectable" classes came somewhat later. Such studies were very discreetly conducted and the topics treated were relatively "external," e.g., place where retail shopping was done, frequency of church attendance, membership in voluntary associations, duration of residence, etc. The respect for scientific research and for universities gave confidence to both the observer and the observed. The former thought himself to be serving the harmonious causes of knowledge and welfare, the observed felt that such auspices justified his participation. Hence, the tradition of direct confrontation of the subject through interviewing became firmly established before there seemed to be any moral problem. The chief problem of this technique of research therefore appeared to be the overcoming of "resistance" to being interviewed, i.e., resistance to the disclosure of private matters.

Nonetheless, the creation of techniques for the direct observation of living persons and contemporary institutions, the deepening of intellectual curiosity about the motives and the very tissue of social life, the diminution of inhibitions on intrusions into other persons' affairs, and the concomitant formation of techniques for perceiving these deeper and subtler things, have precipitated problems of ponderable ethical significance. The ethical values affected by contemporary social research are vague and difficult to formulate precisely. They refer mainly to the respect for human dignity, the autonomy of individual judgment and action, and the maintenance of privacy.

Sociology began by applying its techniques of observation and interrogation to the lower classes; it subsequently extended its range upward in the hierarchy of classes. This coincided with the adoption by academic political scientists of the techniques of sociologists and the extension of the interests of historians to contemporaneous events and persons. The study of "power elites" by political scientists and sociologists coincided with the historians' writing of biographies of recently deceased or retired public figures. The use of the "private papers" of the latter meant that activities and expressions of still living persons, which had not been intended for public disclosure, were opened to public view. In this case, the anonymity of the person studied, which had been respected by the earlier sociologists, could no longer be preserved.

The "muckraking" tradition of American journalism had been specifically focused on the public disclosure of actions and statements of politicians which had been undertaken or made with the expectation that they would be kept out of public view. By the time academic social scientists and historians turned to the study of still or recently living politicians, the muckraking tradition had been firmly established. Considerations of "confidentiality" or "secrecy" were obstacles to this movement of disclosure of thoughts and actions which otherwise would be known only to those who had perceived them when they had occurred.

These disclosures are intrusions into the private sphere of living persons.

II

The sacredness of individuality in the conventional religious sense is based on the belief that each individual human being is a member of a special category of God's creatures, each having in himself or herself a breath of divinity or being capable of absorbing, and of being absorbed into, divinity. The individual's value lies in that relationship to divinity. The so-called secular view omits only the element designated as divinity but retains nearly everything else. The individual human being is the sentient, mindful human being; the experiences of this individual are not just transient events which occur and pass away in time and space but are gathered up in memory and transformed by the powers of the mind into a coherent, judging, choosing, discriminating, self-regulating entity, conscious of its selfhood. In its individuality, the human organism develops an ego, a complex, bounded system into which occurrences in the past are assimilated, the future envisaged and sought, and the present made the object of discriminating assessments in which are contained assimilated precipitates of past experience and judgments and choices about the future. Individuality is not, however, just a cognitive system or a system of cathectic dispositions. It is constituted by the feeling of being alive, consciously and continuously, by the existence of responsiveness which is part of a highly integrated system. Every response of individuality bears the mark of the uniqueness of the system, which is self-creating and self-sustaining in significant measure. Each individuality is a system with its own rules of direction and rest. This mindful, self-regulating core of the life which has its seat in a distinctive and discrete human organism is what is sacred; this core constitutes the organism's individuality. It is this that makes man into a moral entity capable of entering into relationships of personal love and affection, capable of becoming wise, capable of assuming responsibility for his actions and of acting on behalf of a collectivity, be it a family, a civil community, or any other corporate body or aggregate of human beings.

It is the possession of individuality which renders a human being capable of transcending his individuality in love and friendship and in responsible membership in a civil community. He can transcend his boundaries, guided by standards and sensitivities which are integral to the individual. Obviously, there are limitations to this self-regulatory power. The biological organism within which individuality has its seat has its own determinants; the dispositions and capacities developed in interaction with the early social, primarily familial, environment create a framework which it is not easy to leave behind. The weight of cultural tradition, the needs of cooperative undertaking, and the maintenance of social order on a wider scale impose restrictions on the self-regulatory powers of the individual. But they never extinguish it, and the stronger, the richer, and the more elaborate the individuality, the more it can assert its self-regulatory powers.

Individuality requires actual autonomy—not only freedom of action, freedom in the outward movement of the individual, but also immunity from intrusion into areas constituted by the individual's sphere of action. This entails both freedom to move outward and autonomy vis-à-vis externally instigated intrusions or efforts to influence the sphere so defined. The sphere of privacy is built up from memories and intentions, by standards, tastes, and preferences which are attended by self-consciousness and which an individual would share only with intimates, and voluntarily, if he were to share them at all. He might not even be in a position to share these elements of his self because he is insufficiently aware of them, even though they are of constitutive significance for the structure of his self-consciousness. But whether he is aware of them or not, respect for privacy requires that their disclosure must be entirely voluntary and deliberate; otherwise his autonomy is infringed upon. No individual lives in isolation, and so his sphere of individuality is open to those with whom he accepts association, regardless whether the association is prized for its own sake as in friendship or love or whether it occurs in the pursuit of some other end. Disclosure of the content of the realm of individuality to those with whom it is not voluntarily shared for either of these reasons should be based on some knowledge of why the disclosure is elicited and on voluntary assent to the reasons for eliciting it.

Modern liberal society has been the parent of individuality. It could not have developed in a society in which there was no freedom to explore, to experience, and to judge, and in which the individual did not bear some of the responsibility for the consequences of his judgment. The emergence of individuality and the attendant demand for freedom is accompanied, however, by sensitivity and openness to the individuality of others. From this arises one of the problems which modern social research only complicates but does not create.

The individuality of other human beings arouses curiosity; it arouses desire to be in some sort of contact; whether it be entirely cognitive or cathectic (loving or worshiping) can be left aside at this point. It generates a demand for intrusion into privacy far more powerful than the trivial gossip at a distance which is characteristic of less sensitive phases of human development.

The respect for the privacy of the individual has taken its place in the constellation of values of modern liberalism. It is, however, a relatively recent addition. It rested for a long time among the undrawn implications of the liberal position and came to the forefront only with the growth of individuality and its appreciation, and the development of a more widespread personal sensitivity. However lately arrived on the scene, it is now fully incorporated. Like the other values of modern liberalism, it is subject to the affinities and the antinomies of any elaborate *Weltanschauung*. It has its limits in the birth and existence of human beings in families, of their residence in neighborhoods and their membership in corporate groups like schools, workshops, ecclesiastical bodies, political associations, and civil societies.

The respect for the privacy of the individual and of the bounded corporations into which he enters rests on the appreciation of human dignity, with its high evaluation of individuality. In this, the respect for human dignity and individuality has a historical connection with the freedom of intellectual inquiry and creation, which is equally precious to modern liberalism. The tension between these values, so essential to each other in so many profoundly important ways, is one of the antinomies of modern liberablism. The ethical problems with which we are dealing here arise from the confrontation of autonomy and privacy by a free intellectual curiosity, enriched by awareness of the depth and complexity of the forces that work in us and implemented by the devices of an effort to transform this awareness into a more systematic body of knowledge shared with others.

This essay is an effort to explore and to make explicit some of the problems which arise from this confrontation. It does not claim to be more than a first approximation, with respect to both the issues raised and the standards by which they should be treated. It tries, in a tentative way, to indicate some of the general standards which should enter into the investigator's response to these problems, rather than to promulgate specific rules. Where principles are in conflict, only the exercise of reasonable judgment, following reflective consideration of the issues, is in order. Moralistic rigorism would be injurious to the crucial values of liberalism and above all to our self-understanding and our self-control. Callow scientism would be pernicious.

III

In contemporary sociology, social anthropology, social psychology, and in those other related branches of social inquiry influenced by these disciplines, it is generally thought desirable that our knowledge of human thought and action should rest primarily on information gathered by looking at and listening to living human beings in the immediate presence of the investigator. These procedures are called interviewing and observation; the latter includes both "participant" and manipulative—experimental—observations as well as the more conventional type of casual observation gathered in the course of ordinary social life. Interviewing consists in eliciting information about the self of the person interviewed, about his past activities which occur outside the interviewer's range of observation, and about other persons with whom the interviewed person has been in contact.

Interviewing seems, at first glance, to be, ethically, the least problematic of the techniques of research in the social sciences. It seems to be little different from conversation. It is, however, conversation which does not arise from the immediate desire for conviviality; it has primarily a cognitive end in view, and an end which is that of one of the parties to it. This makes it different from ordinary conversation. It seems to leave the subject's autonomy intact, and although it does enter into his private sphere without the legitimation of intimacy, it does so only with his consent. It is impossible for a social scientist to interview a person without his consent and willing cooperation. When this requirement of respect for autonomous action is met, one of the major ethical obstacles to social research is apparently overcome. Manipulation of an adult person denies his autonomy by deceiving him, i.e., by depriving him of his power of reasonable decision, and by directing his action towards an end alien to his own consciousness; it is therefore ethically reprehensible. Consequently, an interviewer who requests the prospective interviewee's permission to conduct an interview, giving in the course of the request some explanation of the intent and nature of the inquiry, therewith avoids manipulation and the moral onus associated with it.

Yet, there would seem to be nothing morally problematic about this. What, after all, can be more unexceptionable morally than increasing the stock of human knowledge? And what is wrong with having a conversation with another person in order to add information about the person and generalizations formed on the basis of that information to this valued stock of human knowledge? Why should it not be thought by a person being interviewed that it is his obligation—and privilege—to contribute something from himself to the process of enlargement of the stock of human knowledge?

Whatever may be the obligations of a social scientist or historian to a dead person, there can be no doubt that he has obligations to the living ones whom he studies at firsthand. Whatever their differences in education, social status, intelligence, and political belief, the social scientist and the person he studies, belonging to the same species and having the same categories of capacities, have moral obligations to each other. These obligations include respect for individuality and for the private sphere, respect for the capacity to recognize the truth. It should also be said that, alongside these obligations, the asymmetrical character of the relationship made up by an interview does not allow to the interviewer the prerogatives of family or friendship. In a sense, the interviewer is a "foreign body" within the private zone of the individual interviewed.

Yet it is essential that the research worker recognize that he himself and the person he is studying both live in an identical moral realm. But why should the interviewer treat the interviewee as within his own realm? Are not the observance of the usual decencies of courtesy, such as attentiveness, and the expression of gratitude for cooperation sufficient? I do not think so, and my doubts are connected with a fundamental position regarding the fucntion of social science. Social science is a body of knowledge about human beings. The effort to make the knowledge of human beings more scientific in a broad sense imposes discipline, detachment, and orderliness of procedure; it might even end up by becoming more like a science in the sense of natural science. None of this can, however, transform the nature of the subject-matter, which must always remain human beings to whom the interviewer has moral obligations as he has to any other human beings. In eliciting information from the person whom he interviews, and even prior to that, the interviewer has the obligation to respect the interviewee's autonomy. Even though valuable information can be gained by deception in many situations, deception is contrary to this obligation.

Moreover, the knowledge gained by social science, if it is to find application in a more or less liberal democratic society, must have the function of collective self-clarification, of increasing collective self-understanding. Now while it might well be questioned whether it is desirable for an individual to be as clear about his motives as a psychologist or sociologist could conceivably make him, or for an institution to understand itself "completely," there can be no doubt that if such serious knowledge as is achieved by social science is to enter into "practice" in a liberal democracy it should do so by being shared, by the formation of rational opinion in the wider public. The alternative is for it to be "used" by rulers on those they rule.

What is true of the "consumption" of knowledge in the social sciences is true also of its production. The truthful sharing of the interviewed person's knowledge with the interviewer imposes on the interviewer an obligation to be truthful in his dealings with the person interviewed. This is the reason why the indispensable detachment of the interviewer from the person he interviews must be combined with acceptance of the moral obligation of common membership in the same moral realm. This is why the interviewer is obliged to explain to the person he is to interview not just his own personal end, e.g., to write a doctoral dissertation, but also what he is trying to do intellectually. This is not always easy but an honest effort should be made. Questions ought to be justified by the explanation of what the answers will contribute to the clarification of the problem being investigated. Naturally, it is not necessary that each particular question should be so explained, but groups or types of questions asked in an interview should be explained in this way. I appreciate the difficulties which stand in the way of observance of this standard, and, in many cases, the interviewed person himself will not care to have the explanation. Often he will not be able to understand the intentions of an elaborate piece of research, and, furthermore, the limited time which the interviewee is willing to grant might be excessively consumed by the explanation. The standard is nonetheless valid and should be adhered to at least as a guiding principle.

How "informed" must "informed consent" be in order to meet the standard? What is an "explanation of the intent and nature of the inquiry"? Is a perfunctory explanation which is enough to get the interviewer's foot in the door adequate? Is a general explanation which truthfully covers the early part of the interview sufficient, if the latter part of the interview, once "good rapport" has been established, moves far beyond the original assertion of aims? Why should not consent alone be decisive and sufficient without the requirement of "explanation" or "information"?

Sociological investigators certainly do not always inform their interviewees of the true intention of their inquiries. Some deliberately falsify their roles as sociological investigators and tell less than the whole truth or something quite other than the truth, in order to avoid arousing resistance to the disclosure of the information sought. In interviewing on controversial questions, some interviewers simulate agreement with the expected attitudes of the interviewees; others falsify the intentions of their research, claiming, for example, to be working on housing needs while actually seeking to observe family life or "leisure-time activities." The simulation of "warmth" is widely recommended in manuals of research techniques; it is probably also widely practiced and not always hypocritically.[1] These practices are often inexpedient from the point of view of gaining the cordial cooperation of the interviewee, particularly at later stages of the inquiry when further cooperation is required. Sometimes their spurious explanations or misleading identifications embarrass the research worker and even impede the further progress of the inquiry. The interviewee sometimes becomes suspicious of the motives of the interviewer. The falsehoods are also occasionally damaging to the dignity of and the public regard for social research, as well as being morally offensive by their mendacity and their pettiness; they also breed a cynical attitude among graduate students of the social sciences. Yet, their very triviality is their salvation; most of these misrepresentations are really peccadillos. They seldom harm the interviewee, who is often pleased with the experience of being interviewed. Nonetheless, quite apart from these latter considerations, which are entirely secondary, such falsehoods are improper, in principle, because they introduce deception into the process of scholarly and scientific discovery which postulates the value of truth.

Social scientists, whose disinterested quest for serious knowledge certainly must be acknowledged—even though it frequently does not produce results commensurate with the intention—may claim the privilege of permitted entry into the private sphere. Privacy, like free-

1. Social scientists who find the "pseudo-friendliness" of salesmen and businessmen offensive seem not to mind the beam in their own eye. The following passage is characteristic: "if the interviewer's task is to obtain information about some aspect of the respondent's habits—marital relations, for example—it would be necessary for him to establish a deeper kind of personal relationship with the respondent. In general, we can say that the more intimate, emotionally charged, or ego-involved the topic of the interview, the more delicate the job of establishing the relationship becomes and the deeper that relationship must be" (L. Festinger and D. Katz, *Research Methods in the Behavioral Sciences* [New York: Dryden, 1954], p. 357).

dom, can be restricted for good reasons, but it is essential in our outlook that the diminution of privacy should be for very good reasons; it should be voluntary and retractable. Just as a free man has not the right to sell himself into slavery or to establish an irremovable dictatorship, so the particular privacy which an individual suspends by making particular disclosures to another (in this case, the interviewer) must be reinstated by the treatment which the disclosed private information receives. The privacy should be restored by the obliteration of any connection with the person who disclosed it; this means that the interviewer must never disclose the connection to anyone, orally or in writing. The particular confidences must be respected; they must not be transmitted in their particular form and in their relationship to the particular individual to anyone else; they may be introduced into the public sphere only by generalization and anonymity.[2] In the main, this is the practice of sociological investigators.[3] Few investigators actually go so far in their respect for the privacy of the persons interviewed that they submit a draft of their research report to the persons on whose confidences they have drawn. This would enable them to ascertain whether they have disclosed anything which the interviewed person on subsequent thought decided he would like to withdraw or would, at least, like to see withheld from further diffusion.[4]

2. The corporate privacy of voluntary bodies is as much a part of our system of rights as is individual privacy, and deceptive intrusion into their interior affairs is unjustifiable in principle. At the same time, like the events which occur in the private sphere of the individual, it is a legitimate object of reasonable sociological inquiry. Such inquiry, however, depends for its conduct on a knowing and voluntary suspension of the barriers which maintain privacy. In its publication particular truths must make many concessions to privacy, as long as these concessions do not make inroads into the general truths discovered by the inquiry.

3. The jurisprudence of privacy, in so far as it existed at all, until recently confined its discussion to the protection of privacy from a far-flung publicity which permits the individual whose privacy has been infringed upon to be identified. Then with the development of computerized records, the concern with privacy shifted to the protection of information given to one private institution or department of government, to keep it from being disclosed to another authority on the same level; it has also been concerned with the amalgamation of separate pieces of information into a single record which would constitute a new and unauthorized observation and therewith an unauthorized infringement on privacy. Social scientists, when they are cautious to maintain the confidentiality and anonymity of the information which they obtain, place themselves beyond the reaches of a substantial part of the criticism of the penetration of privacy in contemporary life.

4. The privilege of entry into the private sphere of an individual by a sociological investigator naturally also entails a strict exclusion of any improper use of the fiduciary relationship into which they have entered by the very act of conducting the interview, e.g., to establish sexual relations with one of the participants, or to derogate or otherwise give publicity to one of the persons into whose private sphere they have been admitted. I mention these infringements on standards of propriety because certain cases are known to me.

The obvious differences between the critical, even destructive, treatment of the published work of an author and the divulgence of information given in an interview, accompanied by the name of the person who has given it, deserve some further reflection. The author of a published work has already attached his name to the work, and by the conventions of the literary and the learned worlds he has made his work available for whatever assessment anyone who reads it cares to make of it. The act of publication of a work is a renunciation of the privacy of a work—but it is not a renunciation of its author's privacy in other respects. If someone criticizes his work and censures the deficiencies of his accomplishment, he may claim no redress— assuming that the criticism is not libelous or is made by a qualified judge. In contrast with this, a person who has given information to an interviewer under the assurance that his name will not be disclosed and that he will not be identifiable does have a justified grievance if these conditions are not adhered to. He has indeed a multiple grievance: his privacy has been infringed on, the infringement has been aggravated by the identification, and he has also been deceived. (A person whose conversations with a friend who is also a novelist, if they are repro- duced in a work by the novelist in a way which permits the friend to be identified, is also the victim of a multiple impropriety: his private conversations with a friend are reproduced without his consent, he has been recognizably identified, and he has been deceived as well.)

The mere existence of consent to be interviewed or observed does not exempt the social scientist from the moral obligation of respect for another's privacy, no more than does the fact that priests, lawyers, physicians, and psychiatrists receive the confidences of other persons automatically resolve the issue for the social scientist. The priest receives confidences and grants absolution as part of a scheme of cosmic salvation to which the confessing person is committed; the lawyer receives them because the confiding person needs his aid in coping with an adversary under the law; the physician and the psychiatrist receive them because they offer the prospect of a cure to troubles of body and mind. The social scientist has, according to the traditions of our intellectual and moral life, nothing comparable to offer.

To intrude into privacy solely for the sake of a possible contribution to the general understanding of man's nature and of society's is unprec- edented in history.[5] The conflict between an aspiration to contribute to knowledge and some belief in and attachment to sacred things is not

5. The novelty is not, of course, evidence of an insuperable anomaly; it only indicates the need to study the problem carefully and honestly and to be aware of the need to make amends for the infringement by contributing seriously to knowledge rather than just contributing to the literature of the social sciences and the size of the population of doctors of philosophy.

new in history; what is new here is the kind of knowledge sought, the mode and the motives of its acquisition, and the particular sacred value with which it comes into conflict. The tension of the present conflict is aggravated by the legitimacy of the claim to enhance our stock of understanding; it is a claim which must be put forward with great circumspection. Especially in the present situation, when the attainments of the social sciences are rather modest in relation to their scientific aspirations, it is no justification for the infringement of an important right of the individual. Since most social research contributes little to general understanding, theoretical or empathic, and since its practical value in contributing to human well-being is less than that of medical research which experiments with human beings, it is very needful to be circumspect in intrusions on privacy. Even more to be censured are deception and divulgence of identity.

The moral problem is somewhat lightened by virtue of the satisfaction which being interviewed gives to many persons. It is not often in a busy society that one finds a person who will listen for several hours to an account of one's thoughts, sentiments, and experiences. Unburdening oneself, especially to an amiable stranger, often gives considerable satisfaction. Then too, among the neglected and the forgotten of our great societies, an interview is a cornucopia of attention and conviviality. All of these points render the intrusion into the privacy of the persons interviewed more supportable, but they do not eliminate the problems it engenders. We would not be justified in interfering with a person's choice of his friends or his occupation just because he enjoys submission, and our disapproval of prostitution does not depend on whether the prostitute finds it unpleasant; no more are we justified in forgetting that privacy is a right conjoint with freedom and that its voluntary suspension, although it might further the progress of social science, does so in a morally problematic way.

IV

Not all interviewing approaches the interviewed person simply as an informant about his own experiences and the experiences of others with whom he has been in contact. This complicates the situation. Much interviewing is intended to lead to observation. It is often an attempt to manipulate the subject into "revealing" aspects of himself which he does not knowingly articulate. Questions are often asked not because of the genuine interest of the investigator in the manifest content of the answer but because of his interest in the overtones of the answer, in the disclosures of experience, sentiment, and mood which occur inadvertently and in which the interviewer has not initially avowed an interest. The interviewee is manipulated into disclosing aspects of himself which have not been openly solicited. This is an important feature of projective tests, which are "manipulative interviews" that seek to elicit manifestations of dispositions and sentiments of which the interviewed person is presumably unaware. A projective test is an invitation to an interviewed person to allow himself to be observed in the unwitting manifestation of properties of which he may or may not be aware; he does not know what it is that he is disclosing. In responding to the test, he produces responses the content of which he must be ignorant, not only because he has not perceived them in his own thought and conduct or because he lacks the technical knowledge adequate to their interpretation, but also because their assessment is done outside his presence. Projective tests almost by their nature must go beyond the informed assent of the person tested, and they go moreover into areas generally conceded to be private. They fall into the class of what some social scientists have ingenuously called "unobtrusive observation," meaning thereby penetrations into privacy without authorization.

The same applies to the participant-observer technique which was once highly esteemed and which is still one of the more productive techniques of sociological research. It seems to me to be susceptible to considerable ethical abuse. It is plainly wrong for an inquirer obstensibly to take up membership in a community with the primary intention of conducting a sociological inquiry there without making it plain that that is what he is doing. His disclosure of his intention might occasionally hamper the research he is conducting, but the degree of injury suffered by his research does not justify the deviation from straightforwardness implied by withholding his true intentions. It may be mentioned in passing that since sociologists, like most other people, have a certain strength of moral scruple, their subsequent interviewing and observation in the group or community is likely to benefit from having an easy conscience.

There is, in principle, nothing objectionable about much of the observation of the conduct of other persons; it is inevitable as well. Life in any case is unimaginable without it; it is inevitable as long as human beings live together. It is, moreover, the source of reflective wisdom, and those who do not practice it at all abstain only because they are morally or intellectually defective. The observation which is part of the normal course of life, however, usually is not sought on false pretenses. It is integral to the process of living together, and when it is focused on actions in which the observer has no immediate part it is directed to actions which the persons observed perform in the pursuit of their own ends. The observations of everyday life are conducted in relationships which have arisen out of other than scientific or scholarly intentions. The observer has not created the relationship merely for the purpose of observing the other person; to the extent that he has done so he is guilty of manipulation, which, however frequent, remains nevertheless morally obnoxious, nor does it lose its obnoxiousness by virtue of its triviality or harmlessness.

Observation which has within it a large element of manipulation— and this is also common to certain kinds of interviewing and participant-observation and to most projective tests—seems to me to be morally questionable on two grounds. First, on account of the wrongfulness of manipulated self-disclosure and, second, on account of the private nature of the subject-matter of the disclosures which the manipulating interviewer tries to precipitate. It is an effort to intrude, without a person's consent or his knowing cooperation, into the reserved sphere of the individual.

V

Observation which takes place in public or in settings in which the participants conventionally or knowingly accept the responsibility for the public character of their actions and expressions, for example, in a parliamentary chamber or in a public meeting, is different from observation which seeks to enter the private sphere unknown to the actor. The person who takes on himself the responsibilities of public life, like the writer of a novel or a scholarly or scientific work, has to some extent made a certain part of his activity public property, although in the case of the mixed public-private situation, e.g., a university seminar or a restaurant, the moral right of privacy should limit the freedom of observation.[6]

The open sphere—the sphere in which the individual by his career has committed himself to publicity—is a legitimate object of observation, as it is of interviewing; the right to observe and to interview in this sphere is justified by the postulate of each individual's responsibility for the actions he undertakes in public places and in public roles. What of the conduct, the participants in which believe to be private to themselves, and which they would even like to keep secret? The answer depends on whether the action is properly in the public domain. Even though he tries to keep it private or secret, the politician who takes bribes as well as the one who does not, the administrator who favors a kinsman as well as the one who does not, and the person who commits some crime cannot rightfully claim that his privacy is invaded if a governmental investigator or a newspaper reporter or a university research worker observes his professional actions or ob-

6. There are situations in which such unadmitted observation is necessary, e.g., in the pursuit of criminals, spies, etc. The necessity of such situations on behalf of social order does not diminish their morally objectionable character; it simply outweighs it.

tains the relevant information by interviewing him or another person about them. Even though every man is entitled to withhold his views from public expression, citizens' views on public issues, if observed without deception, raise no problems about the invasion of privacy. On the other hand, the quiet conversation of two friends in a restaurant or bar, the spontaneous intercourse of a family within its own home, a discussion in a university seminar, the confidential discussion of a governmental committee or the deliberations of a jury are, for a variety of reasons, not equally in the open sphere, or even in the open sphere at all. In each of these, important events occur which are certainly interesting subject-matter for the analyses of the social scientists. Yet are social scientists justified in penetrating into this sphere through surreptitious observation?

The propriety of their entry into the sphere which is not public rests in part on the extent to which they do so with the approval of the persons observed. If the social scientists observed what occurred in the relationship but did so with the knowledge and permission of the participants, then the intrusion into privacy could at least be justified by having been granted the assent of the observed. If a sociologist observes what goes on in a restaurant or in a concert hall, the situation is somewhat different because the participants know that they are in a public place in which they are observable. Privacy, and even secrecy, are positive rights, but the obligation to respect them may properly be suspended if the actions to be observed are voluntarily disclosed to the observer by those who may legitimately do it. If the knowledge is sought solely for the sake of increasing our general intellectual understanding of human conduct, the moral objectionableness might not be so great. Likewise, if it is impelled by considerations of public good—and not public curiosity or professional accomplishment.

Although there might be some uncertainty regarding the propriety of entering, by permission, into the private sphere, there seems to me to be no doubt at all about the impropriety of unauthorized entry when the persons are observed in situations which they legitimately regard as private to themselves as individuals, as friends, or as a corporate body. The development of new mechanical devices for observation, such as small, soundless, motion-picture cameras, small, unnoticeable microphones, and other undiscernible sound-recording equipment, have precipitated a very urgent issue, and it is desirable that social scientists should take a very unequivocal position. They should make perfectly clear that they regard as utterly reprehensible any observations of private behavior, however technically feasible, without the explicit and fully informed permission of the persons to be observed or of those who are entitled to represent them. Such an intrusion into privacy could be justified only as an emergency measure necessary for the maintenance of public order, or the protection of the society as a whole, which might otherwise be severely threatened.[7] The growth of sociological, anthropological, and psychological knowledge scarcely falls into this class of emergencies, because the real and immediate benefits which it can bring are so small and problematic.

Although the incarceration of individuals who have committed crimes is justified by the necessities of social order, high scientific curiosity would provide no justification for similar measures. *Mutatis mutandis*, the same principle applies to the invasion of the private sphere of the individual or of groups. It is true that in the case of the successfully surreptitious invasion of privacy, no physical harm is done, and none might ever be done, and if the persons observed remain permanently ignorant of the process of observation, they are not even, in fact, embarrassed or inconvenienced. Nonetheless, the intrusion is not to be justified. Nor is it justified even if anonymity is maintained. Nor, given the low probability of intellectually significant results, does it have the justification of contributing to the understanding of human conduct. Nonetheless, quite apart from consequences, it is a contravention of our moral standards and must not be undertaken.

In the latter part of 1955, a furor arose in the United States over the installation, by sociological investigators, of microphones in a jury room in Wichita, Kansas. The jurors were not informed of the existence of the microphones or the recording apparatus. It was done with the permission of the trial judge and the lawyers for both litigants. The tape on which the record was made was kept away from any situation in which the individual jurors could be identified by any parties involved in the litigation, their associates, or journalists, and in the typewritten transcript their names were changed so that no particular attributions could be made for any assertions made during the proceedings of the jury. The social scientists involved disclosed nothing of the recorded proceedings to anyone on their own initiative, except to members of the team of investigators. The only breach of complete secrecy in custody of the recording and transcription was committed at the request of the bench.

There are several issues involved here. The first is the infringement on the confidentiality of collective deliberations which in this case were part of the machinery of adjudication; the second is the deception of the individual members of the jury who understood that their deliberations were confidential; and thirdly, there is the question of

---

7. I do not mean to imply here that the police should be perfectly free to use these devices to observe the conduct and conversation of any suspected criminal or any person suspected of espionage. On the contrary, in these instances too the use of these instruments must be subjected to the strict control of the courts and the highest levels of political officialdom.

the appropriateness of the scrutiny of major institutions by social scientists. The questions of the infringement on confidentiality and the deception are, in principle, quite simple. The concealment of microphones which would record discussions which the jurors had good reason to believe were not being recorded is contrary to honest dealing, and, even if the judge and the two lawyers had a crucial responsibility, the social scientists are not thereby exempted from their share of the blame. Let the judiciary and the bar look after the integrity of their own members; social scientists are responsible for their own professional morals.

Does it make any difference that the subject-matter of the deliberations was not in the personal-private sphere of the jurors? The jurors' proceedings were undertaken with the understanding that, although performing public functions, they were performing them with the guarantee of confidentiality,[8] like those with which personal-private relations are conducted. It was therefore an invasion of the confidential sphere in the same way in which newspapermen invade the confidential sphere when they interview jurors or when they attempt to get government officials and legislators to say what went on in confidential or secret meetings, or when they purloin and cause to be published secret documents, private or governmental. It differs from the observation of occurrences within a family or between lovers, if their permission to observe them had not been obtained in advance, which are clearly intrusions on privacy, only with respect to the fact that the jury system, like a cabinet meeting, is of genuine public interest and not just amusing to public curiosity.

There are other reasons to be considered for denying the permissibility of such action, even if the jurors had agreed in advance to the observation and recording of their deliberations. The confidentiality of jury proceedings is traditionally justified by the desirability of completely free discussion as a means of reaching a collective decision; and by the necessity of avoiding pressure on jurors by nonjurors, which might occur if the course of deliberations were to become known by nonjurors, e.g., litigants, their lawyers, friends and kinsmen of the litigants. The confidentiality of the jurors' deliberations is not quite the same as the confidentiality of personal private affairs, and the argument for maintaining it must therefore be somewhat different. The invasion is an infringement on a convention which, it is claimed, sustains an important public institution.

It might be maintained that no harm would be done to the effective-

8. This confidentiality is not, however, always strictly adhered to by jury members and the press, once the deliberations are completed. Again, it is for social scientists to look after their own morals and not to seek the most common denominator to justify themselves in the assessment of improprieties.

ness of the jury process, if the record, once taken without the knowledge and permission of the jurors, remained sealed up under the strictest custody of the trial judge until after any period during which appeals could be made, if the control and custody of the record and the transcript were sufficiently rigorous to protect the jurors from pressures or reprisals from persons who might have suffered from their judgments, and if members of subsequent juries, knowing that their deliberations might be recorded, were given absolute assurance by the judge—which they accepted—that no record whatsoever was being made.

Nonetheless, although the free discussion within the jury might not be damaged if observations of this sort with these safeguards were made, they would still possess an element of impropriety because they involved the deception of the jurors.

If all the jurors had been informed of the arrangements for recording their deliberations and of the secure provision for preventing any breach in confidentiality, if all of them had agreed to the arrangement, then it might have been permissible.[9] Unfortunately, however, there is no absolute security of such provision. There would be a risk that one or more of the jurors would talk to an outsider about the recording, as jurors sometimes do about the proceedings themselves, and this might be exploited by one of the lawyers in seeking a reversal of the decision; but as jurors cannot be called as witnesses about deliberations in hearings on appeals from decisions by lower courts, so the records of their discussions could likewise be given the same immunity.

The case of the recorded deliberations of the Wichita jury raises questions not only about the permissibility of deception in social research and the right of privacy in private and public roles. It also raises questions concerning the propriety of detached inquiry into the working of the institutions of society.

VI

The public discussion of the affair of the jury in Wichita devoted little serious attention to the problems involved in the invasion of the jurors' privacy and not much more to the possible influence of the recording or the research on the effectiveness of the jury system. Mostly, the response was a very passionate and unreflective denunciation of the sociological and legal investigators who had had the effrontery to "tamper" with the jury system. Quite apart from the responses and motives of the congressional committee which conducted

9. A question remains of the moral right of all the members of a jury to agree to waive the confidentiality of their deliberations when they are acting in a public capacity. They do not have the same rights as individuals in a private capacity.

the hearings and of the officials of the Department of Justice, there was a widespread feeling of abhorrence for the very notion of a detached scrutiny of the interior of a "sacred" institution. The abhorrence, although "irrational," is not on that account to be condemned out of hand.

The nominally secular modern state has no avowedly "sacred" sphere, and the churches no longer have the power to prevent anyone outside their jurisdiction from turning an empirically analytical eye onto their sacred beliefs and actions. Nonetheless, there is a sacred area of even secular societies, and much sentiment is aroused by whether this area should be open to all eyes or whether observation and publicity about it should be restricted. The detached and realistic observation of the actual working of certain institutions and arrangements or of certain beliefs arouses feelings approaching horror and terror in some persons, just as it exercises the fascination of sacrilege in others. For the secular state, what goes on in these institutions or what is contained in these beliefs is sacred; social scientists, like journalists, are eager to penetrate into this sphere, and there are others who would like to restrict their penetration. The powers of these two antithetical tendencies fluctuate. In the United States, there have been rather extreme variations since the Second World War. The general trend is towards the abolition of secrecy, especially the secrecy of authority,[10] and towards the wider opening to observation. Yet the movements are ambivalent. For example, there is much resistance against the opening of the distribution of genetic qualities in the population to scientific scrutiny and, above all, against the study of the genetics of the intelligence of ethnic groups for fear that certain beliefs which have become sacred will be placed in doubt.

It would be misleading to account for this horror of penetration into the "secrets" of vital institutions solely to expediential calculations, such as the guarantee of secrecy necessary for national security or the protection of bureaucratic or political skulduggery or, the maintenance or enhancement of the effectiveness of the institutions in question. Of course, the secular state does not confine its tendency towards closure solely to those matters in which secrecy is necessary

10. The fact that there are so many "leaks" of secret information, utterly unconnected with espionage, is no argument against the interpretation given in the text. The eagerness to penetrate and disclose secrets is not just motivated by professional journalistic pride and democratic concern for the common good, but it is also the product of an urge to be in contact with the sacred zones of authority and to give public evidence of that contact. Likewise, the readiness in the United States of administrative officials and congressmen to "leak" the proceedings of secret meetings is in part a product of political tactical considerations and an act of conciliation towards the powerful journalists. Yet it is also the product of a desire simultaneously to give evidence of being in contact with sacred zones and to degrade it by disclosure to the uninitiated. The populistic ethos is nurtured by such sentiments.

for national military security. The meetings of cabinets, the president's meetings with his advisors, the deliberations of the chiefs of staff, the caucuses of party leaders have in the past been closed to scientific inquirers, just as they have been closed to journalists. It is not so just because public knowledge of them would necessarily harm the state or subvert public order or diminish the prestige or effectiveness of politicians and administrators, but because many persons who wield great power feel a deep urge to keep their deliberations from external knowledge.[11] Laws to guard "official secrets" guard not only knowledge and intentions which ought to be kept from foreign enemies but internally "sacred" things as well. There are also things which are not officially secret, such as the discussions among the justices of the United States Supreme Court.

Even where the society is as populistic as it is in the United States, where the journalists are so inquisitive, and where politicians enjoy and seek the bright light of publicity, social investigators have been denied entry into such spheres. In fact, social scientists usually have not even sought such entry, partly because they believed it would be denied them and partly, I believe, because they themselves stood in such awe of the majesty of the powerful. This has begun to change.

Good arguments can be made against continuous publicity about public institutions. It could be claimed that extreme publicity not only breaks the confidentiality which encourages the imaginativeness and reflectiveness necessary for competent decisions, but also it weakens—especially when it selects and emphasizes improprieties of conduct—the respect in which political institutions should, at least tentatively, be held by the citizenry. The former argument is purely empirical and has a reasonable probability of being right. It stands in contradiction to the liberal-democratic and particularly to the populistic-democratic principles of "the eyes of the public" constituting the "virtue of the statesman." It would also restrict the freedom of social scientists. The second argument is genuinely conservative, since it implies that the institutions of authority should have some aura of the ineffable about them. It denies a postulate of liberalism and of the social science which is a part of liberalism, both of which have on the whole believed in the value of unlimited publicity and an easygoing irreverence or conscious hostility towards authority.

To what extent is it justified to refuse social scientists the right to penetrate into zones of public conduct which had been regarded as confidential? What harm can it do, what good can it do? Is it necessary for social science; is it necessary for the enlightenment of opinion

11. Such is the ambivalent nature of human beings that the need for secrecy is often accompanied by the equal and concurrent need for publicity about what is secret.

to which the social sciences might contribute? If we accept that the press should be entitled to disclose many things about the interior of institutions of authority, why should not social scientists do so? In principle, it is right for the press to go as far as it can, although there are as many or more instances of useless and vulgar disclosures by the press—almost always with the aid of some persons within the circle of authority. Much of the divulgence of secrets by the press is really the divulgence of secrets—of "leaks"—by individuals within government to the press either for political ends or for personal ones or both. Should the social sciences engage in this kind of activity? One argument against their doing so is that they become thereby an instrument of the designs of politicians and civil servants to achieve their ends and to vindicate their past actions. It may also be said that in allowing themselves to be "used" for political purposes, they would involve the social sciences and the universities in politics. It tempts social scientists into the melodrama of journalism; it even makes social science identical with journalism and thus makes itself superfluous by doing what journalists have already done. It would be especially superfluous if social scientists seek primarily to "expose" and to discredit the institutions of authority in liberal-democratic societies. In any case, the instances in which social sciences have acquired improperly divulged material regarding the internal processes of governmental institutions are very rare. Most academic study of governmental institutions does not acquire data illicitly, and it does not use such data unless they have already been published, although their original divulgence might well have been illicit.

It seems to me obvious that social scientists should not engage in the purloining of "classified" documents for the purposes of their research, nor should they allow themselves to be exploited by officials who wish to undo or discredit their rivals within the government. I do not think that any good intellectual or social purpose is served by the zeal of social scientists and contemporary historians to gain access to the documents of recent governmental transactions which have been recently declassified or which still await declassification. It is part of the tendency to turn social science into journalism; it bespeaks an unseemly desire to be "in on" secrets. As far as the damaging consequences for social order and the respect for institutions is concerned, publications based on illicitly obtained confidential or secret documents are not to be taken very seriously. There are not likely to be very many. For the rest, which depend on recently declassified, formerly secret documents, neither harm nor benefit can result from this practice. Except for jargon and footnotes, they are indistinguishable from journalism.

I myself see no good reason, therefore, other than expediency, why these "sacred" secular subjects should not be studied by social scientists, or why they should not be studied by legitimate research techniques. I can see no harm that can come from such inquiries, carried on with judicious detachment and presented with discretion. I can see no moral issue here, such as I can see in the case of manipulation by interviewers and observers or in the case of intrusions on privacy.

VII

As the methods of observation of human conduct became better controlled and more precise, and the effort to discern correlations in a more exact form emerged, the logic of intellectual development dictated the desirability of experimental studies. The experimental investigation of man as a moral and social being has an old history. It began on a large scale with experimental psychology in Germany in the second half of the nineteenth century. The prototype of the experiment on human action is still the psychological experiment carried out with controlled stimuli, divorced from the world of real experience. The introduction of experimentation into the study of social relations adhered quite closely to its point of origin. As a result of this background and because of its greater practicability, social-psychological experimentation was confined largely to the study of small groups in face-to-face relationships or of individuals in school classes, camps, etc.

There has thus far been very little experimentation with larger collectivities. Social scientists have served as administrative officials or advisors to such officials concerned with the organization of communities such as displaced persons camps, prisoner of war camps, rehabilitation centers, prisons, settlements of unemployed workers and impoverished farmers, etc. In these instances, however, experiments of a genuinely scientific nature were seldom carried out; the social scientists engaged in these activities were counselors speaking in the light of their general understanding of the situation and not as scientific experimenters. Their scientific procedures were usually not brought into play. It was rather a precipitate of the knowledge which they acquired in their earlier studies which entered into their judgments and their consequent counsel or decisions. Their advice and judgments in these situations were usually formulated with an administrative end in view; the concern of the social scientist in administration was, like that of all administrators, to achieve or maintain a given condition of order and a certain level of individual satisfaction rather than the enhancement of knowledge as such. In what used to be called "action anthropology", the aim of the anthropologist was usually the achievement of certain social conditions in the attainment of which anthropological understanding would be employed. The aim was not the enhancement of knowledge through controlled observational experiments but rather the utilization of generalized, previously attained, knowledge in conjunction with the power to achieve a practical end.

Such experiments as have been carried on in these circumstances are usually part of the ongoing administrative process. They take a form in which a new measure which is being considered for comprehensive application is tried first in one area, while the previously used measures are retained in another area. These "experiments," in so far as they are conducted by legitimate governments and do not contravene properly enacted laws or general moral standards, are like any other administrative actions carried out in pursuit of the purposes of a legally constituted government. The administrator's authority to command comes from his role as a civil servant, charged with particular practical responsibilities. This does not mean that governments are morally empowered to design experiments which might be anticipated to do damage to those over whom they exercise authority. To the extent that they do, they behave reprehensibly. Still, the authority and the necessities of governments are different from those of social scientists, and it is with the latter that we are concerned here.

There is nothing in the nature of the knowledge offered by the social sciences or in the moral status of the social scientist, nor in the benefits which their research can provide, which confers the authority to command or to manipulate, or to deceive, or otherwise to use human beings as means to the scientist's own ends.

Most of the experimental work in the social sciences which is aimed at the increase of knowledge does not raise moral issues. In the first place, the groups on which experiments are carried on are small. The situations are very often no more than quasi-real at best. They are contrived by the experimenter; they are seldom recurrent, and they are usually of rather brief duration, falling mainly between a half-hour and two hours. The stimuli or the variables in the situation are rarely of great significance to the experimental subjects, and as far as is known—it has never been followed up—leave no lasting impression on the personality or outlook of the subject. Since the groups which are the objects of the experiment usually have had no anterior life of their own, they disappear from memory with the end of the experiment. The experimental subjects are moreover ordinarily informed of the purpose of the experiment.

A full account of the experiment is not always given, in part because the subject does not seek it and, in further and more important part, because it does not seem necessary to the experimenter and because occasionally an element of unself-consciousness is thought necessary to the success of the experiment.[12]

The ethical issues arising from experimentation are the following (1) the propriety of the manipulation and deception of adult, normal human beings, even for the progress of knowledge, by social scientists; (2) the propriety of possible injury to a human being on behalf of scientific progress and the progress of human well-being; (3) the depth and permanence of the effects of the experiment on the individual subject.

Experimentation often involves manipulation and deception, although it need not always do so. Manipulative experimentation involves the exercise of influence for an end which is not fully shared between experimenter and the experimental subject. Such experimentation is not a relation between equals; it is a relationship in which power is exercised, at best within a framework of consent and mutual good will, but the actual relationship between the experimenter and the manipulated and deceived subject is not a relationship of consent.

Authority is exercised throughout society, and most of us still regard it as something reasonable to accept in many situations. Authority is exercised by legislators, physicians, priests, teachers, and civil servants. In all these relationships, the end striven for by the person exercising authority is not as clearly perceived or equally shared by the person over whom it is exercised. That is in the nature of authority, and its inevitability renders it acceptable, even though it should be recognized that the exercise of authority often falls very far short of the highest ethical standards. But apart from its inevitability, we regard it as proper by virtue of the common commitment to membership in the civil community. Membership in the civil community is by no means entirely voluntary. There are many situations in which the exercise of civil authority shades off into manipulation, i.e., when the ends of the required action become more and more opaque to the person over whom it is exercised; there is also much coercion or the threat of it to reinforce the commands of legitimate authority. The authority of the experimenter has none of the claims of the civil authority; it is more like a contractual relationship, with the limitation on the right to contract away one's will or dignity or to serve unforeseen purposes of the experimenter. The less the experimental subject appreciates or desires the ends sought by the experimenter and the less intelligible to him are the means used for eliciting his obedience, the more problematic the experimentation becomes ethically. As consen-

---

12. Sometimes the experimental subjects are actually deceived about the experimenter's intention.

sus becomes attenuated, manipulation increases. This is the kind of power exercised in the operation of a sociological experiment. The subject of an experiment will practically never know as much about the experiment and its meaning as the designer of the experiment; if he did, it might prejudice the desired outcome. The problem which remains, therefore, given the irreducible trace of the ethically problematic in social-psychological experimentation, is whether it is kept down to a minimum in its pernicious effects. Here, on the whole, the record of social science experimentation seems to be unexceptionable. Its acceptability, however, might be partly a function of its inconsequentiality. If it studied more important variables which touch more deeply and lastingly on the life, conduct, and outlook of the subjects, it might perhaps have acquired more scientific substance, but it would do so at a much greater ethical risk.

Some years ago a group of anthropologists of Cornell University came into control over a Peruvian hacienda of two thousand persons on whom they wished to use their authority to institute large-scale and long-range changes. They undertook to rule the lives of men and women without the legitimacy which any government, even a tyranny, possesses, but with the legitimacy of a large landowner. If we assume that they introduced no measures except what they thought beneficial for their subjects, then they were benevolent despots. If, as seems to have been the case, they attempted to establish democracy there, to raise the standard of living, to increase education and civic responsibility, their position was little different from that of the conventional liberal reforming landlord, except that they were also trying to observe precisely the results of their efforts. They had two claims to justification: one, the enhancement of welfare; the other, the increase in knowledge of how the changes in general came about—but as far as I can gather, no measure was instituted exclusively for cognitive purposes. Although I have not seen any detailed reports on this unprecedented undertaking in which the Peruvian government has rented two thousand of its citizens to a foreign landlord, the dominant impression I receive is that the Cornell group is trying to apply its already available knowledge to the practical task of improving the life of a hitherto impoverished and suppressed group, increasing their self-respect, their desire and capacity for self-government, their productivity, their understanding and skill. There seems to have been no experimentation in the precise sense. Whether academic social scientists should undertake to run a plantation far from their own society is problematical, but this view has nothing to do with manipulation.

Since the Cornell-Peru scheme, experimentation on a large scale has repeatedly been recommended by social scientists testifying before governmental bodies regarding the contributions which social scientists can make to the attainment of the ends of government. Very little attention has been given to the ethical problems of social experiments by social scientists.

By and large, as the result of a historical accident, experimentation by American social scientists has been influenced by a liberal, humanitarian attitude. This is to some extent attributable to the influence of Kurt Lewin. The anti-authoritarian attitude which is inherent in the culture of American social science and which has concerned itself with the discovery of the consequences of emancipation from authority and particularly from repressive or manipulative authority has also had some influence on the manipulation characteristic of experimental social psychology. The experimental groups have usually been relatively indulged as compared with the control groups, which have been dealt with in the manner which is conventional in existing institutions. In the studies conducted under the inspiration of Kurt Lewin and his students and disciples at the Universities of Iowa and Michigan and in the work of the Tavistock Institute of Human Relations (London) which arose from a tradition of medical therapy, the independent or experimental variables have frequently been decentralized authority (as contrasted with the conventional centralization of authority in the control group) and discussion and enlightenment as means of instituting changes in the behavior of subordinates (in contrast with the conventional technique of command in the control group).

This has by no means always been the case. There are many instances of the use of traumatic stimuli by the experimenter; this is clearly reprehensible ethically. Moreover, the deeper the level of the person whom he attempts to influence, the greater is his ethical responsibility, and the more objectionable the introduction of a traumatic stimulus. It is said that these manipulations, deceptions, and possible injuries are excusable because the objective is the advancement of knowledge. When an investigation is embedded in the discipline with a tradition of genuinely scientific accomplishment and is not just a product of an individual frivolousness or destructiveness, the argument for experimental manipulation is said to be strengthened. When the investigation is motivated by a genuinely therapeutic desire or is embedded in a genuinely therapeutic culture, it appears to be more justifiable. At present, however, much experimentation in social science possesses neither the therapeutic nor the genuinely scientific qualifications. Even if it did, that might not outweigh the objectionableness of manipulation as such. Its ethical acceptability, which is marginal, rests on the peripheral nature of the stimuli and the transient character of the effects introduced.

More serious experimentation by social scientists in the present state of their disciplines must be viewed very cautiously. Many restraints must accompany its recommendation or execution. In medicine, where knowledge is admittedly fragmentary, although undoubtedly less fragmentary than in the social sciences, experimentation has been generally guided by a strongly rooted therapeutic tradition and is almost always a link in a continuing sequence of scientific activity. One of the chief features of research in the social sciences today is the absence of both therapeutic intent and a tradition of cumulative scientific growth. This renders more doubtful the scientific value of the results attained by experimentation which would deal with the more vital features of individual or corporate life.

Furthermore, because the therapeutic tradition of medicine is lacking, the possibility that sociological experimentation on more important variables might have harmful consequences is greater. Even in medicine, this moral restraint in experimentation is sometimes lacking. Nonetheless, the professional ethos formed by the weight of a powerful tradition and inculcated in medical schools where a sense of ethical responsibility has been one of the best precipitates of a course of study, which includes much that is not technically necessary for the medical practitioner, is still lacking in the social sciences. This ethos is not by any means just a product of scientific maturity, although the latter does make a positive difference. It flows from a deeper solicitude which is still lacking in the scientific study of man.

VIII

Ultimately, the ethical quality of the relationship of the investigator to the person he interviews or observes is derived from the social scientist's relations, as a person and as a citizen, with his society and with his fellow man. Respect for the privacy of those he studies will be related to his general appreciation of privacy. The care for the good name of other persons will be related to his respect for human beings generally. The newly possible techniques of research which would permit the destruction of the spheres of autonomy and privacy, through infrared films, concealed cameras, microphones and recording apparatus, and chemical and psychological manipulation, become dangerous when the ethical outlook of the social scientist is hostile towards society and diabolical in its curiosity. Unfortunately, the prospect is not entirely unequivocal.

About a half-century ago, a German social scientist said that sociology began as an *Oppositionswissenschaft,* a discipline impelled by the spirit of opposition to the then contemporary society. In France, the positivist sociology of Comte and St. Simon arose as a scientistic criticism not only of the society of the ancien régime but of the modern bourgeois society. In Germany, the Romantic reaction against the French Revolution and against the spirit of commerce and citizenship of the French bourgeoisie and the *philosophes,* moved in the same direction of hostility toward contemporary society, a hatred of individualism, distrust of the central institutional system, and a deep dissatisfaction with the insufficient integration of the central value-system of the emergent large-scale society. This element in the tradition of sociology has never been lost. In Tönnies, in Simmel, and in Durkheim, it occupied a central position, and even in the work of Max Weber, who was less enthusiastic about the desirability or possibility of a totally integrated society, it is not entirely absent.

Nor did the European alienation come to an inhospitable soil when it was brought into American sociology. The most fertile figures of American sociology before the great upsurge which began just before the Second World War were William Graham Sumner, Robert E. Park, William I. Thomas, Charles H. Cooley, and William F. Ogburn. With the exception of Sumner, who expected nothing reasonable from any society and demanded only individual freedom and who accordingly found himself quite at home in the vigorous capitalistic America of the turn of the century, all of these sociologists were critics of modern society. They regarded modern Western and particularly contemporary American society as individualistic and uncongenial to stability. They flourished in the traditions of muckraking and populism and shared many of their attitudes toward traditional authoritative institutions. Even Professor Ogburn, who by no means shared the intellectual tradition of the others, was a persistent critic, from a scientific point of view, of the failure of modern institutions through their incapacity to eliminate the "cultural lag" created by the advances of modern technology.

In the Great Depression after the Second World War, the critique of contemporary society current in the older generation of sociologists received reinforcement from the various currents of European thought of the 1920s and the 1930s which began to flow through the intellectual classes in the United States. These adaptations of Freud, Marx, Pareto, Durkheim, and Weber began to play an important role among American sociologists. These new influences resulted in new subject-matters and new approaches to the older subject-matters. New problems of sociological inquiry came to the foreground in the last part of the 1930s and throughout the 1940s: the psychoanalytical interpretation of ethnic hostility, beginning with Dollard and moving on to the Horkheimer circle, the studies of industrial relations which, leading from Mayo through Warner and Whyte, stressed the anomic character of modern industrial relations, the studies of mass communication which began with public opinion studies and then went on to voting studies, with their stress on the dissensual, and the analysis of popular culture, the study of pressure groups in politics; these and many other studies left their imprint on the interpretation of American society. It was an interpretation which gave prominence to the anomic, the irrational, the dissensual, the coercive, and the vulgar elements in our society. The coherence, stability, and continuity of American society were left unattended or taken for granted. It is not unfair to say that much of the work of American social scientists showed a certain measure of distaste and repugnance for their own society. In significant respects they felt alien to their own society and culture which they thought had gone astray or been wrong for a long time.

Now while much in this attitude was fruitful of keen insight, it was also blind to important features of society. More significant, however, was the moral distance which it expressed. This sense of moral distance has not been without dangers for the ethical conduct of social research. In so far as it has expressed a sense of moral disjunction between the investigator and the human beings whom he investigated, it made it easier for him to disregard moral scruples. It freed him from obligations to these persons arising from membership in a common moral community. The objects of his inquiries thereby became mere objects, without valid moral claims. They were accordingly made available for the treatment which any scientist accords to his nonhuman objects. Against the background of such a limited sense of affinity, manipulation and deception become perfectly appropriate means of inquiry, and all spheres of life, provided that it is technically possible to obtain access to them, are regarded as open to psychological and sociological scrutiny and publication.

IX

The reserve forces of Western culture which would inhibit social scientists from seeking to establish a scientistic tyranny over their fellow-men—with benevolent intentions—are multifarious; they are also, however, by no means free from contradictory impulses. On the positive side, there is a very real respect and appreciation for the value of the individual. There is among men of practical experience a distrust, sometimes excessive, sometimes insufficient, for the theorist, for the scientist with his abstract schemes and doctrines. There is also, in the vast majority of the population, a common decency and sense of moral restraint which is common to our Western culture with its tendency towards moral equalitarianism. There remains in varying strength a respect for community derived from religious belief and an attachment to the past; both of these impose restraint on inhumane ingenuity.

On the other side is the scientistic attitude, and the impatience with imperfection which are also parts of our cultural inheritance from Bacon, Condorcet, Comte, Marx, down to Veblen, Bernal, Lundberg, and Skinner, and which has envisaged men of science ruling society, bringing it into order, overcoming man's imperfections by the application of scientific knowledge.

Alongside it, sometimes overlapping with it, sometimes running against it is the humane liberal tradition to which nothing human is alien, the tradition of the British, French, American, and German Enlightenments, of Locke, Adam Smith, Hume, Kant, Lessing, Schiller, Jefferson, Franklin, Voltaire, Diderot, et al., who, even where they have not been read, have continued to exercise a great spiritual influence in heightening the appreciation of the spark of divinity in every living human being. Yet a cranky, embittered alienation and romanticism accentuate the anti-authoritarianism innate to liberalism. This alienation and romanticism cut the individual off from his society and his fellow-man and cause him to despise the triviality of ordinary human beings and the symbols and persons they respect. It is exacerbated by a naive belief in the ease with which men can be improved and the unreflective conviction that social science is the right means to that improvement.

Within the social science professions themselves—from which I except economics—the situation is also quite indeterminate. Unlike in the natural sciences, no great tradition has yet established itself, commanding universal assent. Something more like chaos reigns there. Social resentment and scientific enthusiasm, the desire to legitimize themselves by being useful and influential, the alienation from and the fascination with authority are all forces which potentially could work in the direction of evil. The public opinion which they create among the oncoming generation is not always consistent with respect for the dignity of the individual life or its collective arrangements. Yet it must be remembered that they are integral parts of our culture and also share in its values in one form or another. Moreover, even the very curiosity which prompts the investigator's intrusion into privacy is the manifestation of a breadth of empathic curiosity, an openness to and imagination about other human beings, in their essential individuality, which to some extent provides its own inner curb. Inherent in this scheme of interpretation is a genuine respect for the humanity of human beings.

Finally, and perhaps most important, the social sciences are conducted mainly within and under the auspices of the great universities, which, despite all the deformations of size, fashionableness, and intellectual vanity, still respect an older tradition which they have not cast off. There are therefore strong supports for a self-containing sense of responsibility which will guide intellectual curiosity and imagination amidst the dangerous temptations which modern techniques of research afford.

9   Social Science as Public Opinion

I

Social inquiry, even when most scientific, is a social action; it is, even at its very best, part of a set of social relationships. In recent years, some writers have come to see that there is an underlying social structure in all fields of intellectual work, but thus far they have attended only to the internal social structure of the scientific community. The social relationships which link the objects and subjects of social investigation, i.e., the persons studied and those who study them, have thus far not been seriously considered. The relationships between the student and the studied are not exhausted by the situation of the interview, the questionnaire, or even by the subsequent protection or disclosure of the information provided by the interview. It continues in a generalized form through the more general accounts, of varying degrees of abstraction, which the social scientist formulates. It is widened in its scope so that it becomes an orientation towards whole classes of persons; it becomes a part of the social scientist's relationship to his society, towards specific institutions, groups, and classes of his society. It enters into his action towards those with whom he comes into contact. It becomes a component of his "political" orientation in the deepest sense of that word, i.e., it expresses his orientation towards authority.

Now, the social sciences are only to a small degree sciences. Only parts of the social sciences possess the rigorous methods and results required for admission past the threshold of science, and very little of their beliefs can claim the evidence, the continuity and the generality of genuinely scientific achievement. Quite apart from the unscientific state of most of the knowledge which constitutes the social sciences today, their inevitable involvement in the societies which they study, and of which their practitioners are members, confers on them another physiognomy. Even if the social sciences become "real" sciences in the sense that the physical sciences are sciences, the social sciences would still constitute a set of judgments—cognitive, moral, and appreciative—about contemporaneously relevant past and and recent events. Their judgments, perhaps truer in some respects than many of the judgments of these events made by journalists, politi-

This essay originally appeared in *Minerva,* vol. 15 (1977), ©1977 by *Minerva.*

cians, and interested citizens, would still have much in common with these latter judgments. The social sciences are and will remain a part of public opinion. They are part and parcel of the opinions of the social scientists and they can enter into the opinion of the laity, including those in positions of authority and those who are citizens.

It is true that modern scientific knowledge, i.e., modern physical and biological knowledge, has increasingly become—through formal education and the reading of popular scientific writing—a general possession, more or less understood and assimilated by certain sections of the population beyond the scientific profession. It is, of course, most unlikely that a great deal of the specific content of the natural sciences can ever become very intimately intertwined in the cosmos of sentiments and beliefs which we approximately designate as public opinion. Nonetheless, the diffusion into the broader public knowledge of the discoveries made by scientists and scholars in geology, archaeology, palaeontology, geophysics, astronomy, comparative religion, and textual criticism have certainly had some influence on Christian and Jewish religious belief; they have diminished the acceptance of the accounts of the origins of the universe and man and of the efficacy of divine powers which were proposed in the traditional Christian accounts. A similar process may be seen in Asia and Africa in attitudes towards the cognitive content of Buddhism, Islam, Hinduism, and the pagan religions. Because of the nature of political and social life and the general anthropocentric preoccupations of most human beings—the highly educated and the most intelligent as well as those who are less intellectually developed—beliefs, observations, and assessments of the social sciences are beliefs about objects which lie at the center of public opinion. The objects of public opinion are human beings, as well as the institutions and practices of human beings in their relations with each other and with authority. The relations of human beings with each other, their solidarity and hostility, consist in part of opinions, of beliefs, cognitive and evaluative, about the self and others. The social sciences are beliefs about human beings. This is as true of the "scientifically hard" parts as it is of the more impressionistic parts; it is as true of the specific observations which social scientists make as it is of the "framework" within which particular observations are made.

The perceptions and beliefs of the social sciences, in view of this identity of objects studied by social science and those experienced in the course of social life and because of the social scientist's inescapable membership in his society—whatever the degree of his civility or incivility—are integral to the "larger mind" of the time, one large and amorphous zone of which takes form in "public opinion." More differentiated, more disciplined and more specific than public opinion in the current sense,[1] the social sciences are elaborate, specific, and orderly as compared with the other areas of the "public mind," but they are part of it.

The deeper strata which underlie the entire terrain of the mind of the age also underlie the social sciences. The sensibilities, ethical dispositions, animosities, and sympathies which are comprised in these deeper strata are the matrix of the consciousness which dominates the social sciences. The individual's share in "public opinion" is an integral component of his connection with his society; it is a constitutive element in his activities. The social sciences, or those parts of them which any individual social scientist possesses, are his image of man and society. I do not mean that every specific observation made by a social scientist enters at once into his picture of society. Most of them are washed away but in so far as they are precipitated into stable, however vague, propositions, they are constitutive in his view of society. In so far as the laity—including students—read what he writes or listen to his lectures, his views of man and society can become theirs.

It is true that many social scientists do not wish to think of themselves as addressing anyone except "the profession," meaning other social scientists with similarly specialized concerns. Nonetheless, their audience goes beyond the limits of "the profession." Not all the students of social scientists become professional social scientists, any more than all the students of professors of medicine become professors of medicine. The former enter into all sorts of professions outside as well as inside academic life, just as a majority of the latter enter medical practice, while relatively few remain in academic medical schools to concentrate on research and on teaching. The practicing physician brings with him some of the medical science which he learned; the ordinary citizen who passes from undergraduate studies in social science to become a businessman or a civil servant or a producer of programs for television or a journalist or a lawyer brings with him some of the views of society which he acquired from his studies in social science. Those who do not attend university or who study subjects other than social science do not thereby escape the flow of social science beliefs. They read, hear, or see, at second remove, what others who have absorbed some of the beliefs of social science produce.

Even quite technical social science finds its way into broader pools of opinion. Those professional social scientists who address their colleagues are nevertheless pleased when they see the social sciences

1. Although not necessarily more so than the public opinion of the early liberal epoch, which was the opinion of a delimited, more or less "expert" public of journalists, ecclesiastics, university dons, informed business men, et al.

being "used" by civil officials, military officers, managers of industrial firms, advertisers, directors of civic bodies, politicians in and out of office, etc. They too acknowledge the existence of an audience for the social sciences outside the profession. It seems less demeaning to their professional dignity to have an audience of the powerful who accept social science as a "science" rather than as opinion. So it seems to the professionally proud social scientists. Nonetheless, they are wrong. Even if what they communicated were scientific, it would still be opinion, i.e., a set of beliefs about the world, man, and society.

II

The social sciences have been deeply infused with a number of traditions which are romantically hostile to civility.

Much of recent American social science is conducted from an ethical and political standpoint which is alienated from American society, from the central institutions through which authority is exercised in that society, and from the cultural values which regulate life in those institutions. This does not mean that most American social scientists are radicals or revolutionaries. Most of them are collectivistic liberals; very few of them are revolutionaries, even fewer are conservatives or liberals in the older sense of the word. This does not mean that American social scientists who are collectivistic liberals falsify or distort their observations and analyses in order to obtain results which would conform with a view of American society which is worthy of a negative evaluation. It is not that simple. It would perhaps be closer to the truth to say that they study aspects of American society, the analysis of which leads, given the evaluative standpoint of collectivistic liberalism, to negative judgments. It is the choice of subject-matter rather than a lack of probity in research which sustains their conclusions.

If it is the tradition of sociology to concentrate on dissensus, it is no wonder if the society appears dissensual; if one concentrates on the lowest categories of a distribution, it is no wonder that the society appears to be inegalitarian.

Such preponderance is accorded to the dissensual elements in American life that it is difficult to perceive any elements of order whatsoever.[2] This preponderant emphasis on the dissensual is ac-

2. In the index of an important book published recently by one of the most distinguished of living sociologists, and one who is among the most level-headed and responsible in the entire profession, the dissensual topics outnumber the consensual topics by a ratio of more than seven to one. Is there any reason to believe that dissensual events are seven times more numerous or seven times more important than consensual ones? It is not that the eminent sociologist believes that American society is as dissensual as his distribution of attention would suggest. It is rather that he is a sociologist and, although rather an original one, the weight of tradition was too strong for his curiosity.

companied by the belief, with different degrees of explicitness, that the alternative to a highly dissensual society is a highly integrated one in which there would be practically no dissensus. The romantic ideology of the superiority of *Gemeinschaft* to *Gesellschaft* still remains, despite much sophistication, a postulate of much of the outlook of the contemporary social sciences except for economics.

Many of the leading figures of American social science—in so far as they were not exclusively preoccupied with purely technical or procedural questions—have tended for several decades to see American society—there are important exceptions—as a mass society, characterized by loveless apathy and civic ignorance in most of the population, and a self-interested, ruthless pursuit of power for its own sake and for the retention of what they already possess among the powerful. American society is seen—in contrast with what society could be—as a heap of atomised, lonely, status-preoccupied individuals, isolated from the central institutions of their society by lack of faith, by anxiety and impersonality, and from each other as persons by their egoistic competitiveness. In so far as they participate in corporate action, apart from that necessitated by the requirement of earning a living, their actions are selfish and their interests irreconcilable. American society no longer has any local integrity—an integrity now mourned for—and it also lacks national integration. American society is represented as a "state of nature" where the rule of *homo homini lupus* prevails. This all-pervading fear of one's fellow man makes, as Hobbes said it would, for submission to the commands and demands of authority. Man in America, according to this current of social science thought, has not only renounced his unloved liberty to the elites who dominate "the organization," but he has renounced his inner substance as well. He has lost his individuality and is too fearful to attempt to regain it. Everywhere man is driven by anxiety, nowhere does he find fulfilment. The "successful" are caught in a squirrel's cage, and the faster they run the less satisfaction do they find; the failures naturally have not even the consolations of the squirrel's cage. In this society there is no justice; each man's hand is raised against his fellow citizen.

The masses allow themselves to be drugged by television, radio, and popular press. They become depersonalized and dehumanized. What can the political order of such a society be but a tangle of cynical manipulation and a tug of war among interests? The interests organized in pressure groups are unchecked by any conception of the public interest. The legislative body is the object of these pressures and the resultant legislation registers the relative forces of the contenders. Legislators, seeking only the security and enhancement of their own fortune, and concerned therefore with reelection before all else, must make themselves into the instruments of those who can assure their reelection.

A society which is utterly dissensual, where each man looks after "number one," cannot provide the foundation for a political regime which is any way concerned with the common good. The leaders of such a society are either automata, puppets, or rogues, and in none of these capacities can they merit respect or arouse the fellow-feeling of those who study their actions.

The most prominent piece of social research of the first fifteen years after the end of the Second World War—acclaimed as the most influential work by more than a score of leading social scientists at the Center for Advanced Study in the Behavioral Sciences—asserted that, except for those who accepted a "progressive," collectivistic liberal viewpoint, the population of the United States consisted of authoritarians, proto-Fascist in their outlook. One of the most widely read sociological works of the 1950s declared that the country was ruled by a small circle, dominated by the military clique and the great corporations. One of the most influential of all American sociological investigations of the present century sees a small community, alleged to be representative of the country as a whole, cut across by six separate and distinctive social classes each of which is preoccupied with its own status vis-à-vis the others; it was only after several more volumes had been published that the author discovered a common culture in a patriotic celebration. A brilliant young German sociologist published an article in the United States which asserted that such order as there is in modern societies is a product of coercion; otherwise conflict would be all-pervasive. The article became a basic text for many sociologists of the generation of the 1960s. One of the most admired sociologists of the 1970s produces book after book which portrays all social relationships as efforts to deceive, dominate, and humiliate or to defend oneself from such actions by deception and evasion.

One of the most popular sociological works of the 1950s portrayed American society as a chaos of deeply apathetic individuals without any communal or civic life, impelled only by a need for conformity and left a ready prey to machination and manipulation. One of the most widely acknowledged treatises in political science in recent years, applying an antiquated physical model to the study of social phenomena, sees the political order simply as an equilibrium of forces or pressures. American political studies have increasingly interested themselves in the realistic examination of the distribution of authority and the workings of administrative bureaucracies. In these studies, the image of oligarchy, undemocratic, devious, illiberal, underlies and precedes most empirical studies. The studies of the administrative bureaucracies of corporate bodies repeatedly emphasize the mistakes and self-deceptions of the authorities and the evasions of the subordinates. Frictions and frustrations make up the whole picture.[3] Relatively little attention is given to the fact and the way in which complex jobs get done, despite the many barriers of tension and uncooperativeness, of miscalculation and harshness.

The studies of occupations and professions stress their mythology, their exploitation of this mythology for self-enhancement, their private evasion of publicly proclaimed responsibilities. The instances could be multiplied ad infinitum; the works and authors referred to are both typical of perhaps the dominant undercurrent of feeling about American society among American social scientists today.[4] The alienated, Hobbesian viewpoint which I have roughly sketched is very fashionable at present. It is sophisticated to espouse it, and to interpret one's particular findings in its light.

This interpretation is of course not wholly incorrect. There are traces, even considerable elements, of truth in it. Power is far from equally distributed in the United States, deference is also unequally distributed, pressure groups are influential, there is much crime in the United States, much self-centered hedonism; there is much hypocrisy, much conflict. But this is far from the whole picture. Blindness to consensual elements in American society and sensitivity exclusively to elements of dissensus are major defects of this outlook. This exclusive concentration on the dissensual is by no means a result of a straightforward confrontation with the facts. It is rather another manifestation of a romantic aspiration toward a highly cultured, highly integrated, smoothly functioning society—a cross between a village community, as seen by Tönnies, and the Athenian polis, in the Whig interpretation. Those who espouse this ideal are affronted by the reality of a loose, pluralistic society, rough and vulgar, patriotic, individualistic, energetic, given to waves of enthusiasm and despondency, disrespectful towards authority and yet highly organized. This reality is offensive. The image of American society is formed by juxtaposition with ideal society.

The traditions which carried this image came from European and indigenous sources. They have long histories, both inside and outside the sociological disciplines. Empirical research seems to sustain them.

3. The efforts of certain industrial sociologists to introduce a qualification by stressing the integrative function of personal attachments have been roundly criticized for obscuring the irreconcilable dissensus which overrides everything else.
4. There are also notable exceptions who take up a very divergent view. There are also investigators who are so very particular in their observations or so preoccupied with procedures that such general theoretical orientations are not prominent in their work.

The intellectuals, among whom the social scientists have taken a prominent position, vying with and almost supplanting the man of letters, see the existing society as a horror in contrast with the land of their heart's desire. Elevation of spirit, contact with vital realities, the meaningfulness of existence, a perfect justice, a realm of harmony, are the unspoken ideals which they acquire from their tradition. In their stead, they see damaged lives, lost souls, vulgarity, triviality, unjust power and powerless innocence, incessant conflict and frustration. It is all exceedingly repugnant to them. They cannot make their moral peace with such a society. Nor can they turn their backs on it to look heavenward and to the refinement of small intellectual conventicles. Their traditions, their professional obligations, and their tastes keep their minds set on the frightful present.

III

Social scientists are the contemporary equivalents of the *philosophes* of eighteenth-century France. They are publicists commenting on the current scene in America and the world. (They are diverted from time to time from this activity by "purely scientific" activities which refer to no particular facts of the present social order. Here too, however, they resemble the *philosophes,* who also made excursions into science.) Even the deepest and most abstract of contemporary social scientists are, in no pejorative sense, publicists. They are writing most frequently about contemporary society, and, even when they declare their allegiance to the ideal of an ethically neutral science of society, they quite consistently do not allow that to stand in the way of their ethical judgment and political partisanship with respect to the society which they study. The best among them utter their comment in a wide context and refer to the deepest forces which mold our lives.

The social sciences tend more and more to provide the educated classes with their intellectual response to the world. Underlying this is a greater, more pervasive preoccupation with the state of society and of the condition of its members. Despite the allegations of dehumanization and depersonalization which critics of the modern world direct against modern Western societies, this growth of social sensibility seems to me to be one of the most significant developments of the age. It is partial and deformed and can never be complete. Many human beings are indifferent most of the time about what goes on in the society beyond the radius of their immediate experience. There are some persons in influential positions in the larger society who have only the minimum of interest in the larger society. They are concerned to know only what they need to control, and their wider experience gives them the knowledge which they think they need. In those sections of society, too, a movement towards an extension of the radius of interest and awareness has occurred, but there are resistances which should not be disregarded. There still remain aesthetically sensitive persons who do not care about society but only about works of art; here too a change has occurred in modern times and artists are full of opinions and ostensible knowledge about society. There are still mystics who are concerned only about God, but the clergy and theologians are nowadays more interested in society than they are in divinity. The growth of social awareness and of curiosity about society is thus certainly far from complete. It is certainly not desirable that it should be complete; perhaps it is too great already.

One part of this development is the increased cultivation of the social sciences. They are, in this regard, a manifestation of a heightened consciousness of society. I do not mean to be understood as saying that earlier epochs and other civilizations were indifferent to society. That is emphatically not my view. What I wish to say is that a larger proportion of the population turns more of its attention to perceiving—whether correctly or erroneously is another matter—and judging society than seems to have been the case in other epochs and civilizations. A much larger proportion of the population is active professionally in describing, analyzing, passing judgment on, making decisions about, and attempting to influence society than was the case in other times and civilizations. Perhaps in other times and places, most human beings had to labor so hard and long to maintain themselves physically that they had neither the time nor the energy to open and direct their minds to the wider reaches of a society in which their own experience fell within a very short radius. They had very little means of learning about the things of which they did not have direct experience. Little effort was expended on the part of those who were better placed in this respect to bring such "news of society" to the peripheries. In any case, a great change has occurred. Among the educated, the concern with the gods has diminished, the concern with codes of personal rectitude and self-discipline has diminished; the evacuated space is partly filled by the expanded interest in society.

This is not the place to dwell at length on the extension of the radius of social awareness in previously very peripheral sections of the population. I wish only to stress that the growth of the social sciences should be looked upon as part of this much larger change in the focus of attention of human beings. It is not only part of it; it is also one of its most significant parts. The rest of society, more eager to know about society than it used to be, turns to the social sciences.

There are some special reasons for this turning to the social sciences. With the diffusion of social curiosity and awareness, the social sciences have come to occupy an increasingly prominent position in the courses of study in colleges and universities. The classics have been greatly reduced and the study of the great literary works of the past has retreated before the study of recent works, in their social significance. These works are often only of social significance. The empty space, and the new ones created by postgraduate studies, have largely been taken up by the natural and the social sciences as here understood, meaning sociology, social anthropology, social psychology and political science, which have assumed a great sway. Not only are these social sciences among the most popular subjects of undergraduate and postgraduate study, but they have extended their sway into the study of history. There is resistance in this field but it is resistance to a rising tide. As oriental studies have expanded in the United States and as they have recovered in Europe, with a primary emphasis on the recent political, economic, and social features of those countries—in contrast with the previously preponderantly philological, literary, theological, and archaeological emphases in Indology and Sinology—the sphere of influence of the sociological approach has widened correspondingly. Divinity schools have given more and more attention to the social aspects of the cure of souls, e.g., to pastoral counseling, to marriage guidance, and to civic participation, into all of which the outlook of the modern social sciences penetrates. Medical schools and law schools are striving to open their syllabi and research programs to some sectors of the behavioral sciences. The growth of "general education" on the undergraduate level has likewise opened the way for the sociological outlook to reach persons who enter into every walk of life, and who enter more particularly into the influential positions reserved for the highly educated—into journalism and other media of communication, into administration, private and public, into teaching, and into similarly influential occupations.

Accompanying all these changes in the content of university study and research, there has occurred an expansion of opportunity for higher education, and an increasing presence of those who have availed themselves of these opportunities in the circles which have a weighty influence in opinion and policy. Thus the teachings of the social sciences, and above all their basic orientation, enter as an ingredient into the minds of others through education, through counseling and guidance, through management and advice to managers, through manipulation and propaganda, and through the exercise of legislative and administrative authority.

The social sciences can never supplant direct experience as the basis for assessing concrete situations. They are establishing themselves as a major constituent of modern outlook on society and undoubtedly will come to constitute an increasingly significant component of the practical man's image of the social world. Among practical men who have self-respect, the social sciences can be taken in their stride. The corrective and distorting influence of experience, of

462 *The Ethics of Sociology*

maxims of action, and of traditional wisdom will always reshape, correct, and warp the perception and analysis provided by the social sciences. The greatest successes of the social sciences lie in the slow permeation of opinion, in the provision of a general orientation. Their chief success thus far, and in the proximate future, is likely to be found among the student bodies of the universities. There the younger generation, unsupported by experience, are exposed to the full blast of the social sciences. The social sciences fascinate them; they are their substitutes for the "grand tour," for the inherited wisdom of the ancients. Their contemporaneity makes them all the more alluring. Their alienated, conflict-ridden, anti-authoritarian outlook renders them especially attractive to sensitive young men and women, and even those who are not so disposed, are, at least for a time, overpowered by them. It is from these young persons that the intellectuals of the next generation in the universities, in the press, etc., will come, and it will be on them that modern societies will depend for leadership in the formation of opinion and in the guidance of policy.

IV

The proper calling of the social sciences lies in the illumination of opinion. Even if they become sciences like the natural sciences, that will be their best function—although many problems remain regarding the ways in which scientifically formed opinion might operate in the relations of human beings who possess those scientifically based beliefs. Having their point of departure in opinion, it is their task to return to opinion fortified and disciplined by dispassionate study and reflection. To return effectively—and not injuriously—to opinion, to persuade by sound evidence and rational argument, to aid publicists and politicians and civil servants to see things in the light switched on by systematic observation and analysis, presupposes, however, a state of affinity between the social scientists and the society which they study and interpret and to which they address themselves. The enlightenment of opinion by social science is not the deformation of opinion by social science. The enlightenment of opinion presupposes a readiness to be enlightened and the existence of enlightening truths. Many of the beliefs of contemporary social scientists are not such truths; they are rather precipitates of deep prejudices about modern societies.

The social sciences might or might not becomes sciences in a rigorous sense. Whether they do or do not, they are and remain scholarly disciplines with standards of observation and analysis which can be best appreciated by those who have specialized in their study. As such they are under the control of persons who are equally expert. Documentation, evidence, precision of observation and analysis are required if the author of a social science work is to meet the standards of his colleagues. There are referees and editors of learned journals, there are their colleagues whom they meet daily at their universities and less frequently at colloquia and conferences, there are book reviews and ''reviews of the literature.'' Social scientists in their professional scholarly capacity are kept under the disciplinary scrutiny of their peers. That this is not always good enough is attested by the present state of the social sciences. If political and other unscholarly criteria penetrate into these professional judgments, the intellectual merit of the discipline suffers accordingly.

Since ''professional'' social science is more factual and less interpretative, its biases against existing institutions and society as a whole are less apparent. The social sciences, when they go beyond their small and specific subjects, introduce principles of interpretation which also derive from major traditions of the social sciences. These principles are less visibly present in the more specialized works of research. They tend to be more visibly present in works of macrosociological reference and they also tend to be more present in works which are addressed to a composite of professional social scientists and the laity; in many instances they tend to be of interest to this wider public because they, for the most part, deal with contemporary events of the societies in which they are produced.

What is to be expected in such circumstances? Do the social sciences contribute to a realistic understanding of the particular society and of modern societies more generally and of society as such? Do they concentrate primarily on those features of society which are regarded as morally deficient and which give rise to moral abhorrence, or do they show to the wider public aspects of society which need not call for moral denunciation?

The situation is very unclear and what can be seen of it is generally unsatisfactory. ''Men of letters,'' the book reviewers for the major journals, deriving as they do from the aesthetic and bohemian literary traditions of the United States and Western Europe, generally provide the signposts for the reading of the serious lay audience for intellectual works. They have been inclined in a radical political direction for many years, and academic social scientists who were not under their influence before the Second World War have come to be so since then. The social scientists who write from this standpoint on large topics, of whom C. Wright Mills was the most eminent in his time, tend to receive the most favorable attention. The result is the diffusion into the large lay audience of those works which set forth one version or another of ''oppositional'' social science. The reservations about such works which obtain within the narrower circles of the professional social scientists do not reach the larger audience.

The same situation exists with respect to the activities of social scientists as advisers to governments. Works like Daniel Moynihan's study of *The Negro Family* and Professor James Coleman's *On the Equality of Educational Opportunity* have received careful academic assessment. For the most part, the counsel given by social scientists does not come before their professional colleagues and it does not receive their scholarly assessment. The social scientist as adviser is in the same position as the social scientist as publicist; he is relatively free from the scrutiny of his peers. Civil servants and politicians are in a stronger position than the lay public: they are in positions of authority and they have commitments which enable them to disregard whatever is distasteful or uncongenial to them. The lay public is in principle also free to accept or reject what it reads or sees, but it does not have to make any immediately practical decision about the ideas from social science which it acquires from reading the works themselves or from encountering their views with some degree of meditation. Nonetheless these ideas form increasingly their intellectual environment. As the proportion of the population which has been subjected to the social sciences from secondary school onwards increases, its receptiveness to ideas from the social sciences increases too. The social science which is being taught in many colleges and universities presents a partial and distorted image of man and of contemporary society. It is usually not untrue in its details; partiality and distortion increase as the analysis ascends to greater generality. The result is an allegedly scholarly but untruthful confirmation of radical prejudices.

Societies can be changed through revolution and through radically alienated agitation. Some of the most important changes have taken place in this way. Some of the most massive changes have been advanced through the workings of alienated intellectual opinion. For these modes of change, the outlook which runs through a large part of contemporary social science is the right one. For those, however, who would eschew these procedures and would decide more discriminately about what to conserve and what to change, and who would exercise their influence through reasoned persuasion of their fellow citizens and their representatives rather than through threat, obstruction, and withdrawal, a more realistic conception of society and a more realistic portrayal of the motives of human conduct than are offered by much of contemporary social science are desirable.

10 The Legitimacy of Social Inquiry

I

Western societies in recent times have accorded a higher measure of importance to systematic, secular, empirical, and theoretical knowledge than have societies on other parts of the earth's surface and in other epochs. This kind of knowledge has been esteemed as a good in itself; actions into which this kind of knowledge is incorporated have been regarded as superior to actions without it. It is not wisdom or vision but the possession of secular knowledge which is esteemed. By extension, societies into which such knowledge is infused are thought to be better societies. For the sake of convenience in what follows, I shall call these societies "cognitive societies," although they are no more exclusively cognitive than "traditional" societies are exclusively traditional. Cognitive societies are those in which some of the exercise of authority and, to a greater extent, publicistic and political contention about the exercise of authority have been affected by the belief that such knowledge of the sensible world acquired through rational reflection or analysis of organized and disciplined sense-experience, is necessary to the proper conduct of all human enterprises. The conception of efficiency which underlies, or is honored, at least rhetorically, in modern administration in government and economic life postulates the availability and value of secular knowledge of the consequences of alternative paths of action; it presupposes the estimation and systematic rational assessment of the consequences of action. The modern conception of tolerance includes the prizing of rational and factual discussion among antagonists. Long before the "computer age" and the "information society," the ideal of a rationally conducted society in which myths and superstitions had been cleared away by the expansion of systematic empirical or scientific knowledge had made much progress. In no other societies than those of the West have traditional religious beliefs been so eroded by scientific knowledge and by the scientistic attitude.

Long before modern technology became "science-based," the "scientific" way of looking at things was praised. It did not mean scientific in the sense that the techniques and propositions of scientific discipline were drawn upon, only that judgment was dispassionate, disinterested, considerate of factual evidence, and attentive to rational and factual counter-arguments which involved ostensibly demonstrated empirical propositions. This tremendous shift of the human mind I will call the "movement of cognitive expansion" or the "cognitive movement." The rational and experimental procedures of the natural sciences—especially as understood by publicists of science—were only more rigorous promulgations of the modes of thought commended by the cognitive movement.

It was believed by a growing body of devotees of the movement that no injurious consequences could flow from scientific knowledge. But this was only a corollary of the belief that benefits would inevitably come from the increase in the stock of scientific knowledge. The acquisition and possession of scientific knowledge or of knowledge which was as scientific as possible was itself good, was necessary to the dignity of man. Scientific knowledge was contrasted with "revelation," to the disadvantage of the latter; even "intuitive" knowledge could not be accepted unless it was confirmed by observations gathered through disciplined empirical observation theoretically interpreted. All sorts of virtues were attributed to this kind of knowledge. It was, for instance, said that only on the basis of such knowledge could sound ethical beliefs and a proper moral life be founded. In some parts of the movement, it was even claimed that in the course of time scientific knowledge would replace "value judgments." There would be no problem of man's earthly existence which could not be solved by means of scientific knowledge. These utopian excrescences were the most forward positions of a more moderate, but nonetheless pervasive, appreciation of the supreme value of rational empirical knowledge.

II

The cognitive movement grew along three major lines. The first was the enormous advance of the natural sciences. Curiosity and imagination disciplined by the organized body of the traditions of science, by theory, and by scientific techniques of observation and analysis, and aided, in its later stages, by organized institutional provision and the recruitment, selection, and training of the most talented members of the oncoming generation, produced one grand discovery after another. Knowledge of the universe, of the earth, of man's biochemical nature, natural history, of the animals, minerals, and plants which existed on the earth, went forward into previously uncharted territories.

The understanding of man as a moral and social creature made less progress, but this retrograde condition was regarded as a misfortune attributable to the obduracy of traditional beliefs and one to be overcome by exertion and encouragement. It was never suggested that the knowledge of man's nature as a moral and social being could be harmful; no knowledge could be harmful. How could it be, when the very notion of human dignity comprised a rational understanding of the world and the self? Man and society would become more intelligible as scientific methods were applied to their study. The effort to find and establish the most appropriate "scientific" procedures for the better understanding of man and society preoccupied some of the best minds of the nineteenth and twentieth centuries. The legitimacy of scientific social inquiry was self-evident; the only question was how to make it scientific enough. There was, especially in Germany, a certain amount of criticism of the application of the "methods of the natural sciences" to the study of culture and society. This criticism and the alternative offered did not, however, entail any renunciation of the ideal of *Wissenschaftlichkeit*.

The second major line of the cognitive movement lay in the appreciation and promotion of education. The spread of educational opportunity was the corollary of the growing dominance of the belief in the value of secular knowledge; scientific knowledge came relatively later into the curriculum of the schools, but educational reformers had urged its inclusion much earlier. Scientific studies entered universities on a large scale only in the nineteenth century, and they were assimilated into school syllabuses later than that.

Education was the diffusion into many minds of what a relatively few greater minds had discovered or created. Education was the acquisition of knowledge; no one disputed that, although other consequences of education, such as its contribution to social discipline and the mastery of practical skills needed to earn a livelihood, were variously stressed. But whatever the accents and emphases, the rational and empirical cognitive element was always prominent.

The topography of the cultural realm changed as scientific studies, the rationally and empirically disciplined exercise of curiosity about the sensible world, moved into the center. In the education of children, progressive reformers sought to reduce the burden of old knowledge and to open up the pupils' minds by developing their curiosity for new knowledge based on their own experience. Knowledge freshly gathered to satisfy the "needs" which arise in the course of the individual's development was given precedence over the mastery of the knowledge contained in traditions of past accomplishments. Ancient Western history and languages, their grammar and their great works, were pushed towards the margin. More and more, classical studies became a subject of specialized study, like any other academic specialization, rather than the knowledge possessed by all educated persons. Classical antiquity became the object of scientific historiography; classical literature became the object of systematic scientific philological study. By the middle of the twentieth century, the acquisition of new knowledge as the task of universities grew to such an extent that the transmission of knowledge of the great works and deeds of the past was forced to the side. If these works and deeds were to live at all, it had to be as the objects of systematic scholarly study. Even aesthetic appreciation was compelled to take on scientific lineaments.

Increasingly in the nineteenth century, the universities, which hitherto had not regarded cognitive expansion as their responsibility, took up in earnest the task of producing new knowledge of important things. The greatest university reformer of the nineteenth century thought that the formation of moral character, which had once been thought attainable through religious instruction and through the study of the Western classics and their languages, could be achieved by the discipline of scientific research. In the present century, the idealistic belief of Wilhelm von Humboldt in the benefits conferred by scientific research on the moral character has lost its force, but the conviction about the value of the knowledge it produces has increased.

The third major line of growth of the appreciation of the cognitive function occurred in the sphere of public life. Philosophers of history in the eighteenth and early nineteenth centuries had described the progress of humanity as consisting in the progress of detached, dispassionate, secular knowledge acquired through the senses and disciplined by method and theory and in the reorganization of society through the application of, or in harmony with, that kind of knowledge. The introduction of factual considerations into the preparation and assessment of legislation and the belief that governmental administration required regularly gathered, sound, and truthful information were part of the cognitive expansion. The growth and promotion of public opinion, understood as "informed" opinion, as a factor in the making of political decisions added a new variant to politics.

Politics has always been a struggle about who is to occupy the positions of authority and, to some extent, about the policy to be followed by those who occupy them. But prior to the modern age, there was no organized, constitutionally provided and technologically and economically feasible arrangements for distributing to a wider public, knowledge of the events which were the issue of contention and the immediate matrix of politics. Of course, Athenian democracy and the Roman Senate had open debates, but there was no formal provision for those who did not attend the debates to learn of what transpired in them and to pass judgment on them. This was mainly a phenomenon of the nineteenth century. The enlarged proportion of the population able to read—itself a consequence of this expanded appreciation of the cognitive function—and the development of inexpensive mechanical reproduction of verbal texts coincided, not accidentally, with increased desire in larger proportions of the society to know about, assess, and act in the political sphere.

In the eighteenth century there had grown up a stratum of political pamphleteers, commentators, and correspondents who wrote regularly on particular political events. In the nineteenth century the profession of journalism developed, one of the main functions of which was to supply to the interested public factual knowledge of current political and economic events and opinions purporting to be grounded in facts. The knowledge purveyed was primarily knowledge of the public actions of those in authority; economic journalism had a longer history but it too came into its own only in the nineteenth century. Journalism and parliamentary government went hand in hand. Parliamentary government was an institutional arrangement for justifying and criticizing the actions of governments before large audiences—the members of parliament and the small part of the public which attended to the debates. The justification and criticism were increasingly made in terms of successes and failures in bringing about certain consequences which could be assessed by observation of "the facts." Journalism—political journalism—was an institution and a profession to bring the knowledge of governmental actions and policies and the criticisms of them to a larger public which could not attend the debates. Again "facts," less than moral principles or traditional practices, were in the essential parts of the criticism. Walter Bagehot's designation of the nineteenth century as the "age of discussion" expressed a view that decisions about public issues were to arise from rational discussions in which factual information, gathered by experienced and dispassionate professional journalists, would be of fundamental importance.

The working of royal and parliamentary commissions, congressional committees, and similar bodies was similar in intention to journalism: these bodies were intended to assemble knowledge pertinent to political decisions and public understanding about complex, politically important events. These innovations in the diffusion of factual information about the activities of governments and the things they dealt with were part of the process of limiting the power of governments and controlling their exercise of that power. The observant eye, the knowing eye, of the public was a condition of the virtue of the statesman. Politicians and administrators would be forced into the straight and narrow path by the awareness that the public knew what they were doing or would, in the course of time, find out about it.

All this gave a great impetus to reportorial journalism. It also gave a great impetus to empirical inquiry into social and economic conditions, about which legislation came increasingly to be about. Reformers of the conditions of the poor in the homes, factories, and workhouses aimed to arouse public opinion in support of their aspirations by presenting well-grounded, factual accounts of the actual state of affairs which was to be improved. Surveys of familial relationships, housing conditions, health and illness, employment and remuneration, poverty, criminality, and penal institutions were forerunners of the more numerous and more rigorous investigations of the twentieth century. Their aims were similar to those of reportorial journalism, except that they sought to be more "scientific," i.e., quantitative, systematic, methodical, and reliable.

The state, no less than the public, was preoccupied by the expansion of educational opportunity—not always on its own initiative and more often in response to prodding from the public. It came, in the twentieth century, to support science less from pressure from the public but to make itself more effective in the pursuit of its own domestic and foreign policies. But one cognitive program which it did undertake on its own initiative was to collect information in a systematic form.

The establishment of periodic censuses in most countries was a major step in the cognitive expansion of the state. Governments began to accumulate information in many spheres in which they had not been active in a comprehensive manner: the registration of births, marriages, and deaths, the licensing of business enterprises and trades, the recording of occupations, the description of housing and standards of living, the recording of frequency of illnesses and amounts of income and property, etc. The police, even before the French Revolution, had been great assemblers of information about persons and sectors of society which were suspected of criminal actions or subversive intentions. The assembly of criminal statistics, however, became a common governmental activity only in the nineteenth century in most Western countries. Governmental statistical departments were established and their publications were drawn upon by their own staff members and others for a new series of attempts to construct a body of scientific knowledge about society.

Scientistic rationalism in the ethical sphere was a by-product of the cognitive expansion. The view that the individual would behave better in his relations with other individuals if he learned to face the hard facts of human existence and to assess them in a dispassionate manner is much older than the modern age. The understanding of the niggardliness of nature and of its unresponsiveness to human desires and of the ineluctable fact of mortality was thought to counsel self-restraint. Philosophy might help its adepts to accept these facts, but the facts themselves did not require special study. They would be evident to all who had the courage to face them. The utilitarian view which emphasized the consequences of actions for their contributions to the maximization of utility rather than for their intrinsic value or their dogmatically asserted goodness or wickedness, went further than this. The utilitarians were promoters of social investigation and of the necessity of applying economic theory by government in its own decisions. When the utilitarians spoke of a "science of legislation," they meant that the rightness of laws was to be estimated in the light of their consequences observed or estimated by empirical means. The utilitarian program called for the development of the social sciences. The theory of evolution was also put to work on behalf of a "scientific ethic" which would free man from superstition, i.e., traditional beliefs regarding the efficacy of spiritual powers and from ethical beliefs derived from religious doctrines. The psychoanalytic theory that the laying bare of events hitherto repressed into the unconscious parts of the memory and the bringing of them into clear awareness are the preconditions of release from their deformative consequences is another variant of the scientistic view that scientific self-understanding is a necessity of the right conduct of life. Likewise, the campaign against "Victorian morality," i.e., the reticence which obscured certain spheres of individual conduct, and against the reluctance to discuss "private" things in public, is still another form of the effort to open every sphere of life to public knowledge. It is still another form of the argument for the universal disclosure of the facts of existence.

III

It was against this background that social inquiry in the form in which we now know it came into existence. Observation and reflection on man's conduct in society and on the vicissitudes of societies is a very old activity, and notable works were produced in Western antiquity, in ancient China and India, and in the Islamic Middle Ages. The direct observation of human conduct and the orderly collection of information, each performed in accordance with standards of cognitive accuracy and reliability, and the adduction of the information so gathered in the making of policy, in administration, and in the "agitation" of public opinion, was, however, a development which got under way only in the nineteenth century. Before that, information had been gathered in connection with the concern of governments to know what material resources and manpower they had available to carry out their policies and to forestall subversion. These two practical interests in power, plenty, and order provided inspiration and direction to subsequent investigators. The social sciences which emerged from this background seemed to be equally of service to officials who served existing governments and to those who wished to "use" the knowledge to persuade or otherwise influence governments to institute new policies. Both sides accepted the legitimacy of veracious social inquiry. The legitimacy of social inquiry was a self-evident extension of the legitimacy of the pursuit of scientific knowledge more generally and of the ideal of rational conduct based on such knowledge.

The surveys conducted into the conditions of life of the poor in France and Great Britain in the first half of the nineteenth century by

both governmental and private investigators, seemed utterly unproblematical in the ethical sense. They were self-evidently desirable.
They were intended by those who conducted them to enable governments and private philanthropists to deal more effectively with the
"social problems" of indigency, unemployment, ill health, child and
female labor, prostitution, illegitimacy, criminality, etc. The surveys
were intended to inform the public and to arouse their opinion on
behalf of legislation and private action which would reduce misery
and improve the condition of society. Mayhew's *London Labour and
The London Poor* and its more systematic successors, by Charles
Booth in London and Seebohm Rowntree in York, were regarded by
right-thinking persons everywhere in the English-speaking world as
wholly admirable works necessary for the improvement of society.
There were parallel activities in France and Germany. The knowledge
to be gained was good because it was knowledge and because it would
lead to the ethical improvement of the class of persons studied. The
works of Frederic Le Play and Ernst Engel on family budgets likewise
did not raise ethical questions regarding the collection of data or their
publication. Such inquiries were regarded as justified because they
satisfied legitimate curiosity, because they resulted in additions to
knowledge on subjects in which some persons were interested, and
because some persons thought such knowledge was pertinent to the
improvement of society or to the prevention of its deterioration. Their
conformity with the standards of truthfulness of science rendered
them immune to fundamental criticism. Critics of socialism and of
social reforms, who adduced the results of these investigations to
argue that changes were needed in existing social arrangements, did
not challenge the fundamental legitimacy of the investigations themselves.

In the United States, the hesitant studies of urban housing conditions, which began fairly early in the nineteenth century, led to the
path-breaking Springfield survey and the rural sociological studies of
Charles Galpin in the early decades of the present century, and then to
the more academic and better-conducted surveys of urban conditions
which were produced in Chicago in the early part of the century.
From this tradition came the monumental work on *The Polish Peasant
in Europe and America* by William I. Thomas and Florian Znaniecki
and the subsequent urban sociological works of Robert Park and
Ernest Burgess. The next stage was *Middletown,* in which the "anthropological method" was employed. Early investigations drew
either on data already gathered by officials, supported by the authority of the state, e.g., census-enumerators, or on information assembled by clergymen, policemen, civil servants and magistrates,
teachers, employers, and landowners who in the course of their regular duties had observed the activities of the persons studied.

The surveys in London, York, and elsewhere around the turn of the century were original in their techniques because they conducted interviews with ordinary persons whose mode of life and activities were in fact directly the object in which the investigators were interested. It began to be taken for granted that such inquiries could not be executed unless the investigators went directly to the persons under investigation to obtain information about them which only they possessed.

Sociology at this time was still at the stage of a handicraft, conducted by a single investigator, sometimes with the aid of students and sometimes with the aid of volunteers. Investigations by teams of research workers were rare. In so far as sociology was a profession, it was a profession practiced almost entirely in universities in which teaching was a major obligation and research was carried on as a professionally obligatory but adjunct activity. Some of the leading sociologists of the first quarter of this century were active in movements of social reform; they collaborated closely with social welfare organizations, using their data and making available to them the results of the completed investigations. The social scientists of this period were generally speaking men of the Enlightenment. Even though many of them were Christians, albeit of a new stripe, they were convinced that good and beneficial policies had to be based on what they thought was scientific knowledge, and they looked to sociology as a means of giving reality to Christian, democratic, and humanitarian ideals; others who did not share these ideals to the same extent, justified their activity by invoking the name of science, so that in one very important respect they were as one with their humanitarian colleagues. The method of gathering the needed information by interview and observation was indispensable to the truthful knowledge for which both strove, and was hence ethically unproblematical.

The establishment of the sample survey, which, coupled with the procedures of market research, greatly increased the scale of research, moved things a step further. After the Second World War, sociology became a profession which could also be practiced on a moderate scale as a full-time, nonacademic profession. Sociologists began to be employed by governments, civic and religious organizations, and industrial firms. Survey research institutions grew up alongside universities as nearly self-supporting institutions performing research on a contractual basis. The basis of this research was the interview, in which the opinions of the person interviewed were elicited and in which he reported on those of his activities, beliefs, and sentiments in which the surveyors were interested.

Innumerable surveys were conducted into opinions about institutions, about the political leadership of the country, about trends in society, about the desirability or undesirability and the justice or injustice of particular arrangements and actions. As the institution of social survey research became well established, more and more subjects were brought within its purview. Ethnic attitudes and sexual practices were subjected to study by the survey technique. From religious affiliations and religious observance, surveys moved on to the study of attitudes of parishioners to their priests, and of priests towards their ecclesiastical superiors.

The enlargement of the profession brought with it a greater artfulness or "sophistication" in the technique of interviewing. The simultaneous progress of the techniques of psychological testing and the popularization of psychoanalysis led to closer scrutiny of the mtethods of eliciting information from persons being interviewed or tested. The resistances of those interviewed had to be overcome or circumvented by better techniques. Refusals of persons to be interviewed were not regarded as ethical problems. They were simply challenges to be dealt with by improvement in the technique of interviewing or in the training of interviewers. Refusals to be tested or interviewed were scarcely an issue since the tests and interviews were frequently conducted on school children and on university students who usually accepted the test as one more task set by authority.

Social anthropology, which is closely akin to sociology in the tasks it sets itself, began as a discipline which obtained the information which it needed from the reports of travelers, missionaries, soldiers, and administrators in mostly primordial societies or, as they were then called, "primitive" or "savage" or "preliterate" societies. The costs and inconveniences of travel to these societies at first placed first-hand observation outside the limits of what was easily practicable. In the course of time, this changed. It changed first in the United States, where there were "primitive" Indian societies available within the national boundaries; and where social anthropology first became a subject practiced by staff members of universities and museums; then it changed in France and Great Britain, where there were no "primitive" or "savage" societies within their own national boundaries. Anthropologists who did "fieldwork" in these societies encountered differences among the members of those societies in their capacity and willingness to communicate information. They found some with greater congeniality, fuller memories, and wider experience, and they drew primarily on these "informants" and on their own immediate observation. The informants did not resist: no coercion was employed to gain information. It was necessary, of course, to obtain the approval of the rulers of the "primitive" society, who were of two sorts: the indigenous leaders—chiefs, kings, or elders—and the administrators. This method of obtaining information about the life of these societies was ethically unexceptionable and there was also no alternative if the societies were to be studied at all. There were few or no documents written by members of the society and not enough records or accounts created by administrators. If the societies were to be known, that therefore was how it had to be done.

There was little discussion of whether it was desirable to know about these societies. Those who wished to know about them took it for granted that such knowledge was a good. Since social anthropology arose in many instances in close connection with physical anthropology and paleontology, it benefited from the aura cast by these subjects at a time when scientific knowledge was acquiring a sanctity such as previously only religious knowledge had possessed.

Outside the United States and, much later, Latin America, India, China, and Japan, the primordial societies in which anthropologists worked and lived were usually in continents and in colonial territories which were ruled ultimately by the governments from which the anthropologists themselves originated. Dutch anthropologists did their "fieldwork" in the societies of the Netherlands East Indies; French anthropologists did theirs in societies in the French colonial territories in Africa and Southeast Asia; British anthropologists studied societies in British colonial and imperial territories; Belgian anthropologists studied societies in the Belgian Congo and Ruanda-Burundi. A considerable number of American social anthropologists worked in Latin American countries and, on rare occasions, in Japan, Africa, or Indonesia. If they were aliens to the sovereign state which ruled the territory and even if they were not, they had in most cases to have the approval of the governmental officials who were responsible within the larger territory or in the locality in which they wished to conduct their investigations.

Colonial officials were usually tolerant of anthropology. Sometimes they regarded the knowledge which anthropologists obtained as possibly useful to their own understanding of the societies they ruled; more often they probably did not. But as long as they were not apprehensive of agitational activities which the anthropologists might carry on and were not concerned lest a mysterious stranger cause disruption, they regarded anthropologists as scholars, as men of learning, who were entitled to the prerogatives of pursuing knowledge wherever it was to be found. The traditional rulers of the primordial societies which were under study were usually deferential to the nationals of the alien sovereignty which ruled them and would therefore tolerate the social anthropologists as long as the colonial officials did so. The intention of "writing a book" about their society was a strange undertaking to most indigenous rulers; colonial officials knew what a book was and that itself was a sort of legitimation for the intrusion.

In the sociological and anthropological study of contemporary Western societies with more or less liberal-democratic regimes, no such governmental authorization was regarded as necessary. The governments of these societies did not regard it as coming under their competence to give or to withhold authorization for sociological studies—local, regional, or national. Private, relatively closed corporate organizations took a different attitude: sociologists usually could not study the members of such bodies without the approval of the authorities who governed them. Thus, to study the working of a factory, it was necessary to have not only the approval but also the cooperation of the directors and the trade union leaders; to study the working of a school, it was necessary to have the approval of the principal and the cooperation of the teachers; to study an ethnic community required at least the agreement and cooperation of the leaders, formal and informal, of these communities, such as the secretaries of voluntary associations; to study a Roman Catholic parish would require the approval of the bishop of the diocese as well as that of the parish pastor. In most of these cases, the persons whose agreement was required were usually literate. They knew what a book was, they usually knew that persons from universities wrote books, and although the value of the particular inquiry might be obscure to them, they were willing to accredit it by virtue of its association with entities as dignified as books and universities.

After the Second World War, most of the territories which had been colonies acquired sovereign governments of their own, ruled by persons of indigenous origin. Anthropologists doing research in these countries could no longer depend on the tolerant attitude of colonial officials who were their fellow nationals. To work in a district of one of these countries, it was necessary not only to have a visa from the national government and some explanation of what the investigator intended to do, it was usually also necessary to have the approval and the cooperation of the local administration. Usually, this was forthcoming. The traditional tolerance of administrators towards anthropological investigation continued.

In this same period, sociologists and political scientists who had generally not studied these "backward" countries began to attend to them. They usually concentrated on the urban and "modern" sectors of these societies, unlike the anthropologists, who studied villages and tribes. They too had to have visas issued by competent governmental authority; and, in some cases, where their problem made it necessary, they had to have the cooperation of the local governmental authority, party officials, the custodian of archives of the local party secretariat, etc. Those whose authorization they required were literate persons and often relatively highly educated. Except when they were concerned that disclosures might be made which would do damage to their interests, they accepted the legitimacy of the writing of books. Thus, on the whole, the investigators worked with the same freedom and with the same sense of the justification of their inquiry as they had when they conducted inquiries in their own countries.

In most cases, the cooperation and approval which was needed was in fact forthcoming. Where it was not, the refusal was accepted as a fact, but not as a fact to which ethical significance should be attributed. The cooperation of officials was necessary not only because they had the power to have the investigator expelled from the area but also because they were often important informants; without their aid and information the investigation would probably founder. The occasional refusal of such aid and information, when it happened, was attributed to the retrograde outlook of officials. It was one of those irrationalities evincing an insufficient understanding of the value of social science, or neurotic anxiety, not so very different from the refusal of self-disclosure by an individual who, having received a questionnaire through the post, puts it into his waste basket without answering it. "Nonresponse" had to be diminished by better questionnaires, more authoritative sponsorship, and better "entrée."

With regard to the persons whose conduct and belief were to be investigated, their sensitivity had to be considered primarily for reasons of prudence. The establishment of "rapport" was necessary since, otherwise, no information or false information would be obtained. But there seemed to be no ethical problem involved in treating another human being as a source or object of information. It was not asked whether the human beings who were interrogated or studied had an obligation to lay themselves open to scrutiny or, alternatively, whether social scientists had a right, given by their engagement in a scientific task, to acquire information containing the past and interior or private experiences of other persons. The Kantian injunction to treat other human beings as ends and not as means had not dealt with the use of other human beings as objects of cognition. A negative justification for this kind of knowledge is that it is not obtained by coercion. A more positive justification is that the community can expel an undesired investigator and an individual can refuse to make disclosures; if the investigator is allowed to remain in the community and if individuals answer his questions they do so voluntarily. It lies within their power to put him out or to refuse to speak to him. These considerations may give an improvised legitimacy to social inquiry.

The intrinsic value of the knowledge of society which was sought has been thought to outweigh any other consideration; and there has been, as well, a belief in the ultimate practical value of increased understanding of human behavior in general, and of particular societies or sectors of societies. Publicists, administrators, and legislators often paid lip-service to the social sciences on the basis of benefits which would allegedly accrue from the increase in knowledge of human beings. Governments in almost all of the richer countries began, in the period after the Second World War, to appreciate the prospective contributions of the social sciences to the "solution of social problems." In the United States, governmental departments and agencies commissioned extra-governmental institutions, academic and private research institutes to do research on the "problems" for which solutions were desired. In France, where the universities had not been favorably disposed to the promotion of social research, the Conseil national des recherches scientifiques began, after the war, to make grants for sociological research; in Great Britain, a Social Science Research Council was formed to promote the development of the social sciences by guidance and institutional and financial support. In the Federal German Republic, private research institutes, conducting sample surveys, live from commissions by governmental and private bodies for the conduct of inquiries into problems thought to be relevant to their policies and ends.

The empirical social scientists, taken as a whole, began to approximate to an all-seeing eye—at least in their aspirations. They came to believe that nothing should be hidden from them. Everything was to be observed and enumerated. They took it as their right to penetrate and lay open to the light of public knowledge every obscure corner and crevice of society and of the life of the individual. Only insufficient financial resources, their own intellectual capacities, and their limited numbers inhibited this titanic cognitive aspiration; but as resources and numbers increased, new potentialities were seen. It is true that not all social scientists permitted themselves such luxuriant conceptions of their powers and their prerogatives and that many of those who did have such notions justified them on the grounds that the definitive "solution of social problems" was possible only if the requisite knowledge were available. Not curiosity, but social utility, justified the cosmic sociological eye. Society was to become conscious of itself through the social sciences. The cognitive expansion which had begun and made its most spectacular advances with the study of the external world of nature now turned to engulf the society which was sustaining that great expansion of the mind's possessions.

The idea that something should be withheld from them was an affront to these scientists; it was difficult to believe that any one individual, private organization, or government could reasonably deny the right of a social scientist to study the events which occurred under their respective jurisdictions. Only those who had something to hide would resist the extension of social science into their sphere of life.

The coming of the computer whetted the cognitive appetites of social scientists. Their intellectual powers have been increased through the use of computers; the computers have also increased their aspiration to amalgamate all the pertinent knowledge of their societies into data banks. The data banks would, by accumulation, bring together all that has become known and would make available to every individual social scientist who wishes to have it all that has been learned on the subject of his interest. The data bank would assemble in a single electronic depository the contents of the collectively possessed knowledge of multitudes of social scientists.

IV

This intensification and extension of the quest for knowledge of society and individuals has been sustained by the enthusiasm of trained professionals. Social science was carried at first by scattered amateurs, then the assemblage of social scientists into institutional points of concentration like universities and learned societies heightened interest and made the value of such knowledge appear more self-evident than it had been previously. Social science has in its more recent phases been borne along not only by the older beliefs about the value of science in general and the presumptive practical value of a body of scientific knowledge of society; it has become part of the movement of a broader and deeper desire to penetrate cognitively into every sphere of life and to disclose it to the wider public. This desire to penetrate into reality by empirical means, rather than by communion and contemplation, has extended into the length and breadth of public life and into personal relations as well. The newspaper press, although in most advanced, democratic countries sorely beset economically, has become even more unremitting in its desire to penetrate and disclose. *Arcana imperium,* having been in steady retreat before this extending curiosity, have been almost abolished. The permanent inclination of governments towards secrecy regarding their own proceedings, was given a sharp fillip by the development of nuclear weapons and the fear of espionage, but in the 1960s Western governments, and particularly that of the United States, began to withdraw from the spaces they had once regarded as necessarily secret. The inclination has not disappeared and probably cannot do so. It is not in the nature or exigencies of the exercise of governmental authority to be completely open to public scrutiny, although very great inroads from the outside and capitulations from within have taken place. However much governments might resist the intrusion of the external eyes, they have, under the onwardly rolling wave of the cognitive expansion, repeatedly yielded ground to it. In the nineteenth century, governments conceded the publicity of parliamentary proceedings; in the twentieth century, they have made many more concessions; and even in Great Britain, once the most reserved of countries, the secretiveness of government is being to some extent abandoned under the demand from the outside for knowledge of the doings of authority. The "fifty-year rule" which protected governmental documents has been given up and the "thirty-year rule" is under siege. There are recurrent pressures for the television broadcasting of parliamentary deliberations. In the United States, the movement has gone much further. The television broadcasting of the proceedings of important congressional committees is now well established. The federal government of the United States now acknowledges that it has often "over-classified" documents and that it should be more "open" about its proceedings. Even the discussions of the National Security Council and the activities of what has traditionally been the most secret of all governmental activities, namely, intelligence, have repeatedly been disclosed by "leaks" from within and by penetration from the outside, usually in collaboration with each other. The cultivation of "leaks," which is a characteristic feature of disloyalty to institutions and of the incivility of civil servants, seems to be incapable of being halted. The recent radical demand for the "transparency" of society has only put in a more ideological and extreme form what is a more generally shared desire.

The retreat of governments from the once jealous preservation of their own secrecy is evidence that they have accepted, within the limits which are generated by the very exercise of authority, the rightfulness of the cognitive expansion. At times, of course, they make a counterattack, but it is not usually successful because the courts will not sustain them, and the organs of "public opinion," which are the major carriers of the cognitive expansion outside the universities, give them no peace. President Nixon's ill-fated invocation of executive prerogative, although obstinately insisted on, defeated and discredited him. But despite these counterattacks, which in some countries are in fact successful with regard to military secrets, governments have moved very far from the secrecy which the doctrines of the divine right of kings and of the *raison d'état* permitted and justified.

The cognitive expansion of modern times did not originate in governments. It was only through their uneven and fitful patronage of science that they contributed to it before the French Revolution. It is indeed primarily through their support of science on such a large scale that they have contributed to the rising tide. But they themselves are adjuncts rather than initiators. They are part of the flooded area rather than the flood.

The technological accomplishments which have recently given a further impulsion to the fantasy of an all-knowing collective mind have been taken over by governments. "Data banks," even though they are still a great distance from the ideal of an all-knowing computer mind, have strong proponents and have made some progress.

President Johnson's desire to record conversations which took place in the White House and President Nixon's continuation and broadening of that practice are other instances of this aspiration to omniscience, this belief that everything which has occurred should be known and recorded for the knowledge of future generations. (It is likely that both presidents had additional motives for this profuse curiosity and the recording of its results.) The prodigious proliferation of questionnaires which governments distribute to their citizens produces quantities of information of a sort and on a scale even greater than that assembled by the police of the ancien régime in eighteenth-century France. The emergence of "cost-benefit analysis," of PPBS and of "evaluation studies" and "policy analysis," all postulate the prior existence of huge bodies of information and the creation of more such knowledge, all of which is to be utilized for making governmental decisions and activities more rational, i.e., more scientific. These techniques are the outcome of the strivings of social scientists for many years to enable authoritative decisions to be made in accordance with the findings of scientific research about causal relationships. They give evidence of the readiness of governments to accept them, at least in principle if not in practice. The more scientistic governments are, the more they give their support to science and quasi-science and thus help to create a larger vested interest in its continuance. Most scientists incline towards the ethos of scientism. They think that everything can be made to yield to the "scientific approach" and that all spheres of life should be laid open to it.

V

Man is more than *homo sapiens;* above all, he is more than a being aspiring to empirical omniscience. There are other dispositions in the human mind. There has in fact been powerful resistance to the cognitive expansion through much of the period in which the expansion grew from strength to strength. Some of the resistance came from those who were committed to traditional Christian religious beliefs. The religious mode of knowledge gradually had diminished in its self-evident plausibility and became discredited before the educated classes as some of the particular propositions of the body of Christian knowledge were refuted or were placed in doubt by geological, historical, and archaeological research. Old universities fought hard against the secularization of their teaching and government; churchmen resisted the implied conclusions—sometimes more than implied—of research in paleontology, geology, and history. Governments sometimes refused to tolerate certain scientifically founded beliefs. Practical business enterprisers and inventors decried the prestige of scientists whose theories were remote from the world of everyday life. Certain artists and seers hated the empirical scientific mode of acquiring knowledge. Politicians and powerful private groups sometimes opposed the disclosure by social scientists and journalists of certain classes of facts which might have placed them in an unfavorable light. Social scientists were more harassed in the United States than elsewhere; journalists were more harassed in Central Europe because it was anticipated that their disclosures would be upsetting to order. In the mass of the less-educated population traditional religious beliefs survived, sometimes joined by astrological and magical beliefs; the knowledge acquired through the experience of daily life and the vicissitudes of existence was scarcely challenged by the cognitive expansion. A morality of reticence and a belief in the value of privacy also exercised restraining influences on the forward movement of cognitive expansion. Within the movement itself, there were antinomies; natural scientists looked down on the social sciences; psychoanalysts thought economists too rationalistic. But, by and large, in the liberal countries of Western Europe and North America, the powers of resistance external to the movement weakened. Churchmen, humanists, and artists either desisted or went over to the other side or had to resign themselves to being overshadowed. For twenty years after the Second World War, the opposition was especially weak and the cognitive expansion came to a crescendo.

Since then, the movement has not been all in one direction. The cognitive expansion is once more encountering resistances on a scale which is startling to those whose perspective is confined to the last quarter of a century. It is difficult to know whether the resistance presages a resurgence to the level of earlier ages, or whether it is no more than a transient fluctuation. There is a revulsion in some circles from the stringent discipline of scientific research. It is visible in the attack, at the margins, against technology, which is seen as the poisonous flower which has grown from the root of science. It is visible in the attacks on the possibility of objective knowledge, particularly in the social sciences; it is visible in the self-contradictory assertion that all knowledge and all pursuit of knowledge are "ideologically" contaminated. It is visible in the attacks on universities by the penumbra of publicists and those administrators and teachers who decry the university as an intellectual institution. It is visible in the complaints of disappointed scientists and radicals—scientists and laymen—and the view of academic political scientists that the natural scientists are only a pressure group, like any other, interested in power, wealth, status, and professional advantages. It is evident in the "counter-cultural" renewal of the old attack on science as deforming the balance of human talents, as drying up the springs of emotional sensitivity, and as a destruction of man's attunement to the richness of nature.

In all this skirmishing, the social sciences had escaped relatively unscathed. They suffered two kinds of affront: academic criticism from the natural scientists who thought that they were not really scientific and from the humanists who disparaged their deficiencies in traditional high culture; and criticism from the politicians and businessmen who were offended by the collectivistic liberal beliefs which many social scientists espoused. For many years the reputation and the fortunes of sociology suffered from its identification with socialism. When classical and neo-classical economic theory was criticized by collectivistic liberals, it was not so much because it was untrue as because it seemed to support preference for an economy organized around relatively free, competitive markets. The fundamental legitimacy of social science was not challenged and therefore it was not defended.

Social scientists themselves, long convinced of their present and even more of their prospective utility to the good of society, always took for granted that right-thinking, "progressive persons," especially those opposed to "exploitation," "imperialism," and "capitalism," would acknowledge the truths which they disclosed through their research. Most sociologists and social scientists, especially in the past thirty-five years, have themselves been "progressives"—the cognitive expansion was part of the outlook of the party of progress—and they were particularly concerned, therefore, about the poor and the humble, the outcast and the neglected, the insulted and injured. They took for granted that their research could not do other than bring benefit to such as these members of society. Their research would arouse public opinion to support action to remedy the conditions which they described and their theories of motivation and community would show what conditions had to be installed to abolish existing evils.

The circle has, however, now turned back upon itself. The cognitive expansion is being resisted, allegedly on behalf of the powerless. There has been a parting of the ways. It was always thought in the past that the cognitive revolution would enhance the welfare as well as the dignity of man. Now, however, there are some who say that the dignity and welfare of certain groups in society will be damaged by the continued expansion of knowledge. It is not the powerful and the ascendant who are to be protected by these restrictions in cognitive expansion but, rather, the poor, especially the very poor. It is said in some quarters that the techniques of the social sciences are injurious to the dignity of those they study and that the results of the social sciences can also do harm by making it appear that the sections of the population they study are unworthy.

VI

Sociology had almost from its origins studied those aspects of modern Western societies which the dominant ethical views of the circles of the educated regarded as evils. Yet sociology has become the target of critics who charge that the evils it studies are not the "real" or the "fundamental" evils but only the superficial ones. Sociology has for many years focused much of its attention on "anomie," "dehumanization," "atomization," "social disorganization," the dissolution of primary group ties, corruption, particularistic selfishness, individual self-seeking, conflict between ethnic groups, etc. This was thought to be all to the good. Evils had to be disclosed and faced in order for effective action to be taken against them. The cognitive expansion was always opposed to self-deluding complacency, and, like liberalism, it was no respecter of persons or of what was handed down by authority in the past or in the present. Social scientists prided themselves on the claim that social inquiry destroyed myths, dissolved superstition, abolished ignorance, and showed reality for what it really was. There were some conservatives who did not like this, and who thought that, by dealing so emphatically with those aspects of modern society which brought it into discredit, social inquiry was making common cause with socialism and revolution. (This was one of the reasons for the reluctance to admit sociology as a professional and as an academic subject in certain countries and certain universities.) Nonetheless, the position of sociology advanced because there were honest and good men who, without being revolutionaries, thought that the facts had better be faced and that efforts for the improvement of society could not be effective without a realistic understanding of the nature and magnitude of those aspects of modern societies which were adjudged to be ethically evil.

In the course of these investigations, the chips were allowed to fall where they might. Sometimes aggrieved legislators and businessmen attacked the sociologists whose research put them in an unfavorable light. Some of the infringements on academic freedom in the United States were instigated by such research. The American Association of University Professors (AAUP) was formed to protect university teachers—in the social sciences above all—from attacks by outside groups and by university administrators who agreed with them, for having told truths about particular situations as they discovered them. The success of the AAUP in acquiring a considerable following was evidence that academics, out of professional self-interest and commitment to the cognitive ideal, were not willing to see a check put upon the cognitive expansion. The AAUP, although it dealt mainly with the security of tenure of appointment when it was threatened by anyone and on any grounds, postulated that it was the obligation and right of university teachers to discover and teach the truth.

As sociology and the sociological study of political activities and institutions progressed, especially after the Second World War, many groups in society came under the microscope. Many situations were uncovered which were "imperfections" when compared with the ideal of an egalitarian regime of civility. Malpractices by policemen, the yielding of legislators to the arguments of parochial "interests," the tendency of businessmen's organizations to portray themselves as concerned only with the interests of the society as a whole, the allocation of patronage by politicians for the benefit of their party, the machinations of local politicians in gaining electoral support and in frustrating their opponents—all these and much else were disclosed by sociological investigators. Juvenile delinquency and adult criminality and their correlates in ethnic, class, and occupational characteristics were investigated. Occasionally, indeed, rarely, one result was discomfiture to the small numbers of individuals studied and damage to their standing, or, rather, the standing of their role, occupation, religious and ethnic affiliation, in society, since individuals were usually portrayed anonymously and in terms of statistical aggregates, and general class-names permitted no identification of individuals. This was accepted as one of the occasional risks of sociological investigation; but, like the reluctance to respond to a request to be interviewed, it was not thought by social scientists to raise any question regarding the ethical value of the investigation. In fact, some sociologists thought that such objections only confirmed the rightness of their calling. They had a good conscience about what they were doing.

The reflectiveness of social scientists about the ethical standing of their procedures and about the consequences of the diffusion of their results was no more aroused as they rose on the curve of their prosperity than it was in earlier decades. Generally speaking, they behaved quite properly and they were quite careful to preserve the anonymity of their informants and those they interviewed by giving them pseudonyms and by omitting reference to any idiosyncratic or distinctive characteristic which would permit a reader to identify them. They also attempted to hide the identity of the communities they studied by the use of fictitious names. (When, as in the case of "Middletown" and the "X" family, or in the case of Yankee City, the real name became known, no serious scandal was caused.) On the whole, issues of the identification of individuals did not arise since the communities which sociologists studied in the first third of the century did not include readers of sociological books; in any case it did not occur to sociologists to think about the matter. The safeguard of anonymity was as far as social scientists deemed it necessary to go to meet those small ethical obligations which were incidental to the pursuit of the truth. As far as "primitive" societies in far-off countries were concerned, disguised names of villages were not thought to be necessary because the villagers were even less likely to read the anthropologists' account of their lives than were the persons studied by sociologists; those who did read the anthropologists' monographs were most unlikely to know personally any of the villagers written about.

The various injunctions governing the conduct of investigators vis-à-vis those they investigated were as much matters of prudence as they were of morality. The investigator was abjured not to become involved in partisanship in the groups he studied; he had to avoid illegal activities; he had to be deferential and courteous; and he had to avoid any actions which would bring the profession of social science into disrepute or "queer the pitch" for future investigators.

VII

An enormous change has been taking place in Western societies in recent years. It is a change which is as great as the movement towards democracy which Tocqueville observed. I refer to the increased demand for deference, the increased sensitivity to dignity, and particularly to the increased sensitivity to derogatory reference.

The new states of Asia and Africa are participants in this movement, especially in so far as their relations with other, and with richer and more powerful, societies are concerned. They, or at least some of their sensitive and better-educated nationals, scattered through legislatures, civil services, the press, and universities, developed something like a sense of collective privacy. They seemed to think that being the objects of someone else's knowledge was derogatory to their dignity. They have sometimes thought that their society was placed in an unfavorable light by being regarded as "primitive" and hence appropriate to study by anthropologists whose traditional task it was to study "primitives." Then too, they seemed to resent an implicit condescension in being made the objects of study by nationals of their former colonial rulers or at least nationals of countries of the same category as their former rulers. It was as if the eye of knowledge had become an evil eye. India, which was for many years one of the countries most studied by foreign social scientists, particularly American, began several years ago to put some restrictions on such study; this was done mostly by the control over the issuance of visas. Indian officials, defending the government of India, have variously asserted that foreign scholars have studied only the traditional, archaic parts of India, which exhibited India as a museum of backwardness; or, alternatively, that foreign scholars studied only the pathological aspects of India, e.g., caste and communal conflicts, etc. They have also complained that the investigators "took their knowledge away from India," instead of leaving it there; they appeared to assume that knowledge about a person or a society "belongs" to that person or society. Of course, these arguments and beliefs are not the whole story. Spokesmen for societies want their societies to be well esteemed, and they fear that the truths of social science investigation will result in their societies being thought unestimable; they might also believe that their own social scientists are at a disadvantage compared with the foreign social scientists who are better-supported financially, better trained and more disciplined, and more energetic; and they might want to close the resultant gap by handicapping the foreign social scientists, or by requiring that they be associated with Indian scholars and universities so that their knowledge would be shared and their own stock rise proportionately. They also charged that some of the foreign social scientists were in fact agents of foreign intelligence services which were seeking to penetrate and acquire vital national secrets; they have at times denied that the foreign social scientists are the disinterested scholars they put themselves forward as being. Whatever the amalgam of their motives, one thing is clear: they do not regard the pursuit of knowledge for its own sake as possessing a degree of merit which is sufficient to outweigh other considerations such as national dignity. The upshot is that they do not want to allow their fellow countrymen to be studied.

An approximately similar attitude, *mutatis mutandis*, has been expressed by certain persons in the black sector of American society and among some who have taken it upon themselves to speak on their behalf. As much as some of them extol their own "black culture" and insist on its appreciation, they resent its study by alien, nonblack scholars—again, as if as a result of its being observed, something would be taken away from it. This is especially so with regard to sociological investigations. The belief that only blacks can or should be permitted to study blacks—as some black social scientists have asserted—is a complicated one. In part, it implies that nonblacks will inevitably misunderstand blacks and will produce observations which will be both wrong and derogatory to blacks; in part, it implies that the diffusion of the observations and interpretations made by nonblack social scientists will damage the standing of blacks according to prevailing standards which those making the argument share to some extent. Then there is a vague apprehension that being observed is itself a derogatory action; being in a relationship created for observation, being an object of cognitive activity, is per se derogatory. There is also, occasionally, an overtone of a belief that something is taken away from the person who becomes the object of someone else's knowledge. There are also suggestions of a belief that the knowledge which can be obtained about a person or community "belongs" to that person or community and should not be allowed to go further; this postulates the desirability of a cognitively closed community but it does not answer the question regarding who should decide about the closure. Should it be the government, or self-appointed spokesmen, or should it be the individuals and communities themselves which decide? Quite apart from the locus of authority and the mode of deciding on the closure of boundaries, so that they are impermeable to cognitive penetration, there still remains the problem of whether such closures are rationally justifiable or unjustifiable. Whatever the answers, there is now more resistance to the firsthand study of black society by white social scientists and, also, a little more resistance to the firsthand study of African and South Asian societies by European and American social scientists than there used to be.

The investigation of the social distribution and the relationship of that distribution to the genetic transmission of intelligence is another of the types of social inquiry which has been passionately resisted since the movement of civil rights for blacks acquired force. Elaborate studies of the social distribution of intelligence were undertaken over many years in Great Britain and the United States. They did not arouse much resentment, although they were criticized on scientific grounds; it was said that the results of intelligence tests did not really correspond to native intelligence but only to differences in the culture of the different groups. Against this view it was contended that the differences which were disclosed were genuine differences in intelligence and that they were, moreover, the result of differences in genetic endowment. There were demurrers from this hypothesis, but they were mainly confined to academic and professional circles and there was little anger in the disagreement. No one said that such inquiries should be prohibited.

There has been a change recently in the United States, and to some extent in Great Britain. There has been vehement denunciation and in a few cases violent demonstrations against certain of the proponents of the view that a large proportion of the variation in average intelligence between groups can be accounted for by biological heredity. Professors Arthur Jensen, Richard Herrnstein, William Shockley, and Hans Eysenck have been harassed and threatened and at least one of them has been physically assaulted, because they assert that the black population in the United States has, on average, lower intelligence scores than the white population and that these average differences are genetically explicable. There seems to be a common fear that, if these hypotheses were correct, they would do damage to the cause of improving the civil and economic position of black persons in the

United States. In consequence of this, these scholars have been subjected to grave abuse and the National Academy of Sciences of the United States has refused to recommend a program of research on such matters. This is one of the very few clear cases which has ever come to my attention in which scholars have refused to approve of the study of an issue because they were apprehensive that the conduct of the research would give rise to social disorder and also because they feared that the results might lead to social situations and policies which are abhorrent to them. For example, it is imagined that the social status of blacks might be lowered if it were thought that they were, on average, hereditarily less intelligent than whites; it is also thought that if it were shown scientifically that blacks are, on average, hereditarily less intelligent than whites, the social policies designed to improve their lot in American society would be discontinued and replaced by policies which would be injurious to blacks.

In the case of the study of the social distribution and inheritance of intelligence, the resistance to the cognitive expansion has come, not from remnants of the party of tradition, but from one of the outposts of the party of progress, namely, the National Academy of Sciences. A strange recruit to the party of nescience and misology!

The two instances I have cited are indeed instances of a pattern more widely manifested. Some other elements in the pattern help to give it more influence. One of them is the agitation by radicals now well established as a minority within the academic world which asserts that the prevailing social science is an instrument of constituted political authority and economic power and serves and is even intended to keep the lower classes in bondage. It is on such grounds that it bases its hostility to systematic, dispassionate observation. Like the conservative who years ago fought a losing battle against sociology on the grounds that its discoveries might lead to socialistic conclusions or that its practitioners were socialists, now radicals are fighting against sociology on the ground that its discoveries might lead to inegalitarian conclusions. The stream of thought of which radicalism is one current always accepted the cognitive expansion as an aid to the realization of its program. Present-day radicalism takes the lead in the clamor against cognitive expansion, not only on this issue but also through its hostility towards science and scientific technology. (At the same time, it demands the "transparency" of society.)

One other element in the more critical attitude towards the cognitive expansion arises from a very serious concern to guarantee that the human subjects of experiments in biomedical research are not wantonly misused by investigators. The treatment of human experimental subjects must always have been a latent problem, ever since biomedical experiments were conducted on living human beings. It was, however, not much discussed, partly because the research was conducted by medically qualified persons who benefited from the good repute of the medical profession, and partly because the research was conducted on a scale which was relatively small compared with the present-day scale, and also because the experimental subjects were frequently deferential, lower-class persons who accepted what was done for and to them without public complaint. The Hippocratic oath was generally thought to be adequate to govern the conduct of physicians towards their patients and, by implication, of medically qualified investigators towards their subjects. This situation has now begun to change. The scale of research has been very greatly enlarged; patients, or those who take it upon themselves to speak on their behalf, are much more sensitive and outspoken; and some physicians have become more sensitive to the ethical issues implicit both in old and in new and hitherto unforeseen types of situations. It is not likely that the patients and the spokesmen for "patients' rights" would have made themselves audible if there had not been the encouraging conjuncture of a growing general uneasiness about an unqualified cognitive expansion.

The United States Department of Health, Education, and Welfare, which is the major patron of biomedical research in the United States, decided to intervene. It has done so over a broad front with the general intention of protecting the persons on whom research is done. It has interpreted protection in an extremely comprehensive way. The desire to protect experimental subjects from physical or neural damage and from severe psychic trauma, and to prevent the exploitation of the powerless for experiments in which they cannot refuse their participation, was a desire to caution scientists not to coerce or deceive subjects into serving as objects of investigations. This was a very legitimate concern, whatever one may think of the magnitude of the problem and of the specific institutional arrangements proposed to make the concern effective. It is right that scientists should be reminded that they must treat their human subjects with the respect and consideration due to human beings. Furthermore, the concern is an ethical concern about the consequences of techniques; it does not refer to results or the application of results. It is not a concern to avert in advance certain findings as in the instance of the aversion to investigations into the genetic transmission of intelligence. The concern to protect human subjects which have not yet been born, those who are too young to understand, and those of mature years is about procedural rather than substantive matters. But the momentum generated by this delimited and important concern in biomedical research has been too great in the present atmosphere. The barrier could not hold. The concern flowed into the field of social science and into the sphere of results.

On 8 November 1972 Chancellor Albert Bowker of the University of California at Berkeley presented a document containing the university's response to the requirements set forth in the United States Department of Health, Education, and Welfare *Grants Administration Manual*. The response was accepted by the department "as satisfying current DHEW regulations." The response was concerned, in the words of the spokesmen for the University of California, to protect "any individual who may be at risk as a consequence of participation as a subject in research.... An individual is considered to be 'at risk' if he may be exposed to the possibility of any harm—physical, psychological, or other—as a consequence of any activity which goes beyond the application of those established and accepted methods necessary to meet his needs." The university's statement then went on to deal with social inquiry in a way which was quite original with regard to academic traditions.

> *Social risks* are related in the main to procedures that may place the reputation or status of a social group or an institution in jeopardy. Procedures designed to measure the characteristics of easily defined sub-groups of a culture may entail risk if the qualities measured are ones which have positive or negative value in the eyes of the group. Even where research does not impinge directly on it, a group may be derogated or its reputation injured. Likewise, an institution, such as a church, a university, or a prison, must be guarded against derogation, for many people may be affiliated with, or employed by, the institution, and pejorative information about it would injure their reputations and self-esteem. In evaluating social risk, an investigator should ask himself how the findings will appear to persons belonging to any identifiable group—or affiliated with an institution—studied and reported upon. These cautions are as equally warranted in the case of anthropological field research in distant cultures as in studies performed in domestic settings.

This is not censorship of scholarly or scientific works following publication. It is an announcement that inquiries which have some moderate probability of reaching results of a particular content are not to be supported and, in the present circumstances of social inquiry, are not to be carried on.

VII

The concern is for blacks, "Chicanos," Puerto Ricans—not for politicians, businessmen, civil servants, or lawyers or physicians or school or university teachers; not for farmers or the mass of the industrial working class; not for Protestants of the major and minor denominations or for the Roman Catholic Church; not for persons of Polish, Italian, Bohemian, Slovak, Ukrainian, Greek, German, Croatian, Irish, or Lithuanian ancestry. Such groups have been the subjects of sociological inquiry for a long time. Sociologists have told what truths they could discover about them in many monographs of considerable intellectual value. No harm was alleged to have been done to the Polish-Americans by W. I. Thomas and Florian Znaniecki's *The Peasant in Europe and America,* to the Jews by Louis Wirth's *The Ghetto,* or to the blacks by Franklin Frazier's *The Negro Family in the United States.* It is conceivable that *The Power Elite* by C. Wright Mills did some damage to the standing, among American university students, of American businessmen as a class, as in an earlier generation by Veblen's *The Theory of the Leisure Class,* or as Veblen's *The Higher Learning in America* might have done to the standing of academics. Any attempt to prevent the investigations which resulted in the three former books would have been regarded as an intolerable interference with intellectual freedom in general and with academic freedom in particular. Any attempt to restrict the publication of the three latter books would have been no less offensive to the standards of a decent academic community or to those of a liberal society, and it would have surely led in the course of time to passionate but justifiable denunciation of the attempt as a reactionary and obscurantist effort to interfere with serious intellectual discussion and to hamper the spread of truth. So it was when the cognitive expansion was not distrusted.

But the United States Department of Health, Education, and Welfare and its collaborators in the University of California were carried along on the wave of distrust which broke through the surface in the second half of the 1960s. That is why they were willing to undertake such an infringement on the reasonable freedom of inquiry. They declared their readiness to withhold support from research which they or their advisors might have predicted would have an injurious effect on the reputation of a group or class, however well qualified the investigator and however good the prospects of a sound and truthful piece of research, and even if, as always in the past, the persons studied explicitly or implicitly gave their agreement by cooperating with the investigator. If all that was required was the explicit or implicit consent of the interviewed and studied persons, there would be nothing new. In the past the investigators obtained the "informed consent" of the persons he was studying; otherwise, anthropological and sociological work could not have been done. There have been investigations in which the investigator deceived the persons studied by taking up employment among them; this is not the common practice. In most cases, the investigators present themselves as such and the readiness of those they interview to answer questions about their beliefs and activities is, it would seem, tantamount to consent. Just how "informed" that consent has to be to be "informed consent" is a very ambiguous affair.

The innovation introduced by the United States Department of Health, Education, and Welfare and the academics who at the time accepted it is of a different character. It introduced a new criterion into the choice of topics for investigation. Whereas hitherto the criterion had been interestingness to the investigator, i.e., intellectual interestingness and anticipated social utility, a new criterion of anticipated social disutility was promulgated. Disutility! Any newly discovered truth of immediate or far-reaching scope can be distressing to those who have not shared it previously, and its newness or originality by definition means that it has not been shared prior to its discovery and publication. Any discovery discommodes those who have not participated in making it. It requires, if they have interested themselves in the subject-matter, their renunciation of what they believed previously and this is not always an easy thing to do. Any new truth about society, of a general sort or at the level of the accurate description of what has not been described before, is likely to show that things are not what they were thought to be. Furthermore and not less important, since all societies are, in addition to much else, constellations of interests and distributions of scarce and valued objects, roles, and statuses, an accurate description is likely to uncover frictions, conflicts, falsely based claims, unjustly held advantages, improprieties of conduct, griefs and grievances, and many other features of social life which are in disaccord with widespread moral standards. Of course, an honestly conducted investigation will show much which is not subject to moral censure—although this, alas, is not in the tradition of sociology—but it will also reveal to the public eye features of what is studied which are subject to moral censure. Karl Marx's *Das Kapital* has certainly influenced a chain of thought and events which have caused much distress to private businessmen and to persons who are antipathetic to socialism and communism. Adam Smith's *The Wealth of Nations* in the course of time brought embarrassment to mercantilist officials. Gunnar Myrdal's *The American Dilemma,* to take a work of less intellectual significance but one which is still noteworthy, brought embarrassment to white Americans. According to the new policy, such works should have been nipped in the bud.

A policy of the sort being discussed here—I have been informed that it has, in fact, never been executed at the University of California—would represent an innovation in modern, more or less liberal democracies. It would be an invitation to bureaucrats and self-appointed spokesmen of the prospectively affected groups to render judgment on and to influence decisions as to whether, in view of the possible substance of its still unattained results, an inquiry should be carried on at all. Alternatively, it leaves the decision to intimidated academics. It would clearly be a decision to place intellectual criteria in an inferior position in the administration of a policy of support for the social sciences. It would replace the "reactionary" concern for social order and class advantage at the expense of truth by a "progressive" concern for the status of particular groups at the expense of truth.

As far as I know, the view expressed at the University of California has had no reverberating echo in the United States, and academic social science has continued as before. In the meantime a fairly strong movement has arisen in the United States on the fringes of the academic community demanding a "moratorium" on research into recombinant DNA in view of the inestimable possibility of the creation of an uncontrollable virus. There had been demands in earlier generations for a "moratorium" on scientific and technological research to avoid the once feared "technological unemployment." This earlier demand came to nothing; the present one for a moratorium in research into recombinant DNA has thus far not been successful. There are no precedents for a moratorium on research in the social sciences in liberal countries. They have been largely suppressed in totalitarian countries—in the Soviet Union because they were regarded as rivals to the orthodox Marxist interpretation of society and in Nazi Germany because they had been, so it was thought, carried on by liberals, socialists, and Jews. Nothing like this has happened in Western countries. Nonetheless, the cognitive expansion at least on certain fronts has begun to falter and a counter-movement has begun.

IX

The legitimacy of social investigation is at issue.

Now in so far as the social sciences are sciences, they enjoy the legitimacy of science. The promise that the social sciences would become sciences was what entitled them to claim legitimacy. Except for some progress in economics and some parts of psychology, it cannot be said that this promise has been honored.

The social sciences have also been justified on the grounds of their contribution to the improvement of society, by discovery of laws of society and individual behavior which could be adapted to or set going in ways which were conducive to good social ends. Again, except for economics to some extent and psychology at the margins of physiology, this promise has not been fulfilled. On the other side, descriptive social investigations including economic investigations have been useful to administrators and business enterprisers by showing them the situations which they must reckon with, adapt to, or attempt to change, and they have also been useful in the informing and enlightenment of the opinion of the educated classes regarding the conditions of their own societies. This function has been very unevenly performed. Partly because of unintelligibility, partly because of inaccessibility, the accounts of their own societies which the publications of social scientists have placed before the public are only a small part of what they have done. Not all of these accounts have been truthful; some of them have had a deformity of vision not so different from the uninformed vision which it would have been a justification for the social scientists to cure.

Much of contemporary social science continues and resembles some of the better travelers' literature of earlier centuries. It is like the writing of publicists like Tocqueville, Leroy-Beaulieu, and Dawson, who in the nineteenth century described whole societies in ways which are still exemplary. Social scientists who are not primarily theorists and who are not interested in expounding their analysis mathematically continue the tradition of travelers and publicists, except that their methods of observation are usually more intensive and methodical and that they write more frequently about their own countries.

No one ever raised any objections to these investigations by travelers and publicists except on rare occasions by a tyrannical ruler who thought that his regime was not being presented with sufficient admiration. It was not that the peasants or merchants of these countries were deprived of some of their essential substance, which they alone should possess, through being observed and described in a published work. Sometimes the authors benefited from the conventions of hospitality, sometimes it was the respect for his European background which made the subjects willing to speak to the visitor. The Europeans did not question the rightness of learning about their hosts and of reporting what they had learned to their fellow countrymen. They did not usually think that they were contributing to an emergent science of society nor did they think that what they learned was going to be applied for the improvement of society.

Why should one do historical or archaeological research and write books on these subjects? No science will result from them and they have little practical value. Why write the biography of a minor artist of two centuries ago? If one removes the scientific pretensions and aspirations, and the belief that one's work will influence rulers and electors and make their conduct more reasonable, much work in the social sciences is like historical, archaeological, and biographical research. Its subject-matter is, it is true, contemporaneous and it makes more use of abstract categories—in this respect historical studies, especially in the United States, have come closer to the social sciences. But in its study of contemporary things, the social sciences attempt to evoke the pattern of the present, just as history and archaeology and biography attempt to evoke the patterns of the past. The fact that the historical disciplines study individuals, frequently famous ones, while the social sciences study the relatively common and anonymous life makes a difference. Famous persons by definition belong to a larger public, unknown ones do not. The former have lost much of their privacy, the latter still retain it. The loss of privacy by a deceased person, especially one who wished to be known in the world, raises some questions but not as many as does the loss of privacy of a living person.

Are social scientists who seek information directly from living persons about their otherwise unrecorded beliefs and actions doing something for which there is no justification, putting aside for the moment the justification of contributing to scientific knowledge or providing knowledge necessary for the improvement of society? Their works extend our awareness of our society and of societies outside our own. They heighten the awareness of others, thus extending the contents of individual minds, populating them with the images of other individuals and other societies. They extend our knowledge and they arouse our cognitive sympathies. They fill out and differentiate our picture of the world.

It might be that human beings would be better off if they could remain in a small room. The great sage who counseled that men should do so, himself reached out into the infinite spaces, frightening though they were.

X

The flooding cognitive revolution is in some aspects like the irresistible tide of democracy which Tocqueville saw rising and flooding the Western world in the first half of the nineteenth century. The propagandists of the cognitive expansion believed that the human race would achieve a secular sort of redemption through the growth of rational and empirical knowledge. It was a secularized version of Christian redemption through communion with the divine. It is now evident that this secular redemption is not attainable through scientific knowledge and the technology which has arisen from it.

There is nothing wrong with pointing out the limited powers of the scientific mode of knowledge in many very important categories of human existence. The resistances to the stream of cognitive expansion mentioned earlier are not of the standard of the religious and ethical criticisms of the limits of empirical scientific knowledge as a guide to human life. They fly in the face not only of the tradition of cognitive expansion but of an ethical postulate which asserts the obligation to acknowledge the truth, and its particular Western variant which asserts the obligation to seek it—and to seek it, moreover, in a methodical, empirical way.

Man is many things, but he is *homo sapiens* too. This aspect of man's powers has been impelled into the center of his outlook, pushes forward and legitimates the cognitive expansion. It assumes that man is nothing if he is not a knower. It assumes that everything is worth knowing and that everything which is in principle knowable must be known. In its democratic form, it also includes the further belief that what is known to some should be known to all—or, at least, to all those who have the desire to know.

There is much foolishness in the extreme forms of the cognitive expansion. This applies to social inquiry too. The prerogatives claimed on behalf of social inquiry would be more legitimate if the accomplishments in this field possessed the intellectual standing of the accomplishments of the natural sciences. The occasional pretensions of social science to replace ethical reasoning and judgment by scientific propositions are baseless. The confidence that the truths of the natural and social sciences could provide an adequate regimen for all the moral and spiritual obligations of human beings is likewise misplaced. The same may be said of numerous other facets of the cognitive expansion. There are governmental matters which ought to be kept secret. Not all issues can be settled by discussion, and the better part of statesmanship in these matters is to forestall their being raised. Continuous disclosure and publicity do not always produce better, fairer, or even more democratic decisions. Privacy is an intrinsic value which need not necessarily be inundated by the cognitive expansion, certainly not without some guarantees for the individual and compensations in the larger intellectual and social interest. The consequences of the publication of the results of social inquiry might not always be beneficial, or at least harmless.

Still, after all these reservations, much of the effort and some of the results of social inquiry in the broader sense do partake of the best elements of the cognitive expansion. They do represent a tremendous effort of self-understanding and they continue the great tradition of moral philosophy. Here and there they have helped to illuminate opinion and to improve the lot of men here below. They display man in the use of his cognitive powers in the discernment of order in a relatively uncharted terrain, and the order which is sought is of the utmost "seriousness." They have helped him to see his intimate affinities with human beings whom he would otherwise never know. They have helped to enlarge his world and have furnished his mind.

XI

All these things being said, those instances of recessions here and there in the flood of cognitive expansion, with their mixture of good and problematic motives, give us occasion to think about the costs of the great enterprise of the pursuit of knowledge. I say that without qualifying my affirmation of its intrinsic value. Yet there are costs. It has been taken for granted by the agents and beneficiaries of the cognitive expansion that it was worthwhile and in fact urgently necessary to lay waste the inherited patterns of Christian religious belief and to deprive many human beings of the consolation and fortification which come from faith in an all-knowing, just, and loving deity. It has been taken for granted that it was worthwhile to discredit traditional beliefs and loyalties. Confidence in the "presuppositionless" scientific approach led them to describe beliefs other than "scientific" ones in an idiom of disparagement. It has until recently been taken as self-evident that the privacy of other human beings could with propriety be laid open by social investigation. Social investigation is a part of the cognitive expansion which has been endowed with a progressivistic standpoint which is not inherent in it but which its practitioners have propagated year in and year out. They have assumed that the progressivistic standpoint is so obviously right that they have very rarely tried to examine the costs of a universal diffusion of the progressivism which enfolds and permeates their investigations. They have never really considered whether the spread of knowledge about society can have costs (other than financial ones) as well as benefits.

Neither the benefits nor the costs of social investigation can be calculated. This is no reason why they should not be thought about and more circumspection brought to bear on them.

Social investigation has become an important part of modern intellectual culture. As popular university subjects in a time of mass higher education, the social sciences are now forming the fundamental idiom in which a large and influential minority are interpreting the world and influencing the minds of others. This idiom is accentuated and made more subtle in the conduct of social investigation so that there is a circular process of reinforcement. Social investigation has obtained much of its motive force from being drawn in the wake of the larger cognitive expansion of the modern epoch. It has begun to be self-propelled as an intellectual activity which also has a lay audience, and lay "users," and it needs lay support. It must reassess therefore its own legitimacy more painstakingly than it has done hitherto.